MEDIEVAL FLANDERS

MEDIEVAL FLANDERS

David Nicholas

Longman
London and New York

LONGMAN GROUP UK LIMITED
Longman House, Burnt Mill,
Harlow, Essex CM20 2JE, England
and Associated Companies throughout the world

Published in the United States of America
by Longman Publishing, New York

© Longman Group UK Limited 1992

First published 1992

ISBN 0 582 01679 7 CSD
ISBN 0 582 01678 9 PPR

British Library Cataloguing in Publication Data

A catalogue record for this book is available from the British Library

Library of Congress Cataloging in Publication Data

Nicholas, David, 1939–
    Medieval Flanders / David Nicholas.
        p. cm. –
    Includes bibliographical refererences and index.
    ISBN 0-582-01679-7 – ISBN 0-582-01678-9
    1. Flanders – History.   2. Europe–History–476–1492. I. Title
II. Series.
DH801.F462N53 1992
949.3'101–dc20   91-45256 CIP

Set by 7B in Bembo
Produced by Longman Singapore Publishers (Pte) Ltd.
Printed in Singapore

Contents

List of genealogical tables and maps

TABLES

MAPS

Abbreviations

AESC:	Annales. Economies. Sociétés. Civilisations.
AGN:	Algemene Geschiedenis der Nederlanden, second edition, Utrecht, 1982
AH:	Annalen van de Belgische Vereniging voor Hospitaalgeschiedenis
AHR:	American Historical Review
AM:	Appeltjes van het Meetjesland
ASEB:	Annales de la Société d'Emulation de Bruges
BCRH:	Bulletin de la Commission Royale d'Histoire
BK:	Biekorf
EcHR:	Economic History Review
EP:	Georges Espinas and H. Pirenne (eds), Recueil de documents relatifs à l'histoire de l'industrie drapière en Flandre, 4 vols (Brussels, 1906-24)
HMGOG:	Handelingen der Maatschappij voor Geschiedenis en Oudheidkunde te Gent, new series
IAB:	Inventaire des archives de la ville de Bruges, Section première: Inventaire des chartes, ed. L. Gilliodts-van Severen, 6 v. (Bruges, 1871-76)
IAY:	Inventaire analytique et chronologique des chartes et documents appartenant aux archives de la ville d'Ypres, ed. I.L.A. Diegerick, 7 vols (Bruges, 1853-68).
JMH:	Journal of Medieval History
MA:	Le Moyen Age
MKVA:	Mededelingen van de Koninklijke Vlaamse Academie, Brussels
RBPH:	Revue Belge de Philologie et d'Histoire
RH:	Revue Historique
RN:	Revue du Nord

SAG:	Stadsarchief te Gent [Municipal Archive of Ghent]
TG:	*Tijdschrift voor Geschiedenis*
TRHS:	*Transactions of the Royal Historical Society*, London
VKVA:	*Verhandelingen van de Koninklijke Vlaamse Academie*, Brussels

Preface

The history of medieval Flanders has been the subject of an immense literature. The political power of its enormous cities, their economic structures based on the export of fine woollen cloth, the 'world market' of Bruges, the struggles between workers and employers that were complicated by the rivalries of French and Flemish speakers, the glorious art of the fifteenth century, all are the stuff of legend. It is curious, therefore, that this book is the first modern history of Flanders by a single author in any language. Aspects of Flemish history are contained in the now outdated, albeit classic accounts by the great Henri Pirenne (1862–1935) and in two excellent joint works, the second edition of the *Algemene Geschiedenis der Nederlanden* and the *Geschiedenis van Vlaanderen* edited by Els Witte.[1]

Flemish history is known outside Belgium almost exclusively through works in French and English, particularly Pirenne's studies. For most English and American readers the Flemish language, a dialect of Dutch, remains a dark chasm of the unknown; yet most documents written after 1300 and much of the historical literature are in Middle Netherlandish and modern Dutch respectively. The inaccessibility of the history of medieval Flanders to most English readers is especially unfortunate, because in the Middle Ages Flanders and England had close diplomatic and economic ties that impinged severely on the

1. Henri Pirenne, *Early Democracies in the Low Countries: Urban Society and Political Conflict in the Middle Ages and the Renaissance* (New York, 1963); Pirenne, *Histoire de Belgique*, 1: *Des Origines au commencement du XIVe siècle*, 5th edn (Brussels, 1929); 2: *Du Commencement du XIVe siècle à la mort de Charles le Téméraire*, 3rd edn (Brussels, 1922); *Algemene Geschiedenis der Nederlanden*, 2nd edn (Utrecht, 1982 ff.); Els Witte (ed.), *Histoire de Flandre des origines à nos jours*; *Geschiedenis van Vlaanderen van de oorsprong tot heden* (Brussels, 1983).

policies and alignments of the English monarchs as well as of the Flemish counts and cities. I have done my best to present current opinion on debated questions, and this has sometimes caused me to eschew older accounts for more recent works. At the same time, some modern writing in Belgium has been undertaken from as much an ideological as a scholarly perspective, and I hope to avoid the problems of this approach. This book is thus based on an exhaustive study of the secondary literature and of primary documents that are available in printed editions. I have also used manuscript material for Ghent, the largest city of Flanders and the subject of most of my original research.

Another difficulty in writing about medieval Flanders is that 'Flanders' has meant different things at different times. The tendency has crept into some English historical writing to refer to the entire Low Country region as 'Flanders', but this is imprecise. The core of Flanders was in Carolingian frontier districts along the North Sea. The Scheldt river was a natural frontier on the east and the north; northern Flanders in the Middle Ages was what is now the southern segment of Zeeland. On the east, however, the Flemish counts, to defend themselves against the German emperors, established a march between the Scheldt and Dender in the eleventh century. From this time on, the Scheldt was the eastern frontier of Flanders from Dendermonde north to the sea, while the Dender was the border with Brabant southward to the frontier of Hainault. When the counts fortified this frontier and established themselves in the east, they became vassals of the German emperors.

The southern frontier of Flanders was more nebulous than the eastern. The counts between the tenth and twelfth centuries pushed their frontiers into Vermandois and Artois, far south of the Flemish-speaking area that formed the core of their domains, but they were never able to establish a strong administrative organization there. They were vassals of the French king for these territories, and at the end of the twelfth century they lost most of them to the crown. Except between 1305 and 1369, however, medieval Flanders always had a substantial French component. The ruling dynasty in Flanders was of French origin between 1128 and the end of the Middle Ages. Many of the upper bourgeoisie preferred the French language and manners of their princes to Flemish. Thus, for coherence and convenience, the 'Flanders' of this book is the area ruled by the Flemish counts, although this fluctuated considerably.

A NOTE ABOUT NOMENCLATURE

Virtually all Flemish persons, places and natural features have separate names in Flemish and French, and some have a distinct English version. Any effort to be unfailingly consistent in an English publication about Flanders will founder on the shoals of incomprehensibility. My general rule for places and for foundations such as abbeys has been to adopt the locally used name, such as French Lille rather than Flemish Rijsel but Flemish Oudenaarde rather than French Audenarde. Exceptions are made in the cases of several large cities of Flemish Flanders, notably Ypres, Bruges and Courtrai, which are so well known in English by their French names that to call them Ieper, Brugge and Kortrijk would only occasion confusion. English Ghent is neither French nor Flemish but is close enough to the Flemish Gent to be clear. For persons, most Flemish counts are known in English by French names, such as Louis rather than Lodewijk of Male, and I have retained this usage. For others, I have used a Flemish form except for the nine Baldwins, whose name I have translated since either Flemish Boudewijn or French Baudouin could cause confusion. For kings of France and the counts of Flanders of the Burgundian dynasty, I have used the English version of the name.

Acknowledgements

This book has had an extremely long gestation period and accordingly requires a formidable list of acknowledgements. Professor Bryce Lyon, who directed my doctoral research, first made me aware of the endless possibilities of the Flemish archives and has been an inexhaustible fount of advice, criticism and encouragement since my days under his tutelage. From February 1966, when I first entered the university and archives of Ghent, every Belgian scholar with whom I have had contact has shown me every courtesy, from helping me arrange accommodations on my stays in Belgium to having microfilm and photocopies made and sent to me. Any list of names must be partial at best, but I owe special thanks to Professors Adriaan Verhulst, Walter Prevenier and Ludo Milis and to Mrs Greta Milis-Proost of the University of Ghent and more recently to Dr Marc Boone. I am deeply indebted to the staffs of the History Seminar and the Central Library of the University of Ghent and to the direction and staffs of the City and State Archives of Ghent for their unfailing and cheerful cooperation in giving me full access to their facilities. Outside Belgium I have benefited greatly from the advice and assistance of Professors John H. Munro of the University of Toronto and James M. Murray of the University of Cincinnati. Finally, all research requires financial support. I have received grants at different times from the American Council of Learned Societies, the American Philosophical Society and the National Endowment for the Humanities, and a Maude Hammond Fling Fellowship from the University of Nebraska. Some of these grants were for projects of a more specific nature than this; all, however, contributed to the conclusions presented here and therefore merit my grateful acknowledgement.

CHAPTER ONE

The Sand that is upon the Seashore

FLANDERS UNDER ROMAN RULE

Although the Romans are now known to have occupied the southern Low Countries more thoroughly than was once thought, particularly before the third century AD, Flanders was far less Romanized than either northern France or the eastern Low Countries. As a frontier area along the coast and subject to pirate attacks, it was not densely populated, and Roman governance was skeletal.

The region that became Flanders was mainly swamp. The Roman *civitates* were farther south, along a northeast to southwest road. West of the Roman *civitates* was an alluvial plain that was subject to frequent flooding, with mounds a few feet above the tides that supported a few inhabitants who raised sheep and fished. Still farther south was a somewhat drier area, of 20–25 metres above sea level, with habitable plateaus separated by swampy valleys.

The Flemish coast, which is now straight and considerably west of its medieval location, had several broad river estuaries that fluctuated considerably with the tides. The Zwin, IJzer and Aa were the largest, and a bay near Bergues was already becoming a salt marsh when the Romans came. The coast was separated from eastern Flanders by an area of heavy clay covered with forest and marshes that extended northward from the Scheldt below Tournai toward the mouth of the IJzer. This region would effectively separate the two original nuclei of the medieval county, around Bruges and Ghent, until the second half of the eleventh century.[1]

The population of Flanders at the beginning of the Christian era was primarily Celtic, with some Romans and a few Germans. The area seems to have shared most features of the pre-Roman La Tène culture, except, not surprisingly in view of its flat terrain, that it had few hill forts. There was agriculture and animal husbandry, in which sheep dominated. Fishing was very important, and the fish sauces of the Flemish coastal area became famous and were exported. Although the Celts had towns elsewhere, they did not have them in the Low Countries before the Romans, perhaps because coin was not used in the area, which is notably devoid of usable metals and minerals. Julius Caesar's *Commentaries* give us some information about conditions in the first century BC. Caesar described the *Belgae* as the most ferocious of the Celtic tribes, because they were farthest from the Mediterranean, and merchants rarely got to them to make them effeminate. Along the North Sea coast in the Pas-de-Calais between the Aa and the Canche were the *Morini*, whose name means 'sea folk'. The *Atrebates* ('possessors of the soil') were farther inland in what became Artois and Flemish Flanders as far south as the Canche.

The most numerous tribe in what became Flanders were the *Menapii*, who occupied a swampy area behind the Scheldt that Caesar's army found very difficult to cross. Caesar thought them very powerful, but they seem actually to have had less internal cohesion than the *Morini*. He finally subdued the *Menapii* in 54, but they continued to wage guerilla warfare. He tells us much more about the *Nervii* than about the western tribes. They occupied the area between Scheldt, Rupel, Dijle and Lasne, dominating the smaller tribes of eastern Flanders and regions farther east.

Caesar's discussion shows that the area that became Flanders was backward both economically and politically in comparison to the rest of the Low Countries in the first century BC. Ditches from camps of the first century AD have been found in Courtrai and Tournai. Tournai, which was just across the Scheldt from Flanders proper and would later become the capital of its *civitas*, was already important for quarrying in the first century. But far more public buildings survive from the southern towns of *Gallia Belgica* than from Flanders. Few Roman mosaics have been found, and all but one are in the territories of the *Menapii* and the *Morini*. There are few Roman inscriptions and reliefs

---

1. Norman J.G. Pounds, *An Historical Geography of Europe, 450 BC–AD 1330* (Cambridge, 1973), 267.

north and west of a line running Senlis–Soissons–Saint-Quentin–
Tongeren, all of them except Tongeren considerably south of Flanders. There is not even much evidence of pottery making in Flanders.

The main Roman roads were also south of Flanders. The northernmost was the Boulogne–Cologne route, which went through
Thérouanne over Velzeke and Asse and Tongeren. There was a secondary coastal road that did cross the southern tip of Flanders. It branched from the Boulogne–Tongeren route east of Cassel and went to
Aardenburg, while the Boulogne–Tongeren road crossed the southern
tip of Flanders at Cassel and Wervik. Tournai developed where the
Roman road to Cassel and eventually Courtrai over Wervik crossed
the Scheldt, but its ties were directed more south and west than
northward. Arras, Thérouanne and Bavai were south of the main road
and were more Romanized than was what would eventually become
'Germanic' Flanders. The Boulonnais and Pas-de-Calais, rather than
Flanders, were the areas from which boats set sail for England.

When Flanders became part of the province of *Gallia Belgica* after
Caesar's conquest, the Celtic tribal capitals became the centres of
Roman *civitates*: Thérouanne and later Boulogne for the *Morini*, Arras
for the *Atrebates*, and Cassel on a hill overlooking the Flemish plain on
the southern border of the *Menapii*. It was the only *civitas* in what
would become Flanders proper and served as a frontier fortress to protect the Romans against the northern tribesmen. The *civitates* were
centres of governance and military administration.

In addition to the *civitates*, which were on or near the major links
of communication, there were numerous smaller settlements or villages
(*vici*). Most *vici* were agricultural markets, where farmers sold food and
bought such local manufactures as pottery, bronze, iron work and
leather. Buildings were of wood, half-timbering, or occasionally ma-
sonry. Wool was produced throughout *Belgica*, as indeed in most parts
of Roman Gaul. Salt was refined from sea water along the coast, notably at De Panne and somewhat later near Bruges, where there had
been an Iron Age settlement. More evidence of the Roman presence
in Flanders comes with iron works at Destelbergen, near Ghent, and
Waasmunster, in the northeast. Courtrai and nearby Harelbeke also
had iron working from the mid first century AD until the late third. These
places were still inhabited in the fourth century. The *vici* in the north may
have been somewhat larger than those in the south, probably because the
north had no cities and thus knew a more diffused industrial activity.[2]

2. A. van Doorselaer, 'De Romeinen in de Nederlanden', *AGN* 1: 22, 28, 31,
39–40, 45, 55, 57; Edith Mary Wightman, *Gallia Belgica* (Berkeley and Los Angeles,
1985), 29–30, 50, xii–xiii, 75, 81, 94, 98–99, 133, 138, 139, 149, 164–5, 273.

Although the Roman fortifications along the Rhine were north of Flanders, they may have given security for peaceful development in Flanders, particularly during the Batavian uprising in the northern Netherlands in 69. The Flavian emperors (69–96) strengthened the Rhenish forts, and from their time onward the Flemish coastal area was gradually inhabited and Romanized. The tribes of the south rebelled only under duress, generally preferring the 'Roman peace' to the Germans.

But the area was only superficially Romanized. Picardy was the northernmost area with many Roman villas, and even there there was a substantial decline in the number of occupied sites after the fourth century. There is little evidence of Roman villas at any time in Flanders and only slightly more in the adjacent parts of Brabant. Of about 400 known Roman villas in modern Belgium, only a score were still occupied after the late third century. Particularly in northern and eastern Flanders, where villas existed around Aalst, Waasmunster and Belsele, they reverted to forest.[3]

By contrast, cloth making, which would be the keystone of the medieval Flemish economy, had evidently been practised since prehistoric times, fostered by the ease with which sheep could be raised on the dunes. Caesar mentioned most tribes having sheep herds. The *Morini* grew flax and made linen, and the *Nervii* made jackets. Woollen cloth from Arras was marketed in Asia Minor. A *gynaeceum* where soldiers' uniforms were made was established at Tournai and persisted into the fourth century.[4]

There was also a constant risk of flooding. The first 'Dunkirk transgression' was receding only in Caesar's time, followed by a 'Roman regression' in the first two centuries AD. Agriculture became more productive. *Vici* were established in Flanders between the second half of the first century and the second half of the third at Courtrai, Harelbeke, Wervik, Oudenburg, Wenduine, Bruges, Aardenburg and Ghent, and those at Wenduine, Oudenburg and Bruges had some industry.[5] The most prosperous period seems to have been the second

3. A. Verhulst and D.P. Blok, 'Het Natuurlandschap', *AGN* 1: 116–19.

4. Witte, *Geschiedenis van Vlaanderen*, 16–18; van Doorselaer, 'De Romeinen', 68. On the meaning of *gynaeceum* as a place where wool was worked, most often by women, see David Herlihy, *Opera Muliebria: Women and Work in Medieval Europe* (Philadelphia, 1990), 10–11.

5. Verhulst, 'An Aspect of Continuity between Antiquity and Middle Ages: The Origin of the Flemish Cities between the North Sea and the Scheldt', *JMH* **3** (1977): 178.

century, with many *vici* resulting from the growth of Roman civil administration, especially toll stations along the Cologne road. Navigable interior water and sea routes promoted a thriving trade with England and the Rhineland. Most of the Low Country *vici* did not survive into the fourth century. Those that did, such as Tongeren and Maastricht, had other economic ties to the surrounding rural area, and none of the larger ones was in what became Flanders.

The civil disorders that racked the entire empire beginning in the late second century quickly affected the Roman presence in the northwest, reducing a weak civilian settlement to one that was skeletal and almost exclusively military. Tournai was destroyed in 172, but some settlement continued. The Romans built coastal fortresses around that time at Oudenburg and Aardenburg in response to a growing problem of piracy. Oudenburg had an extensive layout, with both a civilian *vicus* and a military *castellum*.

Nonetheless, the region remained generally prosperous until the Franks broke the Rhine frontier near Cologne in 258–9, then struck the north and west of what is now Belgium before 275. Military engagements became endemic thereafter. Oudenburg was destroyed in 273. Virtually all *civitas* capitals and large camps that have been excavated show massive destruction during the third century. Excavations around Ghent suggest that the *vicus* of Ganda, a settlement with an artisan quarter, had been attacked in the late second century but was not finally abandoned until the last quarter of the third. It was fortified in the fourth century and in the sixth became the site of St Bavo's abbey.[6]

But the Germans were not the Romans' only problem. Roman civilian settlement in the southern Low Countries came between the first and second 'Dunkirk transgressions'. Western coastal Flanders and Zeeland were again being flooded by the late second century and were deserted by the end of the third. Before 400, the area west of the Aa, Leie and Durme rivers had been depopulated, opening the way for the invaders. The flooding continued until around 600.

The Romans incorporated the much reduced coastline into the Saxon Shore, which was based in Britain but included both sides of the English Channel. Maritime Flanders and eastern England were thus a military and administrative unit at this time. The fort at Oudenburg

6. Marie Christine Laleman and Hugo Thoen, 'Prehistory-Sixth Century AD' in Johan Decavele (ed.), *Ghent: In Defence of a Rebellious City. History, Art, Culture* (Antwerp, 1989), 23–35; Verhulst, 'Aspect of Continuity', 186.

was destroyed around 275 but was rebuilt and strengthened in the fourth century. The latest Roman graves at Oudenburg are from the beginning of the fifth century, when the second Dunkirk transgression cut it off from its hinterland. One of the two settlements at Bruges was also not flooded and was repopulated in the fourth century.[7]

The emperor Diocletian (284–305) divided *Belgica* into two provinces. Flanders and northern France were in *Belgica Secunda*, whose capital was Reims, which would be the metropolitan see of Flanders during the Middle Ages. Thérouanne remained the capital of the *civitas* of the *Morini*, but there were three major changes. Tournai replaced Cassel as the chief place of the *civitas* on the southern frontier, while Cambrai became the chief place of what had been the *civitas* of the *Nervii*, whose previous capital had been Bavai. Boulogne also became important strategically and a *civitas*, probably after the partial destruction of Thérouanne in 275.

Since the waterways had provided access for invaders, the Romans built small forts and towers along them, often on the sites of abandoned *vici*. All *civitates* and most *vici* had been fortified by the fourth century, many of them with walls of up to 3 metres or more. Most fourth-century settlements were considerably smaller than their predecessors, and the Romans established garrisons considerably north of Cassel, notably at Ghent, Bruges and Courtrai.

In striking contrast to all other parts of Europe that the Romans had occupied, the Christian churches in the Low Countries did not become nuclei of settlement across the period of the Germanic migrations in Flanders. When Christianity was legalized in the early fourth century, the *civitas* capitals probably became centres of the new faith and eventually bishoprics, as elsewhere. Yet the late Roman Low Countries provide strikingly little evidence of Christianity, which was always centred more in France. Christianity is known to have been practised at Tournai before its bishops first appear in written sources at the beginning of the sixth century, but there is no prior evidence from Flanders proper.[8]

Since most tribes moved southward along the major rivers, there is little evidence through the mid fourth century of Germans in the part of Flanders west of the Scheldt. Between the Scheldt and Leie was still mainly Roman and east of the Dender almost entirely Roman. But

7. Verhulst, 'Aspect of Continuity,' 178–82.
8. Verhulst, 'Aspect of Continuity', 186–9; Heli Roosens, 'Traces de christianisation dans les centres urbains de l'ancienne Belgique', *RN* **69**: 1–15.

this situation changed abruptly. Franks serving as Roman federates occupied the area between the lower Scheldt and the Meuse from the period of Julian 'the Apostate' (361–63). By this time, Oudenburg, Aardenburg and Bourbourg were the only usable Roman forts left in northern Flanders, and of the interior routes, only the road linking Tienen with Courtrai and Cassel was usable, with fortifications at strategic intervals. The Boulogne–Cologne road was a border, with forts that had little civilian settlement.[9] The Vandals, Suevi and Burgundians made a short-lived irruption in 406, then moved on, and northern Gaul had half a century of relative peace. The Romans abandoned the area, and Salian Franks settled in the Leie and Scheldt valleys. Southeast of the Meuse, however, in the eastern Low Countries, most *vici* survived, and it is no accident that this area was much more significant in the trade and industry of Merovingian Gaul than was Flanders.

GERMANIC FLANDERS, FOURTH THROUGH EIGHTH CENTURIES

Landscape and settlement

Medieval Flanders had three broad physical zones. South of a line running from Nieuwpoort to Ghent and south of the Scheldt east of Ghent was sand and loam. This area was colonized by the Franks and included some areas now south of the language frontier. It had been relatively densely settled by the seventh and eighth centuries. It had patches of woods but no coherent forest masses except between the Leie and Scheldt. North of this was the sandy coastal plain, from the IJzer at Diksmuide to the Scheldt at Antwerp. In this region the original forest cover had been cleared and converted to heath by the eleventh and twelfth centuries, and it remained thinly settled even after the medieval clearances. Animals were always raised there, and during the thirteenth century it became important for the production of peat. Finally, the polders, from Calais to the present Scheldt mouth, were constantly subject to flooding. Although the floods were ending

9. Wightman, *Gallia Belgica*, 160, 202, 204–5, 209, 219, 221, 223, 227, 230, 233–4, 245; van Doorselaer, 'De Romeinen', 42, 63, 66, 80–5, 89.

d 600, population stayed low in maritime Flanders into the ninth and tenth centuries. No villages existed before the late ninth century along the coast except southeast of Ostend. There are only occasional references to individual homesteads on man-made mounds. This area was originally used for sheep pasturing.

Thus most of the landscape in western Flanders was man-made after the eighth century. In the east, however, there is more continuity with Celtic and even Roman antecedents. Most Germans seem to have sought areas that already had a core of settlement, but they tended to settle near Roman ruins, although not inside or even directly adjacent to existing habitations. The Romans generally preferred hills, while the Germans tended more towards the river valleys. The newcomers thus generally did not displace existing populations; but they also avoided central interior Flanders, which had been uninhabited under the Romans, and settled along the rivers, especially between the Leie and the Scheldt. The Franks in particular did not undertake massive clearances – they were more interested in animal husbandry – but where they found partially cleared land, they often finished the work. Archaeological evidence shows both Germanic and Romance language groups in this area and thus a considerable continuity.[10]

There are countless variants on these basic themes. Sometimes the Germans took over the memory of a Roman place, such as *Blandinium*, 'the property of Blandius', the only Gallo-Roman toponym at Ghent. A few Roman names persisted, but they are isolated, such as Scheldewiendeke, south of Ghent between Aalst and Oudenaarde. Even more striking is the Roman name of Kaprijke, in extreme northern Flanders, suggesting persistence of an early core of settlement across the turbulent period of the invasions.[11] In other places, the two language groups co-existed. Semmerzake has a cemetery containing both Frankish and Roman remains. In southeastern Flanders around Oudenaarde and Ninove and even as far north as Temse and Drongen there were substantial populations of both Germans and Romans. Des-

10. Verhulst and Blok, 'Het Natuurlandschap', 128; Erik Thoen, 'Een Model voor integratie van historische geografie en ekonomische strukturen in Binnen-Vlaanderen: De Historische evolutie van het landschap in de Leiestreek tussen Kortrijk en Gent tijdens de Middeleeuwen', *Heemkring Scheldevelt* **19** (1990): 8–9; Verhulst, 'Het Landschap' in *Flandria Nostra* **2**: 22; A. Verhulst, *Précis d'histoire rurale de la Belgique* (Brussels, 1990), 18–19.

11. Erik Thoen, 'Historisch-geografische teksten bij het kaartblad Oosterzele', *Project 'Historisch-Landschappelijke Reliktenkaarten van Vlaanderen: Intern Rapports* (Ghent, 1987), 1; Erik Thoen, 'Historisch-geografisch teksten bij het kaartblad Eeklo', *Project*, 40.

pite the exceptions, however, there are fewer than a dozen Roman toponyms in Flanders, most between the Scheldt and the Leie, but only three of them are north of Ghent, which seems to have been at the northern edge of significant Roman settlement in Flanders.[12]

By the Carolingian age, a Romance dialect was spoken in most places on both sides of the Scheldt south of Oudenaarde by a population of Celts, Romans and probably a diminishing number of Germans. Yet the ethnic composition was even more heterogeneous than in the north, to the point where talk of a linguistic 'frontier' is misplaced before the tenth century at the earliest. Some southern settlements took Germanic names, depending on who settled them and when. The farthest expansion southward of Germanic place names, in the tenth century, reached the Saint-Omer vicinity, which is considerably south of the modern linguistic frontier. Although this would change in the north, as territorial lordships stabilized in the Carolingian age, heterogeneity of language remained common in the south, and indeed in the cities of Germanic Flanders language often divided a French-speaking upper class from the Flemish-speaking commoners until the end of the Middle Ages. North of the Scheldt–Leie line, however, population outside the isolated pockets of bilingualism became almost exclusively Germanic and eventually Frankish.[13]

The Tribal Migrations into Flanders

In the second half of the fourth century the Salian ('salty') Franks established scattered settlements between the *silva Carbonaria*, a dense forest extending east–west across the southern Low Countries, along the east bank of the Scheldt and in the Scheldt and Leie valleys. The Ribuarian ('beach') Franks followed in the fifth century. The Ribuarian Franks came by the Cologne–Boulogne road and settled near it, using abandoned Gallo-Roman buildings, in the western Pas-de-Calais. They then crossed the Scheldt, moved northward into western Flanders, and reached the Aa in the seventh century. Southern Flanders and northern France, where Flemish was spoken in the Middle Ages, were thus the regions of early Frankish settlement.

12. Katrien van der Gucht, 'Semmerzake (Gavere, O. Vl.): Merovingische Neder-zettingsceramiek', *HMGOG* **35** (1981): 7; Verhulst, 'Landbouw', *AGN* **1**: 166; Blok, 'Hoofdlijnen van de bewoningsgeschiedenis', *AGN* **2**: 143.

13. M Gysseling, 'Germanisierung en taalgrens', *AGN* **2**: 100–15; C.T. Smith, *An Historical Geography of Western Europe before 1800* (New York, 1967), 128–30.

The Germanic area includes both Frankish regions and areas where the Romance element had been strong.[14]

The establishment of place names gives important clues about the chronology and direction of the migrations. Virtually all pre-Carolingian evidence concerns the coast and the Leie and Scheldt areas. We know little of the central part of the Flemish interior. Some Franks were in the area south of Ghent between the Scheldt and the Dender as early as the fifth century, when the Frankish suffix *hem* ('house, habitation') first appears. The suffix *ingahem* used with a proper name in the genitive ('belonging to X') comes mainly from the seventh century and suggests that the Frankish lords were assuming territorial power by that time. *Heem* ('home') names, which are also Frankish, occur in a band eastward from the Leie and Scheldt and south to the modern French border and somewhat less densely west of the Scheldt, especially in the Bruges area. The area from the Scheldt eastward is precisely where the greatest persistence of Roman place names occurs.

The Ribuarian Franks were then followed in the sixth century by Saxons, Danes and Frisians, who were driven south by flooding. The Saxon movements southward, of which the invasions of Britain were part, were concentrated around Boulogne and the Canche near the port of Quentovic. Names with *ingahem*, which is Frankish, and the Saxon suffix *thun* ('town') are numerous near Boulogne, between the Leie and the Zenne in Brabant, and the vicinity of Tongeren, areas that had had a relatively dense population in the Roman period.

The churches, although latecomers to Flanders, were also involved in the clearance and settlement of vacant lands. Names ending in *zele* point more directly to reclaimed territories and are frequently used with either directions or a church foundation. Some *zele* toponyms are early medieval, although they also are found in the later period of clearance in the eleventh and twelfth centuries. The village forms were more structured in the 'zele' places than in others before the eleventh century; 'zele' and 'hove' indicate large estates and generally come from at least the second stage of the Frankish colonization of northwestern Europe, as the Frankish kings and other great lords fostered colonization as they moved into Flanders when the flood waters receded in the eighth century. Oosterzele, whose name means 'place cleared on the east', is a good example. It was a village in the lordship of the abbey of St Bavo of Ghent. As was often true of these villages,

14. Jan Dhondt, *Les Origines de la Flandre et de l'Artois* (Arras, 1944), 12–13; H.P.H. Jansen, *Middeleeuwse Geschiedenis der Nederlanden* (Utrecht and Antwerp, 1971), 37.

the centre of the abbey's domain was near the church in the middle of the village, while the arable land for peasant tenures was on the western edge of the settlement of the village centre.[15]

Thus the area of the linguistic frontier was relatively densely populated throughout the early Middle Ages. In western Flanders settlement was more sparse, while in the northeast there is very little evidence of habitation except at Temse. The essential demographic configuration of medieval Flanders was thus prefigured by the settlement patterns of the county before the counts established their power. Of interest also is the fact that the area of meeting of races, of productive agriculture, and of dense settlement crossed the eventual political frontier, for it included the southeastern quarter of Flanders and the southwestern quarter of Brabant.[16]

But these are scattered indications. Although there were pockets of dense settlement around Bruges and Ghent, what would become the most densely populated and heavily industrialized part of northern Europe by 1200 was still a largely pastoral area in the seventh century, with a governing structure that has left no trace in the written record. Then, however, tremendous changes began. The Franks, who had originally settled farther south, began moving northward when the sea level declined again in the eighth century. 'Flam' or 'Floem' means 'mounds', whether man-made or natural, surrounded by sea marshes that are subject to frequent inundation. 'Fleming' was probably the Frankish name for the natives of the territories into which they were moving. The term is first found in written sources from the eighth century to refer to the inhabitants of the coastal area between Calais and Bruges, then became used for the region where they lived.[17]

The early Flemish church

We have seen that Christianity came late to Flanders. There were no stable bishoprics until the erection of Arras and Tournai in the sixth century and Thérouanne in the seventh. The first missionaries did not make widespread conversions, and within a generation of their missions Tournai was assimilated by Noyon and Arras by Cambrai, and the location of these bishoprics would be disputed for several centuries. The parts of Flanders west of the IJzer were in the bishopric of

15. Erik Thoen, 'Historisch-geografische teksten', *Project*, 2–8.
16. Blok, 'Hoofdlijnen', *AGN* **1**: 149–51 and map.
17. Verhulst and Blok, 'Landschap en bewoning', *AGN* **1** 109; Witte, *Geschiedenis van Vlaanderen*, 20–21.

Thérouanne. Southwest of the IJzer and east to the Scheldt had recourse to Tournai/Noyon, while southern Flanders east of the Scheldt was in the bishopric of Cambrai/Arras. The Land of Waas and the Four Offices, to use the later names for the extreme north and east, answered to the bishopric of Utrecht in Holland. By the seventh century, spiritual direction thus came from three bishoprics in France and one in the Netherlands.

Christianity first spread significantly north of Tournai in the seventh century. The missionaries who evangelized Frankish Flanders were monks from Ireland, Scotland and France who were sent by the bishops of Tournai. The Frankish King Dagobert also promoted evangelization. He raised Thérouanne to episcopal status and promoted the mission of St Amand. Shortly after Dagobert died in 639, St Omer organized the conversion of the *Morini*. He and his disciple Bertin founded the abbey, later called St. Bertin, near where the town of Saint-Omer would develop. Several abbeys in Artois, including St Vedast of Arras, were also established in this period.

The Aquitanian St Amand is the best known of the early missionaries to Flanders. Typically, St Amand destroyed non-Christian idols and buildings and established a church in the same place, a procedure that did not endear him to the peoples to whom he preached. He founded several abbeys, most notably St Pieter and St Bavo at Ghent. The missionaries apparently followed the mixed monastic rule that was commonly used in northwestern Europe after 816. The great monasteries held immense properties. Although no church in the Low Countries had full immunity, which freed it from secular control, in the Merovingian period, St Bertin later claimed that it had enjoyed immunity since the end of the seventh century. But as late as 900 the only other Flemish church or abbey with immunity was St Pieter of Ghent.[18]

The greatest of the earliest Flemish monasteries were Sts Pieter and Bavo of Ghent.[19] Both were foundations of St Amand, who evangelized the area between 629 and 639. Evidently St Pieter's was established first; located on a hill, it gave Amand protection from the hostile natives in the valley. But as his work made progress, he established a basilica in the Roman ruin of Ganda and bought a domain

18. Dhondt, *Origines*, 17–18; F.L. Ganshof and D. P. Blok, 'De Staatsinstellingen in de merowingische tijd', *AGN* 1: 240.

19. The section on the two abbeys is based on Adriaan Verhulst, 'Early Medieval Ghent between Two Abbeys and the Counts' Castle', in Decavele, *Ghent: In Defence*, 39–55.

nearby to endow it. Before Amand died around 676, the relics of one of his followers, Bavo, who had lived in the area between 648 and 659, were brought to this church, and a monastic community dedicated to Bavo developed. Donations soon made St Bavo's abbey richer than St Pieter's. Einhard, Charlemagne's biographer, was lay abbot of both, which suggests considerable prosperity.

The Norman invasions, however, shifted the material balance of power in favour of St Pieter. St Bavo's was uninhabited between 879 and the 930s, and St Pieter's was thus the only monastery in Ghent during the critical time when the patronage of the Flemish counts was becoming important. It became their burial place from 918. Accordingly, St Pieter's was able to make St Bavo its dependant until 981.

Princes thus played an important role in furthering the material interests of the earliest churches. But since the royal presence in Flanders was not notably strong, the great churches extended their power only rather late and were always subject to a degree of secular control that was unusual elsewhere. This was the era of the proprietary church. Lay abbacy and pluralism were common; Einhard's is not an isolated case. The establishment of power by the counts of Flanders cost the churches considerable independence. The counts became lay abbots of the two Ghent monasteries and of St Bertin while the monks were in France fleeing the Vikings. Of eight abbots of St Bertin between 820 and 883, only one was a monk.

THE FORMATION OF THE COUNTY OF FLANDERS, 600–918

Some understanding of the governance of Merovingian Flanders is essential in order to understand the rapid rise of the counts. Although political units in southern Europe, where the Frankish kings ruled a basically Romance population, were based on the *civitas*, in the north the considerably smaller *pagus* (Flemish *gouw*) or district – the term is untranslatable, but it was usually a subdivision of the *civitas* – was the basic subdivision. Within the *pagi*, local strongmen could exercise real control, and some *pagi* were subdivided into hundreds. The *pagus* of Tournai is mentioned in 580 and that of Thérouanne in 649. Except at Ghent, where one Dotto evidently ruled between 625 and 647, the *pagi* of Germanic Flanders are later: *Bracbatensis* (north of Ghent between the Scheldt and the Dijle) at the end of the seventh century;

13

Rodaninsis (around Aardenburg and the western part of the Land of Waas) in 707; and *Mempiscus* (Flanders west of the Leie) in 723. A document of 831 mentions several others, including *Flandrensis* along the coast, *Medelintensis* (the Lille–Seclin area), Ostrevant (the Douai area west of the Scheldt), Arras, Boulogne and one centred on Quentovic, south of Boulogne on the Canche. Flanders also contained several smaller and probably densely populated *pagi* between the Leie and the Scheldt, and one source claims that the *pagi* between Ghent and Tournai were under a single administration in these years. By the Carolingian period, *comitatus* is occasionally used to designate a group of *pagi* united under a single count; but the prevailing tendency was for *pagi* to be subdivided, not grouped into larger units.

By the late Merovingian age the *comes* (count) was the chief official in the *pagus*. He was the king's representative in all matters, including judicial, tax, police and military. The count summoned the *mallus* (the court of freemen) and received one-third of judicial fines and of the yield of royal estates in his region. In the Merovingian period, local judges called *rachimburgii* rendered verdicts; they were replaced by *scabini* in the Carolingian period.

The Carolingian kings through to Charles 'the Bald' (ruled 840–77) spent little time in the western Netherlands. Royal fiscs in the Low Countries were mainly in the southwest and the Meuse area, and many passed into other hands in the ninth century. The abbey of St Vaast at Arras received several royal visits. Charles the Bald was once at Petegem and Charlemagne once each at Ghent and Boulogne, but only to inspect the state of preparedness of the ships to fight the Scandinavians.[20]

The Scandinavians in Flanders

The county of Flanders took shape in the late ninth century during the period of Scandinavian attacks. The total impact of the Vikings is a tangled question, but it seems clear that the raiders devastated Flanders less than areas farther east and south. They were so severe in the Meuse valley that they contributed to ruining commerce there and thus indirectly fostered the rise of the Flemish cities.

20. A.C.F. Koch, 'Het graafschap Vlaanderen van de 9de eeuw tot 1070', *AGN* 1: 355; Ganshof and Blok, 'De Staatsinstellingen', 232–40; Witte, *Geschiedenis van Vlaanderen*, 24–6; F. L. Ganshof and G. Berings, 'De Staatsinstellingen in de Karolingische tijd', *AGN* 1: 243–63.

The threat from the Scandinavians was serious by the early ninth century. The *Annals of the Frankish Realm* mention that in 820 'thirteen pirate vessels set out and tried to plunder on the shore of Flanders, but were repelled by guards'. Einhard, writing around 834, said that Flemish coastal defences were still intact.[21] It thus seems likely that the strength of the first Flemish counts in their western domains may have been due to a surviving Carolingian defence organization.

The west Frankish king Charles the Bald was no more able than other rulers to defend his frontiers against the Scandinavian attacks. Most northern invaders of Flanders were Danes, with a few Norwegians. The earliest land invasions were sporadic and destructive, but the armies left quickly. They were raiding bands that were detached from main army groups stationed in France. But the Danes also attacked from the north. They raided Antwerp in September 836, then in 846 came through Frisia, sailed down the Scheldt and may have moved as far south as Ghent. The situation became more serious around 850, when an army ravaged Thérouanne and the nearby coastal regions. The main targets of the raiders were churches and monasteries and to a lesser extent commercial settlements. In 851 the Danes again sailed the Scheldt to Ghent and sacked St Bavo's abbey. They were in Frisia in 852, but the next firm reference to them in Flanders is from 860, when they came by the IJzer mouth as far as St Bertin, pillaged the district of Thérouanne, then moved south to the Seine. In 864 they struck the Flemish coast, but local garrisons again drove them off.

There is no direct evidence of the Scandinavians again until 879, when they reappeared in the Scheldt and Meuse valleys. Their most serious activity in Flanders occurred between 879 and 881. They evidently came to the continent after Alfred the Great drove them away from Britain. They attacked Thérouanne, St Bertin and the southwest, then turned north to the Leie and Scheldt valleys. They wintered in St Bavo's abbey in Ghent, then in early 880 moved south, sacked Tournai and the monasteries of the Scheldt valley, and finally went into France. Resistance there was so strong, however, that they had to return north. They wintered at Courtrai in 880 and from there they raided virtually at will through February 881 between the Scheldt, Somme, Aa and the sea. After campaigning along the Somme, they returned to Ghent to repair their boats in the late summer of 881. But

21. *Carolingian Chronicles. Frankish Royal Annals and Nithard's Histories*, Trans. Bernhard Walter Scholz with Barbara Rogers (Ann Arbor, 1970), 107; Blok, 'De Frankische periode tot 880', *AGN* 1: 301.

they directed their campaign of 881–2 towards the Meuse valley. They returned to the Scheldt between the autumn of 882 and late 884, but they concentrated on the southern parts of the river. They again struck the Flemish coast in the spring of 891, attacking the Thérouanne, Saint-Omer and Cassel areas, but in June they went east by the Meuse. The decisive battle that ended their activity in the Low Countries was along the Dijle river near Louvain on 31 August 891.[22]

The first count of Flanders

The political origins of the county of Flanders combine royalty, romance, international intrigue and diplomatic manoeuvring. Eastern Flanders was a prosperous frontier area at the time of the Scandinavian attacks, but the west was barely habitable. Indeed, as late as 1015, when the third Dunkirk transgression was reversing some gains made against the sea during the tenth century, the legend-spinner of the Norman ducal house, Dudo of Saint Quentin, expected his claim to be believed that the Frankish king Charles 'the Simple' (898–922), faced with the need to give the Scandinavians a place to settle, had first offered them Flanders, but they had rejected the place as being too swampy and insisted on having Normandy instead.[23]

The county of Flanders would take its name from the *pagus Flandrensis*, the district around Bruges. Yet the early counts had more real power in the more prosperous and populous east, notably around Ghent. The first known Flemish count was Baldwin I, who was given the nickname 'Iron Arm' in the eleventh century. He was the son of one Audacer, whose name suggests cognates with a family that had furnished three counts of *pagi* between Scheldt and Leie. They were evidently related to the counts of Laon. Baldwin was thus already a count, probably at Ghent, when he established the basis of his family's fortune by eloping around Christmas 861 with Judith, the eldest child of King Charles the Bald. Judith was already the childless widow of two West Saxon kings when she returned to the continent at age sixteen in 860. Alfred 'the Great' was her stepson, and Alfred's daughter Aethelfryth or Elftrude would later marry Judith's son, Count Baldwin II of Flanders.

22. Albert d'Haenens, *Les Invasions normandes en Belgique au IXe siècle: Le phénomène et sa répercussion dans l'historiographie médiévale* (Louvain, 1967), 43–55.

23. Jules Lair (ed.), *De moribus et actis primorum Normanniae Ducum auctore Dudone Sancti Quintini* (Caen, 1868), 168.

The pair fled to the pope, who persuaded Judith's father to forgive them in 863; King Charles insisted that they marry, a detail that they had neglected. In addition to his countship in the east, Baldwin now received the *pagus Flandrensis*. Shortly afterward he was given Ternois, the Land of Waas and the lay abbacy of St Pieter of Ghent. Baldwin's relations with his father-in-law continued to be strained. In 877 he joined the rebellious counts who forced the capitulary of Quierzy on the king and was one of four lay members of a council of ten potentates who were appointed to advise Charles's heir during his father's absence in Italy.

The motive for the series of transcontinental marriages involving Judith may have been to deprive the Scandinavian raiders of ports of call on both sides of the Channel. Certainly they suggest that control of the coastal marshes was coming to be strategically significant. Baldwin I seems to have become especially interested in Flanders proper. Recent scholars have suggested that the legend that he built the church of St Donatian of Bruges has a factual basis, although that honour is still more generally credited to his descendants. While historians have usually considered him the only Flemish count who was simply a royal official and not an independent potentate, this view may need modification.[24]

Baldwin II (879–918)

Baldwin I died in 879; it is unknown whether Judith was still alive. Their marriage had created a prestigious bond of the Flemish counts with both the French and English monarchies. The military exploits of their son, Baldwin II, against the Vikings and his territorial expansion created the real basis of the dynasty's power. Baldwin's reign began inauspiciously, as the Scandinavian invasions were coming to a paroxysm. It is uncertain just how much he still ruled by 883, but he evidently took refuge from the Northmen in the marshes of *Flandrensis*,

24. Koch, 'Graafschap Vlaanderen', 354–61; Rosamond McKitterick, *The Frankish Kingdoms under the Carolingians, 751–987* (London, 1983), 249; Pauline Stafford, 'Charles the Bald, Judith and England' in *Charles the Bald: Court and Kingdom*, British Archaeological Reports, International Series 101 (Oxford, 1981), 137–44; Dhondt, *Origines*,

25. On the question of St Donatian, see G. Declercq, 'Wanneer ontstond het Sint-Donaaskapittel te Brugge?' ASEB **122** (1985): 245–57. The plan was similar to Charlemagne's palace church at Aachen, but it may have been copied from Charles the Bald's imitation of it at Compiègne, with which the Flemish counts were undoubtedly familiar. J. Dunbabin, *France in the Making, 843–1180* (Oxford, 1985), 72.

the territory with which his dynasty was principally associated from that time onward.

Some sources suggest that both Baldwin I and II cooperated at least tacitly with the Vikings who were fleeing from Alfred the Great. After the Normans left, however, Baldwin II occupied three *pagi*: Mempisc, Courtrai and the IJzer. In a series of expeditions beginning in 892, he seized control of the two counties of Ternois and Boulonnais south of the IJzer gulf and also of the Tournaisis, although he did not take the city of Tournai itself. This gave him a base in fertile territory with great domains that was much more densely populated than Flanders proper. Baldwin almost certainly also recovered the *pagi* of Ghent and Waas, which his father had ruled.

Baldwin II also built a network of fortifications on the edge of the coastal plain between 879 and 883. They later became nuclei of castellanies, which were centres of government, justice and militia. In contrast to the *burhs* of his father-in-law, Alfred the Great, most of Baldwin II's fortresses were so small that they were usable only for strictly military purposes and did not evolve into cities. Except for some that were refurbished Roman walls, they were round, about 200 metres in diameter, surrounded by an earthen wall and a broad ditch and spaced about 6-9 miles apart. Other fortifications, perhaps including that of Ghent, were built or rebuilt by other persons at this time but came into the count's hands by the early tenth century.[25]

By the beginning of the tenth century the plural form Flanders (*Flandrae*) was being applied to the entire conglomeration of territories ruled by Baldwin II, and by the second half of the century the singular *Flandria* was used for it, as the counts consolidated their authority. The legal basis of their power was the union of the *comitatus* (comital power in exercising regalian right as representative of the king) with *bannum* (the power to command free persons and to punish). In fact, successful princes throughout northern Europe at this time were able to join several *pagi* and exercise power in their own names, not as delegates of the king. The counts of Flanders held the comital power but not the county in fief of the west Frankish king. The count had authority over his vassals and over the lands in his domain. As succes-

25. A. Verhulst, 'Die gräfliche Burgenverfassung in Flandern im Hochmittelalter' in *Die Burgen im deutschen Sprachraum: Ihre rechts-und verfassungsgeschichtliche Bedeutung* (Sigmaringen, 1976), 268–73; Richard Hodges, 'Trade and Market Origins in the Ninth Century: An Archaeological Perspective of Anglo-Carolingian Relations' in *Charles the Bald: Court and Kingdom*, 225–6; Koch, 'Graafschap Vlaanderen', 361–3; Dunbabin, *France in the Making*, 68–74.

sors of the Carolingian kings, the counts also had the right to *balfart* (labour on forts) or a money payment in its place. They assumed regalian rights, including collecting tolls, issuing coins and especially controlling advocacy or lay abbacy. This was particularly important because Carolingian kings had given the monasteries immunity from the jurisdiction of the counts. Lay abbacy in effect allowed the count to recover complete power. He had the right to approve abbatial elections and perhaps nominations. At the latest by 988, the count's authority over the churches took the form of advocacy, which was a public authority of Carolingian origin.[26]

Baldwin II thus consolidated his authority by usurping church possessions. He got control of the abbeys of Sts Vaast and Bertin. The counts did not have much influence over the choice of bishops until a century later, but Baldwin II's church policies involved him in the quarrel between rival factions for the west Frankish crown, a theme that would haunt early Flemish history. The Capetian Count Odo of Paris was trying to seize the throne after the deposition of Charles 'the Fat' in 888 (his son Charles 'the Simple' was only eight), but Baldwin joined a coalition that tried to interest Arnulf, the east Frankish king, in taking the western crown. When Arnulf refused, Baldwin backed Odo, but he soon fell out with him when the king refused to support Baldwin's effort to become lay abbot of St Bertin over the opposition of Fulk, archbishop of Reims. Odo pursued Baldwin to Bruges but was unable to capture it.

Odo's opponents, including Baldwin, then had Charles the Simple crowned, but Baldwin in 895 changed sides in the middle of a battle and recognized Zwentibold, Arnulf's son and duke of Lorraine, as king of the west Franks. This gave him an excuse for attacking the counts of neighbouring Vermandois, Artois and Boulogne, who were allies of Charles the Simple, but by 900 they had driven Baldwin out of Vermandois, Arras and Artois and killed his younger brother Rudolf. In vengeance for his defeat over the abbacy of St Bertin, Baldwin II had Archbishop Fulk assassinated in 900. He then tried to reconquer the Vermandois, killing Count Heribert II to avenge Rudolf's death.[27]

---

26. Raymond Monier, *Les Institutions centrales du Comté de Flandre, de la fin du IXe s. à 1384* (Paris, 1943), 15; D. Lambrecht and J. van Rompaey, 'De Staatsinstellingen in het Zuiden van de 11de tot de 14de eeuw', *AGN* 2: 77–9; F.L. Ganshof, 'La Flandre' in Ferdinand Lot and Robert Fawtier (eds), *Histoire des institutions françaises au Moyen Age* (Paris, 1957), 2: 364–5.

27. For Baldwin II's reign, see Dhondt, *Origines*, 31–6; Koch, 'Graafschap Vlaanderen', 361–5; Ganshof, 'La Flandre', 344–5.

Most of our information about Baldwin II comes from the *Annals* of St Vaast, which stop in 900, and the next usable chronicle, that of Flodoard of Reims, begins in 919. We know little of the intervening years. It is clear, however, that Baldwin II ruled a territory of 180 square kilometres along the coast between the Zwin and the Canche, including most of what had been the Frankish royal domain areas west of the Scheldt. His cause was probably helped by the fact that his family lands were in northern Flanders, far away from the major sources of royal power. The Canche was a natural frontier, but it was far from the more natural southern frontier, the hills of Artois. The Baldwins were unusual among crown vassals in the extent of their independence from the crown by the early tenth century.

Baldwin II's great prestige was due not only to his territorial conquests, but also to his distinguished lineage. He had married Alfred the Great's daughter Aelfthryth (Elftrude), possibly during a year of enforced exile in England in 883–4. Their children were thus grandchildren of Alfred the Great and great-great-great grandchildren of Charlemagne. Baldwin II died in 918. He wanted burial at St Bertin beside his father; but Elftrude wanted interment beside him, and when the monks refused to allow even a dead woman in their abbey, she had him buried at St Pieter's Ghent, which became the mausoleum of his dynasty.[28]

28. W. Blockmans, 'Vers une société urbanisée' in Witte, *La Flandre*, 50; Koch, 'Graafschap Vlaanderen', 354: Dhondt, *Origines*, 37–8.

CHAPTER TWO

The Economic Development of Early Flanders

FOREST, FIELD AND VILLAGE IN EARLY MEDIEVAL FLANDERS

By the seventh century the tribal situation in the Low Countries had stabilized. Despite the migration of Germanic peoples into Flanders and the establishment of some new settlements, population continued to decline in the sixth century, due in part to a plague that became endemic after 543. But in the mid seventh century there is evidence of population growth, when the appearance of *rodha* and *rodom* names indicates new clearances in the vicinity of Ghent.

The Flemish landscape was dominated by swamps in the west and north and forests in the east. The coast was virtually deserted between the late third and early eighth centuries. At that time, however, herds reappear, often being maintained for abbeys of the interior. Although there was flooding in the northern Netherlands in the ninth century, it does not seem to have affected Flanders before the early eleventh century.[1] While the west was swampy and barely habitable, eastern Flanders was densely wooded except between the Scheldt and the Dender, which had a relatively high population even by the seventh century. Elsewhere, woodland separated the few settlements from each other. The extension of grazing in the far north thinned the native oak and birch forests, but deforestation became significant only after 1000 in

1. Verhulst, *Précis*, 20.

the barren sands of the Flemish interior. The Franks who occupied Flanders knew agriculture and sedentary farm life, but most of their hamlets were unstable groups of cultivated fields separated from one another by forest.

Three main forest zones have been distinguished. In northern Flanders, beyond a line running between Diksmuide and Gavere over Tielt and Deinze, the land was flat and sandy. Between the seventh and ninth centuries there were dense forests between Torhout and Ghent and along the edge of the coastal plain southwest of Bruges. Woods still persisted as late as the twelfth century north of Ghent around Eeklo, between Drongen and Wondelgem, east of Ghent between the Scheldt and the Dender, and between the Durme and the Scheldt downstream from Ghent in the south. The western part of this forest mass was considered a public forest in the early Middle Ages, and much of it had been converted to arable field by the eleventh and twelfth centuries. The section east of Lokeren was protected by foresters, first of the Frankish kings and later of the Flemish counts. This was evidently the origin of a 'royal forest' that occupied most of the extreme northeast in the twelfth century except the fertile river banks of the Scheldt at Temse and of the Durme at Tielrode, both of which had been Roman sites.

Secondly, two adjacent forest masses occupied nearly the entire Leie–Scheldt area between Ghent and Courtrai in the early Merovingian period except along the riverbanks themselves. The massive 'Scheldt Wood' (*Sceldeholt*) in the north reached the outskirts of Ghent. The Scheldt Wood was converted to arable fields in the eleventh and twelfth centuries. Farther south, the 'Methela forest', extending from Vijve to near Courtrai, remained intact until the twelfth and thirteenth centuries. Thirdly, in the sandy loam area of the southwest, three forests surrounded the small settlement that became Ypres.

The extent of forest in early medieval Flanders suggests several conclusions that can help explain its economic development. Flanders had more total forest than neighbouring parts of Brabant. Yet there is no evidence that Flanders ever exported forest products, for its woods were mainly scrub and easily cleared. Of more potential significance is the fact that the Scheldt Wood, between the major rivers of the east, was not subject to strict control and thus was cleared early. This was unsound ecologically but was productive economically, and precocious clearance here may help to explain the rise of Ghent. Although most princes of the time sold their forest rights when they were financially strapped, the Flemish counts gave theirs away, evidently to promote settlement. Although most evidence of this is from the eleventh century, the Flemish counts leased some of their forest rights in the southwest even earlier.[2]

The great estates of early Flanders

Information about early Flemish agriculture is thus extremely sketchy. The Frankish kings were the biggest landowners, although the largest concentration of royal property in the Low Countries was east of Flanders. Some royal fiscs (administrative groupings of several villas) were in the Scheldt–Leie–Dender area, but only one big estate was west of the Scheldt. The great estate was a recent development here, evidently because there had been so few Roman villas and because in the southeast – the only part of Flanders that was fertile enough in the early Middle Ages to support intensive agriculture – population growth seems to have been so sudden and the result of heavy migration that the end product was less often great estates than the establishment of small parcels of independent proprietors. Except for the properties of the oldest and greatest monasteries, most large estates in Flanders date from the ninth century and later.

In the Merovingian period the villas consisted mainly of woodland and arable that was exploited for the lord's benefit by unfree personnel who did not hold tenant farms on the estate. This continued to be true in the northeast into the ninth century; but in the more fertile south, the arable land was gradually extended between the seventh and ninth centuries by the labour of slaves, who in return received tenures on which they would reside, making kind payments and doing labour services on the lord's reserve as rent. The Frankish movement into Flanders was accompanied by a revival of slavery, which had ended temporarily with the decline of the Roman villas. Slaves were sold at Ghent in the seventh century, evidently as part of a Frankish trading network that linked the Cambrai area with Frisia. As late as 1000, Flemish and Irish slaves were sold on the market of Rouen.[3]

Thus many villas, particularly in southern Flanders, changed from a 'single cell' operation in the seventh century to a bipartite structure (involving tenures for peasants and the lord's reserve or demesne) by

2. This section is drawn from M. Gysseling, A. Verhulst and D. P. Blok, 'Landschap en bewoning tot *circa* 1000', *AGN* 1: 99–164, especially the section by Verhulst and Blok, 'Het natuurlandschap', 116–42, particularly 123–4, 126, 128, 134–5.

3. Stéphane Lebecq, 'Dans l'Europe du nord des VIIe–IXe siècles: Commerce frison ou commerce franco-frison?', *AESC* **41** (1986): 385; Witte, *Geschiedenis van Vlaanderen*, 36.

the mid ninth. The exploitation of the reserve of wage-earners and of serfs who did not occupy tenancies declined, while more labour was furnished by tenant farmers who worked as part of their rent. The lords offered protection and used their powers of command to obtain labour from freemen. This policy was furthered by substantial population growth, mainly in eastern Flanders, which created a labour surplus that caused the peasants to be willing to do labour services to get land. On some domains, however, especially the smaller ones, lords still used slaves and wage-earners and may even have thought them more desirable; St Pieter's abbey of Ghent used the services of tenant farmers only when other sources of labour were inadequate.[4]

In the ninth and tenth centuries some great abbeys compiled lists of their tenant farmers and specified their obligations in money rent, labour and goods in kind. Only three of these surveys, called polyptychs, are relevant for Flanders: that of the abbey of St Bertin (844–48), a short one for St Amand and the tenth-century *Liber Traditionum* of St Pieter's abbey of Ghent, which contains documents going back to the seventh century. The St Bertin polyptych mentions eight classic *villas*. All except Poperinge, just west of Ypres, were in areas of substantial Germanic settlement that would no longer be Flemish by 1200. The monks were efficient administrators. The polyptychs show intensive agriculture under a powerful central direction, much better organized and with more densely populated farms than we have any reason to think was usual on lay properties.[5] By the time the polyptychs were compiled, many peasants lived on 'manses', units of land that could support one household but that might house several families. The manse was attached to the lord's reserve farm, which was larger than the tenures and was sometimes fortified, with room for a residence and outbuildings, kitchen, bakery, stalls, huts for serfs who had no land and a place for women to work. Cloth, evidently for use only locally, was woven on the great estates. The *Miracles* of St Bertin, written in the tenth century, show a young weaver who learned the trade in the establishment of a great landholder of the area. The wives of the leaseholders of St Bertin at Poperinge wove shirts for the monks.[6] Small farmers also continued to live outside the great estates,

---

4. Verhulst, 'Landbouw . . . tot *circa* 1000', *AGN* **1**: 166–9, 171, 175, 178.

5. On this important point, see Y. Morimoto, 'Problèmes autour du polyptyque de Saint-Bertin (844–859)' in Adriaan Verhulst (ed.), *Le Grand domaine aux époques mérovingienne et carolingienne* (Ghent, 1985), 125–51, especially 145.

6. Verhulst, *Précis*, 21; Verhulst, 'De Boeren. I: De Middeleeuwen', *Flandria Nostra* **1**: 89; Witte, *Geschiedenis van Vlaanderen*, 32.

often on their edge, and sometimes were numerous enough to form their own villages. Most examples of this are from the earlier developing Walloon regions of Flanders.

The Flemish records suggest important differences from the west Frankish polyptychs from farther south. Although the manse existed in Flanders, it was a recent creation in the eighth century that was probably imposed by the kings and/or the abbeys, and not all the land on the abbeys' estates was divided into manses. Although the polyptychs of the Paris basin distinguish between 'free' and 'unfree' manses, these words were generally not used in the Low Countries, probably because it was assumed that a free tenant held the manse.[7]

The polyptychs give information about agricultural routine, personal status of the farmers and village and field forms and population. But they are notoriously difficult to use, especially for population figures, for they do not distinguish resident from non-resident tenants, and that of St Bertin lists only heads of households. Population was definitely rising at St Bertin as new tenures were being created. Densities ranging from 20–40 per square kilometre have been calculated. The Poperinge estate was very large and consisted of manses of equal size, suggesting recent clearance.[8]

St Pieter's abbey of Ghent owned a modified bipartite villa in the mainly Frankish area of dense population between the Leie and Scheldt rivers south of Ghent. But while the peasant manses were large, comparable in size to those of St Bertin at Poperinge, St. Pieter's reserve, in the southern and western parts of the modern city of Ghent itself, was roughly one-seventh the size of the average reserves of St Bertin.

In contrast to what is found on some other ninth-century estates, no tenement on St Pieter's estates had more than one family, nor were fractional manses found. This situation seems generally to have been true in Germanic Flanders. Although this was by far the most densely populated part of Flanders, the Scheldt–Leie area thus was less inhabited than the Paris region or even the Ardennes or the south-

---

7. Verhulst, 'Landbouw', 175–6.

8. Georges Duby, *The Early Growth of the European Economy* (Ithaca, NY, 1974), 78–9; C.M. Schwarz, 'Village Populations According to the Polyptyque of St Bertin', *JMH* **11** (1985): 31–41, using F.L. Ganshof (ed.), *Le Polyptyque de l'abbaye de Saint-Bertin (844–859): Edition critique et commentaire* (Paris, 1975); H. van Werveke, 'De Bevolkingsdichtheid in de IXe eeuw: Poging tot schatting', 30e congres van het Oudheid-en Geschiedkundige verbond van België (Brussels, 1935). *Jaarboek* (Brussels, 1936): 107–16; Verhulst, *Précis*, 23, 34–5.

western Flemish area occupied by the estates of St Bertin. The juridical condition of the tenants of the manses is not given in the survey, but charters of 941–50 show that the abbey's steward was a serf. Rents and labour services were virtually standardized, suggesting strong central organization by the abbey.

The St Pieter documents thus show several highly interesting features. The small size of the reserve in relation to the tenures confirms other suggestions of recent population growth. Second, tenants of manses owed heavy payments in kind, especially of grain; but even as early as the ninth century, the only labour services demanded on the farms around Ghent itself were of an industrial nature: making posts and planks and weaving linen. No farm labour on the reserve was exacted; indeed, except at Poperinge, labour services on Flemish villas were usually only a few days a year, and some lack them entirely. Third, numerous serfs were simply attached to the reserve and did not occupy separate farms as tenants. It is thus likely that St Pieter's domain was being farmed by a bountiful supply of non-tenant labour, while the residents of the tenures did nothing but industrial jobs for the abbey. The press on resources was already so intense by the ninth century that the abbots evidently found that renting out their lands was more profitable than exploiting them directly. The situation on St Pieter's estates suggests the potential of the early development of an exchange economy in farm products in fertile and densely populated southeastern Flanders, which bordered two underdeveloped areas, the northeast and the coastal areas west of the Scheldt, that provided a market for any surplus. Unfortunately, in the present state of our knowledge, the role of the southeast in a commercial network must remain hypothesis.[9]

Field forms and consolidation

Toponymy has also advanced our understanding of field forms and the situation of the farmers. The terms used for farmland in early medieval Flanders were *accra* or *akker* (field) or *terra arabilis* (arable land). The *akkers* were nuclei, often with a central field and several subsidiary ones, that gradually grew together as clearances progressed. Each *akker* had a name, and the chief field of the hamlet sometimes became

9. For these extremely important points, see F.L. Ganshof, 'Le Domaine Gantois de l'abbaye de Saint-Pierre-au-Mont-Blandin à l'époque carolingienne', *RBPH* **26** (1948): 1038–9; Verhulst, *Précis*, 34–5.

joined to the original name of the place, most often an *inga* or *hem* compound with the name of the village lord. Many of the smaller fields also had the name of a person, probably the individual who had cleared them. Thus the village lord tended to dominate except on the periphery, where small strips held by independent proprietors continued to exist.[10]

By the eighth and ninth centuries virtually all settlements in the interior had a *dries* (common grazing area), but this was later eliminated in areas of intensive agriculture. The original division of the fields may have been into strips, but from the ninth century they were absorbed into compact blocks. Strips persisted only on the outskirts of the hamlets. The shift from strips to larger parcels may show a loss of standing for small free farmers in the eighth and ninth centuries. As population grew, the smaller *akkers* were absorbed by the larger ones and lost their names and individuality. The same thing happened to many primary settlements with compound names of *inga* and a field designation. But the borders of the *akkers* were preserved in a 'closed' landscape pattern, with fields demarcated by hedges, stones or trees that persisted into the modern period, particularly between the Leie and Scheldt. *Akker* may be a transliteration of the Latin *ager* (field), and if so it is still another suggestion of considerable Roman persistence in the Leie valley.[11]

Although *akker* continued to be used in the central Middle Ages in western Flanders, the larger and more centralized village fields thus created were being called *culturae* in the Latin sources by the ninth century. These fields, which were open and unenclosed, are found most often on higher sand areas that were drained naturally and along the Leie and its tributaries. By the time of the great clearances of the twelfth century, *cultura* was being transliterated into Netherlandish as *kouter* in southern and interior Flanders, especially between the Scheldt and Leie; but the name change followed the consolidation of fields by about a century. This expansion in effect created the open-field, nucleated village in densely populated southeastern Flanders. It was accompanied by the spread of three-field agriculture, which had been known earlier in the adjacent regions of northern France, then spread into Flanders, and eventually French terminology was borrowed to

---

10. Verhulst, *Précis*, 24–7.

11. Erik Thoen, 'Een Model voor integratie van historische geografie en ekonomische strukturen in Binnen-Vlaanderen: De Historische evolutie van het landschap in de Leiestreek tussen Kortrijk en Gent tijdens de middeleeuwen', *Heemkring Scheldeveld, Jaarboek* **19** (1990): 10–12.

describe it. The same village might thus have both open fields (the central *kouter*) and smaller enclosed *akkers*.

By the twelfth century the south and east thus had triennial rotation, while two-field agriculture was more usual in northern and western Flanders. Either one village would have three *kouters* or a single *kouter* would have three subdivisions called *slagen*. These older territories were subject to compulsory labour services as rent and to a common agricultural routine that was mandatory for all villagers, in contrast to lands that were cleared later and were not subject to these constraints.[12]

The merging of fields and the establishment of great estates, evidently by using slave labour, were part of a process by which the territorial lords consolidated their power locally as Flanders was being melded into a political unit. The growth of great estates in the late Merovingian and Carolingian periods is explained in part by population growth and clearance, but another element was village lords getting control of scattered lands, whether through gift or purchase, and integrating them into units of exploitation. Some also forced independent farmers to acknowledge their authority, usually by giving them some additional land as an inducement. This change, however, affected only the south between the Scheldt and Dender and farther west between Courtrai and Ypres. In other regions, notably most of northern interior Flanders, the small proprietor held out better.[13]

The 'classic domanial regime' of reserve, tenures and pasture is thus found only in southern and eastern Flanders, and it was not generalized even there. Elsewhere, particularly in the coastal areas, the fields were smaller and the domains bipartite rather than tripartite. There is scarcely any evidence of peasant labour services on the reserve as rent in northern Flanders. In maritime Flanders, which was unsuitable for agriculture until the late tenth century, even the bipartite domains are lacking. Smaller exploitations were developed, some of them from subdivisions of larger estates.

In most parts of Flanders, the count's domains were extensive by the tenth century and probably earlier, and the populations living on them were free. In the south and east, particularly around Aalst, private lordships of nobles and churches are more common. Clearly, there were great changes in Flanders even before the onset of

12. Pounds, *Historical Geography*, 202; Erik Thoen, 'Historische evolutie', 16–19; Verhulst and Blok, 'Landschap en bewoning', 116–19, 156–60; Erik Thoen, 'Kaartblad Oosterzele', 9–12.
13. Verhulst, *Précis*, 31–2.

commercial change and a more structured political organization beginning in the eighth century.

TRADE AND TOWNS

Although the urban life and commercial economy of Flanders grew more rapidly later, important antecedents can be traced to the period before the first counts. Sheep had been raised for their wool in Flanders during the Roman period, and Flemish cloth was exported to distant regions of the empire. The relationship of Frisian trade to the commercial development of Flanders in the early Middle Ages is a thorny problem. Merovingian Frisia, an ill-defined region of the Netherlands north of the Lek, produced textiles that were sold in England and at the Frankish royal court, but Flanders' later domination of the export woollen market led Pirenne to assume that the cloth marketed by the Frisians must actually have been made in Flanders. Recent archaeological excavations at Hamwih/Southampton give some support to this view, but the Frisians were also exporting textiles made elsewhere. The Frisians are also known to have used the Scheldt ports, particularly Ghent and Cambrai, for their trade in slaves.

Early medieval Flemish commerce seems to have fallen between two major networks. North of Flanders, Dorestad served trans-Channel trade and provisioned the Frankish royal court at Aachen. On the south, Quentovic on the Canche linked the Seine river trade with England. The Scandinavian attacks destroyed both emporia, but Dorestad had passed its peak before the Viking attacks became serious. Its earlier growth evidently contributed to the commercial flowering of the Meuse towns in the seventh and early eighth centuries. They declined from the mid ninth century, just as the Scheldt centres were beginning to grow significantly.[14] Thus Flanders, far from being a successor of Frisian trade, played a very minor role in it and owed its later

14. Verhulst, 'La Vie urbaine dans les anciens Pays-Bas avant l'an mil', *MA*, 1986: 189, 192, 194.

commercial prominence to circumstances that developed after Frisian commerce had passed its peak. With the decline of the Carolingian monarchy, the rise of new territorial principalities diffused not only political authority but also markets.[15]

We must examine the physical origins of the Flemish towns and the beginning of their specifically urban functions of trade and industry. Flanders had no Roman *civitates*, which elsewhere frequently became the nuclei of cities. Furthermore, while a dual nucleus around a church and a commercial settlement was a common form of urbanization elsewhere, Arras and to some extent Ghent are the only Flemish examples. The major Flemish towns, including Ghent, developed around comital castles, and the others had a single nucleus. This is especially pronounced with places that developed around the circular forts erected by the counts in the late ninth and early tenth centuries.[16]

References to commercial *portus* (ports) and *emporia* (markets) multiply from the end of the eighth century and throughout the ninth more rapidly in the Low Countries than in any other region of Europe. Some were inside or just outside the walls of a prince's castle or a Roman ruin, but others were free standing. Tournai had a *portus* inside the Roman wall, while one is mentioned in 865 at Ghent, at which wool was being traded with Tournai by the end of the tenth century. A 'port of the IJzer', probably Veurne, is mentioned in 861, then disappears. Veurne's circular wall may have hindered its growth, since only in the eleventh century did urban development resume

15. On the question of Frisia and its relation to Flanders, see Lebecq, 'Dans l'Europe du nord', 361–77; Richard Hodges, *Dark Age Economics* (Ithaca, NY, 1982); Richard Hodges and David Whitehouse, *Mohammed, Charlemagne, and the Origins of Europe: Archaeology and the Pirenne Thesis* (Ithaca, NY, 1983), 93, 95, 115–18, 163; Michel Fixot, 'Une Image idéale, une réalité difficile: les villes du VIIe au IXe siècle' in G. Duby (ed.), *Histoire de la France urbaine*, 1: 525–27; A. Verhulst, 'Der frühmittelalterliche Handel der Niederlande und der Friesenhandel', in *Untersuchungen zu Handel und Verkehr der vor- und frühgeschichtlichen Zeit in Mittel- und Nordeuropa*, 3: *Der Handel des frühen Mittelalters* (Göttingen, 1985): 381–91; Jan Dhondt, 'L'Essor urbain entre Meuse et Mer du Nord à l'époque mérovingienne', *Studi in onore di Armando Sapori*, 1 (Milan, 1957): 55–78; Dhondt, 'Steden in het landschap en stedelijk landschap', *Flandria Nostra* **1**: 55–85; and the summary discussion by D. Nicholas, 'Of Poverty and Primacy: Demand, Liquidity, and the Flemish Economic Miracle, 1050–1200', *AHR*. **96** (1991): 23–4.

16. Verhulst, 'Aspect of Continuity', 191–2; Verhulst, 'Zur Entstehung der Städte in Nordwest-Europa' in *Forschungen zur Stadtgeschichte. Drei Vorträge. Gerda Henkel Vorlesung* (NP, 1986), 30, 46; A. Chédeville, 'De la Cité à la ville' in Duby, *Histoire de la France urbaine*, 2: 81.

there with the establishment of a merchant settlement outside the wall.[17]

Despite the great rivers and the high water table that facilitated canal construction, however, overland routes were extremely important in the development of all Flemish towns. Aalst, for example, developed at a crossing of the main road from Brussels with the main route along the Dender north from Hainault. Dendermonde, at the mouth of the Dender at its confluence with the Scheldt, was at the crossing of the Mechelen road and the river. Both roads led to Ghent and Bruges. Even Bruges, which later would live by seaborne trade, developed first on the land route leading to Ypres.[18]

While no conclusive evidence has been presented that the former Roman settlements in Flanders were inhabited continuously across the Germanic invasions, Ghent and Courtrai were capitals of *pagi* that bore the chief town's name. The *pagus Flandrensis* that would give its name to the entire county took its name from a geographical area rather than its administrative centre, which had probably been Bruges. The recollection that the Romans had used these places as seats of government doubtless contributed to their growth but cannot explain it completely. Towns do not originate as entities apart from an agricultural environment; yet early medieval Flanders was poor except between the Scheldt and Leie, and the great reclamation works in Flanders postdate the basic urban configuration of the county except for Ypres and Lille.

The functional origins of the Flemish cities thus must be sought in conditions in the countryside. Germanic primary settlement centred on two areas: small coastal enclaves, principally around Bruges, and the Dender, Scheldt and Leie valleys. The area between them was colonized only in the eleventh century. The western coast was sandy and covered with heath in the early Middle Ages, and the inhabitants raised animals. A similar soil type is found north of Ghent, and this area also was pastoral even in the late Middle Ages. East of the Scheldt–Leie area there were three nuclei of settlement, around Aalst, Ninove and Geraardsbergen, all of which became important secondary centres. Despite the river junction, there was little settlement in the area of Dendermonde, probably because the sandy coastal plain bends

17. A. Verhulst and R. de Blok-Doehaerd, 'Nijverheid en handel', *AGN* 1: 211.

18. J.A. van Houtte, *An Economic History of the Low Countries 800–1800* (New York, 1977), 25; D. Nicholas, 'Medieval Urban Origins in Northern Continental Europe: State of Research and some Tentative Conclusions', *Studies in Medieval and Renaissance History* 6 (1969): 96.

abruptly south at Ghent to include much of the territory between the Leie and Scheldt near Ghent but then follows the Scheldt farther east. The most important areas were along rivers that were important for grain production and transport. The pattern is clear: large towns developed a) at the junction of fertile farmland with the less productive sandy coastal plain, and b) downstream from the grain supply. Dendermonde, however, failed to develop into a major centre, although it was always important as a satellite, because Ghent developed first and controlled downstream traffic on the Scheldt.[19]

The origins of Ghent have been the most completely examined of the Flemish cities.[20] The ruined Roman fortification at the *vicus* of Ganda, on the left bank of the Scheldt, continued to be used at least into the ninth century. Ganda was the site of the abbey of St Bavo and of the *municipium* of Ghent mentioned in the eighth century. A Roman secondary road reached the right bank of the Scheldt directly across from Ganda. The first settlement in the city proper was along the left bank of the Scheldt near the seventh-century cell of St Bavo that was the origin of the church of St John. This was the site of the merchant *portus* mentioned in 865. This area was included in a *vicus* that had at least three quais surrounded by a semicircular moat. Ghent's shipyard was important enough by 811 to attract a visit from Charlemagne. Ghent thus grew around several shrines near the intersection of the main land route between Bruges and Cologne (the later Brabantdam) with the Scheldt. This settlement was destroyed during the Scandinavian attacks of the 870s and 880s.

At the latest by 939, a Flemish count, probably Arnulf the Great, built a wooden rectangular fortification on an island in the Leie, which by then was linked to the Scheldt by the Ketelgracht canal. This fortress, which was later called the Oudburg, had an area of about 4

19. D. Nicholas, 'Structures du peuplement, fonctions urbaines et formation du capital dans la Flandre médiévale', *AESC* **33** (1978): 502–7.

20. For early Ghent, the classic work of Hans van Werveke, *Kritische Studiën betreffende de oudste geschiedenis van de stad Gent* (Antwerp, 1933) can still be used with profit. The basic studies of the early development of Ghent are now, however, the monumental works of Adriaan Verhulst. Readers should begin with his 'Die Frühgeschichte der Stadt Gent' in *Die Stadt in der europäischen Geschichte: Festschrift Edith Ennen* (Bonn, 1972), 108–137, then proceed to his more specialized studies: 'The Origins of Towns in the Low Countries and the Pirenne Thesis', *Past and Present* **122** (1989): 3–35; 'Saint Bavon et les origines de Gand', *RN* **68** (1986): 455–70; and 'Early Medieval Ghent' in *Defence of a Rebellious City*, ed. Johan Decavele (Antwerp, 1989), 49. Verhulst's analytical framework should be supplemented by Nicholas, 'Structures du peuplement', 510–14, in which the origin of Ghent as a rural market on the edge of the densely populated area between Leie and Scheldt is explored.

hectares and contained an agricultural settlement and a population of leather workers. This suggests that at this time the economy of Ghent was directed towards pastoral northern Flanders. But while the castle was the single fortification at Ghent still in use after the Vikings, there were now two *portus*. The earlier one on the Scheldt had been re-populated, while a second one existed by 941 on both sides of the Leie outside the castle. The inhabitants of the Oudburg would have traded at the *portus* on the Leie, and it thus seems that it originated in local trade, while the earlier one on the Scheldt handled long-distance trade.[21]

The three food markets (Grain, Friday and Fish) eventually became centres of banking as well as of most non-textile merchandising in Ghent. They were just outside the walls of the fortification, suggesting that the main business of the city was in provisioning the suburbs with grain and other necessities and only secondarily provisioning the castle. The port of Ghent was on the Leie, where settlement was denser than along the Scheldt, backing upstream away from the castle; for with Tournai and Cambrai farther downstream on the Scheldt, the grain was pre-empted there, while there were no large towns upstream from Ghent on the Leie. By the mid tenth century the two *portus* were linked by the Hoogpoort street, which became a nucleus around which settlement would develop.

Ghent thus originated as a trading centre. The earliest references to cloth making there are from the late tenth century, evidently in the Hoogpoort. By that time, Tournai was supplying Ghent with wool. But the textile quarters of Ghent would develop mainly in the subur-ban areas, not in the sections of the town that were being settled between the eighth and tenth centuries. The Scheldt area was not thickly settled until the twelfth century, and parts of it were annexed only in the thirteenth. Clearly, the cloth workers came after the traders. The greatest industrial centre of medieval Flanders originated

21. On this point, see Nicholas, 'Structures du peuplement', 512; H. van Werveke and A. Verhulst, 'Castrum en Oudburg te Gent', *HMGOG* **14** (1960): 56–7. Leather workers also lived in the fortification at Bruges. At both Bruges and Ghent, the term *Oudburg* was used for the settlement that developed adjacent to the fortress. A. Ver-hulst, 'L'Historiographie concernant l'origine des villes dans les anciens Pays-Bas depuis la mort de Henri Pirenne (1935)', *Cahiers de Clio* **86** (1986): 112; Verhulst, 'Origins of Towns', 26.

as a grain market. We shall see that it was reverting to this situation at the end of the Middle Ages.[22]

During the tenth century Ghent continued to grow, mainly at the expense of the two great abbeys. The term *portus* would refer by 1000 to the entire settlement entailed by the linkage of the two original *portus*. Our discussion of early agriculture on the estates of St Pieter has shown small parcels of land in the later city even in the ninth century and a suggestion of merchandising. A text of 949 shows a regular division of portions of this area into tenancies. The oldest fair of the medieval Low Countries developed in St Bavo's abbey village, perhaps by the ninth century.[23]

The early history of Bruges confirms the patterns observed at Ghent. Bruges shows little before the twelfth century to suggest its later greatness. The frequent alterations in the hydrography of Bruges have made reconstructions of how and when its internal waterways and harbours developed very difficult. The high water level between the fourth and eighth centuries linked Bruges to the sea on the north by a deep creek and on the west by a bay. Thereafter, except briefly in the eleventh century, Bruges was inland and was joined to the coast by canals, most importantly the Zwin and Old Zwin.[24]

Like Ghent, Bruges originated around a Roman ruin, the seat of the *municipium Flandrense*. Government thus preceded commerce at what would be medieval Flanders' chief port. Its name, attested in the ninth century, is from the Old Norse *bryggia* (landing bridge or quay),

22. For the concentration of markets and wealth along the Leie, see D. Nicholas, *The Metamorphosis of a Medieval City: Ghent in the Age of the Arteveldes* (Lincoln, Nebr., 1987), 67–119. In view of this, I cannot accept Professor Verhulst's arguments that the settlement along the Scheldt was more important, even though he is undoubtedly correct that the centres of Roman and medieval government were there. Verhulst, 'Probleme der Stadtkernforschung in einigen flämischen Städten des Früh- und Hochmittelalters' in Helmut Jager (ed.), *Stadtkernforschung* (Cologne and Vienna, 1987), 281–86.

23. A. Verhulst, 'Leie en Schelde als grens in het portus te Gent tijdens de Xde eeuw', *Naamkunde* **17** (1985): 413–17; Verhulst, 'De Heilige Bavo en de oorsprong van Gent', *MKVA*, Kl. Letteren, 47 (Brussels, 1985), 75–90; Verhulst, 'Kritische studie over de oorkonde van Lodewijk IV van Overzee, koning van Frankrijk, voor de Sint-Pietersabdij te Gent (20 augustus 950)', *BCRH* **150** (1984): 274–327.

24. Marc Ryckaert, 'De Brugse havens in de middeleeuwen', *ASEB* **109** (1972): 5–27, especially 9, with summaries of the voluminous literature. See also J. Noterdaeme, 'De Vroegste geschiedenis van Brugge, 3: De Burcht van Brugge', *ASEB* **112** (1975): 171–204, especially 190, 195; Noterdaeme, 'De Vroegste geschiedenis van Brugge, 6: Een ander "Oudburg" te Brugge', *ASEB* **114** (1977): 211–338, especially 233–4; Noterdaeme, 'De Vroegste geschiedenis van Brugge, 1: S. Salvatorskerk. II: O.L. Vrouwekerk,' *ASEB* **112** (1975): 5–59, especially 19–20.

but the explanation of the name may not be trade; for the nearby abbey of Torhout, where the counts would establish a fair in the eleventh century, was a centre for missions sent to Scandinavia from 829.

As at Ghent, churches were nuclei of civilian settlement at Bruges. Its oldest parish church, St Salvator, was founded on the Frankish royal domain and came to Baldwin I by his marriage to Judith. Baldwin himself founded the Church of Our Lady nearby. The Bruges churches were built on the outskirts of parishes, not at their centres, and this suggests that substantial agrarian settlements were already present when they were established. Both churches were about 400 metres southwest of the counts' castle, which was established before 892 near the church of St Donatian, on the site of the present city hall. The remains of St Donatian go back to about 861. It was outside the late medieval centre of the city, which developed around a merchant settlement that postdated the churches, north of the market and the fortress. The suburban area between the churches was residential. It was southwest of the count's castle and outside it. This area was later known as the *Oudeburg* quarter, which suggests that its origin was similar to that of the Ghent *Oudburg*.[25] The chief public buildings of Bruges, including the cloth hall and wool house, were eventually constructed in the *Oudeburg*. But while the *Oudburg* at Ghent remained tied closely to the count's castle, at Bruges it was transformed into an autonomous merchant settlement and had a wall distinct from that of the comital fortress.

The volume of trade along the Scheldt was greater than along the coast in the tenth century, perhaps because the interior was better protected, perhaps because the coast was too marshy for harbours. Before the eleventh century, the modest foreign trade of western Flanders was probably concentrated on the 'port of the Ijzer'. The two major roads from Bruges, leading to Ghent and Courtrai, leave from the *Oudeburg*. The marketplace was near the linkage of the *Oudeburg* and the castle. Bruges thus seems like Ghent to have originated in local trade, but it remained confined to it longer, for its links to the

---

25. The word 'burg' has given rise to some confusion. It resulted from a conflation of the late Latin *burgus* (small fortification), with the Germanic *bur* (an unfortified community of peasants or merchants). The early medieval *burgus* was generally an unfortified settlement with a market outside a fortification that preceded it. See Walter Schlesinger, 'Burg und Stadt', in *Aus Verfassungs- und Landesgeschichte: Festschrift zum 70. Geburtstag von Theodor Mayer* (Lindau and Constance, 1955), 2: 97–150; for Flanders, see Hans van Werveke, *'Burgus': Versterking of Nederzetting?* (Brussels, 1965).

sea were severed by the retreat of the waters. A *vicus* is mentioned at Bruges around 900, perhaps in reference to the *Oudeburg* settlement, but Bruges did not have a *portus* until the early eleventh century, when the comital castle was rebuilt and a sea link was re-established north of the city. The medieval city developed between the fortress and this new harbour. The *Encomium of Queen Emma* describes the arrival of the Norman-born English queen dowager in exile at Bruges in 1037 in glowing terms, showing that the city was a port that was accessible to warships but also used other communities as outports. It was considered something of a frontier place by foreigners.

> And so, having enjoyed favourable winds, they crossed the sea and touched at a certain port [probably Oudenburg] not far from the town of Bruges. The latter town is inhabited by Flemish settlers, and enjoys very great fame for the number of its merchants and for its affluence in all things upon which mankind places the greatest value. Here indeed she was, as she deserved, honourably received by Baldwin, the marquis of that same province, who was the son of a great and totally unconquered prince, and by his wife Athala (a name meaning 'most noble'), daughter of Robert, king of the French, and Queen Constance. By them, furthermore, a house in the above-named town, suitable for royal outlay, was allotted to the queen, and in addition a kind offer of entertainment was made . . . [She was followed by her son Harthacnut] Thereupon, the wrath of the sea having subsided, and the storm having dropped, he spread his bellying sails to the favourable winds; and thus, having enjoyed a successful voyage, he touched at Bruges. Here, having moored his ship with anchors and rods, and having commissioned sailors to look after them, he betook himself directly with chosen companions to the lodging of his mother.[26]

Bruges thus was transformed into the only Flemish city that was clearly oriented towards the sea and long-distance trade, although initially settlement had backed down an artery that was better suited to local than to long-distance trade.[27]

The counts of Flanders had less power in the south than around Bruges and Ghent, but their situation in the Saint-Omer area was based on a substantial domain. Yet, while natural advantages of site favoured the growth of Bruges and Ghent, Saint-Omer developed in

26. Alistair Campbell (ed. and trans.), *Encomium Emmae Reginae*, Camden Society, Third Series, 72, Royal Historical Society (London, 1949), 47–51.

27. Verhulst and Blok, 'Handel en Nijverheid', 209; Verhulst, 'Probleme der Stadt-kernforschung,' 291–3; Verhulst, 'Origins of Towns', 30; Verhulst, 'Aspect of Continuity', 193–4; Verhulst, 'Vie urbaine', 204–8.

the least promising physical location of any Flemish city, on a butte surrounded on three sides by marshes; the only access by firm land was from the southwest. Until the late ninth century, the abbey of St Bertin was the only settlement there.

But the marshes of Saint-Omer were also a defence; the town needed to be fortified strongly only on one side. Baldwin II was able to take refuge from the Northmen at Saint-Omer because they could not pursue him. The area was infertile, but Saint-Omer developed at a contact point between the trade of Flanders and Artois, for the land route linking Arras and Calais crossed the south and western marshes. The Aa, leading to the coast, was the only river, following the course of the present canal. The major streets led from the top of the butte, where the market for Artois grain was, to the gates. Saint-Omer's first trade was probably to the grain-poor north, based on the surplus produce that the abbey took as rent from its tenants. The Flemish counts attached considerable political importance to St Bertin, which became a power base from which they tried to conquer areas farther south. With the decline of Thérouanne, Saint-Omer's market, at the gate of the castle that the counts erected, became the only significant emporium in the region. Saint-Omer's wall, built around 1000, was the earliest of any Flemish town except for castle complexes.[28]

Although the Flemish towns were clearly growing in the late ninth and tenth centuries, most of their trade was internal, concentrated on agricultural goods and low-grade cloth, and was handled by barter or in foreign coin. Flanders does not have native supplies of precious metals. It was still less developed commercially than the northern Netherlands and less developed industrially than the Meuse valley. Coin evidence suggests a commercial shift towards the Scheldt during the Scandinavian invasions, and Flemish mints were back in operation soon after 883. Still, their circulation was mainly local. Although much has been made of the presence of coins of the late tenth- and early eleventh-century Flemish counts in Baltic hoards, they comprise only 1 per cent of the total. England had far more mints than Flanders, and English coins in Swedish hoards outnumber Flemish by 80 to 1.[29]

Similarly, although cloth continued to be made in Flanders, there is little evidence to support the idea that the Flemish cities had strong

28. Alain Derville (ed.), *Histoire de Saint-Omer* (Lille, 1981), 11–30.

29. D.M. Metcalf, 'Coinage and the Rise of the Flemish towns' in N.J. Mayhew (ed.), *Coinage in the Low Countries (880–1500): The Third Oxford Symposium on Coinage and Monetary History*, British Archaeological Reports, International Series 54 (Oxford, 1979), 2–10.

industrial components before the mid eleventh century. Most industry was in the rural areas in the early Middle Ages. The 'old *Burg*' settlements in both Ghent and Bruges had leather workers, but they precede the earliest references to cloth workers by about a century. On St Bertin's domains in southwestern Flanders and Picardy, both free and unfree women owed flax payments to the abbey. Flax and manufactured shirts were owed from the manses of St Pieter at the beginning of the ninth century, and St Bavo around 800 got cloaks from its vassals in Zeeland. Most cloth made for sale was of linen, the textile of preference, since wool was still considered too coarse for fine fabrics.[30] Flanders was thus beginning to develop an important commerce in the early tenth century, and its cities, particularly Ghent, were growing rapidly, but its industrial greatness was still very much in the future.

30. Verhulst and Blok, 'Nijverheid en handel', 183–4.

CHAPTER THREE
The Counts and the County, 918–1071

ARNULF THE GREAT (918–65)

Baldwin II's domains were divided between his two sons. The older, Arnulf, got Flanders proper, while Adalolf got Boulogne, the lay abbacy of St Bertin and other territories in the southwest.[1]

Arnulf I 'the Great' was responsible for a tremendous expansion of Flemish territory southward. Between his inheritance from his father and his own acquisitions, Arnulf eventually had a territory three or four times the size of the *pagus Flandrensis*. While Baldwin II's major opponents in southward expansion had been the Frankish kings, Arnulf's were other territorial princes of northern France.

Baldwin II's state lacked natural frontiers. Arnulf I encountered little resistance in Ostrevant, which gave him the junction of the Scarpe with the Scheldt. To control Artois he needed Montreuil-sur-Mer, the capital of Ponthieu, which controlled the Canche, the natural frontier of Flanders on the southwest. But the Normans wanted Montreuil for the same reason Flanders did, and Arnulf's expansion southward thus placed him on a collision course with the Scandinavians who were consolidating their power in what became Normandy. The chronicler Flodoard of Reims, the source of much of our information about Arnulf's reign, attributes much of this to ethnic hostility, for he sees the

---

1. The most convenient sources for the reign of Arnulf I are Rosamond McKitterick, *The Frankish Kingdoms under the Carolingians, 751–987* (London, 1983), 249–54, and Koch, 'Graafschap Vlaanderen', 354–5, 365–9.

Flemings as Franks and the Normans as Danes. The Carolingian king was Arnulf's natural ally, and in 925 Arnulf and Adalolf thus joined King Raoul's expedition against the Normans. The Flemings took Eu and massacred its garrison, but the French then had to call off their part of the invasion. The Normans turned their full attention to the Flemings but were beaten badly in 926.[2]

Arnulf's great rival was thus William Longsword of Normandy, with whom he disputed Montreuil and Ponthieu. In 932 he seized the abbey of St Vaast and soon afterwards took Douai, the chief place of Ostrevant. When his brother Adalolf died in 933, Arnulf seized the Boulonnais and Ternois, thus disinheriting his nephews, who would eventually become counts of Boulogne and Saint-Pol. This acquisition, however, gave him a border with Heribert II of Vermandois. In 934, to secure his southern frontier while he fought the Normans for Ponthieu and Montreuil, Arnulf took Heribert's daughter Adela as his second wife.

William Longsword opened hostilities and invaded Flanders; Arnulf and King Louis IV, who had used Flemish ports to return to the continent in 936 from an exile in England, invaded Normandy, and Arnulf seized Montreuil. Herluin, count of Ponthieu, got Norman aid and retook Montreuil. In 942 Arnulf tricked William into an ambush at a peace conference and had him murdered. William left a young son, and Louis IV became his guardian. When Heribert II died the next year (943), his territory was divided between Odo 'duke of France' and Arnulf. The Normans refused to accept this arrangement and for the rest of the decade fought the Flemings and the king for Montreuil, but Arnulf's possession seemed secure after 949. Despite occasional diplomatic marriages, the rivalry with Normandy would dominate Flemish foreign policy for the next century.[3]

Arnulf I was the first of his dynasty distinguished for patronage of the church, which had suffered in the Scandinavian attacks. In 937 the relics of St Bavo, which had been taken to France for safety from the Vikings, were returned to the abbey. King Odo had made his brother

2. While there may be an element of truth in the notion of ethnic hostility, it is absurd to carry it to the extent of Eleanor Searle who, evidently on grounds of Arnulf's seizure of Eu, portrays the Flemings as brutal Franks who subjugated and reduced to slavery the peaceful Normans who settled among them. Count Arnulf becomes 'the Flemish–Frankish ruler over subjects who were the abject descendants of free northern sailors'. Eleanor Searle, *Predatory Kinship and the Creation of Norman Power, 840–1066* (Berkeley, 1988), 50–1, 82. In fact, the Scandinavians did not settle in Flanders except in the Guines area, southeast of Boulogne, in the tenth century. Dhondt, *Origines*, 14.

3. Dhondt, *Origines*, 40–5; Searle, *Predatory Kinship*, 151.

Robert lay abbot of St Pieter's of Ghent, and the need to assert his control over this important abbey, which was the comital mausoleum, may explain some of Arnulf's reformist impulses. In 941 Arnulf made the noted reformer Gerard of Brogne abbot and restored some of the abbey's possessions that his father had taken as lay abbot. There was opposition, for Arnulf's introduction of the Benedictine rule to St Pieter's transformed a chapter of canons into a monastery, and most left rather than submit to the rule. St Bavo's also was reformed about this time, but Arnulf seems to have taken lands from most abbeys except St Pieter to give to his vassals. Arnulf soon spread the Benedictine rule to the other great abbeys in his domains, most of them in the French south, in the face of continued resistance by the canons and neighbouring populations. Gerard of Brogne claimed the right to choose abbots. Arnulf sheltered English exiles, including St Dunstan, who took refuge at St Pieter's in 956 and became acquainted with Gerard of Brogne's monastic reforms, which he later introduced into England.[4]

Arnulf I is now called 'Arnulf the Great', but his prestige and advanced age – he was about eighty when he died – caused contemporaries to call him variously 'Arnulf the Rich', 'Arnulf the Old' and eventually 'Arnulf the Lame'. After the conquest of Montreuil, he enjoyed peace until 961 except for minor troubles. Arnulf impressed his contemporaries primarily as a conqueror, but he was also one of the richest princes of the region. Arnulf I became ill around 930 in St Pieter's abbey and feared death, A text inserted around 1036 in the *Liber Traditionum* of the abbey, but which has reference to material contained in the unquestionably genuine donation of 941 that we have noted above, claims that he made an important concession to Gerard of Brogne in return for his cure:

. . . Regarding the possessions that God has given me in gold, silver, clothing, horses, mules, cattle, food, grain, cheese, and all that appears to be of my power, be it known to my faithful men that if I should die suddenly and be unable to distribute them according to my will, my wife and children should have half, while the other half should be given for the redemption of my soul by the holy monasteries to the churches that are on my land for buildings, pilgrims, the sick, widows, orphans and the poor.

And know also, my faithful men, that I give to the abbey of St Pieter, on

4. On the church reforms, see Dhondt, *Origines*, 47–8; McKitterick, *Frankish Kingdoms*, 249–54; Koch, 'Graafschap Vlaanderen', 366.

the place called Blandinium, where my father and mother lie buried, land where one hundred sheep can be pastured, located in the estate of Maldegem, and whatever income is owed from them each year.

I also pray in the love of almighty God and his saints that you, my faithful men, in the fidelity that you have rendered to me, give two-thirds of the money that I gave by the hand of the monk Gerard to almighty God to the aforesaid shrine of St Pieter, where St Amalberga, the virgin of Christ, lies, and one-third to thirty monasteries that I have named to the aforesaid Gerard, so that none of my kinsmen nor my wife presume to do anything with this treasury, given to me by the Redeemer, unless I myself order it. And if anyone presumes to do anything [against this], let him incur the wrath of almighty God and feel to all eternity the anger of all the saints and of St Pieter, the keeper of the keys of heaven. The aforesaid monk Gerard and my treasurers know where this bequest is kept under seal.[5]

This text shows not only Arnulf's considerable wealth, but also that large herds of sheep were being raised near Ghent. The advocacy of numerous monasteries was a critical aspect of the count's power. He had a well organized council of retainers that could be used to counter usurpations by the count's own relatives. Arnulf had treasurers and a treasury that did not follow him about and was moved under his seal.

But Arnulf's last years were clouded by his efforts to provide for the succession. He evidently gave administration of the south to his son Baldwin III, who predeceased Arnulf in 962 leaving a young son, the future Arnulf II. The situation was complicated by the hostility of another Arnulf, the older son of the count's brother Adalolf. Arnulf I turned to the Carolingian king Lothair IV, who made peace by awarding Boulogne and the Ternois to Arnulf son of Adalolf. At the beginning of the eleventh century, the northern part of the Ternois (the Aire and Saint-Omer areas) became part of Flanders, while the rest became the county of Saint-Pol. Before 988, the independent county of Guines also broke off from the Boulonnais. By 1065 a county of Hesdin had been detached from Saint-Pol, but it included parts of former Ponthieu and the Amiénois. All of these were held in fief of the counts of Flanders except Saint-Pol, which was held of Boulogne and thus was a rear fief of Flanders. Lothair agreed to protect young Arnulf's succession in his ancestral lands, but Arnulf I had to surrender his conquests to the king, notably

---

5. This text is mentioned by Dunbabin, *France*, 49–50. I have translated the document from the edition of A.C.F. Koch, 'Gérard de Brogne et la maladie du comte Arnoul Ier de Flandre', *Revue Benedictine* **70** (1960): 126.

Artois, Ostrevant, Ponthieu and Amiens.[6]

Flanders was seen increasingly as a coherent unit. No charters survive from Baldwin II's reign, so we do not know what title he used, but the Lotharingian chronicler Regino of Prüm described him as leader of a *ducatus* (duchy). Folcuin of St Bertin called Flanders a 'march' and called both Baldwin II and Arnulf I marquis, the term used for them in contemporary royal acts. The king called Arnulf I, but not Baldwin II, 'count and marquis'. Marquis by this time had lost its connotation of frontier lordship and was simply a personal distinction given to powerful persons as a sign of royal favour. By 941 Arnulf I was styling himself 'marquis by the aid of God's mercy', suggesting that his title was not owed to the king. The succession settlement of 962 is notable in giving Arnulf I the title 'prince' (*princeps*), which had previously been held by Count Hugh the Great. All feudal bonds in Flanders went through the prince, including counties such as Boulogne that were or would be formed within Flanders.[7]

ARNULF II (965–88)

Arnulf was succeeded by his four-year-old grandson Arnulf II, who began to govern on his own only in 976.[8] Arnulf II was not a mean figure, but his extreme youth meant that the counts' power underwent a severe crisis during his reign. The barons rebelled, and the count and the churches were the chief losers. The nucleus of many noble patrimonies was probably established in these years as potentates built castles, particularly in southern Flanders. Some nobles assumed the regalian rights that had previously been the counts' monopoly to raise troops, hold courts, exercise *bannum* and name officials. Arnulf I had left Baldwin Baldzo, son of his brother Adalolf, as guardian of Arnulf II subject to the king, and Baldwin made himself count of Courtrai. The child-count's maternal uncle, Thierry of West Frisia, took Ghent and Waas. King Lothair, acting under the terms of 962, entered Flanders as the young count's protector and occupied the southeast. He

6. Dunbabin, *France*, 73; Ganshof, 'La Flandre', 348.

7. Dunbabin, *France*, 48, 73; McKitterick, *Frankish Kingdoms*, 249–54; Gysseling and Koch, *Diplomata Belgica*, 144.

8. For the reign of Arnulf II, see Koch, 'Graafschap Vlaanderen', 370–2; Dhondt, *Origines*, 51–3.

got most Flemish nobles to submit but was not able to eliminate the counts of Courtrai, Ghent and Waas.

After the crisis of 965 the opposition to Arnulf II within Flanders died down. However, the emperor Otto II (973–83) began taking an active interest in Flanders. The early tenth-century border was the Scheldt, which caused a complication; for Ghent, the largest town of Flanders, was west of the Scheldt, but its abbey village of St Bavo was east of the river and thus in the empire. Furthermore, the Scheldt had been diverted from an initial location east of its present bed so that it would come to the very edge of the central city. Otto II evidently had a canal dug from Ghent to the western Scheldt. Later called the Ottogracht, it became the border between 'royal' and 'imperial' Flanders. Otto thus claimed not only St Bavo's abbey, but also the Land of Waas in the northeast.[9]

To counter a perceived threat of invasion due to Lothair IV's considerably increased power in Flanders, the emperor established marches on the right bank of the Scheldt, from Valenciennes in the south to Antwerp in the north, with a midpoint fortress at Ename. Otto II's efforts so occupied Arnulf II in the east that he could give little attention to western Flanders. After Baldwin Baldzo died, his territory was lost to the ruling house. By the time Arnulf died in 988 he had no effective control over the Boulonnais, Ternois, Cambrai, Ghent and Waas.[10]

Yet the Flemish counts were important figures, for they had held the balance of power between the kings of France and the dukes of Normandy and now were thought to have this role between the French and German monarchs. Finally, they had the most distinguished lineage of any non-royal house in Europe. Thus Arnulf II at his majority in 976 was able to marry Rozela, the daughter of King Berengar II of Italy. Unfortunately, he died in 988 and left his widow with a daughter Matilda and an eleven-year-old son Baldwin IV. The result was the second succession crisis within a generation.

Part of the problem was obviously that in a period when 'institutions' of government were in their infancy, rulers had to control their domains by a delicate balancing act of acquiring land and gaining the loyalty of the great nobles; but one of the ways they gained that loyalty was by giving them land. The count was the greatest allodial land-

9. Koch, 'Graafschap Vlaanderen', 365; on the canal, see K.G. van Acker, 'De "libertas castrensis operis" van Antwerpen en de Ottogracht te Gent', *HMGOG* **41** (1987): 1–9.

10. McKitterick, *Frankish Kingdoms*, 252–4.

owner in Flanders, but his possessions were concentrated in the north, in an area bordered by Bruges, Ghent, Lille and Saint-Omer. He derived most of his income from this area and exercised power directly. But he claimed power in the north outside his domains, and in the south his dynastic ambitions were more extensive still. The first two Baldwins had established the central area. But by the time Arnulf I began in earnest to expand his frontier southward, the period of unrest and migration was over and the Flemings had to move against firmly established settlements and a local nobility whom the Flemings wanted to tie to themselves through vassalage. The counts, however, lacked the manpower to rule their southern conquests, most of which involved Romance populations, on the same basis as their ancestral lands in the north, where an institutional structure would develop during the critical reign of Baldwin IV.

BALDWIN IV (988–1035)

Thus the still considerable domains of the Flemish counts were divided after Arnulf II's premature death. The growing power of the Capetian kings and the dukes of Normandy meant that there would be no more significant Flemish territorial acquisition on the southern frontier.

The reign of Baldwin IV was to be one of the most important in the history of medieval Flanders, but in the beginning his tender years left Flanders open even more than before to royal influence.[11] If Baldwin had died without heirs, Flanders would have reverted to the crown. Apparently as a reward for Flemish help in the Capetian revolution of 987, King Hugh Capet had recognized Baldwin's claim to all of Flanders, including the part taken by Lothair IV in 965. But according to a twelfth-century source, many nobles saw this as an opportunity to convert the lands that they had held in fief of Arnulf II into allods, an allegation that suggests a high degree of feudalization.[12] The situation was particularly grave in French Flanders, where in the

11. For Baldwin IV's reign, see Dhondt, *Origines*, 54–61; 'Koch, Graafschap Vlaanderen', 371–6.
12. The text in question is the *Life* of Bertulf of Renty, written by a monk of St Pieter's abbey of Ghent between 1083 and 1088. See discussion in Koch, 'Graafschap Vlaanderen', 371; and for the reliability of the source, d'Haenens, *Invasions normandes*, 242–3.

early eleventh century numerous local lords became virtually independent save in judicial matters.

In 989 King Hugh arranged the marriage of the count's mother Rozela to his son Robert, later called 'the Pious'. She then took the name Susanna, but Robert repudiated her in 991. Rozela returned to Flanders and helped her son against the nobles, but the Capetians kept Montreuil, which had been her morning gift from the Flemings. They reacted to this provocation by joining a noble rebellion against Hugh. The result was that Ponthieu stayed with the crown while Artois and Ostrevant returned to Flanders. When the separate comital dynasty in Ternois died out in the early eleventh century, Baldwin IV managed to keep northern Ternois, including Saint-Omer and Aire-sur-la-Lys, while the south eventually became the county of Saint-Pol. Except for Robert the Pious's support of the emperor Henry II's invasion of Flanders in 1020, Baldwin IV's relations with the French crown were generally peaceful after the 990s. He affianced the future Baldwin V to Robert's daughter and arranged for her to be raised in Flanders.[13]

While previous Flemish counts had concentrated on expanding their southern frontiers, Baldwin IV was the first to expand east of the Scheldt, probably to eliminate Otto II's marches. He campaigned in Lotharingia in 995 and captured the march of Valenciennes briefly in 1006. The next year the emperor Henry II recovered it by invading Flanders and seizing Ghent. Baldwin then switched to an alliance with Henry II, helping him to install a new bishop at Cambrai in 1012. In gratitude, Henry II enfeoffed him with the islands of Zeeland, then added Valenciennes in 1015. Their alliance was brief, however, and Henry II again invaded Flanders in 1020. Nothing is known of how the matter was settled, but Baldwin's initiatives eastward had led to invasions from the empire that were at least as serious as the threat from the Capetian kings and the Normans. In the time of Baldwin V (1035–67), Valenciennes was returned to Hainault, but the Flemings extended their power to the Dender–Scheldt line.[14]

Internal administration under Baldwin IV

Baldwin IV's period is also important for internal administration. The term *comitatus* (county) is first used in a territorial sense for Flanders

13. Dunbabin, *France*, 208.
14. Ganshof, 'La Flandre', 349.

during his reign.[15] The old Carolingian *pagi* in Flanders may have become administrative districts under comital functionaries as early as the time of Baldwin II. These local potentates gained much independence after 965. In 993 Baldwin divided most of Flanders into large units called *comitatus*, amounting to castellanies and not to be confused with the use of that term for all of Flanders. Texts of 993–4 mention castellanies at Ghent, with the old *pagus* of Waas as a subordinate jurisdiction; Courtrai in a single district with Tournai; and 'Flanders' (the Bruges region), which was assuming increasing importance as the sea level declined and serious reclamation began. Later evidence suggests that the castellany of Saint-Omer was established at about this time.

The Flemish castellan held his office in fief of the count, but not the fortress from which he exercised his power or its territory; in these he exercised military, governmental and judicial rights in the count's name. He was a person of high standing, not, in contrast to the later bailiff, a transferable civil servant. He led the militia of the castellany, but it was the count's army. He also presided over the comital court of the *scabini*. There is no evidence that the administrative reorganization of 993 was extended to French Flanders.

Although the older and larger castellanies originated in 993–4, the newer and smaller ones are not attested until the 1070s and 1080s. The second group included districts that were initially subordinated to a larger castellany but were being separated. Most were on the northern frontiers of the castellanies of Tournai (from which that of Courtrai split) and Saint-Omer (from which Ypres, Veurne, Bergues-Saint-Winoc, Bourbourg and Cassel divided at different times).

There were twelve castellanies by 1070–5. Although the castellan exercised justice everywhere in theory, the court structure was not uniform. Bruges had a classic Carolingian model, with twelve *scabini* meeting under the castellan's presidency. The castellany of Ghent lacked a central college of *scabini*; courts were held in the rural areas by colleges of seven *scabini*, presided over by a local official called the *schout* or *meier*, but the castellan acted as an itinerant justice for important cases. Saint-Omer had a central college of *scabini*, but in the districts on the north that would eventually break away, the local *schout* had more independence than in the castellany of Ghent.[16]

15. A.C.F. Koch, *De rechterlijke organisatie van het graafschap Vlaanderen tot in de 13e eeuw* (Antwerp, n.d.), 16; Dunbabin, *France*, 244.

16. Ganshof, 'La Flandre', 380–1; A.C.F. Koch, 'De Ambtenaren in de mededelingen' in *Flandria Nostra* **5** (Antwerp, 1960): 319–42; A.C.F. Koch, 'Die flandrische Burgschaften' in *Zeitschrift für Rechtsgeschichte. Germanistische Abteilung* **76** (1959); and especially Koch, *Rechterlijke organisatie*, passim.

Baldwin IV and church reform

Baldwin IV continued his predecessors' limited furtherance of church reform. He intervened frequently in episcopal elections and ejected a new bishop chosen at Thérouanne in 1029–30 against his wishes. Although he initially opposed appointing the reformer Richard of Saint-Vannes abbot of St Vaast, they were reconciled by 1012. Thereafter Baldwin promoted monastic reform, albeit in the by now traditional pluralistic form. As had been true of Gerard of Brogne's reform, the changes of Richard of Saint-Vannes were essentially reflections of his personal character and did not long survive him.[17]

The Flemish churches had less temporal power than did most in France and Germany, but they were wealthy, and the counts' privileges to them hindered local nobles from using the advocacy of local churches to build powerful lordships. Baldwin IV tried to limit the advocates, who were usually powerful nobles. He was recognized as chief advocate of all monasteries of Flanders, which gave him the right to intervene in their affairs and 'protect' them from others. Baldwin bought out the seigneurial rights of several advocates over church lands. In the second half of the century, the role of lay lords in nominating abbots was reduced, and the counts abandoned lay abbacy. Baldwin IV often allowed monks to choose their own abbots, subject to his approval. The counts also nominated the provosts of many collegiate churches. But except for the bishoprics, which were obviously important for the Flemish heartland, the counts of Flanders did not intervene in church patronage in the south as long as their rights as feudal overlords were respected.[18]

The end of the reign

In 1028 the future Baldwin V was married to Adela, the daughter of King Robert 'the Pious'. But the royal marriage went to the youth's head, and he led a party of nobles in rebellion. It was initially successful, and his father had to take refuge in Normandy. Since Baldwin IV had campaigned mainly in the east, he had good relations with the

17. Koch, 'Graafschap Vlaanderen', 378.

18. Raymond Monier, *Les Institutions centrales du comté de Flandre du IXe siècle à 1384* (Paris, 1943), 13–14, 16–17.

Normans. After marrying the daughter of Duke Richard of Normandy, Baldwin IV returned to Flanders with reinforcements. His son quickly submitted but was allowed to rule jointly with his father. The duke of Normandy mediated the peace, and a conclave including nobles and clergy from throughout Flanders was held at Oudenaarde in 1030 to finalize arrangements and to settle the eastern frontier. The count and the bishop of Tournai got the oath of all Flemish knights to live according to the peace of God, which had initially been proclaimed for six years by the archbishop of Reims in 1024. Baldwin V and Bishop Drogo of Thérouanne jointly proclaimed the peace in 1042–3.[19]

BALDWIN V (1035–67)

Baldwin V, called 'the Bearded' and 'of Lille', was a political consolidator, not an innovator, but his economic measures, which we shall discuss separately, resulted in the reclamation of large tracts of land and contributed substantially to the eventual pre-eminence of Flemish trade.

Baldwin continued his family's church policies. He intervened in the diocese of Cambrai, allying with the castellan of the city against the emperor's bishops. He continued the monastic reform of Richard of Saint-Vannes, but little progress was made after Richard died in 1046. Baldwin also founded collegial churches in the interior, not just the peripheries, where they could be useful strategically. His wife Adela, the king's daughter, was especially active in church affairs.

Baldwin V was the first count since 918 who was of mature years when he took power. His only serious foreign problem was with the emperor Henry III. He continued his father's expansion eastward and consolidated control between the Scheldt and the Dender. The 1030 meeting at Oudenaarde, on the Scheldt frontier, may have been intended as a provocation, for in 1034 Flemish troops crossed the Scheldt and devastated Ename, then established a fortification at Oudenaarde.

Initially, relations between the new count and Henry III were friendly, for Henry needed Baldwin V's help against the princes of Lorraine. Baldwin had even sent his son to be educated at the imperial

19. Ganshof, 'La Flandre', 380.

court. Henry made the boy a knight and gave him the march of Antwerp in fief in 1045, thinking to get Baldwin V's help against Duke
Godfrey of Lower Lorraine. Instead, initiating an adventure that could
easily have been more disastrous than it was, Baldwin allied with Godfrey, and the coalition was joined by King Henry I of France, Baldwin's brother-in-law, who was preparing an invasion of Germany in
1047. Henry III was simultaneously facing an invasion of Utrecht by
Count Thierry of Holland, and he had to retreat. But in 1048 he detached Henry I from the alliance by promising him part of Lotharingia.
In 1049 the emperor returned to Holland, killed Thierry, and Godfrey
submitted. Baldwin V was left alone. The king of Denmark blockaded
the Flemish coast, and Edward 'the Confessor' of England, annoyed at
Baldwin's habit of sheltering English exiles, joined the coalition. Baldwin
was fortunate that he lost only the march of Antwerp.[20]

By 1050 the originally imperial march of Ename was part of Flanders. This gave the Flemish counts the land between Scheldt and Dender. This area had been densely populated, although less so than
between Scheldt and Leie, since the Frankish occupation of Flanders
and perhaps earlier. The local nobles were powerful. Most of their
lordships were composed of allods, over which the count had less control than fiefs. The counts had little territory between Scheldt and
Dender even after 1050. They thus had to buy land to counteract the
pretensions of the nobles. A good example is the purchase of Geraardsbergen by Count Baldwin VI (1067–70).

There was also no castellany organization in the Scheldt–Dender
area. Baldwin V organized it into the four great seigneuries of Bornem, Dendermonde, Aalst and Marke and gave them in fief to nobles
of the Ghent area. The counts had rights in these lordships only over
the lands that they held in domain. Aalst was the largest, almost
amounting to a county of its own. From 1071 to 1082 the lords of
Aalst, who were also advocates of St Pieter's abbey of Ghent, also held
the Land of Waas and the seigneurie of Drongen in fief from the
Flemish counts. This composite lordship of Aalst was returned to the
counts in 1165. A lordship on the border with Hainault was given to
the lord of Pamele, who commanded the count's castle at Oudenaarde. The Flemish counts also claimed Zeeland, but they enfeoffed it
to the counts of Holland.[21]

20. G.P. Cuttino, *English Medieval Diplomacy* (Bloomington, Ind., 1985), 33.

21. A.C.F. Koch, 'Het Land tussen Schelde en Dender vóór de inlijving bij Vlaan-
deren (met een opmerking over het ontstaan van Oudenaarde)', *Handelingen van de
Geschied- en Oudheidkundige Kring van Oudenaarde*, Feestnummer 1956, 56–73; Ganshof,
'La Flandre', 351.

But Baldwin V's dealings with the empire were not yet consummated. In 1051, in an astonishing diplomatic coup, Baldwin married his son, the future Baldwin VI, to Richilde, widow of Count Herman of Hainault. A secret agreement excluded Herman's two young sons from the succession in Hainault. This posed immense dangers to the emperor, and in 1054 Henry III invaded Flanders and wreaked considerable havoc but had to retreat. In 1055 both Baldwins joined Duke Godfrey in attacking Antwerp, but a combined land and sea assault failed. In 1056 Henry III's widow agreed that Baldwin V would hold the Scheldt march in fief of the empire. His son became Count Baldwin I of Hainault.[22]

Baldwin V's two other children also made distinguished marriages. Robert in 1063 married Gertrude, widow of Count Floris I of Frisia, and governed there in the name of her children. Eight years later he would usurp the countship of Flanders and would identify himself in official acts by the nickname that has adhered to him, Robert 'the Frisian'.[23] Baldwin's daughter Matilda married Duke William of Normandy. Baldwin's marriage diplomacy extended Flemish power west from the Dender and from Holland to southern Hainault. Only the southern frontier continued to be problematical. Although the counts continued to have vital interests in the southwest and were among the greatest of princes of France, their only real chances of expanding their domains through dynastic union after Baldwin V's reign were in Hainault and Holland/Zeeland, both of which were in the empire.[24]

Baldwin V's prestige was immense. He was called 'prince of the fatherland' in Flemish texts. The title 'marquis' was still used but would be abandoned in the next century. It is uncertain whether the early counts were genuine royal vassals of the French or simply 'faithful men' or peers. When Henry I of France died in 1060, however, Baldwin, as the late king's brother-in-law, became guardian of the eight-year-old King Philip I.[25]

22. Dunbabin, *France*, 209.
23. Charles Verlinden, *Robert Ier le Frison, comte de Flandre: Etude d'histoire politique* (Antwerp, 1935), 14.
24. Dhondt, *Origines*, 74–7; Koch, 'Graafschap Vlaanderen', 376–82.
25. Monier, *Institutions centrales*, 16.

The succession crisis of 1067–71

The possibility of a union of Flanders and Hainault, in combination with the conquest of the English throne in 1066 by Duke William of Normandy, threatened a fundamental alteration in the balance of power in northwestern Europe, but it was not to be. Baldwin V was succeeded by his elder son Baldwin VI (ruled 1067–70), who had ruled Hainault since 1051; but his younger son Robert the Frisian had other ideas, although he swore loyalty to his older brother 'regarding Flanders'.

Baldwin VI died in 1070. He was succeeded briefly by his son Arnulf III (ruled 1070–1), who would rule only a few months before his uncle Robert the Frisian overthrew him in a revolution that struck even contemporaries as peculiarly callous. Robert the Frisian was to be one of the memorable Flemish counts, but the circumstances of his accession were unpromising. Galbert of Bruges, writing in 1128, claimed that Baldwin VI on his deathbed got Robert to repeat the oath that he had given to Baldwin V, but this time he also swore loyalty to Baldwin VI's sons.[26] Robert nonetheless invaded immediately from Frisia. Most foreign powers preferred Arnulf, including King Philip I of France. Arnulf's greatest strength was in maritime Flanders, but a party in Ghent was favourable to him. The power of Richilde, the young count's mother, was in the south. Arnulf was killed in a battle near Cassel on 22 February 1071. Thereafter there was no organized opposition to Robert the Frisian in Flanders. Robert apparently got Philip I to invest him with Flanders in return for ceding Corbie, which had come to Flanders as a dowry of Adele, Baldwin V's wife. Philip then married Bertha of Holland, Robert's step-daughter. Richilde and her younger son Baldwin kept Hainault, and the two principalities were separated until 1191.[27]

Flemish relations with England before 1071

Although the most pressing political problems of the Flemish counts were on the continent, the maritime location of Flanders and quickening

---

26. Galbert of Bruges, *The Murder of Charles the Good, Count of Flanders*, trans. with an introduction and notes by James Bruce Ross (New York, 1959, 1967), 233.

27. Verlinden, *Robert le Frison*, 16–17, 44, 63–4, 71; T. de Hemptinne, 'Vlaanderen en Henegouwen onder de erfgenamen van de Boudewijns 1070–1214', *AGN* 2: 372.

commercial ties during the eleventh century brought Flanders into growing ties with England. We have seen that the dynastic bonds go back to the first counts of Flanders. Although Flanders was Christianized by Gallo-Roman and Frankish missionaries, ecclesiastical relations began early with England. Two eighth-century abbots of St Bavo's of Ghent had English names, and the Englishman Fridegis was abbot of St Bertin between 820 and 834. Although the justly famed wool trade between Flanders and England becomes significant only in the twelfth century, there had always been exchange, first over Boulogne, then Quentovic, then Wissant and later Calais in the south and Bruges in the north. Flemings were mentioned around 1002 in the Billingsgate/London tolls along with Normans and other Frenchmen. Flanders probably exported cloth to England, and the *Miracles of Saint Winnoc* suggests traffic in slaves in the tenth century. The establishment in eleventh-century London of a parish of St Vedast (Vaast), a saint associated almost exclusively with Arras, suggests some ties with that city. But the weight of the evidence suggests that Flanders and England both traded at least as much with Scandinavia as with each other before 1066.[28]

Ecclesiastical relations continued active in the tenth century. The English and Flemish courts gave refuge to each others' fugitive clergy and monks, and it was through his exile in Flanders that Dunstan became familiar with the Lotharingian monastic reform movement, which he fostered in England once he had been restored to favour. At his request, King Edgar in 964 gave St Pieter's Greenwich and Woolwich and confirmed the abbey's possession of Lewisham in Kent, a gift of Count Baldwin II's English wife in 918.[29]

While cultural ties flourished, political bonds were rockier. The confusion of renewed Scandinavian attacks on England after 978 may have hindered normal relations, but with the return of peace in 1016 the Flemish rulers tried to maintain ties with both sides of whatever controversy might swirl around the English throne. King Cnut (1016–35) maintained friendly relations with Flanders; but after he died in 1035, relations became strained because Flanders shielded several English exiles, most notably Emma, the Norman princess who was queen

---

28. Philip Grierson, 'The Relations between England and Flanders before the Norman Conquest', *TRHS*, Series 4 (1941): 73, 77, 80–1, 104–6. Grierson's work remains the basic study of its subject. On St Vedast, see C.N.L. Brooke assisted by Gillian Keir, *London 800–1216: The Shaping of a City* (Berkeley, 1975), 142.

29. Grierson, 'Relations', 89–94, 105–8; Gaston G. Dept, *Les Influences anglaises et françaises dans le comté de Flandre au début du XIIIe siècle* (Ghent, 1928), 14–15.

successively of King Ethelred II (978–1014) and of Cnut. Bruges was the headquarters where English exiles, led by Emma and Harthacnut, her son by Cnut, assembled ships for an invasion in the winter of 1039–40.[30]

With the accession in 1042 in England of Edward the Confessor, the opponent of Emma and Harthacnut, relations with Flanders became worse. When Edward exiled the Godwines in 1051, Earl Godwine himself went to Bruges. Baldwin V allowed the Godwines to embark for their return to England from the mouth of the IJzer, which at that time was a deeper port than the Zwin at Bruges. The restoration of Godwine in 1052 ended hostilities between Flanders and England until 1065.

The Flemish court was the centre of a variety of intrigues connected to the Norman conquest of England. Baldwin V of Flanders was both the father-in-law of William the Conqueror and the brother-in-law of Tostig, younger brother and rival of Harold Godwineson, the last Saxon king of England. When Tostig was expelled from England in 1065, he went to Saint-Omer. Flemish mercenaries, evidently with Baldwin's permission, served in William's conquering army. Although Baldwin officially maintained neutrality, there was definitely a pro-Norman tilt in his policy.[31]

The Flemings who served William in 1066 came from all social strata. Some held substantial amounts of land after the conquest. Domesday Book mentions fifteen tenants-in-chief, fourteen individuals and St Pieter's abbey. Gilbert of Ghent, son of the lord of Aalst, and Gerbod the Fleming were among the most prominent. Gerbod was given the county and city of Chester, but the natives harassed him so much that he got William's permission to return to Flanders by 1071. There was a considerable Flemish element among the local landowners, particularly in Yorkshire, Lincoln and Somerset, both among the tenants-in-chief and the mesne tenants. Most of the Flemings were described simply as *Flandrensis*, and their continental backgrounds cannot be reconstructed, but most whose place of origin is known came from French Flanders. One of the tenants-in-chief, Walter of Douai, had large numbers of sheep, although it is impossible to say whether

30. Grierson, 'Relations', 95–7, 99–101.

31. Grierson, 'Relations', 109; Dept, *Les Influences,* 15; Dunbabin, *France,* 208; Robert H. George, 'The Contribution of Flanders to the Conquest of England, 1065–1086', *RBPH* 5 (1926): 81, 84; Emile Varenbergh, *Histoire des relations diplomatiques entre le comté de Flandre et l'Angleterre au Moyen Age* (Brussels, 1874), 43, 46–7.

he was exporting wool to Flanders. The other Flemings did not have significant wool operations.[32]

Flanders thus was playing an increasingly important role in international diplomacy by the last third of the eleventh century. To the bonds with France and England that had inaugurated the county in the ninth century were now added a Norman alliance and an uneasy truce with the emperor. The next century and a half would witness both the political and diplomatic rise of Flanders to a position of eminence from which it would decline with shocking rapidity, and the economic growth that would make Flanders the leading producer of luxury cloth and the chief marketplace of northwestern Europe.

32. George, 'Contribution of Flanders', 86–7; Johan Verberckmoes, 'Flemish Tenants in Chief in Domesday England', *RBPH* **66** (1988): especially 726–7, 735, 753; Dept, *Les Influences*, 31; D. Nicholas, 'Of Poverty and Primacy', 29.

CHAPTER FOUR

The Apogee of Flemish Power, 1071–1206

ROBERT I 'THE FRISIAN' (1071–93)

Robert the Frisian was the first of a series of remarkable counts who would take Flanders to the zenith of its political power by the early thirteenth century. Both the central administrative organization of Flanders and the strongly urban and textile–industrial character of its economy first became apparent at this time. The Norman conquest of England also confronted the Flemish counts with new diplomatic problems that were exacerbated as Flemish cloth makers became dependent on imported English wool. Finally, the tie with the German empire became less important for Flanders from the late eleventh century.

Robert the Frisian moved quickly to legitimize his coup, which led to wars with Hainault and Lotharingia. A party of nobles plotted to replace him with Baldwin II of Hainault in 1082. Robert's prestige was nonetheless high. In addition to the royal marriage of his step-daughter Bertha of Holland, his daughter Adela was married to King Cnut of Denmark; her son would be the famous Count Charles 'the Good' of Flanders. Another daughter, Gertrude, married Thierry II, duke of Upper Lorraine. Their son, known as Thierry of Alsace, became count of Flanders in 1128. Robert the Frisian's son and heir, Robert, was married to Clementia of Burgundy, whose family was of Carolingian ancestry. [1]

---

1. De Hemptinne, 'Vlaanderen en Henegouwen', 372–4; Verlinden, *Robert le Frison*, 81, 86, 106–7, 165.

Baldwin V had been the first count of Flanders who enjoyed peaceful bonds with Normandy, but matters returned to normal with Robert the Frisian. Flanders became a refuge for English opponents of William I after 1071. When William stopped an annual rent of 300 marcs that he had given to Robert's two predecessors, the count gave asylum in 1078 to William's rebellious son, Robert Curthose. Relations reached their nadir in 1085 when Robert the Frisian and his son-in-law Cnut of Denmark planned a naval attack on England, but the enterprise ended when Cnut was assassinated in 1086. When King Philip I repudiated Bertha, however, Robert retaliated in 1093 by allying with William Rufus.[2]

Robert the Frisian continued his ancestors' policy of fostering church reform when it was politically advantageous. After Baldwin IV had made himself supreme advocate of the Flemish churches, there were few problems with local advocates. Robert showed no interest in promoting monastic asceticism; he made donations, limited advocates' rights and installed abbots. He gave charters of liberties to several abbeys and churches, most of them in the thinly populated belt of forest in central Flanders that was being cleared during this period.[3]

Robert rarely responded to Gregory VII's communications about simony and clerical marriage, but Gregory was satisfied that Robert was an enemy of the empire. The count's relations with Pope Urban II were more problematical. Over Urban's protests, Robert rigorously enforced regalian right on the goods of deceased clerics. Yet the pope and Robert agreed on the separation of Arras from Cambrai; both wanted to weaken the empire, and Robert wanted an entirely Flemish bishopric. In 1093 Robert the Frisian supported Rome's candidate for that bishopric against a citizens' commune. A series of wars turned out so well for Flanders that the emperor Henry V in 1107 had to enfeoff Count Robert II with the castellany of Cambrai. Thereafter, however, the Flemings quickly lost control of the bishopric, and by the thirteenth century it was no longer in their sphere of influence.[4]

2. David C. Douglas, *William the Conqueror* (Berkeley, 1964), 225–9, 205–21; Verlinden, *Robert le Frison*, 77, 107–12.

3. Ganshof, 'La Flandre', 372; Koch, *Rechterlijke organisatie*, 41–7, 52.

4. Ganshof, 'La Flandre', 350; Verlinden, *Robert le Frison*, 100–1, 113–29. On the efforts of Counts Thierry and Philip of Alsace to control Cambrai, see Ferdinand Opll, *Stadt und Reich im 12. Jahrhundert (1125–1190)* (Cologne, 1986), 55–61. In 1184 Frederick Barbarossa gave a diploma to Cambrai that is very close to the wording of the Flemish comital charter for Saint-Omer in 1163.

ROBERT II 'OF JERUSALEM' (1093–1111)

The old count had associated his son with him by 1080 to assure the succession. Robert II is associated with a number of policy initiatives, particularly crusading and the peace movements. He was more active in church reform than his father. This was due in large measure to the influence of his wife Clementia of Burgundy, whose brother would become Pope Calixtus II. She avidly promoted the monastic movement and had the Cluniac rule, which previously had been unknown in Flanders, introduced in several abbeys. While Robert was absent on crusade in 1099, she helped displace the bishop of Thérouanne in favour of the reformer Jan van Waasten.[5]

In the Treaty of Dover of 1103 Robert II, following his father's lead, accepted a money fief of £500 sterling annually from Henry I of England. The count agreed to support Henry I against all men, reserving his fealty to King Philip of France. He agreed to try to dissuade Philip if he planned to invade Normandy; if he invaded anyway, Robert would personally accompany him with as small a force as he could without risking forfeiture of his lands. This meant that in case of Franco-Norman conflict, Robert would furnish 980 knights to the English while serving personally with twenty knights on the French side. In fact, Robert II aided Henry I in conquering Normandy from the king's older brother, Robert Curthose, and the alliance of 1103 was renewed in 1110. Yet the long-range interest of Flanders was to separate England from Normandy, and Robert's successors returned to the traditional policy of joining the French against the Anglo-Norman bloc.[6]

BALDWIN VII (1111–19)

Baldwin VII became count as a youth and died prematurely after a chaotic reign. When he refused to return his mother Clementia's marriage portion, she instigated a rebellion of the south Flemish barons,

---

5. Verlinden, *Robert le Frison*, 129–30.

6. The treaty of Dover has been edited by Pierre Chaplais, *Diplomatic Documents*, 1: *1101–1272* (London, 1964), No. 1. See discussion by Philippe Contamine, *War in the Middle Ages* (Oxford, 1984), 49–50. See also G.P. Cuttino, *English Medieval Diplomacy* (Bloomington, Ind., 1985), 36; Dhondt, *Influences*, 19–20.

aided by the count of Hainault; but the towns supported Baldwin VII, and she had to submit. The influence at court of Charles, son of Robert the Frisian's daughter by Cnut of Denmark, grew rapidly. Baldwin took the side of William Clito, Robert Curthose's son, as duke of Normandy. When Henry I refused to recognize him, Baldwin invaded Normandy but was wounded and died of infection. On his deathbed the childless count designated Charles his successor.[7]

Violence, government and the public peace

Flanders continued to be an extremely violent place, particularly in the west, where some of the most important domains of the counts were found. When Robert the Frisian ordered a record made of the homicides committed around Bruges, it led to an assassination plot. Maritime Flanders resisted the count's peace until the end of the twelfth century.[8] The *Life* of Arnulf, bishop of Soissons, written around 1121 about a saint who died in 1087, said that at Gistel 'there lives there a type of men as given over to atrocities as the Scythians'.[9]

The eleventh-century counts relied on church courts for matters that were secular concerns by the 1120s. Baldwin VI refused to take jurisdiction when a husband abused and eventually murdered his wife, referring the victim's father to the bishop's. The church was rather tolerant of homicides committed during private war, but it was harsher about parricide, which did not include the murder of one's spouse, who was not a blood relative. Flanders has a dozen cases of spectacular penances set for parricides by church authorities, and there is no reference to the Flemish counts playing any role, although parricide came by extension to include the murder of one's lord or an abbot.[10] When the counts managed to apprehend a malefactor and were willing to take jurisdiction, they imposed gruesomely exemplary punishments. Baldwin V burned alive a knight who had stolen two cows from a farm woman and hanged ten others who had robbed

7. For the reign of Baldwin VII, see de Hemptinne, 'Vlaanderen en Hene-gouwen,' 376–7.

8. Verlinden, *Robert le Frison*, 148–9. It is true, as Jean Dunbabin notes (*France*, 255), that the domain of the Flemish counts was unusually large and compact, but there is no evidence that this facilitated administration at least until the time of Philip of Alsace.

9. *Monumenta Germaniae Historica, Scriptores*, 15–2, 889.

10. H. Platelle, 'La Violence et ses remèdes en Flandre au XIe siècle', *Sacris Erudiri* **20** (1971): 101, 120, 145–69.

merchants at the fair of Torhout. Baldwin VII personally hanged ten knights who had violated the peace of the fair and had another one boiled in oil.[11]

As protector of the public peace, Robert the Frisian tried to control private war. In 1092 he swore to uphold the truce of God. He forbade castle building without his authorization and protected roads, merchants, widows, orphans and travellers.[12] But such measures had little practical impact. An incident of 1084 shows how powerless the counts were even to enforce their much-discussed peace of the fairs. Robert the Frisian in effect made a judicial whitewash of a faithful knight's role. The impromptu meeting of the count's followers, as related in the *Life* of St Arnulf, is replete with coarse humour:

> Around the festival of St John [24 June], when one Zeger had chanced to come to the fair of Torhout to buy clothing, William struck him in the neck with a very sharp sword without drawing blood. He did not kill him but threw him instead into a basket full of clothes. The whole fair was in an uproar, and there was an outcry and outrage among the people because someone had presumed to break the count's peace. They went to the count, who was then in his house at Torhout. They told him contemptuously that a man who could not protect his celebrated fairs counted for nothing. Count Robert came forward in a savage mood and ordered the assailant and the victim to present themselves immediately. Meanwhile, he heard from his knights that Big Bill [Willelmus Longus] had been the perpetrator of this bold deed and was disturbing the fair to avenge the killing of his son. Then the count, mollified to a degree, responded: 'I cherish Big Bill as a brave knight and son; but I condemn it that he has avenged again the death of a son, for the deed has been pardoned and pacified by the holy bishop Arnulf.' Meanwhile the victim was brought into his presence, fearful but unharmed. His neck appeared not to have been struck by a sword but looked almost as if it had been bound by a red cord. Then the count said to William: 'I am amazed at your temerity, but I deplore your great weakness even more. If perhaps you did not wish to spare him, why do you not blush to hit a man so amateurishly that it appears that a woman's hand, not the right hand of a man, appears on this neck. Therefore be it known that since the cause was neither a sword nor a right arm, it was done on the orders of almighty God, who does not permit wounding of a neck that has agreed to the peace freely, on the example of such a holy man.' Then the count,

11. Ross, 'Introduction' to Galbert of Bruges, p. 45; D. Lambrecht and Jan van Rompaey, 'De Staatsinstellingen in het Zuiden van de 11de tot de 14de eeuw', *AGN* **2**: 80.

12. Raymond Monier, *Les institutions centrales du Comté de Flandre, de la fin du IXe siècle à 1384*, (Paris, 1943), 18-19.

his nobles and knights declared that whatever St Arnulf had pacified would remain firm and inviolable according to the will of God.[13]

More progress was made under Robert II. At a council in 1099 he proclaimed that since all forts in Flanders were held of the count, he could lawfully seize all others, even during truce. In 1111 he repeated his father's decree that no one could build fortifications without the count's authorization and issued the peace of God in his own name. Robert II, who allied with the towns against the nobles, also proclaimed a market peace and punished violations severely. Charles the Good extended the peace to include the 'weak and the tillers of the soil' and prohibited bearing arms on marketplaces or in towns. An important step was taken in 1127, after which any knight who wished to offer scutage (shield money) in lieu of military service could do so.[14] Charles was a notable defender of church liberties. Every one of his thirty-four known charters involves donations of land to ecclesiastical institutions, regulations of conflicts between churches or between churches and laypersons to the benefit of the churches, or confirmations of church liberties.[15] Yet all chronicles and saints' lives continue to show endemic violence in Flanders, and the violence in 1127–8 surrounding Charles's murder shows that the peace movement had made little impact on private warfare and noble feuds.[16]

---

13. *Monumenta Germaniae Historica, Scriptores*, 15–2, 889 (my translation). My understanding of this important text, which thoroughly undermines sanguine interpretations of the count's justice, has been enriched by discussions with Professor James Murray. In an often cited article, Charles Verlinden cited this document but used only the part up to 'present themselves immediately'. This quotation out of context left the impression that Robert the Frisian was enforcing the peace of the fair strictly. The complete text shows unambiguously that the knights whom the count consulted included the perpetrator of the deed himself and that the victim was brought in only to hear the rigged acquittal of Big Bill. See Charles Verlinden, 'Marchands ou tisserands? A propos des origines urbaines', *AESC* **27** (1972): 403.

14. R. Bonnaud-Delamare, 'La Paix en Flandre pendant la première Croisade', *RN* **39** (1957): 147–52; Platelle, 'Violence', 118, 150; Ganshof, 'La Flandre', 371; de Hemptinne, 'Vlaanderen en Henegouwen', 212; Dunbabin, *France*, 263, 278, 321.

15. Total calculated derived from F. Vercauteren (ed.), *Actes des comtes de Flandre, 1071–1128* (Brussels, 1938), 209–92, supplemented by A.C.F. Koch, 'Actes des comtes de Flandre de la période de 1071 à 1128', *BCRH* **122** (1957): 272–7.

16. See especially Geoffrey G. Koziol, 'Monks, Feuds, and the Making of Peace in Eleventh-Century Flanders', *Historical Reflections* **14** (1987): 531–49, who however interprets the sources, in my opinion against the entire sense of these narratives, to mean that conditions were improving due to the preaching.

THE CRISIS OF 1127–8

Baldwin VII was succeeded by his cousin Charles of Denmark, called Charles 'the Good' after his martyrdom. For Charles's reign and the social and constitutional crisis provoked by its termination in 1127, historians rely principally on the magnificently detailed account by the notary Galbert of Bruges.[17]

Although some have assumed that many of Charles's problems resulted from his unfamiliarity as a Dane with conditions in Flanders, he had been at the Flemish court since 1086, when he could have been no older than five. He was a minor court figure under Robert II but had close relations with Baldwin VII. The new count faced a revolt immediately, when his predecessor's mother Clementia supported the candidacy of William of Ypres, who although illegitimate was the last descendant in the male line of Robert the Frisian. A severe famine struck Flanders in 1124–5, and the count's efforts to combat it by releasing grain from his storehouses were well received. Charles extended the count's peace and made increased use of courts to settle disputes. He followed carefully the proceedings of castellany courts. Galbert claims that his observations showed him that in important cases, free men refused to answer suits of the unfree. This comment shows that serfs were suing in the public courts and that Charles saw nothing remarkable about it.[18]

The crisis that led to Charles's martyrdom came from his evident desire to ascertain exactly what belonged to him in human and material resources. Since 1089 the provost of St Donatian's church in Bruges had been chancellor of Flanders and thus the chief financial officer of the count's domain. After 1091 this office was held by Bertulf, a member of the Erembald clan. Although Charles had been in Flanders for some forty years, Galbert says that he was surprised when a court informed him that the Erembalds were serfs, and he accordingly decided to disgrace them. It seems clear that their status was an open

17. I shall use basically Galbert of Bruges, *The Murder of Charles the Good, Count of Flanders*, trans. with an introduction and notes by James Bruce Ross (New York, 1959, 1967). Ross's superb introduction is also extremely valuable. The translation is based on Henri Pirenne (ed.), *Histoire du meurtre de Charles le Bon, comte de Flandre (1127–1128), par Galbert de Bruges* (Paris, 1891). See also R.C. van Caenegem, 'Galbert of Bruges on Serfdom, Prosecution of Crime, and Constitutionalism' in Bernard S. Bachrach and David Nicholas, eds., *Law, Custom, and the Social Fabric in Medieval Europe: Essays in Honor of Bryce Lyon* (Kalamazoo, 1990), 91–2.

18. Galbert, *Murder*, 96–7.

secret among the other potentates and that none was particularly bothered by it until Charles raised the issue. Indeed, after discovering the problem with the Erembalds, Charles summoned his councillors, many of whom were related to the provost, which means that there were serfs in the council and that the count knew it. Thus, while the 'old guard' whom the count wished to destroy were of servile origin, some officials of the central court were free 'new men' who incited Charles against the Erembalds.[19]

To forestall the count, the Erembalds assassinated him in the church of St Donatian on 2 March 1127. They evidently expected the other magnates, who shared their own problematical ancestry, to rise in support of their deed, but they were sadly mistaken. Party warfare had divided the nobles, and the side taken by one clan would cause its opponents to adopt the other. The attitude of the citizens of Bruges was ambiguous. In addition to the castellan, Bruges had a town government that could speak for the citizenry; for while their rulers allied with Gervase of Praat, a knight who led the resistance to the assassins, many of the citizens seem to have favoured the Erembalds, whom they considered 'their own lords'. When Gervase's men arrived, the citizens acted jointly to require them to swear to respect the safety of the town before admitting them. Ghent also had its own militia organization, 'men with a name for conflict and battle who knew how to demolish defenses in sieges'.[20]

The Erembalds were besieged in the count's castle at Bruges. Galbert gives most of the credit for breaking the revolt to the citizens of Bruges. Although they worried that the martyr's remains would be spirited off to Ghent to St Pieter's abbey, that did not prevent them from looting the houses of the count and provost after the castle was stormed on 19 March. There was no discipline; when the men of Ghent and Bruges started fighting over the count's body, the defenders attacked them both. Several of the Erembalds escaped – Bertulf to his properties at Veurne – but to a man they were hunted down and killed.[21]

The problem thus arose of a successor to the childless count. The early Flemish counts had chosen their own successors. Baldwin II had stipulated that his sons would rule jointly, but thereafter the eldest son had succeeded his father until 1119. But Charles the Good had not

19. Galbert, *Murder*, 105, 125–6.
20. Galbert, *Murder*, 146, 150–8, 160, 181.
21. Galbert, *Murder*, 174–9.

designated an heir, and the question arose of whether the right to choose a new count rested with the barons, who normally ratified the preceding count's choice, or the king, who invested him.[22]

The conspirators had offered the countship to William of Ypres, who had disputed the succession in 1119, but he abandoned the Erembalds when it became clear that they would lose. The Flemish succession gave Louis VI of France a golden opportunity to extend his influence beyond the royal domain and gain an ally against Normandy. As the feudal overlord of whoever was count of Flanders, Louis summoned the Flemish barons to Arras, where on 21 March they elected as the new count William 'Clito', nephew and rival of Henry I of England and Normandy. In separate actions taken in assemblies of their regions as well as in the cities proper, the towns also ratified the choice of the new count, but only after extracting concessions from him.

> There was also read the little charter of agreement reached between the count and our citizens about the remission of the toll and the ground rent on their houses. As the price of their election and acceptance of the person of the new count, they were to receive from the count this liberty, that neither they nor their successors in our place should pay toll or rent henceforth to the count or his successors. And having been granted this liberty in perpetuity, as it was written in the charter of agreement, they should receive confirmation of this same liberty by an oath which they demanded of both king and count, to the effect that neither king nor count, either in person or through their agents, would any longer disturb our citizens, or their successors in our place, about paying the toll and rent but would respect inviolably the privileges of the canons as well as the remission of tolls and rent, honestly and fairly, without reservation. Binding themselves to accept this condition, the king and count took an oath on the relics of the saints in the hearing of the clergy and the people. Subsequently the citizens swore fidelity to the count, according to custom, and did homage and pledged loyalty to him, as they had done formerly to his predecessors, the lawful princes and lords of the land. In order to make our citizens well disposed towards himself, the count granted to them in addition the right freely to correct their customary laws from day to day and to change them for the better as circumstances of time and place demanded.[23]

The king enfeoffed William Clito with Flanders, but William had no genealogical claim on the countship. Henry I intervened against his

22. Monier, *Institutions centrales*, 30, 32.
23. Galbert, *Murder*, 186–9, 193–4, 198–9, 201, 203.

nephew and bribed his adherents, with particular success in Ghent and eastern Flanders. Lille rebelled on 1 August, when Clito violated the peace of his own fair by trying to seize one of his serfs. In September Clito alienated Bruges by rescinding the toll exemption granted in the 'little charter'. Saint-Omer rebelled on 8 February 1128 over its dislike of a newly appointed castellan.[24]

The barons who spoke for Ghent then claimed that Clito had not fulfilled his agreements to respect the liberties of the cities. At a general assembly in Ghent, they demanded that the count call a meeting of his own court at Ypres to judge whether he could continue as count 'without violating the honor of the land'. If the count is a deceiver and perjurer, he should 'give up the countship . . . to us so that we [sc. barons and Ghent] can entrust it to someone suitable and with rightful claims to it'. Clito agreed to this, but the meeting never occurred, and Ghent thus renounced him.[25]

The new claimant was Thierry of Alsace, son of Robert the Frisian's daughter. He agreed to respect the privileges that Clito had given to the towns. Rivalries between towns and nobles, within the towns and between different towns produced chaos in the spring of 1128 that was complicated by the machinations of the French and English kings. Bruges recognized Thierry on 30 March 1128, and Gervase of Praat, whom Clito had made castellan of Bruges, switched sides and became Thierry's vassal. Most of the nobles still supported Clito, who had considerable military success in the spring and summer of 1128. But after he died of a battle wound on 28 June, Thierry was recognized as count everywhere.[26]

The events of 1127–8 show that the Flemish nobility was assuming an increasingly institutional and corporate role in the affairs of the principality. But Flanders was not governed solely by nobles and the count. King Louis VI waited at Deinze 'for the men of Ghent who were to accept the new count, William Clito, according to his order and the election of the barons of the land'. Then 'our [Bruges] men and the men of Ghent' agreed to accept Clito. By 31 March 1128, 'citizens' of Bruges had met 'with the men of Flanders' (Galbert restricts this term to persons from the *pagus Flandrensis*; the Franc or castellany of Bruges thus was holding assemblies). They decided to

24. Galbert, *Murder*, 203–4.
25. Galbert, *Murder*, 267.
26. On the end of the crisis, see de Hemptinne, 'Vlaanderen en Henegouwen', 378–9.

send a delegation of twenty knights and 'twelve of the older and wiser citizens' to confer with the men of Ghent. Burghers of the 'cities and fortresses' of Flanders 'were pledged to each other in loyalty and friendship' to do nothing except in common regarding the election. Thierry of Alsace, bidding for the support of burghers and barons, granted 'to his barons and to the people of the land, the right to amend all the laws and judgments and customs and usages of the inhabitants of the land in matters concerning the common welfare and the honor of the land'. The burghers had a consultative role, even this early, although the mechanisms by which it was exercised are unclear. No one could function as count in Flanders from this time on without the consent of the towns.[27]

The counts and the nobility

The events of 1127–8 illustrate a complex and changing social structure. Countless stories demonstrate the Flemish counts' problems with their turbulent nobles. As elsewhere, the criteria of noble status in Flanders were initially a combination of blood, power and proximity to the prince. Ernest Warlop's standard account holds that nobility, as distinguished from knighthood, was always transmitted by blood and that until the late thirteenth century, when large numbers of townspeople entered the nobility by intermarriage, Flanders was unusual in requiring that both parents be noble to produce a noble offspring. There are problems with this interpretation even for the twelfth century, however, and from about 1200 a distinction was made in Flanders between nobles from the paternal and maternal sides.[28]

The first counts of Flanders had been ennobled as affines (in-laws) of the Carolingian kings, not through their own blood line.[29] Their example also shows how important officeholding was in the constitution of nobility. Some sources suggest that the Flemish counts picked their own officials from persons who were already noble, but in other cases, such as the Erembalds, a person of low birth could be considered noble by virtue of holding an office. Possessors of these powers

27. Galbert, *Murder*, 199, 279, 284–5.
28. E. Warlop, *The Flemish Nobility before 1300*, 4 vols (trans. J.B. Ross and H. Vandermoere) (Courtrai, 1975), 1: 102; Philippe Godding, *Le Droit privé dans les Pays-Bas méridionaux du 12e au 18e siècle* (Brussels, 1987), 53.
29. J.M. van Winter, 'Adel, ministerialiteit en ridderschap 11de–14de eeuw', *AGN* 2: 128.

had 'comital' power. Genealogical research suggests that the Flemish castellanies may have been established on the basis of territorial units called 'counties' that were formed after the confusion of 988. At Ghent, Courtrai, Saint-Omer, Bergues, Bourbourg and Ypres, the comital and eventually castellan families came from nobles who had held estates and public authority in these areas since the establishment of the Baldwins. At Bruges and Veurne, however, 'comital' power was held by the Erembalds, who were 'serf knights' (*ministeriales*) from the Veurne region. The singularity of maritime Flanders may have been due both to the fact that conditions there were more fluid and the nobility less entrenched and to the consolidation of a new group of nobles who were rewarded for helping Robert the Frisian's coup in 1071.[30]

We have seen that most land in early medieval Flanders was allodial, but this changed to a degree during the central Middle Ages. Far from being synonymous with decentralization of government, as is sometimes still maintained, feudal relations could be used by princes to gain control over territories. The Flemish counts used the fact that the lord owned the fief and the vassal had only use as a means of gaining control over territories. Most of the great men who were being called 'noble' or 'baron' by the early twelfth century were in fact vassals of the count;[31] we shall see that an aspect of this was their establishment as hereditary castellans and tenants of important offices that had begun as service positions in the counts' court. From about 1170, and especially in the thirteenth century, the Flemish counts were able to force some allodial landholders to become their vassals and fiefholders. Allodial land was held both by smallholders and great men, but most large allods that were being created in the twelfth and thirteenth centuries seem to have been going to churches.[32] With the spread of landholding by feudal tenure, courts for vassals evolved. The count's central court may have been one initially, although it was becoming a public court in the twelfth century. Courts of fiefholders appear in the castellanies of Ypres, Aalst, Bruges and Courtrai between 1210 and 1220.[33] The development of feudal relations thus has important implications for the establishment of a noble estate in Flanders.

---

30. Warlop, *Flemish Nobility*, 1: 106, 208, 114, 121–8, 136.
31. Karen S. Nicholas, 'The Role of Feudal Relationships in the Consolidation of Power in the Principalities of the Low Countries, 1000–1300' in *Lyon Essays*, 115.
32. Godding, *Droit privé*, 153–5.
33. Monier, *Institutions centrales*, 63.

Galbert's remarks about the nobility in 1127–8 show a group that is difficult to define, but he always distinguishes 'peers', 'princes' or 'barons' from knights. A charter of Robert II in 1111, regarding how nobles and peasants should take oaths, each with their peers, shows that knights (*milites*) and nobles (*nobiles*) were grouped together in relation to everyone else.[34] By 1127–8 the elite included most holders of high justice as it was then conceived in the baronies and counties of east Flanders, the group of great vassals who claimed the right to elect the count in 1127–8 and some officials of the count's household. Many of them were involved in the assassination plot, evidently because Charles had favoured 'new men' such as knights. But then they formed a sworn association, negotiated with the king, and avenged the count on the Erembalds, until they were forced to share power with the burghers. The knights were more heterogeneous, and in fact had constant contact on a virtually equal footing with the nobles, but they had less self-consciousness as a group than either the burghers or the barons.[35]

The *ministeriales* (knights), another group whose basic function was service, were thus an important component of the Flemish nobility. This term was applied to both free and unfree persons in the Carolingian period, but by the eleventh century it meant unfree persons who served in a lord's entourage. The count's *ministeriales* did castle guard and were functionaries in the central household. They originally did not do homage as vassals, since they were already dependants of their lords, but in the twelfth century they were doing so and thus losing the taint of serfdom.[36]

Some *ministeriales* were also called *milites* in the Latin sources. This ambiguous term can mean 'knight' as a social distinction, but it also was applied to ordinary soldiers. Nobles, who were members of old families of undisputed blood line, *ministeriales* (who were becoming a newer nobility) and soldiers of lower rank were all called *milites* in the twelfth century. Galbert's chronicle shows clearly the distinction between the noble families and the *ministeriales*, who were newer and in some cases had more power over the count.

The Erembalds, the villains in the murder of Charles the Good, were *ministeriales*. Ernest Warlop has argued that the discovery of their low birth caused the Flemish nobility to define itself more rigidly than

34. Vercauteren, *Actes*, 126.
35. Ross, 'Introduction' to Galbert, 29–34.
36. Van Winter, 'Adel', 130.

before. After 1127 there were no *ministeriales* among the Flemish nobility. Yet we have seen that it is most improbable that the other nobles, some of whom were married to Erembald women, would not have known their ancestry.[37] It thus appears much more likely that a conspiracy of silence about ministerial origins knitted the Flemish nobility together after the nearly fatal embarrassment of 1127. After that, birth, not service, and complete ancestral freedom were the mark of all Flemish nobles.

Flanders thus had a numerous knighthood, probably of about 1500 individuals in the early twelfth century. The nobility, however, was a much more restricted group, of about 130 families.[38] The nobles were recognized as a group apart by being distinguished from others in witness lists, but in other respects the Flemish nobles had only the privileges enjoyed by other free men. The rapid rise of the towns in the twelfth century seems to have compromised their power seriously. While elsewhere the nobles were having financial problems from the second half of the thirteenth century, it happened earlier in Flanders and probably contributed to their willingness to serve foreign princes.[39]

The peers of Flanders

The 'peers (*pares*) of Flanders' were a powerful subgroup of the nobility. They probably originated in the *principes* and *optimates* mentioned in tenth- and eleventh-century texts: rich, landholding nobles living in castles or towers, vassals of the count for one or more fiefs, but holding most of their land and definitely the castle as allod. The peers are first mentioned in 1067, when Baldwin VI called the 'peers and barons' to hear Robert the Frisian's soon-to-be-broken oath. Galbert says the peers were 'second to the count'; by 1128 there were nine. Although the college underwent some personnel changes in the shake-up after 1128, all peers were entrenched in imperial Flanders and on the southern frontier; none was in an area where a powerful castellan family provided defence. In the name of the Flemish people, the peers elected the count and sat as a court in judgement on him if he failed in his duties. Cases involving the peers themselves were judged by the college. The number and importance of the peerages

37. Warlop, *Flemish Nobility*, 1: 107, 205–15.
38. Warlop, *Flemish Nobility*, 1: 100; Nicholas, 'Feudal Relationships', 115.
39. Godding, *Droit privé*, 52–5.

declined sharply in the thirteenth century. Several passed by inheritance to the counts; this and the territorial losses to France had dropped
the number to four by 1300, all of them in the southeast. They had
social prestige, but little political or military role.[40]

FLANDERS UNDER THE ALSATIAN COUNTS (1128–91): THIERRY OF ALSACE (1128–57/67)

Thierry of Alsace was the first of a series of French counts of Flanders
that would last until 1482. He issued an amnesty, married his daughter
to a Flemish noble, did homage to Louis VI and enfeoffed his half-
sister, the countess of Holland, with Zeeland west of the Scheldt.
Although Thierry's reign was generally successful, it seems to have
been due to the burgeoning prosperity of Flanders and the strength of
the central administration, for the count was largely absent. Only in
1148, when Baldwin IV of Hainault invaded Flanders, was there a
serious crisis with a foreign power.[41]

Thierry preserved official neutrality between France and Eng-
land/Normandy. In the English civil war, Thierry declared for Matilda
rather than Stephen; he was the husband of an Angevin princess, and
William of Ypres, pretender to the Flemish countship in 1119 and
1127, led Stephen's army. The many Flemings who had fought for
Stephen had reason to fear the accession of Henry II, who in 1154
forced all Flemings who were not involved in commerce to leave
England. The by then aged William of Ypres retired to his castle at
Loo, and William of Aalst, whose family was likewise involved in the
events of 1127–8, also returned to Flanders. Some Flemings went to
Scotland and Wales rather than return home, and as Henry became
more secure he gave money fiefs to numerous Flemish nobles. There
was clearly a considerable cross-channel traffic in nobles, who maintained ties and property in both England and Flanders.[42]

---

40. Lambrecht and van Rompaey, 'Staatsinstellingen', 80–1; Warlop, *Flemish Nobility*, 1: 139–42, 150–1, 224–30; Monier, *Institutions centrales*, 51.

41. For the reign of Thierry of Alsace, see de Hemptinne, 'Vlaanderen en Henegouwen', 381–2. See also Dunbabin, *France*, 291–92.

42. Emile Varenbergh, *Histoire des relations diplomatiques entre le comté de Flandre et
l'Angleterre au Moyen Age* (Brussels, 1874), 73–9; Dept, *Influences*, 29–30.

Crusading enhanced the prestige of the Flemish counts. Robert the Frisian made a much publicized pilgrimage to the Holy Land between 1086 and 1090. Robert II had participated in the First Crusade but spent little time outside Flanders. The Flemish involvement with the East becomes more serious with Thierry of Alsace. In 1134 he married Sybilla, daughter of Fulk V of Anjou, king of Jerusalem. He went to Palestine four times, in 1138–9, 1147–9, 1157–9 and 1164–6. His son Philip's interests were more European, but he went on crusade three times, in 1173, 1177 and 1189.

PHILIP OF ALSACE (1157/67–91)

When Thierry went to Palestine in 1157, this time accompanied by Sybilla, he evidently thought seriously of staying in the East permanently. He had his eldest son, the fourteen-year old Philip, installed as count before he left. Despite his youth, Philip of Alsace directed policy while his father was gone. He issued charters in his own name, which Thierry did not bother to confirm after his return. He kept some of his father's advisors but also named some of his own people, notably the chancellor Robert of Aire. When Thierry returned in 1159, embittered and alone – Sybilla entered a convent in Jerusalem – he attended increasingly to ceremonial duties, while Philip handled most actual administration.

Philip of Alsace was probably the most remarkable ruler of medieval Flanders. He undertook major administrative changes, relying at the beginning of his reign on Robert of Aire, to Thierry's considerable distaste. Robert, son of a smith of Chartres, first appears in 1157 as provost of Aire and in the next ten years accumulated other offices. When he was chosen bishop of Cambrai in 1174, Philip had to ask the church authorities to delay his ordination, for he had too much still to do in Flanders. Robert was murdered shortly afterwards, evidently with the connivance of Jacques of Avesnes, who was then the leader of the anti-Flemish faction in Hainault.[43]

Philip of Alsace's wife Elizabeth, the sister of Count Ralph V of Vermandois, had inherited that county in 1164 but soon had to assign

---

43. H. van Werveke, *Een Vlaamse Graaf van Europees formaat: Filips van de Elzas* (Haarlem, 1976), 35–7.

it to her husband, probably as punishment for adultery.[44] Philip's state thus became the largest territory ever ruled by a Flemish count, extending to within 25 kilometres of Paris. Relations with Hainault, which had been troubled since 1071, were repaired in 1169 when the future Baldwin V of Hainault (1171–95) married Philip's sister Margaret. Their son, who would be Baldwin VI of Hainault and Baldwin IX of Flanders, was born in 1171, and the alliance was renewed in a mutual assistance pact directed against all parties except their mutual overlords, the French king and the emperor. The alliance with Hainault was natural geographically; despite the rivalry of the ruling houses, some nobles had lordships in both Flanders and Hainault.[45]

The marriage diplomacy of the Alsatian dynasty continued when Philip's younger brother Matthew in 1170 married Eleanor of Beaumont, Elizabeth's sister, who stood to inherit Vermandois after the deaths of Philip and Elizabeth, who were childless. When Matthew died in 1173, Philip got his youngest brother, Pieter, who was bishopelect of Tournai but had not yet been consecrated, to renounce holy orders and accept knighthood. Two years later Pieter married the widow of the count of Nevers, but he died soon afterwards. Philip's heir would clearly be his nephew of Hainault.[46]

The addition of Anjou and Aquitaine to the English/Norman empire changed the balance of power. Philip of Alsace understandably saw Henry II as a greater threat than the Capetian king. He tried to maintain correct relations with England, however, and in 1163 renewed the Treaty of Dover with Henry II. Philip tried to arbitrate the quarrel between Henry and archbishop Thomas Becket, but he gave Becket asylum in 1164 over Henry's protests. Philip supported the conspiracy against Henry II in 1173. He allowed the young King to use Flanders as a base and invaded Normandy. Young Henry is alleged by English chroniclers to have promised Philip the earldom of Kent and the castles of Dover and Rochester. In 1174 Flemish

44. An English chronicler relates that Philip punished one of her lovers by ordering him beaten to death with a mace, then displaying the body hanging upside down into a privy from its seat. *The Historical Works of Master Ralph de Diceto, Dean of London*, edited by William Stubbs, 2 vols (London, 1876), 1: 402. My attention was called to this scabrous reference by Professor John Bednar of Clemson University.

45. Hans van Werveke, 'La Contribution de la Flandre et du Hainaut à la troisième croisade', *MA* **78** (1972), 57.

46. For the reign of Philip of Alsace, see in general van Werveke, *Filips*; de Hemptinne, 'Vlaanderen en Henegouwen', 382–90. The implications of the Vermandois marriage for France and Flanders are discussed in John W. Baldwin, *The Government of Philip Augustus: Foundations of French Royal Power in the Middle Ages* (Berkeley, 1986), 8.

mercenaries led by Hugh Bigod burned Norwich but were quickly besieged there and allowed to return to Flanders. An invasion of England from Scotland led by one Jordan the Fleming also failed.[47]

Philip of Alsace and Philip Augustus

The French tilt to Philip of Alsace's foreign policy made him the dominant figure at the royal court during Louis VII's last illness. Although he was not the official guardian of the new king, Philip II 'Augustus', he was able in the summer of 1180 to negotiate Philip's marriage to Isabella, daughter of his sister Margaret and Baldwin of Hainault. This move would have enormous consequences for both Flanders and the French crown; for Philip gave her in dowry an area roughly equivalent to what soon would become the county of Artois, including Arras, Bapaume, Saint-Omer and Aire, on condition that Philip of Alsace keep the use of these places for his lifetime.[48]

Few people stayed allied with Philip Augustus for long. When Elizabeth of Vermandois died in 1182, her county was inherited by her sister, Eleanor of Beaumont, but Philip of Alsace refused to surrender it. The next year Philip remarried Theresia (called Matilda in Flanders), daughter of King Alfonso I of Portugal. To get this royal marriage, Philip gave her a widow's portion that included land in the dowry of Isabella of Hainault. Philip Augustus understandably claimed that this violated his rights. When the Fleming ignored a summons to the royal court, Philip Augustus announced his intention of repudiating Isabella of Hainault.

Although the king backed down from this threat, he fed the distrust between Philip of Alsace and Baldwin V of Hainault. When war broke out between Flanders and the king, Baldwin of Hainault took the royal side, perhaps in fear for Isabella's safety. Philip of Alsace was quickly beaten. The peace of Boves in July 1185 gave Philip of Alsace the title of count of Vermandois for life but awarded Eleanor most of the land. When Queen Isabella died in 1190, her son, the future King Louis VIII, inherited her dowry of Artois.[49]

The hostility between Flanders and France then diminished for the rest of Philip of Alsace's life, but Flanders and Hainault were reconciled

---

47. Van Werveke, *Filips*, 20–5; Varenbergh, *Relations diplomatiques*, 81–2.
48. Baldwin, *Government of Philip Augustus*, 15–16.
49. The most convenient account of the French–Flemish problems of 1180–5 is Baldwin, *Government of Philip Augustus*, 17–26. See also van Werveke, *Filips*, 29–31, 38; van Werveke, 'Contribution', 73–4.

only in 1190. In his last years Philip returned to the domestic policy interests of his youth, which we shall discuss separately. A prince of 'European format', Philip of Alsace joined the emperor and the kings of France and England on crusade in 1189. He died at Acre on 1 June 1191, aged only forty-eight.

BALDWIN VIII (1191–4)

The death of Philip of Alsace precipitated another ambiguous succession. He had designated his brother-in-law Baldwin V of Hainault as his successor, but Philip Augustus claimed that Flanders had escheated to the crown in default of male heirs, and he had some support in Flanders, notably at Ghent. The archbishop of Reims mediated an arrangement that was formalized in the treaty of Arras. On 1 March 1192 Baldwin was enfeoffed with crown Flanders for a relief (inheritance duty) of 5000 silver marks, then did homage for imperial Flanders to Henry VI.[50]

Baldwin VIII faced several problem nobles, including some of his own castellans. The most serious threat was from the dowager countess Matilda, who received a widow's portion in southern and coastal Flanders, where she increased taxes so much that she provoked rebellions at Veurne and the castellany of Bourbourg. Disorders continued until 1221 throughout the southwest between the Ingrekin and Blauwvoet parties.[51]

Baldwin VIII's major preoccupation was recovering the dowry of Isabella of Hainault. The loss of Artois was a severe blow.[52] Baldwin sided with Philip II while Richard of England was being held for ransom and even permitted him to recruit Flemish mercenaries for a

---

50. Monier, *Institutions centrales*, 34.

51. De Hemptinne, 'Vlaanderen 1070–1244', 390; Warlop, *Flemish Nobility*, 1: 261–3. Although this has been portrayed as a social conflict between the noble Ingrekins and the free farmer Blauwvoets, there were actually persons of high and low birth on both sides.

52. Baldwin, *Government of Philip Augustus*, 249. Koch, *Rechterlijke organisatie* (32–7), has argued that Philip of Alsace's donation of this territory in dowry was an implicit recognition that he could not govern it; for by this time, most of the rest of Flanders had been integrated into a court structure strictly subordinated to the counts, but the extreme south, where the princes had little land, remained outside it. Philip's successors clearly did not see it that way.

planned invasion of England,[53] but this policy of accommodation was short lived. Since Baldwin VIII was count of Flanders by marriage only, when his wife died on 15 November 1194 their son succeeded her in Flanders. When Baldwin VIII died the next year, Hainault and Flanders were united under one ruler.

BALDWIN IX (1194–1206)

The new count had been raised at the German court and was more independent of France than his father. Baldwin IX was one of the most remarkable of his dynasty. His tragic demise on crusade was a catastrophe from which Flanders never recovered. Baldwin IX was the first great prince whose feudal obligations to the French crown were specified in writing. He had to do liege homage and swear to aid the king against all persons and oppose all his enemies except the emperor and the bishop of Liège. He agreed that violation of this arrangement entailed automatic excommunication of the count and interdict of Flanders by the archbishop of Reims. The relief for the countship was to be equal to a year's income of the fief.[54]

Baldwin IX quickly undid much of the damage of the Treaty of Arras. He catered to Philip Augustus until he did homage for Flanders and Hainault, but in September 1197 he allied with Richard of England, and war broke out with Philip Augustus. By the end of 1198 Baldwin's armies had overrun northern Artois; but when the French captured Philip of Namur, Baldwin's brother, the count had to agree in the treaty of Péronne (January 1200) to give up his alliance with England, although in return he got Saint-Omer, Aire and Guines. Philip Augustus kept the rest of Artois. Matilda's widow's portion was to return to Flanders after her death.[55]

The period of Baldwin IX saw the beginning of a new development in count–noble relations: international politics played a considerable role. Flemish nobles had done military service in England by the eleventh century. By 1163 three Flemish peers, three hereditary court officials, and six castellans had accepted money fiefs from Henry II.

53. Cuttino, *English Medieval Diplomacy*, 36.
54. Baldwin, *Government of Philip Augustus*, 264.
55. De Hemptinne, 'Vlaanderen 1070-1244', 292; Baldwin, *Government of Philip Augustus*, 91–2, 95–6.

Most counts before Baldwin IX had generally favoured France but had not tried to stop English recruitment among the Flemish nobility. But Baldwin was strongly pro-English. The formation of an English party in Flanders, which would continue as a theme in Flemish politics through the fifteenth century, now became a policy supported by the counts. Richard and John made land grants and spent immense amounts on money fiefs for Flemish nobles. Flemish noble families continued to hold lands in England. While most Flemish nobles with English ties had previously been from the south, prominent nobles from Germanic Flanders began joining the English party with the loss of Artois, while nobles who opposed Baldwin gravitated toward France.[56]

In 1200 Baldwin IX's countess, Marie of Champagne, gave birth to their first child, Joan. In 1202 the grateful count took the cross. His wife followed after giving birth to their second daughter, Margaret, but she died before reaching her husband. Flanders was governed by a regency council consisting of the chancellor (Baldwin's uncle, Gerard of Alsace) and two castellans, presided over by Baldwin's brother Philip of Namur and the dowager countess Matilda. Baldwin IX was crowned emperor at Constantinople on 9 May 1204, but he was taken prisoner in 1205 and killed shortly afterwards by the Bulgarians. Even before news of his death reached Flanders, Philip of Namur had to do homage to Philip Augustus, promising to marry Philip Augustus's daughter and not to betroth his nieces without the king's consent. When word of Baldwin's death reached Flanders in February 1206, the king assumed his right as feudal overlord to wardship of the two young Flemish heiresses. Rumours began almost immediately that the count was really alive. Some of the most tragic episodes in the history of medieval Flanders were about to unfold.[57]

56. Dept, *Influences*, 24–5, 54–63; Warlop, *Flemish Nobility*, 1: 261.

57. De Hemptinne, 'Vlaanderen 1070–1244', 395; Baldwin, *Government of Philip Augustus*, 202–3; Robert Lee Wolff, 'Baldwin of Flanders and Hainault, First Latin Emperor of Constantinople: His Life, Death, and Resurrection, 1172–1225', *Speculum* **27** (1952): 290–1.

THE GOVERNMENT OF FLANDERS IN THE TWELFTH CENTURY: THE TRANSITION TO THE ADMINISTRATIVE STATE

The central court

The Flemish central administration made immense strides during the twelfth century, particularly under Philip of Alsace. Although the counts probably had a central organization by the time of Arnulf 'the Great', the court of great domestic officers became an organ of government only under Baldwin V, when the counts were in regular contact with the Capetian court. Members of the court witnessed charters or acts, made rulings on custom and judged cases concerning fiefs held directly of the count. The court met on the count's summons. Its composition depended to a great extent on where it was meeting, but it generally included peers, castellans, great household officers, the count's chief advisors, the provost of St Donatian and occasionally other prominent ecclesiastics. The clerical element was much weaker at the Flemish court than at either Paris or Westminster.[58]

The early counts' court rarely acted in a judicial capacity except when acting as a supreme feudal court, trying cases between vassals and between the count and his vassals. The court became a more formal tribunal during the twelfth century, rendering verdicts and arbitrating, although most often in cases when one litigant was a vassal of the count. Before comital courts were established in the castellanies, the central court evidently exercised high justice over particularly severe crimes, such as murder, arson, rape and breach of the peace. By the thirteenth century these would be 'reserved cases' for the count, as they had been for the English king since 1166. The court investigated the facts before ruling, and some cases of the early thirteenth century show it investigating the authenticity of written documents used to support claims.[59]

Thus, while most court officers were probably servants at first, the growing complexity of the court's business and the prestige attached to comital service meant that they were generally nobles or at least

---

58. Monier, *Institutions centrales*, 53; D. Lambrecht and J. van Rompaey, 'De Staatsinstellingen in het Zuiden van de 11de tot de 14de eeuw', *AGN* **2**: 85; Ganshof, 'La Flandre', 85.

59. Lambrecht and van Rompaey, 'Staatsinstellingen', 86–7.

knights by the mid eleventh century. Initially the central court offices were appointive, and most of them had several simultaneous titularies. They were all hereditary and held by nobles by the period of Thierry of Alsace, who also designated certain officials as '[office] of Flanders' or 'of the count'. These individuals assumed priority over others holding the same title.[60]

The great central offices soon became fiefs. The first to become hereditary was the constable, which is first mentioned in 1089 and was held by the lords of Harnes by the 1120s. By Thierry's period the lords of Grammene were hereditary chamberlains and the lords of Wavrin seneschals. The position of steward was first held by the lords of Eine-Oudenaarde, then the lords of Gavere. The lords of Bailleul and Vichte each had the office of marshal. In the twelfth century the holders of these offices performed their functions personally, but they became honorific in the first half of the thirteenth century. They still had some financial perquisites, and the counts accordingly bought out the rights of most of them.[61]

The chancery (writing office) in Flanders has excited considerable admiration. In what was undoubtedly his most famous enactment, Robert the Frisian in 1089 had made the provost of the church of St Donatian of Bruges his chancellor, probably because the count's largest domains were near Bruges, and St Donatian's clerks were already keeping records of them. This was a domain office, not a central chancery. The chancellor's main job was placing the count's seal on documents. The chamberlain, not the chancellor and the notaries under him, was the most important figure in the administration of the domain until the mid twelfth century. Roger, Bertulf's successor as provost of St Donatian, was less often called 'chancellor' than were technocrats of the chancery.

Nonetheless, the counts were making increased use of written instruments. In a reign of twenty-two years, Robert the Frisian issued fifteen charters that have survived. In eighteen years Robert II issued thirty-six, while Baldwin VII in eight years issued forty-two charters that have survived, surpassing even Charles the Good.[62] Notaries be-

---

60. Warlop, *Flemish Nobility*, 1: 157–60, 167–74, 178.

61. Lambrecht and van Rompaey, 'Staatsinstellingen', 82; Ganshof, 'La Flandre', 379–80, 385–6.

62. Totals compiled from Vercauteren, *Actes*, and Koch, 'Actes', 261–78. I regret that Th. de Hemptinne and A. Verhulst in collaboration with L. de Mey, *De Oorkonden der Graven van Vlaanderen (juli 1128-september 1191) II, 1: Regering van Diederik van de Elzas (juli 1128-17 januari 1168)* (Brussels: Royal Commission of History, 1988) actually appeared too late for use in this book.

came more numerous and the writing office became a real focal point of administration during the last years of the frequently absent Thierry of Alsace. Yet even this date places Flanders half a century ahead of its neighbours in the development of chancery activity. Under Philip of Alsace's chancellor Robert of Aire, the chancery became the administrative centre of the domain. Robert was 'chief notary' and 'master of the count' by 1163. From 1164, the notaries whom he supervised became the chief financial officers of the increasingly rich comital domain. In 1168 he became provost of St Donatian, linking this ancient office and the chancery, and held it until his assassination in 1174. Between 1183 and 1205 the count's natural brother, Gerard of Alsace, was chancellor, and the position became even more influential thereafter.[63]

In addition to documents prepared in the central chancery, the Flemish counts in the late twelfth century often had documents written by the resident officers of the individual domains. Lower-level chancery officials were laymen by the twelfth century, although the chancellor himself was a clergyman through the first half of the fourteenth. The Flemish chancery was issuing about twenty acts annually by 1200, in addition to accounts, land and rent books and other administrative documents.[64]

The counts' financial administration

The Flemish counts developed a sophisticated financial apparatus during the twelfth century that helped to make them among the richest princes of Europe. In the late eleventh century they lived almost exclusively on the proceeds of their domains. The feudal aids gave them some additional income in the early twelfth century but dwindled into insignificance during the thirteenth.[65] During the twelfth century the counts developed new sources of revenue, in which money incomes predominated, but they still collected more in kind. Galbert's chronicle suggests that in 1127 there was a bipartite financial administration: the

63. Our understanding of the Flemish chancery during the twelfth century has been enhanced considerably by A. Verhulst and T. de Hemptinne, 'Le Chancelier de Flandre sous les comtes de la maison d'Alsace (1128–1191)', *BCRH* **141** (1975): 267–311, esp. 273–99.

64. W. Prevenier, 'De Laat-middeleeuwse vortelijke kanselarijen als exponenten van een modern of archaisch staatsapparaat', *TG* **87** (1974): 202–10.

65. A. Verhulst, 'L'Organisation financière du comté de Flandre, du duché de Normandie et du domaine royal français du XIe au XIIIe siècle' in *L'Impôt dans le cadre de la ville et de l'état* (Brussels, 1966), 41.

provost of St Donatian supervised accounts and the expenses of local offices, while the chamberlain handled actual disbursements for the count himself and was in physical control of the treasury.[66]

The general domanial account of 1187 gives considerable insight into Flemish administration.[67] A central account was compiled annually by notaries under the direction of the chancellor/provost. It summarized the particular accounts (*brevia*) of local officials, which have not survived separately. Until at least 1157, finances were simply handled in general sessions of the count's court, but the accounting thereafter became a special session.[68]

The Flemish counts had very little domain land south of a line between Saint-Omer and Lille. They had two sources of income. The account of 1187 was for the 'old domain' or *reneghe*, which was organized into more than forty territories (*ministeria* or *officia*). Several of them correspond closely to castellany borders, notably Bruges. The receivers of districts that contained several *officia* sometimes met together; by 1190 the Franc of Bruges had 'chief receivers' who met under the presidency of the provost/chancellor. The general account of 1187 was submitted to such a group. Roughly half the domains were administered in 1187 by notaries, who were in holy orders, but the others were in charge of laymen. By 1232, if not before, the lay receivers held their offices in fief of the count.[69]

The old domain had four types of bureaus: *spicaria* collected mainly payments in grain but also some money in the larger centres, *lardaria* animal products, *vaccaria* dairy goods, while the *brevia* or *scaccaria* handled payments in money. Some places had more than one of these types.[70] The old domain was probably organized when *spicaria* were established in the chief place of each castellany around the mid eleventh century and collected all revenues that were owed to the count in the castellany. This organization suggests that the count's domain was especially strong at that time in the castellanies of Veurne, Courtrai and the western part of the Oudburg of Ghent, and the

---

66. Bryce Lyon and A.E. Verhulst, *Medieval Finance: A Comparison of Financial Institutions in Northwestern Europe* (Providence, RI, 1967), 13–14.

67. A. Verhulst and M. Gysseling (eds), *Le Compte Général de 1187, connu sous le nom de 'Gros Brief', et les institutions financières du comté de Flandre au XIIe siècle* (Brussels, 1962).

68. Lyon and Verhulst, *Medieval Finance*, 27.

69. Verhulst and Gysseling, *Compte Général*, 100–1, 106, 120–1; Lyon and Verhulst, *Medieval Finance*, 23–7.

70. Verhulst and Gysseling, *Compte Général*, 74–7, 90–7.

Franc of Bruges. *Brevia* were added later in areas where a strong
money economy developed; but the older centres, which had longer-
standing commercial significance, paid both money and grain into the
spicaria.

The counts' major incomes in the old domain were from land. By
the second half of the twelfth century, special receivers were collecting
revenues that were more lucrative than those in the General Account
of 1187. The chancellor audited only the old domain revenue, while
the new incomes went into the treasury in the chamber, which thus
became more important. By the early thirteenth century, however, a
separate clerk was beginning to supersede the chamberlain. He soon
took the title 'receiver of the count' and eventually 'receiver general'.
The provost/chancellor remained in control of the old domain, which
produced the count's 'regular' income. The expenses of local officers
were deducted from what they rendered to the treasury. Much of the
count's profit was converted into money at market prices.[71]

The basic categories of receipts and expenditures of the General
Account had not changed much by 1255, when the next one survives.
The revenues of the old domain were already becoming outmoded in
1187. Although most of the payments were still in kind in 1187, by
1255 they were converted into money, varying according to yearly
prices of the goods that were owed. Just as the growing use of money
and more effective administration revolutionized the counts' finances
in the twelfth century, the growth of 'public' incomes in the late
twelfth century established the basis of a financial structure based on
judicial profits and an increasing reliance on taxation in the thirteenth.

The 'new domain' was organized on a non-territorial basis and was
subordinated directly to the count. It amounted to revenues coming to
the count in his capacity as chief of state: the profits of justice, particularly those from Philip of Alsace's reform of the penal law, loans, tolls,
feudal rights, seigniorage, sales of vacant lands on which the count was
increasingly exercising regalian rights, and taxes, levied chiefly on the
towns or approved by them. By the late thirteenth century the old
domain yielded about £7000 per year, while the five great cities alone
paid aids of £6000. But although new sources of income were added
in the thirteenth century, they were less effectively managed than in
the twelfth. Local officers went into arrears for several years at a time,
and we shall see that princes had to borrow heavily.[72]

71. Verhulst and Gysseling, *Compte Général*, 43–4, 54–7, 64–5, 122–4; Lyon and
Verhulst, *Medieval Finance*, 17–20.
72. Verhulst, 'Organisation financière', 29–41; Verhulst and Gysseling, *Compte
Général*, 126–7; Lyon and Verhulst, *Medieval Finance*, 65.

Flemish territorial government in the twelfth century: the castellany

A network of local officials was thus at the base of the counts' domain administration by the late eleventh century. They probably descended from the hundredmen who were deputies of the counts of the *pagi* in the Carolingian period. At the bottom of the hierarchy was the *meier*, called *amman* at Ghent, Courtrai and in the Franc of Bruges and the three maritime castellanies. They were domanial agents who began as summoners and enforced local agrarian routines, but some held courts for petty offences in the rural areas in the late Middle Ages. The *ammans* in the cities amounted to jailers. The *schout*, the next level in the hierarchy, also represented the count of the *pagus* in local territories and summoned the local court. Some *schouten* became castellans, while others remained very minor officers.[73]

The basic comital territorial organization was based on the castellany and was in place by the 990s. The Flemish castellanies may have simply continued the borders of Carolingian *pagi* or more probably the 'offices' (*ambachten*) or 'ridings' (*roeden*) into which some were subdivided. Some of the subdivisions preserved their own characters, notably Waas and 'Four Offices' in the castellany of Ghent.[74] At various times there were at least eighteen castellanies. Four were lost to France between 1191 and 1212. The castellany organization was found originally only in crown, not imperial Flanders, although it was eventually extended there.[75]

The largest castellanies, which originated as mergers of several Carolingian *pagi*, were the oldest – Bruges and Ghent as originally constituted. That of Bruges was called the Franc (Freedom) from the thirteenth century. Some smaller ones were more recent creations, notably the five that were formed from that of Saint-Omer by Robert the Frisian. There were only minor changes in the borders of the western castellanies after 1100.[76]

There were more serious shifts in eastern Flanders. The primitive castellany of Ghent was divided at the end of the twelfth century into

73. A.C.F. Koch, 'De Ambtenaren. 1: De Middeleeuwen', *Flandria Nostra* **4**: 322–5, 329–30, 333.

74. Verhulst, 'Burgenverfassung', 275; Lambrecht and van Rompaey, 'Staatsinstellingen', 109; Ganshof, 'La Flandre', 398, 400.

75. Van Werveke, *Filips*, 23; Ganshof, 'La Flandre', 395–6.

76. Ganshof, 'La Flandre', 396–8; Koch, *Rechterlijke organisatie*, 87, 132; Verhulst, 'Burgenverfassung', 278.

subsections having the same functions as other castellanies. The Four Offices, a union of jurisdictions in northern coastal Flanders, got a now lost constitution from Philip of Alsace that was confirmed and extended in 1242. When the Land of Waas in the extreme northeast got a comital constitution in 1241, the castellany of Ghent became confined to the Oudburg and the office of Zomergem. The castellany of Oudenaarde was formed from the eastern part of the castellany of Courtrai in the second half of the thirteenth century, but it had no castellan and was directly under the count's bailiff.[77]

The castellany originated as a military creation, centred on a comital fortress at which the count's vassals owed guard duty. Strategic considerations were paramount in the establishment of the southern castellanies, whose chief places were roughly the same distance apart. But economic considerations probably weighed more heavily in the erection of the forts that gave rise to newer castellanies at Ypres and Lille, places where the trade routes leading from the coast reached the point at which a river became navigable. All castellanies of the north coincided territorially with districts or groups of districts of the comital domain and thus became centres for economic administration. From the second half of the eleventh century the castles were used for delivery and storage of goods, although this function was generally given to priests or canons of the parish church that the count had founded in the fort, rather than to the noble castellans.[78]

The counts' justice

About half a century after the castellanies are first mentioned as military centres, benches of aldermen (*scabini*) appear, mainly in the castellanies between the Aa and the Scheldt, where the count had a large, compact domain. In the south, where the domain was small or nonexistent, some castellanies were not given central courts until later, and they evolved as purely allodial courts for property questions.[79]

The judicial institutions of the castellanies reflect their diverse origins. The castellan came to preside over a central court that handled both civil and criminal actions. He took one-third of the court fines. A major limitation of his jurisdiction was that he could not prosecute

77. Lambrecht and van Rompaey, 'Staatsinstellingen', 110–11; Koch, *Rechterlijke organisatie*, 121–2, 136.

78. Verhulst, 'Burgenverfassung', 275–80.

79. Verhulst, 'Burgenverfassung', 278.

cases unless a plaintiff had complained. In Carolingian *pagi* that were named after a central place (such as Ghent), rural districts were generally subordinated to the central court, and this was continued in the later castellany organization. In those named for regions (Flanders, Waas and Mempiscus), the subordinated areas were usually independent of the central court. They often had their own benches of aldermen; in the case of Ghent, this meant that there was no central board of aldermen in the Oudburg. The castellany of Bruges, the old *pagus Flandrensis*, began with a twelve-man bench called the 'aldermen of Flanders', but the twelfth-century counts erected seven districts called *vierscharen*, each with seven aldermen, in the polder areas. They joined the twelve in a sixty-one-member board of aldermen for the Franc of Bruges that was the only one of its type in Flanders.[80]

The castellany organization began to decline from the mid-twelfth century, especially when the bailiffs, who were instituted in the last years of Philip of Alsace, assumed the castellans' more important judicial functions. The towns also limited the competence of their castellans. As payments in kind were replaced by money, the castellans' function as domain administrators was weakened. By the thirteenth century some castellans' offices were being sold. Most were purely honorific by the fifteenth century.[81]

During the twelfth century the judicial organization of the Flemish counts was thus breaking out of the Carolingian mould. The Carolingian fine for crimes incurring high justice – those involving spilling blood, arson, theft, robbery and rape – was 60 shillings. This is a ridiculously low sum in twelfth-century coin, but it was the highest fine that early eleventh-century Flemish counts could levy.[82]

In the late twelfth century, however, 60 shillings became the highest fine that could be levied by courts holding low justice, which judged fist fighting and other assaults without bloodshed. High justice became divided into 'high' and 'middle' or 'theft' justice. This meant a revolution in Flemish judicial practice at the local level. Courts exercising middle justice could levy fines of £10, while the highest fine, now £60 rather than 60 shillings, was reserved to the count. By 1170–80 a number of lords who had exercised high justice in the Carolingian scheme were now confined to middle, for they did not possess the delegated regalian right of the count. In Germanic Flanders

---

80. Lambrecht and van Rompaey, 'Staatsinstellingen', 108, 112; Koch, *Rechterlijke organisatie*, 151–7.

81. Ganshof, 'La Flandre', 401; Verhulst, 'Burgenverfassung', 280–1.

82. Koch, *Rechterlijke organisatie*, 17, 26.

the introduction of the 'blood ban' or high justice as a comital monopoly around 1175 meant that most seigneuries – those that had neither aldermen nor a feudal court – ceased to form enclaves where the castellan had no authority. The count's monopoly of blood justice was enforced by the bailiffs, new officials whose territorial sphere was the castellany but who were superimposed on the castellans and given far more extensive powers.[83]

Since castellany courts with aldermen existed only in the parts of Flanders where the counts had a large domain, chiefly in the towns and the coastal areas, there was a judicial vacuum in the interior. Around 1200 the counts partially filled it by establishing courts of feudal vassals to exercise high justice. They met in the castellanies under the presidency of the bailiffs. These courts, however, exercised public jurisdiction as well as feudal, thus assuming functions that in areas where the domain was stronger were handled by the castellany and town courts. They became especially powerful in the Oudburg of Ghent, Oudenaarde, the land of Aalst and Douai. The only court in Flanders that was limited to feudal cases was the 'Burg' of the Franc of Bruges.[84]

Town courts seem to have developed from rural courts, and their aldermen (*scabini*), who fulfilled many of the same functions as *jurés* ('sworn men') in places that were more independent of the town lord in the beginning, were comital officials. The abbey of St Vaast at Arras had its own aldermen, but the town aldermen of Arras of 1111, the earliest known in Flanders, were a comital court, evidently the result of Baldwin VII simply seizing rights of blood justice from the abbey in that year. Aire-sur-la-Lys got its own town court by 1111, while Ypres had aldermen with territorial jurisdiction by 1116, Douai between 1111 and 1119, and some of the others got them in the 'little charters' of 1127–8. Curiously, Galbert does not mention that Bruges had aldermen. Ghent may not have had them until 1169.[85]

Philip of Alsace as lawgiver

Philip of Alsace was perhaps the most important legal innovator ever to be count of Flanders. Until his time most constitutions and

83. Koch, *Rechterlijke organisatie*, 21, 28–32, 38–9, 202.
84. Lambrecht and van Rompaey, 'Staatsinstellingen', 128–9.
85. Lambrecht and van Rompaey, 'Staatsinstellingen', 116–17; Koch, *Rechterlijke organisatie*, 68–70.

ordinances had a local or regional application, but he tried to legislate for the entire county, especially in penal law and criminal procedure. In smaller places that evolved organically into towns, such as Oudenaarde, Courtrai and Veurne, there were no town aldermen until his time. In 1163 he founded Nieuwpoort with a constitution that provided aldermen, and this document became a model for his other town foundations. Most importantly, Philip forced the large towns to accept uniform constitutions that provided severe penalties for most crimes (see discussion in Chapter Five).

The practice of *hoofdvaart* (*chef-de-sens*), in which a lower court is obliged to seek the advice of a higher in disputes, was present in the thirteenth century and may have been initiated by Philip of Alsace. Towns that were founded were usually given the law of a previously existing town and did *hoofdvaart* to it. Subordinate jurisdictions within castellanies had recourse to the central courts of their districts. It was unusual for a town to be the judicial 'head' of a rural district, but it happened with Ghent, which was the head of the Four Offices. The heads would later use this practice to gain juridical footholds in the smaller communities.[86] The aldermen of the great cities in their turn together constituted a superior court, the 'aldermen of Flanders', to which all Flemish urban courts had recourse when they could not reach verdicts. This helped to unify Flemish urban law, but it also perpetuated the domination of the great cities, particularly as the counts' power became weaker during the thirteenth century.[87]

Flemish courts also used advanced procedures and methods of proof. Written evidence was used in secular courts during the twelfth century, although it has been argued that the idea was borrowed from the church courts.[88] The *waarheden* were sessions of the aldermen acting as witnesses rather than as judges in land actions. They thus amounted to a sworn inquest. This was called a *stille waarhede* when the aldermen heard the sworn testimony of others about cases that had not yet been tried. Since all adult males owed attendance at local courts, they were summoned to tell judges whether crimes remained

---

86. David Nicholas, *Town and Countryside: Social, Economic, and Political Tensions in Fourteenth-Century Flanders* (Bruges, 1971), 142–9; Monier, 'Le Recours au chef-de-sens, au moyen-âge, dans les villes flamandes', *RN* **14** (1928): 5–19; B.H.D. Hermesdorf, 'Ten hoofde gaan', *Vereeniging tot uitgaaf der bronnen van het oudvaderlandsch recht: Verslagen en Mededeelingen* 11 (Utrecht, 1954), 17–50; Koch, *Rechterlijke organisatie*, 192–3.

87. Blockmans, 'Vers une société urbanisée', 65–6.

88. M. Vleeschouwers-van Melkebeek, *De officialiteit van Doornik: Oorsprong en vroege ontwikkeling (1192–1300)* (Brussels, 1985).

unpunished. The lists of witnesses thus became the basis for the agenda of the next court session, called the 'general inquest' (*doorgaenda waarhede* or *durginga*), which was being held at least from the twelfth century but could hear only cases involving fines of up to 3 shillings. Eventually the count's bailiff had the responsibility of proclaiming the general inquest. The *durginga* was held thrice annually on the occasion of the general pleas *(placita generalia)*, when civil cases were brought to trial in local courts.[89]

The bailiffs

The Flemish bailiff originated in the period of Philip of Alsace in the merging of the functions of several other public and domain officials, although the title 'bailiff' seems to have been brought from Hainault and applied to the Flemish officials by Baldwin VIII.[90] The bailiff's justice was to be the linchpin of the Flemish court structure for the next 200 years.[91] A suggestion that Philip of Alsace was moving towards a system of bailiffs even before he became sole count is found in his charter of 1163 for Nieuwpoort, which established a 'justice' who held the pleas of the count, divided fines with the aldermen and could not try burghers without the aldermen's consent. Veurne had a similar officer by 1170.[92]

The bailiffs were salaried officers with judicial, military, financial and police functions. They were superimposed on the castellans to handle cases involving blood justice in areas where the count had had little power before. They presided over aldermanic courts in the cities and rural territories, and everywhere over the count's newly established feudal territorial courts, but they were not judges. After Philip

89. Koch, *Rechterlijke organisatie*, 184–6; Henri Nowé, *Les Baillis comtaux de Flandre: Des origines à la fin du XIVe siècle* (Brussels, 1928), 318.

90. Officials similar to the bailiffs whom Philip of Alsace introduced into Flanders had also appeared in Vermandois in 1167 (Baldwin, *Government of Philip Augustus*, 135–6). Although the bailiff originated under Philip, the 'Ordinance on the Bailiffs' is now thought to have been issued by Baldwin IX, since it modifies some of Philip's rules and uses the term 'bailiff'. It had specific reference to Ghent (R.C. van Caenegem, 'Considérations critiques sur l'ordonnance comtale flamande connue sous le nom d' Ordonnance sur les baillis'", *Actes du Congrès International de la Société Italienne de l'Histoire du Droit. Venise 1967* (Florence, 1971), 138–49).

91. Louis M. Degryse, 'Some Observations on the Origin of the Flemish Bailiff (*Bailli*): The Reign of Philip of Alsace', *Viator* 7 (1976): 293.

92. R. Degryse, 'De Nieuwpoortse justiciarius en zijn opvolgers 1163–1302', *ASEB* 90 (1953): 131–9.

of Alsace established *ex officio* prosecution of crime, the bailiff summoned, prosecuted, held inquests on request and at his own initiative, imposed truces in feuds and gave safe conduct. He collected income owed to the new domain, the feudal aids and incidents, mortmain, the right to the best chattel owed by serfs, the property of bastards who died without legitimate children of their own, rights of succession to foreigners' estates when no heirs could be found, and treasure trove.

The bailiffs swore to respect and preserve the liberties of the places to which they were assigned. They enforced the verdicts of local aldermen, but they also acted as the count's viceroy, receiving the oaths of magistrates and supervising roads, waterways and public works. The bailiff rendered accounts thrice yearly for the incomes that he collected, initially to the chief notary, then in the second half of the thirteenth century to the Receiver of Flanders. He deducted his expenses, notably his own and his deputies' wages and the cost of collecting fines and enforcing laws.[93]

The Flemish bailiff exercised his functions in the territory of the castellany. The territorial term *baillivia* (bailiwick) is first used in 1251. The bailiwick borders were fixed by 1255, and the only changes thereafter resulted from subdivisions, as more localities got their own bailiffs. The castellan continued to function independently of the bailiff but was limited largely to military matters and guarding the count's castle. Most earlier territorial magistrates – provosts, *schouten*, *meiers* and *ammans* – became the bailiff's deputies, holding their offices in hereditary tenure unless the count had bought them out. The bailiffs also had 'underbailiffs', and there were also separate bailiffs by 1249 in Four Offices, Waas and the Oudburg. Such local officials could exercise considerable discretion in all matters except finances.

The bailiffs served at the count's pleasure, without fixed term. The constitution of most bailiwicks forbade a native or even the husband of one to serve in the place where he or she was born, and this was generally respected until the early fourteenth century. The majority were rotated after only a year or two. Most bailiffs were initially from knightly families whose members were vassals of the count, although by the fourteenth century most came from the town patriciate.[94]

The institutional developments of the twelfth century revolutionized government in Flanders and provided a solid underpinning for the counts' diplomatic manoeuvring. They are also paralleled by an

93. Degryse, 'Bailiffs', 248–51; Nowé, *Baillis*, 41, 119.
94. Nowé, *Baillis*, 24–5, 60–2, 72, 81–7, 110–14.

economic growth that transformed Flanders from backwater to commercial and industrial leader.

FLEMISH CULTURE BEFORE 1206

Just as the economic and political development of Flanders was not precocious, so its cultural life was slow and still essentially derivative of French. Of the early Flemish counts, only Philip of Alsace was noted for his cultural patronage. All involved themselves to some extent in the affairs of their churches but for political rather than religious reasons.

Even in the early Middle Ages there was a language problem. The heartland of the area ruled by the Flemish counts spoke a Germanic dialect, but the counts also ruled in the south where French was spoken. There was no Flemish bishopric, and most of the upper clergy in Flanders were Frenchmen. Around 900, Archbishop Fulk of Reims would describe the people of the diocese of Thérouanne, most of whose inhabitants then spoke Flemish, as 'of barbarous . . . savagery and language'. The Flemings were legendary in France and England for their backwardness and crudity. In the late twelfth century Richard of Devizes instructed a young man who was about to travel in England that he should 'for such qualities [ignorance and boorishness] always look on Cornishmen as we in France consider our Flemings'.[95] Preachers such as Lambert, abbot of Lobbes (d. 1149), could speak in both French and Flemish, but this was clearly unusual. The upper Flemish clergy were educated at the cathedral school at Tournai, and Galbert mentions 'our students who at that time were studying in Laon'. The Flemish abbeys maintained primary schools, but they were far behind their Lotharingian counterparts in curriculum and influence.[96] The important Flemish authors were from the lay world rather than the church, even by the twelfth century.

The small size of the Low Countries and the fact that Flemish nobles participated in tournaments in France, Hainault and Brabant, and were active in England, which was ruled by a French-speaking aristocracy, shows that many of them were at least minimally bilingual.

95. John T. Appleby (ed.), *The Chronicle of Richard of Devizes of the Time of King Richard the First* (London, 1963), 64; examples cited in Nicholas, 'Poverty and Primacy', 20–1.

96. Koch, 'Graafschap Vlaanderen', 368–9; Pirenne, *Histoire de Belgique*, 1: 159, 165; Galbert, *Murder*, 114.

Medieval Flanders

Since Flanders was so dependent on imported French grain even in the twelfth century, and since so much Flemish cloth was exported through the Champagne fairs, it is virtually certain that the wealthier merchants were as well. By the thirteenth century it was absolutely essential for Flemish merchants to be able to understand oral and written French. Yet even this had its limits. As late as 1175 Pope Alexander III confirmed the 'ancient custom of the Gentenars to plead church cases before their own dean rather than at the court of the official of Tournai, because the language used there was foreign to them'.[97]

The Flemish church

The Flemish church had considerably less influence over temporal affairs than even in neighbouring principalities of the Low Countries. Since the Flemish counts, at least before Robert II, were such lukewarm supporters of church reform, most of the quarrels over church discipline that were such burning issues in France had little impact in Flanders. Monastic life in Flanders before the eleventh century was centred in the great establishments of Saint-Omer, Arras and Ghent. Ename, Mesen and Oudenburg were founded in the eleventh century. Most Flemish monasteries were Benedictine. Except briefly for St Bertin, none took the Cluniac rule. The Cistercian order was important mainly in the southern Low Countries, although Ter Duinen, in west Flanders, was a Cistercian establishment that had begun as a hermitage.[98]

Only three chapters of canons existed in Flanders as early as 900. Nineteen new ones had been founded by 1000 and another twenty-eight by 1100. Richard of Saint-Vannes had a considerable influence on this development. There was none in the first half of the twelfth century, probably because by then the reform movement was concentrating on changing earlier churches into formal chapters of canons under a rule. There were twenty-six new foundations in the early thirteenth century. The process of reformation could take a considerable time. The church of St Veerle at Ghent, outside the count's

97. Pirenne, *Histoire de Belgique*, 1: 343; document in A.E. Gheldolf, *Coutume de la ville de Gand* (Brussels, 1868), 1: 406.
98. See in general Ludo Milis, 'De Kerk tussen de Gregoriaanse hervorming en Avignon', *AGN* 3: 167–74, 181–2; C. de Clercq, 'De Seculiere geestelijken, mannelijke en vrouwelijke religieuzen te lande', *Flandria Nostra* 4: 47.

castle, probably existed by 920–30, but the chapter of canons there was established only at the beginning of the thirteenth century. Characteristically for Flemish church life, no chapter of canons was founded by a bishop, although some bishops did confirm them. Most were founded by laypeople, eleven by the Flemish counts. Of over fifty chapters established, only eight were in Flemish Flanders or the Lille–Douai area.[99]

The eremetical movement was also important in Flanders. Around 1052, one Everelmus established himself on an island in the Reie river at Bruges. The community that developed there called themselves 'poor men of Christ' in the twelfth century. The cell of Ailbertus at Rolduc gradually evolved into a monastery. Many of the early hermits were laymen, such as Gerlach of Houtem, a knight who had a conversion and undertook a pilgrimage to Rome and Jerusalem, then lived in a rotted-out tree in his home area. Eventually a Premonstratensian abbey was established on the site.[100]

Religious life in frontier Flanders thus often assumed forms that were less formal and structured than are found elsewhere. Wandering priests abounded, including Wederic, a monk of St Pieter's of Ghent, who circulated between 1076 and 1083 in Flanders and Brabant, allegedly with papal permission. Norbert of Xanten, who founded the Premonstratensian order, was active in Flanders. Antwerp, just across the Scheldt in Brabant, was the home of Tanchelm, a renegade priest who is alleged to have thought himself a risen Christ in the early twelfth century. Hordes of poor Flemings are known to have participated on the First Crusade, where they acquired a reputation for being fierce fighters.[101]

Church governance in Flanders fits the standard pattern for northern France. The bishoprics were subdivided into deaneries containing numerous parishes. The dean, who was nominated by the bishop, collected payments, but he had no independent jurisdiction. The deaneries were grouped under archdeacons, who expanded their powers into the thirteenth century by visiting dependent parishes, granting benefices and holding synods. The nomination of archdeacons gradually escaped the bishops, for they were generally named

---

99. G. A. Declercq, 'Sekuliere kapittels in Vlaanderen, 10de–begin 13de eeuw', *De Leiegouw* **28** (1986): 235–7 and Appendix; Declercq, 'Nieuwe inzichten over de oorsprong van het Sint-Veerlekapittel in Gent', *HMGOG* **43** (1989): 49–50; Milis, 'Kerk', 182–5.

100. Milis, 'Kerk', 178–80.

101. L.A.M. Sumberg, 'The "Tafurs" and the First Crusade', *Medieval Studies* **21** (1959): 225–6.

in chapters, sometimes under papal reservation. Only at the end of the twelfth century did the court of the official expand its jurisdiction as the chief court of the bishop.[102]

Literature in Flanders through the twelfth century

Most evidence of intellectual life is found in churches and chapters until the twelfth century. Latin literature was devotional and hagiographical. Thierry of St Truiden, while at St Bavo's abbey around 1090, wrote a *Life* of St Bavo. An anonymous *Life of St Macharius* was written after 1067, inspired by the rivalry between Sts Pieter and Bavo. A *Translation of Lievin of Flanders* and a *Life* after 1050 concern St Lievin, who was widely venerated in Flanders. The *Annals* of St Bertin and of St Pieter's abbey of Ghent, the *Chronicon Centulense* of Hariulf, together with such didactic works as the *Liber Floridus* of Lambert of Saint-Omer are examples of early literature produced in Flanders.[103]

Count Arnulf I evidently inspired a semi-official chronicle of his reign. By the early twelfth century the counts were having genealogies compiled to emphasize their links with the Carolingian past. Historical writing improved. The *History of the Counts of Guines* by Lambert of Ardres has interesting evidence for the county of Wijnen (now Pas-de-Calais). It still had a Flemish population in the twelfth century, and the nobles and counts knew little French, in contrast to the Alsatian rulers of Flanders. But the works of literature that Lambert mentions at the court of Guines were tales of the crusades, epics and love poetry, and there is no proof that any of it was translated into Flemish. Historical writing also is more in evidence in the Germanic north after 1100, although it remains far behind the south in quality and quantity. Galbert of Bruges and Walter of Thérouanne both wrote histories of the murder of Charles the Good.[104]

Hendrik van Veldeke, arguably the first great figure in Flemish literature, was a Brabantine knight rather than a Fleming, born in the first half of the twelfth century. He spent time at Frederick Barbarossa's court and thus was influenced by German rather than French

---

102. Milis, 'Kerk', 192–3; Vleeschouwers-van Melkebeek, *De officialiteit van Doornik*.

103. L. van Acker, 'De Latijnse literaire cultuur in Noorden en Zuiden van *circa* 1050 tot *circa* 1350', *AGN* 2: 331.

104. J. van Mierlo, *Geschiedenis van de Oud- en Middelnederlandsche Letterkunde* (Antwerp, 1928), 35, 41; van Acker, 'Latijnse literaire cultuur', 340–1.

traditions in his courtly stories and love poems. His version of the legend of St Servatius of 1170 is the first Flemish vernacular work that can be dated.[105] Poetry in a classical form was written around 1100 by Petrus Pictor of Saint-Omer, especially a lyrical *Praise of Flanders* (*De laude Flandriae*) of 1110–11, expressing longing for the fatherland. He also wrote satires of clerical fiscality and crime and poems about the alleged depravity of women.[106]

Some works of fiction were also being produced in Flanders. The increasingly literate townsmen were drawn to satirical *fabliaux* and fables. Master Nivardus, who either was a native of Ghent or spent time there, around 1149 wrote a Latin beast epic, the *Isengrimus*, which is set on the Blandijnberg, the hill south of Ghent where St Pieter's abbey was located. The tale has twelve episodes that the author uses to comment on church conditions.[107] Because it was written in Latin, Nivardus's poem was not widely read. The first Flemish version of *Reinard the Fox* goes back to the late twelfth century and is a composite work by several authors: Arnold, followed by William, who was probably a monk of St Pieter's or the nearby abbey of Drongen. The court of King Nobel, whom the Fox tricked into releasing him with prospects of a treasure, may be a parody of that of Philip of Alsace. William had read *waelsche boeken* (French books) for his basic story, but he gives it a Flemish cast and situates it around Ghent and in the Land of Waas, which he called the 'sweet land'. It features among other luminaries a French-speaking dog named Courtesy. Isengrim the wolf and his clan testified in court that Reinard's crimes against them were so numerous that 'if all the cloth they make at Ghent were turned into parchment, they could not write it all thereon'.[108]

Philip of Alsace was the first Flemish prince noted as a patron of culture. He was famed for his piety and specifically for his relic collection. Although heretics are mentioned in Antwerp in 1112, the first direct reference to them in Flanders is from the 1160s, when they were fleeing to England and Cologne. Philip participated personally in a heresy trial in 1182 at Arras. The English chronicler Ralph of

105. A. van Elslander, 'De letterkundigen', *Flandria Nostra* **3**: 72; van Mierlo, *Oud-en Middelnederlandsche Letterkunde*, 92–8.

106. Van Acker, 'Latijnse literaire cultuur', 339.

107. Van Elslander, 'De Letterkundigen', 73; Pirenne, *Histoire de Belgique*, 1: 352.

108. Van Mierlo, *Letterkunde*, 104; Pirenne, *Histoire de Belgique*, 1: 356; Van Elslander, 'Literature' in Decavele, *Ghent: In Defence*, 397. A convenient translation of Reinart is found in E. Colledge (ed.), *Reynard the Fox and Other Mediaeval Netherlands Secular Literature* (London, 1967); for these references, see pp. 57, 58, 121.

Coggeshall claims that he was the most relentless persecutor of Cathars of his time, although no other information links the Flemish heretics with the Cathars.[109]

Philip's court was renowned for its large number of literate laymen. An English chronicler described him as 'a most eloquent man, with a tongue on which he set a high price'. Philip could read and write Latin and French and was a patron of French poets and authors, including Chrétien de Troyes, who dedicated *Perceval* or *Le Conte du Graal* to him. He also patronized Gautier de l'Epinal and other poets. His first wife, Elizabeth of Vermandois, had a 'court of love' that, as we have seen, may have included practical experience. Court patronage thus fostered French literature, which affected mainly southern and western Flanders, while in the north and east Netherlandish literature was developing. Flemish literature at this point was strongly influenced by French models; courtly epics were virtually literal translations from the French. There is no direct evidence that Philip of Alsace knew any Germanic tongue, including Flemish, the language of most of his subjects. Some Flemish was probably used at court, however, for Baldwin of Hainault, who knew no Flemish himself, sent his son, the future Flemish count, to the imperial court to learn the language.[110]

The bilingualism of the Flemish court at the end of the twelfth century was a harbinger of the times. Diederic van Assenede reworked his version of the legend of Floris and Blancheflor for 'those who do not know French', which shows that even by the early thirteenth century part of the nobility knew only Flemish.[111] Charters and business papers were being written in French by the beginning of the thirteenth century and in Netherlandish by mid-century. By then the comital court was an anachronism in a principality dominated by Flemish speakers.

Art and architecture

We have little evidence for Flemish church architecture, given the ravages of fire and time. There is some information for St Bavo's abbey, begun in 985 and consecrated in 1067. The transept was relatively small, not jutting out far, but this was more usual in monastic

109. Van Werveke, *Filips*, 66–7; *Radulphi de Coggeshall Chronicon Anglicanum*, ed. Joseph Stevenson (London, 1875), 122.

110. Appleby, *Chronicle of Richard of Devizes*, 26; van Werveke, *Filips*, 78–81; Pirenne, *Histoire de Belgique*, 1: 348–9.

111. Van Elslander, 'Letterkundigen', 72.

churches than in cathedrals. An exterior crypt was added in 1148. The style was strongly Romanesque. The abbey church of St Pieter's of Oudenburg was of the same basic type but smaller and of a more unitary construction, perhaps due to the more rapid building; begun in 1056, it was consecrated in 1070. It had three aisles with a transept that was no wider than the naves. The total effect was an almost square rectangle with a small choir. The famous church of St Donatian is the only known Flemish example of a rotunda. At the west there was a massive tower, divided in the upper part into two smaller steeples.[112]

We know little of town architecture at this time except for city walls. Galbert described fortified houses of nobles near Bruges, but they evidently lacked mottes and stone walls; they had a palisade, trench or moat, approachable only by a bridge, which was demolished when there was danger. They could be of wood or stone. Such a fort at Oostkamp resisted a siege of six days. The count's castle at Bruges was surrounded in part by water, and had four gates, towers, and walls 15 metres high. Inside the wall was the count's palace, a two-storey donjon type. A gallery of wood and stone linked it to the church of St Donatian.[113]

The castle of Merkem is described in similar terms in the *Life* of John of Thérouanne.

> It is the custom of all the richest and most noble men of this region . . . to construct, piling up the earth, a motte as high as they are able, digging all around it a ditch as wide and deep as possible, and fortifying it on the outer side of its enclosure with a palisade of planks solidly joined together in the form of a wall. They furnish the circuit with as many towers as possible and on the inside they build in the centre a house or rather a fortress which dominates everything else, set up in such a fashion that the entry into the dwelling is only accessible by means of a bridge which, starting on the outer edge of the ditch and resting on a series of pillars, grouped in twos or, even, threes and placed at the appropriate spot, slowly rises over the ditch, sloping in such a way that when one reaches the level of the platform of the motte, the bridge has attained the same level directly before the gateway.[114]

---

112. André Verplaetse, 'L'Architecture en Flandre entre 900 et 1200, d'après les sources narratives contemporaines', *Cahiers de civilisation médiévale* **7** (1965): 28, 30; Joseph Mertens, 'The Church of Saint Donatian at Bruges', appendix to Galbert, *Murder*, 318–20.

113. Galbert, *Murder*, 302; Verplaetse, 'Architecture', 32–3.

114. Philippe Contamine, *War in the Middle Ages* (Oxford, 1984), 45. A fortress of this primitive type is on the Bayeux tapestry.

Until the mid twelfth century, only the richest built in stone. In addition to Tournai black marble and 'yellow stone' of Boulogne, brick is mentioned a few times, although Flanders became important in brick making only in the thirteenth century. Bricks were used at Saint-Omer in a subterranean building in the ninth century and in the vault of St Donatian of Bruges at the beginning of the twelfth. This is the oldest large vault known in Flanders, although there had been small vaults in crypts earlier.[115]

The development of the plastic arts in Flanders came from Tournai and its cathedral, begun in 1140. Tournai gave rise to a neo-French architectural style known as 'Scheldt Gothic', with a central nave and side aisles but less profusely ornamented than the churches of Burgundy and the Ile-de-France. The cathedral at Tournai was begun in 1140 with a Romanesque nave and transept but continued with Gothic elements later in the century and with a gabled choir begun in 1243. The best example of Scheldt Gothic in Flanders is the church of St Nicholas of Ghent. In the late twelfth century several churches, notably St Bavo's of Ghent, St Pieter's of Ypres and Dudzele, adopted the German style of extending the western end of the church beyond the nave, usually with a single- or double-towered facade. The Norman type with double-towered facade is also found in St James's church in Ghent.[116]

115. Verplaetse, 'Architecture', 39–40.
116. H. Baeyens, 'De Bouwmeesters', *Flandria Nostra* **2**: 81; Jean Bony, *French Gothic Architecture in the Twelfth and Thirteenth Centuries* (Berkeley, 1983), 108–10, 386–7.

CHAPTER FIVE

The Social and Economic Transformation of Flanders in the Eleventh and Twelfth Centuries

During the central Middle Ages Flanders underwent an economic revolution. The reclamation of interior Flanders was virtually completed during these centuries. Maritime Flanders was drained and converted first to sheep runs, then to arable. By 1200 Flanders was the most densely urbanized region of Europe, with cities that specialized in exporting fine woollen cloth. But Flanders also became severely dependent on imports, from France for food and from England for wool. The crossfire produced by these problems — for France and England were usually enemies — would plague Flanders' rulers for the rest of the medieval period. The dilemma was to become painfully apparent after Baldwin IX's death; 1206 is as clearly a turning point in the economic as in the political history of Flanders.

THE AGRARIAN ECONOMY

The expansion of the arable: maritime Flanders

Flanders was reclaimed later than the neighbouring parts of France but before the rest of the Low Countries. Not until the third quarter of the twelfth century did it reach the density of rural habitation that Picardy had around 1000. Although there were dense nuclei of Germanic primary settlement around Bruges and between the Scheldt and Leie rivers, there is little evidence of reclamation or population growth during the tenth century. Rapid clearance of the interior began in the eleventh century, and most of it was over by 1200 except in the extreme northeast. In the central and eastern Low Countries, it began in the twelfth century and lasted through the thirteenth. The fact that Flanders, a natural gateway to the Low Countries of goods from northern France and England, was operating at its agricultural peak this early undeniably contributed to its precocity in trade.[1]

We have seen that the swamps of southwestern Flanders were suitable only for sheep raising and had little human habitation. The IJzer mouth was a deep bay, called the 'gulf of Loo'. The shepherds erected dikes, represented on the modern map by *werf* and *wal* toponyms. Some habitation was established in the polders in the tenth century, and comital fortifications became nuclei of villages. Yet, although the sea level was receding by the late tenth century, new floods in 1014 again made some polders uninhabitable, especially along the IJzer around the later area of Nieuwpoort. The flooding lasted until 1042, but the inundations of the eleventh century were less catastrophic than those of the early Middle Ages, for large areas were spared, notably much of the coastal plain southwest of the IJzer between Bredene and Blankenberghe. A great dike erected along the Bruges–Blankenberghe line protected this area, which gradually was dried between about 1050 and 1150. Expansion was particularly notable around Veurne and in the Ypres–Diksmuide area, where much of the growth came not only from draining but from cutting the previously protected comital forest of Houthulst, until then the largest in Flanders.

The counts gave the coasts to the abbeys on condition of diking and turning them into agricultural or pasture land. As the area was turned into polders, many villages originated with names ending in *kapelle* (chapel) or *kerke* (church). Their layout shows that the expansion was planned, probably by the counts, for the dikes were in concentric circles. In the beginning, however, the alluvial deposits were suitable for little except raising sheep. Settlements in this area were islands in the midst of waste and woodland.[2] As the gulf of Loo silted,

1. Robert Fossier, *La Terre et les hommes en Picardie jusqu' à la fin du XIIIe siècle* (Paris, 1968), 1: 163; Nicholas, 'Structures', 506–7.

2. Geert Berings, 'Het oude Land aan de rand van het vroeg-middeleeuwse over-stromingsgebied van de Noordzee: Landname en grondbezit tijdens de Middeleeuwen', *HMGOG* **39** (1985): 39–41; A. Verhulst, 'Die Binnenkolonisation und die Anfänge der Landgemeinde in Seeflandern', *Vorträge und Forschungen* **7–8** (Constance, 1964): 448; P. Callebert, 'Ontstaan en vroegste geschiedenis van het kapittel te Eversam (1091–1200)', *ASEB* **107** (1970): 174–6, 186; F. Blockmans, 'Vers une société urbanisée', in Witte, *Histoire de Flandre*, 45.

however, a new harbour was created by the late 1120s at Diksmuide, which was linked by canals to Veurne, Ypres and the Zwin. Diksmuide was probably the first outport of Ypres, a fact that doubtless explains why its textiles were marketed widely in the twelfth century. But by the mid twelfth century the IJzer was silting, and Diksmuide remained a small inland town.[3]

The central part of the Franc of Bruges was better protected by dikes and was continuously inhabited from the ninth century. The area north and northeast of Bruges was dried in the second half of the eleventh century. Beginning in 1134, a great new dike was built to protect against floods along the Zwin, and new polders and smaller dikes were established in the last quarter of the twelfth century and throughout the thirteenth. The dikes were strong enough to withstand inundations except northeast of Hoeke, where a network of creeks developed. This area was characterized by the street village type of settlement and isolated farmsteads separated by marshes, many of which contained peat deposits.[4]

Reclamation continued here in the thirteenth century, but its character and focus changed. Many of the twelfth-century polders in the southwest had been drained by the great abbeys, evidently with the intention of using the land for sheep runs. More drainage was undertaken during the thirteenth century in the north and northeast, notably in the Maldegem, Eeklo, Zelzate, Moerbeke and Wachtebeke areas, but the entrepreneurs were financed by city patricians who were looking for *moeren* (places where peat had formed).[5]

The counts were the chief beneficiaries of the early stages of the reclamation movement. They had regalian right on flooded lands and simply kept it as it was reclaimed; thus they became more powerful in the west than in the interior, which had many strong noble lordships. In patronizing the reclamation efforts of the great churches in the west, the Alsatian counts granted them immunity, which weakened the local nobles still more. They also established collegiate churches in the newly cleared areas and may have used the canons as notaries in

3. R. Degryse, "'s Graven Domein te Nieuwpoort', *ASEB* **85** (1948): 70–1; Degryse, 'Oude en nieuwe havens van het IJzerbekken in de middeleeuwen', *ASEB* **84** (1947): 10–14.

4. François–Louis Ganshof and Adriaan Verhulst, 'Medieval Agrarian Society in its Prime: France, the Low Countries and Western Germany' in *The Cambridge Economic History of Europe: The Agrarian Life of the Middle Ages*, 2nd edn (Cambridge, 1966), 1: 295.

5. Verhulst, 'Occupatiegeschiedenis', 87–8; Verhulst, 'Het Landschap', 28.

Medieval Flanders

their administration. The IJzer river network over Bruges and Mesen
linked the Leie–Scheldt and Zwin networks and facilitated both trade
and administration. Before the second half of the eleventh century,
Bruges was the only important town in the west. There were only
traces of settlement at Torhout, Ypres, Mesen and Lille, but by 1150
all were thriving commercial towns.[6]

The rural and commercial economies were linked by a network of
canals. Due to the marshiness of western Flanders, small boats could go
virtually anywhere. As the land was reclaimed, creeks and artificial
waterways linked the domains of princes and abbeys. Access to interior
markets was much easier in Flanders than in its neighbours; and as
Flanders became overpopulated, this was critical in making the place
attractive to foreign traders.

Waterways in the Franc of Bruges were supervised by the central
bench of aldermen, which by the time of Philip of Alsace was delegat-
ing power to 'water associations' in the *vierscharen*. The water associations had a sluice master, dike aldermen and an assembly of
inhabitants. Virtually all of maritime Flanders was always navigable except for the area north of Bruges, and that was made more accessible
from the eleventh century. The Lissewege waterway, for example, was
being used by the abbey of Ter Doest by the late eleventh or early
twelfth century. In the late thirteenth century it was linked by another
canal to Dudzele, which was probably used to transport peat. By 1297
it had been diverted to link with the Ieperleet. Northeastern Flanders
had been crossed by canals since at least the tenth century. A navigable
canal extended Ghent to Ertvelde and thence to Biervliet, where the
city's merchants sold cloth and bought peat and English wool.[7]

Although animal husbandry remained very important in maritime
Flanders throughout the Middle Ages, it was yielding from the twelfth
century to agriculture, but not to the classic manor. The General Account of 1187 shows that oats, which do well on light soils and on
those recently reclaimed from forest, were the major grain crop grown
in western Flanders, where farms were relatively large and enclosed.

6. Jan Dhondt, 'Développement urbain et initiative comtale en Flandre au XIe
siècle', *RN* **30** (1948): 145, 150–4; Verhulst, 'Binnenkolonisation', 449–50. This interpretation is disputed by Berings ('Oude land', 64–5), who argues that the extent of
independent church and Merovingian–Carolingian noble possession of land in this area
has been underestimated, while that of the counts has been exaggerated.
7. S. Astaes, 'Het Waterwegennet ten noorden van Brugge van de XIe tot de XIVe
eeuw', *HMGOG* **18** (1964): 3–17; Verhulst, 'Binnenkolonisation', 459–60; van Acker,
'Ottogracht', 1–9. A systematic geographical study of the canals of medieval Flanders is
urgently needed.

100

Yet Galbert's account of the famine of 1124–5 shows that the bakers of Bruges normally made bread from oats only during emergencies.

> The count...was feeding one hundred paupers in Bruges every day...And likewise in his other towns he had made the same provision. In the same year the lord count had decreed that whoever sowed two measures of land in the sowing time should sow another measure in peas and beans, because these legumes yield more quickly and seasonably and therefore could nourish the poor more quickly if the misery of famine and want should not end in that year...He also prohibited the brewing of beer because the poor could be fed more easily and better if the townspeople and countrypeople refrained from making beer in this time of famine. For he ordered bread to be made out of oats so that the poor could at least maintain life on bread and water...In this time of famine, in the middle of Lent, the men of our land living near Ghent and the Leie and Scheldt rivers ate meat because bread was completely lacking. Some who tried to make their way to the cities and towns where they could buy bread perished of hunger along the road, choking to death before they were halfway. Near the manors and farms of the rich and the strongholds and castles, the poor, bent low in their misery as they came for alms, fell dead in the act of begging. He ordered a fourth of a measure of wine to be sold for six pennies and not more dearly so that the merchants would stop hoarding and buying up wine and would exchange their wares, in view of the urgency of the famine, for other foodstuffs which they could acquire more easily and which could be used more easily to nourish the poor. [8]

This passage suggests that grain was imported. Wheat was grown in northern France and the Scheldt regions of Flanders. Estates were small in northeastern Flanders and grew mainly and in some cases exclusively oats. Farms were larger and their sowing patterns better balanced in the Leie–Scheldt areas, and wheat dominated on some farms there. [9]

The expansion of the arable: the interior

The Leie–Scheldt–Dender area had always been more densely populated than maritime Flanders and the northeast, although the interior areas with 'field' toponyms such as the Scheldeveld were so infertile that they were not put under the plough until the agricultural revolution. [10] Most population growth in the east in the early eleventh

---

8. Galbert, *Murder*, 85–9.

9. Norman J.G. Pounds, *An Historical Geography of Europe, 450 BC–AD 1330* (Cambridge, 1973), 285–6 and Figure 5.6.

10. Blockmans, 'Vers une société urbanisée', 47.

century was between the Leie and Dender. The new clearances were a response to the sudden growth of population and created smaller parishes than most in the west and north.

The clearances became more rapid at the end of the eleventh century, with the church joining the counts in some ventures. Some clearances began when a lord founded a new village in the midst of a forest, and it became the nucleus around which the forest was cleared. This systematic promotion of clearance lasted into the late twelfth century but slowed markedly thereafter, probably in response to temporary population decline after the severe famine of 1196–7.

While most reclamation in the eleventh and early twelfth centuries was in the Franc of Bruges and the southwestern castellanies, where the counts perceived vital political and governmental interests, the scene shifts after 1200 to the north and northeast, which they had previously ignored. Northwest and east of Ghent, thick forests hindered expansion before the thirteenth century. Then the abbeys of St Bavo and Boudelo cleared the area between the Durme and Scheldt, forming a landscape of small enclosed fields and street villages that even today show a planned character.[11]

Major clearance of the Four Offices and eastern Land of Waas thus began only in the thirteenth century. The area was hard to drain, for bays of the western Scheldt penetrated far inland, and substantial forests also remained, of which the largest was the 'Royal Forest' between the moors of Hulst and Durme. Making the land profitable required considerable money. The abbeys initiated diking and poldering, followed in the twelfth century by lay lords, particularly the counts and their family, then in the thirteenth by comital officials and some rich townsmen.[12]

In areas that had been settled since the early Middle Ages, fields were elongated and regular, grouped along the roads and radiating out from the centre of the village. In the interior clay areas, clearances were often by individual initiative, resulting in irregular fields and dispersed habitations. The clearances of the twelfth and thirteenth centuries, particularly in the sandy areas, which were more often the result of planning and a major investment by a public authority or church, produced oblong fields that were often surrounded by hedges. Except

11. A. Verhulst, 'Occupatiegeschiedenis en landbouweconomie in het Zuiden, *circa* 1000–1300', *AGN* **2**: 83–6; Dhondt, 'Développement urbain', 133–56; Bryce Lyon, 'Medieval Real Estate Developments and Freedom', *AHR* **63** (1957): 47–61; Verhulst, 'Het Landschap', 1: 27– 30.

12. Verhulst, 'Het Landschap', 42, 51.

along the Durme and around Tielrode, which were occupied in the early Middle Ages and had a *kouter* structure, Waas characteristically had street villages along clearance roads leading into the woods.[13]

The Leie valley tended toward dispersed settlement, resulting from the *kouter* structure, while villages and grouped habitations are found more often in the Scheldt and Dender areas. Gullegem, near Courtrai, had at least forty-four walled habitations. Erik Thoen has attributed this to the considerable power that the Flemish counts exercised as landlords, not simply as princes, at an early stage in the Leie valley. Other lords seem to have lacked the means to enforce conversion to the open fields and enforced triennial rotation found farther east, where the counts had less power.[14]

We have noted that in the early Middle Ages, *akkers* had been arable fields that were separated from one another by uncultivated land and thus were not integrated into a rotation of fields; each *akker* was worked individually. The *kouter* was a French form that was imported into Flanders, although Flanders by the ninth century had similar structures that lacked only the *kouter* name. The French *culturae* were generally subjected to a mandatory triennial crop rotation. There is some evidence of this in Flanders during the eleventh and twelfth centuries, when new arable lands – generally two fields of equal size – were opened alongside older cultivated areas. By the thirteenth century, as space between fields was brought under the plough, some fields that had previously been called *akker* changed their names to *kouter* suffixes and were converted to three-field rotation.[15]

Kouters are found mainly around Ghent, Oudenburg and Tielrode and in the Leie–Scheldt area east of Deinze and towards the Dender. Farther southeast, the *kouter* yields to longer strips in a still basically open-field structure. The example of Oosterzele, a clearance village between Ghent and Oudenaarde, can be instructive. Parts of its area had been inhabited before the reclamation of the central Middle Ages, but then *zele* (clearance), *veld* (field), *heide* (heath) and *bos* (woods) names spread. The newly cleared fields followed the direction of the local relief. Most were open, while fields in older settled regions were enclosed. North of Oosterzele, the clearances produced a mainly enclosed landscape.[16]

13. Blockmans, 'Vers une société urbanisée', 47.
14. Thoen, 'Historische evolutie', 21–8.
15. A. Verhulst, 'Note sur l'origine du mot flamand "kouter" (lat. *cultura*, fr. *couture*)', *Studi Medievali* **10** (1969): 261–7.
16. Thoen, 'Oosterzele', 13–16.

Farther north and west, on lands that were cleared in the twelfth and thirteenth centuries, enclosed fields (*kampen*) dominated the landscape. The *kampen* form was newer than the *kouter* or the strip open field. It first meant an isolated, hedged, compact and small piece of land, usually with one owner. It was usually squarish but irregular in shape and was much smaller than the *kouter*. The field was often a pasture, paralleling the strong rise in animal husbandry, since enclosures made it easier to keep animals. As there was a single owner, there was no compulsory agrarian routine. Dispersed settlement is not a consolidation of the existing hamlets but rather is a new form associated with late medieval *kampen*. Where the *kouter* persisted, so did the hamlet; when the *kampen* developed beside the *kouter*, the village became dispersed. *Kouters* and *kampen* are sometimes found together, with the *kouters* as the central fields and the *kampen* on the outskirts separated by waste in a structure similar to the earlier *akkers*. *Kampen* were built along existing roads and often used them or other natural features as boundaries. They are often in originally waste areas, the result of drainage or clearance, with a pastoral economy.[17]

Lords and tenants

The changes of the central Middle Ages clarified and generally diminished lords' financial rights over their tenant farmers. The Flemish peasants, particularly in the maritime areas, were freer than their neighbours in France even in the early Middle Ages, and the clearances accelerated emancipation. The movement for clearance in Flanders was more spontaneous than in France, and accordingly fewer villages were deliberately founded and endowed with charters of privileges. Lords generally had little physical control over the lands of their tenants, who paid a small ground rent. Forced labour on the reserve was unusual.

The situation of serfs in the early twelfth century is elucidated by Galbert's account of the events of 1127–8. The status was hereditary and was widespread even among powerful persons in the west. Female serfs gave the rank to their husbands, not just their children, after a year. Serfs were not entitled to trial by combat and thus were not procedurally equal to the free. Masters could use the count's courts to

17. Verhulst, 'Het Landschap', 43–50; Verhulst, 'Le Paysage rural en Flandre intérieure: son évolution entre le IXème et le XIIIème siècle', *RN* **62** (1980): 12–13, 17–18. The clearest summary of these complex developments is Verhulst, *Précis*, 46–57.

reclaim runaway serfs. Although the towns were powerful, they were not yet 'islands of freedom'; migration to the cities cannot be explained as a desire to escape servile exactions. For the notion that 'town air makes a man free', which had originated in Spain, had not yet reached Flanders; if it had, the Erembalds would have been free. This principle first appears in Flemish law in Philip of Alsace's charter of 1163 for Nieuwpoort and thereafter was inserted in the major urban constitutions.[18]

Just as the Erembald case shows the ambiguity and fluidity in the Flemish social structure, so the situation of Arras, the largest Flemish city before its loss to France in 1191, shows the complexities in questions of freedom and serfdom and causes us to be wary of facile formulas. Freedom and economic advantage cannot be equated. The exemption of the abbey of St Vaast from toll was so lucrative that merchants of the city were surrendering their freedom to become the abbey's serfs and enjoy financial benefits of bondage. In 1111 St Vaast sued one Ingelbert, demanding that he prove that he was a serf. Ingelbert had been in charge of collecting the head tax each year from the serfs of St Vaast and from numerous inhabitants of Arras who wanted to be counted as serfs to get the exemption. Ingelbert, supported by the citizens of Arras, had argued that an individual could prove his servitude solely with his own oath, but the abbot objected. The count's court ruled in 1122 that an oath was insufficient without proof of origin, and two later counts confirmed this. Serfdom, however, had its disadvantages. In 1115, when Arras already had municipal aldermen, Robert II ruled that the bakers of the town were still bound to mill their grain at the abbey's mill, despite the aldermen's protests.[19] After 1127–8, the economic advantages of serfdom were definitely outweighed by its legal disabilities.

Labour services on the reserve were rare for both serfs and free tenants and were completely absent from the lands that were reclaimed in the twelfth century and later. As population rose and a labour market was created, wage labour became cheaper and more efficient for lords than tenant labour. Charters did not alter the economic situation of the peasant much – labour services on the reserve had never been

---

18. R.C. van Caenegem, 'Galbert of Bruges on Serfdom, Prosecution of Crime, and Constitutionalism (1127–28)' in *Lyon Essays*, 90–1, 94–6, 98; Raymond Monier, *Les Institutions judiciaires des villes de Flandre des origines à la Rédaction des Coutumes* (Lille, 1924), 121.

19. The documents are in Vercauteren, *Actes*, 248–51, 161–2; see summary in Monier, *Institutions centrales*, 58–9.

significant even in the older settled areas with three-field agriculture – but they did give him some political influence.

The favourable conditions enticed many settlers. Peasant emancipation was especially rapid from the second half of the twelfth century. Serfdom became rare during the central Middle Ages except in imperial Flanders, where all peasants of the land of Aalst at the end of the Middle Ages who were direct subjects of the count were still considered serfs. Yet even there, labour services were rarely required. Even in the Carolingian period there is little evidence of rent payments in the form of forced labour in Flanders except in the French part, which was more fertile than the north and had the highest incidence of obligatory triennial rotation.[20] Furthermore, while French serfdom was usually imposed as a condition of tenure, binding the farmers to the soil, it was personal in the Frankish law that dominated Flanders. Serfs such as the Erembalds thus had freedom of movement.[21]

During the thirteenth century, the counts removed most of the remaining obligations of serfdom. In 1232 the free farmers on the count's domains in the Franc of Bruges, which by then included most of the territory, were freed from the obligation to surrender the best beast as a death duty. For the unfree, the count in 1252 converted their obligation to pay half their chattels as a death duty into a best-animal obligation. Apart from the counts' approval of especially favourable conditions for the tenants of the abbeys that were diking land, the emancipation of the maritime Flemish peasants resulted less often from comprehensive charters of franchise than from remissions from individual obligations.[22]

From their free tenants, most lords were entitled to a death duty and to a ground rent (*cens* or *cijns*), a payment in money, kind or both that is closer to the modern land tax than to 'rent'. Most Flemish ground rents were fixed by custom or written charter before or during the twelfth century, and inflation of the coin thus cut into lords' profits. Land held for ground rent was hereditary; as term leaseholds began to replace hereditary tenure in the thirteenth century – the first example is from St Bavo's domain at Lochristi in 1228 – the ground rent came to be worth much less to the lords than the leases. The lord's consent was required for the tenant to alienate his land, but this was normally granted for a fee. The lord was entitled to entry fees and

20. Verhulst, 'Boeren', 97; Godding, *Droie privé*, 49; J. Mertens, 'De Landbouwers in het Zuiden 1100–1300', *AGN* 2: 107.

21. Godding, *Droit privé*, 48–9.

22. Verhulst, 'Binnenkolonisation', 451–2.

'issue', which were owed by new and existing tenants respectively when properties changed hands. When entry and issue fees were calculated as a percentage of the sale price, they were an important source of income for lords; when they were figured as a percentage of the ground rent, they were economically insignificant.

Particularly to attract tenants to areas being reclaimed, lords offered the inducement of a fixed ground rent, usually at a rate per unit of land that was far below the rental value. The ground rents, however, rose dramatically in the late twelfth century, as population pressure grew, and the ground rent on new clearances was often vastly higher than on older land. On some domains of the abbey of St Bavo near Ghent, newly cleared land was given a 'new ground rent' in the second half of the twelfth century of 1 shilling per *bunder* of land, which was roughly equivalent to the yield in kind of ancient domanial tenures. By the second half of the thirteenth century, the rate was 10–12 shillings per bunder, but as a lease rather than a ground rent.[23]

There is some evidence that great domains were being subdivided and rented out, but the problem was probably less severe in Flanders than in its neighbours, since most of the reserves had always been farmed with more wage-earners than tenant labour services. Small tenancies were being created in the eleventh and twelfth centuries for serfs who previously had been attached directly to the reserve, but the tenancies were often so small that the serfs were unable to support themselves and had to hire themselves out as labour on the reserve.[24]

The growing population of Flanders

The population of Flanders was clearly growing, but there are no statistics. Chroniclers by the first half of the eleventh century were under the impression that Flanders was overpopulated, but they based this on the fact that so many Flemish mercenaries served abroad. There is less evidence for emigration of farmers except to Britain. We have noted Flemish participation in the conquest of 1066, and some Flemings were settled as military colonists on the Scottish and Welsh frontiers.

23. Verhulst, 'Occupatiegeschiedenis', 104; Verhulst, 'Boeren', 100–1; Godding, *Droit privé*, 163; Verhulst, *De Sint–Baafsabdij te Gent en haar grondbezit* (Brussels, 1958), 216–18, 255–6, 305–7.

24. Ganshof and Verhulst, 'Medieval Agrarian Society', 310–11; Verhulst, 'De Boeren. I: De Middeleeuwen', *Flandria Nostra* 1: 99; Blockmans, 'Vers une société urbanisée', 49.

Medieval Flanders

Between 1086 and 1110, Flemings helped drain Romney Marsh. But since these were people with special skills, it does not necessarily mean overpopulation in the homeland. William of Malmesbury relates that Flemings were driven to England in 1111 by floods, and Henry I settled them in the north. They built the mountain route of Pembroke, called Flemingsway.[25]

Flanders had had pockets of dense settlement since the Germanic migrations, but they were isolated and much of the land was too sandy, salty or marshy to be productive. There were still large amounts of uncleared land in Flanders in the thirteenth century. Galbert's account shows that western Flanders was importing food by the early twelfth century and that in the Leie–Scheldt area grain was available in the cities, presumably because they imported it from France, although not in the pastoral rural areas; but the farmers had plenty of meat, probably a reflection of the still pastoral economy of most of rural Flanders.[26]

The Flemish food supply was increased as the newly reclaimed swamps were desalinized and converted from sheep runs to arable; but this diminished the wool supply that the urban textile industries needed. Furthermore, famine was endemic. Vague references to scarcity, dryness and hunger abound. Even in the twelfth century, a period of general economic growth, there were two severe famines, in 1125 and 1197, and less severe shortages are reported in thirteen other years between 1106 and 1202. The famine of 1124–5 is known chiefly through its impact on food prices, not supplies on the rural markets, and the commercial character of the Flemish economy was accentuated during the twelfth century. The famine of 1196–7 was probably even more severe; in 1195 the price of wheat was ten times the normal in Flanders, and the last grain reserves from the inadequate harvest of 1196 were exhausted before the 1197 crop could be harvested. The yield of 1197 was good, and prices gradually returned to normal.[27]

Overpopulation in rural Flanders thus almost certainly caused some emigration in the twelfth century, especially in its second half, to the marshy areas along the Weser and to the Harz mountains and Thuringia. Stendal was founded by Flemish colonists, and Flemish and Brabantine weavers were at Magdeburg in 1179. Count Leopold of Austria

25. Cited by Varenbergh, *Relations diplomatiques*, 69–70.
26. Galbert, *Murder*, 80–8; for the implication of the passages concerning the food supply, see Nicholas, 'Of Poverty and Primacy', 31–3.
27. Hans van Werveke, *De middeleeuwse hongersnood* (Brussels, 1967), particularly 10, 15.

gave a privilege to Flemish weavers at Vienna in 1208. Lübeck and Kiel had Flemish districts, and Wismar, Dessau and Gdansk had prominent Flemish families. A substantial number of Flemings settled in Saxony after 1160 and became renowned for their cloth making. They kept their peculiar customs in Germany, and a popular song, evidently contemporary, told of them going to the east in search of 'a better place'. If the emigration was due to overpopulation in Flanders, the chronology thus suggests that population was growing substantially after about 1050, and the pressure on native resources was worst at the beginning and end of the twelfth century, perhaps connected to the great famines of 1124–5 and 1196–7.[28]

The question of why and to what extent Flanders was unable to support its population is tied to two problems: the growth of cities, which derived their income in large part from sources outside Flanders, and the per capita productivity of Flemish agriculture. Seed yields were rising everywhere in the central Middle Ages. By the thirteenth century they were probably double those of the tenth, although by modern standards they were still low. Three-field crop rotation and enforced agrarian routines make more efficient use of farmland than two-field structures and individual initiative, but they were never generalized in Flanders. Flemish agriculture seems to have had relatively low per capita yields on grain until the mid thirteenth century. Thereafter, Flanders became more productive in response to prior population increase and not as a cause of it. Most parts of Flanders were still getting lower yields in the early fourteenth century than farmers in Picardy got in the second half of the twelfth. The 'Flemish' farming techniques that were later taken to England actually originated in northern France and were not widely used in Flanders until the fourteenth century.[29]

28. Louis de Baecker (ed.), *Chants historiques de la Flandre 400–1650* (Lille, 1855), 156–7; Renée Doehaerd, 'Handelaars en Neringdoenden. I. De Romeinse Tijd en de Middeleeuwen', *Flandria Nostra* 1: 366–7; Verhulst, 'Occupatiegeschiedenis', 93–4; Nicholas, 'Of Poverty and Primacy', 31.

29. Verhulst, 'The "Agricultural Revolution" of the Middle Ages Reconsidered' in *Lyon Essays*, 17–28; Ganshof and Verhulst, 'Medieval Agrarian Society', 296; Verhulst, 'Occupatiegeschiedenis', 93, 99–100.

COMMERCE AND INDUSTRY

The new towns: the link of the rural and urban economies

The Flemish counts are famed as founders of new towns on their domains, most of them in western Flanders. Two of them, Ypres and Lille, developed into major cities. Much of their initiative resulted from the simultaneous retreat of the coastline and the use of large boats that required deep bays and high quais. Philip of Alsace accordingly evolved a master plan to provide the Flemish coast with ports that could be linked with interior towns such as Bruges, which would continue to provide brokerage and customs. Gravelines and Nieuwpoort were founded in 1163 as the outports of Saint-Omer and Ypres respectively. Philip established Biervliet in 1183, probably to serve this function for Ghent, although that did not materialize. In 1180 he hired Dutch labourers to build a dam across the Reie, which led northeast from Bruges to the sea at Kadzand. This became the city of Damme, which became Bruges' outport, although Bruges was still accessible by the Zwin to seagoing vessels for most of the twelfth century. None of the great cities of Flanders was a natural port by 1200. A major theme of the economic history of the coming centuries would be the use of political power by the great cities to create monopolies for themselves in actual hindrance of free trade, for they placed their ports under stringent controls.[30]

The only charter of a Flemish 'new town' that survives is that of Nieuwpoort. Personal freedom was guaranteed after a year and a day. The charter did not specifically give the freedom to alienate land, a standard clause of burgage tenure, but there was a tax on land transfers. All burghers got freedom from toll in Nieuwpoort itself, and this exemption was gradually extended to merchants of most communities of west Flanders, who gained access to the ports by canal.[31]

The coinage

The Flemish counts maintained a generally stable coinage until the

---

30. Blockmans, 'Vers une société urbanisée', 45; Doehaerd, 'Handelaars en neringdoenden', 378; Pounds, *Historical Geography*, 424; Alain Derville, 'Les origines de Gravelines et de Calais', *RN* **66** (1984): 1051–52.

31. Monier, *Institutions judiciaires*, 99; Degryse, 'Graven Domein', 72–9, 91; *IAY* **1**: 6, 9.

fourteenth century. During the twelfth century the silver content of
the Flemish coin was reduced; but instead of adding copper alloy to
keep the weight steady, they maintained fineness but made the coin
lighter. After a devaluation of one-quarter to one-fifth between 1137
and 1141, the coin remained stable until a reduction of 11 per cent in
the early 1180s. Thereafter, Flemish money remained stable until the
late thirteenth century.[32]

The development of trade furthered minting in Flanders. The
powerful local lords of southern Flanders coined money from the late
eleventh century. During the twelfth century, the most active Flemish
mints were at Saint-Omer and Arras. Although the counts controlled
the mints in the cities, each town had its own mint design. All the
coins were legal tender throughout Flanders, but actual circulation was
localized, in contrast to England, where the coins had the same type
even if coming from different mints.

After 1180, about 90 per cent of the total coinage came from five
major mints, at Lille, Ghent, Aalst, Ypres and Bruges. The importance
of Aalst was probably due to its border situation; it was the first Flemish town through which goods from Germany would pass. Similarly,
after Arras was lost in 1191, trade from the Champagne fairs entered
Flanders through Lille. Except for coins of Duisburg and Aachen,
which were allowed to circulate in Flanders under an agreement of
1173 with the emperor, only Flemish coins were legal tender in Flanders at this time, although this would change dramatically later.[33]

The fairs of Flanders

The counts also fostered commerce by establishing fairs. They had
established fairs by 1127 in their new or revived settlements of Ypres,
Lille, Mesen and Torhout; the fifth 'free fair', at Bruges, came later.
All were west of the Scheldt and depended on the economy of Bruges
rather than of Ghent. Flanders was the only region of northern Europe
that had important fairs this early; those of Champagne developed only
during the twelfth century. Galbert of Bruges noted that foreign merchants, including Italians, fled the Ypres fair at the news of the count's

32. Françoise Dumas, 'Comparison between the Political, the Economic and the
Monetary Evolution of the North of France in the Twelfth Century' in Mayhew,
Coinage in the Low Countries, 35–48.
   33. D.M. Metcalf, 'Coinage and the Rise of the Flemish Towns' in *Coinage in the
Low Countries*, 10–15.

assassination, since they could no longer enjoy his protection. This suggests a fair that was already well developed, perhaps going back to when the town was established in 1066. It also shows that foreigners enjoyed privileges that denizens evidently did not possess and that the natives resented them.[34]

Each fair lasted thirty days. They were held in a staggered cycle from the end of February through to the beginning of November, with intervals of two to four weeks between fairs that would allow merchants to go to neighbouring regional fairs in northern France and England as well as the international fairs in Champagne. A 'peace of the market' protected merchants en route to and from the fairs. Although evidently intended to build the local economies of the places in which they were founded, the fairs were also instrumental in the growth of the rest of Flanders. Tolls were levied, but the citizens of privileged towns – Bruges, Veurne, Diksmuide, Aardenburg, Oostburg, Oudenburg, Gravelines, Ypres, Ghent and Oudenaarde – paid much less than others.[35]

Changes in transportation facilitated the development of the fairs. Land routes first became competitive with rivers as commercial arteries in the eleventh century, with the invention of four–wheeled carts. Merchants also began using horse teams with collars, which could carry 500–600 kilogrammes of grain 40 kilometres per day. Many Flemings thus began going overland to the Rhine markets, although some of them still went around Zeeland and the Rhine channels. The Roman road from Boulogne to Cologne, which crossed southern Flanders, was less often used than a new route that was opened in the twelfth century from Cologne through Brabant to Aalst and thence to Ghent and Bruges. The change increased the value of Flanders as a point of entry for French and English goods en route to the developing markets in Brabant and Germany.[36]

The textile industry

Demand for goods from France, England and Germany in naturally poor Flanders created a vast interior market. But Flanders also

34. Dhondt, 'Développement urbain', 155; Pounds, *Historical Geography*, 299; Jansen, 'Handel en Nijverheid', 158; Galbert, *Murder*, 123–4.

35. Jansen, 'Handel en Nijverheid', 158–60; Jan Dhondt, 'Bijdrage tot het cartularium van Meesen (1065–1334)', *BCRH* **106** (1941): 145.

36. A. Derville, *Histoire de Saint-Omer* (Lille, 1981), 35; Jansen, 'Handel en Nijverheid', 161.

re-exported the imports after local needs had been satisfied, and the mechanics of that re-export produced significant revenue. Flanders also paid for the goods it imported by exporting cloth of all types. Pirenne maintained that the sudden growth of Flemish woollen cloth for export began when fine English wool was imported, for which the first documentation is the early twelfth century. Yet Flanders had textile manufacturing as early as the Roman period. Flanders and Artois had clay for fulling earth and grew dyestuffs, which are mentioned at the toll of Arras in 1024 and 1036.[37]

But the basis of the early Flemish textile industry was the large domestic production of fine wool, which was supplemented by the English product as local supplies became inadequate during the twelfth century. The reclamation of maritime Flanders nurtured a textile industry that was already thriving throughout Flanders – not only in the towns – by providing new grazing lands for sheep. Some urban drapers raised sheep on their rural estates as early as 1120. Except for a reference of 1013 to a Tournaisien taking a boatload of wool down the Scheldt for sale at Ghent, all evidence suggests that Flanders first began importing foreign wool in the early twelfth century.[38]

Even before the conversion of pasture in western Flanders to arable and the loss to France of the pastures of Artois, both in the late twelfth century, Flanders imported large quantities of English wool; but native wool was still used in export clothmaking at all the large cities except Ypres, which was the most exclusively directed towards luxury cloth of the major cities and required English wool for all export textiles. Bruges developed an important textile industry that used local wools for imitations of the speciality fabrics of other cities. Although Bruges would later be the major port of Flanders and may have been so already, it did not manufacture luxury cloth until later, despite its proximity to the source of wool in England.

Although Flanders came to specialize in luxury cloth making, it made all types of cloth from all types of wool, and its domination of overseas manufacturing was not as total as once was thought. Considerable cloth was sold at the Flemish and Champagne fairs, and Italian records show that although Ghent and particularly Ypres sent much cloth to the Mediterranean at the end of the twelfth century, the

37. Georges Espinas, *La Draperie dans la Flandre française au Moyen Age,* 2 vols. (Paris, 1923), 1: 25, 30.

38. Unfootnoted statements in this discussion of native wool in Flanders are taken from Verhulst, 'La Laine indigène dans les anciens Pays–Bas entre le XIIe et le XVIIe siècle: Mise en oeuvre industrielle production et commerce', *RH* **96** (1972): 281–322.

smaller Flemish towns, notably Diksmuide, Bailleul and Geraardsbergen, together with those of Walloon Flanders and northwestern France, seem to have taken a greater share of the southern market than did Ghent and Ypres, whose trade was directed towards England and Germany. Prices from Genoa, which re-exported raw Flemish cloth to other Italian towns for finishing, suggest that cloth of Diksmuide was of medium grade, while fabrics of Ypres and Arras were expensive. By 1200 Ypres was generally the best represented of the large Flemish cities, followed by Ghent, with Lille a distant third. The trade of Saint-Omer was directed mainly towards England; there is little evidence of its cloth at Genoa. Ghent lagged behind several French centres, notably Amiens, Tournai and Montreuil-sur-Mer, and English cloth was also an important competitor on the Genoese market for the Flemish product before 1200.[39]

The textiles of the early Middle Ages had been called by various names, most often *pallia*, but all had been made on primitive, vertical looms that amounted to stretching frames, similar to what the Romans had used, in which the woof threads were inserted manually by a nail or pin across the warp. Most weaving was done in the rural areas and was a largely female occupation.[40] Although Flanders was noted for its cloth before the mid eleventh century, so were neighbouring parts of northern France and western Germany, and an eleventh-century German source suggests that Flanders was better stocked with cows than with looms, for it was famous for its dairy products.[41]

In the late eleventh century, however, Flanders became renowned for its *panni*, longer and heavier cloths that were made on a treadle horizontal loom that was operated by either men or women. This device is first attested in Champagne in the mid eleventh century, but it quickly spread to Flanders. It eventually yielded to the heavy horizontal broadloom, which required the labour of two people, almost always males, and was used only in the towns where the labour supply

39. Sivery, *Histoire de Lille*, 166–7; Verhulst, 'Laine indigène', 291–2, 311; Nicholas, 'Of Poverty and Primacy', 34–5; Patrick Chorley, 'The Cloth Exports of Flanders and Northern France during the Thirteenth Century: A Luxury Trade?' *EcHR*, ser. 2, **40** (1987): 349–79; Hilmar C. Krueger, 'The Genoese Exportation of Northern Cloths to Mediterranean Ports, Twelfth Century', *RBPH* **65** (1987): 722–50; Robert L. Reynolds, 'The Market for Northern Textiles in Genoa 1179–1200', *RBPH* **8** (1929): 840–47.

40. Herlihy, *Opera Muliebria*, 77–92.

41. A. van de Vyver and Charles Verlinden, 'L'Auteur et la portée du *Conflictus ovis et lini*', *RBPH* **12** (1933): 59–81, but the authors' interpretation of this text cannot be accepted.

was more abundant than in the rural areas. The new loom produced a heavier cloth than the varieties made during most of the twelfth century, and thus the technological change by 1200 was accentuating the demand in Flanders for English wool. The growth of Flanders' population, together with the availability − if only briefly − of an adequate supply of fine wool thus created the basis both of the famed Flemish textile industry of the Middle Ages and of the shift of cloth making from the rural areas into the cities.[42]

For whatever reason, Flemish cloth making became a mainly urban occupation and expanded tremendously between the periods of Robert the Frisian and Baldwin IX. Cloth of Flanders was traded throughout the known world. Woollens of Ypres are found at Novgorod by 1130. Flemish merchants are attested in 1143 at Saint-Gilles-du-Gard at the mouth of the Rhône and at the fair of Poitiers in 1180. By 1262 a toll exemption that had previously been given to the merchants of Aardenburg in the areas of Brunswick and Magdeburg was extended to all Flemish merchants. Ghent cloth is mentioned in the Baltic region in the twelfth century, probably getting there through Cologne, where its merchants had special privileges. Ghent had an organization of merchants who regularly went to 'the emperor's land'. They complained to Frederick Barbarossa that Cologne merchants were preventing them from traversing the Rhine south of Cologne, alleging that a privilege of St Bavo's abbey permitting it to do business in the entire empire applied to them. Barbarossa in 1164 confirmed the 'customary rights' of the Gentenars. He gave free circulation to Flemish merchants in the entire German empire and ordered that cloth halls be built for them at Aachen and Duisburg, where they visited the fairs. By 1197 the German trade was extensive enough to require an agreement between Cologne and the Flemings on court procedures to be used for prosecuting Flemish debtors and criminals.[43]

42. Nicholas, Of Poverty and Primacy', 36; van Werveke, 'Introduction historique' to Guy de Poerck, *La Draperie médiévale en Flandre et Artois: Technique et terminologie*, 3 vols (Bruges, 1951), 1: 7–11; Jansen, 'Handel en Nijverheid', 156–8; P. Vàczy, 'La Transformation de la technique et de l'organisation de l'industrie textile en Flandre aux XI–XIIIe siècles', *Studia Historica Academiae Scientiarum Hungaricae* **48** (1960): 3–26.
43. Blockmans, 'Vers une société urbanisée', 57–60; W. Stein, 'Der Streit zwischen Köln und Flandern um die Rheinschiffahrt im 12. Jahrhundert', *Hansische Geschichtsblätter* **17** (1911): 187–215. The agreement of 1197 is translated in Roy C. Cave and Herbert H. Coulson (eds), *A Source Book for Medieval Economic History* (Milwaukee, 1936), 222.

The English trade with Flanders

England and Flanders were trading partners before 1100, but nothing suggests the volume of trade that developed thereafter. The growth of the Flemish export textile industry in the twelfth century would have been impossible without the stimulus of English wool. By 1127 trading ties were so frequent that the death of Charles the Good was known in London two days after it occurred. English financial bonds with Flanders were particularly close early in Henry II's reign. The cloth merchant and moneychanger William Cade of Saint-Omer had a house in London. He was involved in the London money market and was one of the earliest Flemish merchants who bought wool from the Cistercian abbeys and paid in advance. He lent money to various officials and to Henry II himself both before and after he became king. Although there is no direct evidence that Cade lent money to Becket, both fell from favour in early 1164. The king borrowed no more from Cade and seized his assets in England in 1166, presumably when Cade died.[44]

Anglo–Flemish trade quickened especially from the late twelfth century, but it was totally at the mercy of relations between the two ruling dynasties. Interruptions were frequent, and merchants had to seek special privileges. When Philip of Alsace supported the Young King's revolt in 1173, substantial quantities of wool and woad belonging to Flemings were seized. The English also seized Flemish boats, wine – which the Flemings evidently brought to England from France – and grain. After 1176, Flemish merchants in England were unmolested until 1194, when the government confiscated the year's wool clip, for which Flemish merchants had already paid, to finance Richard I's ransom. The Flemings were also hurt by the first English national customs levy, a tax of one-tenth on overseas trade. Thereafter, except during Baldwin IX's brief alliance with Philip Augustus in 1196, the English kings generally maintained good relations with Flanders until after 1206, but always with the threat of reprisals if the Flemish counts did not adhere to the alliance against the French.[45]

44. Galbert, *Murder*, 113; Hilary Jenkinson, 'William Cade, a Financier of the Twelfth Century', *English Historical Review* **28** (1913): 209–27, 731–2; see also discussion in Christopher N.L. Brooke assisted by Gillian Keir, *London 800–1216: The Shaping of a City* (Berkeley, 1975), 228–30.

45. Dept, *Influences anglaises*, 27–8; T.H. Lloyd, *The English Wool Trade in the Middle Ages* (Cambridge, 1977), 7–9.

The Flemings, who seem to have controlled much of England's continental trade in the twelfth century, also visited the English fairs and conveyed English goods to Champagne. Through the late twelfth century, Flemish traders bought wheat and wool in England and sold wine and almost certainly cloth, although the sources do not say so explicitly; Flemish cloth was definitely sold in England in large quantities by 1220. By the end of the twelfth century, Ypres and Douai had overtaken Saint-Omer and dominated the Anglo–Flemish trade at the English fairs.[46]

The continued growth of Flemish urban life

Although Flanders had commercial settlements before the economic upsurge that began in the mid eleventh century, its urban and commercial development lagged behind that of England and northern France, although it was the most advanced area of the Low Countries. With the phenomenal growth during the twelfth century, however, the urban density of Flanders became the most extreme in Europe, surpassing even Italy. The Flemish towns were no more than 60–90 kilometres apart; Tournai, Douai, Ypres and Courtrai were within a radius of 25 kilometres of Lille. 'Every great Italian merchant city controlled a territory as large as Flanders.'[47] The configuration was striking. All the major Flemish cities except Geraardsbergen, Aalst and Dendermonde were between the sea and the Scheldt where it bends east at Ghent; and all were south of the Ghent–Bruges line. The northeast and southwest were agricultural. Paralleling their population growth, the great cities were walled in the late eleventh century. Bruges got a first wall around 1100, but the second, enclosing large suburban areas involving four new parishes, was built only between 1297 and 1300. The walls of Ghent were extended seven times in the thirteenth and fourteenth centuries.[48]

We have discussed the early history of Ghent and Bruges, the greatest towns of Germanic Flanders, and have noted their role in the dramatic events of 1127–8. Saint-Omer had also developed precociously. From unpromising beginnings near the abbey of St Bertin, it was the seat of a comital court by the tenth century, with an 'urban

46. Ellen Wedemeyer Moore, *The Fairs of Medieval England: An Introductory Study* (Toronto, 1985), 30–1.

47. This important point, statistics and quotation are made by Sivery, 'Histoire économique et sociale' in *Histoire de Lille*, 164–5.

48. Blockmans, 'Vers une société urbanisée', 53–6.

judge' (*praetor urbanus*) and probably aldermen and free burgage tenure. Saint-Omer also had a confraternity whose statutes suggest that they are very old; clerics and laymen were joined in the cult of St Omer for prayers, friendship, drinking and funerals. The brotherhood was called a merchant guild in the eleventh century. It helped members who were fearful of distant travel and assured them rights to pre-empt sales on the market of Saint-Omer. Members furthered 'common utility', maintenance of streets, gates and walls and relief of the poor and lepers. The guild had some governmental power initially, but it lost it with the consolidation of the aldermen's powers in the charter of 1127.

Textiles may have occupied half of Saint-Omer's workforce in the High Middle Ages. It was the most prominent Flemish city in the English trade before 1191. Like Ypres, it benefited from the flooding of the early twelfth century, which cut a gulf at Gravelines. But by 1160–70, Saint-Omer was becoming landlocked as the waters receded. At the initiative of Philip of Alsace, Saint-Omer dug a new canal along the bed of the Aa, the 'Great River', to Gravelines. Saint-Omer remained its proprietor and had a staple on the Aa by the late twelfth century, forbidding anyone to discharge cargo between Saint-Omer and Gravelines. Bruges dug its canal to Damme at about this time, but big sea vessels could never get through to Bruges, while Saint-Omer remained a seaport that could handle boats with a capacity of up to 600 tons, with no worse obstacle than the sluice of Gravelines.[49]

While these three were 'organic' towns that developed gradually in the absence of an act of foundation, Lille and Ypres grew on the sites of new castles of the eleventh century that were evidently part of the Frisian counts' plans to promote trade and link their eastern and western domains. Lille would have great political power by the thirteenth century as one of the 'good towns' of Flanders, but economically it was essentially a farm market. Ypres, by contrast, became one of the greatest industrial centres of medieval Europe.

Lille developed near a Carolingian fisc, but its early economic development has never been explained satisfactorily. Baldwin V had a castle there by 1054, but it was probably built to protect a merchant settlement that was already present. Lille had a market by 1066 and the fair by 1127. Although the topographical expansion of the city was south from its origin at the castle, trade was more important by river with the north than overland towards the south. Lille's *portus*

---

49. Derville, 'Gravelines', 1054; Derville, *Histoire de Saint-Omer*, 36–45.

developed on the south bank of the Lower Deûle, at the point where the river becomes navigable and cargoes are thus recharged. The Deûle linked Lille to the Leie and Ghent, and Lille was at the point where the road to Arras and Cambrai would later divide and where the land roads to Ghent and Ypres crossed the river. Lille thus had more advantages of site than Saint-Omer. The fertile soil of the area made it a grain exporter, but the town area was marshy, and its development was due more to the frequent presence of the counts' government than to economic factors. Lille picked up some of Arras' trade after 1191, but it was never as dependent on textiles as the other cities. It was more significant as a comital residence than for its trade until the modern period.[50]

Ypres was the most successful of the planned foundations. Baldwin V built a castle there on the shore of the Ieperleet canal, near one of his estates. By 1066 he had surrounded the castle with a navigable moat. The town developed east of the island thus formed, as a dual nucleus formation from the market outside the comital church of St Martin and the originally rural church of St Pieter, around which merchants congregated. The Bruges–Torhout–Mesen–Lille route crossed the market by 1127 and joined those coming from Poperinge and Diksmuide at the point where the Ieperleet ceased being navigable. In contrast to Bruges and Ghent, Ypres had a rectangular street layout, suggesting a plan. It grew into a major city in half a century, probably benefiting from the flooding that gave it canalized access to the coast. It is now an inland city, and the silting of its water links became a problem even in the late twelfth century; but at the outset of the economic revival it had at least as good a location for overseas trade as did Bruges.[51]

Urban law in the twelfth century

The early sworn associations of burghers called themselves 'friendships' (Aire, Lille and Diksmuide) or 'peace' (Arras), for they were established to guarantee the peace to their inhabitants. The argument has

50. Louis Trenard (ed.), *Histoire de Lille*. I: *Des origines à l'avènement de Charles Quint* (Lille, n.d.), 11–74; Sivery, 'Histoire économique et sociale' in Trenard, *Histoire de Lille*, 147–9, 152, 154, 191ff.

51. A. Verhulst, 'De vroegste Geschiedenis van het Sint-Maartenskapittel en het onstaan van de stad Ieper', *HMGOG* **11** (1957): 31–48; van Houtte, 'Ieper door de eeuwen heen', in O. Mus and J.A. van Houtte (eds), *Prisma van de Geschiedenis van Ieper* (Ypres, 1974), xi–xii.

been raised that this sworn association or 'guild' was the first town government, but this tangled question is impossible to answer satisfactorily. Certainly merchant elites dominated the early cities. The aldermen met in the merchants' hall at Saint-Omer, although the building was the count' property until 1157.[52]

The count gave evidently similar 'little charters' in 1127 to all the Flemish cities, although only that for Saint-Omer has survived. There were local variations. Saint-Omer received fixed ground rents. The charter made allods of the land at Bruges, where the count himself was lord except for the lands of St Donatian. This had occurred at Ghent in the late eleventh century, when the burghers had bought out the abbeys' rights to ground rent. The count gave Bruges the right to modify its own laws. Saint-Omer and probably Ghent also enjoyed this privilege.[53]

The Saint-Omer charter, which was given on 14 April 1127 by William Clito and later confirmed by Thierry of Alsace, remains the fundamental starting point for a consideration of Flemish urban law.[54] The aldermen, who were evidently functioning before this time, could act as a court to judge all cases arising in the town, even those in which the count was a party. The city government was allowed to sequester the property of anyone who defaulted on a debt to a townsman, but only if the debt had been acknowledged before persons who owned land within the *portus*. The 'landowners' became a separate estate in most Flemish cities from this time. If the debtor denied the obligation, judgement would be given according to the testimony of two aldermen or two 'sworn men'. The burghers were required to do military service outside the town only if a hostile army invaded Flanders. A 'guild' of citizens, obviously merchants, was freed from all tolls at the ports of Diksmuide and Gravelines and from specific tolls at Arras. The burgesses were freed from arbitrary taxes, the head tax and payments to the advocates of the abbot of St Bertin. The count recognized the 'commune' or sworn association of Saint-Omer and imposed a duty of collective vengeance if a citizen's injuries at the hands of an outsider were not redressed.

Count Philip of Alsace, a legal innovator in so many other respects, also tried to standardize urban law in Flanders. Only from his time is it proper to distinguish urban law as a distinct type from the essentially

---

52. Monier, *Institutions judiciaires*, 68–79, 84.
53. Galbert, *Murder*, 201–2 and Ross's comment.
54. The charter is printed by Vercauteren, *Actes*, 299–302. For a convenient English translation, see David Herlihy, *Medieval Culture and Society* (New York, 1968), 181–4.

Frankish law of rural villages that had special privileges. The urban
magistracies in Flanders were aldermanic, outgrowths of Carolingian
judges (Lat. *scabini*, Fr. *échevins*, Fl. *scepenen*). *Jurés*, representatives of the
sworn association, dominated the towns of the eastern Low Countries
and existed in Flanders, but they were weak and did not develop into
the chief magistracy of any city.[55]

While Philip fostered the economic growth of the larger cities, he
resisted their efforts to gain autonomy. The growth of the cities during
the twelfth century spread the already endemic violence into an environment where it was even harder to control than in the rural areas.
In 1179 the archbishop of Reims condemned powerful persons in
Ghent, 'insolent because of their wealth and their fortified houses,
[who] rebelled against the Church and usurped the jurisdiction and
authority of Count Philip'.[56] The Gentenars had been notoriously bel-
licose since at least Galbert's time. Evidently hoping to overawe them,
Philip of Alsace rebuilt the earlier comital castle in the Oudburg into
the famous *Gravensteen* that, considerably reconstructed, dominates the
modern central city.[57]

A charter that Philip introduced at Arras, probably in 1163, was
then extended in a revised version to Bruges, Douai, Ghent, Ypres,
Lille and Saint-Omer between 1165 and 1177. It was then given with
further revisions to several smaller communities.[58] Although he called
the charters 'law and custom', they are in fact new laws. They provided more uniform justice for the cities than for rural areas in criminal matters. Whereas earlier urban law, as we have seen from the
disorder, had emphasized arbitration of disputes among lineages,
Philip's statutes entailed more severe penalties for criminal acts and
enlarged the count's share of fines. The ordeal was abolished in judicial
inquests in favour of investigation by the aldermen. The death penalty
was provided only for forgery and theft in the Arras charter, but rape
and homicide were added in the later ones. The use of the sworn
inquest to name persons suspected of crime had been known by 1127
at the latest and was now expanded. For major crimes the entire fine,
notably the £60 fine for blood justice, went to the count, while for

55. Monier, *Institutions judiciaires*, 105–8.
56. R.C. van Caenegem, 'Criminal Law in England and Flanders under King
Henry II and Count Philip of Alsace', *Actes du Congrès de Naples (1980) de la Société de
l'Histoire du Droit*, 250.
57. Van Werveke, *Filips*, 10–12.
58. Unfootnoted references to the charters are taken from R. C. van Caenegem and
L. Milis, 'Kritische Uitgave van de "Grote Keure" van Filips van de Elzas, graaf van
Vlaanderen, voor Gent en Brugge (1165–1177)', *BCRH* **143** (1977), 207–57.

lesser crimes the older system was kept, in which fixed percentages went to the count, the victim, the town and the castellan.[59]

Philip's charters for the cities mention a 'count's justiciar' who exercised the functions that would be associated with the bailiff by century's end: adjudicating complaints that the aldermen had given false judgement, confiscating criminals' property, consenting to measures that the city used to raise money and holding the count's pleas. Prosecution normally depended on the public outcry or private initiative of the parties, but the count's bailiff could prosecute house-break *ex officio* and quickly did so for other offences.[60] Prosecution *ex officio* was perhaps Philip's most important legal innovation. Under some circumstances, notably those involving blood justice with the £60 fine, the aldermen could not refuse to summon an accused person to trial or pardon him without the count's consent. Although the aldermen could render verdicts in capital cases, only the bailiff could enforce a sentence involving death or mutilation. Levels of violence remained high. No fine was incurred for any action in self-defence or for killing an exile, who was already an outlaw. Trucebreak, which involved violation of an agreement between families, entailed the £60 fine, as did theft. There were fines for using insulting language, from which many fights broke out. Only merchants and other transients might carry swords within the walls; but if anyone entered the city intending to stay, he had to leave his weapons in the suburbs. Citizens about to face the world outside could carry weapons en route to leaving town.[61]

Later evidence shows that the authorities were utterly unable to enforce these provisions, but the position of the aldermen in the city was nonetheless strengthened. They had been purely judicial officials before, but these constitutions gave them some administrative responsibilities. They continued to be essentially representatives of the count rather than of the association of burghers. Although the citizens evidently chose the magistrates – the mechanism is unclear at this time – the count by this constitution would choose the successor of an alderman who died in office. The aldermen were to pacify dissensions, saving the count's rights, and the £60 fine was automatic for not accepting a peace imposed by the aldermen or denying their right to

59. Van Caenegem, 'Criminal Law', 235–9; van Caenegem, 'Serfdom' in *Lyon Essays*, 101; Galbert, *Murder*, and Ross's comment, 258.

60. Degryse, 'Bailiffs', 266–70; Nowé, *Baillis*, 44.

61. Van Caenegem and Milis, 'Kritische uitgave', 232–7, chapters 1–2, 4–6, 10, 19–20; Monier, *Institutions judiciaires*, 134.

adjudicate. The aldermen had no authority to alter the constitution without the consent of the count or his representative.[62]

In 1178 Philip issued supplementary rules for Ghent and dispensed with the fiction that they were customary, calling them 'precepts that the lord count establishes'. Although the charters of 1127–8 had evidently given the towns that got them the right to legislate, Philip's constitution of 1178 permitted this only with the consent of his bailiff. Proof was to be by rational means, through formal inquest conducted by the aldermen. If the count's representative demanded that anyone give him a hostage for good behaviour, presumably in an attempt to limit a feud, the £60 fine was to be exacted for refusal. A curious provision prohibits anyone from having 'another man' at Ghent except in connection with a feud or a fief, evidently to hinder the formation of paramilitary clienteles. Persons sentenced to a £60 fine had to pay the count in full within three days or suffer lifelong outlawry.[63]

62. Van Caenegem and Milis, 'Kritische Uitgave', 234–5, chapters 14–15, 21, 24, 28; Monier, Institutions judiciaries, 104, 111.

63. Van Caenegem, 'Criminal Law', 231–54, esp. 245; van Caenegem, 'Recht en politiek: de "precepta" van Graaf Filips van de Elzas voor de stad Gent uit het jaar 1178' in Recht en Instellingen in de Oude Nederlanden tijdens de Middeleeuwen en de Nieuwe Tijd: Liber Amicorum Jan Buntinx (Louvain, 1981), 51–62; van Caenegem and Milis, "Precepta", 5, chapters 1–2, 7, 11–12. In 1191, after Philip of Alsace died, Ghent forced a more favourable charter on his widow, but Baldwin IX withdrew it and added some more severe penalties; van Caenegem and Milis, 'Kritische Uitgave', 216.

CHAPTER SIX

Economic Growth and Cultural Flowering in the Thirteenth Century

RURAL ECONOMY AND SOCIETY IN THIRTEENTH-CENTURY FLANDERS

Many of the developments that we have seen in the twelfth-century rural economy become more pronounced during the thirteenth. Pressure was redoubled on resources in rural Flanders. Although great lords were in financial trouble, large estates still occupied roughly two-thirds of the land surface in Flanders. Even this early, most peasants in the Ghent area held only 2–3 hectares of land, although this might sustain a small household. Small farms were most numerous in areas of old villas that had declined; on the coast, farms were larger than in the interior, but by the fourteenth century a farm as large as 5 hectares was unusual even there. Farmers thus had to supplement their incomes by becoming wage-earners on the great estates or taking work from textile entrepreneurs in the cities. Others went into construction work; many of the less skilled jobs in the cities were taken by farmers of the environs whose plots of land were simply too small to require their full-time attention.

Flemish farmers normally used the wheeled plough. Flanders was definitely precocious in using the horse as a draught animal. It was much more efficient than the ox, and the soils of Flanders were light enough not to need the ox's strength. Yields in Germanic Flanders were respectable but despite some improvement continued to be considerably lower than in Picardy and Artois. The area around Lille, which may have had 20:1 on cereals in the fourteenth century (about 2200 litres per hectare), was probably the most prosperous in Europe. Mixed farming now dominated. Rye, which was hardy and could withstand cold, was the most common winter grain and often constituted one-third of the summer crop as well. Oats was the principal summer grain. Wheat was scarcely ever grown alone; maslin, a mixture of wheat and rye, was more common.[1]

From the mid thirteenth century and perhaps earlier, crops rich in nitrogen – beans, peas and vetches – were cultivated along with summer grains, chiefly oats, in the second field. As early as 1259, a lease of St Pieter's abbey of Ghent obliged the tenant to plant vetches, which were normally fed to horses, on the parts of the estate that previously had lain fallow. This is an important innovation, with the fodder crop the result of a separate sowing rather than intermixed with the spring planting. By raising a new crop rather than allowing the land to rest for a year, the farmers not only made it more fertile but also made it possible to support more animals for ploughing and transport. The peasants of overpopulated areas were also the earliest to grow plants for industrial use. Madder, used for red dye, was being cultivated extensively from the end of the twelfth century in maritime Flanders, but between 1244 and 1270 it was alternated with grains on a two- to four-year cycle near Merelbeke, south of Ghent. Woad, which produces blue dye, was being grown by the mid thirteenth century on estates that formerly had been given over exclusively to the grains that were paid as kind rents to the abbey. The diversification of Flemish agriculture thus dates from the mid thirteenth century and was an important response to the growing problem of fragmentation of plots and overpopulation.[2]

Although the movement of land clearance slowed in Flanders after 1175, it resumed after 1215 with the poldering and clearance of the infertile wastelands of the north. Much of the motive for clearance in the north was the growing use of peat as a fuel. Philip of Alsace and his successors encouraged peat production, which was a regalian right, but the princes were not in a position to exploit the bogs directly. Beginning with Countess Joan, they thus sold and leased them. These

1. Verhulst, *Précis*, 86, 64–6; Verhulst, 'Boeren', 112–13; Verhulst, 'Occupatiegeschiedenis', 101; Nicholas, 'Of Poverty and Primacy', 27–8 and literature cited.

2. Verhulst, *Précis*, 70; A. Verhulst, 'L'Intensification et la commercialisation de l'agriculture dans les Pays-Bas méridionaux au XIIIe siècle' in *La Belgique rurale du moyen-âge à nos jours. Mélanges offerts à Jean-Jacques Hoebanx* (Brussels, 1985), 91–9.

transactions became so numerous that Countess Margaret had to appoint a 'moor master' to handle them. By the second half of the thirteenth century there was a veritable boom in the peat bogs, particularly in Four Offices and Waas, in which most purchasers were burghers of Ghent and Bruges. During the fourteenth century there was a wave of speculation in the bogs. Unfortunately, no quantifiable evidence of peat exports survives, but it is clear that the growing problems of the Flemish textile trade were compensated for to some extent by the export of peat.[3]

The exploitation of the peat bogs tells us much about the reclamation movement and the administrative faculties of the Flemish rulers in the thirteenth century. The moor of Aardenburg is already mentioned in the count's General Receipt of 1187. The name *Meetjesland*, which is still used for the area around Eeklo, is an early medieval toponym indicating division of the land into measures (*meten*) for peat exploitation. A text of 1313 shows that the bog between Aardenburg and Kaprijke was divided into parcels of standard size, which shows considerable administrative sophistication. The peat plots were separated by a network of drainage ditches that were dug in the thirteenth century by the count's officials, then linked to the major canals to take peat to the cities. A dike, mentioned in the thirteenth century, separated the moors of Eeklo and Aardenburg. Today it divides two water courses and is a parish border. As the peat bogs played out, canals lost their usefulness, and dikes were converted to land roads. Sheep could also be raised in the peat areas, and cloth making became important.[4]

The economic expansion of thirteenth-century Flanders brought significant profits to some churches and hospitals, but perhaps not enough to compensate for the immense expenses that they incurred in bringing the land into production. This was not necessarily the result of faulty calculation; few could have foreseen the economic downturn after 1275. It is clear, however, that the economic growth of the thirteenth century did not benefit most great lay lords. Much of their problem was due to mismanagement and poor calculation, particularly making life grants of properties to their own domain agents and to lesser lords for an annual sum in kind or money and granting fixed rents. After 1215 some tried to retrieve their domain lands from the leaseholders but without much success.

Virtually all lords began keeping more written documents, including inventories, lists and transfers. There was an even greater use than before of wage labour; tenant labour services were totally ended or

3. Nicholas, *Town and Countryside*, 290–1.
4. Thoen, 'Oosterzele', 42–4.

limited to a few days per year. They also introduced fees for using their mills, breweries and other equipment. As population growth drove up the price of land, even waste, lords leased land that had been common. They also controlled the increasingly scarce woodland.

The early thirteenth century was an inflationary period, although before 1275 it was caused by demand exceeding supply rather than coin debasement. To compensate, some lords began converting rental contracts from hereditary ground rent to term leasehold (*bail à ferme*), usually for nine-, six- or three-year terms. By 1281 St Pieter's abbey of Ghent received over six times as much from leases as from ground rents. The leases were generally for an entire large domain. Since few individual farmers usually had enough capital to assume such a lease, townsmen often did it, then sublet to the farmers. Contracts often were very specific about what was to be done during the term, protecting both the actual farmer and the investor.[5]

Most early conversions from ground rent to term leasehold are in the interior. In maritime Flanders, the abbeys and the count held large farms that they exploited directly into the late thirteenth century. Term leaseholds spread from entire demesne farms to individual parcels in the fourteenth century. Only in the newer polders in maritime Flanders were individual parcels systematically given out for a short-term money lease from the time they were cleared in the late thirteenth century. By the fourteenth century, most small farms were composites that contained both land held at ground rent and a piece of land detached at term leasehold from the older domain farm.[6]

The churches were slower than lay lords to adapt to the term leasehold, but they were forced to adopt it everywhere by the early fourteenth century. Many overextended in the land boom of the early thirteenth century and had to retrench after 1275, as yields declined, marginal land went out of cultivation and costs and wages rose. Thus the abbeys reduced expenses by either giving up direct exploitation or converting to term leases.[7]

As lords' problems mounted, there is increased evidence in the thirteenth century of conflicts between them and village associations. In

---

5. Verhulst, *Précis*, 75; Mertens, 'Landbouwers', 107; Verhulst, 'Occupatiegeschiedenis', 102; Ganshof and Verhulst, 'Medieval Agrarian Society', 322–3; Verhulst, 'Boeren', 102–3. The estate of the Cistercian abbey of Vaucelles at Zaamslag, in maritime Flanders, illustrates these characteristics and trends; Stéphane Lebecq, 'Les Cisterciens de Vaucelles en Flandre maritime au XIIIe siècle', *RN* **54** (1972): 371–85.

6. Verhulst, 'Boeren', 105; Verhulst, 'Occupatiegeschiedenis', 104.

7. Verhulst, *Précis*, 76–8; Verhulst, 'Occupatiegeschiedenis', 103.

1266 the inhabitants of Destelbergen fought St Pieter's abbey of Ghent over the abbey's plan to reclaim the waste of Haenhout. It was judged by the countess, who allowed the abbey to reclaim part of the disputed area and left the rest as common pasture to the villagers. There are references in the second half of the thirteenth century to guards of woods and of harvests, named by the community. Communal regulation of waste and common lands became customary in the thirteenth century, sometimes gained by purchase from the lord, sometimes by gradual assumption of rights. But only after 1300 were such lands generally the corporate possession of village associations.[8]

THE CITIES

The towns and the rural areas

The growing activity of the burghers in the countryside signals an important change. Townsmen were interested in rural areas as an investment. Most simply bought land, then gave it out in ground rent or term leasehold, frequently to the person who had sold it to them; some sale and rental arrangements thus amount to concealed mortgages. But they were interested also in protecting the environment so that it could be used in the future. Much has been made of the environmental consciousness of the Flemish counts, but their concern seems to have been limited to their forested hunting preserves.

Townsmen, however, took great care in their rural land leases to specify that the land would be left in the same or better condition as found. They also built dikes. From the thirteenth century most diking in western Flanders was undertaken by patricians of Bruges, hospitals and comital agents who acted on their own initiative rather than on the countess's orders. Burgesses of Ghent also had dikes constructed in Four Offices and Waas, especially around Hulst, Aksel and Saaftinge, although the abbeys were also active. In the polder areas the owner of the land kept the tithes, which became sources of immense kind rents. Diking continued in the northeast until around 1300, considerably later than in the gulfs of the IJzer and Zwin; indeed, later floods submerged some of the newer polders. The extraction of peat, otherwise

8. On this important point, see Mertens, 'Landbouwers', 121.

so profitable, lowered the soil level and made it more subject to inundation.[9]

The canals

Although the counts had sponsored most canal construction before 1200, initiative passed to the great cities during the thirteenth century. Ghent from 1251 built the Lieve, which linked the city with Damme and connected inland Ghent to the burgeoning Zwin trade. Ghent bore the entire cost of construction and acquired several houses on the quais at Damme, as well as lands along the canal. Ghent rigidly controlled access and channelling into the Lieve, which provided linkage not only to Damme but to the canal network of northern Flanders along which the peat trade moved. Ghent also controlled most of these subsidiary canals, into areas where its burgesses owned peat bogs, and may have built them.

Bruges and Ypres were faced with silting of their water links with the sea as reclamation continued to push the coastline westward. Damme, originally a port, was an inland town by the mid thirteenth century. Thus in 1280 Bruges and the count founded Sluis as the new port. The city maintained the Zwin and the smaller streams that joined Bruges with Damme and Sluis. Like Ghent, Bruges had extra-territorial jurisdiction over lands adjacent to the canals and controlled the sluices in the outports. Although Bruges would begin constructing canals in the Franc soon after 1302, it did not as far as is known directly control other canal construction during the thirteenth century.

Ypres's water problems were the worst, although the city kept canal links to the sea at Bruges and Nieuwpoort. After a new canal to Nieuwpoort was completed in 1265, maintenance, dredging and fighting sabotage by farmers who resented the city's privileges and particularly its expropriation of farmland occupied a substantial part of Ypres's budget. In 1290 the count permitted Ypres to build a canal across the land of the abbess of Mesen, with whom Ypres had a running battle throughout the late Middle Ages, but they were to pay her an indemnity and reimburse her for damages already sustained.[10]

9. Pirenne, *Histoire de Belgique*, 1: 309–10; Verhulst, *Précis*, 53–7.

10. For the canal-building activities of the city governments, see Nicholas, *Town and Countryside*, 125–37; *IAY* 1: 89–90, 104–5, 110, 111, 133. The original charter of 1275 confirming toll freedom at Nieuwpoort was given in Latin but also existed in a Flemish translation in the Ypres archives, perhaps an indication of the inability by that time of the magistrates of Ypres to understand Latin.

129

The physical expansion of the cities

All the major Flemish cities experienced tremendous growth in the thirteenth century. We have no population figures for Ghent or Bruges, but Ypres in 1247 alleged to the pope that 200,000 persons inhabited the city. More realistically, in 1258 the cathedral chapter of St Martin used a figure of 40,000.[11]

By the thirteenth century Ghent and Ypres had a ban mile, a territory outside the wall in which the law of the town ran and from which it drew much of its temporary workforce. These areas were largely rural but also housed craftsmen, most of them unskilled, who took occasional jobs in the city. It was not the same juridically as the town, but the town had extensive privileges there that were gradually extended until by the fifteenth century the city courts had cognizance over virtually all criminal cases in the ban mile, although not civil, which were still regulated in the courts of the enclaved lordships.[12]

The large number of noble town houses complicated the task of the town magistrates. The inner city of Ghent at one time contained no fewer than fifty-six fortifications. Apart from the count's castle, the most famous is that associated with the Ghent castellan Gerard 'the Devil'. It had been built by 1254 on the Scheldt border with imperial Flanders at the foot of the Brabant bridge. The city used the castle for storage of military equipment in the fourteenth century.[13]

Each large city annexed most of the suburban territories that were under lay proprietorship during the thirteenth century, and Bruges and Ghent extended their walls on the erroneous assumption that population growth would continue. Thus Ghent in 1254 and 1270 bought out the countess's right on the Brabant quarter, also called 'Over Scheldt', and on the Oudburg, the area controlled by her castle. In 1270 and 1274 Margaret negotiated agreements between the city and the two great abbeys, by which the city agreed to fortify the abbey villages in return for a tax. The 'Great Charter' of Ghent of 1297 obliged the abbeys to promulgate all regulations made at Ghent by the

11. *IAY* **1**: 64–5, 82.

12. Hans van Werveke, 'La Banlieue primitive des villes flamandes', *Etudes Pirenne anciens élèves*, 389–401.

13. See map in Milis, 'The Medieval City' in *Ghent: In Defence*, 68; K.G. van Acker, 'Geraard de Duivel: Poging tot belichting van een duisterfiguur', *HMGOG* **38** (1984): 3–15.

aldermen and the count's bailiff. By 1311 Ghent was levying fines and taxes in the abbey villages that were owed to the count and the French king, and soon thereafter it began assessing municipal taxes in the villages. In 1274 and 1299 the city bought out the suburban seigneuries of the castellan and a local noble. A trench around the city to mark the outer limits of its jurisdiction was begun in 1270, but the fortification network of Ghent remained incomplete except for the old centre until the 1380s.

Ypres had less trouble than Ghent with enclaved territory, although some noble properties did remain outside the town's control. By 1283 the city had acquired most of the territorial rights of the larger churches. As at Ghent, the countess ceded substantial areas. Ypres, however, did not incorporate these territories into the system of town walls, fearing insurrection by the artisans living in the suburbs. Ypres, more than Bruges or Ghent, became a dual city, with an aristocratic centre and proletarian suburbs.

Bruges acquired only one significant enclaved ecclesiastical lordship, but the immunity of the provost of St Donatian remained outside the city's jurisdiction and became notorious for brothels and pawnshops.[14] Bruges had more trouble than did Ghent and Ypres, however, with isolated rights of lay lords that hindered commerce. In 1293 the town bought the lord of Gistel's rights on land where the crane was located. Bruges had a long quarrel with the lords of the Gruuthuuse, who held in fief the right to a tax on *gruit* (spices used to make beer) and did their utmost to hinder hop beer from getting into the Flemish market. In 1298 the constable of France, who was governing Bruges at the time, disallowed Gruuthuuse's claim of an import prohibition but substituted a tax that the city had the right to buy out.[15]

14. Nicholas, *Town and Countryside*, 58; R. de Roover, *Money, Banking and Credit in Mediaeval Bruges: Italian Merchant-Bankers, Lombards, and Money-Changers. A Study in the Origins of Banking* (Cambridge, Mass., 1948), 113–15. The large cities were not the only jurisdictions in Flanders where lords' immunities caused problems of law enforcement. As late as 1374 the butchers of Tielt claimed that people from various parishes were coming to the fief of Lord Daniel van Mullem's wife in Tielt, setting up stalls, selling uninspected meat and not paying the count's toll. N. de Pauw (ed.), *Bouc van de Audiencie: Acten en Sentencien van den Raad van Vlaanderen in de XIVe eeuw*, 2 vols (Ghent, 1901, 1903), 1: 625.

15. For the territorial unification of the major cities, see Nicholas, *Town and Countryside*, 54–65; *IAB* 1: 31, 58–9; and more generally van Werveke, 'Banlieue primitive', 389–401.

Urban society in the thirteenth century

Much has been made of the fact that the cities of medieval Flanders were dominated by merchant oligarchies in the thirteenth century and from 1302 by artisan groups that became increasingly oligarchical. In fact, the contrast between the regimes is less stark than has been portrayed.

We have seen that the early cities were corporate sworn associations. There were caritative and religious guilds and a merchant guild in many cities that seems to have controlled foreign trade. The aristocratic character of the guilds was accentuated in the late twelfth century. At Bruges aldermen had to belong to the Hanse of London, and membership on the council at Ghent was also reserved to the members of the merchant guild, who bought wool and fixed weavers' wages. The constitution of Saint-Omer of 1127 noted a group who owned land within the city. In legal actions, members of the merchant guild were believed on their own testimony, while others had to have two landowners as witnesses after 1218.[16]

Although Arras had associations of artisans in the eleventh century, they are not mentioned in Flemish Flanders until the thirteenth. Bruges had several craft guilds, but no artisan guild was autonomous until after 1302. The only group of craftsmen in Ghent who are known to have had a formal organization before 1302 were the smiths, who by 1273 had a brotherhood dedicated to St Eligius. Although most references to artisan discontent are after 1270, False Baldwin (see Chapter Seven) had a great initial success among the craftsmen. The workers rose at Douai in 1245. At Ghent the fullers and weavers revolted against the merchant drapers in 1252, and they left the town as a group in 1274. The town rulers made agreements with the elites of other cities to deny admission to the strikers. The revolutionary potential was much stronger among the weavers and fullers than among the 'small guildsmen' of the non-textile trades, since the textile workers were salaried by the merchant entrepreneurs, while the small guildsmen were independent and sold their products directly to their customers.[17]

16. R. Märtens, *Weltorientierungen und wirtschaftliches Erfolgsstreben mittelalterlicher Grosskaufleute: Das Beispiel Gent im 13. Jahrhundert* (Cologne, 1976), 158; Blockmans, 'Vers une société urbanisée', 66–7.

17. Blockmans, 'Vers une société urbanisée', 66–7; Milis, 'Medieval City', 68; W. Prevenier, 'La Bourgeoisie en Flandre au XIIIe siècle', *Revue de l'Université de Bruxelles*, 1978/9, 424.

The 'patriciate' of Ghent has been the most thoroughly investigated of the Flemish urban oligarchies. In a classic study, Frans Blockmans argued that wealth rather than landholding was the original criterion for participation in the magistracy but that during the thirteenth century, when the patricians were threatened by newly rich persons, they developed new criteria, notably the exercise of governmental authority. Various terms were used early for the ruling group, in which 112 families have been identified, but from 1228 *viri hereditarii* was customary. These were 'men who hold *hereditates*' (allods), not persons who have inherited social position. The 'patrician' government of the thirteenth-century Flemish cities was thus a government of landowners. Just as possession of allods created a presumption of nobility outside the city, so it created a patriciate inside it. The ancestors of the thirteenth century patricians were thus tenants of the two abbeys whose ground rents had been commuted in the central city in the eleventh century. At least eighteen of the 112 allodial families, including six whom Blockmans thought representative of the group that first became wealthy in commerce and only then invested in land, migrated to the town from the rural environs of Ghent after the mid twelfth century. Thus it was possible to acquire land in the central city; the landowners were never a closed group.[18]

The landowners developed a group consciousness against other wealthy persons who were excluded from the rigidly cooptative magistracy of Ghent. Antiquity of lineage was crucial, although the terminal point must be the early thirteenth century rather than the twelfth. Such a figure as Walter van der Meere is indicative. He was a 'new man' who owned land, farmed comital tolls and lived extremely well, but he could not enter the patrician ranks and remained a commoner. But while opposition to the hereditary town councillors included families of newly rich who were excluded by their recent ancestry from the magistracy, several older families of 'hereditary men' sided with them as a result of personal rivalries. The 'social' struggles were thus to equalize opportunity for public office among merchants, not to enfranchise the workers.[19]

Officeholding was critical to the perpetuation of the wealth and social position of the urban elites. The magistrates of Ghent held office

18. Blockmans, *Het Gentsche Stadspatriciaat tot omstreeks 1302* (Antwerp, 1938). See the important discussion by Märtens, *Weltorientierung*, 141–3.

19. Blockmans, 'Peilingen nopens de bezittende klasse te Gent omstreeks 1300. I: Twee typen: Gilbert Utenhove en Wouter van der Meere', *RBPH* 15 (1936): 496–516; Märtens, *Weltorientierung*, 152–5, 215, 249.

for life in the twelfth century. In 1212 Count Ferrand forced the city to accept an annual rotation of the magistracy to avoid concentrating power too narrowly. In 1228, however, he had to accept the XXXIX, the most closed oligarchy ever to exercise power in the medieval Low Countries. There were three boards of thirteen members each: aldermen, councillors and 'vacationers'. Each year the boards rotated with the aldermen becoming councillors, the vacationers becoming aldermen and the councillors taking a year out of office. Vacancies caused by death or removal were filled by cooptation. Except for a temporary suspension between 1275 and 1280, this system remained in effect until 1301. The personnel of the XXXIX was changed in 1297 but not the mechanism.

At Ypres there was annual cooptation within the ruling group from 1209. At Bruges the count appointed aldermen, although after 1241 he agreed to rotate them. At Ghent and Ypres, therefore, the patriciate chose the governing organ of the town without the intervention of either the commoners or the count. The privilege of 1241 at Bruges and extended to Damme denied access to the council to any labourer unless he gave up his trade for a year and a day and became a member of the Hanse of London. At Bruges a council functioned alongside the aldermen from 1241, and aldermen and *jurés* are mentioned in the same charter of 1258 at Ypres. Some Flemish cities had a burgomaster, but he was a weak figure limited largely to ceremonial functions.[20]

Pirenne also argued that the Flemish patriciates were made up almost exclusively of merchants in the beginning, and he also saw the older patrician families dropping out of commerce in the late thirteenth century to live on their rents and invest in land. There are several problems with this hypothesis. First, ground rents were so low that few if any town patricians could have lived solely on their rents. The evidence of burgher landownership in the Flemish countryside is skeletal before 1250 and becomes much more abundant thereafter; but as early as 1227, Ferrand exempted from the land tax all land held in the castellany of Ypres by burghers of the city. Ypres had the most rural hinterland of any of the great Flemish cities; and for the problem of tax liability, which would plague the city's relations with the castellany in the fourteenth century, to arise this early, landholding

20. Prevenier, 'Bourgeoisie', 416–17; A. de Smet, 'De Klacht van de 'ghemeente' van Damme in 1280: Enkele gegevens over politieke en sociale toestanden in een kleine Vlaamse stad gedurende de tweede helft der XIIIe eeuw', *BCRH* **115** (1950): 1–2; R. van Uytven, 'Stadsgeschiedenis in het Noorden en Zuiden', *AGN* **2**: 230–1.

by burghers must have been extensive even in the early thirteenth century.[21] Furthermore, many great town families had rural origins, and it is most unlikely that they would not have kept lands in the countryside. At Lille most lineages whose ancestors can be traced evidently began in small-scale rural marketing. Such men as the Le Borgne and the Sequedin were on the city council within a few years of being tenant farmers.[22]

Law, government and courts in the Flemish cities

The urban courts were also regularized in the thirteenth century. Aldermen could judge any case occurring on their territory except when the defendant had personal exemption, such as by being a burgess elsewhere. 'Quarter sessions' (*vierscharen*) were held in both the towns and rural areas, originally four times per year, but this was inadequate to handle litigation. By the mid to late thirteenth century most small towns held the *vierschaar* every two weeks, while the larger ones met two or three times a week. The aldermen acted as judges in the presence of the count's bailiff. At Ghent and Bruges the jurisdiction of the aldermen was not limited to the quarter sessions. They could assemble in 'chamber' without formalities, from which decisions could be appealed to the *vierschaar* at Ghent, although not Bruges. In practice this usually amounted to routine cases being handled by two aldermen. By the late thirteenth century the strictly regulated cloth halls had their own courts under 'hall lords', where sales and purchases of cloth and disputes arising from this were heard. There were also 'arbitrators' on the major markets to adjudicate petty civil disputes. Other special courts, notably guild tribunals, appear after 1302.[23]

The Flemish cities were torn apart by vendettas between extended families, which as a point of honour tried to settle matters by bloodshed and avoid the jurisdiction of the courts, whose role was often confined to declaring truces and arbitrating. Thus in 1241 Countess Joan ruled that when the aldermen of Ypres established a truce, the parties must respect it or be compelled by countess's justice.[24] Justices of the peace as a separate board of the magistracy appear at Douai in 1268, at Ypres by 1270 and at Ghent in 1297.

21. *IAY*, **1**: no. 41, p. 38.
22. Sivery, 'Histoire économique et sociale' in *Histoire de Lille*, 191–2.
23. Monier, *Institutions judiciaires*, 181–6, 194–5, 200–1, 223.
24. *IAY* **1**: 57.

Burgesses had the inviolable privilege of being tried only in their own home courts in cases involving blood offences. Naturally, this caused problems with the smaller communities, which were victimized by gangs of city people. The defendant in these cases could choose trial at the court where the suit was brought or in his home court, although most towns except Ghent punished those who did not insist on trial in the home town. Debt litigation, by contrast, was handled by the aldermen before whom the debt had been contracted. Some towns made arrangements among themselves to return the burgher who was sued for debt to his home town.[25]

We have seen that Philip of Alsace issued unitary constitutions for the Flemish cities, but they developed peculiarities in the thirteenth century. Ypres is unusual in that Philip's original Latin charter has been lost, but two later French versions of it exist. Both, particularly the second later version written between 1270 and 1310, change important clauses to enhance local autonomy. The monetary fine for theft was replaced by execution. The wife's own property and her share of common assets were freed from confiscation for her husband's misdeeds. Aldermen who were found guilty of perjury were tried by their peers, no longer by the count. While local aldermen could not exercise legislative power without the count's consent, this becomes a formality. The charter extended the power of the town government to divide the rural estates of deceased townsmen and gave the aldermen the right to judge all criminal cases between burghers of Ypres, even when the misdeeds occurred outside the town area.[26]

Changes in Flemish law and nascent capitalism

There were thus significant developments in Flemish law during the thirteenth century, as well as in governmental administration. Philip of Alsace's constitutions had substituted the sworn inquest in the cities for the judicial duel, and this spread to the rural areas in the thirteenth century. Flemish property law also had made a significant evolution. Particularly around Ghent, Flemish custom was basically Frankish. The family was the repository of its members' goods, and there were

25. Nicholas, *Town and Countryside*, 69–75; Monier, *Institutions judiciaires*, 216–17, 219–20.

26. R.C. van Caenegem and Ludo Milis, 'Edition critique des versions françaises de la "Grande Keure" de Philippe d'Alsace, comte de Flandre, pour la ville d'Ypres', *BCRH* **147** (1981): 1–44, esp. 1–11.

restrictions on alienating it. Widows always had full disposition over the dowries given them by their husbands in Germanic Flanders, but French marriage contracts from the tenth century tended to restrict this, especially if there were children. In the twelfth century the dowry was thus transformed completely in France and southern Flanders into a life use right of the widow on a portion of her husband's estate. One of the earliest examples in the southern Low Countries of this change involves the marriage portion of Clementia, widow of Robert II of Flanders, in 1112.[27]

But a new property regime, called 'universal community', was customary by the 1050s at the latest in Germanic eastern Flanders and was enshrined in Flemish written law in Baldwin VI's constitution for Geraardsbergen (1067–70). The Geraardsbergen code provided that when either spouse died, the survivor received the entire estate if a child had been born of the marriage; and if children had received marriage endowments, they had to return them to divide with their siblings when one parent died. Widows thus kept their dowry rights, but also came to control a substantial part of the property coming from their husbands' sides, even if there had been no children to inherit the joint estate. This situation was absolutely reciprocal, applying equally to widows and widowers. It soon spread to west Flanders; the infamous castellan Erembald murdered his predecessor, then married the widow and used her property to obtain the castellanship. Philip of Alsace's constitution for the Franc of Bruges provided that when either spouse died, money (although not land), regardless of the side from which it had come, would be divided between their respective sets of kindred.

It is thus clear that Flemish property law came to be strongly oriented towards the nuclear family during the central Middle Ages. It gave much less power to the patriarch of an extended family to control the lives and property of his children. Each time a marriage took place or someone died, a substantial amount of property could change hands. Immovable property, most obviously land, was difficult to seize for debt; but in the thirteenth century, evidently as a result of the desire of townsmen to recover debts owed them by nobles, 'chattels', which are movables, came as a legal notion to include everything on the land that was perishable, including trees, crops in the ground and even the buildings. Such property could be attached for debt.[28] Thus

27. Godding, *Droit privé*, 262–3.
28. For this argument, see Nicholas, 'Of Poverty and Primacy', 38–9, based partly on Godding, *Droit privé*, 142–4, 246–7.

from the thirteenth century debts were easily recoverable and property entered the marketplace much more frequently in Germanic Flanders than in neighbouring areas, including Walloon Flanders, and doubtless contributed to the favourable climate that Flanders presented for merchants.

Social services and the patrician ethic

The cities also began a tradition of social services in the twelfth century that by the fifteenth would include a comprehensive system of poverty relief. But while elsewhere the churches played a major part in poor relief and care of the sick, by the thirteenth century these were lay concerns in Flanders.

A leper hospital was established in the western suburbs of Ghent around 1146. Later called the *Rijke Gasthuis* (Rich Inn) because of its patrimony, it was under civil administration by 1300. It was only for persons of substantial property, who were expected to give up their possessions on entry. Poor lepers were maintained at the city gates and in huts and open fields and thus were known as 'field sick'. Lepers wore a special uniform, notably a noisy clapper, to distinguish them from the healthy and warn others of their proximity.[29]

The aldermen of Ghent governed all hospitals. They controlled their property, oversaw accounts and legislated. They normally appointed guardians, usually prominent burghers chosen for a one year term, most often from the magistrates who lived in the neighbourhood of the foundation. The master, who was in fact usually a mistress, was appointed by the guardians from the healthy brothers and sisters for life. The urban patricians seem to have viewed such activities as an obligation incumbent on them by virtue of their position, and most of the politically prominent families of the large cities became active, at least perfunctorily, in poor relief.

Before 1200 Ypres also had a leper hospital and a hospice of ecclesiastical origin dedicated to the Virgin. Four more were added in the thirteenth century, all of them founded by wealthy burghers whose families were frequently in the magistracy. From 1212 the town government handled civil administration in all but one. Characteristically, the exception was not Our Lady but the hospice 'Belle', founded and

29. This discussion is based on C. de Coninck and W. Blockmans, 'Geschiedenis van de Gentse leprozerie "Het rijke Gasthuis' vanaf de stichting (*ca.* 1146) tot omstreeks 1370', *AH* **5** (1967): 3–44.

controlled by the family of that name. Holy Ghost Tables, parish organizations under lay control that accumulated endowments whose income was used for poor relief within the parish, may have existed at Ypres in the thirteenth century, but the first firm evidence is from 1315.[30]

FLEMISH CULTURAL LIFE IN THE THIRTEENTH CENTURY

The bishops

The secularism that characterized Flemish intellectual life in the previous centuries continues in the thirteenth, with stronger evidence of anticlericalism and the development of a vibrant vernacular culture.

The Flemish church was hampered by the fact that it was not really Flemish. The first bishop of Tournai who came from Germanic Flanders was Philip Mus of Ghent in 1274. During the thirteenth century the jurisdiction of the official, who held the bishop's court, was gradually extended. Although he claimed the right to intervene in questions between clergy and laypersons, it was unusual even for persons in holy orders to go to the official before trying their luck in the lay courts, since the churches could not enforce temporal penalties and the Flemish counts were rarely willing to do it for them. The churches fought in both the count's and the official's courts to retain their rights of justice over the tenants in their villages. Tithe rights were an especially serious point of contention between churches and secular lords, and some of the cases show the conflict between oral and customary forms of proof and more 'modern' criteria. An action of 1254 between the cathedral chapter of Tournai and several Flemish nobles has the church claiming that custom running longer than the memory of man had attributed the collection of tithes at Moorslede, near Ypres, to the local pastor, while admitting that the defendants in the action had in fact collected them for twenty years.[31]

---

30. O. Mus, 'Rijkdom en armoede: Zeven eeuwen leven en werken te Ieper' in *Prisma*, 10–12.

31. Vleeschouwers-van Melkebeek, *Officialiteit*, 69; Vleeschouwers-van Melkebeek, *Documenten uit de praktijk van de gedingbeslissende rechtspraak van de officialiteit van Doornik: Oorsprong en vroege ontwikkeling (1192–1300)* (Brussels, 1985), 32–3.

In 1246 the press of business in the church courts and growing nationalism in Flanders forced a division of the bishopric of Tournai into two archdeaneries, Tournai and Flanders. By 1272 Flanders was further subdivided into the archdeaneries of Ghent and Bruges. The Flemish part of the diocese of Thérouanne was in an 'archdeaconate of Flanders'. At the century's end the Flemings tried in vain to get Pope Boniface VIII to make Flanders into a separate diocese on grounds that 'most of the county uses a Teutonic idiom and cannot profit from the instruction of its bishops, who do not know their language'.[32]

Monastic life and the mendicants

Flemish monastic life remained largely Benedictine. The wealthy older abbeys increasingly became a religious establishment controlled by wealthy local families and out of touch with the spiritual needs of most believers.

The association often made between the new 'mendicant' orders of the thirteenth century and urbanized areas, however, certainly holds true for Flanders.[33] Not only the Franciscans and Dominicans but also the Augustinians, Brothers of the Sack and Carmelites, along with several smaller groups that emphasized apostolic poverty found a strong reception in the Flemish cities. Most mendicant foundations were in urban locations, and the mendicants seem to have preferred commercial to purely industrial environments. Of twenty-six convents founded before 1350, fifteen were in Bruges, Ghent or Ypres.

The Franciscans were in Ghent and Lille by 1226, in Bruges by 1233 and by 1252 in Douai, Lille and Oudenaarde. Between 1225 and 1234 the Dominicans had establishments at Lille, Ghent and Bruges. There was a lag of a generation before they expanded to Ypres and Douai in 1268–9. Joan and Margaret preferred the Dominicans, while the Franciscans had the patronage of the city governments.[34]

---

32. Vleeschouwers-van Melkebeek, *Officialiteit*, 125–6; James M. Murray, 'The Failure of Corporation: notaries public in medieval Bruges,' *JMH* 12 (1986): 155–66; Pirenne, *Histoire de Belgique,* 1: 343–4.

33. In saying this, I do not imply adherence to the absurd thesis of Jacques LeGoff that the level of urbanization of a place can be measured by counting the mendicant cloisters. See Jacques LeGoff, 'Ordres mendiants et urbanisation dans la France médiévale', *AESC* 25 (1970): 924–46, decisively refuted by Walter Simons, 'Bedelordenvestiging en middeleeuws stadswezen: De Stand van zaken rond de hypothese-Le Goff', *Tijdschrift voor Sociale Geschiedenis* 12 (1986): 39–52.

34. Walter Simons, *Bedelordekloosters in het graafschap Vlaanderen. Chronologie en topografie van de bedelordenverspreiding vóór 1350* (Bruges, 1987), 31–62, 68–75, 80–2.

Most mendicants, like the monks, evidently came from the urban upper orders, although evidence is scanty. The Bruges convents were the largest: in 1340 there were about ninety Dominicans, seventy Carmelites and sixty Augustinians. Ghent's were smaller: in 1297 the Dominicans in Ghent included about forty-nine friars, the Franciscans forty-four, the Augustinians seventeen, the Carmelites twenty-two and the Brothers of the Sack twelve. Even by mid-century the Flemish mendicants were relaxing their practice of poverty, and by 1270 they were acquiring rents and other properties. After 1300, gifts to the mendicant friaries became more numerous and usually did not go through the formality of using an intermediary who would own the property in use for the convent.[35]

Nunneries were never strong in Flanders. The church frowned on associations of pious women, among other reasons because they required a priest to administer the services and the authorities feared that the males might be contaminated. Only four convents of Poor Clares and two Dominican nunneries were established in Flanders. They were patronized by the counts and were even more aristocratic than the male mendicant houses.

The Beguines, however, offered some consolation to women who wanted to lead lives of quiet piety.[36] They remained laywomen, which probably explains why they became suspect. The Dominicans helped to found the larger Beguinages, although they refused to accept permanent positions as chaplains. The argument has been raised that Beguinages were established because there was a surplus of females over males in the Flemish cities, and dowry funds for them were thus lacking.[37] Yet, although the thirteenth-century foundation charters say that they were founded because there were too many women, confirmations of those charters more than a century later use the same language, which makes it highly unlikely. Furthermore, the Beguinages never included enough women to have a serious impact on population. St Elizabeth's of Ghent, which was probably the largest one in the southern Low Countries, had 400 inhabitants at the end of the sixteenth century and may not have been much smaller in the late

35. W. Simons, *Stad en Apostolaat: De vestiging van de bedelorden in het graafschap Vlaanderen (ca. 1225–ca. 1350)* (Brussels, 1987), 152.

36. On the Beguine movement in the Low Countries, see in general Ernest McDonnell, *Beguines and Beghards in Medieval Culture, with Special Emphasis on the Belgian Scene* (New Brunswick, 1954); Alcantara Mens, *Oorsprong en betekenis van der Nederlandse begijnen- en begardenbeweging* (Antwerp, 1947); L.M.J. Philippen, *De Begijnhoven. Oorsprong, geschiedenis, inrichting* (Antwerp, 1918).

37. Herlihy, *Opera muliebria*, 66–70.

Middle Ages. Others were much smaller. The Beguinage of Champ-fleury in Douai had about a hundred residents in 1273, while Ter Hooie of Ghent had forty-eight and that of Courtrai forty-six in the second half of the fourteenth century. Furthermore, far from being poor, most early Beguines came from propertied families, although this was less true after 1260.[38]

The earliest Beguines lived in their parents' homes, but small communities (Beguinages) were soon formed under the direction of the clergy. Concern to protect the Beguines from robbery, sexual harassment, abduction and forced marriage led to the establishment of the communal or 'court' type of Beguinage, which is rarely found outside the southern Low Countries. Separate parishes were also very typical of Flemish Beguine life. Yet many Beguines continued to live at home even after the Beguinages and independent parishes were established.

The Beguines provided genuine poor relief to needy women. By the 1270s a second Beguinage had been founded in some Flemish towns, but it usually remained smaller and was populated by Beguines of lower social origin than lived in the first foundation. In 1284 the Beguinage of St Elizabeth at Ghent asked the count's permission to acquire more property because the number of destitute Beguines had grown to about 300. Almshouses for poor Beguines were being founded by the century's end. The rapid decline of the textile industry after 1270 may have adversely affected single women such as the Beguines, many of whom were employed in cloth making. From about that time, the first municipal laws began restricting Beguines' activity in producing and selling cloth.[39]

Popular religion

Although the great churches and monasteries were no longer the focal point of devotions for many, this does not mean that the Flemings

38. Walter Simons, 'The Beguine Movement in the Southern Low Countries: A Reassessment', *Bulletin van het Belgisch Historisch Instituut te Rome* **59** (1989): 71, 80. Simons admits the argument of a surplus of women in the southern Low Countries but says that it was confined to the cities and to the age group between five and twenty-five. In the older age groups, the ratio was reversed because of higher infant and adolescent mortality among males. Another problem in evaluating the population-response thesis is that the Beguinages actually drew more inhabitants from outside the cities in which they were located than from within.

39. Simons, 'Beguine Movement', 84–5, 89–90, 94–7, 100; C. Declercq, 'De seculiere geestelijken, mannelijke en vrouwelijke religieuzen te lande', *Flandria Nostra* **4**: 69.

were not religious. They seem also to have been essentially orthodox. Although in the next century heresy was imputed to some Beguines, most heretical movements are found farther south. Reverence for local saints, such as Lievin, Bavo and Amand, became even stronger, as local festivals and processions celebrated their anniversary days. A local cult of Charles the Good developed after his assassination. Charles was canonized less than a month after his murder, following testimony that his body had no odour and that a miraculous healing allegedly occurred at his grave. As was true of most Low Country saints, his cult remained confined to the region where he was buried.

Preaching became a more important part of religion in the thirteenth century. The mendicants were a major influence in this expansion of the church service towards the laity. Preaching was generally in the vernacular, since by the thirteenth century most laypeople no longer understood Latin and the church frowned on vernacular translations of the Bible. The *Rhymed Bible* of Jacob van Maerlant, which is actually a translation with revisions of the *Historia Scholastica* of Peter Comestor, was enormously popular, but the church disapproved of it.[40]

Education, literacy and language

Education in Flanders was in principle a monopoly of the churches, but it was being contested everywhere during the thirteenth century. Although the count's church of St Veerle had been given sole charge of the municipal school at Ghent in 1191, by 1300 private instruction was available in Flemish, and several other churches of the city had schools. The cathedral of St Martin of Ypres received a monopoly in 1195 similar to St Veerle's, and in 1253 the pope confirmed the chapter's excommunication of those aldermen and other citizens who had sent children to unauthorized schools. Later that year, however, the city and chapter agreed that there would be three superior schools whose teachers would be appointed by the chapter. The fees that the instructors could charge for instruction and materials were strictly limited. But all citizens were guaranteed the right to hire private tutors for their own children as long as they did not teach outsiders, and anyone could keep an elementary school without the licence of the aldermen or the chapter. In 1289 the number of superior schools was

40. A.H. Bredero, 'Het godsdienstig leven *circa* 1050–1384', *AGN* **2**: 224–5, 242.

reduced to two, and it was forbidden to send children outside the home to other professors for grammar and logic.[41]

Official records continue to be in Latin through most of the thirteenth century, although in the lower courts, which were less likely to have trained clerks as personnel, the vernacular is found earlier. In 1249 the earliest surviving administrative act in Dutch/Flemish was issued by the aldermen of Boekhoute. Flemish documents from Velzeke survive from 1254 and 1257. From 1260 many more are found from throughout Flanders, at all levels from court to village. A substantial party among the urban patricians preferred French, reflecting their political orientation; we have noted that the counts' Latin statutes were translated into French during the thirteenth century so that the magistrates could understand them. Even the churches had to make accommodations to the times. In 1236 the bishop of Tournai issued statutes for the leper hospital of Ghent in Dutch rather than Latin. The oldest vernacular document in Dutch from Ghent itself records a dispute in 1253 between St Bavo's abbey and one of its local deputies. The earliest municipal account of Ghent, from 1280, is in Flemish, while the bailiff's accounts remain in French. The accounts of Bruges are in Latin until 1300 and thereafter in Flemish. French replaced Latin at Ypres between 1256 and 1325.[42]

As would be expected in such an environment, there is not much evidence in Flanders of libraries, which tended to preserve religious and philosophical works. The most important libraries outside private hands in Flanders were in the oldest abbeys and the chapter of St Donatian at Bruges. The cathedral of St Martin of Tournai, where many Flemings were educated, had a fine collection. The monasteries had writing offices that produced some manuscripts, but the overall corpus is not large. One of the glories of early Flemish art is the *Viel Rentier* of Oudenaarde, a rent book illustrated with scenes of daily lives of peasants and burghers. It was the property of the lords of Pamele-Oudenaarde at the end of the thirteenth century.[43]

There is not much evidence this early of Flemish attendance at the universities. The Dominican William of Moerbeke between 1260 and 1285 provided the first complete translation of the works of Aristotle from the original Greek into Latin. But he and the great scholastic theologian Henry of Ghent are exceptions. The major employers of

41. *IAY* 1: 73–5, 130–1.

42. Milis, 'Medieval City', 79; Blockmans, 'Vers une société urbanisée', 72–3.

43. D. Dhanens, 'De plastische kunsten in het Zuiden 1100–1384', *AGN* 2: 268–70.

persons with degrees in the arts, law and theology were the churches –
which were weak in Flanders and purveyed what most Flemings considered a foreign culture – and the towns, which developed sophisticated record-keeping only after 1250.

Nonetheless, there are harbingers of the future. Flemish students
were attending the university at Orléans, presumably studying law, by
the 1290s. The testaments of several Flemings attached to the church
of Tournai set up endowments to support needy Flemish students in
theology at Paris. But even the phraseology of the grant of Nicholas of
Bruges, at different times official of Tournai and archdeacon, shows
how Flanders was regarded as a sort of peculiar stepchild of western
Christendom. The university of masters at Paris gave Nicholas permission to situate annually in the Sorbonne five masters studying in
theology 'who have a good knowledge of the Flemish idiom, which is
known to be the native language in his archdeaconry'. After the archdeacon's death, the bishop of Tournai or the archdeacon of Flanders,
'if he shall deem him fit therefor', might make the appointment.
There was already rivalry between Flemings and Walloons abroad.
The testament of Pieter van Harelbeke, archdeacon of Tournai, in
1278 provided that a stipend would go alternately to a French speaker
and Flemish speaker, while Bishop Michael of Warenghen (1284–91)
left his house at Paris to his successors as bishop on condition that they
pay £20 yearly to two masters, 'only Walloons', who would study at
Paris.[44]

Flemish literature in the thirteenth century

After 1200 little original literature was produced in Latin in Flanders,
even for theology and religion. A Latin translation of the Dutch *Rein-
aert* made in the 1270s by 'Baldwin the Younger' from the environs of
Bruges is a cultural anachronism.[45]

The comital family continued to patronize writers of French chivalric fiction and poetry. Joan was partial to the grail legend; Manessier
wrote a conclusion to Chrétien's *Conte du Graal* for her. Margaret
preferred didactic poetry; Baudouin de Condé's *Conte de l'Eléphant*
is dedicated to her. Guy of Dampierre (1278–1305) was the most

44. Lynn Thorndike (ed.), *University Records and Life in the Middle Ages* (New York,
1944), 74–5, 124–5; Vleeschouwers-van Melkebeek, *Officialiteit*, 73–4.
45. L. van Acker, 'De Latijnse literaire cultuur in Noorden en Zuiden van *circa*
1050 tot *circa* 1350', *AGN* 2: 341.

important patron, keeping numerous minstrels at court. The Latin *Genealogy of the Counts of Flanders* was translated into French during the first half of the thirteenth century. By 1300, serious patronage of French works was restricted largely to the counts and their relatives.[46]

There is considerable evidence of creative writing in Flemish as well as French during the thirteenth century, although much of it was simply translation. Most French chivalric romances became popular in Flanders and were imitated there. Zeger Dieregodgaf of Ghent, who translated selections from the *Roman de Troie* of Benoît of Saint-Maure into Netherlandish, and Diederic van Assenede, who translated *Florence and Blanchefleur* at the end of the thirteenth century, are representative examples. The Arthur and Alexander cycles also were available in Flemish in the thirteenth century, as were prose and epic versions of Bible stories.[47]

The greatest figure of thirteenth-century Flemish literature is Jacob van Maerlant (*c.* 1235–*c.* 1300). He was born near Bruges, probably at Damme, where he lived after 1266. Later legend makes him clerk of the aldermen there. His reputation was so high that Jan Boendale, the great Brabantine Flemish writer who flourished in the early fourteenth century, used Maerlant's *Spieghel Historiael* in his own *Brabantsche Yeesten* and called him the 'father of German literature'.[48]

Maerlant's earliest works are Flemish adaptations in rhymed couplets of the works of French chivalric authors. He wrote an *Alexander* and *Torec*, but his most complete romance was *History of Troy*. His *Secret of Secrets* (*Heimelicheit der Heimelecheden*) is a translation of the *Secreta secretorum*, a treatise for princes on the secrets of rule that was thought in the Middle Ages to have been the work of Aristotle.[49]

But Maerlant came late in life to disdain these works, going so far as to write that 'what is French is false', and he took pride in basing even his derivative works on Latin rather than French models. He thus moved into didactic works of theology and history, drawing heavily on the works of Vincent of Beauvais, Peter Comestor and Thomas of Cantimpré. He intended to make available to the laity, in its language, the knowledge that until then had been the nearly exclusive province

---

46. W. van Hoecke, 'De Letterkunde in de Franse volkstaal tot omstreeks 1384', *AGN* 2: 379–80; Pirenne, *Histoire de Belgique,* 1: 351.

47. Pirenne, *Histoire de Belgique,* 1: 355; C. de Bruin, 'De Letterkunde in de Nederlandse volkstaal tot omstreeks 1384', *AGN* 2: 350–1, 355.

48. Jan te Winkel, *Maerlant's Werken, beschouwd als Spiegel van de dertiende eeuw,* 2nd edn. (Ghent, 1892, 1979), 227–8, 435, 503.

49. Te Winkel, *Maerlant's Werken,* 48–9, 59.

of the clergy. His two most famous works are the *Rhymed Bible* (*Rijmbijbel*), after Peter Comestor's *Biblia scholastica*, and the *Mirror of History* (*Spieghel Historiael*), after Vincent of Beauvais's *Speculum Historiale*. They were adaptations, not literal translations, with a considerable admixture of original material. Maerlant was an inveterate critic of clerical immorality, complaining of bishops' fine clothes, participation in politics and hunting. He joined the chorus of complaints everywhere about sin in the abbeys. His works became enormously popular and one of them, the dialogue *Wapene Martijn*, became the first work in Dutch to be translated into French. One of his last works, *Van den Lande van Oversee*, is a call to free the Holy Land.[50]

Maerlant's influence on Flemish literature was immense. Later chroniclers frequently cited him. Inventories of property of prominent burghers of Ghent in the fourteenth century show copies of *Spieghel Historiael*, the *Rijmbijbel* and some of the romances. He left the *Spieghel Historiael* unfinished. Philip Utenbroeke of Damme took up the story but also died himself before finishing it. Lodewijk van Velthem of Antwerp finished it in 1314–15. Neither of the continuators wrote at Maerlant's level of inspiration. Maerlant is a towering exception to the general statement that vernacular literature in Flanders was both less original and less quantitatively significant than in any other region of the Low Countries in the thirteenth and fourteenth centuries except Holland and Zeeland. Yet except for five years that he spent at Utrecht, there is no reason to think he studied outside Flanders, and he thus must have had books available there from which he derived his vast body of knowledge. How many others used them we can only speculate.

Flemish art in the thirteenth century

Just as 'Flemish' literature flourished more outside Flanders proper than in it, so Flanders was not a centre of the plastic arts, and the styles were derivative from models that originated along the Meuse or the upper Scheldt. As was true of philosophers, some Flemings of artistic bent made a fine career in France. The famous architect Villard d'Honnecourt was probably from Courtrai.[51]

---

50. On Maerlant's career see in general van Mierlo, *Letterkunde*, 164–72; Blockmans, 'Vers une société urbanisée', 73 provides a convenient summary; de Bruin, 'Letterkunde', 359–61; Te Winkel, *Maerlant's Werken*, 191–4, 198, 221. Pirenne, *Histoire de Belgique,* 1: 356–60 is useful but characteristically exaggerates Maerlant's admiration for French culture.

51. Dhanens, 'Plastische kunsten', 251.

The Flemish cities have some sculpture in the Gothic style. The northwest portal of the church of St Nicholas at Ghent has an early Gothic passion relief, and Romanesque reliefs are also found in the city. Flanders also produced some baptismal fonts in the Tournai style, adorned with expressive sculpture.

Ghent was already becoming known as a centre for the manufacture of funerary sculpture in the thirteenth century. The monument of Hugh, lord of Heusden and castellan of Ghent, who died in 1232, is especially impressive. His figure rests on a slab with four animals under it. It was done probably by one of the de Meyere sculptor dynasty of Ghent, using Courtrai limestone. It was in a Romanesque style, but the tombs of the castellan Gerard 'the Devil' and his wife, which survive only in drawings, were Gothic.[52]

The development of architecture in Flanders was hindered by the fact that virtually all building material had to be imported. In view of this, the number of castles in the region by 1200 and the advanced tradition of public building that developed in the thirteenth century are quite remarkable. Through most of the tenth century wood was the only material used, even for churches. During the eleventh some churches were rebuilt in stone, but wood continued to be used for many churches and for most fortifications through the twelfth century, although with some admixture of stone. Even in the thirteenth century, the stone front often went only to the first storey above ground, the rest being in wood.[53]

Flemish architecture in the twelfth and early thirteenth centuries was based on the northern French and Tournai styles, which evolved into a 'Scheldt Gothic' during the thirteenth century. The preferred building material was Tournai marble. St Nicholas of Ghent, the church of the merchant guild in the heart of the city on the major marketplace, is the finest surviving example of Scheldt Gothic. In the early thirteenth century a new nave and crypt replaced the previous Romanesque structures; then a transept was added with pointed arches. The church at Pamele is a simpler version of this style. Begun in 1234, it had a central nave and two side aisles and the transept was topped with an octagonal tower. The influence of this style was also felt in churches at Lissewege and Damme.[54]

52. Dhanens, 'Plastische kunsten', 275; Dhanens, 'Sculpture and Painting before 1800' in Decavele, *Ghent: In Defence*, 189–265.

53. A.J. van de Walle, *Het Bouwbedrijf in de Lage Landen tijdens de Middeleeuwen* (Antwerp, 1959), 133, 48–9.

54. F. van Tyghem, 'De Gotische bouwkunst in het Zuiden 1150–1500', *AGN* 2: 289.

Considerable brick was used for building after 1200. St John's hospital of Bruges had its own brick works in 1290, and the city owned a kiln at Ramscapelle by 1331 where it manufactured both bricks and paving stones. Some churches as well as secular structures in west Flanders were built of brick. This led to the development of the 'hall church', first at Tournai then in Flanders, where it became common west of the Leie by the late thirteenth century.[55]

Town halls were generally in an ornamented Gothic style. The earliest known, that of Aalst, is from around 1225. It has a rectangular plan, ornamented pointed arch windows and a steep roof with round pointed towers at each corner. The castle of Gerard the Devil at Ghent shows similar features. The Cloth Hall of Ypres, which was rebuilt with the aid of photographs after World War I, was begun in 1230 and was one of the glories of Flemish secular architecture. It was 132 metres long, with ribbed portals, crenellations and a 70-metre high central belfry. There was an unroofed interior courtyard. The Cloth Hall of Bruges is in a similar style but less grand, as is also the Butchers' Hall of Ypres. The hall of the grain staple at Ghent was rebuilt in stone in a severely Romanesque style in the twelfth century. It is the earliest surviving urban stone hall in northern Europe. The earliest belfries evidently were of wood, such as that of Bruges, which burned in 1280 and was quickly rebuilt in stone. The new belfry of Bruges was 80 metres high, with two lower levels originally and a third added in 1296.[56]

55. Blockmans, 'Vers une société urbanisée', 69; L.F. Genicot and H. van Liefferinge, 'De Romaanse bouwkunst in het Zuiden, 1000–1150', *AGN* **2**: 286; van Tyghem, 'Gotische bouwkunst', 293.

56. Blockmans, 'Vers une société urbanisée', 68–9; van de Walle, *Bouwbedrijf*, 186–7; Milis, 'Medieval City', 168.

CHAPTER SEVEN

Foreign Trade, Diplomacy and Dependence: The Catastrophe of Medieval Flanders, 1206–74

Even as Flanders reached the height of its economic prosperity during the thirteenth century, the Flemish counts were coming into a humiliating dependence on the French crown. The seeds of the disasters of the half-century after 1275 were sown in the age of grandeur.

Through the twelfth century, the Flemish counts' power had expanded, paralleling the rise of the cities. Philip of Alsace was one of the greatest princes of Europe, perhaps the most powerful in real terms after Henry II and Frederick Barbarossa. Despite reverses in Philip's last years, the prestige of Baldwin IX, who was also count of Hainault, was high enough for him to be made emperor of Constantinople. The counts continued to acquire some territory in the thirteenth century. Flanders and Hainault had the same ruler until 1280. Count Guy of Dampierre was also marquis of Namur between 1263 and 1297, and he acquired Béthune and the lordship of Dendermonde by his marriage. His son, Robert of Béthune, inherited the county of Nevers in 1262 through his wife, Iolande of Burgundy.

But after 1206 the Flemish counts struggled with ever less success to stave off French royal control. The towns used the external weakness of the counts to good advantage in domestic matters. The count had to accept the large cities as a corporate body, the 'Five Towns', without whose assent he could not govern. The 'aldermen of Flanders' (*scabini Flandriae*) may have been created by Philip of Alsace as a delegation of the seven great towns of the county (Arras, Bruges, Douai, Ghent, Lille, Saint-Omer and Ypres) with whom he would deliberate.

150

This dropped to five with the loss of Arras and Saint-Omer. The aldermen of Flanders frequently dealt directly with the count in important questions of foreign and domestic policy. While the towns had played off count against count in 1127–8, their field of action was enlarged to the point where they could pit count against king after 1275.

JOAN (1206–44)

When definite word of Baldwin IX's death reached Flanders in February 1206, the regency for his daughter Joan was continued. Although the towns had favoured England in the conflict that led to the Capetian conquest of Normandy the preceding year, there was a large pro-French party among the nobles, who used the weakened countship to further their own ambitions. With the capture of Normandy, Flanders became the major goal of French diplomacy. No less than 49 per cent of the money fiefs that Philip Augustus granted were in Flanders. The regent Philip of Namur held one, as did three of the great household officers and the castellans of Bruges and Ghent, who were traditional supporters of the French; but King John, who had a richer treasury than Philip, was able to maintain the English party by the same tactic.[1]

Philip of Namur was a weak figure and an outspoken Francophile. He permitted encroachments on the authority of the counts, and not solely from the French ruler. Philip in 1209 gave annual aldermen to Ypres, the most pro-English of the towns, and even recognized the suzerainty of the duke of Brabant over Aalst in 1209. But the major threat was Philip Augustus. The king had charged Baldwin VIII a relief of 20,000 *livres* in 1192, the same amount paid by King John for his French fiefs in 1200, but Philip insisted on an enormous relief of 50,000 *livres* from Joan's regents. As the overlord of an heiress, he had the right to exercise wardship, then to marry her to a person of his choosing who would perform the services that she owed for her fiefs. He thus demanded that Joan and her sister Margaret, aged six and four respectively, be sent to Paris until they were of marriageable age. He promised Philip of Namur not to marry them without his consent

---

1. Baldwin, *Philip Augustus*, 274–6.

before their majority, but Philip agreed not to oppose a match at that time. Contemporaries considered it treachery; the arrangement was especially odious in Hainault, which was not a fief of France, and whose heiresses should not have been turned over to the king, whatever one might argue about Flanders. The regency lasted until January 1212, when Philip married Joan to Ferrand, the third son of King Sancho I of Portugal and nephew of Philip of Alsace's widow Matilda.[2]

By the Treaty of Péronne (1200) Baldwin IX had managed to undo most of the French annexations of 1191. But as Joan and Ferrand were en route to Flanders, crown prince Louis captured them and occupied Aire and Saint-Omer. To obtain their release they had to agree, in the Treaty of Pont-à-Vendin of 25 February 1212, to ratify this conquest. Their entry into Flanders was thus something less than a triumphal procession. Ferrand was received by Bruges and Ypres, but he had to seize Ghent. Nonetheless, on 9 August 1212, Ferrand gave Ghent the much-desired privilege of having annually chosen aldermen.[3]

Philip Augustus had expected Ferrand to be his puppet, but he was soon disabused of this notion, for Ferrand exiled several prominent Francophiles and opened negotiations with England. When Philip planned to invade England in 1213, Ferrand refused to participate on grounds that his homage did not extend to service outside the kingdom. He also threatened to renounce his homage if Philip Augustus refused to return Saint-Omer. Philip dismissed him from the court, got Ypres and Bruges to submit, and prepared to besiege Ghent.

Most Flemish nobles had accepted money fiefs from the French in 1207–8, but the towns, which were by now cripplingly dependent on the English wool trade, remained pro-English. On 13 September 1208 the governments of all the large Flemish cities swore allegiance to John, saving only their fealty to the young countess. Hugh Oysel of Ypres became a citizen of London, and Simon Saphir of Ghent and Martin Compin of Arras got the title 'merchants of the court', which gave them royal protection even if the general safe conduct given to Flemish merchants should be withdrawn. Despite the alliance the position of other Flemish merchants in England remained precarious, for John violated his promises and hindered the wool export, as the English initiated the regrettable policy of regarding Flemish merchants as

2. Dept, *Influences anglaises*, 49; Wolff, 'Baldwin of Flanders and Hainault', 292; de Hemptinne, 'Vlaanderen 1070–1244', 396; Baldwin, *Philip Augustus*, 203, Table 10, 278.

3. Wolff, 'Baldwin of Flanders and Hainault', 203; Dept, *Influences anglaises*, 91–4.

Frenchmen at any time their prince took action displeasing to the English.[4]

But Ferrand's position among the nobles was strengthened by the fact that the French conquest of nearby Normandy meant that military service outside Flanders threatened to become an annual affair for them; the French money fiefs, which earlier would have involved military service only if the French invaded England, thus lost much of their attractiveness. Furthermore, many Flemish nobles continued to be little more than soldiers of fortune. The English party after 1208 had consisted mainly of younger sons and poor knights. A number of them went to England in 1210 and got fiefs. From the beginning of 1212, Renaud de Dammartin, count of Boulogne, breathed new life into the English party among the Flemish nobility. The towns also renewed their bond with John in April 1213.[5]

When Philip Augustus sent a fleet against Flanders, Ferrand formally allied with King John on 10 July 1213. Bruges, Ghent and Ypres, acting independently, guaranteed the treaty. Ferrand was to occupy Philip in the north while John invaded from Poitou. Bishop Goswin of Tournai predictably took the French side, excommunicated Ferrand and interdicted the part of Flanders in the bishopric of Tournai. The allies caught the French fleet at Damme and destroyed it, although the French burned Damme in revenge. The French army, however, devastated Flanders, took Tournai, seized Cassel, Lille, Bruges and eventually Ghent, then took hostages from the governing elites of the towns. Ferrand fled to Zeeland but quickly returned, and a united Flanders enthusiastically supported John and Ferrand. English agents dispensed money liberally in Flanders, and Ferrand was received magnificently in England in early 1214. But the euphoria was ephemeral. Ferrand and the party of the Flemish nobles who allied with him were captured in the rout of the English forces and their allies at Bouvines on 27 July 1214. Ferrand was taken to Paris and not released until 1226.[6]

Philip Augustus then forced the Treaty of Paris of 24 October 1214 on the young countess. The major fortresses of southern Flanders, at Ypres, Cassel and Oudenaarde, which might have blunted a French invasion, were to be razed and others left in their present state. No

4. Baldwin, *Philip Augustus*, 203; T.H. Lloyd, *The English Wool Trade in the Middle Ages* (Cambridge, 1977), 13–14.
5. Dept, *Influences anglaises*, 69, 64–5, 71–4, 108–10, 115–16.
6. Vleeschouwers-van Melkebeek, *Officialiteit*, 49; Dept, *Influences anglaises*, 126–9; Varenbergh, *Relations diplomatiques*, 102–3, 105, 108–9.

new ones could be erected without the king's consent. French partisans among the Flemish nobility would have their property restored; some compensated themselves at the expense of the comital domain. Philip released his prisoners slowly, negotiating for their release individually. Most were back in Flanders by 1217 except Ferrand, whom the king kept prisoner, using the excuse of non-compliance with the treaty of Paris; indeed, the repatriated nobles became Joan's chief councillors, led by Jean de Nesle, castellan of Bruges. In effect, Flanders was ruled from Paris.[7]

Within a month of Bouvines, the English government began considering Flemish merchants Frenchmen and taking reprisals against their persons and property. By September 1215, however, John was writing to Philip Augustus that French merchants were welcome to trade in England, and in November he gave new advantages to the towns, merchants and lords of Flanders. Trade grew after John's death, since *Magna Carta* guaranteed free trade, but there was a continual war of nerves on the merchants; for since Ferrand was no longer a political ally, the slightest complaint against a Fleming by an Englishman after 1214 would lead to sequestration of Flemish property. In the decade after John's death, the English party in Flanders became almost exclusively urban and would remain so until the 1290s. In 1215 John had had to dismiss the Flemish lords who had served him in England, and it was impossible for those who held English money fiefs to do military service in Flanders. During Henry III's first decade, most money fiefs to Flemings gradually stopped, causing embarrassment to the nobles, who were being hurt by inflation.[8]

The towns accordingly gave Countess Joan no trouble, and she extended their privileges, especially Ghent's. In 1216 the city got the right to have taxes paid according to sworn estimates of wealth. She confirmed the privileges of Dunkirk, Mardijk and Poperinge. Biervliet received annual aldermen, burghers of Ypres were exempted from direct taxes in the castellany, and Bruges was assured that its aldermen would not be changed by the count except for false judgement. Joan bought the castellanships of Cassel in 1218 and Bruges in 1224 from their holders. In a policy that was continued by her successor, Joan tried to promote the fortunes of Courtrai, perhaps as a capital that would serve as a counterweight to Ghent and Bruges, by giving life-

7. Dept, *Influences anglaises*, 138, 145, 153, 170; de Hemptinne, 'Vlaanderen 1070–1244', 396.

8. Lloyd, *Wool Trade*, 14; Varenbergh, *Relations diplomatiques*, 113, 114, 116–17, 120; Dept, *Influences anglaises*, 157–8, 174–6.

time exemption from direct taxes in 1218 to all foreigners who would settle there. In 1224 she freed from taxation fifty men who had come to Courtrai to work wool.[9]

Joan made every effort to gain Ferrand's release. Philip Augustus, however, made matters impossible for her, even refusing to negotiate until she agreed to annul her marriage to Ferrand, to whom she was genuinely attached, and marry Pierre Mauclerc, count of Brittany. Matters eased after the king died in 1223. The next year Joan faced the worst domestic crisis of her reign with the appearance of the 'False Baldwin', the hermit Bertrand de Rains, who claimed to be her father escaped from captivity. A famine, the rivalry between the Dampierre and Avesnes families (see below), and the general weakness of the government all contributed to the False Baldwin's initial success. It is unclear whether he was deliberately inspired by nobles who were opposed to Joan or whether they conveniently attached themselves to something that was potentially embarrassing to her after it arose independently.

The man who was discovered near Valenciennes in February 1224 initially denied that he was Baldwin when interrogated by nobles who had heard rumours; among the nobles was Burchard of Avesnes, an embittered enemy of Joan, his sister-in-law. Everyone whom the authorities could find who had known Baldwin IX personally was confronted with the hermit, and none thought him genuine; but the masses thought otherwise. The man now seems to have convinced himself that he was Baldwin. A civil war followed; all Flemish cities supported False Baldwin, and Joan had to flee to Paris. During her absence False Baldwin made a triumphal procession through Flanders, issued charters, and used a seal calling himself count of Flanders and Hainault and emperor of Constantinople. The turning point came when 'Baldwin' met King Louis VIII on 30 May 1225, was unable to answer Louis's obvious questions and fled. The nobles who had initially supported him deserted. When 'Baldwin' was captured and executed, the agitation stopped.[10]

In Paris Joan had agreed to repay Louis VIII's expenses up to 20,000 *livres* in return for his help. To pay this she levied such heavy indemnities on the towns, which had supported 'Baldwin', that she was able both to pay Louis's minimal expenses and to ransom her husband. By the Treaty of Melun of 1226 she was released from Pierre Mauclerc, took Ferrand back, and paid a ransom of 50,000 *livres*.

9. Dept, *Influences anglaises*, 147–8.
10. Wolff, 'Baldwin of Flanders and Hainault', 294–9.

155

There were to be no new fortresses west of the Scheldt, and all knights and burghers had to swear fidelity to the king of France. All Flemings had to agree to renounce their loyalty to any count who opposed the French king.[11]

Thus Ferrand returned to Flanders in 1227. The premature death of Louis VIII in 1226 and the long regency for his successor freed Ferrand to take action against neighbours who had made trouble for Joan. He forced the count of Holland to do homage to Flanders for Zeeland west of the Scheldt, and he forced Philip of Namur's heir to do homage for Namur. But Ferrand died prematurely in 1233, leaving Joan with an infant daughter. Louis IX demanded that she be sent to Paris to be raised as his orphaned ward, as his grandfather had done with Joan. Louis intended to marry her to his brother Robert of Artois, but the sainted king's plans to couple Flanders to France were foiled when she died. In 1237 Joan married Thomas of Savoy, whose sister was the mother of the queens of England and France, but he returned to Savoy, after assuring himself of a pension, when Joan died on 5 December 1244.[12]

MARGARET (1244–78)

While most of Joan's problems were not of her own making, the disasters of the reign of her sister and successor, Margaret, were due largely to the ruler's incompetence. She antagonized the English without taking a firmly pro-French posture, and the complications of her first marriage were to plague Flanders until 1323.

When Joan returned to Flanders in 1212, Philip Augustus had arranged Margaret's marriage to Burchard of Avesnes, a noble of Hainault who was also a vassal of the Flemish counts. He was about forty and a subdeacon, and whether the ten-year-old girl was in a position to consent to the match, as was required under canon law, is unclear. The Avesnes had long supported French interests in Flanders. Joan and Ferrand did not object to the marriage at first, but when Burchard demanded part of Baldwin IX's inheritance, Joan complained to Pope Innocent III that the marriage was illegal because Burchard had taken

11. Dept, *Influences anglaises*, 148–54, 177–8.
12. Henri Nowé, *La Bataille des éperons d'or* (Brussels, 1945), 20; Varenbergh, *Relations diplomatiques*, 133–4.

orders in his youth. The fourth Lateran Council in 1215 declared the marriage invalid, and Popes Innocent III and Honorius III both annulled it and excommunicated Burchard. But the pair continued to live together and had two children, John and Baldwin. Joan captured Burchard in 1219 and kept him prisoner for two years, finally releasing him on condition that they separate. Margaret was thus at Joan's court, separated from her Avesnes children, from 1219. In 1223, while Burchard was still alive, she married William of Dampierre, a Champagne nobleman, by whom she had several more children. Her Avesnes sons spent years in France under protection and came to loathe their mother.[13]

When Margaret became countess of Flanders in 1244, the Avesnes, as her oldest children, claimed the inheritance of both Flanders and Hainault. Although it hinged on church law, the question was referred to Louis IX, who in 1246 gave Flanders to the Dampierres and Hainault to the Avesnes, but neither party accepted his verdict. Margaret had her eldest Dampierre son, William, do homage to Louis IX for Flanders in October 1246. Louis could rule only for crown Flanders, so the Avesnes concentrated on imperial Flanders. John of Avesnes married Aleid, sister of Count William II of Holland, a bond that would form the basis of the dynastic union of Holland, Zeeland and Hainault in 1299. The Avesnes tried unsuccessfully to get imperial recognition of their claims to Flanders, and when the emperor received Flemish homage for imperial Flanders in 1248, the Avesnes had to accept the decree of 1246.

Margaret, thinking that the troubles were over, then made the mistake of having the pope legitimize John and Baldwin of Avesnes. In 1251, however, William of Dampierre died, and the German king William of Holland changed his mind about imperial Flanders. The Flemings then blundered in an attack on Holland in 1253, and numerous nobles, including Guy of Dampierre, who had succeeded William as co-ruler with his mother, were captured. They were ransomed in 1256, and Louis IX confirmed his arbitration of 1246. The death of John of Avesnes in 1257 put a temporary halt to the costly internecine quarrel.[14]

13. The most convenient brief explanations of these complex proceedings are Jansen, *Middeleeuwse Geschiedenis*, 84–5; M. Vandermaesen, 'Vlaanderen en Henegouwen onder het Huis van Dampierre 1244–1384', *AGN* 2: 399; and Wolff, 'Baldwin of Flanders and Hainault', 293–4.

14. The material on the Avesnes–Dampierre feud in the 1240s and 1250s is taken from Vandermaesen, 'Vlaanderen en Henegouwen', 400–1.

THE COUNTESSES AND THE NOBLES

As in the twelfth century, many of the counts' problems came from within their own families. The counts had always given substantial dowries to their daughters and apanages to their sons. Clementia, widow of Robert II, had been given a marriage portion that included twelve fortresses, some of which were centres of castellanies. She tried to keep it in her second marriage, but it was returned to Flanders after her death. Totally apart from the dowry of Artois that Philip of Alsace gave to his niece on her marriage to Philip Augustus, he gave his second wife, Matilda of Portugal, much of southern Flanders, and she kept it until her death in 1218. The possessions of foreign nobles were a vexation. Between 1196 and 1421, the counts of Namur, who were related to the Flemish counts through the Hainault connection, had great influence in Flanders. They held Harelbeke and Biervliet and transmitted them by marriage to the future Philip VI of France, who returned them to Flanders only in 1337. Even after the detachment of Hainault, they controlled the seigneurie of Wynendale from 1298 and the town and port of Sluis, the town and castellany of Béthune and miscellaneous polders around Bruges and Damme and between Sluis and Biervliet at various times.[15]

Provision for the ruler's progeny became a drain on finances under Margaret, who had eight children by the time she was twenty-nine. Guy of Dampierre in turn spent vast sums, most of them obtained from his mother, acquiring lands for his many children. Guy in 1265 gave his son and heir, Robert of Béthune, an apanage consisting of the old lordship and now castellany of Béthune and the lordship of Dendermonde. The counts did, at least, keep some powers in the apanages.[16]

The prohibition of private war limited the nobles' influence and worked to the advantage of the counts and of public order. After 1127 any knight who wished to pay money instead of providing military service could do so. But although the population of Flanders had grown enormously and was more concentrated, and armies everywhere were larger than in the twelfth century, the counts still had only 1500 knights. Flemish armies had no problem defending their

15. Jean Bovesse, 'Notes sur Harelbeke et Biervliet dans le cadre de l'histoire des Maisons de Namur et de France', *BCRH* **150** (1984): 453, 436–7, 465–6.

16. Ganshof, 'La Flandre', 407.

land against foreign invasion before 1180, but Philip of Alsace then sustained humiliating reverses.[17]

Although feudal relations were strong in Flanders during the twelfth century, the prince's right to the aid and counsel of his vassals was not a significant aspect of his centralization of power, in striking contrast to what happened with the English and French monarchies. Flemish centralization was administrative and tax-related and had minimal linkage to the feudal aids and incidents; for the towns were so wealthy so early that they provided money far in excess of what the count could realize from the much weakened landed nobility. Although some noble properties were extensive, particularly those held by castellan families, countless sources relate the growing financial troubles of the Flemish nobles in the thirteenth century. Marriage and purchase of lordships and hereditary court offices by the counts and later by townsmen weakened the Flemish nobles. Despite the restrictions on alienating fiefs, many nobles were doing so after 1150. The ransoms that many nobles had to pay after Bouvines hurt them financially. Furthermore, as prices rose from the late twelfth century, they were caught with incomes that were generally in the form of fixed rents on land. While the counts, who also gave fixed rents, were developing sources of revenue to compensate for this, notably the profits of justice and trade, these were both comital monopolies by 1191, and the nobles had no alternatives.

The nobles also did not always make intelligent use of what they had. They commuted many of the valuable kind payments owed them as rent into fixed payments in money. But while their English counterparts took intelligent advantage of market forces when faced with this problem, the Flemings did not. When the property of John III of Gistel was confiscated in 1302 for rebellion, he was owed twenty large sheep, commuted at the rate of 2s 2d each. Yet a few years earlier the Flemish counts had paid 9–10s per sheep. The Flemish lords thus did not reckon with the development and rising value of agricultural products and animals. Most nobles provided their daughters with dowries in money and their sons with land to keep estates intact. But to get money for the girls, they frequently had either to sell lands and thus split their estates, or borrow. It is undeniable that the desire to transmit land to their sons makes the nobles appear poorer than they actually were, but the fact remains that they were in serious financial straits.[18]

17. Warlop, *Flemish Nobility*, 271–4.
18. Warlop, *Flemish Nobility*, 270, 279, 281–4, 291, 297, 304–7, 310.

We have seen that the nobles had tried to compensate for the debacle of 1127 by requiring noble parentage on both sides to produce a noble offspring. But there is some evidence from the early thirteenth century that a noble mother, although not a noble father, sufficed to carry the status to a son (this does not hold true of a noble father who married a commoner). By the mid thirteenth century wealthy burgher families were marrying into the nobility without causing the noble family derogation of status, and the genealogical purity of the Flemish nobles was a thing of the past within a generation. As early as 1268 Margaret forbade burghers to hold fiefs so that the military service owed by the fief would not be weakened by the burghers claiming exemption on grounds of their privilege as townsmen from offensive military service, but the prohibition remained a dead letter.[19]

A sign of the changing nature of noble status in thirteenth-century Flanders is the gradual assumption that knighthood was the equivalent of nobility, which had not been the case in 1127. Noble and non-noble knights gradually merged in the thirteenth century into an undifferentiated 'knighthood'. All knights now had the right to use the title *dominus* (lord). Heredity of knighthood, originally a purely personal distinction, also appears in the thirteenth century. The knights had to do military service for the lord who provided land or other benefits, but in the thirteenth century the service was often commuted for a fee, the 'knight's penny'. It was sometimes stated expressly that holding a particular fief did not involve a military obligation. A book of fiefs of 1325 for the Franc of Bruges lists 553 fiefs held of the count by nearly that number of vassals, but only 87 of them owed military service, most of them for forty days. A total of 172 were held by burgesses of Bruges, the prohibition notwithstanding. The count's cavalry was inadequate for his needs, and he had to rely on urban militias.[20]

Status considerations aside, knighthood was expensive, and the number of knights declined. The Flemish counts made no effort, in contrast to the English kings, to constrain wealthy freeholders to have themselves dubbed knights, for they were not dependent on them for local government. Many nobles never became more than squires, and squires even commanded some army units. Knightly status was being acquired by burgher families in the late thirteenth century as a means of working their way into the nobility. While the class consciousness

19. Warlop, *Flemish nobility*, 317–20.

20. Dunbabin, *France*, 321; Warlop, *Flemish Nobility*, 300–2; Ganshof, 'La Flandre', 373–4, 417; J. de Smet, 'Le Plus ancien livre de fiefs du Bourg de Bruges, vers 1325', *Tablettes des Flandres* 3 (1950): 69–87; Nicholas, *Town and Countryside*, 280–1.

of the nobles had been so strong as late as 1214 that at Bouvines they had refused at first to fight against a squadron of commoners, by the century's end they were becoming indistinguishable from the upper bourgeoisie.

Thus the power of the nobles was weakened by the growth of the Flemish cities, which eroded their economic and then their political power. The comital monopoly of blood justice from the time of Philip of Alsace, then the institution of the bailiffs, also hurt them. Thus, while nobles still sat on the count's council, they were gradually limited in government as it became more administrative, an area in which most nobles simply lacked expertise. The Flemish nobles were unruly before 1200, but thereafter they were less powerful in Flanders than in neighbouring principalities.[21]

GOVERNMENT DURING THE THIRTEENTH CENTURY

The Flemish government was the most thoroughly secular in western Europe by 1200. Local government continued to be based on the bailiff, whose powers did not change appreciably during the thirteenth century. The number of bailiffs grew, however, as many of the larger towns got individual bailiffs. The feudal courts of comital vassals alone were functioning by the early thirteenth century alongside those of the castellans. In some castellanies they went on circuit with the count's officer at the great annual general inquest into crimes committed. Particularly in the rural parts of eastern Flanders, the vassals' court absorbed that of the aldermen and became the sole comital tribunal.[22]

The central court and the counts' finances

The financial attributes of the Flemish central court seem to have been elaborated earlier than the judicial. Professional jurists entered the count's council only in the second half of the thirteenth century, and appeals from lower jurisdictions in Flanders to the count's court, as opposed to claims of denial of justice, appear only in the late

21. Ganshof, 'La Flandre', 408–9; Warlop, *Flemish Nobility*, 326, 323.
22. Ganshof, 'La Flandre', 372, 402–6, 412.

fourteenth century. Yet the admission that the French king was the feudal overlord of the Flemish counts meant that appeals were made from the count's court to what would soon be called the *parlement* of Paris, despite the count's efforts to hinder the practice. The king in turn declared the principle that during an appeal, the subject was exempt from the count's court.[23]

Flanders was the wealthiest principality of northwestern Europe in the thirteenth century. The revenues that Margaret realized from Flanders were twice those from Hainault. The counts derived most of their income in the thirteenth century from the 'new domain'. This included tolls, farms of the domain, income from the sale and lease of reclaimed land, and the income of the bailiffs. Apart from this, they had the right to service on military campaigns, including perquisites of clothing, shoes, goods, animals and transport. They also had income from tolls, although many of them were farmed out or had heavy assignments on them that diminished revenues.

Before 1200 the counts' profits from coinage were negligible, but they realized some income from reminting the coin in the thirteenth century. They also had the right to license moneychanging tables and charge fees from the changers, most of them Lombards and Cahorsins. The incomes from lay abbacy and advocacy were by now insignificant, as were feudal incomes except those that could be collected at the feudal courts in the castellanies. The count also received a £500 annual money fief from the English king. During the thirteenth century the 'good towns' occasionally approved taxes to meet exceptional needs at the prayer (*bede*) of the prince; the taxes thus became known as *beden*.[24]

Margaret's finances have been studied more thoroughly than those of the other Dampierre rulers.[25] Her 'old domain' incomes were collected in forty-three offices in 1255. Most were in money, rather than the kind that had dominated in 1187. The notaries of 1187, who had been territorial receivers, had been replaced by laymen and comital clerks. The old domain and the chancellor, who controlled it, lost importance. The 'new domain' incomes escaped the chancellor's control and were supervised by a chief clerk, first Egidius van Bredene

---

23. Monier, *Institutions centrales*, 21, 94.

24. Ganshof, 'La Flandre', 422–5.

25. For this and what follows, see Theo Luykx, *De grafelijke financiële bestuursinstellingen en het grafelijke patrimonium in Vlaanderen tijdens de regering van Margareta van Constantinopel (1244–1278)* (Brussels, 1961).

from 1241, then from 1255 Jan van Mont-Sint-Eloi. Egidius was chief clerk of an accounting department; but administration of finances was not separated from other business, for the countess also used him to settle jurisdictional questions. The first receiver-general, appointed around 1262, was Philip of Bourbourg, lord of Verlingehen, a knight who had been a bailiff for some years. He was called 'receiver of Flanders' in 1271, and he also undertook missions having nothing to do with finances, as Egidius van Bredene had done. Lille, Margaret's favourite residence, became a central accounting bureau and probably a treasury from his time.

The income realized from the old domain was about £7,000 yearly. From the new domain, including the bailiffs' profits, she received another £21,000. Other income, notably the profits of coinage and the irregularly paid English money fief, brought her ordinary revenues to about £30,000. This sufficed for normal administration and her court, but she had extraordinary expenses. Joan had left a debt of £164,000, and between 1244 and 1256 Margaret incurred debts of at least twice this fighting the Avesnes.

The countess resorted to selling large properties, mainly reclaimed 'new' land, forest and peat bogs, which gave her both the sale price and an annual ground rent. The land sales brought her about £150,000 for the whole reign. But ultimately she could cope only by levying *beden* on the towns and borrowing from bankers of Arras and later the Italian cities. Figures from Douai and Ghent suggest that she got more than £200,000 from the five large towns. She incurred most of the loans between 1265 and 1278, when Philip of Bourbourg was handling her finances. Though the contracts do not specify a rate of interest, in obeisance to the usury prohibitions of the church, she evidently had to repay a larger sum than she was given. Some of them were extremely short-term loans and had a daily penalty that amounted to interest. Yet Margaret seems to have been reducing her debt in the last years of her reign. When she abdicated on 29 December 1278, the accounting between her and her son Guy showed a debt of only £57,703.[26]

---

26. Vandermaesen, 'Vlaanderen en Henegouwen', 402.

THE TIES WITH ENGLAND

The counts' diplomatic position was inevitably linked to foreign trade. The English rulers understandably considered the Flemish counts after Baldwin IX French puppets. As long as English relations with France were smooth, Flemish traders in England did not suffer. In periods of Anglo-French hostility, trade was often interrupted. The history of Flemish trade with England in the thirteenth century is thus traceable in large measure through safe conducts given to Flemish merchants by the English government, since before 1270 most Anglo-Flemish trade was handled by Flemish shippers. Although most of the safe conducts and trade were for wool and cloth, England also exported food to Flanders. Flemings also got some Gascon wine through England, although the Flemings by the early thirteenth century were sailing to La Rochelle.[27]

Whenever war erupted with France, Flanders was included in reprisals. Shortly after the English war with France resumed in 1224, English property was seized. But there were English merchants in Flanders against whom the Flemings could retaliate; to ensure their safety, the government freed the merchants of Ghent, Bruges, Ypres, Aardenburg and Damme who had been detained at the Winchester fair, but on condition that they guarantee the safety of English subjects in Flanders. This worked, for other Frenchmen were not released. With bewildering inconsistency, the English government sometimes classified the Flemings as Frenchmen, sometimes not.

Concern with national frontiers can give a distorted picture, for contacts were constant and rapid; cloth could reach the St Ives fair in eastern England from Douai in about a week. Most Flemings went personally to England to inspect wool before purchase, then exported it on Flemish boats. After the first English wool custom was proclaimed in 1202, the English government could control the trade, and the Flemish towns had to seek individual privileges. The trade wars were only intermittent; the sale of wool was too important to England for the government to let hostilities drag on for long. Flanders was not the only dependent trading partner. The English needed to sell cloth and food abroad, and they required woad from Picardy, which came through Flanders and Normandy.[28]

27. Jansen, 'Handel en Nijverheid', 171; Varenbergh, *Relations diplomatiques*, 96–7; van Houtte, *Economic History*, 41–2.

28. Jansen, 'Handel en Nijverheid', 172; Moore, *Fairs*, 12; Lloyd, *Wool Trade*, 16–17, 19.

Another problem was the practice of shippers on both sides of the Channel of transporting goods belonging to persons other than their own nationals; thus an entire cargo might be impounded to see whether it had goods that were subject to permanent seizure. In November 1231 Henry III asked Countess Joan to provide credentials to Flemish merchants who had been damaged in England, so that they could have their claims settled. Instead, the Flemings confiscated English property then in Flanders, which triggered reprisals against Flemish shipping.

The parties agreed to general arbitration in May 1235. Although the basic issue was trade, the English demanded repayment of loans that John had made to burgesses of Ghent and Ypres in 1213–14, while the Flemings demanded compensation for English piracy. The commission of arbitration in 1236 awarded compensation to both sides, but the merchants of Flanders as a group agreed to assume the Flemish debts in return for a safe conduct given in perpetuity, to be honoured even if English merchants were arrested in Flanders or the Flemish count served with the French in anything less than a direct attack on England.[29]

The settlement of 1236 began a period of friendlier relations and trade growth. Conditions worsened briefly when the Anglo-French truce expired in 1242, but open hostilities were averted when England and France made a truce that lasted until the Treaty of Paris in 1259.[30] Beginning with Ypres in 1233, individual towns also got charters of privileges for their merchants in England. The habit of negotiating with cities became even stronger as the counts became more attached to France. Ypres's privilege of 1233 was confirmed in 1259, followed by one to Ghent and the next year to Bruges and Douai. The Ghent and Douai charters gave freedom from toll and confiscation and freed the Flemish merchants from liability for debts of their fellow-citizens except those for which they had stood surety personally, but charged their home governments with protecting English property.[31]

During the thirteenth century most Flemish merchants bought wool in the north directly from the monasteries. They established a virtual Flemish colony in London, which became a base from which they

29. Lloyd, *Wool Trade*, 20–3.

30. Lloyd, *Wool Trade*, 20–3; Lloyd, *Alien Merchants in England in the High Middle Ages* (New York, 1982), 99–101.

31. Varenbergh, *Relations diplomatiques*, 128, 135–6. The Douai charter is printed in A.E. Bland, P.A. Brown and R.H. Tawney (eds), *English Economic History: Select Documents* (London, 1914), 192–3.

could trade at the English fairs. The most important fair for the Flemings was that of St Ives, on the Ouse near Huntingdon. It was held at Easter, perhaps timed to follow the Lenten fair of Ypres. The fact that the *scildrake* (second-in-command) of the Hanse of London had to bring merchandise that had not been sold in England back to Flanders to the next fair, where it was to be disposed of 'by common counsel', shows that the timing of the Flemish and English fairs was linked.[32]

The merchants travelled to the fairs in convoy accompanied by inspectors who got their authority from the aldermen of their home cities. They had absolute authority over their communities once the groups were on English soil. They judged legal actions and decided when the sale of Flemish cloth would begin at each fair to give them time to inspect the cloth thoroughly. Their court also heard cases against Englishmen accused of false trading practices and had the power to exclude them from further dealings with the Flemish community. The rules for each group of traders were drawn up and changed only with common consent; they were proclaimed before the 'community' at the beginning of each fair. The Flemings forbade merchants to sell cloth other than that produced by their own companies, evidently to prevent outsiders from getting a foothold in the export trade. Group solidarity was a major concern, although some contracts survive involving joint investment or business partnerships between Englishmen and Flemings.[33]

The Hanse of London

Probably by 1200 and certainly by 1241, the Flemish merchants in England had an umbrella organization that has become known as the 'Hanse of London'. It included traders from twenty-two communities by 1250. It is not to be confused with the Hanse of the Seventeen Towns, an organization of Flemish and Artesian cities whose merchants traded at the fairs of the Champagne.

Comparison of two surviving versions of the statutes of the London Hanse, both probably dating from the third quarter of the thirteenth century, shows that Bruges was the dominant member, from which the 'count of the Hanse' was chosen. Ypres was second in power and

---

32. Varenbergh, *Relations diplomatiques*, 153–5; Moore, *Fairs*, 13–14, 299; van Houtte, *Economic History*, 35; H. van Werveke, ' "Hanze" in Vlaanderen en aangrenzende gebieden', *ASEB* **90** (1953): 16.

33. Moore, *Fairs*, 96–9.

thus became the collective spokesperson for the other members. The organization of the London Hanse shows that even Bruges had a far more important position in Flemish overseas trade than the evidence of the English fairs suggests; but it was evidently not due to the precocity of its textile industry. Merchants of Bruges could 'gain' the Hanse in Bruges without going to England, but those of Ypres had to trade in England and join the organization there, for the textile oligarchy at Ypres was considerably more rigid and wealthy than at Bruges. Members of the Hanse had to be members of the *caritas* (merchant guild) of their home towns and pay an entry fee. Thus the Hanse was not a federation of guilds, for not all members of the local merchant guild belonged.[34]

Although the Hanse of London has been seen as an organization designed to keep control of Flemish foreign trade in a few hands, the contrary conclusion is suggested by the list of names of new members of the Bruges Hanse in that city's municipal accounts of 1282–9. Of 191 new members, 72 joined fathers who were already in the Hanse while 119 were newcomers, paying six times the entry fee of the first group. A few paid even more, but only because they were not yet members of the merchant guild, which was required before one could join the Hanse of London. Although most new members whose professions are traceable were drapers, wool merchants and hostellers, there were also stocking makers, shoemakers, brewers, spicers, bakers, dyers, mercers and even a Beguine. The Hanse of London at Bruges was thus more open than at Ypres, where merchants had to go to England in order to join. The Hanse of Saint-Omer shows a structure closer to Bruges than to Ypres and suggests that 10–15 per cent of the total population of Saint-Omer was being supported by the English trade.[35]

In addition to the Hanse of London, members of drapers' guilds in different cities made mutual assistance agreements: Ypres with Douai in 1240, and Ypres, Ghent, Diksmuide and Cambrai with Douai in 1261. Saint-Omer had controlled the import of English wool in the twelfth century, but it was dominated by Ypres and Douai after 1215. These two made agreements to control the market from 1240 onwards, then in 1261 let Ghent, Cambrai and Diksmuide enter the

34. Van Werveke, 'Hanze', 10–16, 28.
35. Carlos Wyffels, 'De Vlaamse Hanze van Londen op het einde van de XIIIe eeuw', *ASEB* **97** (1960): 5–30; Carlos Wyffels, 'Hanse, grands marchands et patriciens de Saint-Omer', *Société Académique des Antiquaires de la Morinie: Mémoires* **38** (Saint-Omer, 1962): 14–16.

association, while still excluding Bruges and Lille. The document of 1261 concerning wool purchases was a private arrangement addressed to the aldermen of the cities concerned from 'all the merchants from those places who are associated with the buying of wool from abbeys'. All texts show that the fairs were the principal marketplace for Flemish goods in England.[36]

Shifts within the Flemish economy during the thirteenth century are also reflected in patterns of trade at the English fairs. The balance of economic power shifted northward away from the Walloon cities. By 1250 only Douai of the southern cities still held its old position, and by the fourteenth century it would be more important as a centre for the grain trade than for its cloth. Until about 1220 Ghent and Lille were also important in the English trade along with Douai and Ypres, but then the latter two outstripped them. Between 1233 and 1250, thirty-nine merchants from Douai and Ypres received letters of protection from the English government, while only twenty-nine went to merchants of all other cities in Flanders and Brabant. Taking the century as a whole, some forty families of Ghent got licences for trade in England, operating abroad through resident agents (*homines*) whose status and function is unclear, although most businessmen themselves sometimes appeared in person.[37] The Wardrobe, which procured cloth for the royal court, patronized no Flemish merchants except Yprois and Douaisiens, perhaps because their cloth was excellent, perhaps because their merchants were willing to loan money to the kings. They were the only foreigners who rented municipal booths at the fairs of St Giles and St Ives, but merchants of Ghent, Poperinge and Lille, as well as Douai and Ypres attended the St Ives fair in 1270. Ypres and Douai dominated the Flemish trade at the Champagne fairs, but Cambrai, Ghent and Arras made a stronger showing there than in England.[38]

THE GERMAN TRADE

The statistics from the English fairs confirm other evidence suggesting that Ghent's considerable cloth export was more turned towards

36. Sivery, 'Histoire économique et sociale' in *Histoire de Lille*, 171; Moore, *Fairs*, 95, and edition of the document of 1261, 301.
37. Märtens, *Weltorientierungen*, 60–1, 73, 79.
38. Moore, *Fairs*, 31, 34, 284; Bland, Brown and Tawney, *Documents*, 193.

Germany, whose archives have been investigated less fully than the French and English, and that the city gained considerable income by reconsigning French and English goods to destinations farther east. The important land routes from the Rhineland all came over Ghent, which came to dominate the German trade of Flanders. Ghent had a Hanse or merchant organization by 1199 that was directed towards the Rhine trade; its members received preferential treatment at the toll of Dendermonde, at the border of Brabant.[39]

But while Cologne had been the major centre for Flemish trade in Germany in the twelfth century, the Hanse cities of Bremen, Hamburg and Lübeck, which provided better and cheaper transport with large boats, assumed the lead in the thirteenth. In 1268 Ghent merchants got the privilege that their goods could not be confiscated at Hamburg for the debts of co-burghers or other Flemings. They were permitted to do business in Hamburg without going through native merchants. This charter shows that Flemings were selling their own cloth and French wine at Hamburg and were taking Holstein grain on the return trip. Flemings are mentioned at Kiel in 1273 and shortly afterwards in the Baltic cities of Wismar, Stralsund and Greifswald. The rise of the German Hanse limited Flemish activity from the late thirteenth century; the Hanse forbade the Baltic to Flemish boats in 1285.[40]

COMMERCIAL TECHNIQUES

The organization of the Hanses of the Seventeen Towns and of London shows that the frontiers of Flanders were no barrier to the establishment of common interests and governing regulations. Unfortunately, our knowledge of the precise mechanisms by which the Flemings transferred goods in France and England is sadly deficient. Flemish textile artisans emigrated in the thirteenth century, sometimes on invitation from the local authorities, but less often than in the fourteenth. Shearers from Ypres and Diksmuide are found in Genoa, and in 1234 the burgomaster of Bordeaux invited Flemish weavers there to make cloth in the Flemish, English and French

39. Van Werveke, 'Hanze', 22.
40. Jansen, 'Handel en Nijverheid', 172; Doehaerd, 'Handelaars en Neringdoenden', 380–1.

manner. Weavers from Bruges, Ghent, Veurne and Poperinge worked at Provins.[41]

In view of the region's reliance on foreign trade, there is surprisingly little evidence until the late thirteenth century that Italian and southern French financiers were active in Flanders, even as creditors of the counts. There is even less evidence of Jewish financiers apart from 'Jew Streets' in some of the larger cities, which in itself suggests that they were active in financing an ill-documented phase of urban growth. The Lombards, who were essentially pawnbrokers loaning on pledged security, were present in all the larger towns, but later evidence shows them more active in neighbouring Hainault than in Flanders.[42]

Princes and urban governments prohibited usury, which at this time means interest of any sort, in private contracts, but enforcement was half-hearted. A loan was made at Douai in 1229 at a weekly rate of 4s on £17 15s, or 58 per cent for a year, but it was stated as a penalty for delay in repayment and thus was not usury. Contracts from Ghent show similar patterns. Furthermore, most Flemish town governments themselves borrowed at concealed rates of interest from their citizens; although the town formally engaged to repay only the nominal sum borrowed, the actual repayment was sometimes as much as 16 per cent higher.[43]

As elsewhere, most borrowing in Flanders was done by manipulating the exchange rate, which permitted borrowing with an element of risk, since the rate could move in either direction. Moneychanging developed early, at Arras by 1100 and in all major cities in the thirteenth century. There were twenty-eight changers' booths at the Torhout fairs. At Bruges three exchanges were held in fief of the count shortly after 1200, a fourth in 1224, and a fifth in the fourteenth century. There were also twelve unlicensed moneychangers by 1300 who paid a fee to the licensed changers. A similar organization but with fewer moneychangers existed at Ghent. The financiers of Arras held the Flemish authorities in their collective pockets by the late thirteenth century. In 1278 Countess Margaret owed them £18,600, and Guy of Dampierre owed them £65,000 by 1295. Town governments were also in debt. By 1275 Ghent owed a debt of £38,500, mainly to Arras financiers, and in 1299 Bruges owed the Crespin of Arras £110,000.[44]

41. Doehaerd, 'Handelaars en Neringdoenden', 394.
42. Van Houtte, *Economic History*, 55; Jansen, *Middeleeuwse Geschiedenis*, 199.
43. Godding, *Droit privé*, 474, 476.
44. Van Houtte, *Economic History*, 52–4.

Businessmen of Ghent lent large sums to the English kings, although this diminished during the thirteenth century as the English came to rely more on Italian financiers. But the financial transactions of Gentenars with the English kings were tied to commerce, especially the wool trade. A few Gentenars lent money to their own city government in the thirteenth century, but not to other cities, and the practice was exceptional for them, in contrast to those of Arras. Ghent businessmen ordinarily subordinated finance to merchandising and lent only when the risk was low and potential return was high. We do not have enough information about the lending practices of the merchants of Ypres and Bruges to permit firm conclusions.[45]

Even in the thirteenth century city governments were obtaining credit by selling life annuities (rents) to wealthy investors. The buyer advanced a lump sum to the seller, who in turn was obliged to pay a stated sum annually to the buyer.[46] The element of risk was present, satisfying the church; for if the buyer died before his original investment was recovered, his family's resources would be diminished. The practice was quickly extended to the hereditary rent, and by the fourteenth century it was not only the wealthy who bought life rents; they became similar to the modern bond issue and were sources of investment for persons of moderate means as well as the rich.

Only for Flemish business techniques at the Champagne fairs are we reasonably well informed. A collection of 'fair letters' survived for Ypres for the period 1249–91, and some were published before the archives were destroyed in 1914. The fair letters first appeared in the Mediterranean around 1200. They were obligatory letters that were not endorsable, but they could be transferred between parties orally before witnesses. They could be made payable to the bearer for easy transferability. Substitution of both creditor and debtor was possible. The letters gave the names of the principals, the amount of the debt, when it was due, personal and property sureties, and the aldermen as witnesses and the date. Three copies were made – one each for the creditor and the debtor, with a third to the town hall for security.

Some fair letters involved repayment in a coin different from that in which the original obligation was incurred, a harbinger of the slightly later bill of exchange. They were repayable at another fair, either Flemish or Champagne. The fair letter made it possible for goods to

---

45. Märtens, *Weltorientierung*, 86–99.

46. See for example *IAB* **1**: 5–6, a case of 1265 in which Bruges owed a life rent to two men of Arras.

be paid for without transferring large amounts of specie. A relatively small number of merchants visited the fairs, and few of them specialized in a single item. The linkage of the three fair systems of Champagne, England and Flanders meant that the merchants would act as buyers and sellers of different commodities in several different locales. A system of deferred payment, with the final fair of the year acting as a clearing house (although debts could be transferred across calendar years), thus developed. Although fair letters have not survived from other cities, the Ypres collection mentions one involving a Gentenar done before the aldermen of Bruges in 1274, and another text mentions one done at Torhout for an English merchant. All but four of the Ypres fair letters are in French, a strong indication of the extent of merchant literacy in the vernacular.[47]

The fair letters reveal numerous partnerships. The fairs were the major although not the only avenue of contact between the Italian and North Sea markets. In 1206 one Euroinus de Cogino of Reims recorded two contracts at Genoa, in each case with a Fleming as his partner. Such arrangements were risky for the creditor, for there was no principle of limited liability for joint debts. The merchant usually had a personal guarantor, but some creditors demanded that goods be provided as a pawn, usually land, cloth, wine or wool. The clause 'one payment guarantees the others' is found in some acts, declaring forfeiture of payments already made in case of default on a later payment.[48]

The fair schedules were staggered so that the same person could visit at least some of the fairs in each cycle, although doing all the fairs in France and England would have been difficult, and evidently only some Italians tried it. Champagne and western Flanders were so close, however, that contacts were constant. Exchanges were particularly active between the first Troyes fair and those of Torhout and Lille. Business at Torhout was so heavy that the city of Bruges bought a house there. Later evidence shows that considerable Flemish cloth was marketed at the five fairs of Flanders; it is thus tragic that the fair letters are the only records surviving from the Flemish fairs that shed light on their patterns of trade.[49]

47. G. Des Marez, *La Lettre de Foire à Ypres au XIIIe siècle: Contribution à l'étude des papiers de crédit* (Brussels, 1900), 7–8, 11, 13, 15, 25, 33, 35, 60–1; see comment by Jansen, 'Handel en Nijverheid', 173.

48. Des Marez, *Lettre de Foire*, 40–1, 51, 56; P. Desportes, *Reims et les Rémois aux XIIIe et XIVe siècles* (Paris, 1979), 97.

49. Des Marez, *Lettre de Foire*, 75–86; *IAB* **1**: 40; Desportes, *Reims*, 105; D. Nicholas, *The Metamorphosis of a Medieval City: Ghent in the Age of the Arteveldes, 1302–1390* (Lincoln, Neb., 1987), 141, 152–3, 184, 195.

THE FLEMISH TEXTILE INDUSTRY

We have noted that a major reassessment is needed of the role of textiles in the Flemish economy. Although indigenous forces gave rise to cloth making in Flanders, the Flemings were severely dependent on English wool from the late twelfth century. The large quantities of silver used to buy it came from new supplies, especially from the new Freiburg mines, that became available at the end of the twelfth century. Another reason for the growth may be a change in sartorial taste. In the second half of the twelfth century, the cloth coat, made of wool, gained definite ascendancy over linen as the preferred dress of the rich. The Flemings thus tried to capitalize on a burgeoning market in which demand was exceeding supply. More, however, is needed to make cloth than a wool supply, least of all one that was insufficiently elastic to meet growing demand. Flanders had a bountiful labour supply in the cities, but it depended on Italian and French merchants for many dyes. Indeed, much of the Flemish export to the Mediterranean was undyed cloth that was finished in Italy, particularly at Florence.[50]

We have also seen that Flemish domination of the international trade in luxury woollens was not as comprehensive as was once thought, for the entire northwestern corner of Europe was becoming a textile-industrial zone. Although 'Flemish' cloth virtually disappeared from Mediterranean markets after 1202, the reason was almost certainly that the Italians were now buying Flemish textiles at the Champagne fairs and calling them 'French'. When the direct maritime tie between Genoa and Bruges was established, first in 1277 and more regularly after 1318, the Italians resumed precise nomenclature for Flemish cloth.[51]

It is clear furthermore that cloth making was less patrician dominated in the thirteenth century than was once thought. By the mid thirteenth century the older families of textile entrepreneurs in the cities feared competition from newer lineages, which were generally excluded from participation in the town councils. Texts began distinguishing 'drapers' from 'weavers', and a Douai statute of 1248 prohibits partnerships between them. The drapers, who exported cloth and sold it in rented stalls in the cloth hall, must also be distinguished from

---

50. Peter Spufford, *Money and its Use in Medieval Europe* (Cambridge, 1988), 138–9; Desportes, *Reims*, 103; van Houtte, *Economic History*, 34; Jansen, 'Handel en Nijverheid', 173.

51. Sivery, 'Histoire économique et sociale' in *Histoire de Lille*, 168–71.

the more aristocratic members of the merchant guild, who were actually work givers who bought raw wool directly from the suppliers and had it worked into cloth by weavers.[52]

There are shifts in the geography of the Flemish textile industry during the thirteenth century. Most west Flemish centres, which used the domestic wool available in such abundance locally, declined as their sources of supply were converted to arable. The smaller centres of the Leie valley, notably Courtrai and Wervik, which did not begin making cloth until the thirteenth century, differed from them in using foreign and particularly English wool almost exclusively. A third group of small textile towns of eastern Flanders – Oudenaarde, Aalst, Ninove and Dendermonde – made only 'good' cloth in the thirteenth century but in the late fourteenth would free themselves from the influence of Ghent and began making cheaper grades from local wool and wool imported from places other than England. The shift eastward of rural textiles was clearly connected with the growing importance of the export luxury product.[53]

Yet the Flemish textile statutes of the late thirteenth century mention native as well as Scottish and Irish wool. Even the entire English wool export, which did not go to Flanders, could never have been enough to provide Flanders' needs. Moreover, each Flemish town made a great variety of textile types. The distinction between *saies* (worsteds) and *draperie* (fine woollens) has been exaggerated. Both were a 'wet' cloth, greased on the frames to produce a smooth fabric. Their dimensions might be the same, and the price was comparable on worsteds and the cheaper woollens. Striped cloths, which were among the specialities of the Flemish cities, have also caused confusion, for many grades and dimensions were made. Their chief common characteristic was that they were cheaper than both *draps* and worsteds. They were exported especially to England. The cheaper grades were also not confined exclusively to a domestic market. In terms of both total volume and percentage of total value, the cheaper types of northern cloth were more important on the Mediterranean markets than were the luxury textiles.

The cities in the Hanse of the Seventeen Towns, which sold at the fairs of the Champagne, thus produced a wide variety of cloths. The

52. For these arguments, see the extremely suggestive article of Alain Derville, 'Les Draperies flamandes et artésiennes vers 1250–1350', *RN* **54** (1972): 353–70, esp. 353–9; and more generally Herman van der Wee, 'Structural Changes and Specialization in the Industry of the Southern Netherlands, 1100–1600', *EcHR* **28** (1975): 203–21.

53. Verhulst, 'Laine indigène', 292–4.

high-quality 'coloureds' were virtually monopolized by the greater cities of Ghent, Douai, Cambrai, Ypres and Châlons, and to a lesser extent Lille and Provins. The cheaper types (*rayes*, stanforts, *saies*) were sold by virtually all, including the smaller centres. Although Ypres and Ghent exported luxury cloth, they also produced the cheaper grades; the fact that they tried to stop the smaller towns from making *strijpte halflakene*, an inexpensive ray, at Poperinge and Dendermonde in the 1340s shows that they were making the cloth themselves.[54]

SIGNS OF CRISIS

Although the Flemish economy was generally prosperous during the thirteenth century, there were structural problems suggesting the beginning of a cyclic economy.[55] As inflation worsened in the late twelfth century, lords of tenures yielding fixed rents had serious problems. There were major price variations on grain even within the same region. English grain had a high price at the end of the twelfth century, and much was exported to the Scheldt basin. There was a sudden jump in grain prices in 1225–6 in the Meuse valley, which also sent grain to Flanders. Although we have seen that the drop in the Mediterranean market for Flemish cloth has been exaggerated, the reception given to the False Baldwin by cloth workers suggests a problem. In 1245 the first textile workers' strike occurred at Douai, and grain prices at Lille jumped 300 per cent. Interest rates at the Champagne fairs, normally 16–30 per cent, dropped in 1245 to 5 per cent and never recovered their previous levels. Some Italian banks ordered their representatives in Champagne to borrow there, where interest was low, and lend the money in the northwest where rates were high.

The structural weakness of the Flemish economy is shown in the fact that, despite the stability of Flemish money in the early thirteenth century, considerable foreign coin was now used in Flanders. German silver pennies circulated widely after the agreement of 1173 between

54. Patrick Chorley,'The Cloth Exports of Flanders and Northern France during the Thirteenth Century: A Luxury Trade?' *EcHR*, 2nd series, **40** (1987): 367–70, 350, 359–61, 362–6.

55. This section is based on Gérard Sivery, 'Les Débuts de l'économie cyclique et de ses crises dans les bassins scaldiens et mosans, fin du XIIe et début du XIIIe siècle', *RN* **64** (1982): 667–81.

Frederick Barbarossa and Philip of Alsace. English trade with Flanders was essentially one-sided; although England was flooded with Flemish silver to pay for massive wool imports after 1180, there is little evidence of English coin in Flanders until the mid thirteenth century. A major reason was that Flemish cloth exports were so dependent on the Champagne fairs and France, which excluded sterling. After 1250, and particularly after the English trade embargo of 1270 diverted much of the wool trade to Brabant, the circulation of English coin throughout the Low Countries grew enormously. The strong French coin, at least until the debasements of the 1290s, also circulated in Flanders, apparently at parity with the native Flemish issue.[56]

Flemish coins, although a comital monopoly and stable at 0.45 grammes silver to the penny, circulated only locally, since Flanders imported so much more than it exported. Confusion between Flemish and Artesian money begins from the period of Philip of Alsace, and it was compounded after Arras became a French royal mint. A new Artesian was minted in 1237, of the same weight as the Flemish penny, and this worsened the confusion. Texts from 1260 make the Flemish penny the equivalent of the parisis of Arras, although they were not of the same weight. By the late 1260s foreign coins were being accepted at a rate higher than their intrinsic value. The countess was losing seigniorage income, and there was a metal drain from Flanders. By that time the aldermen of Flanders were advising the countess on monetary matters. The greater prestige and diffusion of French royal coinage, not its intrinsic weight, contributed to undervaluation of the Flemish coin and led to eventual devaluation in response to French action at the end of the century.[57]

THE CRISIS OF 1270–4

Anglo-Flemish relations underwent a crisis after 1270 that would be catastrophic for the Flemish economy. England was the cornerstone of Flemish trade, for Flemings bought wool and other goods in England

56. Spufford, *Money*, 195; P.D.A. Harvey, 'The English Inflation of 1180–1220', *Past and Present* **61** (1973): 26–8; N.J. Mayhew, 'The Circulation and Imitation of Sterlings in the Low Countries' in *Coinage in the Low Countries*, 55–9.

57. Carlos Wyffels, 'Contribution à l'histoire monétaire de Flandre au XIIIe siècle', *RBPH* **45** (1967): esp. 1113, 1117–18, 1120–8, 1130–5.

and channelled French goods from the fairs of the Champagne into England. A contract of 1277 between John de Redmere of Appleby and Jacques le Roy of Diksmuide – the involvement of men of small towns rather than major cities is most suggestive – is probably typical in showing the interdependence of the two national economies. The Fleming sent cloth, spices (presumably from the Champagne fairs) and other merchandise to England; John de Redmere was to sell it and absorb three-quarters of the profit or loss. John in turn sent wool to Flanders, which Jacques was to sell and likewise have three-quarters of the profit or loss.[58] The north German towns were beginning to cut into this market to some extent, but it remained a largely Flemish preserve.

In 1270 Countess Margaret precipitated a rupture by confiscating English property in Flanders, allegedly to retaliate for non-payment of her money fief. By the time the crisis had ended four years later, Flemish merchants were largely excluded from overseas shipping in England and had been replaced by other suppliers. Although Flanders remained dependent on English wool, it no longer compensated by controlling the carrying trade.[59]

Although the money fief was the major irritant, another was the fact that the English assize of cloth was extended to include foreign woollens. As early as 1253 Henry III had complained of the length and breadth of the luxury fabrics of Douai and threatened that cloth not meeting English specifications would be confiscated if brought to the English fairs. Flemish cloth came in many different sizes, and the requirement that it be of standard length was burdensome, since length was the chief differentiating characteristic of the manufactures of each Flemish city. Foreign merchants, not only Flemish, immediately resisted enforcement of the assize. Henry III did not pursue the matter, but Edward I returned to it in 1270 by granting licences to foreigners on condition that they abide by the terms of the assize. Hostilities were then precipitated when Flemish property at the St Ives fair was seized in 1270 on the complaint of a burgess of Lynn that his wool had been seized at Bruges in 1265. This was a breach of the long-established principle that Flemish merchants could be arrested only for their own debts. The exact date of Margaret's order for the seizure of English goods is not known, but it was before the end of September 1270, when all Flemish merchants and their goods in England were arrested.[60]

58. Case cited by Lloyd, *Wool Trade*, 307.
59. See the remarks of Lloyd, *Wool Trade*, 25.
60. Moore, *Fairs*, 133–4; Lloyd, *Wool Trade*, 28–9.

Negotiations were fitful, even when the English tried dealing with individual towns rather than Margaret. Part of the problem was that, perhaps because of the trouble over the assize of cloth regulation or because Flemish merchants had advance warning of the countess's intention, Flemish property seized in England in 1270 was worth much less than English property taken in Flanders. Thus the English had no leverage except their embargo on wool exports to Flanders, and the king gave many licences of exemption. Some English and German merchants were allowed to import Flemish cloth to England, even if it did not conform to the assize, in violation of the embargo. Smuggling was so rampant that plenty of wool reached Flanders. The change was more subtle and devastating. For although, in contrast to what would happen after 1336, the Flemish textile industry was not being starved for wool after 1270, the export licences were issued not to Flemish merchants but rather to denizens and to foreigners other than Flemings.[61]

Flemish merchants thus no longer dominated the carrying trade, taking the profit of selling to others. The Italians seem to have been the chief beneficiaries. Within a few years they had a near monopoly on wool raised by the English Cistercian abbeys, for they were better able to pay them in advance than the Flemings. Others also benefited, notably English nationals, some of whom seem previously to have been innkeepers for Flemings. Numerous Brabanters also got licences to export wool. There was a dramatic decline in the number of Flemish merchants at the St Ives fair after 1270 and a corresponding rise in attendance from Brabant. The wool export from England in 1273 was handled 34.9 per cent by Englishmen, but 24.4 per cent by Italians, 16.2 per cent by persons from northern France and 11.2 per cent by Brabanters. Duke John II of Brabant married King Edward I's daughter, and Edward began directing English wool and leather exports towards Antwerp. The loss of the carrying trade raised the price of wool in Flanders, which contributed to a growing problem that high-grade Flemish textiles were being undersold in foreign markets. There is some evidence that in the aftermath of the English wool embargo and especially after 1300, Flemish estate owners went over more to sheep raising, but such measures could not compensate for the decline and increasing unreliability of the English supply. Civil conflict in Flanders after 1280 then exacerbated the problems.[62]

61. Lloyd, *Wool Trade*, 30–2.
62. Moore, *Fairs*, 211, Table 18; Jansen, 'Handel en Nijverheid', 174; Blockmans, 'Vers une société urbanisée', 60–1; Lloyd, *Wool Trade*, 39–40, 56; Verhulst, 'Laine indigène', 303.

The Treaty of Montreuil of 28 July 1274 obliged each ruler to satisfy the claims of his/her own subjects, but the difference would be paid to the ruler who had lost more. The commissions set up to investigate – four English merchants chosen by merchants of Flanders and four Flemings chosen by the English – ascertained that English damages were 3.3 times as great as Flemish. This meant that Margaret had a substantial debt to Edward I, while her own subjects were pressing her for reimbursement for additional losses that had not been accounted for in the arbitration. Although trade was resumed in 1275, diplomatic feints and wool stoppages continued until in 1278 the burgesses of Ypres, Douai, Diksmuide and Poperinge agreed to pay £2022 of the remaining debt in return for guarantees that they had no liability for the remainder outstanding. The Flemish government continued to welsh on promises to pay the debt until in June 1285 the English forced the issue by demanding the Flemish hostages who had been provided for in the treaty of Montreuil. In February 1286 the count agreed to pay in quarterly instalments and did so by 18 November 1287.[63]

---

63. Lloyd, *Wool Trade*, 35–9.

CHAPTER EIGHT
A Half-Century of Crisis, 1274–1317

The aftermath of the Anglo-Flemish rupture of 1270–4 deepened the problems. The financial settlement was finalized only in 1287. As overseas trade declined, hostility to the countess and of non-patrician burgesses to the urban oligarchies grew.

THE DOMESTIC SITUATION TO 1285

The town governments had increasing problems keeping control. In 1275, in response to complaints from the 'commons', Margaret tried to replace the XXXIX of Ghent with an annual magistracy of thirty members. The XXXIX appealed to the court of her overlord, the *parlement* of Paris, that this violated Ferrand's constitution of 1228. In 1280 the *parlement* restored the XXXIX on condition that they submit to external financial control. More ominously, although there is no evidence this early of efforts to regulate immigration, Ghent in 1286 became the first Flemish city to take the 'issue' tax from persons emigrating or otherwise leaving the tax competence of the city. This probably reflects a problem with wealthy town families moving outside to their rural estates.[1]

1. Godding, *Droit privé*, 57.

The troubles of 1280

The aged Countess Margaret abdicated on 29 December 1278 in favour of her son Guy of Dampierre, who had shared rule with her for some years. The misfortunes of Guy's last years have detracted from the considerable achievement of this prince, who was already in his mid fifties when he became count of Flanders.[2]

In 1280 Guy of Dampierre was faced with major internal rebellions in the three large cities and some smaller communities of Germanic Flanders. There was unrest throughout the north, not only in Flanders. Fullers were imprisoned at Tournai in mid 1279 for having 'hindered and disturbed' the trade. This was followed by a weaver rebellion in 1281. There were also disturbances at Douai and Saint-Omer in September and October 1280. Uprisings also began in the smaller towns. Since 1266 Damme had had taxes on bread, wine, beer and madder, which were extended in 1278 to rents and commercial transactions. The commons of Damme in October 1280 alleged maladministration of the taxes and demanded an equal voice with the aldermen when the levies were collected. They complained of illegal courts and detentions and alleged that the aldermen were choosing deans and arbitrators of the guilds from outside the guild memberships and specifically were appointing their kinsmen and guests. The complaint was apparently ignored.[3]

Although the 'Cokerulle' of Ypres pitted the cloth workers, most of whom lived in nearby villages but worked in Ypres, against the city's rulers and the textile magnates, the rebellions at Bruges and Ghent were between factions of wealthy patricians. The Bruges uprising was directed specifically against the count. Disturbances, later called 'Moerlemaye' by the inhabitants, racked Bruges in two stages between 1 October 1280 and August 1281. Bruges was less firmly textile-industrial than Ghent and Ypres. Even the term 'patrician' causes problems there, for possession of a town allod did not change one's legal status,

2. For the period of Guy of Dampierre, see Vandermaesen, 'Vlaanderen en Henegouwen', 403–10; Pirenne, *Histoire de Belgique*, 1: 389–435; and particularly Nowé, *Bataille des Eperons d'Or*.

3. A. de Smet, 'De Klacht van de "ghemeente" van Damme in 1280: Enkele gegevens over politieke en sociale toestanden in een kleine Vlaamse stad gedurende de tweede helft der XIIIe eeuw', *BCRH* **115** (1950): 1–15, esp. 5–7; see also the comment of J.F. Verbruggen, 'Beschouwingen over 1302', *ASEB* **93** (1956): 41.

as it did at Ghent. At Bruges the ruling elite included drapers, merchants, artisans and less wealthy wholesalers as well as the very rich.

Bruges depended on English trade and blamed the rupture of 1270–4 on the countess. The government refused to participate in peace negotiations or contribute to the indemnity. Another problem was control of the weight at Bruges, which was a fief held by the Gistel and van der Woestijne families. Their inequitable administration caused foreign merchants to ask the countess to give them their own scales. Guy supported the Germans and made the aldermen responsible for punishing violations. When they refused, Guy on 26 August 1280 gave the Germans weighing privileges at nearby Aardenburg.

The count left for Paris in late September and was gone for five months, leaving his eldest son, Robert of Béthune, in charge in Flanders. In early October, mobs aroused by the aldermen took control of Bruges, imprisoning the count's adherents who did not flee. The commons in their turn asked Robert to review all laws of the aldermen and to give them seats on the board of aldermen and the council. The guild masters were in the government of Bruges for eight months. But the leaders of the rebellion were virtually all aristocrats, just as was true of the count's partisans; this was a power struggle within the aristocracy. The masses and the mid-level patricians, given mob scenes and the efforts of the commons to get a voice in government, supported the rebellion but did not lead it.

Order was quickly restored. In the spring the count imposed upon Bruges an enormous cash indemnity, a rent, and compensation of £4000 for property damages sustained by the count and his adherents. He also replaced the charter of Philip of Alsace, which had been lost when the belfry burned as the disturbances were beginning, with one that limited the city's autonomy. Punishments were now 'in the count's grace' for most deeds of violence, and crimes against the church or the coin were reserved to him. All customs were abolished, and only the count could alter the laws. He did grant one point to the commons: a yearly accounting to the count and representatives of the commons. Characteristically for Bruges, of 328 persons who had to do surety to keep the peace, only 158 were guildsmen, and of these only 34 came from textile trades.

Little is known of a second uprising in the summer of 1281. The count imprisoned the persons named hostage after the first rebellion and beheaded five of them; at the burial place in the chapel of St Andrew, their descendants later erected the 'Chapel of the Five Lords'. The leaders' families left public life for years, with some returning only in 1288 or even 1296.

Except for retention of the annual audit, the long-range results were minimal. By borrowing from bankers of Arras and the city government of Lille and raising the assizes on consumer goods, Bruges had paid off the cash indemnity by 1287. The rent was discontinued after 1296. In January 1297 King Philip IV withdrew Guy's charter of 1281 and restored that of Philip of Alsace. Evidently to pacify conflicts between the drapers and guildsmen, the count revised the textile statutes of Bruges after 1280. The Germans returned to Bruges in 1282, and other foreigners quickly followed. The weights were entrusted to sworn officials.[4]

The situation at Ypres, which was the most purely textile-industrial and probably the fastest growing Flemish city in the late thirteenth century, was more complicated than at Bruges or Ghent. Much of the confusion in the historiography of the Flemish textile industry is over the word 'drapers', who were small operators who gave work to individual cloth makers but were not members of the merchant oligarchy that ruled the city. In 1281 the count distinguished 'aldermen and merchants' from 'drapers, weavers, fullers and shearers'. Only after 1280 do the Ypres sources speak of 'master weavers'.

The aldermen and the count issued two separate regulations in September 1280 that evidently led to the uprising. One was a wage scale that the drapers were to pay to master fullers and what the latter were to pay to their journeymen. The draper who paid more was fined, and the master fuller who accepted more lost his profession for a year. The second ordinance regulated the wages and work conditions of the shearers. The fullers, weavers and shearers already had professional organizations, for the three constituted a committee to meet thrice yearly with the aldermen to judge violations of this regulation.

Guy of Dampierre issued a third regulation, in favour of the drapers, from Paris on 30 September 1280. It took the form of a concord between the aldermen and the 'makers of cloth' (weavers) and the drapers. It mentions them bringing their cloth into the city from the suburbs, where most lived. The drapers got the right to buy wool overseas, which broke the monopoly of the Hanse of London, but they were forbidden to exercise another trade while making cloth. If a draper married a woman from another trade, they both kept their professions. Municipal accounts were to be audited, but in contrast to

---

4. C. Wyffels, 'Nieuwe gegevens betreffende een XIIIde eeuwse "democratische" stedelijke opstand: de Brugse "Moerlemaye" (1280–81)', *BCRH* **132** (1966): 37–142, esp. 39–40, 43–58, 62–72, 73–5, 78–94.

other towns the drapers and other commoners made no effort to be present at the audit. Decisions of the aldermen could be appealed to the count; earlier constitutions punished those who refused to accept the judgement of the aldermen. Most of these provisions were repeated in a new charter that Guy gave to the town on 1 April 1281, after the revolt.

The troubles at Bruges began on 1 October 1280 and at Ypres on 6 October. Our information about events comes from the inquest held after the rebellion. A military expedition had been launched against Ypres from Poperinge, 10 kilometres west of the city. Virtually the entire population of Poperinge consisted of textile artisans working for employers in Ypres. The insurrection was less a civil struggle within Ypres than a revolt of Poperinge against Ypres; the other small centres did not participate. Two rich Yprois had been at Poperinge, called the artisans together, armed them and marched on Ypres. They got aid in the unwalled suburbs but could not penetrate the city centre. Although there was much disorder, only two aldermen or former aldermen were killed. The count's authority was re-established by 6 November. The rebels included one baker and one butcher, while the others were textile artisans.

The judgement was moderate. Assemblies of more than ten persons were forbidden. All claims for damages were ruled to cancel out, but the count confiscated one-quarter of the drapers' property. The law of 30 September was confirmed except for a clause that had given the count the right to modify the customs and laws of Ypres at his pleasure. The apprentice weavers were fined 4d per month until 1283, since their real masters were drapers. The aldermen of Ypres were back in the count's grace by 2 July 1281, and he did his best, in contrast to his attitude towards Bruges, not to make things difficult for them. He honoured a promise that he had given in 1279 to ask no more money from Ypres for seven years. In 1294 guildsmen became aldermen of Ypres for the first time.[5]

Ghent had the weakest artisan organizations of any major Flemish city, but even there the craftsmen had militias and treasuries, which were evidently used for charitable purposes. Political struggles in Ghent in the late thirteenth century were between factions of the landowning elite. In 1280 at Ghent the anti-XXXIX faction of the

5. This account of the Ypres disturbances is based on G. Doudelez, 'La Révolution communale de 1280 à Ypres', *Prisma Ieper*, 188–294, esp. 191–2, 203–7, 209–14, 223–6, 231, 235–41, 247–53, 259, 265, 272. The article appeared originally in *Revue des questions historiques*, 1938, 58–78, 3–25; 1939, 21–70.

patricians asked the count to abolish hereditary tenure of the aldermen, grant representation in the city government to the occupational guilds (their allies against the entrenched group), guarantee freedom of all to import wool without joining the Hanse of London and restore the privileges of the counts' bailiffs, which had been restricted on the demand of the XXXIX in 1279. The demands were rejected, and the craft guilds had no political rights at Ghent until after 1302.[6]

Public finance and social services

The fines assessed in 1281 exacerbated the growing inability of cities to meet the fiscal demands placed on them. They were overpopulated, disorderly and facing economic downturn. No Flemish city had healthy public finances before 1302. The city governments of Walloon Flanders collected some direct taxes in the thirteenth century, but they were extremely unpopular and were rarely used by the century's end. They borrowed heavily from bankers, particularly at Arras. This in turn caused resentment among the commoners, who suspected, not without reason, that the magistrates were lining their own pockets and demanded that they render regular accounts. Particularly after 1302, when the major burden of the war with France fell on the cities, they resorted to forced loans in emergencies. To meet less pressing expenses, the cities sold annuity rents.

Most Flemish cities also realized some income from orphan money in the thirteenth century. When either parent died, the child's share of that parent's property was detached from the surviving parent's portion. In the thirteenth century the guardians had to deposit the actual value of the orphan money with the city government, which paid 10 per cent interest. At Ypres, Lille and Saint-Omer the money was kept in a separate account, but at Bruges it went directly into the town treasury. The town spent the money, evidently thinking to guarantee it on the fiscal integrity of the town, which was already seriously in debt. Orphan money was the largest single item in the town receipt in the thirteenth century; in 1281–2 it was 29.85 per cent of the town income, while 18.46 per cent came from ordinary receipts and the other 51.68 per cent was borrowed. In 1301 the city defaulted on the orphan debt; it was still repaying it in 1408.[7]

6. Pirenne, *Histoire de Belgique*, 1: 389–90.

7. The repayments amounted to a life annuity at 10 per cent and are very close to the *Monti* or dowry funds established by some Italian cities. J. Marechal, 'Het Weezengeld in de Brugse stadsfinanciën van de middeleeuwen', *ASEB* **82** (1939): 1–41, esp. 32–7, 23–7.

However, the cities derived most of their ordinary income by century's end from taxes on consumption of food, beer, peat, wool and other foods and industrial raw materials. Naturally, these levies were extremely controversial. They were first used in 1228, but Guy of Dampierre authorized new taxes and raised the rates for Ghent in 1288 to help put municipal finances on to a firmer footing.[8] They would be a major issue in the coming conflicts with the French.

The counts in their turn were placing their finances on a different footing. The basis for the count's finances had long since ceased to be his old domain, and now even the new domain of tolls and commercial revenues brought him less than two other sources. The late thirteenth-century counts borrowed heavily, but after 1305 they turned increasingly to aids, which had to be levied with the consent of the five, later 'three cities'. In 1312 Philip IV 'transported' back to Flanders the rent owed under the peace terms of 1305. The Transport of Flanders became a tax owed to the count and became his first regular source of income apart from the domain. The rate of assessment was supposedly assigned on the basis of the ability of each unit to pay; the very fact that such an assessment was attempted shows that the counts had much more sophisticated records of local income and property-holding than have survived. The Three Cities in combination paid nearly two-fifths of the Transport assessment, with Bruges the richest and Ypres, at about two-thirds Bruges's rate, the poorest; but since the cities and the count by then were the real government of Flanders, with other groups having little power, it is likely that they were in fact underassessed.[9]

THE CONFLICTS WITH THE FRENCH

Flanders versus Philip the Fair, 1285–1314

A new chapter opened in Flemish relations with France with the accession of Philip IV, 'the Fair' (1285–1314). Not since Philip Augustus had the Flemish princes met as determined and unscrupulous an

---

8. Hans van Werveke, *De Gentsche Stadsfinanciën in de Middeleeuwen* (Brussels, 1934), 27, 199 ff.

9. Nicholas, *Town and Countryside*, 155–6, after W. Prevenier, 'De Beden in het Graafschap Vlaanderen', *RBPH* **38** (1960): 361–3; Ganshof, 'La Flandre', 425.

enemy in Paris. Philip the Fair evidently hoped to bring all of crown Flanders under his control, perhaps even to annex it. The other great feudatory whom Philip hoped to weaken was Edward I of England, who held Gascony from the French crown.

Philip allied with whatever group in Flanders would help him. His main foreign allies were the Avesnes of Hainault, the descendants of Countess Margaret's first marriage. Guy of Dampierre tried to forestall the Avesnes by marrying his daughter Margaret to Floris V of Holland in 1279, but later he had difficulties with Floris over Zeeland, and after 1290 Floris allied with the French. The emperor enfeoffed John of Avesnes with imperial Flanders but lacked the means to enforce it. Imperial Flanders stayed out of the conflicts between Guy and Philip and would later refuse to help crown Flanders pay the fines owed to the French after 1305.

Philip the Fair's major diplomatic initiatives, however, were among the Flemish nobles and townspeople. Eager as they were to put municipal finances on a sounder footing, the commoners disliked paying taxes. Philip responded to the public outcry over the taxes of 1288 by installing a French officer in Ghent as regent to control the count, allegedly to provide relief from a despotic prince but actually to put Flanders under royal administration. The XXXIX thus came to depend on the crown. Royal guardians were soon appointed at Bruges and Douai. Appeals were encouraged to *parlement*, bypassing the Flemish courts.[10]

Flemish relations with England had been rocky since 1270, but in 1290 Guy of Dampierre issued new privileges for English merchants in Flanders. But Guy lacked the means and perhaps the acuity to play the kind of diplomatic games at which both Philip IV and Edward I were such masters. Shortly before Guy was to arrive in England to arrange a final peace in 1292, the English embargoed the export of wool to Flanders, but this was a ploy and was lifted as part of the settlement. Forced by continued French provocations to deal with the quixotic English, Guy of Dampierre opened negotiations for a political alliance in 1293. Yet in May 1294 Edward revoked his safe conduct to Flemish merchants as subjects of the French king, evidently hoping to force the Flemings into a firm anti-French alliance.[11]

By the Treaty of Lier of 31 August 1294, however, Guy arranged the marriage of his daughter Philippina with the future Edward II of

10. Vandermaesen, 'Vlaanderen en Henegouwen', 405; Pirenne, *Histoire de Belgique*, 1: 396–7.

11. Lloyd, *Wool Trade*, 74; Lloyd, *Alien Merchants*, 101.

England. By then, France and England were already at war. Using the pretext of an appeal from the XXXIX of Ghent, Philip summoned Guy before *parlement* and incarcerated him and two of his sons. He only released him four months later, after he had renounced the agreement with England and agreed to send Philippina to France to be 'educated'; she died in Paris in 1306. Philip also forced Guy to follow him in a trade embargo with England, contrary to the economic interests of the cities, and required the exclusive use of French coin in Flanders. Then, in another switch, Philip on 10 June 1295 gave Guy the duty of enforcing the embargo and the right to take the proceeds of confiscations.[12]

Coinage now became a matter of international diplomacy. The French were debasing their issue to pay the high costs of their diplomacy and warfare in cheap coin. The exchange rates on other coins circulating in Flanders were set artificially to favour the French, for the king ordered Guy to undervalue the English esterlin and forbade circulation of money of the empire. In 1295 the king demanded that all precious metals in Flemish possession be surrendered to him in return for a compensation much less than their market value, and French coin was revalued against the Flemish. Flanders was thus flooded with French coins.[13]

Philip realized by early 1296 that his intransigence was driving Flanders into an English alliance. He thus coupled his prohibition of Flemish trade with England with a concession that Flemish cloth would be freed of all foreign competition in the realm and declared a two-year moratorium on debts of Flemish burghers and the count to himself. He limited the competence of his sergeants in Flanders and restricted Flemish appeals to *parlement*. He took the cities under his protection and thus *de facto* ruled Flanders directly; yet the cities supported the king because he confirmed their privileges. For although for a time Guy's resistance had given the French-born comital dynasty a popularity borne on nationalist sentiments, the count had dissipated this on 6 January 1296 by agreeing to the king's imposition of a 2 per cent property tax in Flanders on condition that the count get half. Except for Ghent, the cities escaped this by agreeing to pay a 'free will' contribution to the king for less money, but the count got nothing.[14]

12. Pirenne, *Histoire de Belgique*, 1: 399; Nowé, *Bataille*, 36–7.

13. Monier, *Institutions centrales*, 98.

14. Pirenne, *Histoire de Belgique*, 1: 401; Lloyd, *Wool Trade*, 75; Vandermaesen, 'Vlaanderen en Henegouwen', 406–7.

But Guy's worst blunder came in March 1296, when he accepted an invitation from Valenciennes, the chief city of Avesnes Hainault, to rule the city and declared it annexed to Flanders. In June the five great cities of Flanders were again placed under royal guardians, and Guy was summoned to Paris. John of Avesnes invaded Flanders from Holland. Guy asked for trial by his peers rather than *parlement*, which had been guaranteed by the treaty of Melun of 1226, to settle his grievances with the king. Philip refused, going so far as to hold the trial in the presence of representatives of the five great Flemish cities. Guy's fief of Flanders was declared confiscated, then restored for a fine. An exception was made of Ghent, which was then the chief bastion of French influence in Flanders and which the king continued to rule directly. Guy swore not to retaliate against Flemish townsmen who were allies of the king, and the king expressly kept the right to put his own officers in any 'good town' to oversee the count's conduct.[15]

Back in Flanders, Guy of Dampierre began to move closer to the alliance network that Edward I was creating in the Low Countries. On 20 September 1296 he refused another summons to *parlement*, again banished the XXXIX of Ghent and made overtures to the commoners. He renounced his feudal contract and allied openly with England on 9 January 1297, in a long letter in which he enumerated his grievances and accused the king of violating his duties towards a loyal vassal. Transcending the official rhetoric that often accompanied such declarations, Guy's renunciation of homage is a genuinely moving document, the cry of a man on the rack. Philip's response was a conference at Courtrai, where he offered the count trial by peers! The English alliance permitted the wool trade, which had been interrupted since 1294, to resume. Guy immediately abolished the XXXIX and replaced them with a new group, also of thirty-nine members, comprising mainly patrician enemies of the XXXIX, who were exiled in April. On 8 April 1297 he issued Ghent's 'Great Charter', a comprehensive code of criminal and civil law that would govern the city for the rest of the medieval period.[16]

Most Flemish nobles sided with the count in the early stages, but England provided little help, and Guy was unprepared for war. The French made a lightning strike into Flanders on 15 June 1297. Edward I used Ghent as a base, but the west quickly fell. The truce of Sint-

15. Pirenne, *Histoire de Belgique*, 1: 403–4; Nowé, *Bataille*, 9–10; Monier, *Institutions centrales*, 100.

16. Pirenne, *Histoire de Belgique*, 1: 406–7. Nowé, *Bataille*, 44; Lloyd, *Wool Trade*, 82.

Baafs-Vijve between England and France was sealed on 9 October 1297 and was extended to 6 January 1300. It left Guy of Dampierre without an ally. Claiming allegiance to the supreme overlord in Paris, but really facing the practical reality that Flanders had no effective independent government, many nobles defected. Financial difficulties also drove them into the French camp, particularly during the rampant inflation of the 1290s. Their purchasing power had declined, perhaps as much as 25 per cent, and they were selling their military service to the highest bidder. The king promised that they might hold all lands, offices and perquisites under the same terms as they had previously done under Guy of Dampierre. He lent them money and gave them property confiscated from Flemings loyal to the count. By 1302 barely one hundred Flemish nobles would fight in the 'national' cause.[17]

Parties in the cities: Claws and Lilies

The Flemish nobility had been divided into English and French parties since the period of Baldwin IX. By 1290 this split had spread to the cities, where 'Lily' (*Leliaert*) factions loyal to France fought the 'Claws' (*Clauwaerts*), who preferred the Flemish counts. The names are derived from the *fleur-de-lis* (lily) on the royal coat of arms and the lion on that of the Flemish counts. The two parties were not aristocracy versus commoners. Although the Lilies were largely patrician and noble, the Claws included prominent personal opponents of the Lilies as well as artisans. Records of property confiscated in 1297–8 at Ghent show that the Lilies were a very rich group consisting almost entirely of patricians.[18]

Yet even at Ghent the patriciate was not unified, and even some families were divided. The most conspicuous example was Philip uten Hove, who furnished the count with a complete inventory of the property of his Lily brother Gilbert.[19] The division within the elite about the magistracy did not correspond exactly to the Lily–Claw division; we have seen that there were separate groups of XXXIX in 1297, all of them patricians. People also changed sides. John uten

17. Vandermaesen, 'Vlaanderen en Henegouwen', 408; Walter Prevenier, 'Motieven voor leliaardsgezindheid in Vlaanderen in de periode 1297–1305', *De Leiegouw* **19** (1977): 274–7.

18. Prevenier, 'Leliaardsgezindheid', 277–85; Prevenier, 'La Bourgeoisie en Flandre au XIIIe siècle', *Revue de l'Université de Bruxelles* 1978/4, 423.

19. W. Blockmans, *Een middeleeuwse vendetta: Gent 1300* (Houten, 1987), 75.

Hove, Wasselin Haec and John uten Dale were Claws in 1297, Lilies by 1302.[20]

The elite of Bruges was more evenly divided between the parties than that of Ghent. Separate lists of townsmen whose wealth obliged them to do mounted military service for the town in 1292 and who lent the town money in 1297 are almost evenly divided between the parties, perhaps with the Claws holding a slight advantage.[21]

From Sint-Baafs-Vijve to Courtrai

The treaty of 1297 divided Flanders into comital and royal zones. In 1299 John of Avesnes became count of Hainault, Holland and Zeeland, on which the Flemings had had to abandon all claims. As soon as the truce expired on 6 January 1300, the French invaded again. By May Philip the Fair had absorbed Flanders into the royal domain, taken Guy and his sons to prison in France, and appointed a royal lieutenant, the Flemish noble Jacques de Châtillon, who soon made himself odious.

The king then made a triumphal tour through Flanders. He agreed to abolish the unpopular taxes on consumption at Ghent, thereby making considerable trouble for the city government, although he reinstated the Lily aldermen who had been exiled in 1297. For not only had public finance become based on the yield of these levies, but the king's patrician allies farmed the taxes and 'were used to making profit from the said exaction'.[22] In the edict of Senlis of 1 November 1301, the king replaced the XXXIX with two boards of thirteen aldermen, annually rotated but chosen by electors appointed by the prince and representatives of the city government. This structure, which restored the patrician monopoly initially but could also permit broader participation, would continue at Ghent for the rest of the medieval period.[23]

Philip seems to have been lulled by the magnificent displays that accompanied his triumphal tour and the obsequiousness of the Flemish magistrates into thinking that there would be no resistance to the

20. Haec fled to Paris after 1302, was entrusted with the confiscation of Claw property in France and amassed great wealth in this and in merchandising; Märtens, *Weltorientierung*, 244–6, 250–1.

21. J.F. Verbruggen, 'Beschouwingen over 1302', *ASEB* **93**, (1956): 38–40; see also J. de Smet, 'Brugse Leliaards gevlucht te Sint-Omaars van 1302 tot 1305', *ASEB* **89** (1957): 146–52.

22. Hilda Johnstone (ed.), *Annales Gandenses: Annals of Ghent* (London, 1951), 13.

23. Pirenne, *Histoire de Belgique* 1: 414. Prevenier, 'Bourgeoisie en Flandre', 425.

French annexation. But the tax issue caused a rebellion in Bruges, where Philip had not abolished the consumption levies, as soon as the king had left Flanders. The Lily magistrates incarcerated the commoners' leaders, the weaver Pieter de Coninck and the butcher Jan Breidel, but a mob released them and took control of the city. Châtillon and the garrison of Courtrai marched on Bruges and insisted that the city's walls be destroyed. Shortly afterwards, the count's sons John and Guy of Namur, the only members of his family still at liberty, restored a skeletal administration in Flanders around which the anti-French forces could rally. A mob inspired by de Coninck halted work on the destruction of the fortifications. A Claw magistracy was installed at Bruges in the spring of 1302.[24]

The tax question also continued to vex Ghent. The year 1302 was one of famine, and the rural regions, which supported the count's sons while the city government supported the French king, boycotted the food supply. With Châtillon's permission, the Lily government restored the food taxes on 1 April 1302, and the artisans declared a general strike for the next day. The result was an armed conflict in which, after trapping several hundred Lilies in the count's castle, the mob killed two aldermen and eleven other patricians and injured numerous others before the French could restore control.[25] Agitation continued in the countryside and at Bruges. To keep Ghent from joining it, Jacques de Châtillon agreed on 11 May to abolish indirect taxation, punish the magistrates who had reinstated it with his prior permission, and guarantee free commerce for all Gentenars.

The new Bruges government submitted to Châtillon on 17 May 1302. But at dawn the next day his forces were ambushed in the 'Matins of Bruges' when, at what seems to have been a prearranged signal (the cry 'Shield and Friend'), the Claws, strengthened by numerous exiles who had been let back into the city during the night, massacred the French and their sympathizers. The resistance was quickly joined by most of Flanders except Ghent.[26]

The battle of Courtrai (11 July 1302)

The French quickly invaded to put down the uprising, as 'popular'

---

24. Pirenne, *Histoire de Belgique*, 1: 416–17; J. Bovesse, 'La Régence comtale namuroise en Flandre (juillet 1302–mai 1303)', *Liber Buntinx*, 139–40; Nowé, *Bataille*, 65.

25. *Annales Gandenses*, 28; Nowé, *Bataille*, 65–6.

26. Pirenne, *Histoire de Belgique*, 1: 418–19.

governments replaced the old oligarchies throughout Flanders and confiscated Lily property. The interdict was renewed. The nationalist aspect of the conflict sharpened. The Franciscan who wrote the *Annals of Ghent* reported that the French troops began terrorizing civilians in 1302 only when they 'entered Flemish-speaking Flanders'. The battle was joined at the Groeninge brook outside Courtrai on 11 July 1302. The bulk of the army was from Bruges, west Flanders and the rural areas of the east. Ypres sent only about 500 men; although Ghent was officially for the French, the dissidents of the city sent a contingent of about 700 men under Jan Borluut. The Flemish army consisted largely of infantry, while the French force was cavalry; the *Annals of Ghent* state that there were no more than ten knights in the entire Flemish army at the battle.[27] The terrain was both swampy and full of trenches, totally unsuited to the cavalry charge that the French employed. The Flemings barricaded themselves behind a row of pikes anchored in the ground. The result was a total French defeat, with the commander, Robert of Artois, dead and the rest put to flight. By 14 July John of Namur was received at Ghent as its prince and held power in Flanders until the return of his younger brother Philip of Thiette from Italy in May 1303.[28]

The battle of Courtrai has entered legend as a milestone in the Flemish national struggle and as the first major battle in which urban infantry defeated cavalry led by nobles. Germanic Flanders was never to be part of France. The French could not believe what had happened; rumours swept Paris, evidently based on Pieter de Coninck's name (which means Peter King), that the Flemings had ejected King Philip IV and crowned a weaver as King Peter.[29] The conflict became known as the Battle of the Golden Spurs, a reference to 500 pairs of golden spurs taken from the aristocratic French victims who fell in 1302 and kept in the church of Notre Dame at Courtrai.[30] It may also have been the first of several in the late Middle Ages in which the swampy Flemish terrain and rainy climate played an important defensive role. The *Annals of Ghent* mention marshes frequently, including 'a dyke between two marshes, protecting the county of Flanders and dividing it from the county of Artois'; an incidental benefit of the

27. Johnstone, *Annales Gandenses*, 28, 29.

28. Pirenne, *Histoire de Belgique* 1: 420–1; Bovesse, 'Régence comtale', 140–2.

29. Pirenne, *Histoire de Belgique*, 1: 425.

30. When King Charles VI heard this story in 1382, he demanded an indemnity and burned the town. Verbruggen, 'De Historiografie van de Guldensporenslag', *De Leiegouw* **19** (1977): 245–72.

amputation of Artois was thus the establishment of a more easily defensible Flemish frontier on the south.[31]

A satirical gospel was composed at Bruges in the autumn of 1302, most of it concerning the battle of Courtrai. It was intended for an audience of Flemish clergy, who were generally anti-French, despite the attitudes of their superiors, and seem to have enjoyed bawdy humour.[32] The 'Passion' takes the form of an epic, with the French commander Robert of Artois and the chancellor Pierre Flote against Pieter de Coninck. It begins with a standard liturgical 'in that time' and ends with the French in the position of the Magi, who 'returned home by another way'. It is full of puns. Regarding Charles of Valois, Philip IV's brother, *Pater Noster, qui est in caelis* (Our Father, who is in heaven) becomes *frater meus, qui est infelix* (my brother, who is un-happy). Robert of Artois, who perished at Courtrai, is made to ask de Coninck not to kill him with a pun on *Pater*/Pieter: 'Father/Peter, let this cup pass from me'.[33]

The patrician regimes at Ghent and Ypres were overthrown within a few days of the battle, and the corporate existence of craft guilds was recognized. Although the claim that the new governments were 'democratic' is exaggerated, they included a broader segment of the propertied groups than their predecessors. The guilds had the most extensive rights at Bruges, which had led the rebellion. Although guilds were not given the right to specific seats on the town govern-ment there, the thirteen new aldermen included nine who had not been in previous governments and were probably guildsmen. A fuller became the new burgomaster.[34] But the older families again ruled the major cities by 1312, and only much later was the composition of city councils in Flanders determined by reserving seats for particular guilds.

31. Johnstone, *Annales Gandenses* 34, 37.
32. On 23 October 1302, the Flemish clergy authorized an aid to help the war effort. Bovesse, 'Régence', 164 n. 75. The Flemish sympathies of the Franciscan author of the *Annals of Ghent* have often been noted. Johnstone, 'The Annalist' in *Annals of Ghent*, xi–xii; Hermann van Goethem, 'De Annales Gandenses: Auteur en kroniek. Enkele nieuwe elementen', *HMGOG* **35** (1982): 49–59.
33. The parody survives only in a copy made by the English historian Adam of Usk during a visit to the abbey of Eeckhoute in 1406. See discussion by J.M. de Smet, 'Passio Francorum Secundum Flemyngos: Het Brugse Spotevangelie op de nederlaag van de Fransen te Kortrijk (11 juli 1302)', *De Leiegouw* **19** (1977): 289–319.
34. Verbruggen, 'Beschouwingen over 1302', 43; Prevenier, 'Bourgeoisie', 425.

After Courtrai

While the French lost the battle of Courtrai and suffered further reverses through 1303, they won the war in 1304. A French navy crushed the Flemish force at Zierikzee, and on 18 August an indecisive land battle was fought at Mons-en-Pévèle. The Brugeois and others were winning when the contingents of Ghent, Ypres and Courtrai left the field, a pattern that would recur and plague concerted Flemish military actions for the rest of the medieval period. The French held the battlefield, but they were too damaged to pursue the Flemish army.[35]

After a new Flemish army appeared before Lille, negotiations were opened that led to the peace of Athis-sur-Orge of June 1305. The terms obliged the Flemings to pay an enormous indemnity within four years and a perpetual rent of £20,000, provide the king with an army of 600 men, and destroy the fortifications of the major cities, although the cities' privileges were confirmed. As punishment for the Matins, Bruges had to send 3000 citizens on pilgrimages.[36] The count, nobles and towns and all Flemings aged fourteen and above swore eternal fidelity to the king and not to make any alliance that would compromise this. Until the peace was fulfilled, the count placed the castellanies of Lille, Douai and Béthune and the castles of Courtrai and Cassel in pledge to the king. All Lilies who had been damaged for their loyalty to the king would be compensated. The interdict was lifted, but it would be reimposed automatically for any violation and would be removed again only at the king's request. Robert of Béthune, the new count – the aged Guy of Dampierre died in 1305 – did get two major concessions: he was justiciable before his peers rather than before *parlement*, and Holland/Hainault was not included in the peace, leaving him free to pursue his war in Zeeland against the Avesnes.[37]

The military situation did not warrant such an unfavourable treaty, and the cities refused to accept it, accusing the count, his family and the nobles of complicity with the French. No artisan had been in the negotiating party, and the townsmen expected a patrician restoration.

35. Verbruggen, 'Historiografie', 245.

36. To put this figure into perspective, the city militia of Bruges in 1338 contained 7234 men. D. van den Auweele, 'De Brugse gijzelaarslijsten van 1301, 1305 en 1328: Een comparatieve analyse', *ASEB* **110** (1973): 120.

37. See in general Pirenne, *Histoire de Belgique*, 1: 427–9.

The cities had incurred enormous debts from the war, leading to forced loans, high taxes and the sale of rents. The cities also suffered from the immigration of refugees that they were in no position to assimilate. This can be measured statistically only at Lille, which between 1302 and 1311 received nearly double the annual average of fifty new burgesses that the city had absorbed between 1291 and 1301. From a population of 10–12,000 when the wars began, Lille grew by 1310–20 to 15–20,000.[38]

Dissension arose in the count's family. Robert of Béthune showed little independence until 1309, but his eldest son Louis I of Nevers opposed all concessions with France. Philip IV confiscated Louis's principalities of Nevers and Rethel, and the court of peers had him jailed him in 1311. He escaped and ensconced himself in imperial Flanders.

The alliance of convenience between the town governments and the count also disintegrated. In 1307 the king commuted the pilgrimages owed by 3000 Brugeois to £300,000, but the decision to exact it by taxing the entire county was resented. The Flemings also disliked compensating Lilies for their lost properties. Bruges continued to be a centre of resistance and abused some returning Lilies, which set automatic fines into effect. After rebellions in the cities and in Waas in 1309 against the peace terms of 1305, the king decided not to insist on vigorous enforcement of the treaty, specifically not demanding the destruction of the cities' fortresses. The town governments adhered to the treaty later in 1309.[39]

Robert of Béthune began to adopt a more independent posture towards the crown after 1309, but he was unable to get the same level of support in the towns as had been there in 1302. Bruges was still the most anti-royal of the large cities, and the others gradually made separate treaties with the French. Thus the count had to agree in the Treaty of Pontoise of 11 July 1312 to abandon Lille, Douai, Orchies and Béthune to the crown, where they would remain until 1369. In return, as we have seen, the king 'transported' to the count half the rent provided by the peace of Athis.[40]

Robert protested that the treaty was unenforceable, and Louis of Nevers tried to arouse national sentiment in Flanders. By the peace of

38. *Annals of Ghent*, 86; Sivéry, 'Histoire économique et sociale' in *Histoire de Lille*, 193–5, 198–9.
39. Vandermaesen, 'Vlaanderen 1244–1384', 415; *Annals of Ghent*, 96–7; Pirenne, *Histoire de Belgique*, 1: 428–31.
40. Pirenne, *Histoire de Belgique*, 1: 432–3.

Arras (July 1313), Courtrai and its castellany were placed under French rule as a guarantee of the Treaty of Pontoise. The next year Robert broke off dealings with the French, ejected them from Courtrai and besieged Lille. In 1315 Philip's heir, Louis X (1314–16), allied with Hainault for an invasion of Flanders, but his army was stopped by torrential rains that made troop movements impossible.

While the king's chaplain was preaching that it was just as meritorious to fight the Flemings as the Muslims, the Flemish cities opened negotations with the peace party at Paris. The Treaty of Paris (1 September 1316) essentially confirmed the status quo but worsened the financial obligations of the Flemish cities. The Lily and Claw parties revived. Most Lilies had left Flanders after 1302, but some took advantage of the amnesty after 1302 and again in the peace of 1316 to return.[41] After 1316, however, the troubles of King Philip V (1316–22) with the French nobles, who were unhappy with Philip the Fair's domestic measures, gave Flanders a respite.

The troubles in the comital family now became critical. Robert of Cassel, the count's younger son, began making trouble over his presumed exclusion from the succession in favour of Louis of Nevers. In compensation for his claims he got a rent of £10000 secured in imperial Flanders. In 1319 Robert of Béthune was preparing to attack Lille, but Ghent spoiled his campaign by refusing to send its militia across the Leie. The next year the 'regime of the captains' restored a largely Lily patriciate to rule at Ghent. On 5 May 1320 the Treaty of Paris renewed Robert of Béthune's fidelity to the crown and arranged the marriage of his grandson and eventual successor, Louis of Nevers the younger, to Philip V's daughter.[42]

The crisis of public order

In the wake of constant upheaval and military action, public order, never Flanders' strong point, simply broke down. By the late thirteenth century the status of burgher of the major cities, particularly the freedom from trial except in the city even for offences committed outside the town, became a serious problem. Military prowess in the fight against the French could get instant support for virtually any kind of behaviour.

41. Vandermaesen, 'Vlaanderen', 416; Prevenier, 'Bourgeoisie', 426; Pirenne, *Histoire de Belgique*, 1: 434.

42. Monier, *Institutions centrales*, 105; Pirenne, *Histoire de Belgique*, 1: 434–5.

A certain brother William of Saeftingen, a *conversus* of the monastery of Ter Doest, near Bruges, a man of great strength . . . severely wounded the abbot himself, and most cruelly killed a certain aged cleric monk who held the office of cellarer. . . . He fled to the tower of the church of Lisseweghe, near the aforesaid monastery, and was besieged in it by certain friends of the abbot and monks. He was brought out from the tower, after the besiegers had been put to flight, taken to Bruges, and restored to liberty, by John Breidel, a butcher of Bruges, the son of Peter de Coninck, once a weaver, now a knight . . . and about eighty men, well armed, from the commonalty of Bruges. The reason for the friendship and good feeling between (William) and the commonalty was as follows. When the battle of Courtrai . . . was close at hand, the said *conversus*, tall, strong and well armed, was in Courtrai with the men of Bruges. He noticed that one man in the Flemish army had a certain very strong oaken cudgel, with a plate of iron bound about it at the top, into which was inserted a very sharp blade. . . .He bought it, giving in exchange for it an excellent horse which he had brought with him from his abbey, and while fighting manfully in the battle, laid low a host of Frenchmen with the said cudgel. On this account, although he did not belong to Bruges by birth, ever after he was acceptable and in favour with the commonalty of Bruges, and therefore they delivered him from death, or at the least from perpetual imprisonment.[43]

Conditions were confused everywhere, particularly in the cities. Disturbances at Ypres in late November 1303 were judged by Philip of Thiette and the other four 'good towns'. Seven aldermen and councillors had been killed by 'the people' because of misdeeds committed against the commune. The 'people' alleged that thirty present and past magistrates had taken an unauthorized tax. The matter was evidently complicated, for a ruling was given only the following May. Forty-four persons were executed for murder and five for robbery and theft. The aldermen were to do justice to those who complained of extortion since the murder. Significantly, the agreement of Ypres to accept the verdict was made under the seal of the town and the 'five guilds': the weavers, fullers, shearers, butchers and fishmongers. The seals of the two captains of the city were apposed for all the other guilds. Each guild was to choose a captain from among its members to keep the peace.[44]

43. Johnstone, *Annales Gandenses*, 9-2. The episode of 1308 was part of a general rebellion of the lay brothers to news that a plan had been discussed at a meeting of Flemish abbots to make a comprehensive shift to indirect exploitation of their domains. C. Dekker and J.G. Kruisheer, 'Een Rekening van de abdij Ter Doest over het jaar 1315', *BCRH* **133** (1967): 282–6.

44. *IAY* 1: 184–5, 190–4.

The Borluut–van Sinte Baafs feud at Ghent

The Lily–Claw feuds deepened personal hostilities and family factionalism in the cities. Although the great cities were very powerful vis à vis
the counts, they were unable to keep order within their walls. The
best-documented example, because of the survival of an inquest record, is the Borluut–van Sinte Baafs feud in Ghent. It is an example of
so many problems that we have been discussing that it warrants extended discussion.

The Borluuts had sustained serious financial losses since the English
trade stoppage of the 1270s and were being shoved to the margins of
the ruling elite. Hostilities between them and the van Sinte Baafs went
back to a broken engagement in 1282 that had outraged the family
honour of the Borluuts and led them to murder. The families had
made peace after the homicide. But in 1286, when the alderman
Gerelm Borluut died, his colleagues violated custom by passing over
his son in favour of Matthew van Sinte Baafs, who was not technically
an allodial man of Ghent, for he had a fortress and numerous clients in
St Bavo's abbey village, across the Scheldt in imperial Flanders. The
Borluuts thus moved more towards the 'popular' party within the patriciate.

In 1294 a nephew of the alderman Matthew van Sinte Baafs ver-
bally provoked Jan Borluut, son of the man bypassed for office in
1286, into breaking the truce by attacking him. Trucebreak without
wound or mutilation entailed an enormous fine of £100; but at the
request of their colleague, the aldermen condemned him in addition to
ten years' exile. The Borluuts then decided to murder Matthew van
Sinte Baafs, and Jan led a band of armed youths under cover of dark-
ness to St Bavo's village. In the mêlée he killed not the patriarch but
Matthew's nephew, the village bailiff. Borluut declared that by this
action he had worked his revenge, and he and his band returned to
their fortress in Ghent.

Borluut's father got his brother Fulk, the prior of the Franciscan
convent and confessor to no less a figure than Countess Margaret, to
give his son sanctuary. The Borluuts and an armed guard, who
prevented the bailiff from arresting Jan, made a triumphal procession
to the convent, where Jan stayed for several weeks. Uncle Fulk let a
brother write love letters on Borluut's behalf to his fiancée and even
suggested that the cloister's librarian translate into Flemish an erotic
Latin poem that was used as a morality exercise for novitiates.

When Borluut finally went into exile at Tournai, Pieter de Visschere, brother of the abbot of St Pieter's, declared that he was calling on the Borluuts' other friends to kill another of the van Sinte Baafs to avenge Borluut's unjust exile. But he urged the perpetrator to do his work in St Pieter's village, so that the abbot could shield him through his immunity. Three weeks later, de Visschere's minions ambushed and killed a servant of Eustace van den Kerchove, a nephew of the van Sinte Baafs. They got a lenient sentence from the abbot's court.[45] But killing a servant was insufficient revenge. When de Visschere learned that Jan Staes, nephew of the murdered bailiff of St Bavo's, was going to France to buy wine, he alerted the exiled Borluut, who ambushed him.

With these actions, and because Matthew van Sinte Baafs as alderman could undertake no illegal actions personally, the parties arranged a three-month truce in October 1295, but no one was satisfied. On 7 January 1296 Pieter de Visschere was killed in a riot that erupted at a funeral that was being attended by virtually the entire patriciate. Eustace van den Kerchove, a van Sinte Baafs kinsman, was primarily responsible. When Jan Borluut got the news at Tournai, he came to Ghent in disguise and attended the funeral under abbot Jan de Visschere's protection. A few days later he knifed a nephew of Eustace van den Kerchove in the back, then returned to Tournai, pausing en route to kill yet another unsuspecting relative of Matthew van Sinte Baafs.

Since the Borluuts had been the leaders of the Claw minority within the patriciate that opposed the XXXIX, they had considerable support among the craftsmen. The van Sinte Baafs were Lilies and left the city for France in 1297. The Borluut party asked the aldermen to condemn the van Sinte Baafs because the truce of three months was still in effect when Pieter de Visschere was killed. After two succeeding boards of aldermen failed to reach a unanimous judgement, they referred it to the 'good towns', who ruled in favour of the Borluuts.

With the French victory in 1300 the van Sinte Baafs returned, and Lilies controlled the government of Ghent until after the battle of Courtrai. Jan Borluut, however, returned from exile as far as Courtrai and sent word that Gentenars who wanted to fight the French could join him there. His role as leader of the Ghent contingent at the battle made him a hero.

---

45. Ghent was not alone in having clergy involved in blood feuds. In 1293 the official of Tournai, acting on a complaint by the aldermen of Ypres, ordered the dean to compel his clergy to give hostages to guarantee truces. *IAY* 1: 138.

The Lilies were again ejected from Ghent after the battle but were allowed to return under the peace terms of 1305. The son of the bailiff murdered in 1294, now an adult and taught to seek revenge, failed in two attempts to kill Jan Borluut but finally got him as he left a drinking bout in the town hall in December 1305. The two sides agreed that both benches of aldermen and the count would arbitrate. The normal penalty for homicide was a pilgrimage to some distant location and payment of a blood price, but the severity of the punishment hinged on whether the deed had been done during a truce arranged privately, or a truce arranged by the aldermen, or was done outside truce, and also on the personal quality or social standing of the person killed or injured. The settlement of 10 June 1306 was not one-sided in favour of the Borluuts, although Jan Borluut's cowardly killing of Jan Staes, who unlike his killer was not a landed man of Ghent, was atoned with a simple money payment. The Borluuts had to send fifteen men on pilgrimages and the van Sinte Baafs twelve; the Borluuts paid slightly more in blood prices and personal injury claims, while the reverse was true of judicial fines. The families were collectively responsible for carrying out the terms.[46]

The Borluut–van Sinte Baafs feud shows that both the 'Flemish nationalism' and 'social class' explanations of the disorders in Flanders between 1274 and 1317 are inadequate. The pervasive sense that any kind of violence was legitimate and that retaliatory violence was mandatory, the high consciousness of family, and the control of offices in the city government and even the local churches by persons who used them to advance their families' private interests are all involved. Flanders remained a frontier society with rude manners and ruder mores in the late thirteenth century.

The gains of the guildsmen

The period of the French wars witnessed the development of a strong Flemish national consciousness, but the argument has also been raised that the political changes heralded 'social' or 'democratic' changes, and here the issue is clouded. Although the leaders still hated the French, their heroism was a path to social advancement. The leaders of the

46. The story of this feud is recounted in detail in Blockmans, *Middeleeuwse vendetta*. Blockmans, however, insists that the villainous conduct of Jan Borluut was heroic, giving a Marxist social class interpretation to the events that in my opinion has no basis in fact.

revolt of Bruges were made knights, and Pieter de Coninck got an annual pension of £1000 par. from the Flemish counts.[47]

John of Namur began the deliberate policy of linking his family's interests to the democratic movement in the cities. On 1 August 1302 he gave Bruges a charter prohibiting higher ground rents and inheritance taxes and granting perpetual freedom from all tolls in Flanders. On 23 August 1302 he gave Ghent a much-coveted charter forbidding the manufacture of woollen cloth within 5 miles of the city except in places with a comital charter granting that right. On 18 October 1302 he gave the aldermen of Bruges the right to name the aldermen of smaller towns of the Franc of which Bruges was judicial head. Bruges already had the right to demand military service of these towns. In November 1302 he permitted the inclusion of the suburbs of Ypres within the walls.

John of Namur also confirmed the power of the guildsmen. On 2 December 1302 he guaranteed absolute heredity of mastership to the butchers' guild of Bruges and probably to that of Ghent. The fullers, shearers and brokers of Bruges received statutes in 1303. The guilds of Bruges evidently had their own militias by the time of the battle of Courtrai, even though they were not formally recognized as corporations until after the battle. The weavers, fullers, shearers, butchers and fishmongers of Ypres had seals and probably captains before 4 May 1304. To entice foreign merchants back to Flanders, John of Namur and the city government of Bruges gave a charter to the brokers and fixed the rate owed on various goods subject to brokerage.[48]

The statutes of the Bruges fullers, shearers and brokers, and of the shrine workers and coopers of Ghent from 1303 and of the mercers from 1305 show that the guilds had courts, for they mention fines for infractions going to the guild, and the mercers already had a dean and arbitrators (*vinders*). Numerous guilds of Ghent later claimed to have received corporate privileges in around 1302; in 1400 the fishmongers noted 'an old book, ninety-five or more years old'. The fact that it takes a sober tone and does not mention the battle of Courtrai suggests that the claim was genuine.[49]

The charters of the butchers of Bruges (2 December 1302) and of the smiths of Damme (early 1303) were issued jointly by the count's representative and the town government. Both guilds got the right to

47. Verbruggen, 'Historiografie', 272.
48. Verbruggen, 'Beschouwingen', 44–5, 48–9; Bovesse, 'Régence comtale', 143–8.
49. Nicholas, *Metamorphosis*, 255.

choose a dean and councillors with legislative and judicial powers in cases affecting guild members. The butchers' charters always had numerous detailed quality-control provisions, such as prohibitions against selling 'stinking meat' or meat from animals that had died without being slaughtered. The Bruges charter also forbade sale of meat within a mile of the town area except in other chartered towns. This is similar to the extraterritorial privileges being given to the weavers' guilds at this time and suggests a general desire to protect the local market, rather than industrial protectionism to benefit only the guild members. Even this early, many master artisans in this hereditary trade were transacting business through their journeymen; for the master butcher was responsible when his 'journeyman who is a merchant' stood surety for someone. The guild courts, which met every ten weeks, were used for debts owed to the guild or guildsmen, and the person convicted lost his stall in the meat hall.[50]

The peak and decline of the Flemish textile industry

We have seen that the Flemish export textile industry reached its peak in the late thirteenth century and started to decline. Yet it is impossible to measure the extent to which the foreign textile trade was really the basis of Flemish wealth, for the domestic market, on which we have no statistics, was clearly enormous. The aldermen regulated the cloth halls more closely after 1280 than before; but the halls not only handled foreign sales but also contained booths, which were frequently leased to women, where coarser grades of cloth were marketed.[51]

The wars disrupted normal trading patterns. From the 1290s the English began raising the custom on wool exports, and this drove the market prices of Flemish cloth upward. The relations of Ypres with England, its major customer, are revealing. The English customs accounts show an extensive trade, with the Yprois importing wool mainly from Hull, London, Southampton and particularly Boston, usually in boats from Nieuwpoort and Lombardzijde. The wool trade

50. The section on the Bruges guilds is taken from Carlos Wyffels, 'Twee oude Vlaamse ambachtskeuren: De vleeschouwers van Brugge (2 December 1302) ende smeden van Damme (eerste helft 1303)', *ASEB* **87** (1950): 93–105.

51. Doudelez, 'Révolution communale', 278–80; D. Nicholas, *The Domestic Life of a Medieval City: Women, Children, and the Family in Fourteenth-Century Ghent* (Lincoln, Neb., 1985), 102–3.

made a rapid recovery between 1302 and 1305, but then a long-term decline set in. The Ypres wool trade was now much less aristocratic than before, for drapers were buying directly in England. The number of seals placed on textiles at Ypres grew by 25 per cent between 1308 and 1312, and the 1308 figure was seven times that of 1306. The cloth seal evidence suggests continued growth until 1315.[52]

The course of trade

Flanders remained dependent on foreign imports. But while trade had been conducted at regional fairs and those of the Champagne for most of the thirteenth century, the revolution caused by the first Genoese seaborne voyage to Flanders in 1277 soon had a profound impact. Foreign merchants established resident colonies at Bruges, and the Italians handled the bulk of Mediterranean merchandising in the north, which now bypassed the fairs in favour of the sea route. Thus the role of Flemish merchants in freighting southern French wines to Flanders and England declined. In 1282 the Germans became the first foreign nation to receive a collective charter of privilege at Bruges. The Castilians, most of whose trade with Flanders had been through the fairs, quickly began cooperating with the Germans, and the two groups handled each other's business with the magistrates of Bruges.[53]

The beginning of regular galley voyages from Italy to the North Sea ports thus redirected considerable trade towards Bruges, Flanders' major port, that had previously been conducted at the Champagne fairs. While the decline of the fairs forced a redirection of Flemish commerce and undoubtedly hurt some merchant families that were closely bound to them, they brought considerable trade directly to Flanders that would not otherwise have been there. This change in trading patterns thus cushioned the decline of the textile industry by giving Flanders a considerable income in customs and brokerage.

The economic rise of England also forced changes. While in the thirteenth century foreign merchants had visited England and bought

52. Hans van Werveke, *De omvang van de Ieperse lakenproductie in de veertiende eeuw.* *MKVA*, Kl. Letteren, IX, No. 2 (Antwerp, 1947); Pirenne, *Histoire de Belgique* 1: 431–2; O. Mus, 'Het Aandeel van de Ieperlingen in de Engelse wolexport, 1280–1330' in *Prisma Ieper*, 332–42, originally in *Economische Geschiedenis van België: Behandeling van de bronnen en problematiek. Handelingen van het colloquium te Brussel, 17–19 November 1971* (Brussels, 1972), 333–59.

53. Lloyd, *Alien Merchants*, 90; Jules Finot, *Etude historique sur les relations commerciales entre la Flandre & l'Espagne au Moyen Age* (Paris, 1899), 21, 29.

their wool by inspecting it personally on the abbey estates, the kings were now centralizing their customs service. They also began experimenting with 'staples' on wool, having the entire clip sent to an official location where foreign merchants would have to come to buy it. This gave the kings a more regular customs revenue and regulated the amount exported; English wool exports were declining by the 1290s. The English were generally willing to sell exemptions from the obligation to go to the staple; for example, in 1320 Edward II authorized a group of Italian merchants to bypass the staple, which was then at Saint-Omer, by exporting wool to Bruges and transferring it to Venetian galleys. The beneficiaries of this concession had to pledge to ship the wool directly to Venice and not to sell it anywhere in the 'three lands of the staple' (Brabant, Flanders and Artois). Although more wool also reached Flanders directly than has been thought, the staple was nonetheless a major annoyance.[54]

France and England had technically been at peace since 1297. Although this removed the problem of satisfying simultaneously two powerful political rivals who were also commercial partners, it left Flanders without a major foreign ally against the threat from France. Piracy in the English Channel became a persistent problem from the 1290s and would continue to trouble Flemish diplomacy and shipping through the early fifteenth century. Understandably upset at being left alone in 1297, the counts generally ignored English claims against Flemish pirates, who were rarely punished more severely than having to restore the value of the property seized or destroyed. In 1306 two English merchants were authorized to seize Flemish goods at Boston to compensate for a robbery at sea. The English were now seizing Flemish boats that they caught dealing with the Scots, and in December 1310 an entire Flemish fleet was burned at Graunzon in Brittany. Although Flemish relations with England improved as they worsened with France in 1314, Edward II sent ships to aid the French in the summer of 1315. The Flemings finally broke off negotiations in July 1319.[55]

Despite the political problems, large numbers of Flemings were residing at least semi-permanently in England by the late thirteenth century. Foreigners were disliked intensely; attacks on them in London in

54. Jean de Sturler, 'Le Passage des marchandises en transit par le duché de Brabant aux XIIIe et XIVe siècles: L'importance commerciale et maritime du port d'Anvers', *Annales du 30. Congrès de la Fédération Archéologique de Belgique* (Brussels, 1936): 163.

55. Varenbergh, *Relations diplomatiques*, 258–9, 262, 268–9; Lloyd, *Alien Merchants*, 103.

1311–12 caused many to leave the capital for other English ports. But in England as in Flanders, foreigners were becoming so numerous that the local export trade depended on them. Although aliens were permitted to keep hostels if they had local sureties and certificates of good behaviour from their place of origin, eight Flemings and Brabantines, as well as some Italians, Provençals and Germans, were prosecuted in 1298 for keeping a hostel and using the premises to conceal customs violations.[56]

On balance, the late thirteenth-century crisis was more factional and political than social or economic in Flanders. There was overpopulation and economic distress, but there is no direct evidence linking this to a decline of the Flemish textile industry. Flanders did not even come close to having a monopoly of the international trade in woollen cloth. The drop in the overseas trade was not as catastrophic as it would necessarily have been if the Flemish economy had been as dominated by export textiles as was once thought. The wealth and political power of the Flemish nobility was declining, but the urban elites remained very rich. Much Flemish cloth was sold on an internal market swollen by overpopulation, as evinced by statutes of Ypres and Ghent forbidding their citizens to buy cloth except that of the home city. Although the city governments of the fourteenth century seemed to be under a different impression, textiles were not the only source of wealth for Flanders. The grain trade, peat exports, brokerage and other forms of manufacture were also important. Furthermore, although the textile industries of the large cities were declining, it is not at all certain that Flanders taken as a whole produced less cash value in cloth in 1400 than in 1300; for, as we have seen, there are signs of development of rural and small-town cloth making in the late thirteenth century, and this becomes a major theme of Flemish economic development after 1300.

The economic crisis of 1315–17

The political crisis of Flanders was exacerbated by a plague and famine between 1315 and 1317. The climate had generally been favourable during the thirteenth century. The year 1224–5 was the first bad one after 1197, but the next rise in food prices that a chronicler thought worth noting came in 1296. But then the climate began to change. Harvests were poor after 1310, and the rains that stopped the French

56. Lloyd, *Alien Merchants*, 13, 19, 22–4, 53.

invasion of Flanders in 1315 also wiped out the harvest in that year. The result was a Europe-wide famine, but it seems to have been more severe in the southern Low Countries than elsewhere. Grain prices trebled at least, and sometimes reached twenty-four times the normal. The Liege chronicler John of Hocsem, writing of the events of 1316 while living in Louvain, claimed that the barns of that area were full of grain even as the dead were multiplying, for the grain was being taken to the coastal areas, where the scarcity was even worse. But this also suggests that the grain merchants had supplies and were able to control the market.[57] The chronicler Jan Boendale described the situation in Antwerp, just across the Scheldt from Flanders, most graphically.

> In the year of our lord 1315 began the three plagues that will always be remembered, that God sent against mankind. The first plague was the rain, that began in the month of May and lasted a year, so that most of the harvest and grain was lost. The second plague followed without interruption in the same year. That was the horrible expense. I want you to know that such an expensive time has not been seen since God banished Adam from the earthly Paradise. Not only bread, but all food was so expensive that the like has never been seen on earth. A quarter of rye in Antwerp, I can assure you, cost 60 royal grooten. The people were in such great need that it cannot be expressed. For the cries that were heard from the poor would move a stone, as they lay in the streets with woe and great complaint, swollen with hunger and remaining dead of poverty, so that many were thrown by set numbers, sixty and even more, into a pit. Thus God did to men on earth for their sins. The third plague, great and severe, followed this in the next year. This was the plague, which bore heavily on poor and rich, for no one was so healthy that he could escape death at that time. . . . It was said that a third of the people died. Dancing, games, song, all revels were done away with in these days.[58]

In the first known massive transport of grain from southern to northern Europe, since the galleys normally carried luxury products, Italian merchants brought grain to Flanders. The magistrates of Bruges sold at cost first to their citizens and then to others, but this was only a palliative. The next year the biologically weakened population was visited by plague. At Bruges 2000 bodies were carried from the streets

57. John of Hocsem, *Chronique* (ed. Godefroid Kurth) (Brussels, n.d.), 162. Sigebert of Gembloux had complained of usurers who profited from the local grain scarcity of 1095; van Werveke, *Middeleeuwse Hongersnood*, 15.
58. Translated from Jan Boendale, *Brabantsche Yeesten*, 442–3.

into mass graves, and 2800 at Ypres, meaning a population loss of about 5 and 10 per cent respectively.[59] Evidence of how well the crisis was overcome is inconclusive and will be discussed in coming chapters.

59. W. Prevenier *et al.*, 'Tussen crisis en welvaart', *AGN* **4**: 56; Henry S. Lucas, 'The Great European Famine of 1315–1317', *Speculum* **5** (1930): 343–77; H. van Werveke, 'La Famine de l'an 1316 en Flandre et dans les régions voisines', *RN* (1959): 5–14; van Werveke, 'Bronnenmateriaal uit de Brugse stadsrekeningen betreffende de hongersnood van 1316', *BCRH* **125** (1959): 431–510.

CHAPTER NINE

A Delicate Balance: The End of Dampierre Flanders, 1317–84

BETWEEN THE ABYSS AND THE PRECIPICE

The century between 1270 and 1385 was a period of nearly constant turmoil in Flanders. The chronology of military actions and civil discords is a numbing list of virtually annual foreign attacks or serious internal violence.

The clouded succession, 1317–23

The last years of the aged Robert of Béthune were troubled by the quarrel of his two sons. Louis I of Nevers, the elder, inherited Nevers from his mother and acquired Réthel by marrying its heiress. They passed to his son, Louis II, who united them with Flanders as its count. French historiography has smeared Louis I as a vicious man who wanted to dethrone his father to pursue a strictly Flemish policy. Fearing Philip the Fair, Louis opposed his father's decision to seek peace with France in 1312. He was reconciled in 1315 with the crown, hoping to use the anti-monarchical reaction under Louis X to secure Nevers and Réthel. Unfortunately for his reputation, at that moment his father was resisting the French, but he had to contend with peace parties in the towns, composed mainly of repatriated Lily patricians. In 1318 King Philip V proposed to marry his own daughter to Louis of Nevers' son, evidently hoping that this would bring Flanders under the crown. Young Louis had been raised in Paris as a hostage, scarcely knew his father and grandfather, and did not understand Flemish. The succession was regulated in favour of the boy, disregarding the claims of Robert 'of Cassel', Robert of Béthune's younger son. Louis I, however, refused to agree to this until the military and diplomatic situation became impossible for his father in 1320. At this Robert of Cassel, who now opposed all compromise with France, persuaded his father to imprison Louis. He died in exile in France on 22 July 1322, shortly before his father.[1]

After Louis was imprisoned, Robert of Cassel provoked a rebellion in Bruges by arresting a leader of his brother's considerable following. The textile guilds and the radical Claw faction generally favoured Robert, but no guild was united; prominent figures of 1302–5 are found on both sides. The count asked Ghent and Ypres to arbitrate, but meanwhile he gave Robert full power to crush the uprising at Bruges. By January 1322 Ghent was accusing the count of violating its liberties, evidently because he had levied toll on the Lieve canal, a possession of Ghent. Ghent and Bruges allied on 8 March 1322 to defend their liberties and guarantee free trade. Bruges later accused Robert of Cassel of permitting favoured merchants to export food, which the count had forbidden, and of trying to corner the market in strategic goods, including alum.[2]

Robert of Béthune died on 17 September 1322. He had persuaded Robert of Cassel to renounce his claims on the succession by giving him £10,000 and the western castellanies as a non-heritable apanage. Robert nonetheless tried to raise support to exclude his nephew, but had to yield. The cities supported Louis II of Nevers in return for his confirmation of Ghent's textile privilege of 1314 and the grant of similar monopolies to Bruges and Ypres. In January 1323 *parlement* rejected a challenge to Louis by Mahaut, Countess of Artois, sister and mortal enemy of Robert of Bethune. Louis of Nevers was imprisoned for a few weeks, evidently just to show him who was boss. The king confiscated Flanders provisionally before returning it to Louis and forced him into a peace with Hainault on 6 March 1323 that settled the Avesnes–Dampierre feud; Louis renounced all claims on Zeeland, while William I of Hainault renounced imperial Flanders.

The royal war of nerves worked on the naive prince. Louis of Nevers (1323–46) returned to Flanders convinced that the French had

---

1. This account of the palace conflict is taken from Pirenne, *Histoire de Belgique*, 2: 88 and especially H. van Werveke, *Lodewijk, graaf van Nevers en van Rethel, zoon van de Graaf van Vlaanderen (1273?–1322): Een miskende figuur*, MKVA **20** No. 7 (Brussels, 1958).

2. J. Sabbe, 'De Opstand van Brugge tegen graaf Robrecht van Béthune en zijn zoon Robrecht van Cassel in 1321–1322', *ASEB* **107** (1970): 217–49.

actually saved his countship. The Three Cities refused to confirm his treaties with France and complained of the influence over Louis of his own francophile kinsmen and of King Charles IV's advisors. The new count was the most dependent of his dynasty on the French crown. His most serious blunder was his determination, reversing his grandfather's policy, to enforce the financial penalties owed under the peace of Athis.[3]

The Three Cities

During the thirteenth century consultation with the counts was limited increasingly to the large cities represented by the aldermen of Flanders. But the aldermen had advised the prince chiefly on domestic issues and had generally stayed out of foreign policy. The 'five towns' as such played little role in the anti-French agitation after 1290. They also had not attempted to extend their influence over the rural areas of Flanders except as judicial heads of some rural communities.

The cities' right to bind the rest of Flanders was not undisputed. At the beginning of the fourteenth century there was still a strong notion that 'estates' or social orders, rather than cities, were or should be represented. When the counts were in a strong position they negotiated with the 'Common Land', which included delegates of the smaller communities; when they were weak, the Three Cities (Ghent, Bruges and Ypres) or after 1395 the Four Members were in control. The success of the great cities in dominating Flanders can be explained in considerable measure by their financial strength. Around 1325, the annual ordinary revenue of Ghent surpassed the count's. The count could tap extraordinary sources, but many of them were paid by the cities or their burghers.[4]

The Three Cities became the recognized defenders of the liberties of Flanders, but in so doing they began to carve out spheres of influence for themselves in the countryside, starting with their position as judicial heads and later by their textile monopoly privileges. The first references to 'external burghers' (*haghepoorters*) are from the late twelfth century. These were persons who lived outside the cities but

3. Monier, *Institutions centrales*, 36–8; Pirenne, *Histoire de Belgique*, 2: 9, 77; Vandermaesen, 'Vlaanderen en Henegouwen', 420.

4. Ganshof, 'La Flandre', 376–7; Blockmans, 'Vers une société urbanisée', 92. For an assembly of 1306 in which the right of the cities to act for the entire county was challenged, see *IAB* 1: 204–5.

purchased burgher status in one of them. The first references are to persons who had to be out of the city and did not want to lose their citizenship thereby. But many farmers simply had themselves enrolled in a register of burghers or matriculated in a guild. The constitution of Ghent of 1297 mentions fullers and weavers living outside the territorial area of the city. External bourgeoisie conferred various advantages: the right to trial in criminal cases in the city rather than in the locality where the deed occurred and in some cases to exemption from tax on their properties in the castellanies; for external burghers paid Transport with the cities, which were underassessed, and urban-owned property was furthermore subtracted from what the castellanies could tax. By 1322 the abbot of St Pieter's of Ghent alleged that he could no longer find enough persons to staff an aldermanry in his village in the suburbs of Ghent. In 1335, when the count protested, the town claimed the right to give citizenship status to whomever it wished. A shaky compromise was reached that the person's 'principal' residence had to be in town. The city accounts show that Ghent had enrolled many knights of northeastern Flanders as its burghers and was probably using them as a militia to cow the rural areas.[5]

The rebellion of maritime Flanders (1323–8)

Coastal Flanders, still only two centuries out of the swamp, had a free peasantry and, by Flemish standards, large and fertile plots of land. The farmers of west Flanders supported the anti-French movement of 1302. The return of banished Lily nobles, the lords of many tenant farmers, was disliked, as was the requirement of ransoming the nobles taken prisoner to France. The farmers also hated the indemnity provision of the Peace of Paris of 1320. Finally, the dikes in Four Offices broke in 1321, inundating several villages.

There was also resentment at the power of the city of Bruges. In 1289 Guy of Dampierre had limited the exclusive right of Bruges to try its burghers, and in 1318 a new arrangement regulated seventeen points of contention with the Franc. Bruges agreed not to arrest persons inside the town for debts contracted before the magistrates of the Franc and not to tax merchandise imported from the Franc. Judgement in most criminal cases was to be rendered at the site of the deed,

5. Pirenne, *Histoire de Belgique*, 2: 77; J. Decavele, 'De Gentse poorterij en buitenpoorterij', *Liber Buntinx*, 65; Nicholas, *Town and Countryside*, 110–11, 170–1, 237–43.

regardless of the juridical status of the persons concerned, a clear limitation of Bruges's right to try its own burgesses. The city also agreed that all trades practised in the Franc before the French war could continue. The Franc was given independence from Bruges in military actions.[6] Despite these discords, the farmers of the Franc were willing to ally with the Brugeois against the count after 1323.

The urban component of the rebellion of maritime Flanders was a violation of Bruges's commercial privileges by Louis of Nevers. By the late thirteenth century, Bruges had an informal staple or monopoly on most goods entering the Zwin. By 1320 the city was a world market, with large resident colonies of English, German, Italian and Castilian merchants. But at the beginning of 1323 Louis of Nevers violated Bruges's privileges by giving his kinsman John of Namur lordship over the streams at Sluis, Bruges' outport. Bruges retaliated by imprisoning the count, burning Sluis and capturing John of Namur. Thus, on 4 April 1323 Louis of Nevers had to withdraw John's privilege and give Bruges a coveted privilege that made the staple obligatory and exclusive on most merchandise entering the Zwin.[7]

Disturbances erupted in the Franc in the winter of 1323. Louis of Nevers went to France upon his release from Bruges, apparently not understanding the gravity of the situation. Rumours circulated that he was going to exchange Flanders for the county of Poitiers. His interests were defended by his uncle Robert of Cassel and his chancellor Artaud Flote who, with the aldermen of the Three Cities, conducted an inquest and on 24 April 1324 proclaimed a general amnesty and made local magistrates personally responsible for claims of financial peculation.[8]

Another phase began at the end of 1324, in a struggle that assumed overtones of class conflict between peasants and aristocracy. The rebels expelled comital bailiffs and appointed captains, burned nobles' castles

6. Pirenne, *Histoire de Belgique*, 2: 86; Nicholas, *Town and Countryside*, 159–60; *IAB* **1**: 325–8. Curiously, as late as September 1322 the Franc still lacked a common seal, although it held meetings and appointed delegates to treat with the count. *IAB* **1**: 335.

7. Nicholas, *Town and Countryside*, 161.

8. Vandermaesen, 'Vlaanderen en Henegouwen', 421. Much of the count's unpopular French policy would eventually be laid at Flote's door. Louis's bride accused Flote of bewitching her husband so that he would be unable to consummate their marriage. He was also accused, perhaps unjustly, of embezzling Ghent's share of the Transport payment. Maurice Vandermaesen, 'Artaud Flote, abt van Vézelay en raadsheer van de graaf van Vlaanderen: Triomf en val van een hoveling (1322–1332)', *HMGOG* **43** (1989): 116, 120–4.

and massacred. Bruges, by now under the control of a weaver and fuller party, took direction of the revolt from the peasants, who in fact were being led by Clais Zannekin, an exterior burgess of Bruges. The rebels' ability to continue the conflict for five years is conceivable only in the light of the city's involvement. A war of propaganda began, as monks and preachers told the masses that a new era had come and that they were the equals of the aristocrats.[9]

Louis of Nevers then marched on Courtrai and arrested some citizens of Bruges, prompting the militia of Bruges to attack Courtrai. In a blunder that seems characteristic of the hapless count, Louis's forces destroyed the bridges and burned the suburbs of Courtrai north of the Leie to block the Brugeois. But it was so windy that the fire spread to the central city, destroying much of it, and this caused the Courtraisiens to join the rebellion. Louis was captured a few days later and taken to Bruges. The patrician government of Ypres was then toppled by a weaver party, aided by Zannekin's troops, and Ypres thus joined the rebels' side.

Louis of Nevers' problems were complicated by the rivalry of John of Namur and Robert of Cassel. Louis may have made John of Namur regent on 12 June, immediately after being taken captive (the document is suspect);[10] but the Bruges government then forced him to appoint Robert of Cassel regent on 30 June. Ghent responded by appointing John of Namur regent, and in late September the count switched and again appointed John of Namur. At this, war erupted between Robert of Cassel, who was supported in his apanage lands in the west, and John of Namur, supported by Ghent and the nobility. In September John of Namur tried to garrison the towns between Leie and Scheldt. He was unable to take Geraardsbergen, so he returned to Ghent around 23 September, where he and the captains who ruled the city put down a weaver uprising and installed garrisons throughout the Oudburg and Waas. For the last time in the fourteenth century, Ghent

9. Vandermaesen, 'Vlaanderen en Henegouwen', 422; Pirenne, *Histoire de Belgique*, 2: 90–3.

10. Although regencies were customary for counts of Flanders who were minors, Louis's action is the first known appointment of a regent by an adult prince. The practice became common. Simon Mirabello was nominated regent when Louis of Nevers left Flanders in 1340; the Ghent rebels nominated Philip van Artevelde in 1382; after his death, they made Frans Ackerman regent. The English named Jean Bourchier regent in 1384, using Richard II's claim to be king of France as justification. Ganshof, 'La Flandre', 358–9; J. Bovesse, 'Le Comte de Namur Jean Ier et les événements du comté de Flandre en 1325–1326', *BCRH* **131** (1965): 401–10, 416–17.

had resisted an opportunity to make trouble for the counts.[11]

The French, alarmed at the count's capture, had the rebels placed under an interdict, confiscated the goods of Robert of Cassel in France and prohibited trade between Flanders and France. Robert of Cassel switched sides and joined the king. The more moderate rebels got the count released on 30 November 1325, but his actions betray utter confusion. On 19 April 1326 the peace of Arques was sealed. Forts built during the rebellion were to be destroyed, fines paid to the count and to France, while 'innovations' introduced by the rebels, notably extra-legal captains, would be abolished. King Charles IV accepted Robert of Cassel's protests of honourable intention in taking a rebel-approved regency from the count and pardoned him.[12]

But the captains did not give up power, and troubles recommenced. In 1327 Louis of Nevers tried to seize territories in Robert of Cassel's apanage. The rebellion became more radical under the leadership of Jacob Peit, a peasant of the Bergues district and, like Zannekin, an exterior burgess of Bruges. Propagandists attacked the church, and terror reigned in the countryside. Nobles were forced to execute their own relatives in public spectacles. Peit executed anyone who refused to declare openly for the 'commons'.

Moderates deserted the peasants' cause. When Peit was assassinated, the weavers of Bruges, who had no jurisdiction in the matter, held an inquest into the murder. The count fled to Paris. French intervention was delayed by the unexpected death of Charles VI, but the new king, Philip VI, was ready to move by June, perhaps speeded by the prophetic suggestion of William de Deken, burgomaster of Bruges, that Edward III of England be recognized as king of France. The royal and rebel armies met near Cassel on 23 August 1328. The Flemings were in a strong position on a hill, but they grew impatient when the French failed to strike and attacked them in the plain. The rebels were routed. The king received the submission of the rebel castellanies and of Bruges and Ypres the next day.

There was a severe repression accompanied by judicial executions and confiscations. All charters were withdrawn, and the count gave 'evil charters' to the rebel communities that were revoked only in 1338, when he needed allies against a different threat. The position of the count's bailiff was strengthened and Bruges's competence as

11. Bovesse, 'Comte de Namur', 389–96, 399–400; Vandermaesen, 'Vlaanderen en Henegouwen', 423.

12. Pirenne, *Histoire de Belgique*, 2: 93–4; Bovesse, 'Comte de Namur', 418, 424–5.

judicial head was restricted, although the city's economic privileges were left untouched. The Franc lost its unitary magistracy and was divided into three separate areas. Bruges and Ypres were ordered to demolish their walls and fill in the moats. There is more evidence after 1328 of direct involvement by the count's men in renewing the urban magistracies and auditing town accounts. Chancery registers appear, and the Chamber of Accounts and the central court (*Audientie*) took shape. Louis began relying on abler advisors, the chancellor William of Auxonne and the Master of the Accounts Peter of Douai.[13]

The rebellion of maritime Flanders has given rise to Marxist interpretations of class struggle. Some of the peasants' rhetoric lends credence to these views. Yet Flanders seems to have experienced a revolution of rising expectations rather than a rebellion of the oppressed. Bruges had begun hostilities over a point of commercial privilege. The chief centres of the rebellion were more in the southwestern castellanies than in the Franc of Bruges. Bruges appointed captains in the Franc, but in essentials it continued the count's administration without the bailiffs. Although weavers were in the Bruges magistracy, they did not dominate it until the concluding stages of the rebellion; and the 'weavers' were actually wealthy guildsmen. Bruges simply seized an opportunity to weaken the count. Analysis of the hostages taken after 1328 shows that while the weavers were the most revolutionary group, there was substantial support for the rebellion in all crafts. And while many artisans of Bruges were implicated, so were the oldest patrician lineages of the city. Records of property confiscated from peasants or their heirs show that most had substantial assets.[14]

13. Pirenne, *Histoire de Belgique*, 2: 96–8; see also F.W.N. Hugenholtz, *Drie Boerenopstanden uit de veertiende eeuw: Vlaanderen, 1323–1328. Frankrijk, 1358. Engeland, 1381. Onderzoek naar het opstandig bewustzijn* (Haarlem, 1949), 17–34; Monier, *Institutions centrales*, 106; R. van Uytven, 'Stadsgeschiedenis in het Noorden en Zuiden', *AGN* **2**: 200; Vandermaesen, 'Vlaanderen en Henegouwen', 424.

14. For the aftermath of the battle of Cassel, see J. Mertens, 'Les Confiscations dans la châtellenie du Franc de Bruges après la bataille de Cassel', *BCRH* **134** (1968): 239–84; J. Mertens, 'De Economische en sociale toestand van de opstandelingen uit het Brugse Vrije, wier goederen na de slag bij Cassel (1328) verbeurd verklaard werden', *RBPH* **47** (1969): 1131–53; D. van den Auweele, 'De Brugse gijzelaarslijsten van 1301, 1305 en 1328. Een Comparatieve analyse', *ASEB* **110** (1973): 105–67; Nicholas, *Town and Countryside*, 163–5 and literature cited.

The aftermath of 1328

The major victor in the rebellion of maritime Flanders was Ghent. The count had looked weak and foolish, while Bruges and Ypres were humbled in defeat. Ghent, like Bruges, had been gaining control over its environs. The city completely dominated Oudenaarde and to a lesser extent Courtrai, which looked to Ghent for defence of its privileges. Waas, the Oudburg and Four Offices were linked to Ghent through the bailiwick. During the fourteenth century Ghent began extending its domination into imperial Flanders. Its law was the basis of that of Dendermonde, and its textile monopolies extended to that town and Geraardsbergen. During the war of the 1320s Ghent, accompanied by the count's bailiff, installed local officials and garrisons throughout eastern Flanders. There is no evidence, however, that Ghent exercised functions of the comital government outside the Oudburg after 1329. It also did not attempt to tax other parts of east Flanders until the military emergency of 1357–8.[15]

But hostilities mounted between Ghent and the count during the 1330s. The city government felt that it had not profited sufficiently from its loyalty during the rebellion. Ghent had refused to hand over its accounts for audit, as Bruges and Ypres had done. More importantly, the count had allowed Ghent in 1324 to capitalize its share in the Transport, but he and the king now argued that this arrangement was invalid. When Ghent refused to yield, the count revoked the city's right to take the indirect taxes that were the basis of its ordinary revenue. A treaty of November 1335 left the essential issues unresolved. The activities of Ghent's external burghers were also arousing the count's suspicions. The count's incompetence did nothing to aid his cause. He needlessly provoked a war with Duke John III of Brabant over the city of Mechelen, then sustained a humiliating defeat.[16]

The van Artevelde revolt and its aftermath, 1336–49

No single figure of Flemish history has so captured the imagination of collective posterity as Jacob van Artevelde, who led Ghent into

15. Nicholas, *Town and Countryside*, 168–70.
16. Vandermaesen, 'Vlaanderen en Henegouwen', 425; Pirenne, *Histoire de Belgique*, 2: 177.

domination of Flanders and Flanders into rebellion against Louis of Nevers and his overlord, King Philip VI of France. Although van Artevelde's posthumous reputation as a democratic reformer is grossly exaggerated, several important developments that would dominate Flemish history in the coming generations took firm shape or were accentuated during his ascendancy: the domination of each great city over a 'quarter'; the hegemony of Ghent over the other Flemish cities; the essential agreement among persons enjoying the franchise on the manner in which Flanders should be governed; a regime in the cities based on occupationally or genealogically determined 'members'; an 'anglophile' party in the cities that would urge the counts to renounce their fealty to the French in favour of an alliance with the more distant English king, who also controlled the wool supply on which the textile manufactures of the cities depended; and a growing sense of Flemish nationalism against a French count.[17]

Ghent remained as dependent on France for food as on England for wool. But a second imperative was now added to the need to feed the city's own population: much of the income that Ghent was losing as its textile industry declined was compensated by the development of a grain staple. Although the staple was once thought to have originated in 1357, a charter of 1323 mentions 'the old grain warehouse, which used to stand on the Leie' and which the city had demolished 'to make a vacant space needed for the grain staple'. The staple had thus existed for a considerable time before 1323; the evidence of Galbert of Bruges and the twelfth-century construction of the grainmongers' hall suggest that it may have been two centuries old. During the next century and a half, Ghent would not only require farmers of the environs to bring their grain to market in the city, but it would also derive considerable income by re-exporting grain that was not needed in the city down the Scheldt through the Dendermonde toll, and on to Antwerp or into interior Brabant through Rupelmonde and Mechelen, a city with which Ghent developed substantial trading links in the fourteenth century. Even Bruges, which had other sources from the Baltic, got some grain in Ghent, and both Bruges and Ypres would later feel

17. For the political events of the van Artevelde period, see Pirenne, *Histoire de Belgique*, 2: 101–35; Nicholas, *Town and Countryside*, 175–200; H. van Werveke, *Jacques van Artevelde* (Brussels, 1942); Paul Rogghé, *Vlaanderen en het zevenjarig beleid van Jacob van Artevelde: Een Critische–historische studie*, 2 vols (Brussels, 1942). Henry S. Lucas. *The Low Countries and the Hundred Years War, 1326–1347* (Ann Arbor, 1929). For the interpretation of van Artevelde, see David Nicholas, *The Van Arteveldes of Ghent: The Varieties of Vendetta and the Hero in History* (Ithaca, NY, 1988), 1–71.

the wrath of Ghent when they tried to channel canals into the Leie south of Ghent to avoid having to buy grain through the city.[18]

Flanders was thus caught between the imperatives of two powerful neighbours, each of which provided essential goods for this importer economy. In 1327 King Edward II of England had been deposed by a coalition led by his wife Isabella, daughter of Philip the Fair of France, in favour of her son Edward III (1327–77). When the Capetian dynasty became extinct in the male line the next year, Edward III, as the grandson of Philip IV, was excluded from a claim to the throne only by the spurious 'Salic Law' which was invented by lawyers at the French court. Edward initially accepted this and even did homage to Philip VI for his fiefs in France, but relations between England and France worsened through the 1330s.[19]

As war threatened, a party developed in the Flemish cities that favoured recognizing Edward III as king of France. Hoping to pressure Louis of Nevers into an English alliance, on 12 August 1336 Edward III placed an embargo on wool sales to Flanders and insisted that no other Netherlanders who bought it sell to the Flemings. English merchants were seized in reprisal at Bruges on 26 September 1336.[20] The Flemish cities soon were suffering from the wool shortage and the loss of an important foreign market, and domestic and French supplies of wool were inadequate to keep the looms busy. On 3 January 1338 Jacob van Artevelde was made the chief of five captains. Although the aldermen continued to function, van Artevelde in fact dominated the other captains, and the captains dominated the aldermen.

Jacob van Artevelde's only previous appearance in the government of Ghent had been in 1326, when he was a receiver of the fine levied on the rebellious weavers. He was a landowner and broker with ties to the brewers and owned land in northeastern Flanders. Despite his role in 1326, other members of his family were known as friends of the weavers by 1334.

Van Artevelde immediately consolidated his position by associating persons of all guild affiliations in the magistracy, including the weavers, the most numerous and revolutionary of the textile trades, who had

18. For the grain staple of Ghent, see Nicholas, *Metamorphosis*, 241–2; Nicholas, *Town and Countryside*, 122–5.

19. On Edward III's reign, see most recently Scott L. Waugh, *England in the Reign of Edward III* (Cambridge, 1991).

20. The embargo was not a reprisal for a prior seizure of English merchants, as Pirenne (*Histoire de Belgique*, 2: 107) thought. See E.B. Fryde, *William de la Pole, Merchant and King's Banker (d. 1366)* (London, 1988), 46, 58, 75.

been excluded from the government since 1320 in favour of the more tractable fullers. He quickly placed his partisans in all city offices, dispersed an enclave of opponents at Biervliet and forced the leaders of the castellanies and smaller towns to accept one of the Three Cities as its leader. Parties loyal to van Artevelde took control at Bruges and Ypres. His regime was especially resented in southwestern Flanders, which remained loyal to the counts, and in the smaller towns of the east, which resented Ghent's hegemony. Van Artevelde had ended most resistance to his regime by late 1339, although he had to repress revolts at Courtrai in 1340 and Oudenaarde in 1342.

Philip VI urged Louis of Nevers to negotiate. In late 1338 the Flemings were acquitted of all sums still due to the French crown from the peace of Athis. Louis repealed the 'evil constitutions' of 1328–9. Philip VI ordered the entire French wool clip sent to Flanders to make up for the loss of the English supply. Van Artevelde tried for a time to maintain neutrality between France and England, but he moved towards an open English alliance after Louis of Nevers fled to France in December 1339. The wool embargo was lifted, and on 26 January 1340 Edward III entered Ghent and was acclaimed king of France. He promised to return Walloon Flanders and even Artois to Flanders, to issue a coinage that would be valid in England, France, Brabant and Flanders, to give customs exemptions to Flemish cloth in England and to pay enormous subsidies.[21] Edward's famous son John 'of Gaunt' was born in Ghent that spring. Trade with France immediately ended, but English money flowed into Ghent. The wool staple was moved from Calais to Bruges. Van Artevelde seems to have developed a personal friendship with Edward III, who treated him as the prince of Flanders, and the king's lavish payments to the tribune of Ghent gave credence to the claim his opponents would soon be making that he was simply an English agent.

Yet the military significance of the English alliance was minimal. The English decimated the French navy in a battle near Sluis in June 1340. Although an army besieged Tournai in the autumn of 1340, it had no chance of success after Duke John III of Brabant withdrew his forces, evidently after receiving a personal insult from van Artevelde. There were no further actions in Flanders involving foreign troops until 1346. The emergency that had brought van Artevelde to power had ended.

21. Vandermaesen, 'Vlaanderen en Henegouwen', 427; Pirenne, *Histoire de Belgique*, 2: 124.

His regime had been deprived of any pretence of legality by the flight of Louis of Nevers in late 1339. The rebels had maintained the fiction that they were really acting in the count's name; indeed, when he returned briefly to Flanders in October 1340 they forced him to ratify what they had done and promise that he would govern in the future only with the consent of the Three Cities. But van Artevelde needed a puppet regent, and he found a convenient candidate in Simon of Mirabello or van Halen. Mirabello was the bastard son of a merchant of Asti who had come to the Low Countries around 1300. The Mirabellos operated a lending establishment at Ghent by 1307 and owned property throughout Flanders and Brabant; Simon was simultaneously burgher of Ghent, Dendermonde and Mechelen, owning substantial properties in each and lending money to the counts and city governments. Ghent was his preferred residence, and he bought the castle of Bornem from the countess of Bar for the benefit of the city. His daughters married into the Ghent aristocracy, one of them to van Artevelde's nephew. He was killed in 1346, evidently in a feud arising from one of his loans.[22]

On 21 June 1343 the Three Cities formally divided Flanders into quarters. That of Ghent included all territory east of the Leie, together with Four Offices, Waas and the Oudburg. Bruges was supreme in the Franc, while Ypres ruled its own castellany and the 'Westland'. Two years later Edward III recognized that the cities spoke for their quarters. Since the rebellion began, the cities had installed captains throughout Flanders, and the arrangement of 1343 formalized this. Later evidence suggests that the cities also claimed that no assemblies could be held or taxes collected in their quarters without their consent. The cities controlled the coinage and audited accounts. They arbitrated quarrels, particularly in their own quarters, assumed control over foreign policy and raised armies. Although they repressed dissent vigorously, inquests testify to their willingness to punish misbehaviour of their officials in the smaller towns. By 1346, if not before, they levied extraordinary taxes on the rest of the county. Ghent was the unquestioned master of Bruges and Ypres, installing magistrates and frequently arbitrating quarrels, particularly labour disputes. Ghent

22. Paul Rogghé, 'Simon de Mirabello in Vlaanderen', *AM* **9** (1958): 1–52. Mirabello's suburban residence at Ghent had been sold to the count by Mirabello's widow by 1349 and already was under the guardianship of the marshal of Flanders. It later became the Prinsenhof, the main residence of the counts at Ghent in the fifteenth century. T. de Limburg-Stirum (ed.), *Cartulaire de Louis de Male, comte de Flandre: Decreten van den grave Lodewyck van Vlaenderen, 1348 à 1358*, 2 vols (Bruges, 1898–1901), 1: 45.

intervened whenever the power of one of the other cities seemed inadequate, particularly in the case of Ypres in the Westland.[23]

Continuation of the English alliance was a life-and-death matter for van Artevelde; he would have been sacrificed in any peace with France. The French grain embargo was having its effect, and by 1342 Ghent was trying to get food in eastern Flanders, not the best of sources. A party favouring accommodation with the count had gained adherents, and the count himself returned briefly between August and December 1342. Louis simply did what the cities told him, confirming such old privileges as the textile monopolies. Troubles began in Bruges, where van Artevelde was never popular and his partisans had to maintain their hold by force, sometimes with help from Ghent. In January 1343 a rebellion at Ghent briefly toppled van Artevelde from power, but he was reinstalled by troops from Bruges.

Personal enemies of van Artevelde now appeared in the city government, and industrial disturbances weakened him (see Chapter Ten). He was deposed from his captaincy around 23 March 1345, when the Three Cities decided to recall Louis of Nevers to Flanders. Discord mounted in Ghent as the unitary regime that van Artevelde had established in 1338 broke down. On 'Bad Monday', 2 May 1345, the weavers defeated the fullers in a pitched battle on the Friday Market. The scene was described graphically by an anonymous chronicler, who probably lived at Ghent.

> In the year 1345, on the first day of May, which is called 'Bad Monday', the weavers fought the fullers and small guilds on the Friday Market at Ghent, because the fullers wanted to have four grooten more than the weavers wanted to give them. One Gerard Denijs, dean of the weavers, had come with his guild to the Friday Market at Ghent, and Jacob van Artevelde followed the weavers. When John de Bake, dean of the small guilds and captain of the fullers, heard this, he came with a great throng of fullers and other guilds to the Friday market, and there was such heavy fighting there that the Holy Sacrament was carried between the two sides, but to no avail. John de Bake and all his boys perished there. The fullers sustained the greatest losses, but the small guilds also lost large numbers. And the weavers were in the ascendant, and about a thousand men were killed. On this account there was great discord in Ghent, but the magistrates of Ghent, Bruges and Ypres made peace.[24]

23. Nicholas, *Town and Countryside*, 178–87; Blockmans, *Volksvertegenwoordiging*, 124.

24. Translated from N. de Pauw (ed.), *Cartulaire historique et généalogique des Artevelde* (Brussels, 1920) 246.

Jacob van Artevelde continued to be used for his expertise and foreign contacts. The chronicler continues:

> On the seventh day of July, the king of England came to Sluis with 180 ships, and he summond Jacob van Artevelde, who came to him at Sluis, and revealed the situation in Flanders to the king, complaining about the city of Dendermonde, since it had joined Count Louis, and he asked the king's assistance. The king of England said to Jacob van Artevelde that he wanted all the cities of Flanders to hand over the land of Flanders to him eternally for himself and his heirs, and he wanted Count Louis to do him homage for the countship of Flanders, or he would make his son, the prince of Wales, count of the county of Flanders. And Jacob van Artevelde agreed to this and pledged to do his best for it. And Jacob sent word to all cities of Flanders, thus deputized in the name of the English king. But when Jacob was promoting this desire in Ghent before the entire community of the city, there was total astonishment. Then Gerard Denijs, dean of the weavers, who was also an enemy of Jacob van Artevelde, said that he would never be involved in 'unsealing' the legal heir from his land, for this would be the most odious treason that had ever been seen in any city, and he continued: 'This Jacob is trying to deceive us. It is clear, for he is lying, since he once told us that if he ever married his children to gilded spurs, or had towers made, or rode about on great horses, or accumulated great treasure to become rich, that no one should ever trust him again or consider him part of the community. And he is found guilty on all of these counts.' All the people of Ghent supported Gerard Denijs, and Jacob withdrew disgraced and angry towards his house, for he realized that he could not accomplish the pledge that he had made to the king of England. Thus Jacob went home and was taking a meal with his personnel. Then Gerard Denijs understood the entire situation of Jacob van Artevelde and learned of a restorer of old shoes living in the Paddenhoek [a small street behind van Artevelde's residence, in the Kalandenberg street], whose father Jacob van Artevelde had killed, and Gerard Denijs came with an angry mob of his weavers before Jacob's house with standards and banners, and they screamed 'Kill the false sealer, who wants to unseal the land from our rightful prince.' And they forced their way into the house, and Jacob had to try to escape through his stable, but the shoe restorer ran after him and cleaved his head with an axe, and thus avenged his father's death on him.[25]

The circumstances led van Artevelde's sons to believe that he had been enticed treacherously back to Ghent by persons in the city government, a deed for which they held the perpetrators and their male descendants responsible.[26]

25. Translated from de Pauw, *Cartulaire des Artevelde*, 247–8.
26. Nicholas, *van Arteveldes*, 38–69.

Although many in Ghent favoured an accommodation with the French, the magistracy that toppled and killed van Artevelde did not. The English alliance was confirmed within days of his death and maintained in the coming years. But the English could not defend Flanders from invasion. Louis of Nevers was killed fighting for the French at Crécy on 25 August 1346. He was succeeded by his sixteen-year-old son Louis 'of Male' (1346–84), perhaps the ablest of the Dampierre counts. Louis of Male immediately did homage to Philip VI and made his Joyous Entry into Flanders on 12 November 1346, confirming his subjects' privileges and receiving their oaths of fealty. Although he would later show himself quite willing to deal with both sides, he escaped Flanders for France when it became clear that the cities were going to force him to marry a daughter of Edward III. On 1 July 1347 he married Margaret, second daughter of John III of Brabant, and used Brabant as his base for retaking Flanders. When he invaded in September 1348 there was little resistance, as civil war raged in the cities against the weavers and throughout rural Flanders against the domination of Ghent. Louis mended his fences with Edward III in the peace of Dunkirk of 25 November 1348 and got Edward's assistance in blockading Flanders. The rebellion was ended when Louis's troops stormed Ghent on 'Good Tuesday', 13 January 1349. Even in Ghent a faction favoured the count, consisting mainly of some fullers and most fishmongers, shippers and butchers, the count's most trustworthy allies. This political configuration would continue to dominate Ghent in the coming years, with the van Arteveldes and the weavers leading an anglophile party against the food guilds, which favoured the counts and an accommodation with France.[27]

The rule of Louis of Male (1346–84)

The proscription after 1349 was severe. On 5 August 1349 the count ordered an inquest. He confirmed the cities' privileges, but he exiled the van Artevelde family and countless of their humbler adherents. The total number of exiles is not known, but in 1359 Louis pardoned a total of 566 Gentenars, and this did not include those who were unable to furnish an enormous bond of £300. He installed regimes in all cities that excluded the weavers, forbade them to assemble in groups of three or more and relied on the fullers and small guilds to

---

27. Vandermaesen, 'Vlaanderen en Henegouwen', 429.

staff the councils. The weavers were assessed an indemnity that was collected until 1375. The textile industry of Ghent, which was already suffering by being priced out of the market and by its dependence on English wool, began a sharp decline in the 1350s that may have been connected as much to the political situation as to market considerations; for the city was deprived of weavers, whom the magistrates were ordering vainly to return by 1352. Flemish exiles were welcomed in England, where many of them settled in Kent and Suffolk. The numerous exiles who remained in Flanders created a serious problem of order, particularly in Four Offices. On 2 October 1349 Ghent complained that persons exiled by the town government had been allowed to remain in Flanders and that shippers had been sabotaged by stakes and other impediments thrown into the streams. Naturally, the cities were not quiet. There were revolts at Bruges in 1351 and at Ghent in 1353, led by the weavers and millers.[28]

Louis of Male was one of the most masterful diplomats of the fourteenth century. In the beginning he seems to have hoped to increase his power in the Low Countries while preserving good relations with England and distancing himself from France. It is a classic irony that he died in flight from yet another urban rebellion, to be succeeded by a French son-in-law whose descendants would bring to fruition much of the governmental centralization that Louis began.[29]

Van Artevelde had made the return of the Walloon castellanies a precondition of serious negotiations with the French crown. Louis of Male in 1350 refused to go to Paris to renew his homage to King John II unless they were restored. The French could not drive a hard bargain. In the Treaty of Fontainebleau of 1351, they gave Louis substantial funds and forgave him the Treaty of Dunkirk with England. The English played both sides by enticing Flemish weavers and giving pensions to van Artevelde's sons. Deprived of the count himself, the English hoped to marry Louis's young daughter Margaret to one of their princes. John II forestalled this by permitting Louis in 1355 to incorporate the land of Dendermonde, in imperial Flanders, in the

28. Limburg-Stirum, Cartulaire de Louis de Male, 1: 78, 84–5, 348–9, 369, 421; 2: 127, 247–51, 285; de Pauw, Cartulaire des Artevelde, 711–18; EP 2: 471; Pirenne, Histoire de Belgique, 2: 135; Nicholas, Metamorphosis, 5, 135–54. R. Demunck, 'De Gentse oorlog (1379–1385): Oorzaken en karakter', HMGOG 5 (1951): 310.

29. For the reign of Louis of Male, see Fritz Quicke, Les Pays-Bas à la veille de la Période Bourguignonne (1356–1384) (Brussels, 1947); D. Nicholas and M. Vandermaesen, 'Lodewijk van Male' in Nationaal Biografisch Woordenboek 6 (Brussels, 1974): cols 575–85.

comital domain in return for pledging Margaret's hand to Philip de Rouvre, duke of Burgundy.[30]

When John III of Brabant, Louis's father-in-law, died in 1355, his older daughter Joan and her husband, Wenceslaus duke of Luxembourg and brother of the emperor Charles IV, succeeded to the duchy of Brabant. Louis of Male refused to accept his wife's dowry of money, which had never been paid, and insisted falsely that he had been promised Mechelen, which was in Ghent's commercial network and gave an important key to Antwerp. The government of Mechelen recognized Louis as duke in return for his promise to transfer the staple on salt and oats from Antwerp to Mechelen.

This act provoked a war. Louis blockaded the Scheldt, then annihilated the Brabantine forces in a land battle at Asse on 17 August 1356. But Louis had ambitions to control only the Scheldt, not all of Brabant. Wenceslaus had to agree in the peace of Ath (4 June 1357) to cede Mechelen outright and give Antwerp to Louis in fief. This situation lasted until 1404, to the considerable detriment of the trade of Antwerp, but it probably cushioned the declining fortunes of the Flemish cities by giving them better access to the markets of Brabant.[31]

The Brabant campaign caused internal problems in Flanders. Louis overextended himself to the point where Flanders had no defences against English piracy. In 1358 the Hanse, outraged at the inability of the Flemings to protect their own waters, declared a blockade, and in 1360 Louis of Male and the cities had to agree to a humiliating peace. Although the cities supported the Brabant war, it was extremely costly. The weavers began to assume a more revolutionary posture, and there were serious disturbances in all cities by 1358. Etienne Marcel, the leader of Paris's rebellion against the royal government, appealed to the Flemings in two letters of 28 June and 11 August addressed to the cities of France, which to him included Flanders, asking the 'commons' for help.[32] His call seems to have made a profound impression in Flanders. By mid-summer 1358 the count was remitting banishments for people involved in the van Artevelde war, and by August 1361 the weavers had been restored to power in all cities.

Louis's marriage diplomacy, however, was more successful. When Philip de Rouvre died in 1361, Margaret of Male, who clearly would

30. Monier, *Institutions centrales*, 107.

31. Pirenne, *Histoire de Belgique*, 2: 184–5; Vandermaesen, 'Vlaanderen en Henegouwen', 431.

32. Letters reprinted in Jacques d'Avout, *Le Meurtre d'Etienne Marcel* (Paris, 1960): 303–10.

be Louis's only legitimate child, was the most desired heiress in Europe. Louis, with the enthusiastic support of the cities, initially wanted a marriage to Edmund of Langley, Edward III's fourth surviving son. The Treaty of Dover (19 October 1364) arranged the marriage and provided a substantial dowry. The French were in no position to compete openly with the English, but they were able to convince Pope Urban V to refuse on grounds of consanguinity to give a dispensation for the marriage. The pope saw nothing incestuous in letting Margaret marry Philip, the new duke of Burgundy and the younger brother of King Charles V, who like Edmund of Langley was related to her in the fourth degree. To achieve this most desirable marriage, which took place in a splendid ceremony at Ghent in 1369, Charles V had to return the Walloon castellanies. But while Louis of Male got a public declaration from the king that the territories were returned in perpetuity, Philip of Burgundy in a secret agreement – which was never implemented – swore that they would be returned to France at his death.[33]

The English were enraged over the Burgundian marriage, and Anglo-Flemish relations predictably deteriorated further when hostilities were recommenced between France and England that same year. The English considered goods belonging to the French or their allies subject to seizure on the seas. In April 1371 twenty-two Flemish boats were sunk by an English squadron in the Bay of Bourgneuf. The Flemings retaliated, and on 26–7 August 1371 the English and Flemings seized each other's property, leading to a commercial stoppage that lasted until April 1372. The Three Cities, which were conducting their own foreign policy apart from the count, protested that they had nothing to do with his anti-English policy. The English were too preoccupied with the French to make much trouble for Flemish shipping for the next several years; indeed, Bruges was often used for Anglo-French peace negotiations in the 1370s.[34]

Bread, water and the 'Ghent War' of 1379–85

For understandable reasons, Louis of Male tended to favour Bruges over Ghent. In 1330 Louis of Nevers had authorized Bruges to dig a

---

33. J.J.N. Palmer, 'England, France, the Papacy and the Flemish Succession, 1361–9', *JMH* **2** (1976): 339–64.

34. Varenbergh, *Relations diplomatiques*, 405–7; Lloyd, *Wool Trade*, 219; D. Nicholas, 'The English Trade at Bruges in the Last Years of Edward III', *JMH* **5** (1979): 34–5.

canal, the 'New Leie', between Bruges and Deinze to link the Leie river with the Bruges network on the Zwin. A century earlier such a canal would probably have occasioned no more controversy than had the Lieve of Ghent. But the New Leie would divert trade from Ghent's grain staple. Although Bruges began digging immediately, continuous work on the canal is recorded only from 1361. In 1379, construction entered the Oudburg of Ghent. The 'White Hoods' of Ghent, a band that had been used largely for terrorizing rural populations, then attacked the workers. The result was yet another civil war.[35]

Shortly after the attack on the Brugeois, the bailiff of Ghent was murdered. Jan Yoens, the dean of the shippers' guild, became captain and began a military expedition through Flanders, installing weaver-dominated magistracies at Bruges and Ypres. Louis of Male was forced into temporary exile; on 1 December 1379 he had to confirm all privileges of the rebel cities and agree to an inquest into the problems that had led to the rebellion. The truce did not last, and Oudenaarde and Dendermonde, the count's only remaining strongholds, soon fell to Ghent. But the rebellion was so unpopular at Bruges, which saw only Ghent's advantage in it, that when the Bruges militia went to Dendermonde to help the Ghent troops, the comital party at Bruges retook control on 29 May 1380, and the rest of west Flanders soon followed its lead.[36]

Following a winter truce, the war was resumed in February 1381. The count blockaded the rivers south of Ghent, depriving the city of its normal supply of food and forcing it to scavenge provisions in eastern Flanders. Ghent was in serious danger of being starved out by late 1381. A substantial party, consisting mainly of butchers and the now repentant shippers, wanted peace with the count, but an even more revolutionary party led by Philip van Artevelde, Jacob's youngest son, took power in December. Philip van Artevelde formally became captain on 24 January 1382 in a scene described by the anonymous Flemish chronicler.

On Saint Paul's Eve [24 January], a letter was found and read at Ghent before the community, which stated that if they wanted success, they should choose for their captain and government Philip van Artevelde, and then they would be successful, just as they had been in the time of Jacob, his father. Otherwise all would be lost. At this, half of the people, who wanted no part of it, left the marketplace. But four or five banners also

35. P. Rogghé, 'De Politiek van Graaf Lodewijk van Male: Het Gents e verzet en de Brugse Zuidleie', *AM* **15** (1964): 388–441; Nicholas, *Town and Countryside*, 138–41.
36. Pirenne, *Histoire de Belgique*, 2: 208; de Muynck, 'Gentse oorlog', 317.

left the marketplace and went to look for Philip van Artevelde. They found him in a bathhouse and brought him to the town hall, and they received his oath. The following Friday four captains whom he chose swore with him, two from among the landowners, one weaver and one shipper. And he chose people from all guilds to go with him. [37]

Philip van Artevelde used his first month in power to pursue family concerns, for, now in control of the city records, he found evidence of the identity of persons whom he blamed for his father's murder, and systematically hunted down and killed the eldest male relative of all of them he could catch. [38]

Philip came to the aldermen on Saturday, 23 January [actually 25 January] and asked why the city was at war. The advocate answered 'We don't know.' But Philip said 'You jolly well do know', and he added 'Tomorrow I'll say it.' Then Pieter van den Bossche [a van Artevelde ally] stood, and he spoke to his colleagues who were Law Aldermen, alleging that on Christmas Day they had handed the city over into the count's hands with the city's seal and their own seals. And Sunday at eleven o'clock Simon Bette, the first Law Alderman, was killed.
. . . And the people took the killing of Simon Bette on themselves collectively . . . The following Thursday [30 January], when the Collacie was meeting, Philip had his clerk read a letter addressed to Gilbert de Grutere [dean of the small guilds] alone, in the presence of the aldermen and the fifty-two deans. It alleged that Gilbert had let the seven villages near Dendermonde compose [pay less than the sum owed] and sent the money to the count of Flanders and released the hostages from Dendermonde. The letter also said that Gilbert had stood in the chamber at Lille with the lords, where the prince had offered him terms, and Gilbert had said he would do it all, even if it cost him his life. He signalled the same thing by throwing his cap under his feet saying 'So be it.' The good man protested his innocence of all of this. Thirdly, they accused him of having had John Perneele and William de Scepene banished from the city and advising the count that he had done it in his honour. Gilbert then said 'I was then first Alderman of the city!' Then Philip said 'You will never again banish one of my men', and he drew a knife, and Gilbert was murdered in the hall of the Collacie. And the people assembled on the Market, everyone under his banner; and Philip said that he had done it for the common profit of the city, and the community took the deed upon themselves. Then Philip had three prisoners, all named John – John de Rommere, John Mayhu and John Sleipstaf – brought to the square in front of the jail and beheaded. [39]

37. Quoted by Nicholas, *Van Arteveldes*, 127–8.
38. Nicholas, *Van Arteveldes*, 120–59.
39. Translated from de Pauw, *Cartulaire des Artevelde*, 351–2.

Turning to public policy from the end of February, van Artevelde rekindled his father's alliance with England. He had, in fact, been receiving a pension from the English government since at least 1362.[40] On 3 May the Ghent militia took advantage of the wholesale inebriation of the population of Bruges, where the procession of the Holy Blood was being celebrated, defeated the Bruges militia and seized the city. Louis of Male was in Bruges and barely escaped to Lille.

Van Artevelde could survive only with English help; but although promised, it never materialized, in part because the lords who controlled Parliament were uncomfortable with supporting a government that seemed to have such social-revolutionary inclinations. The older political parties had disappeared in Flanders. Each side simply called itself the Goods and its opponents the Bads. Van Artevelde styled himself regent of Flanders and adopted the estate of a prince. Seeing little in him to admire even in defeat, his enemies dismissed him after his death as 'Filthy Phil'. Van Artevelde sent haughty missives to the regents of King Charles VI, who with the duke of Burgundy now directed Flemish policy. The French were frightened by the cries of 'Long live Ghent' that were sounded by rebels in the streets of Rouen, Paris and Amiens. On 27 November 1382 the French army slaughtered the Flemish army in a swamp at Westrozebeke and killed van Artevelde himself.[41]

Bruges and Ypres quickly submitted, followed by the rest of Flanders. Supporters of the rebel regime were rounded up, and the property of those who had died at Westrozebeke was confiscated during inquests into what had happened during 'Phil's time'. The count's commissioners in the Franc of Bruges beheaded thirty-eight rebels, including three shippers of Ghent and three pirates. At Bruges itself, 224 persons, not all of them Brugeois, were executed and the property of 281 confiscated. The severity of the punishment varied with one's social standing, but it is clear that the count's men used the general sense of outrage to facilitate collection of a windfall of fines.[42]

Since Ghent did not submit, the commissioners were limited to seizing rural property owned by Gentenars and refugees to the city. The dossiers thus are weighted towards the elite of the city, who

40. Palmer, 'Flemish Succession', 342.

41. Pirenne, *Histoire de Belgique*, 2: 213–14; Nicholas, *Van Arteveldes*, 190.

42. J. de Smet, 'De Verbeurdverklaringen in het Brugse Vrije en in de smalle steden aldaar na de slag bij Westrozebeke (1382–1384)', *ASEB* **95** (1958): 115–36; de Smet, 'De Repressie te Brugge na de slag bij Westrozebeke, 1 December 1382–31 Augustus 1384', *ASEB* **84** (1947): 71–118.

bought rural property as a rental investment. Even with this caveat, however, the confiscations show that although there was some involvement of the masses of Ghent in the rebellion, defence of the city's wealth-generating privileges rather than the aspirations of the poor were the driving force behind the revolt of Ghent.[43]

Ghent appointed Francis Ackerman as the new regent. In the summer of 1383 Richard II's government sent a 'crusade' to Flanders under the leadership of Henry Despenser, bishop of Norwich. But although the Ghent forces retook Oudenaarde and Damme, the English accomplished nothing except the destruction of the unfortified suburbs of Ypres. Louis of Male died at Lille on 30 January 1384 and was succeeded by his son-in-law, Philip 'the Bold' of Burgundy. On 18 December 1385 Philip, realizing that nothing could be gained by intransigence, agreed to the peace of Tournai with Ghent, whose consequences we shall discuss in Chapter Eleven.

THE GOVERNMENT OF THE FLEMISH COUNTS IN THE FOURTEENTH CENTURY

Although Louis of Male has not been treated gently by Flemish historians, and with reason, he was remembered after his death as the only prince of his dynasty who had used his subjects' language in administration, a practice beginning in 1352. Yet even while Louis's accounts were written in Flemish, the auditors' annotations were in French, for the immediate entourage of the count still used French. The count's central court (*Audientie*) kept bilingual records, depending on the region of the litigants; of 690 acts in the 'Cartulary of Louis of Male', an early *Audientie* record, 419 are in Flemish, 264 in French and a mere 9 in Latin.[44]

The use of written material proliferates in the period of Louis of Male. The cities were keeping written accounts in the late thirteenth century, and the aldermen evidently kept records of transactions before them by the late thirteenth century. Those of Bruges for the fourteenth century have disappeared, but the books of Ghent's law aldermen

---

43. Angeline van Oost, 'Sociale stratifikatie van de Gentse opstandelingen van 1379–1385: Een Kritische benadering van konfiskatiedokumenten', *HMGOG* **29** (1975): 59–92.

44. Nowé, *Baillis*, 184–5.

survive from 1339 and of the estate aldermen from 1349. These texts, and the city accounts, were public records that were open for inspection and could be used as evidence. In 1374 a citizen of IJzendike successfully sued its magistrates at the count's court for refusing to give him, at his cost, a copy of the town accounts.[45] The records of the trade stoppage of 1371 show that detailed records and bills of lading were kept and presented to the authorities. Furthermore, Flanders still had numerous internal tolls, at which the citizens of privileged places were exempt or got reduced rates. They must have had proof of identity, although none has survived.[46] Not only were the towns and Flemish counts keeping more records, they were becoming more efficient in preserving them. The counts maintained an archive of their charters at Rupelmonde by 1272 that was inventoried shortly after 1336.[47]

The Flemish counts still disposed of the old sources of income in the fourteenth century, but they came to rely increasingly on *beden*. Feudal rights such as relief still gave the counts some income. They were owed hospitality once a year as well as military service from their vassals, although we have seen that feudal military service was hopelessly confused and difficult to enforce by the fourteenth century. They could also get military service from the towns. They collected 'courtesy', an annual payment from the six great Benedictine abbeys. The princes were also owed transport services and forced labour in lieu of military services, all of which they fiscalized.[48]

The tax structure was very different in the towns and the rural areas. Rural communities taxed land and had parish tax assessors. The basis of urban finance, however, was the indirect taxes on consumer goods. The towns leased from the count the right to take these duties, called assizes, then farmed them to private persons. Apart from this, the cities collected a small amount in ground rents, the issue payment on property leaving their jurisdiction, and occasional forced loans. The

45. N. de Pauw (ed.), *Bouc van de Audiencie: Acten en Sentencien van den Raad van Vlaanderen in de XIVe eeuw*, 2 vols (Ghent, 1901, 1903), 1: 583–4.

46. As an example, in 1370 the tollkeeper of Oudenaarde was accused of demanding toll from men of Biervliet, who were exempt, and had to justify himself before the *Audientie*. He failed to appear, so the case went by default; we do not know how they proved their status. De Pauw, *Audiencie*, 81–2, 95, 117.

47. Maurice Vandermaesen, 'Het Slot van Rupelmonde als centraal archiefdepot van het graafschap Vlaanderen (midden 13de–14de e.)', *BCRH* **136** (1970): 273–317, esp. 273–92.

48. Monier, *Institutions centrales*, 26–8; Limburg-Stirum, *Cartulaire de Louis de Male*, 2: 252; Verbruggen, 'De Militairen', 198.

cities avoided direct taxation whenever possible. The immense sums owed to the count thus came from very different sources in the towns and the rural areas.[49]

Coinage and international diplomacy

Louis of Male also realized considerable income from monetary manipulations. Flemish money had generally followed French issues since the late thirteenth century, and the French had devalued their coins to pay for the English wars. But Louis of Nevers had also devalued at times when the French issue was stable to take the profits of seigniorage. By the early van Artevelde period, so much foreign metal was entering Flanders that the native Flemish coinage was not much used until after 1343.[50]

Louis of Male devalued the coin even more rapidly than had his father. In a classic article Hans van Werveke argued that Louis of Male got roughly one-fifth of his income from seigniorage, and his devaluations hurt Flemish exports, even though they made cloth cheaper overseas. More recent studies have suggested that Flemish industry was damaged more by the increase of export taxes on English wool and by political turmoil, although seigniorage continued to be the count's chief motive.

The devaluations also fuelled inflation. A considerable debate has raged as to the extent of that inflation and the degree to which monetary manipulations caused it.[51] The Flemish silver coinage was debased eighteen times and the gold twenty-two during Louis of Male's reign. The weight of the silver penny fell from 4.55 grammes in 1318 to 2.15 in 1346, 0.97 in 1384 and 0.61 in 1477. John H. Munro, following Herman van der Wee, has compiled a composite price index for a 'basket of consumables' based on Adriaan Verhulst's food price statistics

49. De Pauw, *Audiencie*, 2: 828; *IAY* 2: 224.

50. F. and W.P. Blockmans, 'Devaluation, Coinage and Seignorage under Louis de Nevers and Louis de Male, counts of Flanders, 1330–84' in *Coinage in the Low Countries*, 70–7, 81.

51. For the inflation controversy, see John H. Munro, 'Bullion Flows and Monetary Contraction in Late-Medieval England and the Low Countries', in John F. Richards (ed.), *Precious Metals in the Later Medieval and Early Modern Worlds* (Durham, NC, 1983); Munro, *Wool, Cloth, and Gold: The Struggle for Bullion in Anglo-Burgundian Trade* (Brussels and Toronto, 1972); Munro, 'Mint Outputs, Money, and Prices in Late-Medieval England and the Low Countries', *Trierer Historische Forschungen* 7 (1984); Blockmans and Blockmans, 'Devaluation'; Nicholas, *Metamorphosis*, 120–34; van Houtte, *Economic History*, 112.

for Bruges[52] and more fragmentary records from Ghent. This index rose 96 per cent between 1350 and 1374, more rapidly than the debasement of the coin. The Flemish price index thus clearly reflects high demand and Flanders' dependence on imported raw materials. Furthermore, after 1360 the devaluations were severe only between 1365 and 1374 and between 1386 and 1389, and even these were less serious than the debasements before December 1363. Grain prices rose at a more rapid rate than debasements in the 1360s, then declined after 1370, even as the coin debasements slowed to an average of 0.76 per cent per year between 1365 and 1389. Furthermore, in the 1360s and particularly 1370s new wage agreements were made that more than compensated for the extent of the debasements, although they lagged behind the total rate of inflation.[53]

Court and council

The count's council was still ambulatory in the early fourteenth century. During the thirteenth century the court of barons bifurcated, as a judicial section composed of councillors and great feudatories became a supreme court, while the 'council' became an advisory body. The great change in the council came particularly from the period of Guy of Dampierre, who recruited members regardless of social standing or even nationality and preferred professional jurists with training in canon and Roman law. Before that time, trained lawyers had been used only in the courts of the *officialités* in Flanders.

Although Guy used no Flemish lawyers, Flemings were starting to get legal training at the universities. No legists are mentioned in Flanders between 1296 and 1309, but the count kept at least two permanently attached to his council after 1314. From about 1330, the chancellor was a legist. Robert of Béthune was the first to use Flemings, of whom the best known is Hendrik Braem of Ghent, who was also canon of Notre Dame of Tournai. He was simultaneously the salaried town clerk of Ghent and in the count's service from 1306 to

52. Verhulst, 'Prijzen van granen, boter en kaas te Brugge volgens de "slag" van het Sint-Donatiaanskapittel (1348–1801)' in C. Verlinden *et al.* (eds), *Dokumenten voor de geschiedenis van prijzen en lonen in Vlaanderen en Brabant* (Bruges, 1965), 2: 3–70.

53. Blockmans and Blockmans, 'Devaluation', 77–9; H. van Werveke, *De muntslag in Vlaanderen onder Lodewijk van Male*, MKVA, Kl. Letteren, 10, No. 5 (Brussels, 1949); van Werveke, 'Currency Manipulation in the Middle Ages: The Case of Louis de Male, Count of Flanders', *Transactions of the Royal Historical Society*, Series 4, 31 (1949); summary with new material from Ghent in Nicholas, *Metamorphosis*, 120–34.

1332 except for a brief period when Louis of Nevers began his reign by firing all his grandfather's councillors. The central court quickly became predominantly Flemish. Louis of Male had seven chief councillors, all but two of whom were Flemings. Virtually all of them held several church prebends, which probably explains how the counts and towns got away with paying extremely low wages.[54]

An important theme of government in the period of Louis of Male is the movement of large numbers of burghers of the cities into the count's bureaucracy for the first time. The towns too made more use of personnel with legal training, although few lawyers became aldermen in Flanders, probably because of the strength of customary law. During the thirteenth century the town clerk was the most important paid functionary of the town. The aldermen encouraged the best students from the local Flemish schools to go on to the universities, and many of them became clerks or councillors of the town. Most town clerks by 1400 had at least attended a university course in the liberal arts.[55]

Salaried city counsellors or attorneys appear at Ghent in 1310 and Bruges in 1315. In the beginning they did not live in the town that hired them, but in the town of the court where they functioned. From the second half of the fourteenth century, however, they were often required by the terms of their contracts to live in the employing town. By the late fourteenth century the city attorney was the most highly paid officer of Ghent after the guild deans.[56]

In addition to becoming more professionalized, the count's court assumed an appellate function. The counts before Louis of Male had tried to subordinate lower jurisdictions on a regular basis to the central court, but they were limited by the fact that the 'cities of law' had the exclusive right to try their own burghers, which made regional government impossible. Contemporaries such as the anonymous author of the *Chronique rimée* of the 1380s saw this clearly, adding that Ghent was the worst of the lot in using this to free citizens who were guilty of crime.[57] Furthermore, into the fourteenth century there was no

54. John Gilissen, 'Les Légistes en Flandre aux XIIIe et XIVe siècles', *Bulletin de la Commission Royale des Anciennes Lois et Ordonnances de Belgique*, XV, Fasc. 3 (1939): 120–35, 141–7, 173–5, 221–2.

55. Paul Rogghé, 'De Gentse Klerken in de XIVe en XVe eeuw: Trouw en Verraad', *AM* **11** (1960): 5–142.

56. Gilissen, 'Légistes', 177–93; Nicholas, 'Governance', 249.

57. H. Pirenne (ed.), *Chronique rimée des troubles de Flandre en 1379–1380* (Ghent, 1902), 9–10.

appeal in Flemish courts; a litigant could only claim false judgement. This gradually was absorbed by the *amendement* under Louis of Male, who used it to extend the competence of his central court.[58]

Aspects of the law also fostered disorder in the cities. At Ypres seven witnesses were needed to prove a simple misdemeanour, while seven to fourteen were required for a criminal case involving a £60 fine, and capital cases required the testimony of twenty-one witnesses on each of three days of pleading. The smaller towns were more summary. At Aalst, for example, the bailiff needed to summon only as many witnesses as he needed to prove his case. Parties in feuds were under no obligation to submit to the arbitration of local public authorities unless so ordered by the count's officials.[59]

The Audientie

Sessions of the comital council for judicial business were being called *Audientie* by 1309. The special session was a regular court by 1333 at the latest. Under Louis of Male there were six or seven meetings a year.

The published transactions of the *Audientie*[60] show clearly the possibilities and limitations of Flemish justice. Few cases were handled at a single trial day; most were postponed, in many cases for so long that the litigants either gave up or reached an out-of-court settlement, since no final verdict survives. The counts were encouraging local communities to lodge questions about disputed cases with the *Audientie* rather than going to their judicial heads, usually one of the Three Cities. The court accepted actions by citizens of the smaller towns against their home governments.[61]

But the Three Cities resisted this. They had the right to punish their burghers for appealing to the count's court, since the town had the sole right to try them if it wished; thus, when a townsman came before the *Audientie*, he almost always renounced his burgher standing

---

58. Monier, *Institutions centrales*, 67–8, 72; Jan van Rompaey, *Het grafelijke baljuwsambt in Vlaanderen tijdens de Boergondische periode. VKVA* No. 62 (Brussels, 1967), 31.

59. See case of 1376 in de Pauw, *Bouc van der Audiencie*, 2: 872–3, and in general Nowé, *Baillis*, 288–9.

60. Limburg–Stirum, *Cartulaire de Louis de Male*; J. Buntinx, *De Audientie van de graven van Vlaanderen: Studie over het centraal grafelijk gerecht (c.1330–c.1409)* (Brussels, 1949); de Pauw, *Audiencie*.

61. De Pauw, *Audiencie*, 2: 845.

for the duration of the legal action in question.[62] Of the Three Cities, cases came to the *Audientie* frequently only from Ypres, the politically weakest. As a rule, the *Audientie* would consider suits brought against Yprois by outsiders but not by one burgess against another. The disputes over jurisdiction were not confined to the Three Cities, however, and the *Audientie* was generally punctilious in respecting proper claims when they could be documented in an inquest.[63]

Furthermore, the court preferred parties to handle disputes by arbitration when possible. In such cases, the *Audientie* remanded the case to arbitrators in the town. It generally would not hear an appeal from a blood price arrangement once it had been promulgated by a local court. Despite its reluctance to interfere in family feuds, however, the *Audientie* handled cases ranging in gravity from homicide and jurisdictional quarrels to petty theft. In 1370, for example, Kateline van der Elst of Uitbergen went to the *Audientie* with a complaint that Boudin van den Driessche had seized a cow from her that her mother had given her for caring for her during her last illness. He was ordered to return it, but he got the right to sue if he claimed rights on it. Meanwhile, the bailiff of Dendermonde was ordered to make sure that he returned the cow, but also to try Boudin's countersuit if he made one. But if the bailiff thought 'that Boudin has committed a misdeed against the count in taking matters into his own hands and making himself lord by taking the cow', he should do whatever he thought appropriate.[64]

The bailiffs

The count's chief officer in most localities continued to be the bailiff, who received a constant stream of directives from the count and/or the receiver-general, to whom the bailiffs reported directly. The small size of Flanders made permanent contact possible, and bailiffs were sometimes summoned to consult with the count in person. The receiver-general was head of the comital police and ordered the bailiffs to search for exiles, make certain arrests, hold inquests and even execute

62. This could also happen with the smaller towns. In 1376 a woman who claimed trial only at Courtrai as burgess was coerced into surrendering her burgher standing for this case so that the *Audientie* could handle it. De Pauw, *Audiencie*, No. 1848, p. 882.

63. For representative cases, see de Pauw, *Audiencie*, 1: 30, 305.

64. De Pauw, *Audiencie*, 1: 97. In 1373 the *Audientie* tried a case of swine theft; 1: 459–60.

criminals. From the first quarter of the fourteenth century, the bailiff could not make a financial composition with persons indicted for a crime whose fine was £60 or higher without the receiver's consent. The counts from Louis of Male did not sit on the audit of the bailiffs' accounts, leaving this to the receiver.

The bailiff's functions did not change significantly during the fourteenth century. He normally named his own sergeants, but their number was so small — four at Ghent — that they can hardly have been a serious deterrent to crime. In most towns and many rural areas with governing charters, the bailiff himself could arrest a citizen only with the aldermen's consent unless the culprit was caught in the act. But as the century wore on the bailiff seized persons whom he admitted he could not have convicted in court, then made them pay a fine to be released: 'Indictments for the £60 fine for carrying weapons, and the bailiff let them go for a fine for lack of anything better, since he knew that he had no good proof to support the accusation'.[65] Foreigners were especially vulnerable. The Germans complained that 'many bailiffs and their minions do great injury to merchants in many matters, in that they seize the said merchants en route and in cities for bearing arms, and force them to great expenditure before they prosecute, and in that no atonement is made, they just make it worse every day'.[66]

Most of the bailiffs' income was from profits of justice, except for occasional confiscations of property. They deducted their own expenses, including travel, costs and wages of subordinates, and citing parties and holding trials. Just as the count had assigned pensions and annuities on domain receipts in the twelfth century, so he made the same use of the bailiffs' receipts in the thirteenth and fourteenth. Wages were low, even for the bailiffs of the major cities, and the unmentioned perquisites of office and the chance to rise to a higher position seem to have been the major attraction. The bailiffs were sometimes not paid on schedule, which in its turn led to corruption. When the bailiff's account closed on a deficit, he would be reimbursed, usually from his successor's income.[67]

The earliest inquests into bailiffs' misconduct go back to the mid thirteenth century, but the complaints became so numerous that the count ordered a general inquiry in 1307–8. The allegations included

---

65. Translated from General Archives of the Realm, Brussels, Rolrekening 1368.

66. Nowé, *Baillis*, 240–3; D. Nicholas, 'Crime and Punishment in Fourteenth-Century Ghent', *RBPH* **48** (1970): 300–2. The German complaint is in *Hanserecesse*, 3: 321, cited de Muynck, 'Gentse oorlog', 313.

67. Nowé, *Baillis*, 176–9, 202.

illegal exactions and imprisonments, threats, violence, arson and denials of justice. More complaints came from peasants than from towns, where the bailiffs had to be more careful. For example, the inquest brought serious allegations against the bailiff of Aalst and his underbailiff.

> You lords who are inquisitors for our dear lord of Flanders, here are the complaints and serious suffering of which those of Aalst complain, namely of the bailiff of Aalst, lord William de Bloc, Pieter de Kint and their deputies. First, we complain that in time past the bailiff came by dead of night and took a man, Jan van Zottegem, and his wife, who had long lived in the city of Aalst and were citizens there, in their house in the city. They took them outside and condemned them without court and verdict and against the freedom of our lord of Flanders for his city, and the man and wife were of good reputation.
>
> We also complain of what the bailiffs did in violation of the freedom of the city of Aalst and say to you lords that they seized one Dierkind van den Morthuse, son of the late Clais van Bussenghem, who was a free citizen of our lord of Flanders at Aalst. Thereafter his mother complained to the aldermen of Aalst, to whose jurisdiction Dierkin belonged. The aldermen sent their letters to the bailiff that he should deliver Dierkin, the count's free burgess, from prison. Lords, he would not release Dierkin in response to this letter. Afterwards, his mother complained again to the aldermen. The aldermen came and spoke to Pieter de Kint, the bailiff, and asked him to deliver Dierkin, demanding right from him according to the freedom of the city of Aalst that he had sworn to uphold. The bailiff answered that he would handle it. And on top of this, this same bailiff condemned Dierkin without trial and judgement and against the freedom of the city, and held Dierkin in prison unjustly, against the freedom of the city of Aalst.
>
> Lords, we also complain that the bailiff seized the son of one of our burgesses, Lievin, son of the priest of Bardenghem, and brought him illegally to jail at Aalst, which is against the freedom. His mother complained to the aldermen of Aalst that the bailiff had seized her son. The aldermen went to the bailiff and asked him what his accusation against our burgess was. He answered that he had caught him for theft. The mother responded that her son had satisfied Gillis van Lielaer, who was bailiff at that time, regarding this complaint for which Pieter de Kint had seized him, and that this was known to the persons who were then aldermen. And then Pieter de Kint came before the aldermen and acquitted our burgess's son in view of their predecessors' testimony. But my lords, he then held our burgess's son in a horrible prison [so] that his mother, our burgess, out of the suffering and in fear for her son, had to give Pieter de Kint fourteen pounds or more of her money.[68]

68. Translated from Nowé, *Baillis*, 502–4.

Louis of Male from 1349 regularly heard complaints against the bailiffs on the three accounting days per year, when the bailiffs brought the income of their bailiwicks to the court, but he also ordered general inquests in 1349, 1357 and 1358–61.[69]

Punishments of bailiffs were hardly exemplary. In 1377 a man of Bailleul admitted picking the pocket of a butcher of Ypres but said that the bailiff had promised to let him go if he paid composition of twenty-eight times the amount that he stole. Instead, the bailiff got the aldermen to banish him. The bailiff admitted that he had paid the composition, so the *Audientie* revoked banishment. In 1377 the bailiff of Mardijk broke into the house of a sleeping man and stole £26 9s from his pocket before telling him that he was being accused of a crime. The bailiff claimed that it was only £4 7s, but testimony showed that he lied; yet the record says nothing about punishing the bailiff.[70]

Another notorious case is William Slijp, a native of Ypres who was bailiff of Four Offices, then of Aalst between 1376 and 1380 and of Bruges between 1383 and 1394 and an active member of the count's council. In 1377, shortly after his transfer to Aalst, he was sued by a man of Assenede, who claimed that while bailiff of Four Offices Slijp had claimed wrongly that he was in arrears on his taxes and threatened to burn his house, but that he had withdrawn the threat in return for a bribe. Slijp claimed that it was a court fine, but the *Audientie* ordered him to repay the money out of his own pocket, since he already had paid it to the count as part of his annual reckoning. When the auditors questioned the enormous but unenumerated great expenses that Slijp was trying to deduct from his receipt in 1383, he openly altered his account. But such venial sins as fiscal corruption did not hinder anyone's rise. Slijp's descendants held the comital feudal court of no less a place than Westrozebeke.[71]

In fairness to the bailiffs, they were faced with a stupefying level of violence compounded by jurisdictional exceptions and a crudity of manners and morals that astonishes even the most jaded modern sensibilities. For example, the account of the bailiff of the Land of Waas for 1374 relates that:

William de Boc shared a house with his nephew, Linus de Boc. William

69. Nowé, *Baillis*, 135–7, 143–52.

70. De Pauw, *Audiencie*, 2: 931–2; 984.

71. Nicholas, 'Scheldt Trade', 218; de Pauw, *Audiencie*, 2: 981–2; R.C. van Caenegem (ed.), *Les Arrêts et jugés du Parlement de Paris sur appels flamands conservés dans les registres du Parlement*, 2 vols (Brussels, 1966, 1975), 1: 437–9.

the uncle purchased a girl who lived in the environs, and matters went so far between them that she was carrying his child. Then he told his nephew about the affair and complained that he would have to take the girl and marry her. But the nephew said that he had a bright idea: that he himself would go during the night and lie with the girl. Then his uncle would come and lie down beside her also, so that the uncle would not be forced legally to marry her. So the nephew went and slept with the girl. Then the uncle later came at the appointed time. He found the girl and tried to lie down beside her. But then she became aware that the first one was not her lover, and she cried for help. Then the uncle hit her so hard that she bled, and he threw her to the ground. So the bailiff took all steps necessary to see to it that the girl was assured of her lover. In the name of the prince, he also assessed a fine of £72. [72]

The receiver-general and the sovereign bailiff

Two new officials come to the foreground in the fourteenth century: the sovereign bailiff, who was a judicial specialist, and the receiver-general for finances. Bailiffs and local receivers accounted to the receiver-general in the fourteenth century.

We have discussed Philip of Bourbourg, generally conceded to have been the first receiver-general of Flanders. By the period of Guy of Dampierre, the bailiffs rendered accounts to the receiver. Jakemon of Deinze in the 1290s regularized the ad hoc receipts and distributions of funds, and the first evidence of a permanent cadre of subordinate officials attached to the office comes during his period. Given the princes' dependence on foreign sources of capital, it was natural that they turned to Italian financiers as receivers. Thomas Fini, receiver of Robert of Béthune, had to flee to France to escape prosecution for malfeasance. After Fini's disgrace, the count made appointments for shorter periods. [73]

By 1328, if not before, there was a central accounting body of fluctuating composition but always including the 'master of accounts'. Pieter of Douai, master of accounts by 1335, lived in a house at Courtrai that was owned by the count and probably housed a

---

72. Translated from General Archives of the Realm, Brussels, Rolrekening 2895.
73. Ellen E. Kittell, *From Ad Hoc to Routine: A Case Study in Medieval Bureaucracy* (Philadelphia, 1991), strains to keep from calling Philip of Bourbourg the first receiver-general, claiming that until Fini, the duties of the receiver were too various to constitute duties of a regular office.

Chamber of Accounts, since the count's financial archive would have been too large for the usually itinerant master to transport with him. When Pieter of Douai died, the chancellor occupied the house. Courtrai may have been a financial capital of Flanders in the period of Louis of Nevers, as under Margaret. The office of receiver-general lapsed during the van Artevelde rebellion, but Louis of Male reinstituted it. In contrast to his father, he used Flemings; four of the seven receivers from the first years of his reign were burghers of the Three Cities. By 1352 the receiver-general could remove a case from a lower court to a higher and was the chief judicial officer. A revived office of master of accounts was established in 1350 with a general commission to audit all accounts; only Ghent and Bruges managed to escape this obligation.[74]

Although for most of the fourteenth century the receipts from justice were mixed with other incomes, they were separated in 1369. In 1372 the office of sovereign bailiff was created and assumed the judicial functions of the receiver-general. The sovereign bailiff thus became the first official of the central court who was concerned exclusively with justice. The count was not trying to restrict the receiver-general because he was too powerful, but was trying to relieve him of too great responsibilities; for Gossuin de Wilde, receiver-general between 1365 and 1370, became the first sovereign bailiff between 1372 and 1384. There was confusion in the beginning between their functions. The sovereign bailiff's accounts become completely separate only in 1387, but by the fifteenth century the receiver had lost his judicial attributes.[75]

Changes in city government in the fourteenth century

The cities of Flanders were governed by bodies of two or more councils during the fourteenth century.[76] In Ghent the law aldermen issued statutes, recorded civil contracts, supervised administration and adjudicated many legal actions. The estate aldermen, the lower body, supervised orphans' property and functioned as justices of the peace,

74. F. Blockmans, 'Le Contrôle par le prince des comptes urbains en Flandre et en Brabant au Moyen Age' in *Finances et comptabilités urbaines*, 287–338, esp. 298–300, 311–17.

75. Monier, *Institutions centrales*, 68–71.

76. Basic to this section is D. Nicholas, 'The Governance of Fourteenth-Century Ghent: The Theory and Practice of Public Administration' in *Lyon Essays*, 235–60.

imposed truces and ordered punishments for petty violence, normally at mass trial days (*dinghedaghe*) that were held several times a year. Occasionally before 1360 and invariably thereafter, the cities had receivers or treasurers, normally one per political Member.

After 1302 guildsmen had the right to serve on the town councils, but the dominant voice was still the landowning element that had controlled the patrician regimes of the thirteenth century. Bruges and Ypres had burgomasters, who fulfilled largely ceremonial roles; Ghent's chief of state was the first law alderman. During emergencies, captains were appointed. Larger assemblies sometimes met in crisis periods, although there is more evidence of this in the fifteenth century than before.

Ghent was ruled after 1360 by a magistracy in which power was shared among three political 'Members': landowners, weavers (who included smaller textile trades) and small guilds (the locally based food-mongering and smaller artisan trades, together with the shippers); the fullers were excluded from power. Each individual guild had its own dean and councillors, and each Member had an overdean, a very powerful figure in the town government. Ypres had four Members: the landowners (to whom four other guilds were added), weavers, fullers and small guilds. The privilege of Senlis of 1301 for Ghent gave both the outgoing government and the count a role in choosing new aldermen. At Ypres, however, the aldermen were appointed by the prince's commissioners after 1380.

At Bruges, which was less dominated by the textile trades, there were nine Members. As at Ghent and Ypres, the landowners and textile guilds were apart, but the other seven Bruges Members were groups that were joined in the single Member of 'small guilds' in the other cities. Each Member had its own dean, but in contrast to Ghent there were not two overdeans but a college of sometimes nine and sometimes eighteen deans who governed the town along with the aldermen and captains. By the end of the fourteenth century the count's commissioners appointed the magistrates directly, but with the proviso that the burgomaster and aldermen could veto the choices of those to whom they objected. Only Ghent was able to preserve autonomy in the choice of aldermen after 1400.[77]

Both aldermanic seats and guild magistracies were supposed to rotate annually, but in fact the same names tended to reappear after a year or two; the carpenter Arnoud van der Varent was overdean of

77. Blockmans, *Volksvertegenwoordiging*, 76–7; Pirenne, *Histoire de Belgique*, 2: 65–6.

the small guilds at Ghent for seventeen years in succession after 1360. Yet the formality of annual rotation was generally observed. This and the guarantee of seats on the councils for groups of guilds meant that the smaller guilds were more democratically structured than the larger. This seems truer of Bruges than of Ghent, where the number of Members was smaller.[78]

Although much has been written of the guild composition of the city governments, it does not seem to have had much impact on the actual conduct of administration. At all times the cities were governed by guild aristocracies of affluent persons who shared an outlook. Political factionalism tended to develop over foreign policy considerations, such as relations between the city and the count and alliances, not between guilds except in the case of the textile trades. Continuity was provided by the increasingly large corps of technocrats who served the cities – receivers, clerks, messengers, sergeants and the city attorneys – who generally served for many years at a time except during the 1340s.

The city governments of the thirteenth century had been notorious for peculation, perhaps because there was no regular tax structure. There were few scandals in the fourteenth century. The cities stopped borrowing from professional financiers after about 1320 and gradually paid off their debts to them. Only Bruges continued to borrow much from Italians, mainly residents of the city, and then only during emergencies.[79]

The cities derived between 80 and 90 per cent of their income in most years from the indirect taxes or assizes on goods of consumption. Rates were considerably higher on wine than on beer, grain and other goods more in common demand. The count granted the right to levy these taxes periodically in return for a large single payment, which from the 1360s increasingly was linked to massive annual subventions by the cities. The cities leased the assizes at public auction annually to syndicates of wealthy brokers, who collected them and were

78. J. Mertens, 'De Brugse ambachtsbesturen (1363–1374, n.s.): een oligarchie', *Liber Buntinx*, 189–91; R. van Uytven, 'Plutokratie in de "oude demokratieën" der Nederlanden', *Handelingen der Koninklijke Zuidnederlandse Maatschappij voor Taal-en Letterkunde en Geschiedenis* **16** (1962): 402.

79. Raymond de Roover, 'Les Comptes communaux et la comptabilité communale de la ville de Bruges au XIVe siècle' in *Finances et comptabilités urbaines du XIIIe au XVIe siècle*, 88–90; see also P. Rogghé, 'Italianen te Gent in de XIVe eeuw: Een merkwaardig florentijnsch hostelliers- en makelaarsgeslacht: de Gualterotti', *Bijdragen voor de Geschiedenis der Nederlanden* **1** (1946): 197–226, for an Italian house that lent to Ghent and to the count. Conte Gualterotti was receiver of Flanders 1322–6.

considered employees of the city during the lease term. Profits on the tax farms were extremely low, probably less than 2 per cent at Bruges.[80] At Ghent during the late 1330s the city voluntarily compensated the leaseholders for their loss of income, and the city had to assume direct administration of the taxes on several occasions because leaseholders could not be found.

Ghent sold life annuities or rents, amounting to bond issues, in which the lender paid a lump sum to the city and in return received a fixed payment for the rest of his life. Bruges also used the rent but relied more often on forced loans during emergencies than did Ghent. The cities also realized some income from such payments as the issue tax on property leaving the tax competence of the city (largely a death duty, but it was imposed on donations to churches and on the property of those leaving or marrying someone who was not a burgher) and ground rents on land that was owned by the city corporation. Just as Flemish burgesses bought large amounts of land in the countryside, so they invested heavily in the rents sold by the smaller communities, although usually not those of their home cities.[81]

The period of Louis of Male witnessed a tremendous shift in financial power away from the cities and towards the central government. The count's financial demands could not be met by the cities' sources of ordinary revenue after 1360, and thus most city accounts from the late fourteenth century had a deficit. Furthermore, corruption was a way of life. Although the aldermen were not paid salaries through most of the fourteenth century, this changed in the 1390s and became a major drain on city finances. They also had substantial perquisites of office, notably banquets and gifts of expensive cloth for uniforms and display.[82]

We have no basis for comparison with the previous period, but after 1302 the cities were involved in many enterprises affecting the welfare of their citizens. We shall see in Chapter Ten that governments spent large sums on poor relief and charity. The cities main-

80. James M. Murray, 'Family, Marriage and Moneychanging in Medieval Bruges', *JMH* **14** (1988): 120.

81. Immense life rents on the town of Biervliet were confiscated in 1382 from eighty-eight citizens of Ghent, fifty-one of them women. For political reasons Biervliet seems to have turned to the more limited Ghent financial market than to Bruges. Marc Boone, 'Gentse financiële belangen te Biervliet 1382–1384: Naar aanleiding van een konfiskatiedossier', *AM* **33** (1982): 251–67.

82. W. Prevenier, 'Quelques aspects des comptes communaux en Flandre au Moyen Age', *Finances et comptabilités urbaines*, 126–8, 133–5, 144.

tained surveyors, usually prominent contractors, who appraised the value of disputed property and settled boundary disputes. Sworn municipal appraisers determined the value of chattels involved in inheritances. Ghent maintained between ten and sixteen sergeants as policemen and about twenty *cnapen* who performed messenger and guard duty. The guilds also had militias. The cities also maintained specialists, including a city surgeon and in some cases masters of public works. Particularly after 1360 the cities maintained permanent janitorial corps which kept the market squares clean.

The cities did not have large bureaucracies. Ghent rarely had more than 150 persons in the government at any time before 1385. This figure is somewhat misleading, for in addition to persons who were paid by the city government, the guilds – few of whose records survive – had courts and inspectors and normally judged cases involving their own members. The parishes and wards also had organizations that handled some legal actions. For all the disorder, we cannot say that the cities were undergoverned.

The cities maintained a variety of amenities for their citizens. Bridges – Ghent, an interior city, had over one hundred – and roads were kept in repair. The municipal accounts show immense expenditures on preventive maintenance. The most thoroughly documented public works programme in late medieval Flanders has been that of Bruges.[83] Although most building material except brick (Bruges owned a brick factory at Ramscapelle) had to be imported, between 1332 and 1399 public works at Bruges, including buildings, belfry, walls, bridges, sluices, canals and streets, accounted for 13.9 per cent of the city's expenses. This was not unusual for Flanders; between 1365 and 1376 the share of public works in municipal expenditure at Ghent was never lower than 10.05 per cent, and in 1367 it was 23.79 per cent.[84]

83. J.P. Sosson, *Les travaux publics de la ville de Bruges, XIVe–XVe siècles: Les matériaux les hommes* (Brussels, 1977).

84. Nicholas, 'Governance', 253.

FLEMISH CULTURE IN THE FOURTEENTH CENTURY

The Flemish church in the fourteenth century

The cities' problems with the church were compounded during the fourteenth century, when French-born popes ruled at Avignon rather than Rome. There were at least seven excommunications or interdicts, which went into effect automatically when Flanders fought the French king. Low Country bishops were extremely mobile. Robert of Geneva, who would become the antipope Clement VII, was bishop of Thérouanne, then of Cambrai between 1361 and 1371. The popes controlled the Flemish church by reserving nominations to themselves. During the Avignon period the southern bishoprics had 251 vacancies, of which only 46 were filled canonically. Of 66 archdeacons in the fourteenth century, roughly 40 were foreigners, particularly Italians and south Frenchmen. Reservation of prebends led to pluralism. Many holders, particularly those holding university degrees, were absentees.[85]

The older monastic orders and the Dominicans and Franciscans had little political influence after 1300, although they were more popular with the artisans than were the Benedictines. The lesser mendicant orders spread more rapidly in the fourteenth century. The guilds and religious confraternities often founded their chapels in mendicant convents.[86] The Beguines too were having problems, even though most Flemish Beguines were orthodox, cloistered and closely regulated and enjoyed the patronage of the Flemish counts.[87]

The problem of declining allegiance to the established church was of course not unique to the Low Countries, but even the formal side of religious exercise seems to have been minimal in Flanders. The procession of the Holy Blood was held annually on 3 May at Bruges. In 1310 Pope Clement V gave indulgences to penitents who attended it or visited the chapel of the Holy Blood.[88] Yet religious processions did not assume as much importance in Flanders as elsewhere until the fifteenth century. There were parish processions on Corpus Christi

85. Milis, 'Kerk', 207–8.
86. Simons, *Stad en apostolaat*, 228–9 for examples from Bruges and Ghent.
87. Johanna E. Ziegler, 'The *Curtis* Beguinages in the Southern Low Countries and Art Patronage: interpretation and historiography', *Bulletin de l'Institut Historique Belge de Rome* **57** (1987): 31–70; Simons, 'Beguine Movement', 98.
88. *IAB* **1**: 303.

Day, in which the guilds participated under their banners. The guilds themselves almost certainly had processions on the festival days of their patron saints, although evidence for this becomes clearer in the fifteenth century. By 1330 the small group of Yprois attending the university of Paris had a brotherhood encompassing both laymen and priests that provided an annual banquet, celebration of mass, participation in processions and financial help for poor students.[89]

Apart from the parish and guild festivities, Ghent had no religious processions, although a major expense incurred by the town each year was for uniforms for the magistrates who attended the procession of the Virgin at Tournai each 14 September. Particularly after 1360, Shrove Tuesday festivities became a major celebration everywhere and a concern to the magistrates who had to keep public order. Within a few months of the battle of Westrozebeke in 1382, a thanksgiving procession was made to the site on the third Sunday of each July by delegations from most Flemish communities except Ghent, which had no reason for gratitude on that occasion. Conceivably as early as the twelfth century, an annual procession was made to the village of Sint-Lievens-Houtem from St Bavo's abbey at Ghent, which housed St Lievin's relics. Although other church holidays, such as the Festival of Innocent Children and Epiphany, were also celebrated, they were minor affairs that have left few records.[90]

Although large cities, high unemployment, economic depression and an unresponsive church are virtually a textbook prescription for heresy, there is little evidence of it in Flanders, where the attitude seems to have been indifference rather than open hostility. There are occasional exceptions. In 1375 Ypres exiled Meulin Heertrecht for 'the spiteful, dishonest and unnatural words, blasphemies that he uttered about our lord Jesus Christ and the glorious blessed Virgin Mary'.[91] Yet we have noted the minimal evidence of heresy among the Flemish Beguines. Similarly, although the Flagellants and Dancers visited Flanders in periods of crisis, particularly the plague year of 1349, they originated in the Rhineland or the eastern Low Countries, moved through Flanders, picked up a few adherents in the major cities, then left. Tournai seems to have been their preferred pilgrimage site in the

89. Paul Trio, 'De Statuten van de laatmiddeleeuwse clericale O.L.V. Broederschap van de studenten van Parijs te Ieper', *BCRH* **148** (1982): 91–141.

90. David Nicholas, 'In the Pit of the Burgundian Theatre State: urban traditions and princely ambitions in Ghent, 1360–1420', in Barbara A. Hanawalt and Kathryn L. Reyerson (eds), *City and Spectacle in Medieval Europe* (Minneapolis, 1992).

91. De Pelsmaeker, *Registres*, 332.

western Low Countries. In mid-August 1349, 200 Flagellants came there from Bruges and a week later 450 from Ghent, led by two captains who had been aldermen the preceding year. In September separate groups from Damme, Bruges, Sluis, Deinze, Diksmuide, Oudenaarde and Eeklo went to Tournai. The town governments seem to have patronized the Flagellants at first, providing them with banners, wax candles and crosses. But the magistrates turned against the Flagellants after Pope Clement VI condemned them on 20 October 1349. The next outbreak of Flagellant activity in the Low Countries came in 1400 and affected mainly the Liège region.

The Dancers, who were probably a more extreme group of religious enthusiasts than the Flagellants, came to Ghent in 1374, but after continuous dancing through the streets they were banished by the aldermen. The bailiff of Ghent executed four women as heretics in 1374, and another two were acquitted of allegations of witchcraft in the 1370s; one of these cases seems to have been a slander by her sister-in-law.[92]

Church finances

Most Flemish churches recovered financial solvency to some degree in the fourteenth and fifteenth centuries, although much of this may simply be due to the decline of population relieving pressure on the churches' parish services. St Bavo's abbey had been heavily in debt in the late thirteenth century but centralized its finances in the early fourteenth, consolidating nine services with separate incomes into four, with all important expenses – food, wine and alms – centralized under the abbot. From 1351 the increasingly active almonry lost most of its possessions to the central service, which thus controlled about 95 per cent of the abbey's property. St Bavo's may have been unusual, for 33.1 per cent of the income of St Pieter's abbey was still independent of the abbot between 1432 and 1437. St Bavo's expenses and income were roughly balanced between 1356 and 1373, but thereafter papal taxation caused new problems.[93]

92. Paul Fredericq, *De secten der Geeselaars en der Dansers in de Nederlanden tijdens de 14de eeuw* (Brussels, 1896), 4–11, 32–49; Nicholas, *Domestic Life*, 21.

93. Erwin Pairon, 'De Financiën van de Sint-Baafsabdij in de 14e–15e eeuw', *HMGOG* **35** (1982): 61–79.

Lay culture in fourteenth-century Flanders

As the hold of the church on the population continued to weaken, Flanders' secular and largely lay culture was strengthened. Literacy in Latin was not widespread in Flanders. Most ordinary documents, such as for land transfers, were written in Flemish, even by the churches and abbeys, which used Latin only for papal or other formal records. Most urban aristocrats owned books such as bestiaries, histories and gospels. The abbeys, counts and cities had their own writing offices long before the fourteenth century, but then some lesser lords began issuing their own charters.[94]

The cities kept records during this period whose type would not change in the fifteenth century. The surviving records are composites, made from rough drafts that were entered on rolls or compiled into registers. Internal references show that written receipts as claims for reimbursement of expenses were kept and shown to the magistrates although little of this material has survived. The city, the churches and private citizens kept rent and account books and other types of commercial paper. The town and rural councils also kept written records of proceedings and litigation done before them and would register documents drafted by parties and brought to the magistrates for safekeeping. The destruction of the records of rural courts in the rebellion of 1379–85 caused considerable confusion, for property transfers had to be recorded at the place where the property was located, and most persons did not keep separate records of their own. The amount of material recorded with the magistrates thus grows tremendously after 1385, as property owners became more careful. The most important type of private act was the document attested by two landowners. Although they sometimes recorded their own acts with the magistrates, a transaction done under the seal of two 'landed men' was a binding contract, serving the function that the notarial register fulfilled in southern Europe. Although some notarial acts were used in Flanders, most are found in legal actions before church courts.

In view of the widespread evidence of literacy in the vernacular, it should occasion no surprise that primary schooling was available throughout Flanders. We know scarcely anything about the curriculum.

94. Thérèse de Hemptinne, 'Het Ontstaan van een lokaal scriptorium te Gent-brugge in het 2e kwart van de 14e eeuw', *HMGOG* **23** (1969): 3–12.

Although the churches tried to monopolize schools, we have seen that
this was a dead letter before 1300. Many children of Ghent, and not
just the wealthy, were sent to school. Persons of good family needed
to be bilingual, although the education of the lower orders was restricted to Flemish. Most references to children learning French have
them leaving Flanders for the purpose. For those who went to school,
it preceded apprenticeship in a trade. Girls also received an education
in schools as well as from private tutors in the home, although we are
not certain whether they attended the same schools as the boys. In
Diederic van Assenede's romance *Floris and Blanchefleur*, the queen,
hoping to keep Blanchefleur and Floris out of each other's way, advised the king to send the girl to school, so that she would forget
about love.[95]

In addition to government documents and commercial records,
there is some creative activity in the vernacular tongues, although the
quantity declines. The upper orders in the cities continued to prefer
French. Around 1351 Jean le Long of Ypres or St Bertin collected a
number of geographical treatises into a work entitled *Le Livre des
merveilles*. They may have been used from this collection by the author
of *Mandeville's Travels*.[96] In late 1382 Boudewijn van der Luere wrote
an allegorical poem, *De maghet van Ghend* (*The Maid of Ghent*), concerning the city's struggle with Louis of Male. It is included in a
manuscript of two other works by the same author: *Achte persone wen-
schen* (*Eight Persons Wish*) and *Dits tijtverlies* (*This Loss of Time*). There
are some traces of French literature in Ghent before the fifteenth century, notably Mathieu de Gand's seven *Chansons* and a poem by one
Pierre de Gand. A circle of poets developed at Bruges around the artist
Jan Moritoen and his friend Jan van Hulst. They wrote love songs of
high quality in various poetical forms. John de Weert, a physician of
Ypres, wrote *Nieuwe doctrinael*, a social commentary against corruption
and usury.[97]

There was considerable historical writing in the vernacular languages, although the best of it was not done in Flanders proper. We
have noted the Brabantine continuators of van Maerlant. An anonymous chronicler who evidently lived at Ghent wrote a fascinating

95. Nicholas, *Domestic Life*, 127–9; Louis de Baecker (ed.), *Chants historiques de la
Flandre, 400–1650* (Lille, 1855) 122.
96. J.R.J. Phillips, *The Medieval Expansion of Europe* (Oxford, 1988), 209.
97. Antonin van Elslander, 'Literature' in Decavele, *Ghent: In Defence*, 397–417; C.
Bruin, 'De Letterkunde in de Nederlandse volkstaal tot omstreeks 1384', *AGN* 3: 367–
8.

account of the struggles of the fourteenth century. By 1400 the *Chronicles* of the Hainault-based John Froissart, perhaps the most significant work of history as literature from the late medieval period, had been translated into Flemish by Gerijt Potter van der Loo.[98]

Historical writing in poetic form had a long tradition in Flanders. The war of 1379 received treatment in a very perceptive 'rhymed chronicle'. The anonymous author, probably a clerk in the count's chancery, was a partisan of Louis of Male and saw the source of the conflict in the pride of Ghent and particularly its grain staple, which the city was using to put an economic squeeze on the rest of Flanders. His account of the outbreak of the war is particularly detailed and accurate, focusing on the ambush of the Bruges workmen on the New Leie by the White Hoods of Ghent. Although he informed his readers that he was a 'Flemish Fleming', he wrote by choice in French and dedicated his chronicle to Duke Philip of Burgundy. The surviving version is a fragment that breaks off in June 1380, although the author's introduction mentions in anticipation events through 1384.[99]

The author opens with a panegyric on Louis of Male, who had tried to bring peace and concord to Flanders, but

> He could not render sentence,
> For whatever judgement he rendered
> Another would allege that it violated
> The content of its franchise.
> Everyone wanted to acquit
> Criminals of their misdeeds
> On the basis of the liberties of the city.
> This happened more than a thousand times,
> And especially in Ghent,
> Which led the way,
> Making sure that its burghers
> Having done one deed, or two, or three,
> Would reserve it to their judgement,
> And thus made sure
> That no one could do justice.
> If to fight this evil

---

98. Van Mierlo, *Letterkunde*, 284, 406.
99. Pirenne, *Chronique rimée*. Pirenne, who could imagine nothing more natural than the subjection of Flanders to its cities, thought the chronicle an atavism.

One or two or three were seized outside the town of their citizenship
For the crimes that they committed there,
When the Gentenars heard of it,
They would set out with an armed force.

The count thus transferred his operations to Bruges and permitted the
New Leie

To carry all goods to Bruges by boat,
From the side of France, both wine and grain,
Work was begun, and the trench was big.
When the Gentenars heard
That they would lose the good river
That they loved much and held dear [the author here puns on the economic
and emotional meanings of *chière* (dear)]
They screamed and cried like madmen.[100]

Although most modern historians have viewed Flanders in the fourteenth century from the standpoint of the cities, the countryside
generally supported the counts. Hostility towards Ghent ran high in
Flanders, and burghers were in some danger outside the city limits. In
1371 the magistrates of Ghent punished a man who admitted having
asked a burgess 'where he came from, and when he answered "from
Ghent", [he asked] "Are you a burgess there?" and I gave him a good
thrashing'.[101] A famous example of loyalty towards the counts, written
in Flemish from the perspective of the opponents of the rebels of
1323–8, is the *Kerelslied* (*Song of the Hick*):

We're going to sing of the *Kerels* [Hicks],
They're from bad stock;
They want to give orders to knights;
They wear long beards.
Their clothes are all in disarray,
A little hat is stuck on their heads
And it's on askew.
Their trousers and their shoes are in shreds.
Curds and whey, bread and cheese,
That's what the hick eats [poem switches to singular here] every day.
That's why the hick is such a beast,
He eats more than he can take.
A big hunk of rye bread

100. Translated from Pirenne, *Chronique rimée*, 9–10, 10–11.
101. Translated from SAG, Boek van den Blivene 1371–72, f. 3r.

Satisfies all his needs.
He holds it in his hand
As he goes off to plough.
Then his wife comes to him, the dirty cow,
Spinning with a distaff,
Her mug covered with oakum.
She's going to fix his porridge.
Curdled milk, etc. . . .

He carries a Zeeland knife
In his pouch.
He comes to his wife,
Completely foul, he brings his bottle.
Then she gives him many a dirty curse,
When the hick touches her.
Then he gives her a piece of his pastry,
And peace is made.
Curds and whey, etc.

Then comes the big piper,
And pipes him a turelurelure.
Lord, what a ruckus!
They all start jumping head over heels,
Then her long beard waits,
And they make more noise.
May God give him a bad end.
Curds and whey, etc.

The poem then concludes with a threat to hunt down the hicks and give them a proper lesson.[102]

Jousting and secular processions

The counts of Flanders and the nobles of northern France and Flanders were active in tournaments. They held regular jousts, but the Walloon cities were far more partial to tournaments than those of Flemish Flanders except for Bruges. A war erupted between Lille and Douai in 1284 out of a private quarrel at Douai's annual Festival of the Rose, when jousters of Lille and other towns were in Douai. Tournai had a jousting association of 'Thirty-One Kings', rich citizens who took the

---

102. Translated from de Baecker, *Chants historiques*, 174–6.

names of fictional kings. Citizens of fourteen other French and Flemish cities came to a tourney there in 1330, but the only large delegations from Flemish cities came from Lille and Bruges, and Ghent evidently did not attend at all. The festivals usually lasted one or two days, with feasts, dancing, processions and religious services. A leader was chosen for the festival, such as the King of the Espinette at Lille and the Forester of the White Bear at Bruges.[103]

The Flemish nobility by 1400 had in effect merged with the upper bourgeoisie. Part of this rapprochement took the form of growing interest in jousting in the cities. Although chroniclers mention splendid processions at the entries of such princes as Philip IV of France in 1300 and Edward III of England in 1340 at Ghent, Louis of Male seems to have been the first Flemish prince who consciously tried to win over the cities by holding celebrations in them. The government of Ghent itself incurred significant expenses for festivals between 1360 and 1367, but only when the count was in the city. By far the most important and expensive of these was the marriage of Philip the Bold to Margaret of Male in 1369. Philip the Bold himself sponsored tournaments in Ghent in the early 1370s, and the city also held some jousts. They were discontinued after the war of 1379–85 and resumed only in the fifteenth century.

All cities had festivities when the magistracy was rotated and the town taxes were 'cried' at public auction. The other major secular celebration was when a new count made his solemn entry. This was repeated as he peregrinated through Flanders. Each time he swore to uphold the traditions and privileges of the place in question. The tradition goes back at least to 1127, when Bruges held an entry for Thierry of Alsace. The entries before the Burgundian period, however, were minor affairs in comparison with what transpired beginning in 1384, when Philip the Bold made his Joyous Entry into Bruges and was installed as the new count in a solemn and by now traditional religious ceremony at the church of St Donatian.[104]

103. Desportes, *Reims et les Rémois*, 291, 643; Juliet Vale, *Edward III and Chivalry: Chivalric Society and its Context 1270–1350* (Woodbridge, 1982), 25–33.
104. James M. Murray, 'The Liturgy of the Count's Advent in Bruges from Galbert to the Van Eycks, in Hanawalt and Reyerson (eds), *City and Spectacle*.

The plastic arts

Flemish formal artistic styles showed little originality in the fourteenth century, although this would change under Burgundian patronage. Sculpture in the great churches was essentially traditional, but Flemish artists achieved considerable skill in funeral monuments. The de Meyere family of Ghent was known for both brass and stone grave work. Burghers increasingly followed the noble practice of having their graves adorned with coats of arms. Many monuments had a cover on which a statue of the deceased was placed. The men were in military regalia, the women in fashionable clothing. The funeral effigies of William Wenemaer (d. 1325) and his wife Margaret de Brune (d. 1352), who founded a hospital at Ghent bearing their name, are the outstanding examples of Ghent funerary sculpture.

Sculptures of the princes and of figures from mythology adorned the city streets. From 1371 the Hoofdbrug (Head Bridge, the site of judicial executions) of Ghent had a sculpture of a son whose father had to behead him but whose sword miraculously flew off its hilt. The city gates had sculptures of the Virgin, St Lievin, St George and St Christopher. The Great Meat Hall had images of Our Lady with the Inkpot and St John, while the guild halls usually had carvings of their patron saints.[105]

The interiors of the major public buildings had murals, although few survive. The most impressive known is a Last Supper of 1325–30 painted in the refectory of the Bijloke hospital at Ghent. There were paintings at St Bavo's abbey and several in the chapel of the weavers and the hospice of St James. The hospital of the 'Leugemeete' had a famous painting, now destroyed, depicting the guild militias of Ghent arrayed for battle under their banners in 1346. Descriptions survive of murals in the suburban church of Heilig Kerst, the shippers' chapel, various offices in both town halls, and the belfry.[106]

Most painters employed in Flanders before the Burgundian period came from modern northern France and western Belgium. Jan van der

105. Dhanens, 'Plastische kunsten', 283; Dhanens, 'Sculpture and Painting before 1800' in Decavele, *Ghent: In Defence*, 198–9, 206–7, 226; D. Roggen, 'Gentsche beeldhouwkunst der XIVe en der XVe eeuw', *Gentsche Bijdragen tot de Kunstgeschiedenis* **5** (1938): 51–73; G. Gepts-Buysaert, 'De Beeldhouwers', *Flandria Nostra* **2**: 73–146.

106. M.P.J. Martens, 'Enkele middeleeuwse muurschilderingen te Gent. I: Gegevens op basis van kopieën', *HMGOG* **39** (1985): 84–121; II: 'Gegevens op basis van documenten', 40 (1986): 47–84.

Asselt of Ghent worked in the mid fourteenth century on the chapels of the count at Ghent and at Courtrai. Jacob Broederlam, who made the famous sculpture of Philip the Bold for his grave at Dijon, did the rest of his work at Ypres, where he maintained a shop and apprentices. He was versatile: he made portraits, altars and banners. He painted the coat of arms of Burgundy, designed uniforms for the council of Ypres in 1406 and decorated a boat for the duke in 1378. Other notable figures include Jacob Cavael of Ypres and the Coene family of Bruges.[107]

Fourteenth-century architecture

The Flemish churches did not share in the growth of elaborate ornamental styles that characterized the rest of Europe in the late Middle Ages. The major architectural innovation was the construction of enormous towers, beginning around 1270 with the 124-metre high structure of Our Lady of Bruges. Even in the fifteenth century, Flanders was not a centre of 'artistic' building. Most important master architects who worked in Flanders were from Brabant.

The belfry was a symbol of municipal pride and independence. The belfry of Ghent, at a height of 96 metres and with walls 2.3 metres thick, is the most impressive. The architect was master Jan van Haelst, whose parchment sketch of the building from 1321 survives. The original was a free-standing structure with a rectangular tower, not linked to the cloth hall as it later became. Each storey had pointed-arch windows. Towers were added on the fourth storey and were adorned eventually with sculped guards, one of which survives. In the 1370s a weathervane was added with a legendary dragon on the top. Courtrai and Damme also had free-standing belfries.

Most Flemish domestic building was in stone or brick. Half-timbering became common only in the fifteenth century. The open hearth built into the wall was known, but there were problems of light since the narrow side of most houses faced the street and the back yards were used for outbuildings. The Low Countries were unusual in having the top storey in ledges that are reflected in public buildings on the roof instead of sloping roofs. The construction trades were important in the Flemish cities, which spent vast amounts on public works, but most of it was utilitarian.[108]

107. J.L. Broecks, 'De Schilders', *AGN* 2: 153–6.
108. This section is based on A.J. van de Walle, *Het Bouwbedrijf in de Lage Landen tijdens de Middeleeuwen* (Antwerp, 1959), 31, 48, 135, 187.

Medieval Flanders

In short, the fourteenth century was not a period of great creative activity in Flanders. The cities had dominated Flanders economically by 1200. By 1300 they also dominated it politically. The counts were too busy surviving, and the nobles too impecunious, to give much patronage to aspects of culture not connected to the martial arts. The counts and the cities did foster education in the vernacular, for all needed literate clerks who could keep accurate records. In the late fourteenth century they also needed trained lawyers. The Flemish church, however, was weak. On one level it was seen as a tool of the hated French. At another, so much of its income was spent providing assistance to the poor that little was left over for building or art. Except for the problem of the church, which continued unabated, all of these conditions were ameliorated in the fifteenth century.

CHAPTER TEN

Economic Depression and World Economy in Flanders, 1315-84

THE AGRARIAN SECTOR

The landscape

We have seen that land clearance slowed after 1250, but it did not stop completely. More abundant rainfall caused flooding; yet the streams linking Bruges and Ypres to the sea became a growing concern, although the problem may have been as much the increasing draught of the boats as the silting of the channels. Until the early fourteenth century, Damme was the chief outport of Bruges, but it was then supplemented by Munikerede, Hoeke and St Anna-ter-Muiden, which were nearer the sea, and especially by Sluis, which is first mentioned around 1300 and dominated the Zwin trade by 1330.[1]

The southeast continued to have the highest population density and the most intensive agriculture, while the northeast was notable for dairy farming and peat. The west was less developed. There were clear geographical differences within the Franc of Bruges. The dune areas were poor and subject to inundation. South of Bruges was a region of heath that in 1469 contained only about twenty villages, all poor and with a small population. The eastern part of the castellany of Ypres was sandy and wooded; the west was agricultural. This area had numerous large villages and small towns, notably the textile centres of

1. Pounds, *Historical Geography*, 424; Nicholas, *Town and Countryside*, 120–1.

Poperinge, Langemark and Warneton. The castellany of Bailleul had a generally prosperous agriculture, while Veurne, Bergues and Bour- bourg were plagued by flooding.[2]

Part of Flanders' problem was insufficient attention paid to con- servation of resources.[3] There was concern as early as the thirteenth century about denuding the forest cover, and there were some efforts at control and replanting. Damage to the dunes cost Flanders 1300 hectares of land between the Zwin and Nieuwpoort between 1309 and 1408. Most clearance during the fourteenth century occurred when bogs were drained to permit the digging of peat, which weakened the dikes; only in 1407 was it forbidden to destroy dune vegetation. The Flemish coast suffered severe flooding in 1334, and the Scheldt estuary was affected in 1342. The worst flood of the four- teenth century struck in 1375–6. Numerous parishes in the northeast, including some at IJzendike, Boekhoute and Biervliet, were sub- merged. There were more floods in 1394, and the St Elizabeth Day Flood of 19 November 1404 was a disaster.

The count was gradually assuming central authority over the pol- ders. He leased beaches at hereditary rent to persons who then were permitted to dike a polder or sublet to local landsmen. Some ten new polders were created immediately after the flood of 1375. Diking con- tinued along the coast, and the water associations were given broader powers. Still, the overall depression of Flemish agriculture, as native farmers were being consistently undersold by cheap grain imported by Ghent from France and by Bruges from the German Hanse, left owners of flooded land particularly vulnerable. Many owners let their lands go for back taxes, since they were not worth the tax payments.

These developments are illustrated by the village of Weert, on the Scheldt south of Antwerp, where St Bavo's abbey of Ghent and the van Artevelde family held large properties.[4] St Bavo's bought Weert, then an island in the river, in 1240, then diked and diverted the Scheldt westward, so that Weert came to lie on the east bank, in Brabant rather than Flanders. Weert then suffered considerable damage from the floods of 1334, but the abbey responded quickly and had diked new land by 1342.

2. Summary in J. Toussaert, *Le Sentiment religieux en Flandre à la fin du Moyen Age* (Paris, 1960), 24–9.

3. This overview is based on J. Mertens, 'Landschap en geografie in het Zuiden 1300–1480', *AGN* 2: 40–7.

4. Discussion is based on D. Nicholas, 'Weert: A Scheldt Polder Village in the Fourteenth Century', *JMH* 2 (1976): 239–68.

Jacob van Artevelde had land in both Weert and in neighbouring Bornem. When he diked some land beyond the abbey's at Weert, the property of some of St Bavo's tenants was flooded, and one of them was implicated in the murder of Jacob van Artevelde the younger in 1370. The individual properties had small dikes that were linked to the main dike of the polder. Yet, although the population of Weert grew 43 per cent between 1353 and 1365, the total land cultivated expanded by only one-half of a hectare. The economy of Weert was based on small-scale agriculture, particularly oats, and some fowl and sheep. Peat was dug in the village at some point. There was more flooding in the late 1360s, and by 1371 the number of resident tenants had declined sharply. The next year the abbey complained of poverty and dilapidation at Weert. The floods of 1375 were a catastrophe. Between 1371 and 1395 the number of holdings had declined by nearly one-third. The flooding thus made it impossible for the abbey and other lords interested in the area to continue reclaiming new land.

The farm economy

The great monasteries had overextended their resources in the thirteenth century and were retrenching. St Pieter's abbey of Ghent, for example, had severe debts by 1250 and had to sell domain lands. Typical of its problem, St Pieter's took some beaches in ground rent from the countess; then, lacking money to dike them, it gave them to three Gentenars in ground rent on condition that *they* dike them. St Pieter's changed to indirect exploitation of its domains in the second half of the thirteenth century, usually at term leasehold. The abbey leased individual farms, mills, tithes, and judicial rights as well as land in the second half of the thirteenth century.[5]

By 1267 St Pieter's had to sell life annuities. The sources make the reasons for the crisis clear: gifts stopped, the abbey kept buying land even when it was in debt, its rights were being usurped by bailiffs, other laity and clergy, and it sold too many life rents. In 1281 the bishop of Tournai reorganized St Pieter's finances, but the abbey had new problems when papal taxation became severe around 1285. By

5. Discussion based on Walter Braeckman, 'De Moeilijkheden van de Benedictijnerabdijen in de late middeleeuwen: De Sint-Pietersabdij te Gent (*ca.* 1150–1281)', HMGOG **17** (1963): 37–103.

the fourteenth century St Pieter's had loans with professional financiers and was still heavily in debt as late as 1319.

The movement towards term leasehold during the fourteenth century was accelerated by the rampant inflation, which diminished the value of hereditary ground rents. Owners leased large properties for a substantial sum, often to a local noble or burgher, who acted as an absentee landlord, collected the ground rents and payments in kind owed by the tenants and pocketed whatever he collected above this. The terms were most often for nine years or some other multiple of three, suggesting a three-course rotation as the norm on large estates; this is not true of smaller properties, where the reduction of the fallow in favour of fodder crops shows a considerably greater resilience and response to market conditions. Most contracts specified what crops would be sown in specific fields during particular years, especially the last three years of the lease. Some lords provided equipment for their tenants.[6]

Although the abbeys generally converted to term leaseholds, most lesser landowners continued to exploit their own estates directly into the last quarter of the fourteenth century, and some great lords, particularly hospitals, did so.[7] Most abbeys tried to diversify their holdings. An account of the Cistercian abbey of Ter Doest in the Franc of Bruges for 1315 gives information about nine estates, five of them largely agricultural, three mixed but emphasizing animals, particularly sheep, while the ninth emphasized wood products. Four realized substantial profits from fishing.[8]

Techniques and crops: a pattern of diversification

Flemish agriculture became more advanced technically and developed higher per capita productivity during the fourteenth century, although it was still behind northern France. The light scratch plough, which was suited to the sandy soil, replaced the heavy plough used earlier. The sickle was gradually replaced by the pruning hook and the scythe for harvesting. The shape of the scythe permitted the harvester to cut

6. Nicholas, *Town and Countryside*, 296–7; J. Mertens, *De laat-middeleeuwse landbouweconomie in enkele gemeenten van het Brugse platteland* (Brussels, 1970), 53–5.

7. A. Verhulst, 'Bronnen en problemen betreffende de Vlaamse landbouw in de late Middeleeuwen (XIIIe–XVe eeuw)', *Ceres en Clio, zeven variaties op het thema landbouwgeschiedenis* (Wageningen, 1964), 208–11.

8. C. Dekker and J.G. Kruisheer, 'Een Rekening van de abdij ter Doest over het jaar 1315', *BCRH* **133** (1967): 273–305.

and to shape the sheaves for binding simultaneously; it could also cut closer to the ground, which meant that no second operation was necessary to get the straw.[9]

Red cabbage may have originated in Flanders. Particularly after the Black Death, low prices on local grain in Flanders caused farmers to plant more land in peas and beans, particularly on the peripheries of estates, although this becomes much clearer in the fifteenth century. The demand for meat, butter, cheese and wine was increasing in relation to grains in the fourteenth and fifteenth centuries, and prices on these goods rose. Hops also spread rapidly, especially in the Dender valley. There are signs of a rapid increase of native brewing in the cities after 1360 that may be connected with a revival of native hop culture. Particularly near the cities, fodder crops, reflecting the intensive animal husbandry on burgher-owned estates, replaced the fallow. Grass was sometimes sown alternately with food crops, usually in rotations of three to six years.[10]

Cultivation of industrial crops, particularly dyes, to replace the fallow continued to spread. Flax was introduced in the late Middle Ages around Tielt, Ghent and in the land of Aalst. Woad and madder were grown around Aalst and the vicinity of Oudenaarde and Flemish Zeeland. Madder, from which the Flemish red *scharlaken* textile was made, is found at the end of the twelfth century in the polders between Ostend and Bruges, and by 1300 it occupied as much as 15 per cent of the area of some small farms.[11]

The agricultural depression of the late Middle Ages

It is often difficult to determine whether the depression of Flemish agriculture was due to technological failure or to circumstances beyond the farmers' control, particularly war. Evidence is unclear for the impact of the revolt of maritime Flanders on farm output, but the 'Ghent War' was the worst disaster of the fourteenth century for Flemish agriculture. The tithe incomes of St Pieter's at Ghent, which were geared to farm production, declined more than 50 per cent, the lease incomes

9. Verhulst, *Précis*, 128–9; H. van der Wee, 'De doorbreking van de middeleeuwse landbouweconomie in West-Europa (14e–16e eeuw)' in *Historische aspecten van de economische groei* (Antwerp, 1972), 31.

10. Verhulst, 'Bronnen en problemen', 214–18; Mertens, 'Landbouwers', 112–13; van Houtte, *Economic History*, 68, 70; Verhulst, *Précis*, 122–3; Nicholas, *Metamorphosis*, 262–4; van der Wee, 'De Doorbreking,' 25–6.

11. Verhulst, *Précis*, 119–21.

50–70 per cent. Leasehold terms were lengthened, ground rents remitted and loans granted simply to retain tenants and keep the land in production. Land prices fell by about one-third between 1375 and 1384 in the castellanies of Oudenaarde and Aalst. Prices and rents of the same land seem to be parallel until about 1400, then diverge, with prices stagnating as rents rose. By 1410 the crisis in the east was over, although some smaller landowners had to sell to larger operators.[12]

The dense populations of eastern Flanders were fed mainly on grain imported through Ghent from France. Maritime Flanders was by now primarily a grain producer, although a substantial pastoral element persisted, but local agriculture could not feed the cities. Bruges got some grain through Ghent's staple, and it imported grain from the Mediterranean to meet the crisis of 1315–16, but this was unusual. In the late fourteenth century there is increasing evidence of grain imported from the German east.

Prices on native Flemish grain were low except during periods of scarcity and interruption of foreign supply. The severe inflation of the fourteenth century makes it difficult to use series of nominal grain prices. Wheat prices rose by one-third at Bruges between the 1370s and 1460s, but the Flemish silver penny in 1470 had one-third of its value of 1360, so that the real value of wheat declined by about two-fifths. The low prices benefited city dwellers at the expense of farmers. Grain prices began to decline significantly in the last quarter of the fourteenth century, when some estates in the Franc of Bruges began to experience severe difficulties for the first time. The two estates that St John's hospital of Bruges still exploited directly in 1400 were regularly losing money.[13]

Erik Thoen's case study of the agrarian economy of the castellanies of Oudenaarde and Aalst shows that lease rates, tithes and seigneurial rights were all high after 1270, probably reflecting land hunger as population reached its maximum for the medieval period. Term leases spread, and rents were regularly raised at the end of the term. The reserves became smaller and lease terms shorter. The count had a virtual monopoly of seigneurial justice.

12. Erik Thoen, *Landbouwekonomie en bevolking in Vlaanderen gedurende de late Middeleeuwen en het begin van de Moderne Tijden. Testregio: De Kasselrijen van Oudenaarde en Aalst (eind 13de-eerste helft 16de eeuw)*, 2 vols (Ghent, 1988), 2: 882, 885; Verhulst, 'Bronnen en problemen', 222–3; D. Nicholas, 'Economic Reorientation and Social Change in Fourteenth-Century Flanders', *Past and Present* **70** (1976): 23–4.

13. Verhulst, 'Bronnen en problemen', 229–33; Mertens, *Landbouweconomie*, 50; van Houtte, *Economic History*, 67.

Most of these trends continued from 1310 to 1330–5 except for a slight decline of lease rates. From this time until the 1360s, money leases and rents did not keep pace with a great increase in the cost of living, and landlords thus were in difficulties, perhaps also faced with less demand for land after the onset of the plagues. Lease terms were lengthened, another sign of a buyer's market. Between 1360 and the 'Ghent War', leases gradually rose and came into closer correspondence with the cost of living. Individual parcels of estates were more often leased and for shorter terms. Lease rates declined severely during the war of 1379–85, then gradually recovered. Around 1400 most leases were at their pre-war level and continued upward, while grain prices continued a decline that had been perceptible since 1370. The pressure from the count became worse. Fines and taxes were high but still declined after 1394.[14]

The plagues in Flanders

The precarious equilibrium between food production and population was undermined by war, plague and famine. There has been a long controversy over the impact in Flanders of the great plagues of the fourteenth century, particularly the Black Death of 1348–9. The Walloon areas and Ypres were struck severely, but Hans van Werveke argued, essentially from the silence of the sources, that Ghent, Bruges and the northern coastal regions were spared. The Ghent municipal accounts do not survive from the plague years, which were also a period of political revolution. When they resume, they suggest but do not prove conclusively a decline of economic productivity that may be connected to a population loss. The classic signs of the plague – the appearance of Flagellants in 1349, high prices in 1349–50 and low prices perhaps conditioned by overproduction in 1350–1 – are present at Ghent.[15]

Van Werveke's views were challenged immediately, but the challenges have become the dominant opinion only since his death. The plague at Bruges, evidently brought by seamen, was raging before 15

14. Thoen, *Landbouwekonomie*, 1: 643–5 for a summary of data and arguments.
15. Hans van Werveke, *De Zwarte Dood in de Zuidelijke Nederlanden*, MKVA, Kl. Letteren, 12, No. 3 (Brussels, 1950); Paul Rogghé, 'De Zwarte Dood in de zuidelijke Nederlanden', a review of van Werveke's pamphlet, *RBPH* 30 (1952): 834–7; W. Blockmans, 'The Social and Economic Effects of Plague in the Low Countries 1349–1500', *RBPH* 60 (1982): 860–1; Nicholas, 'Economic Reorientation', 18; Nicholas, *Metamorphosis*, 24, 290.

August 1349, when the count authorized two new cemeteries. A charter of 30 September 1350 from the chapter of St Donatian of Bruges notes that 'the tithes of our aforesaid church are worth less than normal at farm, both because of the extremely high mortality that was raging as well as the discomfitures of wars and even storms'.[16] Nine of the thirteen staff members of the Potterie hospital died between 12 July and 17 December 1349. The medical costs of St Jan's hospital were quadruple the norm in 1349–50. Dr Marechal has concluded, rather conservatively, that at least 10 per cent of the population of Bruges died during the plague months of 1349.[17]

On balance, Flanders may have lost one-quarter to one-sixth of its population during the plague of 1349, which is less severe than most other areas.[18] Flanders was also unusual in suffering more seriously from the later plagues than from that of 1349. There were epidemics in 1358–60, 1368–71, 1374–5, 1400 and 1438. The worst were 1368–71 and 1438.

The plagues of the 1360s have been subjected to statistical analysis. The number of new wardships for orphans established at Ghent during 1360–1 was double the annual average for 1353–8, while the number for 1368–9 was an increase of 245 per cent over the annual average for 1363–7. The number of decedents' estates settled annually averaged 171 between 1350 and 1359, 424 in 1360–1, 187 between 1362 and 1367, 579 in 1368–9 and 293 between 1370–2. The figures after 1361 are the more arresting because they are a larger percentage of a population that had already declined substantially. When Gentenars later spoke of 'the plague', they meant that of 1368–9, not that of 1349.[19]

Despite the losses earlier, references to untenanted farmland commence only after the plague of 1368–9 and become numerous only in the 1380s, when warfare and migration from devastated farms into the cities complicates our economic analysis. Flanders was so densely populated that the losses were never severe enough to cause village desertions there, in striking contrast to what happened in England, Germany and France. The few deserted villages attested in Flanders resulted from coastal flooding, not depopulation from the plagues.[20]

16. Archive of the Bishopric of Bruges, *Acta Capitularia Sancti Donatiani*, Vol. A (1345–69), cited Nicholas, 'Economic Reorientation', 18.

17. Van Werveke, *Zwarte Dood*, 10; Griet Marechal, 'De Zwarte Dood te Brugge, 1349–1351', *BK* **80** (1980), 377–92.

18. This figure is suggested by Verhulst, *Précis*, 91.

19. Blockmans, 'Plague', 839–40; Nicholas, *Metamorphosis*, 24–5, 38–9.

20. Nicholas, 'Economic Reorientation', 23; A. Verhulst, 'L'Economie rurale de la Flandre et la dépression économique du bas Moyen-Age', *Etudes Rurales* **10** (1963): 68–80; Verhulst, 'Bronnen en problemen', 219–20.

The rural population of Flanders

The first survey that has been used to reconstruct total population in
Flanders dates from 1469, but less comprehensive fourteenth-century
sources, mainly estate inventories and confiscation records, show that
Flanders was the most densely populated part of the Low Countries.

Land units were largest on the coast, where a small farm contained
about 5 hectares, the area of a middle sized farm in the interior. The
great domains, which were usually leased, were in the 30–50 hectare
range, although parcels were smaller in the less recently cleared parts of
the northern coast. Most of the wealth of the Franc of Bruges seems
to have been in the small towns, rather than the rural areas; 3.47 times
as much monetary value was seized in the small towns as in the villages after 1382.[21] In the vicinity of Courtrai in 1382, four-fifths of
the farmers whose property was confiscated held under 5 hectares;
many of them supplemented their income with cloth making. On the
lordship of Herzele, in the land of Aalst, one-third of the tenants
around 1390 held 0.6 hectares or less, and half held less than 1.2 hectares. Closer to Ghent, most farmers had between 2 and 3 hectares.
Farther north, in areas that had been cleared only in the thirteenth
century, most contained between 5-10 hectares. The large estates that
were leased to entrepreneurs usually contained between 15 and 30
hectares.[22]

The comital estate of Deinze-Drongen, near Ghent, confirms these
suggestions. Farms there were very small in the fourteenth century and
became even smaller in the fifteenth. Most farmers obviously had to
have a second occupation. But there was also concentration, for much
more land was being given out in large parcels at term leasehold after
the late fourteenth century; as tenancies were left without direct heirs
in the wake of the plagues, lords could convert and consolidate. This
change is shown also in the fact that while plots of arable land were
becoming smaller in the late fourteenth and fifteenth centuries, pasture

21. J. de Smet, 'De Verbeurdverklaringen in het Brugse Vrije en in de smalle steden
aldaar na de slag bij Westrozebeke (1382–1384)', *ASEB* **95** (1958): 115. The Transport
assessment also suggests greater wealth in the small towns, but not to this extent. Nicholas, *Town and Countryside*, 156.
22. Mertens, 'Landbouwers', 107–9; Etienne Sabbe, 'Grondbezit en landbouw,
economische en sociale toestanden in de kastelenij Kortrijk op het einde der XIVe
eeuw', *Handelingen van de Koninklijken Geschied-en Oudheidkundige Kring van Kortrijk*, n.s.
15 (1936), 394–458; Thoen, *Landbouwekonomie*, 2: 849.

shows the opposite tendency, resulting from the growing demand for meat in the towns.[23]

The smallholders essentially farmed for subsistence; fluctuations in grain prices and wages affected mainly the big estates that produced for the market. Especially from the 1360s, when grain prices declined while wages rose, the smallholders sustained losses, some of which were catastrophic by century's end. But middle-sized property owners were the great sufferers from the agrarian crisis. They held composite properties including lands held at term leasehold on which rents could be raised, but they also had to hire labour, and wages rose in the late fourteenth century. They were also oriented toward the market, as the smallest farmers were not, and thus were dependent on grain prices, which were stagnating.[24]

Poverty, prosperity and the standard of living

Historians have spent considerable time in recent years discussing living standards in late medieval Europe. Wages were generally rising in the Flemish cities through to about 1375, stagnating or declining thereafter. The price rise continued until the Burgundian period, then was succeeded by deflation. Although wage increases were often granted, they followed the price rise that had occasioned them – grain prices might fluctuate as much as 25 per cent between years – and thus were inadequate. Nominal wages rose in the second half of the fourteenth century and stagnated during the fifteenth. In terms of real wages expressed in grain prices, both of which were much higher in the cities than the rural areas, this meant a slight elevation to 1400, then a drop to 1439. Furthermore, short-term fluctuations in wages contributed to disorders. At Ghent, the wages of master carpenters in the 1380s were nearly the same as in the 1320s, but there were important short-term variations; between 1350 and 1359, for example, their wages declined 57 per cent, then rose 43 per cent between 1363 and 1377. Furthermore, even a rise in real wages does not automatically translate into a higher standard of living, which would re-

23. Eddy van Cauwenberghe, 'Bijdrage tot de financieel–economische evolutie van een vorstelijk domein in Vlaanderen: Deinze-Drongen (XIVe–XVIIe eeuw)', *ASEB* **207** (1970): 250–68; Herman van der Wee and Eddy van Cauwenberghe, 'Histoire agraire et finances publiques en Flandre du XIV au XVIIe siècle', *AESC* **28** (1973): 1051–65.

24. Verhulst, *Précis*, 117; Thoen, *Landbouwekonomie*, 2: 841–3.

quire continuous employment. Professional stature thus also had a great deal to do with how well one lived; for not only were master artisans paid considerably more than apprentices, journeymen and unskilled labourers, they were more likely than others to be employed continuously.[25]

Methodological problems aside, there can be no doubt that poverty was a serious and growing problem in fourteenth-century Flanders. Unfortunately, there is no workable definition of 'poor'. The church usually used 'poor' to refer only to widows, orphans, the sick, elderly and invalids, who were mentioned in that light in the Bible. By the thirteenth century, a 'working poor' had been created by rising prices and the irregularity of employment, but the church definition did not extend to them. Construction workers were very vulnerable in this respect; for although they got high wages when they worked, they were rarely continuously employed. Furthermore, the numerous festival days and Sundays meant that even a continuously employed artisan worked only 220–240 days per year.

Furthermore, poverty was not always a reflection of market considerations. Food supply and prices were regulated more stringently in the large towns than in the small. All cities prohibited the export of grain until local needs had been met. Ypres had price schedules for beer, butter, cheese, meat and fish. Bakers everywhere were subjected to minute regulations regarding size, weight and types of bread. Such measures in effect provided food for city dwellers at less than its market value. The magistrates of Bruges, but apparently not of other cities, often gave confiscated clothing, shoes and other goods to the poor.[26] In addition, the strong consciousness of family in Flanders meant that families were thought to have an obligation to care for their poorer members, and this deflates the incidence of 'public' poor relief. The cities had orphanages for children whose relatives were unable to care for them, but the number of residents was extremely small. We thus cannot extrapolate from wage and price figures to determine the statistical incidence of poverty.

The city records show little consciousness of economic poverty as a problem before the guild revolutions of 1302. Although the Flemish guilds were more concerned with quality and quantity of production than with charity, six guilds of Ghent maintained almshouses for poor members by 1373, beginning with the weavers in 1302 and the fullers

25. Theon, *Landbouweconomie*, 2: 949–51; Nicholas, *Metamorphosis*, 132; Sosson, *Travaux*, 227; Prevenier et al., 'Tussen crisis en welvaart', 74.
26. Demey, 'Handarbeiders', 206, 232; *IAB* 2: 346.

in 1304. The Weavers' Hall housed only a small number of prebendaries (sixteen in 1375, twenty-six in 1444), and we have no basis on
which to estimate the number of persons who received meals but did
not live there. The Bruges guilds took on this function later; apart
from hospices for incapacitated weavers and smiths in 1346 and 1376,
all were founded after 1415. Some guilds lacked the resources to
maintain a separate house, but they still supported needy guild members.[27]

There was also a considerable growth in private charity, as wealthy
persons established endowments to feed the poor on the anniversaries
of their deaths. Numerous small foundations with tiny endowments
and 'poor tables' also cared for a few indigent people. Daniel Coude-
kueken founded twenty-seven poor tables at Bruges between 1360 and
1374. The table masters were chosen from the people of the parish
and were unpaid. In the fifteenth century the tables took on more
features of the hospices, with rooms or small houses. The focus of
charity in these places in the fourteenth century was on distributing
food and clothing.[28]

'Holy Ghost Tables' in the urban parishes also had endowments
that permitted them to provide poor relief. We do not know the
criteria used for eligibility to receive assistance, but small lead tokens
that could be exchanged for food were distributed to the needy in
some parishes of Bruges, Ghent, Courtrai and Ypres.[29] Little else is
known of the administration of the charities. In 1337 separate foundations were established in the hospice of the Holy Spirit at Ypres for
widowers and widows, which in the fifteenth century housed thirteen
and twenty-three persons respectively.[30]

The best figures for estimating the incidence of poverty at Ghent
are the Holy Ghost records of St Nicholas, a rich parish in the central
city.[31] The Holy Ghost bought shoes, grain and pork and distributed
them to the poor. Purchases were all high through the 1330s, then
decline in the 1340s. The records break after 1348, but when they

27. G. Marechal, *De sociale en politieke gebondenheid van het Brugse hospitaalwezen in de Middeleeuwen* (Standen en Landen 73) (Kortrijk-Heule, 1978), 296.

28. Marechal, *Brugse hospitaalwezen*, 296–8; Ghislaine de Messemaeker-de Wilde, 'De Parochale armenzorg te Gent in de late middeleeuwen', *AH* 18 (1980): 52.

29. William J. Courtenay, 'Token Coinage and the Administration of Poor Relief during the Late Middle Ages', *Journal of Interdisciplinary History* 3 (1972–3): 281–2; *IAB* 3: 309.

30. O. Mus, 'Rijkdom en armoede: Zeven eeuwen leven en werken te Ieper' in *Prisma*, 13.

31. Basic to this section are the data and analysis of Nicholas, *Metamorphosis*, 41–66.

resume in 1360 they show a dramatic decline in all commodities, particularly for shoes. There is some rise in the 1360s, followed by a new decline in the 1370s in the number of shoes purchased but a rise in the amount of grain and the number of pigs. The conclusion is inescapable that the parish was feeding and clothing fewer poor than before 1350 but was making better per capita provision for them. Based on the shoe purchases, St Nicholas was assisting about 230 poor persons in 1317–27, 442 in 1327–41, 190 in 1360–67, 174 in 1368–71, 121 in 1372–4 and 73 in the late 1390s.

Some of the accounts of the 1360s and 1370s distinguish between 'ordinary' shoes and those of women and children; these figures suggest that the hard-core poor were mainly but not exclusively women, for the number of children was only slightly larger than the number of adult males. The St Nicholas figures can be supplemented by several anniversary donations in other parishes to derive a total of no more than 1000 persons, out of a total population of about 35,000 in 1370, who were poor enough to receive parish assistance. This figure finds some confirmation in the fact that beginning in 1390 the almonry of St Bavo's abbey distributed one mite apiece to 1272 poor persons.[32] This is a rate of about 3 per cent, and of course it is entirely too low. It does not account for the poor whose families helped them, nor the dependants of the guild halls or orphanages.[33]

There are several reasons for the evident decline of the number of persons on parish poor relief in the late 1360s and 1370s. A combination of rising real wages and declining population meant that fewer persons would need assistance. More importantly, the guild halls and other hospices were assisting numerous persons. Between 1357 and 1390 the government of Ghent gave donations of peat bricks for fuel to thirty-two foundations. The city government of Bruges also bought

---

32. Erwin Pairon, 'De Financiën van de Sint-Baafsabdij in de 14e-15e eeuw', *HMGOG* **35** (1982): 67.

33. However, I must vigorously dissent from the conclusions of scholars who assume that each pair of shoes distributed by the parish organizations represented one impoverished person and who thus derive poverty rates that are two to three times this high. Considerable evidence from the mid fourteenth century in Ghent suggests that for persons not on relief, three pairs of shoes yearly – they did not have soles – were an absolute minimum, so we should assume no fewer than two pairs for those who were aided by the parishes. W.P. Blockmans and W. Prevenier, 'Armoede in de Nederlanden van de 14e tot het midden van de 16e eeuw: Bronnen en problemen', *TG* **88** (1975): 501–38; de Messemaeker-de Wilde, 'Parochale armenzorg', 53; for the evidence about shoe numbers, see Nicholas, *Metamorphosis*, 52 and accompanying notes.

grain and peat for the poor foundations.[34] The war emergency, however, stifled the magistrates' desire to provide for the unfortunate. After 1385 peat shipments were resumed at Ghent only for the halls of the weavers, fullers and shippers, the three largest guilds in the city.

The hospitals

The increased consciousness of poverty in the fourteenth century and perhaps its increased incidence are reflected in the continued activity of the hospitals, growth in their endowments and heightened parish activity in their support.

The hospitals of Bruges have been the most thoroughly studied. The sick of Bruges went mainly to the hospital of St John, which had neither property nor residence requirements. Patients who inherited property while in the hospital were expected to give it to the foundation or pay for their care when they left. St John did not take people whose condition was incurable, such as the blind or insane or others who were thought dangerous to others, for example lepers, for whom separate foundations were provided. St John had 75-85 beds, some of which were evidently occupied by more than one person. The Potterie, which served mainly long-term patients and the terminally ill, had half to one-third the capacity of St John.[35]

The larger hospitals were established before 1300. In the fourteenth century no new institutions were founded that provided full support, as the older ones did; instead, many small foundations with specialized functions were established. Insane asylums were established at both Ghent and Bruges in the 1390s, the former by private charity, the latter by the city government. Only those who were considered dangerous were confined; the mentally retarded continued to live in the community and occasionally established families. Private charity also established a hospital for the blind at Ghent, which also had several abbey hospitals, the Alins and Wenemaer hospitals for prebendaries only, the hospice of St James for travellers, and the Filgedieusen for reformed prostitutes.[36]

34. Marechal, *Brugse hospitaalwezen*, 298–9. By the fifteenth century thirty-four institutions provided poor relief in Ghent. A.M. de Vocht, 'Het Gentse antwoord op de armoede: De sociale instellingen van wevers en volders in de late middeleeuwen' *AH* **19** (1981): 11.

35. G. Maréchal, 'Het Sint-Janshospitaal in de eerste eeuwen van zijn bestaan' in *800 Jaar Sint-Janshospitaal te Brugge* (Bruges, 1976): 41–75; Marechal, *Brugse hospitaalwezen*, 220–37.

36. Marechal, *Brugse hospitaalwezen*, 239–40, 291–2; Nicholas, *Metamorphosis*, 42.

Most fourteenth-century foundations were small, especially those catering to transients, all of which were lay founded and endowed. Bruges could probably accommodate about 200 poor persons in these places – food and lodging were given for only a single night – and they were exclusively for the poor. When the inns for paying customers are added, Bruges clearly had the capacity to support a large transient population.

Prebendaries were poor persons who were supported by the foundation and those who bought prebends by surrendering all their property or at least use of it to the foundation in return for life support. The hospital got property for its endowment, and the buyers got security. There was no distinction in principle between prebendaries and personnel. Since they had more people wanting to buy than prebends available, the hospitals tended to give them to the richest.

The aldermen oversaw the hospitals, appointing masters and approving statutes, but the church tried to limit the powers of lay authorities. In law the prebendaries were laypeople, but they lived under vows of poverty, chastity and obedience. The main area of contention was the parish. Unless hospitals had a separate parish – three of the Bruges hospitals did, but not the Ghent foundations – the sick had to ask the local parish to establish chapels for them, and the church insisted on controlling appointments of pastors. By the fourteenth century the bishop of Thérouanne often used his right to grant a chapel or chaplain as a legal foothold to extend his control over the entire hospital, but even in these cases the aldermen controlled the temporal goods of the foundation.[37]

THE FLEMISH TEXTILE INDUSTRY IN THE FOURTEENTH CENTURY: COMPETITION AND RETRENCHMENT

The increased incidence of poverty is tied to the broader reorientation of the Flemish economy away from its dependence on producing luxury textiles for an export market and towards locally based merchandising and manufacture. There is both a rural and an urban component to that reorientation.

37. Marechal, 'Sint Janshospitaal', 56–7; Marechal, *Brugse hospitaalwezen*, 248–60, 179–87, 158–69.

The problems that we have noted in the thirteenth century escalated into a serious crisis in the fourteenth. Flanders was beginning to have competition from other parts of the Low Countries, particularly Brabant. The overland routes opened in the twelfth century gave Brabant better access than Flanders to the Rhineland market. Indeed, Brussels became a major centre of reconsignment for cloth of Ghent en route to French and German markets. Cloth from Brabant was preferred to Flemish at the French royal court, perhaps for political as well as economic reasons.[38]

Although the burghers of the great cities bought large amounts of rural land, there is so little evidence of them owning sheep in the fourteenth century that it was clearly exceptional; there is astonishingly little evidence of wool in the post-rebellion confiscations.[39] Despite the high quality of the native product, the Flemings continued to rely on English wool. English exports remained substantial until the outbreak of the Hundred Years War. They were low in times of civil disorder in Flanders, but the rulers' political sparring, which led to confiscations and detainments, do not seem to have diminished the volume of wool exports seriously. The high taxes on wool, which had risen to an average of 40 per cent of the wholesale price from the 1330s, were more important for the Flemings. When freight was added, then more customs after 1363 at the staple at Calais, English wool cost Flemish customers more than twice what it cost English clothiers. English wool accounted for 65–75 per cent of the price of the finished Flemish textile and aside from dyes was the only luxury item it contained. Furthermore, as wool exports declined, English cloth exports rose from 5000 pieces annually around 1350 to 80,000 in 1500 and cut seriously into the Flemish market.[40]

Finally, the organization of the Flemish textile trade was changing after the guild revolutions of 1302. We have noted the appearance in the second half of the thirteenth century of 'drapers' as a sort of middle stage between patrician and industrial artisan. The

38. Henri Laurent, *Un Grand commerce d'exportation au Moyen Age: La draperie des Pays-Bas en France et dans les pays mediterranéens (XIIe–XVe siècle)* (Paris, 1935), 164, 186; Nicholas, *Metamorphosis*, 191; Pounds, *Historical Geography*, 389.

39. Verhulst, 'Laine indigène', 304–8, 310, 318, 321.

40. Lloyd, *Wool Trade*, 126; Munro, 'Monetary Contraction and Industrial Change', 110; van Houtte, *Economic History*, 81. See also E.B. Fryde, 'The Financial Resources of Edward III in the Netherlands', Part II, *RBPH* **45** (1967): 1151. On the costly dyes, particularly kermes, see J.H. Munro, 'The Medieval Scarlet and the Economics of Sartorial Splendour' in N.B. Harte and K.G. Ponting (eds), *Cloth and Clothing in Medieval Europe. Essays in Memory of Professor E. M. Carus-Wilson* (N.P., 1983): 13–69.

weaver/drapers, who produced most Flemish cloth, were not merchants, who organized production. The drapers rented stalls in one of the local cloth halls and sold cloth both of their own manufacture and that made by others. The patrician of the thirteenth century had been both a merchant and an entrepreneur who was active at all stages of the cloth making process. But during the fourteenth century, the role of the merchant entrepreneur in Flanders was virtually taken over by foreigners.

The drapers at Ypres were considerably more modest figures than at Ghent and Bruges. Although the monopoly of the Hanse of London on wool supplies to Ypres was broken after 1289, at some point before 1363 only those drapers who had personally brought their wool from England or Scotland could sell it at the Ypres cloth staple. The drapers thus sank back into a weaver group in the second half of the fourteenth century, though they could give the wool to other weavers, spinners and fullers and were responsible for their work. The drapers had competition from the *upzetters* (contractors) who, although they could not buy wool, bought unfinished cloth on the market, finished it or had it finished, then sold it. In 1418 the *upzetters* lost the right to buy cloth directly and had to go through brokers.[41]

In the other cities the draper group also became smaller in the fourteenth century, but under different circumstances. In the thirteenth century the master weaver had taken work from the merchant, but in the fourteenth he was more often a work giver, not only to the apprentices of his own guild but also to the master fullers and shearers. 'Drapers' and 'master weavers' sold cloth to foreign merchants, particularly the Germans, who came to dominate sales of the cloth of the smaller Flemish centres. Flexibility was fostered in all guild structures, including textiles, by a clause in the Great Charter of Ghent of 1297 that permits 'each burgher of Ghent [to] choose within three days of every 15 August what business he wants to pursue during the coming year'. Thus, although wool workers were forbidden to buy or sell wool wholesale, they could buy it one year as brokers and have it made into cloth the next when they declared a different profession. The same person thus could engage in retailing and wholesaling cloth.

41. J. Demey, 'De Vlaamse ondernemer in de middeleeuwse Nijverheid: De Ieperse drapiers en "upsetters" op het einde der XIIIe en in de XIVe eeuw' in *Prisma Ieper*, 143–56. Orig. in *Bijdragen voor de Geschiedenis der Nederlanden* 4 (1949): 1–15.

Through dual matriculation in guilds that permitted it, he could practise different trades.[42]

The dyers were the artisan group that most frequently branched into wholesaling. In view of the expense of their raw materials, the dyers were among the most highly skilled and wealthy of the textile artisans in Flanders, although evidently not elsewhere. The town authorities tried, but with little success, to keep the dyers out of cloth wholesaling, for they were understandably concerned that the dye supply, most of which was imported, would be controlled by monopolists. Although the dyers got some of their supplies through the hostellers, some prominent dyers of Ghent acquired enormous stores, which they then sold to dyers of the smaller cities of eastern Flanders.[43]

Cloth making in the villages and small towns

Much of the difficulty of Flemish textile merchandising was internal. English cloth did not have much success in the international market until political problems in Flanders interrupted production and left unsatisfied customers.[44] Taxes levied by city governments at various stages of the cloth making process contributed to high prices in the cities and to overpricing Flemish cloth on the international market, and the count's coin debasements could not compensate for this.[45] Finally, the great cities also experienced competition from the smaller Flemish towns and the villages. We have seen that the technological changes of the twelfth century had urbanized what had been a generalized Flemish textile industry. Although the smaller communities still made cloth in the thirteenth century, it was much less important on the international market than the urban products.

42. H. van Werveke, 'Die Stellung des hansischen Kaufmanns dem flandrischen Tuchproduzenten gegenüber' in *Beiträge zur Wirtschafts-und Stadtgeschichte. Festschrift für Hektor Ammann* (Wiesbaden, 1965), 296–304. For a discussion of the Great Charter, see Nicholas, *Metamorphosis*, 144–5. Van Werveke's argument that 'merchant-industrialists' ceased to function in Flanders in the fourteenth century as foreigners got control of the commerce in the raw materials of the textile trade is thus overdrawn, although he was right that 'weaver' and 'draper' often had the same meaning after 1350. Van Werveke, *De Koopman-ondernemer en de ondernemer in de Vlaamsche lakennijverheid van de Middeleeuwen*, MKVA, Kl. Letteren, 8, No. 4 (Brussels, 1946).

43. Nicholas, *Metamorphosis*, 165–8.

44. W. Prevenier, 'Les Perturbations dans les relations commerciales anglo-flamandes entre 1379 et 1407. Causes de désaccord et raisons d'une réconciliation', *Economies et sociétés du Moyen Age: Mélanges Edouard Perroy* (Paris, 1973), 494–5.

45. See for example the comment of G. Espinas, *La Draperie dans la Flandre française au Moyen Age*, 2 vols (Paris, 1923), 1: 352–5.

But this began to change with the problems of the late thirteenth century.[46] The urban artisans now resisted the very sort of technological innovation that had made them prosperous. On grounds that it produced an inferior textile, they refused to use the fulling mill, which was common in England and Normandy and fulled cloth twenty to fifty times faster than the traditional manner of stamping fulling earth into the textile with the feet.[47]

The Three Cities themselves did not make exclusively luxury textiles, but they refused to adapt to new conditions, including changes in fashion. Just as in the eleventh century the wealthy had turned from linen to wool as heavier and more luxurious, they now turned more to silk and velvets, neither of which was made in Flanders, and the spread of linen underwear made heavy woollen outer clothing less needed. Although there had been a substantial Mediterranean market for cheap Low Country cloth in the twelfth and thirteenth centuries, references to such textiles virtually disappear after about 1320. Demand for the coarser grades resumes only in the late fifteenth century.

Thus Ghent and especially Ypres concentrated more than before on the heavy luxury woollens. Since the cities were not able to compete with the smaller communities in producing cheaper cloth, which could be marketed only locally anyway, they concentrated on heavily regulated luxury textiles in which the smaller centres could not compete, and their extremely minute industrial regulations for these textiles find their rational explanation. But there was a substantial market within the cities themselves for the cheaper grades. Of the Three Cities, only Bruges permitted its citizens to buy cloth not made locally, and indeed it exported the lighter fabrics made by artisans of Bruges and sold the products of the smaller centres of Flanders and northern France on its market. The city account of 1389–90 shows that while most cloth used by the city government for uniforms was bought from Brugeois, the aldermen also purchased fabrics of Ypres, Wervik, Comines and Brussels.[48]

The complaints of the Three Cities about competition from the smaller towns have obscured the fact that all parties were making

46. Discussion based on Nicholas, *Town and Countryside*, 76–116.
47. R. van Uytven, 'De Volmolen: Motor van de omwenteling in de industriële mentaliteit', *Alumni* **28** (1968): 62–4 and comment by Mus, 'Aandeel van de Ieperlingen', 332–55.
48. Sivéry, 'Débuts de l'économie cyclique', 678–9; van Houtte and van Uytven, 'Nijverheid en handel', 104; *IAB* **3**: 192–6; and esp. J.H. Munro, 'Industrial Transformations in the North-West European Textile Trades, *c.* 1290–*c.* 1340: economic progress or economic crisis?' in Bruce M.S. Campbell (ed.), *Before the Black Death: Studies in the 'Crisis' of the Early Fourteenth Century* (Manchester, 1991), 111–14.

similar cloth. The 'new draperies' mentioned in the sources must not be confused with 'light draperies' or *saies*, which were worsted. The 'new draperies' were woollen imitations of the luxury cloths but were cheaper, using less and cheaper grades of wool, although all of it came from Britain until the fifteenth century.[49]

Pirenne thought that the Three Cities established quarters in response to the growth of the rural textile industries. The cities supposedly tried to stamp out competition within Flanders and turn the rural areas into places that could provide markets for urban cloth and food to feed the city workers.[50] In fact, the quarters originated more for political than economic reasons. Hostility to rural cloth making was generally confined to cases where the villagers manufactured imitations of cloth that one of the major centres considered its speciality; since these textiles were not subject to the rigorous inspection given by the city guilds, they were of lower quality and thus caused the reputation of the city textiles to suffer when they entered the export market. The Three Cities did not generally try to restrict cloth making in 'free cities of law', which had been given charters by the counts to make specific types of cloth. Robert of Béthune seems to have tried to foster the industries of the smaller centres of Flanders, although most of his enactments are known only through confirmations by Louis of Male. Most were very general, providing only that cloth of a given type might be made in the community but not giving detailed industrial regulations. The count got a fee for each piece of cloth made and a share of fines levied for infractions of industrial regulations.

The geographical diffusion of cloth making in Flanders did not change appreciably in the late Middle Ages. There is very little evidence of rural textiles in the northeast until the time of Louis of Male, and they were never strong there. In the southeast, Aalst had a charter by Robert of Béthune's time, but its earliest surviving industrial regulations are from the early fifteenth century. The industry of Geraardsbergen had a large enough workforce to experience a quarrel between the weavers and their apprentices, which the militia of Ghent settled in 1345. Dendermonde was second only to Poperinge among the smaller centres in the sophistication of its textile industry. It was making cloth by 1221, and by 1311 it had a substantial export trade through the Flemish fairs. The Alberti of Florence bought Dendermonde cloth in 1306, and it was known in Castile in 1369. The town sold a large annuity to finance a new cloth hall in 1337. In 1370

49. Munro, 'Monetary Contraction and Industrial Change', 118–22.
50. Pirenne, *Histoire de Belgique*, 2: 127.

Dendermonde had a population of about 9000 persons, of whom nearly one-third were employed in textiles.[51]

Textiles were not strong in the Franc of Bruges. Oudenburg had a very prosperous industry in the thirteenth century that declined abruptly in the fourteenth. The textile manufacture of Oudenburg was doubtless stunted by the town's profitable business in smuggling English cloth; for despite Flanders' need for English wool, it was illegal to sell English cloth in Flanders after 1346.[52] Cloth was also made at Aardenburg, Oostburg, Maldegem, Eeklo, Kaprijke and Lembeke.

The castellany of Courtrai also had an important woollen textile industry. King Philip VI of France established an industry and a free fair at Harelbeke in 1335. Deinze and Tielt had cloth industries before 1338, and cloth of Menen was exported in the early fourteenth century. The castellanies of Veurne and Bergues had several important centres, which prospered by being outside the monopoly areas of the Three Cities. Nieuwpoort had a small textile industry, but it functioned mainly as Ypres's outport. Veurne itself was more prosperous in the thirteenth century than later. Hondschoote became the great rival of Bergues within its own castellany. Hondschoote received its first charter from Louis of Male in 1374, but it was already producing about 1300 pieces of cloth annually. It became the chief town of the West Quarter in the fifteenth century.[53]

Ypres, the smallest and most completely dependent on the woollen textile industry of the Three Cities, went into a severe decline in the early fourteenth century. Between 1310–20 and the mid fourteenth century, total cloth production at Ypres dropped by more than half, then stabilized, although with sharp annual fluctuations, until the early fifteenth century.[54] Predictably, of the Three Cities Ypres had the

51. Verlinden, *Brabantsch en Vlaamsch Lakens*, 17; Prevenier, 'Bourgeoisie en Flandre', 411.

52. Nicholas, 'English Trade at Bruges', 27–8.

53. Emile Coornaert, *Un Centre industriel d'autrefois: La draperie-sayetterie d'Hondschoote (XIVe–XVIIIe siècles)* (Paris, 1930), 1–17.

54. H. van Werveke, *De omvang van de Ieperse lakenproductie in de veertiende eeuw*, *MKVA*, Kl. Letteren, IX, No. 2 (Antwerp, 1947). Van Werveke calculated this from the number of lead pieces that the city bought annually to seal cloth; he then rejected his own figure because, based on his own statistics for Ghent, he assumed that fullers were only 2.2 per cent of the population of Ypres and could not possibly have made the number of textiles suggested by the seal figures. My work on the population of Ghent (*Metamorphosis*, 19) suggests that the fullers constituted 17.63 per cent of the total population, more than enough to make the number of textiles suggested by the lead seal figures. See also the critique of J. Demey, 'Proeve tot raming van de bevolking en de weefgetouwen te Ieper van de XIIIe tot de XVIIe eeuw', *Prisma*, 157–70; orig. *RBPH* **28** (1950): 1031–48.

279

most serious problem with competition in the environs. Langemark and Warneton had chartered industries and entrepreneurs who 'put out' cloth to artisans for the various industrial processes. Diksmuide also continued to prosper on a limited scale.[55]

The largest textile industry in Flanders outside the Three Cities was at Poperinge, 10 kilometres west of Ypres. We have seen that artisans of Poperinge who worked for textile magnates of Ypres were the cause of the uprising of 1280. Poperinge was in the Hanse of London in the twelfth century, and it was renting a section of the cloth hall of Bruges for exporting its goods by 1283. Its cloth is found in France and Spain, but its major market was in Germany, through the Hanse community in Bruges. In 1469, long after it had passed its peak, Poperinge had a population of 3600, and it contained at least 1560 textile workers in 1517, which would suggest that about two-fifths of its population were involved in cloth making.[56]

Although merchants of the great cities were giving work to rural and small-town artisans in the thirteenth century, probably to save labour costs, they began to restrict this practice in the late thirteenth century. Ypres in 1281 limited to the smaller and cheaper grades the types of cloth that could be taken outside the city for processing. When they could no longer work for the townsmen, the artisans of the smaller centres adopted the simple expedient of counterfeiting the cloth of the great cities.

The counterfeiting problem became so serious that Ghent in 1302 and 1314 was given a privilege prohibiting the manufacture of woollen cloth within 5 comital miles (30 kilometres) of its walls except in towns that had charters permitting them to make cloth. Robert of Béthune's numerous grants of charters may have been a reaction to Ghent's privileges. In 1322 Bruges and Ypres received similar franchises, throughout the Franc and within 3 miles of Ypres. The only areas outside these monopolies were the extreme northeast and southwest, together with parts of the castellany of Courtrai, which were regulated from Courtrai rather than the Three Cities.

But although the privilege of Ypres was directed against counterfeiting, this issue arose in the actions of the city against the smaller towns only from the 1340s. Ypres in the 1320s began proceeding against the largest 'free towns' of its environs, specifically Langemark and Poperinge. Ypres sent the militia to Poperinge in 1326 to smash

55. Van Houtte, *Economic History*, 78.
56. Prevenier, 'Bourgeoisie en Flandre', 411–12.

textile machinery, then asked Bruges for reinforcements. The experience was repeated in 1328 and was extended to Dikkebus, which is not known to have had a textile privilege. The count generally supported the smaller towns, but no final settlement was reached.

Bruges was less antagonistic towards rural and small-town textiles than was Ypres. As a city oriented more towards trade than industry, it profited by exporting their cloth. Bruges repressed the efforts of the towns of the Franc to make cloth for export but elsewhere took a laissez-faire attitude. Its monopoly privilege of 1322 is a literal translation of most parts of the Ghent privilege, but with the important difference that Bruges was more interested in the sale of rural cloth than in its manufacture; cloth could be sold only in the same town where it had been made, unless it was brought to Bruges or one of the five fairs.

Ghent was the most hostile of the Three Cities towards rural textiles. The municipal accounts from 1314 show frequent expeditions into the nearby communities, large and small, 'about the looms'. The chronology of the monopoly grants shows that Ghent was pressuring Bruges and Ypres into adopting a harsher attitude towards the manufacture of cloth in the small centres, instead of simply keeping them out of the export market by restricting them at the city cloth hall. Ghent ruled its entire quarter more strictly than did either Ypres or Bruges. The 'Great Charter' of 1297 forbade the sale at the cloth hall of any cloth not made in the city itself and shows that considerable cloth was being made in the environs. By 1314 spinning was the only cloth making operation that could be done outside the city.

The rural textile question in the 1340s

Until the van Artevelde rebellion, most efforts of Ghent and Bruges were concentrated on eliminating woollen textiles in villages that had no charter giving them the right to make them. But the focus now shifts to their claims that smaller towns that did have such privileges were imitating the luxurious speciality cloths of the cities, alleging that they had only the right to make 'dry', low-grade textiles.[57] But such places as Poperinge and Dendermonde had long-established textile industries that had developed before formal charters were being given and thus assumed that their artisans could make all types. The Three Cities were correct that their textiles were being imitated; whether

---

57. For these arguments, see Nicholas, *Town and Countryside*, 187–99.

they had legal cause for complaint is another matter, but they were able to use their power in the 1340s to enforce their claims.

In 1344 and 1345 Ghent sent the militia to Dendermonde to enforce Ghent's demand that the size of cloth made there be modified. Shortly before van Artevelde fell from power, Dendermonde was forbidden to make the luxurious *strijpe halflakene* that was so cherished at Ghent, while the *strijpte lakene* of Dendermonde were to be no longer than 21 metres. The grievances of Ypres against Poperinge, which were re-inflamed from March 1343, also concerned imitation. The Three Cities ruled that the artisans of Poperinge had only recently begun making 'wet' cloth, although they did not state specifically that they had no right to do this. As with Dendermonde, the judgement ordered Poperinge to stop making *strijpe halflakene*, although it could continue, as could Dendermonde, to make wet cloth of small specification. Poperinge promptly violated this ruling, and in 1344 Ypres, acting alone, confirmed the earlier judgement and imposed fines. Louis of Male in 1348 confirmed the judgements against both Dendermonde and Poperinge. Poperinge, as Dendermonde – which sold *strijpte lakene* to Bruges in the 1360s – continued to make other types of cloth, and the quarrels with Ypres died down until 1373.

Ypres's grievances against Langemark were also renewed, but this one was over the 3 mile privilege, not imitation. Although in 1328 Louis of Nevers had ruled that Langemark was a 'free town of law' and thus unaffected by the Ypres monopoly, in 1342 he had to reverse himself and forbid all cloth making there. In contrast to his attitude towards Dendermonde and Poperinge, Louis of Male in 1348 restored Langemark's old privileges. Significantly, the count thus was sympathetic to the Three Cities' claims of imitation, which could hurt Flanders' overseas trading position, but not to a war of extermination against places that had the legal right to manufacture lower-grade cloth.

The attitude of Bruges towards rural textiles remained ambivalent. In 1339 Bruges restricted Eeklo to low-grade cloth and gave its own guilds inspection rights there. In 1342 Bruges and the Franc agreed that the sale of cloth, but not its manufacture, was forbidden in the Franc. One machine of each type necessary to produce a complete woollen textile might remain in each parish of the Franc where such machinery already existed; each parishioner might make cloth on this equipment for his or her household. Two weeks after this agreement, Bruges sent the militia against Sluis 'and elsewhere in the Franc on account of the drapery'.[58] But references in the city accounts suggest

---

58. Quotation from Bruges city account, cited Nicholas, *Town and Countryside*, 197.

that Ghent had pressured Bruges into taking this action; for some places in the Franc, including Eeklo, were within 5 miles of Ghent. In 1345, again at Ghent's urging, Bruges sent another force to Eeklo. The results were predictable; cloth making would be Eeklo's major source of income by the fifteenth century.

The period of Louis of Male

Louis of Male tried to restrict the independence of the Three Cities; but although he confirmed many older charters of the smaller centres permitting them to make cloth, he founded only one new one, at Aksel in the Four Offices, a community that the militia of Ghent had struck frequently after 1314 on grounds of violations of the 5 mile privilege. Louis often intervened in internal quarrels in the smaller places to protect his financial interests.[59]

The Three Cities were forced to accommodate. In 1359 Ghent's privilege of 1314 was confirmed, and its militia continued to extirpate cloth making in places lacking written charters. Not until 1400 did Bruges again complain that cloth was being made in the Franc against its privileges, and this was the outgrowth of a complaint against cloth wholesalers of Sluis who were practising their trade elsewhere in the Franc.

In 1357 Ypres's monopoly was reaffirmed, but the terms show a drastically changed situation since 1322. The count noted that textiles were being made in many communities near Ypres, then forbade the making of cloth larger than a certain size anywhere within 3 miles of Ypres except at Roeselare, Deinze and Bailleul. Ypres's monopoly, once absolute against places lacking charters, was now restricted to claims of counterfeiting its specialities. The account of the bailiff for 1382–3 shows comital textile inspectors in seventeen villages of the castellany of Ypres, only one of which, Langemark, had a formal privilege for cloth making.

Textiles were spreading particularly in the Leie valley. The accounts of the Datini family of Prato and Florence show Leie cloth destined for the Mediterranean accounting for about one-quarter of the market value of foreign cloth being exported through Bruges. Wervik and Courtrai were the most important centres, but some cloth came from Menen and Comines. The Yprois took action against each of these communities except Courtrai.

59. For this section, see Nicholas, *Town and Countryside*, 203–21.

Wervik was the most prosperous of Ypres's small-town competitors. Its cloth competed with that of the Three Cities on the market of Bruges. Italian firms, including the Alberti of Florence, invested in the industry of Wervik, evidently furnishing some of the equipment to the local artisans, then handling the foreign sale of their product. The Hanse merchants also patronized the cloth of Wervik and the other Leie towns, to the point where considerable distress could be caused when the ever-touchy Germans decided to buy large quantities of the cloth of one town and boycott that of another. The Germans wanted light, cheap cloth, which was sold more easily in the east.

The case of Wervik shows how self-defeating the policy of the Three Cities was: Wervik had been restricted since the 1340s to small textiles that would not counterfeit the specialities of Ypres, and Louis of Male had supported Ypres's claims against the smaller centre; yet Wervik cloth was competing successfully with that of the Three Cities, for theirs simply was not selling well. The old specialities yielded to 'Easterling cloth' and 'Leie cloth'. Although the Germans never followed the Italian example by investing in workshops in Flanders, the dependence of the Leie towns on the Germans became even more serious in the fifteenth century. The Germans then agreed to take the entire cloth output of some towns, notably Poperinge, and the Flemish merchants in their turn agreed to work according to the specifications laid down by the Germans.[60]

Ypres's most famous quarrel was in 1373 with Poperinge. There was no violence, as far as is known; uncharacteristically, Ypres cited Poperinge before the *Audientie*, whose verdict has not survived although it evidently favoured Ypres. Poperinge claimed that it had always had the right to make wet cloth, noting furthermore that it had no competition with Ypres, whose cloth was marketed in Spain while that of Poperinge was sold to Hanse merchants. Ypres claimed that the textiles of the Three Cities were the real foundation of the prosperity of Flanders and had to be preserved at all costs. Poperinge, more correctly, argued that textiles without differentiation were the basis of Flanders' prosperity, which could only be increased as more places made cloth. More correct than either was the view of the Four Members of Flanders as expressed to the count in 1473: 'Flanders is a sterile country, infertile in itself, completely founded on the fact and course

60. Van Werveke, 'Hansischen Kaufmann', 297; Philippe Dollinger, *The German Hansa* (Stanford, 1970), 249.

of merchandise, densely populated with foreigners, merchants and others. . . .'[61]

The Flemish linen industry

The Flemish linen industry was growing as woollens declined. Farmers could weave linen as a secondary occupation, for the technology was simpler than that for woollens. Linen working was strongest in the castellany of Courtrai; it was never significant around Ypres, where the smaller centres continued to make woollens.[62]

Linen working was always stronger in the rural areas of Flanders than in the towns, but it was more active in the cities than was once thought. Douai and Lille initially had stronger linen working than the cities of Germanic Flanders, but this was changing after 1250. The comital court bought table linen at Courtrai by the 1270s, and by 1293 the city was already specializing in the predecessors of damasks. Bruges had a guild of linen weavers by 1299, but most of its linen business was with foreigners. Virtually all towns had linen workers by 1300, most of them living in the suburbs, but they were never prominent politically.

Although the cities produced higher grade linen than the villages, there is not much evidence of linen exports in the fourteenth century. The main exception was the substantial concentration of linen workers and coverlet weavers of Bruges and in the village of St Pieter at Ghent. Those of St Pieter's had an organization separate from that of the central city until 1358. After 1385 the urban linen industry grew rapidly, with guilds attested at Damme, Aalst, Dendermonde, Oudenburg, Geraardsbergen and Sluis by 1441.[63]

THE DIRECTIONS OF TRADE

Despite the problems, far more Flemings held jobs in cloth making than in other lines of artisanry, and thus work stoppages and interruptions

---

61. *IAB* 6: 56, cited Nicholas, 'Of Poverty and Primacy', 41.
62. Discussion of the linen industry is based on Etienne Sabbe, *De Belgische Vlasnijverheid*. I: *De zuidnederlandsche Vlasnijverheid tot het verdrag van Utrecht (1713)* (Bruges, 1943), 39–76, 130–70; for a convenient summary, see Nicholas, *Town and Countryside*, 219–21.
63. Nicholas, *Town and Countryside*, 63–5; Nicholas, *Metamorphosis*, 169–76.

of the wool supply caused hardship. But although contemporaries were under the opposite impression, the real basis of Flanders' wealth in the fourteenth century was trade, rather than industry.

Flemish shipping

Although Flanders was a net importer of food, it exported some locally produced comestibles in addition to reconsigning French grain downstream on the Scheldt. In the pastoral northeast, cheeses were produced that were exported through Antwerp. Numerous Ghent foodmongers, particularly cheese merchants, had property and probably animals in and near Weert. Flanders became the leader in dairy products in the southern Low Countries in the fifteenth century. Curiously, although Flanders had dairy herds, and leather was made elsewhere in the Low Countries, Ghent was the only substantial Flemish producer of leather for export, continuing a tradition that had been present by the tenth century.[64]

Maritime Flanders, both north and west, provided sources of income that cushioned the impact of the decline of the textile industry. Although Flanders imported much fish from the northern Netherlands and from the Hanse, it exported herring to France, particularly after Flemings learned the technique of pickling from the Germans around 1390.[65] Herring was the most important Flemish export for the 'west fleet' in the late fourteenth century. On the return trip from the south, the Flemings obtained wine from Gascony and Poitou, salt from the bay of Bourgneuf, grain from Ponthieu and wool from Calais. They also continued to freight goods for English merchants. Damme had been the most important fish staple since 1324, but after 1372 Sluis was also a market for herring of Schonen, handling an annual average of 20,280 tons between October 1374 and Easter 1380.[66]

Salt extraction was also important on the Flemish coast, particularly at Biervliet, with about 300 pans around 1400. Most of it was exported to England, France and the Baltic. The floods hurt this trade and forced Flanders to import more French salt. Biervliet produced

64. Nicholas, *Metamorphosis*, 276–80; van Houtte and van Uytven, 'Nijverheid en handel', 99, 106; *IAB* 2: 17; Nicholas, *Van Arteveldes*, 96–8.

65. The story that Willem Beukels of Biervliet invented pickling is legend; van Houtte, *Economic History*, 90.

66. R. Degryse, 'De Vlaamse westvaart en de Engelse represailles omstreeks 1378', *HMGOG* **27** (1973): 202–6.

about 7 million litres of salt in 1407–8, but it was down to 1,600,000 litres by the mid fifteenth century. This in turn gave new business to Hulst, Axel and Biervliet in refining the imported salt.[67]

Building tiles were an important Flemish export even in the thirteenth century. Jan Boudewijn of Ypres sold 202,500 'Flanders tiles' for use on the Tower of London in 1278. With the expansion of native brick making in Flanders in the fourteenth century, large quantities of building tiles and flat bricks were sent to England. Flues for fireplaces were often made of Flemish tiles, and English brick making first developed in East Anglia and around the Humber, where Flemish influence was strong.[68]

Considerable recent research has overturned Pirenne's picture of a purely passive Flemish trade after 1300. Normally, several Flemish and foreign fleets left the Zwin each year for the westward journey and would return the next year. Sometimes this was done in convoy, with all Flemish boats going together for safety. Louis of Male tried to ensure safety by ordering Flemish boatmen to sail with the fleet and to stay within sight of one another. In 1377 Louis appointed the first 'admiral of Flanders' to keep the convoys safe (Mathijs Claissone, a boat captain of Sluis who also freighted goods), and in early 1378 the count ordered a militia from the small towns of the Franc to patrol the coastal waters in advance of the fleet. Only after 1450, with the silting of the Zwin and the decline of Bruges, were the Flemings pushed out of the Bourgneuf trade.[69]

Although the market of Bruges and its staple on the Zwin have rightly been emphasized as the major generators of commercial wealth for late medieval Flanders, the other ports were also important. As Italians and Germans came to dominate Bruges and Sluis in the fifteenth century, Dunkirk was the most active Flemish harbour for native boats, at least for the English trade, but Nieuwpoort was also important.[70] The yield of the Nieuwpoort toll gradually rose during the fourteenth century, despite problems of access from the land side. It was the point of entry for smaller boats with cargoes intended for the Flemish internal market and specifically for Ypres. The Ypres municipal accounts show that during 122 days in the winter of 1296–7, at

67. Van Houtte, *Economic History*, 89; van Houtte and van Uytven, 'Nijverheid en handel', 100.

68. John Schofield, *The Building of London: From the Conquest to the Great Fire* (London, 1983), 95; van de Walle, *Bouwbedrijf*, 52.

69. Degryse, 'Vlaamse westvaart', 193–229.

70. G. Asaert, 'Scheepvaart en visserij', *AGN* 4: 128–34.

least 3250 barges and 87 large boats passed through the Ypres locks and paid toll, evidently after passing through Nieuwpoort. Ypres was allowed to take tolls on the canal to Nieuwpoort to compensate itself for its costs in maintaining the stream, and throughout the century it continually dredged the canal and erected dikes to raise the water level.[71] Yet Ypres was never able to dominate Nieuwpoort to the extent of Bruges's mastery over Sluis. Its exemption from the tolls of Nieuwpoort was only partial, and in the fifteenth century Ypres tried to bypass them by building a new canal linking the IJzer and Yperleet near Nieuwendamme. The project failed due to the objections of Ghent, and Nieuwpoort remained the port of the IJzer basin.[72]

Our best evidence of active Flemish trade concerns England. Flanders had imported coal from England since 1273. The Newcastle toll of 1377–8 shows eighty-four coal boats from ten Flemish coastal communities, with the largest number from Nieuwpoort, Dunkirk, Heist and Sluis. The Flemings and Dutch also carried iron, osmundus, cooking implements, wood, salt, linen, tar and tiles, and herring from Schonen to Newcastle to exchange for coal. The Flemish trade accounted for 19 per cent of the business of the Newcastle toll in 1380–1.[73] Of 129 aliens who exported wool from London in 1365–6, only seventeen can be identified by nationality, but six were Flemish. The magistrates of Bruges appealed to Edward III on behalf of merchants of Sluis who had been robbed of their wool in the territory of the bishop of Durham. Of sixty-one cases in the King's Bench to which alien merchants were parties between 1350 and 1377, Flemings were plaintiffs in four, defendants in nine. Six of the cases occurred at London, one in Northamptonshire and two in Norfolk.[74]

Following several years of diplomatic tension and piracy, on 27 August 1371 the English and Flemish governments ordered the seizure

71. *IAY* 2: 103–4, 155–6, 176–7. On the dredging efforts of Ypres, see O. Mus, 'Pieter de Maets, Stadsbouwmeester-ondernemer (Ieper, . . .+1318)', *ASEB* 114 (1977): 339–60.

72. *IAY* 2: No. 484, 92; Degryse, " 's Graven Domein te Nieuwpoort', *ASEB* 85 (1948): 97; Degryse, 'Oude en nieuwe havens van het IJzerbekken in de middeleeuwen', *ASEB* 84 (1947): 5– 40.

73. R. Degryse, 'Vlaamse kolenschepen en Schonense kaakharing te Newcastle upon Tyne (1377–1391)', *ASEB* 122 (1985): 157–88.

74. Alice Beardwood, *Alien Merchants in England 1350 to 1377. Their Legal and Economic Position* (Cambridge, Mass., 1931), 36, 86, 139 and Appendix E, 182–9. See also Marc de Laet, 'De Vlaamse aktieve handel op Engeland in de eerste helft van de 14e eeuw, aan de hand van de Customs Accounts', *Economische Geschiedenis van België: Behandeling van de bronnen en problematiek. Handelingen van het Colloquium te Brussel 17– 19 november 1971* (Brussels, 1972), 223–31.

of each other's merchants' goods. The confiscation dossiers and negotiation records show the importance of Sluis in Flemish foreign trade.
Of thirty-nine boats seized at Sluis, none had an English owner, one
was German and the others were Flemish or Dutch. Many of the
English complaints concern sailors' disputes at Sluis, which evidently
had all the dangers associated with seaports without the amenities of
Bruges. The English also claimed that a Flemish shipper had absconded
with English property being sent to Bordeaux and to destinations in
Spain or Portugal. One interesting case involved John Edrop of London and his associates, who employed Ghijs Cudel, a shipper of Sluis
whose boat was owned by the innkeepers Jacob Crakebeen and Pieter
Croec of Bruges, to carry 160 vats of wine from Bordeaux to London,
but the goods were lost to the French. In another case, Nicholas
Brembre and John Phillipot of London used John Belle, shipper of
Sluis, to carry twenty sacks of wool to Calais. It turned out that Belle's
captain had lost the money gambling in London. Most of the cases
litigated show that the English used Flemish boats but not that they
actually were buying goods in Flanders. Flanders was thus clearly active in the Atlantic carrying trade but was producing little that was
being sold in England in the late fourteenth century.[75]

Wool and cloth in the English trade

Many of the trade problems of late medieval Flanders resulted from
the cities forcing the counts to prohibit the import of some foreign
manufactured items, specifically textiles, while continuing to import
food and wool from the very places whose manufactured goods were
being barred.

After the English established a compulsory staple on wool at Saint-
Omer in 1313, Flemish wool merchants were no longer supposed to
travel in England to obtain their wool, but rather had to go through
the heavily taxed monopolists.[76] But the rigidity of the staple has been
exaggerated. Italian merchants could export directly from Southampton to Italy, and some wool was licensed to join cargoes that were
leaving Bruges. The staple was at Bruges during the 1340s, part of the
Flemish price for an English alliance, but a commons petition in June
1344 complained that the Flemings had banned exports of wool from
Flanders, which hindered the business of the Italians and Spaniards.

75. De Gryse, 'Vlaamse westvaart', 212; Nicholas, 'English Trade', esp. 37.
76. Lloyd, *Alien Merchants*, 108.

When Louis of Male regained control in Flanders, the English had less reason to be accommodating about the annoyances. For a few months in 1348–9 the staple was transferred to Middelburg in Zeeland; in March 1352 the staple at Bruges was ended in favour of home staples, evidently in retaliation for Louis's tilt towards France.

In the intervening years, foreign merchants were given rights to export wool from England that native merchants were denied. Once this policy was ended in April 1357, English merchants shipped so much wool to Bruges that a *de facto* staple existed there before July 1359, when Edward III and the Flemish count restored all privileges previously held by the English community at Bruges, and natives who exported wool were required to take it to Bruges. In 1363, however, the English fixed their wool staple at Calais, where it remained permanently except for a move to Middelburg from 1384–9.[77]

Even after 1363, however, Flemish and foreign merchants continued to buy considerable wool at Bruges from Italians without having to go to the staple. Some Castilian merchants living in Bruges bought wool in Calais, then paid for it through their offices at Bruges. The Spaniards also transported some English wool to Italy either from England directly or from Flanders. Some English merchants also used the banking facilities of Bruges to evade the staple. In 1362 William de la Pole had to answer before the King's Bench for the illegal export of 1000 sacks of wool to Flanders that John Goldbeter of York had in turn consigned to a number of Flemings. Goldbeter was outlawed, but he was pardoned on the request of Louis of Male in 1364.[78]

But while wool was welcomed in Flanders, English cloth was not. Although much cloth used in England was produced locally, most imported textiles in the early fourteenth century still came from Flanders and were traded by Flemish merchants, rather than English. Wool ships en route back to England from the continent brought Flemish cloth along with forest products that the English bought from German merchants in Bruges.[79]

The sale of English cloth was probably prohibited in Flanders by 1346 and definitely by 1359. Woollen cloth remained an exception to later English privileges guaranteeing free trade at Bruges. Smuggling was widespread, and English cloth could be bought

77. Lloyd, *Wool Trade*, 209–10, 230.

78. Nicholas, 'English Trade', 28–33; Lloyd, *Alien Merchants*, 108; Childs, *Anglo-Castilian Trade*, 73; E.B. Fryde, *William de la Pole. Merchant and King's Banker (d. 1366)* (London, 1988), 226–7.

79. Lloyd, *Alien Merchants*, 110–11.

easily at Middelburg and Antwerp, just outside Flanders. It was legal for English merchants to bring their cloth to Sluis en route to other destinations as long as it was not offered for sale in Flanders; brokers of Bruges imported considerable English cloth for reconsignment elsewhere in the Low Countries. Although the Flemish authorities frequently confiscated English cloth, it is hard to detect the principle behind their actions, for they got only a small part of the cloth, and by the 1430s Bruges merchants were doing a good business selling previously confiscated English cloth, much of it brokered through the Italian merchant houses, and the count's officials enforced the right of Flemings to possess it.[80]

The wine trade

The trade in wine, the preferred beverage of the upper classes and a necessity for the Eucharist, was always important and provides still more proof that the traditional view of a passive Flemish trade has been exaggerated. In the early thirteenth century Flemish boats were re-exporting French wine, but probably not in large quantities, to northern Germany. With the establishment of the English in Poitou, the Flemings took over much of the carrying trade of southern France with England until the end of the fourteenth century. During the hostilities of 1315–16, French ships pursued Flemish boats into the Thames.

Wine tax receipts were usually under 30 per cent of the city income of Ghent, but the tax rate was extremely high, and the wine assize was usually the single largest item in the city's income. Much of this is due to an increase in per capita consumption, as population in the city fell while incomes rose; but it is also due to Ghent's expansion as a centre of regional distribution in eastern Flanders of imported wines. The yield of the wine tax declined in the fifteenth century; by 1465–6 Ghent was realizing substantially more money on the beer tax than on wine, although beer was taxed at a much lower rate.

Predictably, given the cosmopolitan nature of the place, consumption of wine was considerably higher at Bruges than at Ghent. The staple on wine coming by sea was at Damme, where it had to be sold

80. W. Brulez, 'Engels laken in Vlaanderen in de 14e en 15e eeuw', *ASEB* **108** (1971): 5–25; J.H. Munro, 'Bruges and the Abortive Staple in English Cloth: an incident in the shift of commerce from Bruges to Antwerp in the late fifteenth century', *RBPH* **44** (1966): 1137–59; Nicholas, 'English Trade', 27–8; van Houtte, *Economic History*, 104.

if it was to be resold elsewhere by someone other than the importer. Importers could sell directly in other towns; the farm of the tax
on wine at Damme yielded considerable income. Damme was almost
certainly the biggest wine market of northern Europe, with between
sixteen and twenty-three brokers specializing in Poitevin wines alone
around 1385.[81]

Most Gascon wine went to England until after 1453, when the
Bordelais was returned to France. Most French wine came to the
Damme staple, while the Scheldt carried Rhenish and Burgundian
wines, which dominated the luxury trade at Bruges and Ghent. Some
94,000 hectolitres of Poitevin wine, which became increasingly a *vin
ordinaire* from the late fourteenth century, were imported yearly to
Damme until about 1380. Although some Spanish and other Mediterranean wine came to Flanders on the Scheldt, even Ghent got most of
its Spanish wine from Damme. Over 35,000 hectolitres of German
wine passed the tolls of Damme around 1380, although more of it
went to the northern and eastern Low Countries. Considerable wine
from the middle Rhine came to Bruges through Hainault, then over
Ghent and the Lieve canal. The counts of Hainault got much of the
southern French wine for their courts at Damme and Bruges.[82]

The grain trade

The grain trade assumes primacy of place in any consideration of the
economic changes of Flanders during the fourteenth century. The
once thriving English grain export to Flanders was diminishing and
rarely exceeded 3000 hectolitres to the entire Low Countries.[83] Apart
from the native product, Flanders got most of its grain in the fourteenth century from northern France, supplementing this source late in
the century with supplies from Germany. Most French grain came
from the west along the Leie and Scheldt, although eastern sources,
notably Hainault, cannot be discounted.

The Hainault grain trade expanded in the fourteenth century,
particularly during the periodic interruptions of French supplies to

81. Jan Craeybeckx, *Un Grand commerce d'importation: les vins de France aux anciens Pays-Bas (XIIIe–XVIe siècle)* (Paris, 1958), 88, 93–7, 6–10, 180.

82. Craeybeckx, *Commerce d'importation*, 18, 25–7, 127, 134; van Houtte and van Uytven, 'Nijverheid en handel', 100; G. Sivery, *Les Comtes de Hainaut et le commerce du vin au XIVe siècle et au début du XVe siècle* (Lille, 1969), 30, 95, 127, 136–7.

83. Lloyd, *Alien Merchants*, 108–9; Alain Derville, 'Le Grenier des Pays-Bas médié-vaux', *RN* **69** (1987): 276–7.

Flanders. The Lombards were more active in Hainault than at any place in Flanders except Bruges. Colonies of Lombards at Aalst and Geraardsbergen were owed large sums by businessmen of Ghent, and a source of 1387 shows clearly that they were intermediaries in the trade in grain across the nearby border with Hainault, which Ghent used when its regular riverine sources of supply were interrupted. The grain evidently went overland from Geraardsbergen to Oudenaarde and thence on the Scheldt to Ghent, where it was taxed. Much of it was then re-exported on the indirect route downstream on the Scheldt from Ghent through the Dendermonde toll, rather than proceeding directly down the Dender from Geraardsbergen to Dendermonde and thence to Antwerp. The power of the Ghent grain merchants in southeastern Flanders, which the city would later claim as part of its grain staple, clearly goes back to the late fourteenth century.[84]

Most grain consumed in Flanders came from northwestern France, where yields on wheat were among the highest in Europe. Most of it came through Lille or Douai. Perhaps as early as the time of Philip of Alsace, Douai, which exported considerable grain to Ghent, had a staple that prohibited citizens from buying grain within 5 leagues (25 kilometres) of the city except on the town market; the restriction did not affect foreign exporters. Smaller towns inside that area had their own local staples, and they were respected. Douai thus drew mainly from the area directly south of it. Douai taxed grain that was being exported, perhaps because so much of its export trade was in the hands of merchants of Ghent rather than natives. Around 1400 Douai exported about 723,000 hectolitres of grain, which given local yields would be the surplus of 48 sq. km, while Douai's staple was only 25 km. The city thus clearly derived much of its income from re-exporting grain that came from outside its immediate staple area. Lille was closer than Douai to the major market at Ghent, which may explain why the grain price at Douai was about 15 per cent lower than at Lille. But what Douai lost on price it gained on volume and taxes, for it was better situated than Lille to get Artois and Picard grain.[85]

Once the grain entered Flanders from France, it fell under the control of Ghent, which derived a considerable part of its income from its

---

84. See in general G. Sivery, *Structures agraires et vie rurale dans le Hainaut à la fin du Moyen-Age*, 2 vols (Lille, 1977, 1982); Sivéry, *Comtes de Hainaut*, 30–1; Nicholas, *Metamorphosis*, 246–7.

85. A. Derville, 'Dîmes, rendements du blé et révolution agricole dans le nord de la France au Moyen-Age', *AESC* **42** (1987): 1411–32; Derville, 'Grenier des Pays-Bas', 267–80.

grain staple. The staple did not oblige farmers of the environs to buy their grain at Ghent, but all inhabitants of the town who left to buy grain for resale had to bring it to the staple. Payments in kind that burghers received as rents on their rural estates were apparently not affected. Only in periods of scarcity did Ghent get much of its grain from eastern Flanders. Shortly after noting a drought in the spring of 1370, the municipal account noted messengers sent to Waas and the Four Offices for over a month to search for grain. Similar expeditions were sent to the Oudburg and the Land of Aalst, and six persons were compensated for riding forty-nine days 'into the land . . . because of people who were in arrears on bringing grain to the market days'.[86] During the shortages of the 1380s Ghent regularly sent armed expeditions to the regions of Aalst and Dendermonde to get grain, including some coming from Hainault and Brabant.

Douai and Ghent disputed their respective rights in the lucrative grain trade, and in 1357 Louis of Male ruled that the Douaisiens could bring it from France as far as the port of Ghent but there had to recharge it on boats belonging to shippers of Ghent.[87] Ghent was definitely making considerable money exporting French grain down the Scheldt after that time; it may have been doing so even by the 1330s. A rate schedule of November 1335 for the tax farms, compared with the grain tax lease the next year, shows that at least 792,489 halsters (425,170 hectolitres) of grain and vegetables passed through Ghent even without allowing for the tax farmer's profit. If some 6.32 halsters (339 litres) were needed per person to sustain life, this quantity would have fed 132,080 persons, or roughly double the size of the population of Ghent at that time. The rest was obviously re-exported.[88]

The staple evidently originated because Ghent needed food, for the farmers of eastern Flanders consumed most of what they grew and hoarded much of the rest. Statutes always forbade re-exporting grain from Ghent until the city's needs had been satisfied. But particularly after the decline in population of the fourteenth century, Ghent usually had larger supplies available than it needed, and the re-export of grain down the Lieve canal towards Bruges and along the Scheldt through the Dendermonde toll and towards Antwerp and Brabant

86. SAG, Series 400, 10, fos 16r, 17v.

87. For this and what follows, see Nicholas, *Metamorphosis*, 241–50.

88. The 6.32 figure is suggested by W.P. Blockmans and W. Prevenier, 'Armoede in de Nederlanden van de 14e tot het midden van de 16e eeuw: bronnen en problemen', *TG* **88** (1975): 502–6. See also Nicholas, 'Structures', 514–18.

became a major source of income for the city elite, for the grain went through Ghent brokerage houses and moneychanging operations. Merchants of other cities came to Ghent to order their supplies. As early as 1357 Mechelen was importing substantial quantities of grain from Ghent, and numerous merchants of Mechelen were business partners of those of Ghent. In 1386–7, when recovery from the war of 1379–85 was only beginning, nearly 220,000 hectolitres of mainly French grain passed the Dendermonde toll. This was enough, assuming a normal consumption of 320–340 litres per person, to feed 66,000 persons, roughly twice the population of Ghent itself at the time, which corresponds closely to the 1335 figure (Ghent's population had roughly halved in the intervening years).[89]

If Flemish grain had been cheaper to acquire and transport than French, the merchants of Ghent would have used the domestic supply. Grain prices on rural markets in Flanders in the 1380s were only about two-thirds the sale prices in Bruges and Antwerp. While transport costs and additional tolls in the cities must be added, an enormous profit clearly went to a small number of persons. The wild fluctuations of grain price between years make generalizations suspect, but it seems clear that after the momentary high of the early 1370s, the poor were paying close to half their wages for grain alone in the 1380s, and the master artisans of the more prestigious trades about one-third.[90]

The Bruges market

The capital generated by industry had traditionally been invested in real estate and textiles in Flanders, but both had problems in the fourteenth century – real estate because of declining rents and low farm prices, textiles with the overall decline of the market. While at Ghent the new forms of investment were smaller industry and particularly shipping and the grain trade, at Bruges the outlets were moneychanging, banking, innkeeping and other service occupations. They attracted many foreigners, not exclusively those who kept their previous nationality.[91]

The location of Bruges made it a natural port of entry for goods coming north from the Mediterranean, particularly after the Italians

89. D. Nicholas, 'The Scheldt Trade and the "Ghent War" of 1379–1385', *BCRH* **144** (1978): 250, 255–60.

90. Nicholas, 'Structures', 518–20; Nicholas, 'Scheldt Trade', 256–8.

91. James M. Murray, 'Family, Marriage and Moneychanging in Medieval Bruges', *JMH* **14** (1988): 116.

began making the annual seaborne voyage to Bruges in 1277, and south from Germany. The Flemish counts gave extensive privileges to resident aliens that denizens did not enjoy, notably in debt recovery. The financial mechanisms of Bruges were so sophisticated that foreigners were generally willing to tolerate the minute Flemish customs regulations, which generated considerable capital for Flanders. A case of 1467–8 shows that the cost of transporting wine from Damme to Ghent was less than the costs of the dischargers, brokers and transporters inside the two towns. In one of the few cases where the extent of potential markup between wholesale and retail price can be calculated – the extra amount added to take account of the risk of piracy is the only unknown – Pieter de Clerc of Bruges complained in 1370 that pirates from Calais had robbed him of £139 worth of silk kerchiefs and fustians, but they had refunded only his purchase price, a mere £34.[92]

James Murray has emphasized in several excellent papers[93] the extent to which Bruges became a service society catering to the monetary and physical pleasures of the foreign communities. There are no firm sources for the populations of the foreign communities at Bruges; a recent estimate suggests about 1000 in 1440. They were certainly wealthy. Foreigners paid 52.47 per cent of a forced loan taken in 1378–9 from 'our poorters, the nations and the small towns'. The foreigners at Bruges had a sense of community against the often hostile denizens. In October 1409 a mass meeting was held of 'all nations of Bruges' to protest the count's imprisonment of merchants of Genoa in retaliation for the Genoese rejection of a French governor.[94]

Bruges had a busy night life, with plenty of taverns, pawnshops, gambling houses, bathhouses and brothels. The area controlled by the provost of St Donatian, which was scattered throughout the city, was the red-light district. In 1353, essentially repeating a directive of 1318, the official of Tournai told the ecclesiastical authorities to hand over to

92. Craeybeckx, *Commerce d'importation*, 192. The case of 1370 is cited by Nicholas, 'English Trade', 58 n. 52.

93. James M. Murray, 'The Commercial Comforts of Late Medieval Bruges', paper read at Midwest Medieval Conference, 1987; Murray, 'Housing, Real Estate and the Prince's Pauper in Fourteenth-Century Bruges', paper read at the 21st Annual International Congress on Medieval Studies, Kalamazoo, Michigan, May 1986. Both are cited with the author's permission.

94. Van Houtte and van Uytven, 'Nijverheid en handel', 90; *IAB* 2: 349–53; A. Zoete (ed.), *Handelingen van de Leden en van de Staten van Vlaanderen (1405–1419). Excerpten uit de rekeningen der steden, kasselrijen en vorstelijke ambtenaren*, 2 vols (Brussels, 1981–2), 1: 404, 407.

the secular arm all criminals who took refuge in the churches of Bruges and its environs and used the right of sanctuary to commit new crimes.[95] In 1351, 131 fines were collected from places of prostitution, but the number steadily declined to nine in 1402. It amounted to an informal licensing system, since the same names reappear every year, and the fine was small. The city fathers also understood the need for lavish entertainments; they held big parties and furnished gargantuan quantities of wine to lubricate the delegations of foreigners whom they were trying to entice back to Bruges from Antwerp in 1493, taking care to give separate parties to groups of foreigners who might fight one another.[96] The services of Bruges even included a corps of uniformed municipal 'dog sluggers' (*hondslaren*), who beat 1121 dogs to death in 1455.[97]

Foreigners could own houses but might give lodging only to persons of their own nationality, since the innkeeper was supposed to vouch for his guests. Beginning in 1382 the innkeepers furnished the city government each evening with lists of foreigners who had entered their establishments. Most foreigners lodged with innkeepers, who stored their goods for them in outbuildings and frequently acted as their brokers. For this, the innkeepers posted substantial bonds annually with the town government. From an early stage the innkeepers hired brokers, who wore the innkeeper-employer's livery, to do the actual buying and selling on their behalf.[98]

There is some confusion between brokers and innkeepers. Many brokers were independent operators, while others were employees of the innkeepers. They began as a less aristocratic group than the innkeepers, but this gradually changed during the fourteenth century. The two were in the same guild from 1323. Some brokers doubled as innkeepers, while others confined themselves to brokerage. Although the brokers had a residence requirement, in fact foreigners frequently became brokers.[99]

Some charters of foreign merchant communities protected them from the misdeeds of their own employees, who were entrusted with

95. *IAB* **2**: 13; *IAY* **1**: 261

96. J. Maréchal, 'Le Départ de Bruges des marchands étrangers (XVe et XVIe siècles)', *ASEB* **88** (1951): 39–40.

97. *IAB* **5**: 484.

98. J.A. van Houtte, 'Makelaars en Waarden te Brugge van de 13e tot de 16e eeuw', *Bijdragen voor de Geschiedenis der Nederlanden* **5** (1950): 1–30, 177–97; Laurent, *Draperie*, 233.

99. Van Houtte, 'Makelaars en waarden', 1–8, 16–18.

business involving considerable responsibility, but the brokers of
Bruges were responsible for the contracts of their own underlings.
Although in principle nothing was supposed to be sold in Bruges that
had not gone through brokers, this was impossible to enforce and by
the end of the fourteenth century was limited to transactions involving
over £5 groot, roughly three-quarters the yearly wage of a continuously employed master artisan. The brokers and innkeepers did surety
for their foreign clients but also seem frequently to have doublecrossed
them. Sureties were responsible for the entire debt unless limited
liability had been declared, a practice not confined to Bruges nor to
professional brokers. Since the innkeepers frequently vouched for
their guests, losses by foreigners thus made the innkeepers' business
dangerous, and the rate of failure was high.

In many cases, the losses thus sustained by foreign merchants
seem to have been unavoidable. For despite the prevalence of written
instruments, much was done on the basis of oral agreements and concealed partnerships of short duration. Smuggling was rampant, and
everybody wanted to avoid customs and brokerage fees. The result was
that brokers, virtually all of whom served many clients, often seem
genuinely to have been uncertain of who owned what. For larger
sums, and when the brokers were handling the business of several
foreigners, book entries would record the transfer of funds from one
merchant's account with a broker or at the exchange to another's.
Some innkeepers catered to guests of particular nations or cities, and
this could facilitate exchanges. Foreign merchants at Bruges also
bought considerable merchandise from persons who were not brokers
but who had obtained the goods from brokers and thus cleared customs. Actual payments were usually assisted by moneychangers, with
whom the brokers were in close contact by the mid fourteenth century.
Some foreigners simply had payments due to them made over to the
accounts of their innkeepers.[100]

The mechanics of brokerage at Bruges are illustrated by the following passage from the confiscation record of 1371, detailing property
that had been sold to Englishmen and changed hands but was being
returned to the sellers in return for the portion of the price that the
English purchasers had actually paid in cash. In some cases the Englishmen had taken possession without making even a partial payment:

100. van Houtte, 'Makelaars en waarden', 181–2, 188.
101. Translated from Municipal Archives of Bruges, Political Charters no. 616, fo
26v.

Item to John Fredus, Spaniard, two bales of wax with this mark, sold to John Scot, Englishman, for 20 lb. groot, unpaid. Broker Jan van Coukelare, and the surety for this is [left blank].

Item to Morvel Dama, Genoese, six bales of almonds with this mark, sold to Richard Datfield [probably Hatfield] for 12 lb. groot, unpaid. Broker of this Jacob Vinne, and surety [blank] . . . .

Item delivered to Half van Schevele, Easterling, nine vats of flax with this mark and two of this mark , sold to William Colin, Englishman, for 37 lb. 2s. 2d. groot, broker and surety Zeger Honin the younger. . . .

Item delivered to Michiel de Butorie, Spaniard, 263 rods of iron, which Pieter de Scuetelare bought on the account of Adam Waermer, Englishman, nothing paid on this account, for 58 [lb.] 4s. 1d. gro., broker and surety Pieter de Scutelare, and the iron had this mark

Item delivered to Thuenise de Barnevoerste 2 pipes of oil with this mark , which he sold to John Chilly, Englishman, and one pipe with this mark , sold to Richard Hatfield, Englishman, all for 12 lb. 12s. groot, unpaid, broker Michiel Steedekin and surety Pieter de Scutelare . . .

Item delivered to Lasare Guynise on behalf of Baldes de Cherin, Florentine living at Florence, 27 bales of woad with this mark . Item 12 bales of woad with this mark sold to Heinric Ghistendorp on behalf of Heinric Stasins, Englishman, all for 80 lb. groot, unpaid, surety Zeger Honin the younger.[101]

The money market of Bruges was the greatest in northern Europe and brought considerable capital into the Flemish economy.[102] The papers of the Datini firm of Prato and Florence, which survive through 1410, show an organized money market in place by 1370, where bills of exchange were negotiated and exchange rates were quoted regularly at Barcelona, London, Genoa, Paris and Venice, sometimes Pisa and Florence, and occasionally Lucca. The value of the money of Bruges and Barcelona and of Bruges and Paris were usually close. London was also under the influence of Bruges, but less so than Paris. The money rates had an impact on prices of goods in international trade, notably spices, which moved similarly at Bruges and Paris. The money market facilitated credit transactions and international trade in a period of tight money supply. In 1408 the city of Bruges bought grain that was stored at Ghent belonging jointly to three Italians. Parisians usually sent funds to London over Bruges or by letter addressed to a banker of Bruges.[103] Since the value of a coin was higher in its place of origin than in the place where it was exchanged, the presence of the money market in Bruges involved a gain in specie for Flanders.

Moneychanging and banking were thus highly developed in Bruges. International finance was entirely in Italian hands, but in Bruges they had to act through local bankers, pawnbrokers and moneychangers. At the end of the thirteenth century, the Italians set up permanent branches in Bruges and left the Champagne fairs. Several techniques made this possible, including partnerships for a term of years rather than for a single venture.[104]

The bill of exchange became the preferred means of speculating on the money market. An Italian bought a bill in his own currency, repayable at Bruges or another foreign port in the local coin. It could then be used to pay debts in the foreign port or to speculate on variations in the exchange rate; for it could be redrafted by a business partner, made payable in the home coin and sent back to Italy. Although the quotation of the exchange rate at the time of purchase

102. See in general R. de Roover, *The Bruges Money Market around 1400* (Brussels, 1968).

103. R. de Roover, 'Le Marché monétaire au Moyen Age et au début des temps modernes: Problèmes et méthodes', *RH* **495** (1970): 5–40.

104. The best one-volume account of the commercial environment of Bruges is still R. de Roover, *Money, Banking and Credit in Mediaeval Bruges. Italian Merchant–Bankers, Lombards, and Money-Changers. A Study in the Origins of Banking* (Cambridge, Mass., 1948).

normally specified a *de facto* interest payment, this could fluctuate downward as well as upward; thus gain was not guaranteed with the bill of exchange, and the church countenanced its use. Although some Flemings began using the bills at the end of the fourteenth century, they were employed normally only by the foreigners at Bruges. Use of the bills became an important means of disposing of the stores of specie that the Italians were accumulating at Bruges and of evading the problems caused by the bullion shortage that became so severe after 1370.[105]

The moneychangers were an important element of the Bruges commercial environment. In contrast to the Lombards, who were petty moneylenders and pawnbrokers found in most communities of Flanders, the majority of moneychangers were native Flemings. The number of moneychangers was strictly limited. The four oldest exchanges of Bruges were hereditary fiefs held of the count, but their numbers were augmented by 'licensed moneychangers', who paid a yearly fee. There were about fifteen changers in Bruges in the mid-fourteenth century, but the number declined sharply in the fifteenth.[106]

The moneychangers were taking money on deposit, refundable on demand, by the late thirteenth century. The modern public bank in Flanders is descended from the medieval exchange. In the absence of a municipal bank at Bruges, the moneychangers often handled the town's dealings with foreigners. The moneychangers invested heavily in textile production, and their contacts with foreign merchant bankers gave them easy access to overseas markets. The account books of the moneychangers Collard de Marke and William Ruweel leave the impression that banking was more important for them than exchange transactions. Book transfers outnumber cash transactions in the money-changers' ledgers. Credit was generally extended simply by allowing customers to overdraw their accounts. Understandably, moneychanging was a high-risk profession, with numerous failures.[107]

The foreign communities at Bruges

The German Hanse. By 1250 the Germans had become the largest

105. R. de Roover, *L'Evolution de la lettre de change, XIVe–XVIIIe siècles* (Paris, 1953).

106. Curiously, Ghent, where exchange facilities were much more restricted, had about ten moneychangers at that time. Nicholas, *Metamorphosis*, 127.

107. Murray, 'Family, Marriage and Moneychanging', 114–25; de Roover, *Money,*

foreign group in the Zwin towns, surpassing the Italians in numbers, although not in wealth. The Hanse, a league of north German cities linking the older economy of the Rhineland with the newer foundations along the Baltic coast, brought grain and forest products to Flanders in return for cloth, salt and wine. Although Bruges was the Germans' major centre, they also visited the Flemish fairs, especially those of Torhout and Ypres.

By 1280 German imports were so essential to Flanders that the Hansards used the commercial blockade and a move to Aardenburg as a political weapon against the city of Bruges. Most other foreigners joined the Germans at Aardenburg, returning in 1282 after Bruges made concessions, including the right to deal directly with other foreigners. When they repeated the manoeuvre in 1306, the other foreigners did not join them, and the Germans returned to Bruges in 1309 in return for a comprehensive privilege. We know little of the organization of the German community at Bruges at this time, but it tended increasingly to act as a unit. In 1347 it drew up its first 'constitution'. The Bruges office was the largest and wealthiest of the four Hanse overseas colonies; an assembly in 1457 included about 600 persons.

The Germans also provided the largest and most reliable overseas market for Flemish cloth. They bought more Flemish cloth than did merchants of other areas, who were shifting towards Brabantine cloth by the fourteenth century and English in the fifteenth. More than 75 per cent of the Hanse exports from Bruges were cloth, but this includes non-Flemish cloth bought at Bruges. They especially patronized the smaller Flemish towns, particularly Poperinge but also Comines and Aalst.[108]

From the mid fourteenth century the German colony was frequently in conflict with the Flemish counts and even more often with the city of Bruges over issues that seem to have been beyond the capacity of the Flemings to ameliorate, notably their utter inability to stop piracy in their own territorial waters. Some Hanse towns were also unhappy about conditions in Flanders, notably coinage depreciation, taxation by the city government at Bruges and the extension of the staple to salt and grain, which foreigners had previously been allowed to sell 'from ship to ship' without going through the brokerage houses. A Diet of the Hanse towns in January 1358 decreed a blockade of Flanders, not limiting it to Bruges. It was surprisingly successful, and Flanders had to

108. Pounds, *Historical Geography*, 422; Dollinger, *German Hansa*, 40–2, 48, 50–1, 103, 248–9.

sue for peace in 1360. Flanders paid an indemnity to the Germans and granted them new privileges, including the right to engage in retail trade. By 1362 Hansards were paying only half the toll demanded of natives on wine and German beer.

With the new civil war in Flanders in 1379, the Germans became vulnerable to reprisals from all parties. After repeated complaints, they left Bruges for Middelburg in 1388 and declared a new blockade. The settlement of 1392 prescribed an indemnity and guaranteed that if a Fleming attacked a German in Flanders, the Three Cities would pay the fine if the attacker was insolvent. If it was done by a foreigner, the count and the Three Cities were to arrest all citizens of the culprit's home town if it refused compensation. But the blockade of 1388 was the last one that worked. The Prussians and Teutonic Knights had opposed it in the league Diet, and as the Burgundian rulers of Flanders extended their power over the entire Low Countries, it became impossible for the Germans to blockade their entire domain.[109]

The Spaniards. The Spaniards got their first privileges at Sluis, Damme and Bruges before 1311. The staples of the trade at this time were saffron, oil, iron, nuts and dried fruits. The Spanish community at Bruges was always dominated by the Castilians, although some Catalans and Biscayans are found. In 1348 Louis of Male gave new privileges to the Castilians at Bruges, putting them on the same footing with the Hansards and somewhat later the English. The Castilians, like virtually all privileged foreigners at Bruges, obtained safe conduct for merchants, boatmen, personnel and their families and goods. They were exempted from tolls except customs at Damme and were freed of reprisals for all but their own debts. The privilege was given in perpetuity but, in recognition of the realities of foreign trading, they had forty days to get out if it were ever revoked! Louis of Male extended this privilege in 1368, promising to have new lighthouses built on the coast and pledging to prosecute absconding Flemish debtors of the Spaniards. Hostellers of Bruges were personally bound to pay for goods bought for their guests, and the city of Bruges guaranteed the debts of moneychangers to Spaniards. The count recognized the intricate network of partnerships and partial payments operating at Bruges; for example, if a Castilian committed a capital crime he lost only his own goods, not those in his possession belonging to other merchants.[110]

109. Dollinger, *German Hansa*, 62–7, 74–8; *IAB* 2: 55.
110. Wendy R. Childs, *Anglo-Castilian Trade in the Later Middle Ages* (Manchester, 1978), 110–11, 117; J. Finot, *Etude historique sur les relations commerciales entre la Flandre & l'Espagne au Moyen Age* (Paris, 1899), 47–8, 55–9, 97–105.

The English involvement in the Castilian civil war after 1369 actually seems to have helped Flemish trade, for Castilian merchants were able to transfer goods in Flanders that would have been stopped had they tried to sell them directly in England. Despite dangers, the Castilians never stopped trading in Bruges. The forced loan levied by Bruges in 1378–9 taxed the Catalans on a level with the Florentines and Venetians. Another loan in 1411 placed the Catalans slightly behind the Genoese and Venetians but ahead of all other foreign groups.[111]

The English. The English were the most politically vulnerable foreign community at Bruges, and their position was made the more delicate by the fact that wool, the major English export that was legal in Flanders, was supposed to be handled at Calais, and their cloth was forbidden for sale in Flanders at all. Thus the English colony at Bruges busied itself chiefly with importing Flemish and other continental goods that came to the Bruges market.[112]

Since England was so close to Flanders, the English colony at Bruges had a more fluctuating personnel than did the Germans and Italians, many of whom stayed for years at a time. The basic regulation was a charter granted by Louis of Male in 1359.[113] It has general similarities to his charter for the Castilians but also some specific points that are peculiar to the English. The English were allowed to buy and resell cloth at Bruges and exchange it for their own products, as long as the cloth was not English. They were given their own weight, subject to the regulation of the government of Bruges. They were given freedom of assembly and had their own court, which could adjudicate all but capital crimes. The magistrates of Bruges were to guarantee security of debts owed to the English, and the usual guarantees were given against reprisals.

The accounts of the water bailiff, who was essentially a customs officer along the Zwin, show the English in a number of violations of the extremely minute customs regulations, particularly by 'overshipping' without paying customs at Sluis, the terminal point for all but very small boats. Some of the goods that the English obtained in

---

111. There were no Germans on the list, probably because their ancient privileges exempted them from tax. Finot, *Etude Flandre-Espagne*, 123–4, 149–56.

112. The discussion of the English at Bruges is based on Nicholas, 'English Trade', 23–61.

113. L. Gilliodts-van Severen, *Cartulaire de l'ancien estaple de Bruges*, 6 vols (Bruges, 1904–6), 1: 226–32.

Bruges were truly remarkable: the pork of eighteen pigs, grindstones and 264 tons of honey were actually smuggled between boats. The water bailiff relied on written bills of lading that specified in detail the contents of cargoes. Merchants had marks on their packages to aid identification. The marks were placed on goods when a first payment had been made or even in some cases where the purchase had been agreed upon in principle and no funds transferred.

The English exported considerable beer and cheese to Flanders, where they exchanged it for Flemish herring and the goods of the other foreign communities. We have seen that considerable English cloth reached Bruges, much of it brokered through Italian bankers. Bruges brokerage houses were intermediaries in the wool trade; although in the fifteenth century Low Country merchants had to go to Calais to get their wool, it was available through Bruges in the fourteenth. At least half of the export of wool to the continent by English denizens seems at some point to have passed through Bruges in the early days of the Calais staple. Much of it, too, came from Italians, who had licences to export wool directly to the Mediterranean from Southampton but in fact took much of it to Bruges, together with additional wool that they obtained at Calais, and sold it there on credit to Dutch and Flemish drapers, receiving one-third of the purchase price at Calais and the rest in deferred payments at one of the fairs, most commonly Bruges or Antwerp.[114]

URBAN SOCIETY

Town populations

Interpretations of very diverse data give a basis for estimating the total population of most Flemish cities in the late Middle Ages. Ghent had a population of about 50,000 in 1357 but it had declined in the wake of warfare and plague to 25,000 by 1385. Thereafter population grew into the fifteenth century. Bruges contained some 46,000 souls between 1338 and 1340. Ypres had 20–30,000 in 1311 but had declined to 10,489 in 1412. In 1338 Aalst had 3600, Dendermonde 9000 and Geraardsbergen 4500; the latter then declined rapidly, reaching 3868 in

---

114. Craeybeckx, *Commerce d'importation*, 196–7.

1395 and 3252 in 1441. Figures survive for Courtrai only for the fifteenth century, but it seems to have been relatively stable at about 5300 between 1440 and 1478.[115]

Figures for total population in a single year freeze in time a situation that in fact was actually extremely fluid. Town populations were increased by migration, which is difficult to measure. The rent books of Ghent, which record only population movement without specifying what caused it, suggest a rate of horizontal mobility within the city of generally under 4 per cent before 1340. This rose to nearly 15 per cent in the crisis year of 1360–1, then stabilized at about 7.5 per cent between 1361 and 1379. Migration to the city was not hindered, although guild restrictions limited the jobs that newcomers could hold. New migrants to Ghent were required only to register with the aldermen within three days of entrance, and scattered information suggests that this statute was enforced. There was massive refugee movement into Ghent during the war of 1379–85, and by the early fifteenth century the city had become such a refuge for the poor seeking alms that the government forbade anyone to come to Ghent and stay for more than one day without the consent of parish officials who were in charge of poor relief.[116]

The municipal accounts of Bruges and Ypres record the names of persons who purchased burgher standing, which of course is not the same as a total migration figure. Migration to both was low before 1315, although Bruges generally admitted about twice the number of new burghers as Ypres, reflecting the approximate difference in size between the cities.[117] From 1332 a distinct pattern emerges. Between 1332 and February 1338, Bruges admitted an annual average of 49 new burghers. From 1338–46 the average was 242, dropping abruptly to 120 between 1346 and 1348. The accounts then break until 1350–1. Migration dwindled to a trickle between 1350 and 1362, averaging 72 per year. There is considerable fluctuation between years during the period 1362–76, after which the figures become more fragmentary, but the average more than doubled, to 158. These figures clearly

115. For the figures for Ghent, which are considerably lower than those generally favoured by Belgian scholars, see Nicholas, *Metamorphosis*, 17–40; for the others, see Prevenier *et al.*, 'Tussen crisis en welvaart', 51 and literature cited.

116. Nicholas, *Metamorphosis*, 36–9; M. Boone, *Gent en de Bourgondische hertogen* ca. *1384–ca. 1453: Een sociaal-politieke studie van een staatsvormingsproces*, VKVA, Kl. Letteren 52, No. 133 (Brussels, 1990), 101.

117. This exposition is based on Nicholas, *Town and Countryside*, 228–34, supplemented by Prevenier *et al.*, 'Tussen crisis en welvaart', 52–6.

parallel other demographic trends that we have noted, with a tendency of migration to increase in periods of civil strife. Most of the immigrants came from western Flanders, and somewhat over half were definitely artisans, although the fact that no trade is stated for many makes it impossible to draw firm conclusions. The cosmopolitan character of Bruges is shown, however, in the fact that 21 per cent of the new burgesses between 1281 and 1417 came from outside Flanders and 26.7 per cent of those between 1479 and 1496.

While earlier emigration from Flanders overseas had been of knights and peasants, it was of artisans in the fourteenth century, as the cities for the first time lost substantial numbers of persons. Edward III established about a hundred Flemish and Brabantine weavers in London and some in York, and offered inducements to attract more, specifically exempting them from the requirement of joining the London weavers' guild. This caused such hostility that in 1355 Edward told the magistrates of London to forbid the citizens to molest Flemish artisans.

Yet although English cloth working expanded under Edward III, foreign emigration was so small – about a hundred foreign weavers lived in London, probably more than for the rest of the realm put together – that it cannot explain the growth. This changed after 1385, when the municipal accounts of Ghent show a vastly increased number of persons paying the issue tax. The destruction of the unfortified suburbs of Ypres by the English army in 1383 caused many textile workers to emigrate, especially to England but some also to Brabant. The Low Country artisans continued to have a sense of national identity in England; within the London guild of foreign weavers, hostility between Flemings and Brabantines was so strong that each had its own bailiff, and they had separate cemeteries until 1421. In Florence in 1448 the brotherhood of St Barbara, an association of the so-called 'Teutonic' immigrants, had forty-eight members, of whom thirty-five were Flemings.[118]

The weaver–fuller rivalry

Much of the turmoil in the Flemish cities involved the embittered rivalry of weavers and fullers, the two largest textile guilds, although

118. Henri-E. de Sagher, 'L'Immigration des tisserands flamands et brabançons en Angleterre sous Edouard III', *Mélanges d'histoire offerts à Henri Pirenne par ses anciens élèves et ses amis à l'occasion de sa quarantième année d'enseignement à l'université de Gand, 1886–1926*, 2 vols (Brussels, 1926), 1: 109–26; Demey, 'Handarbeiders', 203.

this has been exaggerated. The problem was more severe in industrial towns that had a large labour force concentrated in one dominant industry than in commercial cities or towns whose industry catered to a mainly domestic market. The weavers and fullers had generally been united in the struggles to overthrow the patrician regimes of the thirteenth century, but they soon became bitter rivals. Although 'weaver' included a wide range of economic groups, from the prosperous drapers who gave out work to individual artisans to the poorer labourers at the looms, the weavers as a whole were considerably more prosperous than the fullers. They controlled the cloth halls. Many fullers were frequently simply the wage-earning employees of persons who were enrolled in the weavers' guild. Their occupation was dirty, and they were the least mechanized and skilled of the cloth making occupations.

The counts generally favoured the fullers, who were less politically revolutionary than the weavers and who in most cities were about two-thirds as numerous a group as they. We have seen that the weavers were excluded from political participation at Ghent in 1320 but were restored by van Artevelde in 1338. In 1349 Louis of Male instituted regimes throughout Flanders that systematically excluded the weavers from city governments in favour of the fullers. Rebellions began in 1358 that were especially severe at Ypres – the count barely escaped one disturbance with his life – but by August 1361 the weavers had returned to influence, although except at Ghent the fullers seem to have had more political power than they.

The fullers of Ghent were naturally resentful. Those of Dendermonde and Courtrai received substantial wage increases in 1367, evidently exceeding the extent to which the coin had depreciated to that point. Most guildsmen of Ghent did as well; the late 1360s may have been the most prosperous period of the fourteenth century for the urban artisans of Flanders in terms of real wages. In 1373 the fullers struck for higher wages, and many of them emigrated to villages south and east of Ghent and to Deinze and Oudenaarde, where resentment against the larger city ran high. In return for a substantial raise – the last wage increase that they would receive until 1420 – the fullers returned to work until weaver provocation led to fighting in July 1379, a week before the outbreak of civil war.

At the first sign of trouble for Ghent, many fullers left the city. Exiled fullers of Ghent helped identify members of the garrison of Gentenars who were retreating from Bruges after the battle of Westrozebeke in 1382, and others helped in the count's defence of Dendermonde in 1380. Curiously, although the weavers controlled the government of Ghent in October 1382, the Ghent captains arbitrated a dispute between the weavers and fullers of Ypres by giving the fullers a substantial wage increase. The hostility between the groups there seems to have been political rather than economic.

The political power of the Flemish weavers thus seems to have reached its apogee at precisely the point when their economic importance was waning. The textile trades in the cities were still numerous, but their wealth and even their absolute numbers were declining. Although it was once thought that some 60 per cent of the population of Ghent in the 1350s consisted of cloth workers, recent work suggests that it was probably less and that it was definitely declining sharply for the rest of the century.[119]

Guild structures

Even at Ghent, the great political constant was the 'small guilds', the fifty-three locally based trades and six small textile guilds which constituted the third Member of the city. The shippers were the most numerous and powerful, but the butchers and brewers were also important and were guaranteed seats on the city councils. This was an elite of politically recognized organizations; 196 non-textile trades have been identified in Ghent, but only 53 had independent guilds. The others were either too small to have their own organization, were incorporated with other trades, or took form after the political division of the city into Members in 1360.[120]

The nature of the guild structures in the Flemish cities has occasioned some controversy. The privileges of mastership were considerable. Masters had the sole right to train apprentices and own their own shops. They employed journeymen, who were generally hired by the week or month rather than by the day; thus, when market demand was low, the master would work while the journeyman would not. Even masters who lacked enough capital to own their own shops and took work from other masters normally commanded twice the wage of skilled journeymen, who in their turn got 20 per cent more than unorganized labourers.[121]

---

119. Discussion based on Nicholas, *Metamorphosis*, 154–7, 19–20 and Nicholas, *Van Arteveldes*, 177–8.

120. On the guild structure, see Nicholas, *Metamorphosis*, 20. See also Prevenier *et al.*, 'Tussen crisis en welvaart', 67.

121. Blockmans, 'Vers une société urbanisée', 84.

The wage structure, as much as a desire to limit the profits of a diminishing market to fewer persons, thus may explain the zeal of the masters in most guilds to restrict the numbers of new entrants. Although journeymen in textile guilds generally had the right to vote in guild affairs, those in the smaller trades did not.[122] It was further- more not necessary for a young man to pass through a period as journey- man if he had done his apprenticeship and had the means to open his own shop. Journeyman became a necessary grade in most guild hierar- chies only in the fourteenth century, and the masterwork as a sign of technical competence comes into vogue only at the century's end. The names of qualified journeymen were kept in a register by the guild.[123]

The drive to strict heredity was peculiar to food guilds in the early fourteenth century. The butchers, as we have seen, are the most conspicuous example. With the natural attrition of a closed group, the number of butchers declined. Although Ghent had 136 butcher families in 1302, their number had dropped to 14 by 1469. Thus most meat was actually being cut by journeymen, while the master butchers controlled the meat supply in principle. There were some odd gaps, notably in the fact that bakers of the city seem to have had the right to provide pigs to the churches.[124]

But by the early fourteenth century most guilds tried to control, although not close, access to mastership by using entry fees, which were always higher for persons who were not the sons of masters than for 'internal' candidates. By the fifteenth century the difference was substantial. Sons of the master carpenters of Bruges in 1441 paid an entry fee that was the equivalent of 5.2 work days, while outsiders who came from other locations in Flanders paid a fee equal to 101 days, rising to 180 in 1479. For journeymen from outside Flanders, the amount went from 149 days' equivalent to 244.

Despite the high entry fees, some guilds remained open. Between 1375 and 1500, 668 new masters were enrolled as coopers of Bruges, of whom only 145 were masters' sons. The difference in entry fees was less than for carpenters, but it was still substantial; outsiders paid

122. H. van Werveke, *De medezeggenschap van de knapen (gezellen) in de middeleeuw- sche ambachten*, MKVA, Kl. Letteren, 5, No. 3 (1943).

123. Demey, 'Arbeiders', 219.

124. H. van Werveke, 'De Gentse vleeschouwers onder het Oud Regime: Demo- grafische studie over een gesloten en erfelijk ambachtsgild', HMGOG **3** (1948): 3–32. The bakers fed pigs with the waste grits. At Antwerp the bakers had a large share of the meat production of the city; they were allowed to keep up to twelve pigs; Demey, 'Arbeiders', 208; see also Nicholas, *Metamorphosis*, 252–61.

19.46 per cent more in 1477, 56.38 per cent in 1478.[125] Prosopographical investigation shows that most guilds at Ghent were open to outside penetration until after 1385. This is not surprising in related trades, such as families having some members as shippers and others as shipwrights, but there are cases of textile artisans siring bakers, the same man being a brewer and a shearer, and similarly unlikely combinations. Since children sometimes inherited presumptive rights in different guilds from several ancestors, they had some freedom of choice even in avoiding the high entry fees. In cases where one son followed his father in the trade, different provision was made for the other sons, and this was not always a question of the oldest son following the father; interest and aptitude sometimes caused the oldest to enter a different profession. The most restricted trades were those demanding a high level of skill, those with political power more impressive than their numbers and those that controlled some essential service or commodity.[126]

We have noted that some Flemish guilds provided poor relief through almshouses for indigent members. The guild statutes generally regulated entry fees, hours and conditions of work, inspections, length of time as burgess, conditions of mastership and length of apprenticeship, which varied from two years to eight depending on the level of skill demanded in the trade. When a confraternity was attached to a guild, an annual due was owed to it. Wage scales were provided in many statutes, although this fluctuated according to demand for labour and the debasements of the coin. The guilds tried to restrict access to the labour market to those in the guild or affiliated with it, but this required the enforcement of the town government, since guild courts had jurisdiction only over their own members. The statutes forbade assaults on guild brothers and made such offences against incumbent deans or councillors of the guild particularly heinous. Such umbrella organizations as the 'small guilds' of Ghent had a joint court that handled cases arising between practitioners of different trades within the Member, for example between a butcher and a brewer; but legal actions between persons in different political Members, for example between a butcher and a weaver, had to be handled by the town court

125. J.-P. Sosson, 'Die Körperschaften in den Niederlanden und Nordfrankreich: neue Forschungsperspektiven' in Klaus Friedland (ed.), *Gilde und Korporation in den nordeuropäischen Städte des späten Mittelalters* (Cologne, 1984), 79–90; Sosson, 'La Structure sociale de la corporation médiévale: L'exemple des tonneliers de Bruges de 1350 à 1500', *RBPH* **44** (1966): 457–78.

126. Nicholas, *Domestic Life*, 183–6.

or by private arbitration. Some guilds limited the amount of work or the number of apprentices permitted to a single master or provided that a master who had more work than he needed should pass the surplus on to another accredited master who did not have enough.

Urban violence

Pirenne and his followers saw the high levels of violence in the Flemish cities in the fourteenth century in the light of conflicts within the textile industry. In the smaller towns, producing mainly for a local market, the independent artisan predominated, and relations between trades were generally harmonious. In the larger cities, which were dependent on an export market that was diminishing, most artisans were wage earners who were employed only intermittently if at all, and much social conflict resulted. [127]

Yet a Marxist explanation is inadequate even in the cities. Evaluation of the extent of 'class' warfare is made difficult by political structures, which grouped persons of different economic strata into the same guild and then again into Members that fought for power. Even more, the strength of family alliances, particularly at Ghent, confuses ideological and political allegiances. Migration was continuous between the cities and rural areas, and some families, particularly in the victualling trades, appear to have had branches both in the city and in the smaller towns and farm villages.

Family feuds could become prolonged and embittered. The level of violence at Ghent is stupefying even to jaded modern sensibilities. We have noted the cases of the Borluuts and van Sinte-Baafs and of Philip van Artevelde, but the list could be extended indefinitely. Blood had to be avenged with blood, and the senior male of the family had an obligation to exact retribution. Although carrying deadly weapons was forbidden under most circumstances, the laws were not enforced. A case of 1365 at Ghent that began as a fistfight, then escalated into a battle involving a knife and a battle axe, aroused the magistrates' ire only when the man who had been attacked initially pursued his antagonist with an iron morning star, for 'a morning star is not an honourable man's weapon, but rather is forbidden among all decent people'. [128] Ghent was divided into armed camps, whose members identified themselves by 'party' and evidently wore special uniforms.

127. Demey, 'De Handarbeiders', *Flandria Nostra* 1: 196.
128. Nicholas, 'Governance', 248, trans. from SAG,Zoendincbock 4, 1, f. 2r.

The blood prices and many of the damage payments for non-fatal assaults were so high that no ordinary labourer could have afforded them, which confirms an impression that most of the disorder was the result of family pride among the ruling elite, not petty criminality among the oppressed. Since kinship was bipartite, marriage into a family would involve a new member in its often very intricate feuds. There was no notion that homicide was immoral; if a blood price was paid, as arranged by the two sets of kin, justice was done.[129]

While disorder was endemic in the Flemish cities, the rural areas were less than havens of bucolic delight, particularly when city men had interests there. In 1373 a brawl erupted at Eeklo, northwest of Ghent, involving several men of Ghent, most of them butchers, and a band of men of Eeklo, several of whom were related to the Gentenars. In the arbitral judgement reached in early 1374,

> Jacob de Ketelboetere and his brother Willem have acknowledged in advance that they entered the house of Heinric [Parijs] eating and drinking and were discourteous there to Heinric and his household, as will be shown. The de Ketelboetere boys also acknowledge that when Eulaert [Parijs] and his brother Heinric were attending a wedding at Eeklo, they threatened to cut off the foot of Eulaert's manservant and otherwise to mistreat him. In addition, Boudin van Wulfscoet and his helpers, kinsmen of the de Ketelboeteres, came upon one Willem Zuchtinc, against whom they had been involved in a legal proceeding but in which Willem had been acquitted; Willem, who is a kinsman of the Parijses, received open wounds from which blood flowed. Furthermore, as Eulaert went to his estate 'ter Heyden', and from there directly to the parish church, Jacob de Ketelboetere, with a big noisy mob of men armed with bows and arrows, came out of Eeklo at night and went to Ravenscoet, where they found Gerard de Zwaef in a tavern. Jacob de Ketelboetere hit Gerard de Zwaef in the head with a battleaxe, and the wound might have been mortal if Gerard had not been wearing an iron helmet. Jacob de Ketelboetere said furthermore that if he had found Eulaert Parijs there, he would have done the same to him, since he had thought it had been Eulaert when he had hit the other man.

The following is the testimony of Eulaert Parijs and his party. First, Eulaert acknowledges that he came into the Meat Hall at Eeklo, where the de Ketelboeteres were standing, and then the de Ketelboeteres trooped

---

129. Discussion based on Nicholas, 'Crime and Punishment in Fourteenth-Century Ghent', *RBPH* **48** (1970): 289–334, 1141–76; Nicholas, *Domestic Life*, 187–206. For the murder of other political leaders of Ghent in the 1380s, see Andrée Holsters, 'Moord en politiek tijdens de Gentse opstand', *HMGOG* **37** (1983): 89–111.

together and looked around, and Eulaert also looked around. Then Eulaert said that if anyone thought that he had done anything wrong, he had better make amends for it or it would be on his head. Afterwards they came drinking into the house where Eulaert was, and Eulaert acknowledges that he was also at the wedding at Eeklo, and when he and his band tried to protect his manservant, and Eulaert and his brother Heinric were in front of and around Heinric de Ketelboetere's house. And then Heinric Parijs or someone on his behalf came to where one Pieter Hildebrand was. Pieter had been at the scene when Eulaert's nephew had been wounded, and Pieter was hit there once or twice with the fist.[130]

The situation of women in late medieval Flanders

Women enjoyed a position in late medieval Flanders that was more enviable legally and to a certain extent economically than in other parts of Europe.[131] Since the eleventh century Flanders had had a legal regime in which spouses inherited common assets from each other with minimal rights for their two extended families. This meant that property was transferred constantly between lineages, an easy alienability that fostered commercial development.

Inheritances were bipartite and gave no preference to males. This tended to benefit women, who were less likely than men to have a trade. When a married person died, the marital assets went in equal halves to all children of the marriage as a unit, to be held in trust for the minors or distributed to the adults, and to the surviving spouse as common property. The survivor also had the right to dower, or life use, on half the children's half. This provided substantial inheritances and made it possible for women whose husbands had some property to maintain independence in relation to the outside world and even their own children. The fact that half the joint assets belonged to each spouse created a kind of limited liability in Flemish law. The Willem Ruweel moneychanging firm of Bruges was saved from total collapse in 1370 by the fact that Ruweel's widow, who had brought him the exchange as a marriage portion, was liable for only half the firm's debts.[132] This also meant that it was rare for Flemish fathers to provide

130. Translated from D. Nicholas, 'The Marriage and the Meat Hall: Ghent/Eeklo 1373–1375', *Medieval Prosopography* **10** (1989): 49–50.

131. Section based on Nicholas, *Domestic Life*, Part 1.

132. Murray, 'Family, Marriage and Moneychanging', 117.

large dowries for their daughters, as happened in Italy, for only half the marriage settlement would be the woman's property. Aristocratic fathers tried to arrange their children's marriages, but with the lower orders, where little property was involved, the couple themselves chose their partners with minimal parental involvement.[133]

Women thus controlled considerable property in Flanders. Single women or 'independent businesswomen' who had been emancipated by their families could transact business on their own. Married women and unemancipated single women required the consent of their husbands, fathers or brothers for transactions above petty cash. A husband had the right to manage or encumber his wife's property, although he could not normally alienate it without her consent. Women were involved as co-participants in between a third and a half of property transactions recorded before the law aldermen of Ghent in the fourteenth century. In an appeal from Blankenberge to Bruges in 1330, the aldermen refused to preside over any transfer of houses, land or rents by a married man unless he was accompanied by his wife.[134]

Women were not often the victims of violent crime; when it did happen, the perpetrator was almost always a male. There are numerous cases of domestic violence, but also frequent displays of conjugal affection. Flanders conforms to a European-wide pattern in this regard. However, standards of sexual morality were abysmally low in Flanders. For this to be true of males is nothing new, but in Flanders it was also the case with women. Although the law provided strict penalties for sexual offences, court and property records show that both women and men did what they pleased and generally went unpunished by the magistrates and their kin. Sex was so open in Ghent that there is little evidence of prostitution, although Bruges had numerous brothels. There is less evidence for Ypres, but the judgements of the magistrates suggest that while women were not cloistered, statutes against sexual misconduct were much more rigidly applied there, and the control of fathers over their daughters more respected, than at Ghent or Bruges. Flemish prostitutes were familiar in France and England. Casotte Cristal, a bathhouse manager in Dijon, was accused of spying for the

---

133. Martha Howell, 'Marriage, Family and Patriarchy in Douai, 1350–1600'; Marianne Danneel, 'Orphanhood and Marriage in Fifteenth-Century Ghent', both in W. Prevenier (ed.), *Marriage and Social Mobility in the Late Middle Ages. Handelingen van het colloquium gehouden te Gent op 18 april 1988* (Ghent, 1989), 16, 107–8.

134. Nicholas, *Domestic Life*, 72; *IAB* 1: 421.

Burgundians after it fell into royal hands in 1478 because she and most of her girls spoke Flemish.[135]

Flemish women, including those with property, were expected to work outside the home if this was necessary to help support the family. Many married women operated businesses in active partnership with their husbands. Yet we have seen that single women received considerable poor relief in Ghent in the mid fourteenth century. Women were less likely to get professional training than men; they were rarely apprenticed, and most got their expertise from their husbands or fathers. We have no firm information for the period before 1300, but during the fourteenth century many guilds began excluding women from their ranks. Guilds that previously had permitted women to pass on presumptive rights of mastership to their sons now restricted succession to the male line. Women worked as journeymen, rarely as masters, although some guilds permitted widows the life practice of their master-husbands' trade. No woman ever held an office in a guild. Yet practice did not always conform to precept. The dyers of Ghent officially excluded women, but in fact many women worked as dyers and owned dyeries.

Even in trades where women were not numerous, they were influential and prominent. In addition to Margaret Ruweel of Bruges, one of the leading moneychangers of Ghent was a woman, Celie Amelakens. Numerous petty moneylenders were women, including some of the biggest operators of the city. Women were hostellers, which got them into brokerage through standing surety for foreign clients, and cloth wholesalers. Women were less involved in brewing and baking in Ghent than in other cities, but they do appear. As elsewhere, many women, including some of high social standing, entered domestic service. Servant girls were vulnerable. Cases from Ghent show that their wages were frequently not paid for years at a time, in effect binding them to their employers, and they seem to have been particularly liable to the amorous attentions of their masters.[136]

135. P. de Pelsmaeker (ed.), *Registres aux sentences des échevins d'Ypres* (Brussels, 1914), 268, 272, 274, 278, 284; Jacques Rossiaud, *Medieval Prostitution* (Oxford, 1988), 34, 45; Margaret Wade Labarge, *Women in Medieval Life: A Small Sound of the Trumpet* (London, 1986), 202.

136. In addition to Nicholas, *Domestic Life*, see M. Danneel, 'Quelques aspects du service domestique feminin à Gand, d'après les manuels échevinaux des Parchons (2ème moitié du XVe siècle' in W. Prevenier, R. van Uytven and E. van Cauwenberghe (eds), *Sociale structuren en topografie van armoede en rijkdom in de 14e en 15e eeuw: Methodologische aspecten en resultaten van recent onderzoek* (Ghent, 1986), 51–72.

316

CHAPTER ELEVEN

A Change of Direction: Flanders in the Burgundian State, 1384–1467

The accession of Duke Philip 'the Bold' of Burgundy as count of Flanders by right of his wife in 1384 begins a new development in the history of Flanders, but the change was neither sudden nor completely apparent. From contemporaries' perspective, having French lords as counts of Flanders was nothing new. Indeed, the Burgundians' importance was in linking Flanders to the rest of the Low Countries, not to France, for all but the first Burgundian duke fought the growth of power of the French crown. Despite its problems and its loss of economic hegemony, Flanders remained the most populous and wealthiest section of the Burgundian domain, which by 1433 included all parts of what are now Belgium and the Netherlands except the prince-bishopric of Liège. Flanders provided the power base from which the Burgundians were able to extend their might.[1]

Only at Ghent, and there only until 1453, did local magistrates in Flanders manage to keep their privileges inviolate against the inroads of the princes. Yet the new counts' efforts to bypass Flemish institutions of a collective nature were never successful. The power of the Four Members (Bruges, Ghent, Ypres and the Franc of Bruges; for the organization and power of the Members, see below) actually grew

1. W.P. Blockmans, 'De Bourgondische Nederlanden: de Weg naar een moderne staatsvorm', *Handelingen van de Koninklijke Kring voor Oudheidkunde, Letteren en Kunst van Mechelen* **77** (1973): 17.

under the first three Burgundians. While the dukes eventually spent most of their time in the Netherlands, referring to Burgundy as the 'lands thither', Flanders was more than simply part of a larger 'Burgundian Netherlands'.[2] It continued to have a highly individualized history. Each principality ruled by the Burgundian dukes had independent administrations and pursued different economic goals.

PHILIP 'THE BOLD' IN FRANCE AND FLANDERS (1384–1404)

The first Burgundian count of Flanders and his nephew, King Charles VI of France, played a larger role than did Louis of Male in ending Ghent's rebellion. Although Philip had spent considerable time in Flanders before 1379, the rebellion changed his attitude; in twenty years as count he visited Flanders only eight times, directing most of his efforts towards cultivating his interests in Paris and the duchy of Burgundy. During his frequent absences, Philip acted through his wife Margaret of Male as regent.

His earliest acts as count show that he would not be vindictive but also that he would brook no opposition. Rebellions in 1387 and 1391 by splinter groups within the weavers' guild at Bruges and in 1392 by dissidents in Ghent were easily suppressed.[3] To forestall trouble, the count in 1387 permitted taverns to stay open in the Ypres vicinity only along major roads, near parish churches or at other populated places and ordered the bailiff to close locales within a league of the city that were being used for secret meetings.[4]

Another problem was religious division. Since 1378 Europe had had two popes, Urban VI at Rome and Clement VII at Avignon. Most Flemings, including Louis of Male, were Urbanist. The Flemish clergy supported this almost unanimously, and Flanders remained Roman despite pressure from the new counts until after Urban died in 1389.

---

2. This term is used by Walter Prevenier and Wim Blockmans, *The Burgundian Netherlands* (Cambridge, 1985).

3. J. Mertens, 'Twee (Wevers)opstanden te Brugge (1387–1391)', *ASEB* **110** (1973): 5–20; Richard Vaughan, *Philip the Bold: The Formation of the Burgundian State* (Cambridge, Mass., 1962), 175.

4. *IAY* **2**: 258. In 1411 the restriction was made even more stringent; *IAY* **3**: 31–2.

By 1393, however, only Ghent remained Urbanist. Gradually the upper officials in the church were replaced with Clementines.[5]

Flanders had been devastated horribly during the war. Philip provided some money to reconstruct fortifications, obtaining other funds from the Four Members of Flanders. He also continued the centralization of government that Louis of Male had so fostered and that had nearly cost him his countship. In 1386 Philip established a section of his council permanently at Lille, which had again been Flemish since 1369, the 'Chamber of the Council in Flanders', later called the Chamber of Accounts.[6]

There was no administrative union with Burgundy. For at least ten years after Philip became count, most of his civil servants in Flanders were still former officials of Louis of Male. The receivers-general were local men, and the three whom Philip himself appointed were all from Bruges. Some officials at the Chamber of Accounts were French, and French became the official language of government in Flanders, but Philip preferred Walloon Flemings to Frenchmen. Language was a major concern. Philip did not know Flemish, and the countess, although Flemish herself, was not fluent. Although the Flemings repeatedly importuned the counts to reside in Flanders, they had their own definition of their homeland. The 'trips and conferences' section of the city account of Ghent for 1454–5 contains the marginal notation, by auditors writing in French: 'They are even trying to maintain that Lille is outside Flanders so that they can claim higher wages and more horses.'[7]

Relations with England

The peace of Tournai of 18 December 1385 had given a general amnesty, even to the most embittered leaders of the rebellion, but a precondition of peace was that the Flemings abandon their English alliance.[8] Yet the cities wanted free trade with England in everything except English cloth, and anglophile parties formed in the Flemish cities, particularly Ghent.

5. J. van Herwaarden, 'De Nederlanden en het Westers Schisma', *AGN* 4: 379–86; Vaughan, *Philip the Bold*, 184–6.

6. Vaughan, *Philip the Bold*, 63, 169–71.

7. Vaughan, *Philip the Bold*, 209–13, 220; Vaughan, *John the Fearless: The Growth of Burgundian Power* (London, 1966), 127–9. The quotation is from Boone, *Geld en Macht*, 19.

8. Vaughan, *Philip the Bold*, 17–19, 33, 38, 76.

Flanders was thus officially on the French side in the Anglo-French conflict of 1386–9. Philip the Bold put the Flemish fleet at French disposal for an invasion of England, but the presence of a large and unruly French army in the Franc of Bruges in late 1386 – the fifth time in four years that foreign troops had occupied Flanders – led to disturbances that, with bad weather, forced cancellation of the invasion. The English responded when the earl of Arundel defeated much of the Flemish West Fleet in 1387 and opened contacts with Ghent. The anglophiles were deprived of their chief when Francis Ackerman, who had succeeded van Artevelde as the leader of the Ghent rebellion, was killed in a family feud; a year later, Philip the Bold rewarded the killer. In 1388 Philip again tried to use Flemish harbours as a base for attacking England. The climax of anglophile agitation came in 1392, when the the Burgundians discovered a spy network centring on Bruges and Mechelen, where a 'beardless man' operated as a double agent and reported to the bailiff of Bruges. The crucial figure was Claus van Lit, a Brabantine who was an external burgess of Ghent and had been master of the artillery of Ghent during the war. The count respected Ghent's right to try its burgher, but anglophilia soon died down.[9]

The war of 1379–85 had caused serious trade disruptions. Most foreigners had left Bruges after Louis of Male prohibited international trade in Flanders in 1380. Although Philip the Bold gradually restored foreigners' privileges, culminating in a general freedom of trade in Flanders issued on 15 January 1387, the English were the only major excluded group. Flemish ships ceased frequenting Southampton and Newcastle in 1382 and reappeared in much diminished numbers only after 1391. Channel piracy, whose main victims were Bruges and the small towns, picked up after 1387; the Flemings nicknamed the pirates *likedeelers* (corpse dividers).[10] Totally apart from the politically charged problem of piracy involving English and Flemings – the Four Members rarely met without taking up that issue – it is clear that Flemish waters were unsafe for all merchants and that foreigners expected the Flemish authorities to do the impossible and protect them not only from Flemings but also from one another, for many of the diverse foreign customers of the Flemings were bitter rivals of one another.[11]

9. The material on the anglophile movement is taken from Marc Haegeman, *De Anglofilie in het graafschap Vlaanderen tussen 1379 en 1435: Politieke en economische aspecten* (Kortrijk–Heule, 1988), 63, 85–6, 119, 156–71.

10. *IAB* **3**: 461, 463.

11. For representative cases, see Zoete, *Handelingen*, 1: 70, 230, 341, 343, 349–50, 355, 360, 426, 429, 617, 627; 2: 913, 1231, 1235.

While the English and the Flemish cities wanted an agreement, the count did not. Furthermore, the English wanted free trade for all items, including cloth. The English also wanted physical security in Flanders, including guarantees that ships driven into Flemish harbours by storms would be released. The English seem to have understood that their cloth could not legally enter Flanders, but they objected when the Flemings seized English cloth that entered Flemish waters by accident. Desperate as the Flemings were for an agreement with the English in the 1390s that would secure the wool supply, the Flemings would not give way on the issue of cloth.[12]

There was understandable confusion in England about who was in charge in Flanders. Even as the count planned an invasion, the Four Members, led by Bruges, negotiated openly with the English. The Flemings needed the commercial tie more than the English did, and the initiative thus generally came from them.[13] Foreigners understood that the Members were interested in security of trade, while the prince was not, and thus turned to them rather than to the count or his council.[14]

The English were also disturbed because Philip the Bold minted such skilfully debased counterfeits of the English noble that they were passed in England as legal tender. He also prohibited circulation of genuine English nobles in Flanders, despite the protests of the cities, for the English were demanding payment for wool at Calais in their own coin. In 1400 the count finally had to yield to the towns and permit the circulation of English nobles, but on the same basis as his own counterfeits, which were of less value. The Flemish issues thus tended to drive out the English coin from circulation on the continent.[15]

Relations improved after 1396, when a twenty-eight-year truce was sealed between France and England, and privileges were given in Flanders to merchants of several English cities. By 1398 most foreign merchants had returned to Bruges, and the English became more receptive to a treaty, for they also needed the Bruges international market. But piracy continued to vex relations. In 1402 there were several English

12. John H. Munro, 'Industrial Protectionism in Medieval Flanders: Urban or National?' in Harry A. Miskimin, David Herlihy and A.L. Udovitch (eds), *The Medieval City* (New Haven, 1977), 238–9.

13. Haegeman, *Anglofilie*, 210–13.

14. Zoete, *Handelingen*, 1: 451.

15. J.H. Munro, *Wool, Cloth, and Gold: The Struggle for Bullion in Anglo-Burgundian Trade, 1340–1378* (Toronto, 1972), 53, 58.

attacks on Flemish ships. Although Philip recommended reprisals, the Four Members preferred negotiation. The adjudication of the complaints gives important information about the realities of Channel commerce; an English captain claimed that a crew of Flemish herring fishermen from Heist were really Frenchmen from Rouen, then insisted that it had been an honest mistake. Attacks continued in 1403, and in April the count ordered English merchandise at Sluis seized.[16]

But the Members convinced the count to join negotiations a month later. Ghent and Ypres, which were less involved in foreign trade, did not play an active role but did support Bruges's efforts. An agreement was finally reached on 10 January 1407 that provided free passage for all merchants in both Flanders and England. Arms were excluded, but express liberty was given to the merchants of Brabant, Holland and Italy to go to the English wool staple at Calais. The crucial issues of piracy and English cloth were left unresolved, but the treaty of 1407 governed Anglo-Flemish commercial relations until after 1435.[17]

The end of the reign

Tensions erupted late in Philip the Bold's reign. The Four Members filed a list of grievances in 1398 whose contents are known only from reactions to it by a functionary at Lille. A major complaint was the count's continual absence from Flanders. The official responded by noting that the count in 1391 had forbidden the Four Members to meet without his consent or to rule on a case concerning an individual town. He questioned the legitimacy of an assembly that, contrary to the French model with which he was familiar, did not include nobles and clergy. The central administration expressly rejected the claims of the cities to speak for quarters.[18]

The major problem of Philip's last years came in 1402 when Ghent banished the sovereign bailiff of Flanders, Jacob van Lichtervelde, for having tried and executed a burgess of Ghent without the consent of the aldermen. Although the aldermen lacked extraterritorial jurisdiction and could not force van Lichtervelde to leave Flanders, the count

16. S.P. Pistono, 'Henry IV and the *Vier Leden*: Conflict in Anglo-Flemish Relations, 1402–1403', *RBPH* **54** (1976): 458–73

17. Prevenier, 'Les Perturbations', 477–97.

18. W. Prevenier, 'Briefwisseling tussen de Vier Leden van Vlaanderen en Filips de Stoute, hertog van Bourgondië, en diens echtgenote Margareta van Male, over de inbreuken op de Vlaamse privileges door vorstelijke ambtenaren en instellingen (1398–1402)', *BCRH* **150** (1984): 506–18.

was legally obliged to enforce their sentences of banishment. The other three Members supported Ghent's claim, alleging also that van Lichtervelde had levied a tax in the castellany of Ghent without Ghent's consent, a new privilege claimed by the Members. The affair blew over when the count, who had no intention of banishing van Lichtervelde, sent him on a pilgrimage to the Holy Land.[19]

JOHN 'THE FEARLESS' (1404/5–1419)

After Philip the Bold died, his widow, who was the legal ruler of Flanders, spent the remaining year of her life in Arras, then yielded to her son, John 'the Fearless', who gained his nickname on the crusade 'of Nicopolis' of 1396 that his father had largely financed. He was the most completely French of the four Burgundian counts; he did not even visit Flemish Flanders until 1398, when he was twenty-seven.[20]

No sooner had John made his Joyous Entry than the Four Members presented a list of demands, but his attitude was conciliatory. He agreed to reside in Flanders or to leave his wife with plenipotentiary powers and councillors there when he had to be away. He ignored the Members' demand that he abolish the appeal, which was subordinating their individual courts to the Council of Flanders. Indeed, in 1405 ducal judicial officers got the right to intervene *ex officio* instead of waiting for appeals from litigants or the town courts. He also agreed that all requests made to himself or the Council of Flanders by the Four Members would be answered in Flemish. The Members were unenthusiastic about John's request for subsidies, although in the early years the problem was less often his French campaigns than the English threat to the Flemish coast. The Flemings were understandably apprehensive about the possibility of foreign troops being used in Flanders, even to defend it. In 1405 Bruges asked in vain that the garrison defending Gravelines consist of 'people of weapons born in the land'.[21]

19. Prevenier, 'Briefwisseling', 518–22; Marc Boone, 'Particularisme gantois, centralisme bourguignon et diplomatie française: Documents inédits autour d'un conflit entre Philippe le Hardi, duc de Bourgogne, et Gand en 1401', *BCRH* **152** (1986): 49–113.

20. Vaughan, *John the Fearless*, 3–4.

21. P. Godding and J.T. de Smidt, 'Evolutie van het recht in samenhang met instellingen', *AGN* **4**: 172; Zoete, *Handelingen*, 31, 35–8, 39 and *passim*; Vaughan, *John the Fearless*, 14–15.

While his father had ignored Flemish demands, John thus tried to be amenable. During the first four years of his reign he spent a year in Flanders, and the countess lived at Ghent between April 1407 and February 1409 and took an active role in government. In 1411 John installed his son Philip count of Charolais at Ghent as his personal representative in Flanders. Except for two brief periods, Charolais spent the rest of his father's life there. The Members had also demanded that John observe all customs of the Flemings and move the Council of Flanders into Flemish Flanders and have its proceedings conducted in Flemish. In August 1405 John moved the Council to Oudenaarde, then in 1407 to Ghent. The Chamber of Accounts remained at Lille. In 1407 John ordered that while French would be spoken in closed sessions of the Council, each party to litigation would speak and receive responses in his own language in the council chamber.[22]

Ghent had been the centre of sentiment against Philip the Bold. Two risings there in 1406, however, evidently caused the government to alter its posture, and Ghent was won over definitely when the Council was moved there in May 1407 and Simon van Vormelis, the chief jurist of Ghent and its leader in the van Lichtervelde affair, became its head. The national initiative thus shifted to Bruges during John's time.[23]

Disturbances were more serious at Bruges, but the city had no allies by the spring of 1407. When agitation continued, John had a new government installed at mid-year. He permitted the guilds of Bruges to have their own banners but on condition that they be used only under comital command. By now, the counts were taking an annual tax in return for the right to collect the indirect taxes that were the basis of all cities' finance. In a fateful step, John the Fearless in 1407 forced the government of Bruges to pay him one–seventh of the city's revenues from the consumption excises instead of this. A cardinal aspect of the princes' policy from that time forward would be to obtain a regular, unnegotiated tax from each major city to relieve them of their dependence on individual negotiation and particularly on the taxes voted by the Four Members.[24]

John's entire reign was coloured by his family's rivalry with the house of Orléans. On 26 November 1407, after admitting that he had

22. Vaughan, *John the Fearless*, 15–19, 153–4.
23. Boone, *Gent en de Bourgondische hertogen*, 212.
24. W. Blockmans and Walter Prevenier, *In de Ban van Bourgondië* (Houten, 1988), 30; Vaughan, *John the Fearless* 26–7.

instigated the murder of the duke of Orléans, John the Fearless fled Paris. From that time on, John spent most of his time in France fighting for position. He tried to raise troops and money from his various domains; understandably, the Four Members were reluctant to commit Flemish troops.[25]

Only in 1411 did the towns agree to provide a small contingent, but the Flemings caused John's siege of Montdidier to fail by going home after disagreeing among themselves about the order of precedence in the militia. When the militia of Bruges returned home, the soldiers refused to re-enter the town until they had been paid, then presented a series of demands that included abolition of the assize on grain (the *cueillote*), restoration of the annual payment to the count instead of the seventh agreed to in 1407, and above all cancellation of the *calfvel* (vellum), the document of 1407 in which the craft guilds had agreed to be ranked behind the militias of the city and the count. Charolais surrendered the *calfvel*, but unrest continued into 1412. Governments ill disposed to the counts remained in power at Bruges until the revolt of 1437–9. The entire inconclusive episode of 1411 is known as the *calfvel*.[26]

Between the *calfvel* and the count's death in 1419, Flanders was largely autonomous for internal affairs. The military situation was unstable. Disturbances around Gravelines were serious in 1412 and 1413, as the French and Artesians harassed the Westland and hindered trade, particularly when they could strike English property.[27] Having learned his lesson, however, John did not ask the Flemings for soldiers again until July 1414, and even then they refused to fight outside Flanders. When the English invaded France in 1415, John forbade his vassals to take arms without his consent. But the towns favoured the English and kept Henry V's army informed of French troop movements, while a number of Flemish nobles, including John's brothers, the duke of Brabant and the count of Namur, lost their lives on the French side at Agincourt.[28]

A signal triumph of Burgundian diplomacy had been the marriage of John the Fearless's nephew, Duke John IV of Brabant, to Jacqueline of Bavaria, heiress of Hainault, Holland and Zeeland, in 1418. The emperor Sigismund, whose interests in the Low Countries were

25. Vaughan, *John the Fearless*, 67; Zoete, *Handelingen*, 1: 277.
26. Vaughan, *John the Fearless*, 165–9.
27. *IAB* 4: 89; Zoete, *Handelingen*, 1: 643, 698, 700; 2: 760–1.
28. Vaughan, *John the Fearless*, 142–5; Varenbergh, *Relations diplomatiques*, 503–4.

325

threatened, had tried to have the pope declare the marriage incestuous; when this failed, he enfeoffed John's uncle John of Bavaria with the three principalities, thus precipitating war between rival branches of the Burgundian house.

PHILIP 'THE GOOD' (1419–67)

The Bavarian affair was still unresolved when the Orléanists avenged the deed of 1407 by murdering John the Fearless at a feigned peace conference on 10 September 1419. The killing caused an abrupt change of Burgundian policy. While before the counts had been enemies of the English, the fact that the Orléanists controlled King Charles VI caused the new ruler, Philip 'the Good', to ally openly with Henry V, who was at the gates of Paris.[29]

The diplomatic triumphs of the Burgundian dynasty through marriages and fortuitous deceases need not be examined in detail for our purposes. In 1421 Philip purchased Béthune, which had been lost in 1389, and Namur. By 1425 he ruled most of the Low Countries except Brabant and Holland. In 1420 Jacqueline of Bavaria had abandoned Holland to her uncle; her incompetent husband was placed under regency by the Estates of Brabant, and Jacqueline left for Hainault, then England. In 1422, without waiting for a papal decision on her petition for an annulment of her marriage to John IV, she married Humphrey duke of Gloucester, uncle of King Henry VI and rival of his older brother, the king's regent, the duke of Bedford. The death of John of Bavaria in early 1425 precipitated a war of Philip the Good against Jacqueline of Bavaria and Humphrey. In 1428 she had to recognize Philip as 'regent and heir' of Hainault, Holland, Zeeland and Frisia. In 1430 the death of John IV's younger brother left Philip the Good the dukedom of Brabant.[30]

Domestic problems arose with the more active involvement of the count in Flemish affairs. The fullers of Ghent agitated intermittently after 1420 until a major uprising began in 1432, this time mainly of weavers. Disorders continued until a new fullers' plot was unveiled in 1434, then died down. A weaver conspiracy to overthrow the government

29. R. Vaughan, *Philip the Good: The Apogee of Burgundy* (London, 1970), 2–3, 35.

30. Prevenier and Blockmans, *Burgundian Netherlands*, 267; Vaughan, *Philip the Good*, 40.

of Ypres for alleged laxity in enforcing the city's textile monopoly was suppressed in January 1429. There were peasant disturbances in the castellany of Cassel between 1427 and 1431, evidently caused by resentment of the bailiff disregarding local privileges. There were riots at Geraardsbergen in April 1430 against the bailiff and peculation by the aldermen. The aldermen and bailiff of Ghent were called in to 'arbitrate' but actually suppressed the revolt by force.[31]

The peace of Arras and the campaign of 1436

The Burgundian alliance with England was increasingly shaky after 1430, as it became evident that Henry VI's regents could not prevent the French from recovering the north. On 21 September 1435 the peace of Arras settled the differences of Philip the Good and King Charles VII, and England was again a Flemish enemy.[32]

Philip decided immediately to attack Calais, which would upset the wool trade on which Flanders depended, but he seems to have been aware that Flanders would be more hurt by the break with England than his other domains. He may also not have realized that Flanders was less powerful than formerly. Thus, in March 1436 Philip made important concessions to get the adherence of the Four Members to the war effort. He agreed not to change the Flemish coinage for twenty years, extended the prohibition against the sale of English cloth to all his domains, agreed to restore goods seized from Casselers during their recent rebellion, pledged to use only native-born officials in Flanders and permitted the Flemish cities to obtain wools of Calais without hindrance. In return, Flanders provided most of the fighting force for the campaign. This was the last time a joint Flemish militia would take the field.[33]

However, delays in raising the force gave the English time to fortify Calais. A plan to assemble a fleet at Sluis and thence go to Calais to help the army miscarried when the smaller towns of the Franc refused to contribute. Philip began the siege of Calais on 9 July. The fleet finally arrived on 25 July, then left on the 27th. The militias of Ghent

31. Boone, *Gent en de Bourgondische hertogen*, 215–16; *IAY* 3: 136–7, 139–40; Vaughan, *Philip the Good*, 57–8, 85–6.

32. Vaughan, *Philip the Good*, 67, 75.

33. M.-R. Thielemans, *Bourgogne et Angleterre: Relations politiques et économiques entre les Pays-Bas Bourguignons et l'Angleterre, 1435–1467* (Brussels, 1967), 70–2, 90; Vaughan, *Philip the Good*, 75–7.

and Bruges were then defeated by the English in separate sorties from the town, panicked and left the area on the 28th. By the time the English lieutenant, Humphrey of Gloucester, Philip's old enemy in the affair of Jacqueline of Bavaria, arrived on 2 August, the siege had been raised. Humphrey then raided virtually at will in western Flanders. On 15 August he had himself proclaimed count of Flanders at Poperinge, then destroyed the town.[34]

As in 1411, the defeated militia of Bruges refused to disband or re-enter the city until they were paid, and the count's officials sent them on to Oostburg and Sluis to resist an anticipated English landing. They returned to Bruges on 26 August and quickly seized the city. On 3 September Ghent rebelled and captured Philip himself but released him in return for written concessions. That same day, the rebels at Bruges arrested all persons who had been burgomaster, treasurer or town clerk for the past thirty years. Once in rebellion, Bruges tried to assure its hegemony over Sluis and the west Flemish countryside by excluding the Franc from the college of the Four Members, but Ghent objected.

Tensions lessened by the end of October but recommenced in April 1437. In May, Philip evidently planned a military demonstration at Bruges en route with a larger army to Holland. He entered the town with an armed guard, then was trapped in a riot when the gate was shut behind him. Philip escaped by forcing the gate, but many of his soldiers and one of his most trusted captains were trapped and killed. The count blockaded Bruges and gave its commercial privileges to Sluis.

Bruges had little help from the rest of Flanders, and the rebellion was over quickly. In February 1438 peace was made at Arras. Symbolic penalties were imposed on Bruges, and the gate that had been closed against the count was demolished and replaced by a penitential chapel. Ten persons were executed. The city had to pay a heavy indemnity of £480,000; to place this into proportion, in 1440 the entire county gave the prince a subsidy of £280,000, in which Bruges's share was 15.7 per cent. This freed Philip of some of his dependence on the Four Members for taxes. Sluis's subjection to Bruges was ended, and Bruges lost its position as judicial head in disputes between other towns and rural jurisdictions, which now went directly to the Council of Flanders.[35]

34. Vaughan, *Philip the Good*, 77–83.

35. Vaughan, *Philip the Good*, 86–92; Blockmans and Prevenier, *In de Ban van Bourgondië*, 124–5; *IAB* 5: 137–50.

Although Bruges's staple and its rights of inspection at Sluis were restored in 1441, the indemnities provided by the peace of 1438 crippled Bruges for several years. The city sold life rents to pay them, and on 11 November 1438 Philip also permitted the city to collect a tax surcharge for four years and in 1442 to levy a direct tax based on the wealth of the payer. The total receipt of Bruges rose from £27,387 in 1439–40 to £66,157 in 1441–2.[36]

Relations with England were regulated shortly afterwards by the Treaty of Calais of 29 September 1439, with mutual safe conduct for merchants and free commerce except in war materials and English cloth. English pilgrims got free passage through Flanders. Fishermen of both nationalities could seek refuge from storms in each others' harbours. This treaty was confirmed in 1447. The only other serious threat to Anglo-Flemish relations during Philip's rule came in 1449, when English pirates seized Flemish and Dutch salt vessels, and Philip briefly sequestered the goods of English merchants in his lands.[37]

The rebellion of Ghent, 1447–53

On 23 August 1435, just before the peace of Arras, the Council of Flanders sent the count a memorandum detailing violations of his lordship that the magistrates of Ghent had committed since 1385. The timing was hardly accidental. The circles around the chancellor Nicolas Rolin began evoking the spectre of a new uprising of Ghent in the van Artevelde–anglophile tradition. The prince made good propaganda use of the role of Ghent in the failed campaign of 1436. Once he had humbled Bruges, Philip evidently decided to break Ghent as the key to mastery of Flanders. Ghent had wider powers in its quarter than did Bruges and the seriously declining Ypres. The external bourgeoisie of Ghent was widespread, and the city used it to secure its jurisdiction. The Three Members were in firm control in the city, and the prince's efforts to secure a client network there had been fruitless.[38]

The count had long hoped to end his dependence on the Four Members for taxes. Bruges since 1407 had given him one-seventh of the city's annual income instead of payment for permission to levy the

36. *IAB* 5: 175–6, 180–2, 256–7.

37. Vaughan, *Philip the Good*, 108–9.

38. Boone, *Gent en de Bourgondische hertogen*, 220–2; Marc Boone, 'Het Vorstelijk domein te Gent (*ca.* 1385–*ca.* 1453): Speelbal tussen vorstelijke centralisatie en stedelijk particularisme?' *HMGOG* **42** (1988): 92–3; Vaughan, *Philip the Good*, 304–5.

assizes. In 1447 Philip promised to abolish the aids at Ghent in return for a tax on salt, on the model of the French gabelle. He seems to have assumed that since Bruges already paid a permanent tax, the rest of Flanders would fall into line after Ghent, then the rest of his empire would follow Flanders. He convinced the deans of Ghent but the Great Council refused, and Philip accused the deans of treachery for not being able to deliver on their guarantees. When Ghent resisted Philip's personal lobbying, he intervened in the renewal of the magistracy in 1447 and 1449. When Ghent appealed to the Four Members, Philip withdrew his bailiff from the city, then called the Three Estates, which were more favourable to him than the Four Members. The government of Ghent agreed to hold new elections.[39]

Philip then demanded extension of the bailiff's power and, citing the charter of 1297, wanted external burghers justiciable in his courts. On 4 June 1451 Philip ordered the aldermen of Ghent to dismiss three of his leading opponents from the magistracy; when they refused, Philip ordered them to appear before him. Ghent protested this as an infringement of its rights, but the three men were exiled. Philip was evidently trying to provoke a military conflict that he knew he would win. During the winter of 1451–2, the commoners in Ghent rebelled against the aldermen as being the count's tools. An anonymous pamphlet was distributed in October 1451 around the town hall:

You gutless weaklings of Ghent,
Who now hold the government,
We'll no longer report it to you,
But will take our complaint to a new Artevelde.[40]

The count withdrew his officials, and by December the militia of Ghent was occupying communities in the quarter. Disorder mounted in the city. Captains were appointed who abolished the *Collacie* (the meeting of guild deans and aldermen) in favour of mass meetings on the Friday Market. In January and February 1452, the insurgents proceeded against those who had governed the town in the past fifteen years. Philip declared an embargo and ordered all Gentenars arrested. Ghent's appeals for help fell on deaf ears; the city was fighting the rest of Flanders.[41]

39. Vaughan, *Philip the Good*, 307–11; Blockmans and Prevenier, *In de Ban van Bourgondië*, 126–7.
40. Quoted from W. Prevenier and M. Boone, 'The "city-state" dream' in Decavele, *Ghent: In Defence*, 105.
41. Vaughan, *Philip the Good*, 312–13.

For most Flemings feared Ghent. In a manifesto clearly intended to inflame public opinion against Ghent, Philip claimed that the two chief deans had been appointing all the aldermen except those chosen from the landowners, thus violating the privileges of the electoral college. He also complained that external burghers of Ghent terrorized places where they lived. Officials of Ghent were accused of 'going around with their striped caps, asking burghers of Ghent where they could find them if they wanted to sue anybody. He claimed that the city had failed to register new burghers, as was required under the charter of 1297, and had granted burgher status automatically when an outsider registered in a guild. The aldermen of Ghent had also banished persons illegally without the knowledge or consent of the count's bailiff, had built forts in the countryside, fortified roads and established captains and other officials in villages, and had even gone so far as to arrest the bailiff of Waas while he was in the midst of a court case, then had taken him to Ghent and executed him.[42] Independent evidence corroborates the count's allegations.

Military action began in earnest in April 1452. By the end of the month the three captains of Ghent had been decapitated for being insufficiently revolutionary. The count invaded from Brabant, using as bases Aalst, Oudenaarde and Dendermonde, all of which resented Ghent. Philip controlled the northeast by June. In desperation, Ghent appealed not only to Bruges but also to King Charles VII of France. The king saw a golden opportunity to embarrass a mighty subject, and on 19 July Philip was forced to agree to a six-week truce. But when Ghent rejected a treaty drafted by royal mediators in September, Philip broke off negotiations. The battle of Gavere on 23 July 1453 was a mutual tragi-comedy. When a sack of gunpowder was accidentally set aflame at the beginning of the battle, the Gentenars panicked and broke ranks. When the battle was won, Philip, who had been wounded in the engagement, asked a local guide to show him the way to Ghent, but the man instead led him back to Gavere, which meant that Ghent itself was not taken and plundered.[43]

But the city had to capitulate. The regime of choice of magistrates by Member, which Ghent maintained was included in the privileges

42. Quotation in Boone, *Gent en de Bourgondische hertogen*, 175; see also Vaughan, *Philip the Good*, 314–16.

43. Vaughan, *Philip the Good*, 313–31; Marc Boone, 'Diplomatie et violence d'etat: La sentence rendue par les ambassadeurs et conseillers du roi de France, Charles VII, concernant le conflit entre Philippe le Bon, duc de Bourgogne, et Gand en 1452', *BCRH* **156** (1990): 1–54.

confirmed at the peace of Tournai in 1385, was ended in theory, although in fact they continued to be chosen on that basis but less rigidly than before. Ghent was fined £840,000, the amount paid by the entire county to the prince between 1440 and 1443. Surtaxes and rents to pay this indemnity crippled city finances for a decade. After 1453 the aldermen of each of the Four Members had to use the Council of Flanders as judicial head. With these immense new sources of revenue, Philip quietly dropped his demand for a salt tax.[44]

THE GOVERNANCE OF BURGUNDIAN FLANDERS

The Members of Flanders

All Burgundian counts had to deal with the great power of the Members of Flanders. We have seen that representative institutions go back at least to 1127 in Flanders and that during the thirteenth and fourteenth centuries they were dominated by the great cities. Louis of Male began to transform the Three Cities, which had been representing the county, into the Four Members by including the Franc of Bruges, which had occasionally met with the cities as early as 1310, more frequently in deliberations. The Members were privileged corporations that were entitled to consult regularly with the prince, just as differently constituted members governed the cities. The Franc was normally included in meetings of the Members from April 1386, although its recognition became official only in 1437 when the duke quashed a move by Bruges to exclude the Franc. Mary of Burgundy abolished the Franc as a Member at Bruges's pressure on 9 April 1477, but Maximilian restored it in 1485. The Members normally convened at their own initiative in Louis of Male's late years. In 1391 Philip the Bold forbade them orally to meet in the future without his permission or in his absence, but this was disregarded.[45]

Under the Burgundians the Four Members became the major avenue through which the Flemings dealt with their princes. Although Bruges disliked having the Franc as a Member, the Franc and the three

44. Boone, *Gent en de Bourgondische hertogen*, 189–90.

45. Prevenier, *De Leden en de Staten van Vlaanderen (1384–1405)*, VKVA, Kl. Letteren, No. 43 (Brussels, 1961), 236; Vaughan, *Philip the Bold*, 173.

urban Members rarely disagreed on policy. In 737 parliaments held between 1384 and 1405, only once did the Franc favour the count against the cities. The alliance pattern tended to be of the two weaker members (Ypres and the Franc) against the stronger (Bruges and Ghent) or actions by Ghent against the wishes of the other three.[46]

'Estates' as social class groups were weak in Flanders. There are only scattered references to the Staten (Estates) of Flanders before 1384, but they were formally established as an institution by 1405.[47] Members of the Estates, defined in 1417 as prelates, nobility and Four Members jointly,[48] met only when the count convened them, in contrast to the Four Members. Since the clergy and nobles resented the domination of the cities, the count was able to use them to elicit support. Between 1384 and 1404 there were twelve meetings of the Estates, usually convening simultaneously with the Members, but 725 of the Members. In later meetings of the Estates General of the Burgundian domains, the Four Members represented Flanders, and the clergy sent representatives. Only under Charles the Bold did the role of the Estates grow somewhat, and even then there were still only 13 meetings of the Estates against 189 of the Four Members.[49]

Terminological evolution has caused some confusion. The 'aldermen of Flanders' are not mentioned this late, but the 'good towns' or Members were the same thing. 'Common Land' (*gemene land*) is occasionally used by the Three Cities or the Four Members to designate their own assemblies, in the belief or claim that they represented the entire county. In the absence of other information, it is impossible to tell whether in a given case this term meant a general or restricted assembly. Technically, however, the Common Land was a full parliament, including the small towns and castellanies. Such assemblies were rarely called except for financial agendas between 1384 and 1405, and the term went out of use in the fifteenth century.[50]

46. W. Prevenier, 'Het Brugse Vrije en de Leden van Vlaanderen', *ASEB* **96** (1959): 5–63.

47. See in general Prevenier, *Leden en Staten*.

48. Zoete, *Handelingen*, 2: 1186.

49. W. Prevenier, 'De Verhouding van de Clerus tot de locale en regionale overheid in het Graafschap Vlaanderen in de late Middeleeuwen', *Sources de l'histoire religieuse de la Belgique, Moyen Age et temps modernes*, Bibliothèque de la Revue d'Histoire Ecclésiastique 47 (Louvain, 1968), 29–30.

50. Prevenier, *Leden en Staten*, 22, 34, 56.

Medieval Flanders

MEMBERS AND QUARTERS

We have seen that the notion of 'quarters' had taken form in Flanders by the 1340s as a further development of the principle that lesser jurisdictions had recourse to a judicial 'head'. There were some differences, since the quarter was a geographical unit in principle, rather than juridical. By the 1390s the Four Members were addressing correspondence to smaller towns and castellanies of which they were head and which accordingly were their 'subjects'. The subordinate jurisdictions within the quarter did military service with the Member in the fifteenth century, providing men, arms and matériel.[51]

Many meetings of the Four Members were prefaced by intense lobbying for support, and it was expected that subordinate jurisdictions would follow the judicial head. The large towns were even more zealous about protecting their interests in questions over judicial headship than they had been in the fourteenth century. The Members, however, took great care to keep subordinate jurisdictions within their quarters informed of developments. In 1405, delegations of the 'small towns of the castellany of Ghent' were summoned before the aldermen of Ghent, and the 'aldermen of Ghent there informed their small towns of the points that they with the Four Members of the land of Flanders and in benefit of the land' had requested of the count. Subordinate jurisdictions within the quarter were also expected to consult with their own constituencies. Flanders had castellany assemblies in which the landed nobles and two representatives from each parish sat, and quarter assemblies convoked by the Member.[52]

The great towns assessed and collected taxes owed to the counts by their quarters as voted by the Members or the Common Land. We have noted Ghent's protest in 1402 that the count had levied taxes in its quarter without its consent. The Members at times made their own tax policy. In the autumn of 1415 they agreed to the count's demand for a subsidy but decided that each Member would pay one-quarter of it. This violated the revision of the Transport assessment made in 1407, which had reduced the share owed by the coastal communities.[53] In 1407 and 1445 the Members did not pay their share of the count's *beden*, but rather shoved them off on to the castellanies.

51. W.P. Blockmans, 'A Typology of Representative Institutions in Late Medieval Europe', *JMH* **4** (1978): 194; Zoete, *Handelingen,* 1: 402, 586–9.
52. Zoete, *Handelingen,* 2: 765, 984–5, 1021; 1: 15–16; 2: 829, 843.
53. Zoete, *Handelingen,* 2: 1202, 794, 799–800, 987–1008.

The Members also got permission of the prince to levy taxes on their quarters to compensate for their own expenses on behalf of the entire county. Ghent, at least, taxed its quarter on occasion to defray the city's internal expenses.[54]

The issue of tax liability was particularly bothersome, especially in view of the high fiscal demands of the Burgundian counts. While elsewhere the nobility and clergy generally enjoyed tax advantages, the cities did in Flanders. The Flemish towns paid no *beden* between 1433 and 1437 as compensation for damages resulting from interruptions in the English trade. The small centres felt that the Members rigged tax assessments in their own favour, but even they were eager to avoid being taxed with the countryside. The aldermen of Deinze in 1405 went to Ghent to have written down two copies of their privilege that Philip the Bold had given them to the effect that they would be not subject to the annual taxes on the castellany of Courtrai.[55] The tax base of the rural areas was diminished by the tax relief given most external burghers.

Although one may question whether having three large cities and one rural territory representing the entire county was 'democratic', Flanders certainly had the most highly developed system in northwestern Europe of consultation with the prince. It was also unique in the Burgundian Netherlands in giving even this limited representation to the rural areas. During the fourteenth century the cities had usually met twenty to thirty times per year with the count. The Members met 3359 times between 1384 and 1506, an average of thirty times per year between 1385 and 1394 and forty-three per year in Philip the Bold's last decade. They averaged fifty-six meetings annually between 1405 and 1411, then declined steadily through 1477, reaching a low of twenty-four per year between 1465 and 1477. Compensating for the less frequent meetings, however, the conclaves became longer, from a norm of three to six days at the beginning of the fifteenth century to five to thirteen days at its end. Delegates to meetings of the Members were usually aldermen, sometimes accompanied by a town clerk or the city attorney. At Ghent, at least, the choice of delegates seems to have followed the Three Member principle that dominated the city

---

54. W.P. Blockmans, *De volksvertegenwoordiging in Vlaanderen in de overgang van Middeleeuwen naar Nieuwe Tijden (1384–1506)* (Brussels, 1978), 107–18; Nicholas, *Town and Countryside*, 143–7; Prevenier, *Leden en Staten*, 54; Boone, *Geld en Macht*, 154–6.

55. Zoete, *Handelingen*, 1: 14; Blockmans and Prevenier, *In de Ban van Bourgondië*, 103.

government; Flanders clearly had corporate representation at the level of the principality of basic cadres of local populations.[56]

The Four Members were normally not a judicial body, but they could exercise this function. They arbitrated and they handled some appeals from the judicial heads, but increasingly the Council of Flanders did this. The Members legislated on subjects as minute as the kind of nets fishermen could use. Most meetings in the fourteenth and early fifteenth centuries dealt with economic policy matters such as finances, coinage and trade; thereafter, finances and defence predominated.

The Four Members also tried to limit the competence in Flanders of the *parlement* of Paris, the court of the count's feudal overlord, and pressured appellants not to take their cases there. The count and the Members had a community of interest in this. In 1445 a nine-year moratorium was declared on jurisdiction that the *parlement* might exercise over the Four Members' courts, but appeals became more frequent again after 1454. Most appeals to the *parlement*, generally from verdicts of the Council of Flanders, were ordinary civil actions, not political cases. The overwhelming majority came from Walloon Flanders in the early Burgundian period, although this changed somewhat as the Flemish areas were increasingly assimilated.[57]

The Members of course were rivals, and their role was purely advisory. The Four could not bind any of their number to a course of action. Approval of the count's requests for money was frequently tied to satisfactory resolution of questions on which the Members had conflicting interests. The other Members were drawn into the quarrels between Bruges and the Franc. In 1407 the Council settled their disagreement over rural textiles only when the other two Members could not agree. The smaller communities also tried, through the Members, to get the same sort of industrial monopoly that the great cities had obtained earlier from the counts. In 1406 the Franc and Bruges disputed the rights of brewing and baking in each district of the Franc, and the Members again could not reach a verdict. The small towns of the Franc in turn tried to use the other three Members against what they regarded as a jurisdiction dominated by nobles against their interests, specifically regarding efforts by the government of the Franc to tax persons living in the small towns.[58]

56. Blockmans, 'Typology', 198; Blockmans, 'Supplement to "Constitutions" ', 216–17, 223–4; Prevenier, *Leden en Staten*, 55, 257.

57. Blockmans, 'Bourgondische Nederlanden', 18–19; Blockmans, 'Typology', 210–11.

58. Zoete, *Handelingen*, 2: 1056–67.

Ghent was the most likely of the Members to refuse to agree to proposals sponsored by one of the others, but Ghent was not alone in its xenophobia. In 1404 Ghent and Ypres hindered flood relief, since the damage had hit chiefly the Franc.[59] A case illustrating the difficulty of the Members agreeing on any course of action pitted Ghent against Bruges in March 1435. The magistrates of Bruges had banished John Belleman, who had been living at Bruges, for six years. He claimed to be burgher of Ghent, so he went to Ghent instead of going into exile. The aldermen of Ghent tried and convicted their colleagues of Bruges for violating Ghent's privileges. In its appeal to Paris, Bruges claimed that the five towns were independent, with no rights over one another, having only a common subordination to the duke of Burgundy. Thus Ghent could not ignore a verdict of Bruges. The Brugeois claimed that the summons of officials of Bruges to trial at Ghent occurred in a mob scene. If Ghent's point were admitted, Bruges and the 'other smaller towns' would be at the mercy of anyone claiming to be burgher of Ghent. *Parlement* ruled that Ghent was not competent to judge the aldermen of Bruges and, in a striking new departure, went further by ruling that the aldermen of Bruges were competent to judge all misdeeds in their territory, whether committed by their own citizens or others.[60]

The record of the Members in defending the interests of other communities in their quarter is mixed. Bruges, of course, was limited by the privileges of the Franc. In the negotiations leading to the peace of Tournai, the Gentenars demanded not only confirmation of their ancient liberties, but also those of the small towns that had sided with Ghent during the uprising. In fact, Ghent's privileges were confirmed; the others were apparently confiscated but were gradually restored over the next several years. In the tax controversy of 1415, the aldermen of Ghent advised those of coastal Four Offices to pay only the Transport percentage. But this attitude changed within a generation. In 1428 several textile towns of the Ghent quarter – Oudenaarde, Aalst, Geraardsbergen, Ninove, and later Dendermonde – asked the city's help in prohibiting baking, brewing, fulling, butchering and weaving outside free towns, but Ghent did nothing of consequence.[61]

59. Zoete, *Handelingen*, 1: 73; 2: 1023; Prevenier, *Leden en Staten*, 235.
60. Van Caenegem, *Appels flamands*, 1: 360–9.
61. Prevenier, *Leden en Staten*, 53; Blockmans, *Volksvertegenwoordiging*, 510–12, 523.

THE BURGUNDIAN STATE APPARATUS

Much has been made of the alleged modernity of the Burgundian state, but recent research has suggested colossal inefficiency and corruption that surpassed even the conditions of the fourteenth century. The Burgundian court was itinerant until after 1459, when Philip the Good began staying mainly at Brussels. Lille was the financial capital. Although the Council of Flanders was usually at Ghent, it was removed three times, notably to Ypres between 1451 and 1464.[62]

The central court

The Burgundian counts had a central court, called the Great Council, and a separate Council of Flanders, a continuation of Louis of Male's *Audientie*, which was subordinated to the Great Council only after 1440. Appeals could be made from the Council of Flanders to the *parlement* of Paris and later to Charles the Bold's *parlement* of Mechelen. Although individual Flemish communities sometimes bypassed the Council and appealed directly to *parlement*, Louis XI ended this practice in 1468.[63]

In the beginning the competence of the Council of Flanders was purely in 'reserved cases' such as private war, rebellion, counterfeiting, crimes by nobles, attacks on foreign merchants and the prince's officers and misconduct by the prince's officials. But it also took on other cases that could not be handled by the ordinary courts, such as conflicts between towns, castellanies, lordships, parishes or church institutions. It usually did not handle private suits and crimes, although we have seen that some such cases came before the *Audientie*. But in the first half of the fifteenth century the competence of the Council of Flanders was expanded considerably, as persons who earlier would have gone to lower courts went directly to the Council in hope of better and quicker justice. By the fifteenth century the Council regularly heard and amended cases on appeal, first from the smaller towns, later the larger, ending with Ghent in 1453.[64]

---

62. Vaughan, *Philip the Good*, 135–6, 191.
63. *IAB* 6: 1.
64. J. van Rompaey, 'De Bourgondische staatsinstellingen', *AGN* 4: 150–1.

The prince's finances

The Burgundians made considerable progress in centralizing their financial administration under the Chamber of Accounts at Lille. Various calculations have been made from the General Receipt of the total income of the Burgundian state and the share of Flanders in that income, and all must be used with caution. The General Receipt suggests that the first three Burgundian counts enjoyed an annual income of about 350,000 livres, but this more than doubled under Charles the Bold. Flanders' share in the ordinary income of the prince, coming from his domains and the profits of administration, was considerably higher than in the extraordinary income. The total share of Flanders diminished from roughly half under Philip the Bold to 13 per cent under Charles the Bold.[65] In accounting of 1445, Flanders paid 24.0 per cent of the gross income of the count and 18.9 per cent of the net. Even this diminished share is more than the entire 'lands thither' (Burgundy and Franche Comté) and double the gross of Picardy, the next most lucrative province in the north.[66]

Another revealing calculation is the share of the *beden* in the total income of the prince. Due largely to the political power of the cities, the entire county of Flanders was taxed somewhat less severely in proportion to its population and wealth than the other Burgundian domains, and this benefited the rural as well as urban inhabitants.[67] Under Philip the Bold, however, Flanders paid taxes that averaged one-third of what the prince realized from his domains; during 1439–49 it was 84 per cent of the domain income, and after 1454 the *beden* gave him more than the domain. The fifteenth century was thus the period of transition towards taxation and away from the domain as the basis for public finance.[68]

The assessment for the *beden* was based on the Transport of 1325 as enforced by the Members and their subordinate jurisdictions. Conditions had so changed since the early fourteenth century, however, that a new assessment was needed. The flooding of 1404, which inundated several communities and damaged others, made it even more urgent.

65. See summary of literature in W. Prevenier, 'Financiën en boekhouding in de Bourgondische periode: Nieuwe bronnen en resultaten', *TG* **82** (1969): 469–81.
66. Blockmans and Prevenier, *In de Ban van Bourgondië*, 100–1.
67. Thoen, *Landbouweconomie*, 2: 633–4.
68. Boone, *Geld en Macht*, 57.

In 1408 a new commission of seventeen (nine appointed by the count and eight from the Four Members) met at Oudenburg to set the percentages that each jurisdictional area would owe in the *beden*. Each Member prepared a report for its quarter. The inquest emphasized wars, depopulation and natural disasters and was especially detailed for the coastal areas. It is clear that the commissioners were using extremely detailed written records, including the number of *gemeten* of land per district under the old and new Transports. Despite the complaints that the assessment was inequitable, it was a monumental administrative achievement.[69]

The administration of the comital domain

The domain was income that did not result from taxation. It was divided in the fifteenth century into administrative quarters corresponding to those of the Three Cities and included income from the farmland, the watergraves and moormasters, fees paid by larger communities for such privileges as the right to levy assizes, agricultural rents, incomes from weights and scales and other economic rights in the small towns, and the yield of woodlands.[70] In the southern Burgundian Netherlands, domain income made up 15 per cent of the total income of the state, which is considerably higher than in most other regions this late. The domain dominated princely finance in the Netherlands in the early fifteenth century, although this was not true by 1500.

There is little difference in domain receipt and expenditure among the first three Burgundians. Pressures on the domain came mainly in periods when the Burgundian dukes were in conflict with the authorities in Paris and did not get subsidies from the Four Members. John the Fearless centralized domain administration more than did his father. With the ending of the French tie under Philip the Good, intense pressure was placed on the domain. His luxurious court and wars forced him to seek opportunities for *beden*. Essentially, he created without intending to do so a floating debt secured on the domain by defaulting on obligations, notably by failing to pay his officials.

69. W. Buntinx, 'De Enquête van Oudenburg: Hervorming van de repartitie van de beden in het graafschap Vlaanderen (1408)', *BCRH* **134** (1968): 75–134.
70. The section on the count's domain is based on Eddy van Cauwenberghe, *Het vorstelijk domein en de overheidsfinanciën in de Nederlanden (15de en 16de eeuw): Een kwantitatieve analyse van Vlaamse en Brabantse domeinrekeningen* (Brussels, 1982).

Little of the money collected on the domains went into the central treasury, for the counts paid many of their expenses by issuing letters of obligation that were redeemable on various domains. These outlays were deducted when the local receiver rendered his annual accounts at Lille. Thus although the domains often show a negative balance, this is not due to maladministration or because the domain was unprofitable. The financial and judicial administration of the domains was separated on nearly all domains by the second half of the century.

The Burgundians used professional civil servants, removable at will and often with professional or even university training. Wages were so low, however, that they do not compare well even with those of urban guildsmen. The wages sometimes were not even paid at all, when the domain revenues – officials were supposed simply to deduct their wages from their receipts – were low and eaten up by obligatory letters from the central government. The domain receivers were also compensated for their expenses and were exempt from taxes. Local governments sometimes gave them gifts. Although the Burgundian dukes demanded careful accounting from their functionaries, the 'goodwill' gift-giving was so all-pervasive that by modern standards, officials were extremely corrupt. Graft at the domain level was petty, not comparable to the scale of the central officers, and provided some relief from the low wages.

The bailiffs

Mention of administrative corruption leads naturally to a discussion of the Flemish bailiffs. The sovereign bailiff of Flanders was created in 1372, not as head of the ordinary bailiffs but as a separate officer with competence throughout Flanders to prosecute offenders who had somehow escaped other agencies. He could act as sole judge in criminal proceedings. There was no appeal from his judgement – he was both prosecutor and judge.[71]

The sovereign bailiff extended his power over subordinate judicial officers in the early Burgundian period. Although under Louis of Male he had been responsible directly to the count, he gradually became subordinated to the Council of Flanders under the Burgundians. Much of his power came from his right to pardon by letters of grace for severe crimes that were not capital offences. An important and

---

71. Van Rompaey, 'Staatsinstellingen', 153.

much-resented element of the sovereign bailiff's power was his right to remit banishments issued by cities, although he could not permit exiles to re-enter the city issuing the ban or enter others whose magistrates did not wish to receive the persons concerned. The sovereign bailiff pursued criminals and enforced exiles, but the sources leave the impression that his interest was as much financial as peacekeeping. He had to authorize composition for any infraction involving a fine of £60 or more. In the fifteenth century he sometimes composed for crimes committed as long in the past as thirty years and in cases where the accused had been freed by a court and been reconciled with his counterparty.

Understandably, the towns and castellanies, which were unhappy at the general process of centralization under the Burgundians, tried to keep the sovereign bailiff from encroaching on their jurisdiction. In 1442 their pressure forced a general inquest into the conduct of the sovereign bailiff and his subordinates. The count took no corrective measures, although nearly 700 infractions were recorded, most of them involving extortion and peculation. The investigation showed that the sovereign bailiff kept a roll with the names of all persons suspected of misbehaviour. One could get on the roll through no more than rumour, but getting off it took finagling and often a payment. The officials of the sovereign bailiff, who circulated through Flanders holding court, preceded him to a locality to make certain that all who were named on the roll appeared before him. His investigations were often rigged. A representative example is the case of a man acquitted of homicide by the aldermen of Bourbourg, but the sovereign bailiff reopened the investigation and convicted him after taking testimony only from the kinspeople of the victim. The sovereign bailiff furthermore promised yet another investigation if the accused would be willing to 'compose'.[72]

The local bailiffs continued to be an embarrassment. Since no complaints survive about their legal competence, we may assume that they had some legal experience, but it was often of a practical, administrative nature and not the result of formal schooling. Anyone with university law training could rise much farther in the Burgundian hierarchy than bailiff. The old pattern of the bailiff's crookedness and cruelty in dealing with suspects that we have seen earlier became exacerbated, particularly after the Burgundians began farming out the

72. J. van Rompaey, *Het grafelijke baljuwsambt in Vlaanderen tijdens de Boergondische periode. VKVA*, No. 62 (Brussels, 1967), 70, 83–4, 52–5, 95–7, 45–54, 58–9, 63–6.

office and leaving their bailiffs unpaid for long periods. Some complaints eventually found their way to Paris. In a case of 1448 involving Damme, *parlement* confirmed a judgement of the Council of Flanders that a bailiff could be punished for malfeasance by his subordinates.[73]

A flagrant and probably representative case arose in 1466. Ypres had ordinances against gambling houses, which the bailiff refused to enforce and even persuaded the Council of Flanders to force the Yprois to withdraw their ordinance. The case went to the royal court, but when the count learned of it he summoned the bailiff, only to find that he and some aldermen had displayed posters reading 'if you can pay, you can play' and allowed anyone who paid 60 shillings yearly to open a casino. The bailiff's clerk and brother had even mocked the aldermen by gambling in the middle of the town square.[74]

Most bailiffs prosecuted crime *ex officio* in the name of the count, but the bailiff of Ghent could do so only when a citizen lodged a complaint. Only in 1438 did Philip the Good give the bailiff of Ghent *ex officio* jurisdiction over rape cases. Although most bailiffs had served short terms in the fourteenth century, they became local fixtures under the Burgundians. Dankaart van Ogierlande was bailiff of Ghent between 1389 and 1411; and although bailiffs were not supposed to marry into local families, his daughter married Zeger Damman, who was alderman of Ghent five times between 1406 and 1424.[75]

The bailiffs accounted to the Chamber of Accounts at Lille. But even in the period of Philip the Bold the receiver-general began demanding that the bailiffs pay an advance on the anticipated incomes of their next account. By the time of Philip the Good this was a *de facto* loan to the prince, often totalling more than the yield of the office. This in turn led to leasing the office under Philip the Good. Charles the Bold tried to end this practice by a worse expedient, selling either the profits of justice or the office itself.[76]

In fairness to the Burgundian bailiffs, the liberties of privileged communities of judging their citizens continued to hamper effective law enforcement. The varying juridical status of the inhabitants might mean that a single village could have feudal, allodial, seigneurial and public-comital courts, while residents who were external burgesses of a city would not be subject to trial there at all.[77] The large towns were

73. Van Rompaey, *Grafelijke baljuwsambt*, 118–19, 274–5; van Caenegem, *Appels flamands*, 1: 497–8, 553–4.

74. *IAY* 3: 267–8.

75. Boone, *Gent en de Bourgondische hertogen*, 182–3.

76. Van Rompaey, 'Staatsinstellingen', 154–5.

77. W.P. Blockmans, 'De Representatieve instellingen in het Zuiden 1384–1482', *AGN* 4: 156.

still shielding criminous citizens with bourgeois standing. The rural jurisdictions were the major victims, for the Three Cities generally although not invariably respected one another's rights.[78]

The conflicts of Ypres with the count's men continued to be more serious than those of Bruges and Ghent, probably because of the weakness of Ypres. On 31 May 1415 the town and castellany of Ypres made a general pacification. All crimes and misdemeanours in the castellany would be brought to court there, and a first instruction given to the court of the castellany by the aldermen of the place where the deed occurred. Every inhabitant of Ypres who committed a crime in the territory, escaped to Ypres and asked judgement of the aldermen could enter prison there and await their judgement. Tax exemption in the territory was given to all inhabitants of the five villages that comprised the territory of the city. External burgesses of Ypres living in the territor y on their own lands or those of other burghers were given tax exemption, but property of burghers inhabited by non-burghers was taxed with the castellany.[79]

A case showing the incredible complexities of fifteenth-century Flemish jurisprudence arose in 1417. On 22 June the town of Wervik seized the property at Wervik of a burgher of Bruges, despite letters of prohibition from Bruges, and in retaliation Bruges took the goods of two Wervikers. The matter had arisen in connection with what was evidently a civil suit on the enclaved lordship 'ten Steenackere' at Wervik, where Pieter Renier of Wervik was alderman. On 2 July the suit was continued because Bruges insisted that the castellany of Wervik had forced the man who had brought suit against the Bruges man to make accounting to him; but it could not do so, since although he had sued in the court of the castellany, he did not live there. On 24 August the other three Members essentially supported Wervik and summoned Bruges, which refused to answer. On 3 October Bruges imprisoned Pieter Renier, who now turned out to be a burgess of Ghent (whether in addition to or rather than enjoying that status at Wervik is not clear), and on grounds of Ghent's exclusive right to try cases involving its burghers he was ordered to be released from captivity. On 5 October, however, Bruges refused to release Renier. It eventually did so when the other Members threatened to seize citizens of Bruges in retaliation.[80]

78. *IAY* 3: 109.
79. *IAY* 3: 59–62.
80. Zoete, *Handelingen*, 2: 1154, 1156, 1173, 1180, 1182.

How many cases such as this escape the record cannot be estimated; but it is clear that while personal privilege and the archaism of the common law made verdicts difficult to reach in England at this time, the problem in Flanders was the liberties of privileged communities and the exemptions given by particular status from the ordinary workings of the law.

To all of this was added the continuation of the blood feud. Solidarity with members of one's community took precedence in Flemish law over the imperatives of order. In an undated case of the late fourteenth century, Ypres as judicial head fined and banished an alderman of Waarstine for having scuffled with a citizen of his own town while breaking up a tavern brawl in which strangers were involved. Although the cities seem to have been somewhat more peaceful than in the fourteenth century, the reverse was true of the rural areas. In February 1415 the Members heard the complaint that feuds in the Westland were so severe that leaseholders could neither sow or grow.[81]

Although blood justice was rarely exercised in Flanders − the blood feud was the preferred method − the extremely frequent use of banishment, even for petty industrial infractions, meant that the countryside was full of vagabonds who could live only by theft and violence. The Burgundians evidently ended Bruges's practice of giving the town sergeants a bounty of 4 pence per person arrested but the city restored it in 1477. The aldermen of Ghent in 1415 ceased granting pardon to persons who had been banished for breach of the peace, and this meant a substantial fall in income for the city. In the 1420s, faced with serious unrest in the textile sector, the aldermen threatened to have the White Hoods seize and execute exiles whom they found in Flanders. Most of the exiles seem to have stayed in eastern Flanders, particularly around Aalst and Dendermonde, but the White Hoods were active in the West Quarter in 1424. The Council of Flanders forced the bailiff of Ghent to exile some White Hoods who had acted against exiles on orders of the aldermen of Ghent. The situation lasted until 1432, when there was a wholesale recall of exiles.[82]

81. De Pelsmaeker, *Registres*, 218; Zoete, *Handelingen*, 2: 910.
82. *IAB* 6: 142; Boone, *Geld en Macht*, 195−6.

FLEMISH CULTURE IN THE BURGUNDIAN AGE

Questions of public and private morality lead to a consideration of the cultural life of Burgundian Flanders. The fifteenth and early sixteenth centuries are generally considered the golden age of Flemish culture. Much of the flowering was due to the patronage of the Burgundian court and to the cosmopolitan character of Bruges. Much of it also was not specifically 'Flemish'. Artists who were natives of other parts of the Burgundian Netherlands spent time in Flanders and became associated with a 'Flemish school'. Except at Bruges, the arts were less splendid in Flanders than in Brabant. Many of the so-called 'Flemish primitives' were either Flemish-speaking Brabanters or Dutchmen. The 'Flemish school' of painting flourished mainly in the second and third quarters of the fifteenth century, the most economically prosperous and generally peaceful period of the Burgundian age.[83]

Schools

Virtually all churches and abbeys had schools, as did most towns and villages. Latin schooling was available everywhere in Flanders. All major towns had a single Latin school in theory, although in practice private tutoring made the study more generally available. University education, however, remained exceptional among the upper orders in Flanders, perhaps because vernacular culture was so strong there and was associated with the national movement. This is not to say that the cities did not value university training. Beginning in 1404, the city of Ghent regularly sent money to ten local boys who were scholars at Paris.[84] No comprehensive lists of Flemish students at the universities have been compiled, but 76 per cent of the canons holding prebends at Tournai and 64 per cent of those of St Donatian of Bruges in the fourteenth century had studied at a university. Half of the Tournaisiens and two-thirds of the Brugeois had gone beyond arts to study in one of the higher faculties, most often law. Paris was the most frequented, although this began to change after the foundation of the university at

---

83. J.H. Munro, 'Economic Depression and the Arts in the Fifteenth-Century Low Countries', *Renaissance and Reformation* **19** (1983): 235–50. Basing his argument largely on the decline of textile exports, Munro argues that the cultural flowering occurred during a period of economic contraction.

84. SAG, Series 400, 11: 70v.

Louvain, the first university in the Low Countries, in 1425. Clergy were gradually replaced in the central bureaucracy by university-trained laypeople in the Burgundian period, first in Flanders then later in Brabant. A noteworthy example is Philip Wielant (1441–1520), a jurist of Ghent who became a councillor of Charles the Bold and author of legal treatises and chronicles.[85]

The language question

Tensions between the French prince and his Flemish-speaking subjects had relaxed during the period of Louis of Male, then revived under the Burgundians. The reincorporated Walloon castellanies never achieved a political power equal to that of the Germanic areas, but the counts resisted their Flemish subjects' requests that they learn the language and live in Flanders.

In addition to the problem of French- and Flemish-speaking Flemings, there were significant regional differences among the Germanic dialects of the Low Countries. Jan Ruusbroec of Groenendael (d. 1381) wrote a devotional treatise in the dialect of Brabant that had to be translated into Latin so that the Flemings could understand it. Around 1425 a notary of Bruges, who clearly could translate Flemish into Latin, had trouble when English merchants asked him to translate the dialect of Middelburg into Latin. The Flemings seem to have been as sensitive to differences in other Germanic languages as to the problems of using French, which was used by most merchant communities of Bruges as an international language. In 1411 the Four Members responded to an oral communication from Lübeck 'that we were not able to understand their language well, and that they should put their request into writing, as close to the Flemish as they can'.

The regimes of the great cities tended to use the Flemish language as a point of identity against the Burgundians, who responded in kind. Philip the Bold knew no Flemish, but he agreed that his eldest son be given a Fleming as tutor. But the Flemings were extremely sensitive, and the dukes had more problems with them over language than in Brabant, which had been officially bilingual since 1356. John the Fearless permitted Flemish in regional administration, but French was the

85. H. de Ridder-Symoens, 'Possibilités de carrière et de mobilité sociale des intellectuels-universitaires au Moyen Age', *Proceedings of the First Interdisciplinary Conference on Medieval Prosopography Held at Bielefeld, 3–5 December 1982* (Kalamazoo, 1986), 6–7; Prevenier and Boone, 'City-state dream', 96.

central language, and this policy was continued by his two successors.[86]

Flemish literature

There is relatively little new original expression in Flemish during the Burgundian period. Chambers of rhetoric were developing in the towns from the early Burgundian period. The earliest guilds of rhetoricians at Bruges were Holy Ghost (1428) and Holy Trinity (1459). They performed plays, sang masses and composed and read poetry.[87] From 1428 Ypres had a 'Pen' society that was soon converted into a Holy Ghost chamber. It held regular meetings in the house of the provost of the chamber, and the members debated theological topics and questions of public/government interest. The chamber had an oratory in the Dominican church and was ruled by a committee of thirteen sworn persons, including a king, provost, dean and assessors.[88] The chambers of different towns had competitions. At a contest at Ghent in 1440, the chamber of Tournai won a prize for the best composition in French and that of Oudenaarde for one in Flemish; there were separate prizes in each language.[89] The chambers thus were recognized and patronized by the cities. Antheunis de Rovere of Bruges, son of the founder of the Holy Ghost chamber, won first prize in a competition at age seventeen and was given a substantial yearly wage in 1465 by the city for having 'served long years at various times well and courteously . . . and has given much pleasure from plays of good morality and of other honourable entertainments'. He was put in charge of organizing processions and parades for the city.[90]

Painting and sculpture

The painters and sculptors were an interregional group who took

---

86. Zoete, *Handelingen* 1: 554; Thielemans, *Bourgogne et Angleterre*, 355; C.A.J. Armstrong, 'The Language Question in the Low Countries: The Use of French and Dutch by the Dukes of Burgundy and their Administration', orig. in *Europe in the Middle Ages*, ed. J.R. Hale, J.R.L. Highfield and B. Smalley (London, 1965), 386–409, reprinted and cited here in Armstrong, *England, France and Burgundy*, 190–1, 195–207.
87. R. Strohm, *Music in Late Medieval Bruges* (Oxford, 1985), 47, 68–70.
88. *IAB* **5**: 520–3.
89. Armstrong, 'Language Question', 193.
90. Van Mierlo, *Letterkunde*, 324, 338.

work where offered. Some painters had establishments in several towns where apprentices and journeymen did much of the basic work before the master put the finishing touches on the painting. The same organization is found in tapestry workshops and the scriptoria, where miniaturists were employed. Flemish artists were the first to use oil-based paints; Melchior Broederlam of Ypres was using them by 1395. They also perfected the 'pouncing' technique, by which a painting could be replicated by using stencils created by dots through coarse transparent fabric. The work of Flemish artists was exported, especially through Bruges to Italy. The city governments patronized artists, particularly in the late fifteenth century. Between 1488 and 1498 Bruges commissioned various works by Gerard David to hang in the aldermen's hall, and Ghent employed Hugo van der Goes. The chief patrons were the Burgundian counts. Most private individuals who commissioned work in Flanders were the Italian merchants living at Bruges, but there were some exceptions; Hans Memlinc did portraits of several burghers of Bruges.[91]

Jan van Eyck, perhaps the most famous Flemish painter, was born about 1390 at Maaseik, in Brabant. He worked at Ghent in the 1420s, but he spent most of his career in Bruges. Rogier van der Weyden was not Flemish at all; born at Tournai, he was active at Brussels. Diederic Bouts and Gerard David were from the northern Netherlands. Hans Memlinc was born in Germany, studied around 1455 with van der Weyden, then settled in Bruges in 1465. The only natives of Flanders were Hugo van der Goes, who was born in Ghent in 1440 and died near Brussels in 1482, and his friend Justus van Wassenhove, better known as Justus van Gent. In his Netherlands period he painted the crusade tryptych in St Bavo's cathedral, then went to Italy in 1468.

The brothers Hubert and Jan van Eyck were the real founders of the late medieval school of Flemish painting. The Adoration of the Lamb tryptych, begun by Hubert and finished six years after his death by Jan, is the most significant of their works that survive. It is one of the glories of St Bavo's cathedral at Ghent. It was painted in oil on oak panels. The scenes are set in Ghent, although just what sections of the city are portrayed is a matter of debate. The tryptych gives us considerable information about architecture, jewellery, costume and furniture. Although some of the human forms, especially of the women, were conventional, with minimal perspective and rigid features,

91. Prevenier and Blockmans, *Burgundian Netherlands*, 335, 331.

it contains extremely realistic paintings of Joos Vijt, the wealthy burgess of Ghent who commissioned it, and his wife Elisabeth Borluut.

Ghent was less attuned to the fine arts than Bruges, probably because it had fewer foreigners. Philip the Bold patronized some Ghent artists, and in 1413 Lievin van den Clite painted a Last Judgement for the comital castle at Ghent. The van Eycks' masterpiece seems to have caused some demand for works of Ghent-based artists. Painted altarpieces of Ghent were much in demand, peaking in the 1440s. The period between 1460 and 1480, when Hugo van der Goes and Justus van Wassenhove flourished, was the greatest in the history of medieval Ghent art. The arts in Ghent declined rapidly thereafter.[92]

Painters were subject to the same corporate regulations as other artists. They had to enrol in the guild of the city where they worked. Most art was more practical than aesthetic, and painters were regarded by contemporaries as craftsmen rather than artists. This was even truer of sculptors, who were less well paid than most painters. The sculptors of Bruges were in the carpenters' guild until at least 1431, and there were problems of jurisdiction with the grave monument workers, who had a separate organization.[93]

The painters, like other guilds, benefited by captive local markets. The Bruges guild was open to foreigners, but at Ghent the work of foreign artists could be sold in the city only at the two fairs, which constituted a sort of art market. The Shrove Tuesday market, which was held during a celebration that became increasingly wild during the fifteenth century, was the most important. During this fair the painters took over the stalls of the butchers in the Great Meat Hall, but they could sell their work anywhere in the city. There was clearly a considerable market for paintings for private homes; not all painters did timeless masterworks such as van der Weyden and the van Eycks. The painters also adorned banners and buildings for the city governments and painted decorations for the parades and festivals that became increasingly numerous and elaborate from the 1440s. The great Hugo

92. Prevenier and Blockmans, *Burgundian Netherlands*, 332; E. d'Haenens, 'Ghent Painting and Sculpture' in Decavele, *Ghent: In Defence*, 202–3, 222, 230, 254; G. Broecks, 'De Schilders', *Flandria Nostra* 2: 147–226.

93. Els Cornelius, 'De Kunstenaar in het laat-middeleeuwse Gent. 1: Organisatie en kunstproduktie van de Sint-Lucasgilde in de 15de eeuw', *HMGOG* 41 (1987): 97–128, esp. 104–23; M. van Roose, 'Twee Onbekende 15de eeuwse dokumenten in verband met de Brugse "Beildesniders" ', *ASEB* 110 (1973): 168–77.

van der Goes was commissioned to paint coats of arms for Ghent in 1467.[94]

Flemish book illumination was also renowned, particularly at the comital court at Bruges. The patrons of illuminated manuscripts included Rafael de Mercatel, natural son of Philip the Good and successively abbot of St Pieter's and then St Bavo in Ghent. Jan de Tavernier of Oudenaarde and Loyset Loédat and David Aubert at Bruges were especially famous. Most of the illuminators are anonymous, such as the artist who adorned the Cartulary of the Ghent brewers' guild shortly before 15 August 1453. The illumination includes a miniature of Arnold of Tiegem, the patron saint of the brewers, and coats of arms.[95]

Festivals and display

The fifteenth century witnessed an upsurge of pageantry in the Flemish cities, although the argument that the counts used display to reinforce their power, made famous by the classic work of Johan Huizinga, is more convincing for Brabant than for Flanders.[96] Much of the merrymaking was inspired by the counts' court, although of the Flemish cities only Bruges and Lille saw much of them. The main occasions for princely pomp in Flanders were the counts' Joyous Entries. Parades were held, with tableaux laden with symbolism of justice and princely beneficence. Other entries of the prince also were occasions for celebration. When Philip the Bold came to Bruges on 2 April 1398, the town made him immense gifts. Festivities continued through the month. There was jousting, and food was provided at all churches for the poor.[97]

While the popular image of late medieval Flemish culture is derived from the largely biblical and mythological themes of the great art works, Flanders was known in Europe as a bawdy, disorderly place. The Pardoner in Chaucer's *Canterbury Tales* opens his story with a tale of a band of youths who once lived in Flanders. They lived a sinful

94. Cornelius, 'Sint-Lucasgilde', 121; Prevenier and Blockmans, *Burgundian Netherlands*, 316.

95. Prevenier and Blockmans, *Burgundian Netherlands*, 323; Broecks, 'Schilders', 171; d'Haenens, 'Ghent Painting and Sculpture', 229.

96. Johan Huizinga, *The Waning of the Middle Ages. A Study of the Forms of Life, Thought, and Art in France and the Netherlands in the XIVth and XVth Centuries* (New York, 1924 and variously reprinted), 56–107.

97. *IAB* **3**: 398–9.

life and made music to bad language, gambled, honoured the devil, made curses, fornicated and mocked the sins of others, but they were especially known for gluttony.

For although the theme of princely patronage of festivals in Flanders has been overdrawn, city festivals not connected with the counts became more numerous. Most were connected with religious ceremonials. Religion was very active at this level, in contrast to the desultory practice of the sacraments. The festival of the Epinette at Lille on Shrove Tuesday began with the election of a king of the Epinette from among the wealthy citizens. Living tableaux illustrated religious scenes, but often with a theme of role reversal. Then there was an opulent investiture banquet followed by a tournament. In each stage, the burghers tried to mimic princes' manners. The combatants in the tournament came from throughout Flanders and included some princes. The other Flemish cities sent delegations to the tourney of the Epinette, while Lille men were invited to the Festival of the Forester at Bruges.[98] In 1394 a Shrove Tuesday parody of a tournament was held at Bruges in the presence of Philip the Good. Expenses on Shrove Tuesday at Ghent were small until the 1390s, but it then became the major festival held in the city.

Virtually all towns have fifteenth-century references to child or scholar bishops, drawn from the students in the local school. At Aalst he was chosen on St Nicholas's day (6 December); he was taken by donkey to the school chapel, where he celebrated a parodied mass. He then treated his followers to a feast, which meant that the children had to make sure that he always came from a rich family. The accounts of Tielt from 1460 mention for Shrove Tuesday the 'youth society' that 'takes great satisfaction from dancing and smashing sleds and other such things'. At Veurne in 1482 the child bishop and the prince of the rhetoricians joined to lead the same festival. Although the Feast of Fools is most often used, the Donkey Festival is also found. Most festivities spilled over into the whole population, not just the group sponsoring them. In 1470 the rhetoricians of Oudenburg made a procession to Gistel with their donkey pope.[99]

Religious processions were held in all cities. Some were in honour of particular patron saints or were confined to a single parish. Others celebrated special events. At Damme in 1338, sailors found an image

98. Claude Fouret, 'La Violence en fête: la course de l'Epinette à Lille à la fin du Moyen Age', *RN* **63** (1981): 377–90.

99. Herman Pleij, *Het gilde van de Blauwe Schuit: Literatuur, volksfeest en burgermoraal in de late Middeleeuwen* (Amsterdam, 1979), 17, 23–8, 31, 38, 48.

of Christ floating in the water and built a chapel in its honour. On every third Sunday in July, they had a procession to implore God's protection against the perils of the sea. Ypres observed 'Thuyndag' (Garden Day) on the first Sunday of August to commemorate events of 1383, when the English army broke off the siege of Ypres after the inhabitants had erected a barricade of garden trellises on the wall. The statue of the Virgin of the Cloth Hall, who was thought to have saved the city, was rebuilt and placed under the belfry, encircled by a trellis. The Thuyndag procession became rowdy, and the magistrates in 1436 had to order an end to excesses.[100]

Few new religious confraternities were formed during the fifteenth century at Ghent, and most that did develop were short lived. The older and more numerous brotherhoods had processions to the church with which they were affiliated. The city government had supported nine brotherhoods in the fourteenth century by giving them rebates on the tax farm that they had to pay to the leaseholders. The amounts suggest that considerable quantities of wine were involved, and the magistrates themselves attended the banquet of the brotherhood of St Lievin in 1340–1. But city support began diminishing from 1347, and it ceased altogether after 1362. As more brotherhoods were founded in the fifteenth century, the diffusion of effort meant that none had much attractive power or big endowments.[101]

At Bruges, however, some brotherhoods were established through occupational guilds. Before 1450 the tailors' guild had formed the Confraternity of Our Lady of the Snow, sponsoring a festival in her honour each 5 September. The fraternity had several hundred members by 1470 and was not limited to tailors. Nobles, courtiers, some foreign merchants and diplomats and even Count Charles the Bold himself were members. Each year's festival was concluded with a banquet in the guild hall. A fraternity of Our Lady of the Dry Tree (a symbol of the immaculate conception) existed before 1396. Florentines dominated it in the fifteenth century, although there were some other Italians and Spaniards. They paid the Franciscans for a daily mass in their chapel from 1396 and soon hired musicians and sponsored performances.[102]

100. J. Toussaert, *Le Sentiment religieux en Flandre à la fin du Moyen Age* (Paris, 1960), 250–4.

101. Paul Trio, *De Gentse Broederschappen (1182–1580). Ontstaan, naamgeving, materiële uitrusting, structuur, opheffing en bronnen* (Ghent, 1990), 206–10.

102. Strohm, *Music*, 47–8, 71–3.

The festivals of Bruges are the best documented for Flemish Flanders. The best-known 'clergy feast' was that of the 'boy bishop', attested at the church of St Donatian by 1304. It was originally on St Nicholas's day, but in many places it was combined with Holy Innocents' Day and held on 28 December. A schoolboy or the youngest clerk was elected boy bishop. Associated with this was the festival of the Pope of the Asses, originally on New Year's Day but by the late Middle Ages in the week after Epiphany. The pope was the youngest chaplain. St Donatian also staged the Christmas play from 1375, the Corpus Christi from 1458 and a passion play by 1476. The passion play was written by Alianus Groote, whose plays in Flemish were so popular that in 1483 he was allowed to perform them in streets around town. Other festivals were celebrated throughout the liturgical year. The churches of Our Lady (*Onze Lieve Vrouw*) and St Saviour also held numerous festivals and sponsored mystery plays. The festival of the Order of the Golden Fleece was celebrated at Our Lady in 1468 and St Saviour in 1478.[103]

Religion and public morality in late medieval Flanders

We have seen that Flanders was divided among several bishoprics. The appointment of bishops in the Low Countries in the fourteenth century was in the hands of the French king, but in the fifteenth the counts were able to get control of them. They interfered in abbatial appointments, sometimes over the objections of the monks. The Burgundians also got the right from the pope to appoint to some benefices and canonries. At all levels of the hierarchy they appointed their favourites, and when possible family members, which meant a growing problem of absenteeism and of an aristocratic upper group against a more proletarianized lower clergy.[104]

The problems of a largely foreign, often absentee, and generally immoral clergy are not peculiar to Flanders. The dioceses were organized into several deaneries, to which the curates reported. The curates were simply benefice holders who often pursued some other line of work as well and were often if not usually absentee. Priests in their turn were permitted to supplement their meagre incomes by practising other trades. Occupations permitted them included scribe, librarian,

103. Strohm, *Music*, 33–6, 44–8, 50–1.
104. Prevenier, 'Verhouding van de clerus', 30–3.

farmer, gardener, herdsman, baker and tailor. They could not be weavers, fullers, moneylenders, taverners, butchers, brokers or advocates. The priest was named to the parish by its proprietor, whether bishop, abbot or layman. The synodal statutes of Tournai in 1366 prescribed the lives to be led by priests, in themselves a damning commentary on the kind of behaviour that was evidently expected: there were to be no arms or armour, games, theatre including the Feast of Fools, no visiting houses in which there were many women (including Beguinages), and the priests were not to take meals with private persons nor attend wedding banquets.[105] The famous *devotio moderna*, which was established in the Netherlands in the late fourteenth century, had houses in Flanders in the fifteenth century but had little impact on religious practice until later.[106]

Most Flemings seem to have followed the festivals of the liturgical year, but they worried little about other religious matters. The Lateran Council of 1215 required confession to one's own priest at least once a year for all persons above age fourteen. Most Flemings did exactly that and no more. They do not seem to have understood confession or the need for it. Attendance at mass was also low. Infant baptism was universal and, like so many other religious celebrations in Flanders, the occasion of disorder.[107]

The churches had image problems other than their foreignness. There were so many festival days that it was difficult for many to do continuous business without violating a holiday. The churches were also used for secular purposes. Public announcements were always promulgated in the churches, evidently on the assumption, which was demonstrably erroneous, that everyone would attend mass.

We have already noted that the churches' right of sanctuary posed problems for peacekeeping in the cities. Perhaps the most flagrant surviving case of church concern over its legal rights at the expense of justice occurred in 1386 at Ypres. Three men made a pact on the market of Ypres to conduct Michiel Blondeel into a secret place to murder him. To get him to go, one conspirator suggested that they visit a brothel. Then, as two of them went towards another brothel in a different street, the third conspirator, who had stayed behind,

---

105. Toussaert, *Sentiment religieux*, 554–9, 565, 572–5.

106. Carla Morliou, 'De Vroegste geschiedenis van het Gentse St Agneeteconvent (1434–1454): Bijdrage tot de studie van de moderne devotie in onze gewesten', *HMGOG* **38** (1984): 17–33.

107. Toussaert, *Sentiment religieux*, 95–6, 105, 113, 116–17, 164, 170–2.

dispatched the victim with a hammer as the others stabbed him. The culprits then fled to the sanctuary of a church but were apprehended and taken to the town hall for judgement of the aldermen. We are not told the outcome of the case, but summons to the court had to be given by the *schout*, because both the bailiff and underbailiff had been excommunicated by the episcopal court for giving offense to the church, presumably for violating sanctuary.[108]

The secular authorities were conventionally pious. The city accounts of Bruges after 1417 regularly show payments to a clergyman who 'preached the Passion in the castle on Good Friday'. Heresy was a crime involving the secular authorities. In 1420–1 the sergeants of Bruges imprisoned one Matheus van Ysendike 'because he conceived certain things contrary to our belief, by which he intended to mislead the people'.[109] What strikes us about these cases is that they are so infrequent, for moralists complained of bad conduct, and we have seen that they probably had more reason in Flanders than elsewhere. Statutes of Veurne and Ypres forbade the faithful to visit taverns during mass or vespers. The curate of Houtave in 1332 complained that he had trouble celebrating mass because of the noise from a nearby pub. At Bruges, a few days before the Festival of Corpus Domini in 1491, the aldermen ordered the closing of all bakeries and other shops and particularly baths, taverns and gambling houses on Sunday and festival day mornings. They added that nobody was to interfere with the devotions of anyone else.[110] Yet such behaviour does not seem to have aroused suspicion, probably because few, given the atmosphere of carnival religiosity that permeated the church festivals, could afford to have their own conduct and attitudes probed very thoroughly.

108. Pelsmaeker, *Registres*, 338–40.
109. *IAB* **4**: 418–19, 414.
110. Toussaert, *Sentiment religieux*, 142–6.

CHAPTER TWELVE

The Flemish Economy in the Burgundian Period: Redirection and Retrenchment

THE AGRARIAN ECONOMY

We have seen that rural Flanders was devastated by two catastrophes within a quarter century, the war of 1379–85 and the St Elizabeth's Day flood of 1404. There was an even worse flood in November 1421, and another on Palm Sunday 1446. The inundations of the second half of the century were less bad, except for seven weeks of flooding from heavy rain in the winter of 1467 and a flood on 27 September 1477. Between the floods some land was again reclaimed, with considerable help from the count and foreigners at his court and some burghers. The first reference to the windmill being used to suction water from the polders is from 1408. Still, investment in the rural areas, which was less significant in the fourteenth century than earlier, was still declining in the fifteenth. The fact that few settlements were established in newly reclaimed areas shows that they were used largely to extend fields or pasture animals rather than to accommodate population growth. Indeed, although Flanders still had a high rural population density, it was much less than in the fourteenth century. Increasing numbers of Flemish smallholders grew industrial crops, which may explain the absence of a price–wage shear and the fact that

357

the agrarian contraction in Flanders, although perceptible, was less severe than elsewhere.[1]

Erik Thoen's summary of developments in southeastern Flanders has important implications for the rural economy. Between 1410 and 1440 lease rates rose slightly, parallel to or less than grain prices. Townsmen invested less often in rural property than they had done in the fourteenth century, perhaps reflecting the tremendous losses that they sustained after 1385.[2] Between 1440 and 1465, lease rates remained stable or climbed except for a decline just after 1453. Grain prices declined, however, which had an impact on many farm incomes. The last third of the fifteenth century shows considerable distress. Until 1488 leases and grain prices both rose. The indices collapse with the wars with Maximilian, but the prewar levels were again reached by 1500. Grain prices show the same pattern.[3]

The wage curve seems to have been parallel in the cities and the rural areas; although nominal wages were higher in the cities, so were expenses. Real wages were rising after 1385, as prices declined. Purchasing power declined after 1420, although not catastrophically, but from 1440 real wages rose again to a top point between 1460 and 1469, confirming other indices that the period of Philip the Good was a time of general prosperity. Grain prices at both Ghent and Bruges began rising about 1470, peaking in 1480, then again rose to peak in 1489–91, dropping sharply thereafter. Wages did not keep pace, and Flanders thus underwent a severe crisis at the end of the fifteenth century.[4] But the overall late medieval economic crisis was less severe in Flanders than elsewhere. Some of this was doubtless the impact of population decline, which meant that supply of labour less seriously exceeded demand.

Although term leaseholds had spread rapidly since the late thirteenth century, some direct exploitation continued on the great estates into the early fifteenth century. Larger farms were more vulnerable than the small to fluctuations in sale prices, wages and general costs of exploitation, and thus they suffered more relatively. Wages paid to workers were generally 40–50 per cent of the total expense on most large domains, but this problem was less severe on individual family farms.

---

1. Thoen, *Landbouwekonomie*, 1: 532–7; Nicholas, 'Economic Reorientation', 23–4; J. Mertens, 'Landschap en geografie in het Zuiden 1300–1480', *AGN* 2: 41–7; Mertens, 'Landbouw', 14–15, 28–9.

2. On this subject, see Nicholas, *Town and Countryside*, 333–8.

3. Thoen, *Landbouwekonomie*, 1: 645–6.

4. Boone, *Immobilienmarkt*, 68–9.

Many large estates thus ran a chronic deficit after about 1390.[5]

Thus, while small farmers exploited directly, great lords continued to favour term leaseholds. Except just after wars and famines, sharecropping was unusual. In the fourteenth century most lords had specified in the lease contracts what sowing patterns the leaseholder would be required to observe. In the Bruges vicinity a firm rotation pattern was often set only for the last three years of a nine year term, and even this was dropped at the end of the fifteenth century, and a financial calculation made of changes in the value of the land during the term of the lease. The profit margin of leaseholders was not high. The total liabilities from lease price, seigneurial rights and taxes were about 60 per cent of the yield. If a leaseholder needed only his own labour he was all right, but he was in trouble if he had to hire workers, whose costs were outstripping the return on the land. In west Flanders the rent generally was about 6.5 per cent of the sale value of rural land.[6]

Flemish agricultural techniques continued to progress. The first illustration of the single-handed plough, which could be handled by one man without needing another to drive the team, comes in a Flemish Book of Hours around 1430. The fields now had six to ten furrows, which gave better drainage. Yields were still respectable, particularly in the Franc of Bruges, but lower than in northwestern France. In the Oudenaarde region, yields were high in the first half of the fifteenth century but dropped sharply in the second. There is a very complex relation between yields and prices of food; but the link was very weak in late medieval Flanders, because it had such superb facilities for importing grain. Flemish farmers did not benefit much from rises in grain prices except during famine and plague periods, notably after 1437. But once that crisis was surmounted, the classic crisis of overproduction recommenced and a period of low grain prices began that lasted nearly thirty years, as population stagnated and production increased. While elsewhere the decline in farm prices continued into the 1470s, they rose moderately in the Burgundian lands until 1480, then extremely rapidly until experiencing a sharp drop after 1492.[7]

---

5. Thoen, *Landbouwekonomie*, 2: 974; Verhulst, *Précis*, 110–12.

6. Mertens, 'Landbouw', 17–20; J. Mertens, 'Enkele bepalingen omtrent bezaaing, beplanting en behuizing in laatmiddeleeuwse pachtcontracten voor het Brugse Vrije (XVde eeuw)', *ASEB* **108** (1971): 245–60.

7. Van Houtte, *Economic History*, 71; Mertens, 'Landbouw', 29; Blockmans and Prevenier, *In de Ban van Bourgondië*, 110; Verhulst, *Précis*, 98–101, 105; Boone, *Immobilienmarkt*, 28.

The grain trade

The grain trade was the crucial point of linkage of the agrarian, urban and regional economies. The major change in the older patterns was the growing importance of German grain, particularly for western Flanders, after the late fourteenth century.[8] Imported grain was cheaper on the city markets than what came from rural Flanders, which in turn caused distress in the Flemish countryside and led more peasants to migrate into the cities or to branch into other lines of work. The ease with which grain could be imported from one of the most agriculturally productive parts of Europe to Flanders is thus a complicating factor that makes the extent of the agrarian crisis in late medieval Flanders difficult to evaluate.

There were three long-term trends in grain prices. From 1391 the movement is generally upward except for a sudden drop in 1417–18; then the rise continued until 1438. Grain prices fell between 1438 and 1464, then rose until 1492 when a brutal but brief downturn began. Annual price shifts were often in the 10–15 per cent range and occasionally higher. The movements were sharpest on rye, which was imported from Germany, least on oats, which were grown in Flanders, while wheat and barley were intermediate. Yet price series are difficult to use. Flemish rural markets show little difference in price from the cities, perhaps because they were getting some of their supplies through the cities' import facilities. Since cities stockpiled large quantities of grain and imported most of it, prices rose less in years of bad yield and declined less in surplus years than one might expect.[9] Prices even at Bruges were significantly affected by developments in France. During the wars of Louis XI against Charles the Bold, for example, there was a serious rise when the king got control of Artois, from which considerable grain was still coming even to west Flanders.

Paradoxically, while the towns imported, the rural areas exported grain, mainly to Holland and Zeeland, for they could get better prices that way than by selling on the local markets, where the authorities were trying to keep prices low. The large cities insisted

8. M.J. Tits-Dieuaide, *La Formation des prix céréaliers en Brabant et en Flandre au XVe siècle* (Brussels, 1975), 143–4.

9. Tits-Dieuaide, *Formation des prix*, 36, 43, 251–3.

that they bring their grain first to the town markets, and claimed that re-export was raising prices in Flanders. In 1408 the countess agreed to a total embargo on grain export from Flanders, because of 'the great grain scarcity currently occurring because the Hollanders and Zeelanders are exporting' Flemish grain.[10]

Particularly in the case of Ghent, the obligation of farmers of the environs to sell in the city meant that the profit of overseas export would go to urban merchants, not local farmers.[11] Bruges had begun buying food and selling it at cost during the famine of 1315, and this practice was continued and the mechanics improved during the fifteenth century. During the two most serious food shortages of the fifteenth century, of 1436–8 and the 1480s, both Ghent and Bruges stockpiled food. In 1482–3 Bruges in effect established a maximum price by guaranteeing the price it would pay for grain from the surrounding areas. The scarcity of grain was so severe in February 1482 that Bruges bought some from the Spaniards, who were not a normal source, as well as substantial stocks from Zeelanders. Premiums were offered to anyone bringing grain from foreign parts.[12]

The grain staple of Ghent was beyond question the most important source of income for the city in the fifteenth century, cushioning the decline of its textile industry. A text of 1456 calls the staple Ghent's 'principal member'.[13] Ghent did, however, have competitors. Ypres, whose access to the sea was extremely difficult, had established a toll station not precisely at the Leie but at the junction of the routes to Wervik and Mesen, both of which were on the river. When Ypres built a canal and road from Warneton to the Yperleet, it established its own grain staple at a point before the grain came under Ghent's control. By 1424 Ghent claimed that Ypres was violating its monopoly of the Leie trade. In 1432 the count ruled that grain coming to Warneton and thence to the Yperleet could not be taken out of Flanders and that all goods coming upstream on the Yperleet had to be discharged at Warneton. Two officials were to stand guard at Warneton to ensure that no grain reached Ypres along the Yperleet, and Ypres's grain trade was restricted to the immediate locality. Ghent even claimed the right to control other trade on the interior waterways of the Westland.

10. Zoete, *Handelingen*, 1: 225. See also Prevenier and Blockmans, *Burgundian Netherlands*, 66.

11. Tits-Dieuaide, *Formation des prix*, 255–9, compared with Nicholas, 'Scheldt Trade', 256–8.

12. Prevenier and Blockmans, *Burgundian Netherlands*, 62; *IAB* 6: 214.

13. Boone, *Gent en de Bourgondische hertogen*, 21.

On the instigation of Ghent, comital commissioners had piles sunk in the Yperleet near Nieuwpoort, so that large boats could not get through. This affected Bruges as well as Ypres, and the count thus restored Ypres's old trading privileges, while confirming that grain coming down the Leie would not be reshipped by boat from Warneton to Ypres and into the interior. Ypres appealed the case to the *parlement* of Paris, but Ghent refused to recognize its jurisdiction.[14]

Ghent was also claiming both an upstream and downstream monopoly of the Scheldt grain trade, which included Dendermonde, Geraardsbergen, Rupelmonde and Four Offices. It amounted to a claim to monopolize all grain imported into Flanders except through Bruges. But only in 1486 did Ghent get the count to agree formally that all grain entering Flanders by the Scheldt to be re-exported outside Flanders had to come to its staple, including what came from upstream, mainly down the Dender from Hainault.[15]

Bruges got considerable grain through Ghent into the early fifteenth century, even though the German grain trade was growing. In 1409, when the countess prohibited exporting grain from Flanders, Bruges protested Ghent's practice, which other cities also adopted, of keeping half of its imported supply, but Ghent refused to budge; in their petition to the Four Members, the Brugeois did not note that they were not relaxing their right to half the grain entering the Zwin. In 1417 Bruges and the Franc decided to embargo the export of oats to Ghent as long as Ghent hindered the flow of other grain to Bruges. But Bruges's last protest of Ghent's grain policy came in 1425. During the scarcity of 1432–3, Bruges obtained grain from merchants of Rouen and Paris. To avoid the Ghent staple, the Brugeois evidently took the grain along the Seine to the coast and thence to their own port. After 1432, when the count confirmed Ghent's rights on the Leie, Bruges gave up on Ghent and did most of its importing from Germany.[16]

The towns thus discouraged exporting grain. They convinced the count on thirty-nine separate occasions during the fifteenth century, most often on the initiative of Ghent, to impose embargoes. Although the town accounts claim that the prohibitions resulted from high prices, the embargoes did not usually come in periods of scarcity or bad harvest, when the cities continued to export grain. In twenty-two

14. *IAY* 3 160–2, 168–9; Boone, *Gent en de Bourgondische hertogen*, 218; Prevenier and Blockmans, *Burgundian Netherlands*, 66; van Caenegem, *Appels flamands*, 1: 372–83.

15. Prevenier and Blockmans, *Burgundian Netherlands*, 61.

16. *IAB* 3: 368; *IAB* 5: 61; Zoete, *Handelingen*, 1: 366; Tits-Dieuaide, *Formation des prix*, 147–9, 170.

of the embargo years, the only cause of high prices could have been a sudden diminution of imports, not a change on the domestic market, which was not directed towards the Flemish market except when foreign supplies were inadequate. The worst grain price rises of the fifteenth century in Flanders corresponded to periods of export restrictions on Baltic grain, although even in the sixteenth century Baltic grain was only 10–15 per cent of the Netherlands' supply. All interests except the Three Cities thus were opposed to the embargoes, and the cities had to enforce them by installing armed guards at such crucial export depots as Aalst, Dendermonde and in Waas.[17]

External bourgeoisie

Another important link between town and countryside was external bourgeoisie, which reached its greatest extent in the fifteenth century. Since the status generally conferred limited tax immunity for rural property in return for a one-time payment, those who could afford to buy it did so. Those who continued to pay taxes with the castellanies were thus primarily the lesser landlords and the poor.

The exemption of external burghers from taxation in the castellanies was not absolute. Dendermonde's were taxed by the castellany from 1364. The issue of the rural property of burghers who lived in the city could also be embarrassing, but in general the rule of the town applied. In 1398, however, Bruges agreed that the lands acquired by its burghers in the castellany of Courtrai from that date would be taxed there. During the fifteenth century actual residence often became the key in determining the tax liability of external burghers, particularly in the Westland.[18]

External bourgeoisie was not restricted to the great cities. It was probably more widespread in the smaller towns than the larger before 1400. Some persons had maintained bourgeois status simultaneously in their places of residence and in larger towns with more extensive privileges, but the count ended this practice in the early fifteenth century under pressure from the Three Cities. Geraardsbergen in 1396 had 4621 external burghers, almost certainly more than the population of the city itself,[19] and Aalst and Dendermonde also had substantial numbers.

17. Tits-Dieuaide, *Formation des prix*, 182–96; Prevenier and Blockmans, *Burgundian Netherlands*, 66.

18. *IAY* **2**: 22; **3**: 193–4.

19. J. de Brouwer (ed.), *Het Buitenpoortersboek van Geraardsbergen van 1396* (Brussels, 1954).

Courtrai had 7753 external burghers in 1398. External bourgeoisie was an important means by which serfs of the counts and other lords in imperial Flanders became emancipated during the fourteenth century. The count seems in fact to have tried to combat the power of the Three Cities by collecting best chattel from their external burghers but not those of the smaller centres. In 1411 the Council of Flanders permitted best chattel to be taken from two men whom the aldermen of Geraardsbergen had tried to free from it as burghers of Geraardsbergen when investigation showed that the men were actually burghers of Ghent living at Geraardsbergen.[20]

Alone of the Three Cities, Ypres was extremely hostile to external bourgeoisie. Shortly after 1275 a statute had forbidden the admission of anyone to bourgeois status there except those who married burgesses, and statutes throughout the fourteenth century restricted citizenship to persons who lived inside the city. The town on 4 January 1366 ordered that in the future all who wanted to become burghers had to swear to live in the town, and the town was not responsible for protecting them from anything in their background that might cause litigation. Specifically, bastardy or being under the criminal ban meant loss of citizenship. The city did permit some external burghers, however, and in 1383 an agreement with the castellany specified that those who claimed the status were to live in the city except for three forty-day periods, when they might leave to care for the harvest. Elsewhere, the reverse was true: external bourgeoisie was permitted to anyone who would live in the city for three forty-day periods annually. A list of the early fifteenth century names only 242 external burghers of Ypres.[21]

Bruges had a substantial external bourgeoisie, although it was evidently less numerous than those of the smaller centres. In 1318 Bruges and the Franc had agreed that burghers were to live inside the city for three forty-day periods per year. Several leaders of the rebellion of 1323–8 were external burghers of Bruges. External burghers owed military service with the town; in the Carmelite district, those who paid the subsidy for the expedition to Calais in 1436 outnumbered the

---

20. *IAY* 3: 29–30; see in general Erik Thoen, 'Rechten en plichten van plattelanders als instrumenten van machtspolitieke strijd tussen adel, stedelijke burgerij en grafelijk gezag in het laat-middeleeuwse Vlaanderen: Buitenpoorterij en mortemain-rechten ten persoonlijken titel in de kasselrijen van Aalst en Oudenaarde, vooral toegepast op de periode rond 1400', *Machtsstructuren in de Plattelandsgemeenschappen in België en aangrenzenden gebieden (12de–19de eeuw): Handelingen* (Brussels, 1988), 477–80.

21. Pelsmaeker, *Registres*, 385.

resident taxpayers but paid considerably less per capita than did the residents. In 1442–3 the wealth-based tax that the count authorized to help pay Bruges's indemnity produced £4323.75 from resident citizens and £3962.5 from external burghers, who were clearly numerous, rich, overassessed or all of these.[22]

Both immigration to Bruges and external bourgeoisie were involved in a complex arrangement of 1429 between Bruges and the Franc that clarified disputed points of the treaty of 1318, notably concerning conditions under which external burghers or immigrants owed the issue tax to the Franc. They also agreed that burghers who lived in the Franc were free of personal taxes, but they had to pay a property tax of 1.67 per cent to the Franc, whether or not they lived on their lands. In 1458 a complicated new agreement between Bruges and the Franc regarding taxation essentially permitted the ruling element in Bruges to keep their exemption on rural land but ended it for others.[23]

The external bourgeoisie of Ghent was already regarded as a major annoyance by the count in the fourteenth century. By 1432, the chronicler Oliver van Dixmude claimed that Ghent had 5000 external burghers. In 1439 the representatives of the small towns of the quarter of Ghent met at Oudenaarde to protest the tax immunity of citizens of Ghent. Ghent protested the meeting as a violation of its rights as chief of the quarter and quashed the initiative.[24] External bourgeoisie was a major issue in the quarrel between Philip the Good and Ghent in 1450. The aldermen, hoping to preserve the peace, agreed to require residence in the city in a room of which the burgher was the sole occupant. Candidates could not get citizenship by living in an inn, and the city agreed to deny the claim of the fullers, weavers and millers to have non-residents in their guilds. The peace of Gavere of 1453 ended external bourgeoisie, but the privilege of 11 February 1477 restored it on payment of fee and residence in a house for a week from Christmas, Easter and Whitsuntide. Candidates could also get citizenship by joining one of the three privileged guilds. Between 21 March 1477 and 26 December 1481 a total of 7151 persons including wives and children acquired external bourgeoisie. The peace of Kadzand of 1492, however, limited Ghent to external burghers in the Oudburg

22. See general discussion and literature cited in Nicholas, *Town and Countryside*, 235–49; *IAB* 5: 114–15, 257.

23. *IAB* 4: 501; 5: 418–23.

24. Boone, *Gent en de Bourgondische hertogen*, 179–80; Blockmans, *Volksvertegenwoordiging*, 229.

and outside chartered towns, and the importance of the status declined thereafter.[25]

The Flemish nobility

The Flemish nobility was another bridge between the towns and the rural areas by the fifteenth century. Even in the fourteenth century large numbers of nobles had lived in the cities and intermarried with burgher lineages. The lesser nobility in particular experienced serious financial trouble, but they had to maintain symbols of status. Around 1370, Wouter van Zwijnaarde had to sell his windmill to St Pieter's abbey of Ghent to get funds to buy a horse! The Gentenars mocked him with the taunt 'Wouter van Zwijnaarde rides his mill'.[26] The townsmen in their turn were acquiring large amounts of rural land and some seigneuries with jurisdictional rights. The Flemish knights had served the Dampierre counts as bailiffs and other officials and continued to do so under the Burgundians. The growth of the prince's bureaucracy gave new avenues of social advance to the wealthy and educated, most of whom came from the increasingly merged upper bourgeoisie and the nobility.

Flemish feudalism had had no tie with military duty for many years, and when Charles the Bold tried to make fiefholders responsible for service, they resisted. The nobles seem to have regarded the Burgundian dynasty as preferable to subjection to the cities. Yet the Burgundians limited noble privileges more than the cities had ever done, making no distinction in grade between 'our subjects', although Philip the Good's foundation of the famous Order of the Golden Fleece was important for his personal relations with the nobles. The last two Burgundians promoted tournaments, but they hindered the nobles from assembling retainers by granting livery and maintenance.[27]

There was no legal distinction between greater and lesser nobility in Flanders, although the differences in social prestige were considerable. Only the more ancient lineages and those closest to the Burgundian

25. Blockmans, *Volksvertegenwoordiging*, 68; Decavele, 'Gentse buitenpoorterij', 66–74.

26. Jan Buntinx, *De Audientie van de graven van Vlaanderen: Studie over het centraal grafelijk gerecht (c. 1330–c. 1409)* (Brussels, 1949), 421.

27. C.A.J. Armstrong, 'Had the Burgundian Government a Policy for the Nobility?' in *Britain and the Netherlands*, II: *Papers Delivered to the Anglo-Dutch Conference, 1962*, ed. J.S. Bromley and E.H. Kossman (Groningen: J.B. Wolters, 1964): 9–32, reprinted in Armstrong, *England, France and Burgundy*, 213–36.

court had titles. Although nobility was transmitted by birth, it was also possible to be considered noble by one's style of life, an essential aspect of which was possession of land. But most nobles in all provinces of the Burgundian Netherlands lived much of the year in magnificent town houses. The nobles were considered a separate Estate in the provincial Estates and in the Estates General, but they were far less powerful in Flanders than the towns. In the Council of Flanders they had a quota of seats, usually one-third, and they were a majority in the duke's Great Council.

While intermarriage into noble lineages was sought by townsmen for prestige, the nobles themselves found it less important for social reasons than entering princely service, although a burgher marriage might help to repair the sunken financial fortunes of a noble family. Knighthood was not synonymous with nobility in Flanders, but it came to be reserved increasingly for the nobles as French influence heightened under the Burgundians. The English referred to both van Arteveldes as knights, evidently with some exaggeration, but John van Artevelde married the heiress of the lords of Drongen and their daughter married the knight Daniel van Haelwijn. The nobility thus was losing power, and its very existence as a separate group was becoming blurred under the impact of the towns and the Burgundian house.[28]

POPULATION AND POVERTY

We have seen that population declined sharply in Flanders during the fourteenth century due to plagues and warfare. The cycle of plagues slowed in the fifteenth century; there were severe ones in 1400 and 1438. The next serious population depressants came after 1467, with a recurrence of epidemics and nearly constant warfare. There was thus evidently some recovery during the middle years of the fifteenth century.

The fragmentary evidence, however, suggests continued crisis. Although in many regions mortality rates were declining by 1400 from their high points during the plagues, normal annual mortality among the external burghers of Aalst between 1395 and 1431 was 10–16 per

28. Nicholas, *Van Arteveldes*, 73; Paul de Win, 'The Lesser Nobility of the Burgundian Netherlands', in Michael Jones (ed.), *Gentry and Lesser Nobility in Late Medieval Europe* (New York, 1986), 95–118.

cent, which is comparable to England between 1348 and 1352. Life expectancy was then lengthening at Aalst, but it was still only twenty-eight at Petegem at the end of the fifteenth century, which is rather low for medieval populations.[29]

The only source from which implications can be derived for the total population figure for medieval Flanders is a hearth tax survey of 1469.[30] Extrapolating from this record, Walter Prevenier and Wim Blockmans have drawn extraordinarily broad implications. They divide the Burgundian Netherlands into four demographic zones, of which the west, including Flanders, was the most densely urbanized, with 36 per cent of the population living in cities. Using a multiplier of five, they calculate a total population of 660,738, of whom 423,210 were rural and 237,528 lived in the cities. These figures suggest a population density of 78 per square kilometre for Flanders, against 40 for Brabant and 66 for Tuscany. Predictably, the coast and the river valleys were the most densely populated. What distinguishes Flanders from the other regions of the Low Countries was that Ghent and Bruges were so large (only Paris was larger north of the Alps) but that the rest were 'third rank', while the urban centres elsewhere were more comparable in size; for Flanders lacked towns in the 10–20,000 range, and there were no real cities within 25 kilometres of Ghent and Bruges.[31] A separate census from 1485 for Walloon Flanders suggests substantial population increase until 1485, particularly in the castellany of Douai, but then decline during the wars to a lower figure than in 1469. This pattern of increase is confirmed by comparison of data for the castellany of Oudenaarde from 1458 and 1482.[32]

The survey of 1469 shows some communities having households listed as 'poor' and thus exempt from tax, while other places lack this information. The figures for the land of Dendermonde show a high poverty rate. Bailleul, Bergues, Bourbourg, Cassel and Courtrai have complete figures. Nothing survives for the Franc of Bruges outside the enclaved seigneuries, but the only one of those for which poor are given is St Kruis, where all sixteen hearths were poor, which is surely unlikely. Although other indices show that the Westland was not prosperous, Veurne and the castellany of Ypres show relatively few poor.

29. Thoen, *Landbouwekonomie*, 1: 94–5, 117.

30. J. de Smet, 'Le Dénombrement des foyers en Flandre en 1469', *BCRH* **99** (1935): 105–50.

31. Prevenier *et al.*, 'Tussen crisis en Welvaart', 43–50; Prevenier and Blockmans, *Burgundian Netherlands*, 28–34; Blockmans, 'Vers une société urbanisée', 78.

32. Thoen, *Landbouwekonomie*, 1: 36, 39.

The land of Waas has figures surviving for many communities and shows severe poverty, which certainly accords with our other information; yet the adjacent Four Offices has hearth figures that are just as complete but list no poor hearths. The extreme variations between adjacent localities make the entire survey of 1469 suspect as an indication of the extent of poverty.[33]

Prevenier and Blockmans have argued that the description of numerous hearths as 'poor' shows a problem of poverty in Flanders in 1469 that boggles the imagination, particularly in the Walloon castellanies and the northeast, where some parishes had over 50 per cent poor hearths. The average is 25 per cent. Occasionally a high poverty level can be correlated to economic developments. At Diksmuide the linen industry declined sharply after 1400, with the number of seals attached to cloths declining 96 per cent between 1400 and 1420; the census of 1469 gives Diksmuide a poverty rate of over 40 per cent.[34]

Unfortunately, the source of 1469 does not say what was meant by 'poor'. The instructions given to the chancellor say nothing about a poverty inquest, and whether to include that information was evidently left to the persons filing the returns. Some evidently thought that certain households deserved tax relief and said that they were poor, while others simply gave totals. The chancellor then added that he was simply passing on the information. The officials of the Chamber of Accounts then wrote to the count that what was collected 'cannot suffice to know truly all the said villages and even their hearths'. Thus the count on 21 November 1469 asked local officers to get correct information, but he still said nothing about poverty. The areas for which he wanted more information include non-Flemish areas and the castellanies of Lille, Douai and Orchies, all of which have the poverty information. It is thus likely that details, and certainly the poverty figures, were added in the second round of inquests, but nowhere is there a call for a number of poor hearths or a definition of what constituted one.[35]

Scholars have also complicated our understanding of the problem of poverty by out-of-context comparisons. It is indisputable that most persons in the large cities lived in rented housing. Even at Veurne there were only 151 homeowners out of 495 families in 1469. The price of an average house in Ghent between 1483 and 1493 was the equivalent of 4.9 years in wages for an unskilled worker, 1.9 years for

33. De Smet, 'Dénombrement des foyers', 121–44.
34. Blockmans and Prevenier, 'Armoede', 512–13, 529.
35. De Smet, 'Dénombrement des foyers', 145–50.

a skilled labourer. If a skilled worker saved 7.5 per cent of his wages for such a purpose, it would take him twenty-five years to buy a modest house. There are numerous methodological problems with this approach. The 1490s had atypically high prices and low wages. The figures assume that each family had only one wage-earner, which for the lower orders is certainly wrong, and an average of five persons per household, which is probably too high. Furthermore, similar statistics regarding rentals and ownership are still true in the cities; the difference is that with improved credit mechanisms, homes can be purchased by mortgage rather than by saving for one's entire lifetime.[36]

Although there are problems of defining poverty, it is nonetheless clear that many persons lived on the margin of subsistence in Flanders. We have seen that around 1370 poverty was becoming a more recognized but perhaps statistically less serious problem than before. Although the war of 1379–85 caused massive dislocation, after 1400 the amounts spent for relief dropped sharply, probably less because the number of poor diminished than from a feeling that only citizens and the genuinely indigent should qualify. Ghent issued statutes between 1414 and 1428 forbidding begging except by persons who were issued tokens by the masters of the Holy Ghost Tables. In 1432, a year of high grain prices, non-burghers were forbidden to beg. The Holy Ghost Tables stockpiled grain and were able to get through periods of scarcity without diminishing, and in some cases even increasing, their distributions of bread. But in the second half of the fifteenth century there is a massive shift to money and away from kind payments in all Holy Ghost Tables of the region, and the number of poor receiving assistance dropped. In 1491 the aldermen of Ghent cautioned the Holy Ghosts against giving aid to able-bodied men and women. They had to be 'incapacitated, poor, crippled people or blind, who have such defect in their members or senses that they cannot earn their living'.[37]

THE CITIES

The larger cities, for which no totals survive in the 1469 survey, certainly had many poor. In 1449 Bruges ordered 4000 tokens to

36. M. Boone, Machteld Dumon and Birgit Reusens, *Immobiliënmarkt, Fiscaliteit en Sociale ongelijkheid te Gent, 1483–1503*, Standen en Landen, 78 (Courtrai-Heule, 1981): 65–6.
37. Blockmans and Prevenier, 'Armoede', 533, 527, 523–4; Boone et al., *Immobiliënmarkt*, 233–34.

distribute to the poor for peat purchases. In a city of perhaps 35,000 souls, this is a very high rate of indigence. Of 850 households in the Ghemeene Neringhe ward at Ypres in 1431, 51 were categorized as poor and another 38 were living in almshouses, for a total poverty rate of 10.5 per cent. Tax records of Bruges for 1392–4 show that in three out of six wards, only 0.16 per cent were exempt from taxation, but nearly 12 per cent paid a minimal rate. Courtrai had a poverty rate of about 10 per cent around 1440, including paupers who were not burghers. Records of the tax levied in Ghent to pay the indemnity owed to Maximilian have survived for three parishes from 1492–4. Exemption was given to all 'who were very poor or lived on parish relief'. A total of 18 per cent of the inhabitants of the parish of St Jacob received assistance from the Holy Ghost Table, and of the 91 families receiving aid, 11 did not even belong to the lowest tax category. Yet some persons who were exempted from taxation on grounds of their poverty were wealthy enough to own houses! The 1492 figures show the poor of Ghent living mainly in rented shacks, sometimes several per room, especially in the alleys of the suburbs.[38]

Particularly in the large cities, poverty was in large part a question of migrants, since the town gates were often closed to wanderers in times of scarcity. In 1418 a statute prohibited anyone coming to Ghent to seek alms and staying more than one day without the consent of the Holy Ghost Masters and the churchwardens of the parishes in which they wanted to beg. The magistrates distributed charity casually but evidently not regularly. Miscellaneous references from the Bruges municipal account of 1417–18 are probably typical. The city continued to give peat to the major foundations. The aldermen gave small alms to persons who performed charitable acts: a woman who kept a foundling eighteen weeks, another who took care of a mentally ill woman, a poor child whose leg was broken by a cart.[39]

Guilds and the labour market

With the decline of textiles and the growing power of more locally based industries that catered to the needs of a domestic market, guilds

38. *IAB* 5: 186: Boone *et al.*, *Immobiliënmarkt*; R. van Uytven and W. Blockmans, 'De Noodzaak van een geïntegreerde sociale geschiedenis: Het Voorbeeld van de Zuidnederlandse steden in de late middeleeuwen', *TG* 90 (1977): 276–90; Blockmans and Prevenier, 'Armoede', 510–13.

39. Boone, *Gent en de Bourgondische hertogen*, 101; *IAB* 5: 56–9; Prevenier *et al.*, 'Tussen crisis en welvaart', 82.

became as much political organizations as occupational groups. The composition of magistracies hinged on groups of guilds as Members having the right to given seats on the urban councils. It was possible in the fifteenth century, as earlier, for a person to be a master in more than one guild, to change guild affiliations from one year to the next, and to be a master in a trade that he did not actually practise. The most prestigious guilds were not always the largest, but rather those that had obtained heredity in law or in fact, those that generally favoured the Burgundian regime and negotiated in their own interests directly with the prince, and the food-providing guilds.[40]

Virtually all guilds rigidified their fourteenth-century statutes giving preference in mastership to the sons of masters already in the guild. Most raised entry fees for outsiders and limited the number who could be admitted. This placed a ceiling over the head of many would-be masters, even those who had good professional training. Journeyman associations were established from the late fourteenth century and proliferate in the fifteenth. Mastership in a guild became reserved, at least in the wealthier trades, to persons who owned shops and hired journeymen to do the actual work, although the aldermen of Bruges in 1477 ruled that a person who was matriculated in two guilds might be an officer only in the one actually exercised. The same ordinance forbade artisans to buy entry into a guild without completing the term of apprenticeship.[41] The trend in most guilds was away from craftsmanship and towards control of labour and supplies. Even when this was not the case, the guild membership was generally so small that personal acquaintance sufficed. By 1500 only five guilds of Lille required a masterwork, including smiths and barbers. In other cases the master simply certified the apprentice, whose work had doubtless been observed by most masters in the guild anyway.[42]

Urban government in Burgundian Flanders

In most Flemish cities the composition of the governing elite and sometimes its statutory formation became narrower. Tax records confirm the wealth of the ruling groups throughout Flanders, including the smaller centres. It was not unusual for the richest 10 per cent of

40. Boone, *Gent en de Bourgondische hertogen*, 58, 79–80.
41. *IAB* 6: 144.
42. G. Sivéry, 'Quelques aspects des institutions Lilloises au moyen âge' in Trenard, *Histoire de Lille*, 301.

taxpayers to fill one-third to half the aldermanic seats.[43] The upper officers of the town were a group apart, well educated, highly mobile, associating with the princely court and sometimes using town office as a springboard to higher positions. At Ghent, at least, the magistrates used their position for financial advantage. Most of the aldermen of Bruges were at the top of the taxpayer lists in a forced loan in 1490–1, but all their peers at Ghent except the first two law aldermen avoided paying.[44]

Boards of aldermen continued to be chosen by political Member, as in the late fourteenth century. In addition to the two boards of aldermen, Ghent had a Great Council (*Collatie*) consisting of the deans of the individual small guilds and dependent textile trades, ten landowners and the overdeans of the weavers and small guilds. Although the *Collatie* met only in emergencies before the Burgundian period, considerable business was transacted there in the fifteenth century. Voting was by Member, while the aldermen voted as individuals, and cases could be appealed to the *Collatie* from the aldermen. Delegates to meetings of the Four Members reported to the *Collatie*. The government of Ghent was thus more democratic but more subject to violent upheaval – as contemporaries clearly recognized – than the regimes of the other cities.[45]

The major magistracies of Ghent, including aldermen, guild deans and receivers, rotated frequently; Ghent's constitution gave guildsmen a much greater voice in government than in any other town of the Low Countries, although landowners still dominated. More than one-third of the fifteenth-century officeholders served only once, and two-thirds held no more than three positions. But the third who served more than three years held two-thirds of the positions, and the 17 per cent who served more than five years held 44.9 per cent of the offices. Thus there was concentration and continuity. While some families were 'political', others, equally wealthy, were not. Old landholder families had many members in the magistracy, but part of this is due to the reservation of five of thirteen seats on each bench of aldermen for this small group; fifteen families held one-seventh of the total offices available. The pattern of rotation became much more rapid after 1477,

43. R. van Uytven, 'Plutokratie in de "oude demokratieën" der Nederlanden', *Handelingen der Koninklijke Zuidnederlandse Maatschappij voor Taal- en Letterkunde en Geschiedenis* **16** (1962): 389.

44. W.P. Blockmans, 'Het Wisselingsproces van de Gentse schepenen tijdens de 15de eeuw', *HMGOG* **41** (1987): 77; Boone et al., *Immobiliënmarkt*, 215, 222, 226–7.

45. Boone, *Gent en de Bourgondische hertogen*, 28–33.

when the cities attempted to undo as many as possible of the Burgundian restrictions on their autonomy.[46]

The basis of city finance continued to be indirect taxes on consumption. They were leased to tax farmers who were drawn in the fifteenth century from an ever-narrower group. Although aldermen normally could not hold tax farms during their terms of office in the fourteenth century, this was less true in the fifteenth, and the elite monopolized public contracts increasingly.

The burdens of Burgundian taxation on the cities became insupportable even as early as Philip the Bold. The counts realized that Ypres was beyond hope; even Charles the Bold commuted payments for the stricken city.[47] But they placed impossibly high demands on Bruges, their richest city. By 1400 Bruges was already selling city property below cost to pay the count, because the loss was less than the interest that would have been paid to borrow the money outright.[48] From 1407 Bruges paid the count one-seventh of the city's revenues, but by 1413 the prince was asking Bruges for a loan against his seventh, to which Bruges responded that it was already in debt for loaning that amount to him. Instead it offered him an advance on the next subsidy voted by the Four Members, and he accepted. The municipal accounts of Bruges were balanced only four times between 1435 and 1467; the city even instituted a lottery in 1439.[49]

Ghent shows continuity of public administration but with a more rigid application of basic principles of participation in the fifteenth century. Membership on the town councils was chosen by Member: the landowners, the weavers and their dependants and the small guilds. Not only were the higher offices chosen rigidly by Member, but so were such lesser offices as clerkships and the city police. Although the aldermen were chosen formally by a college of electors appointed by the count and the outgoing aldermen, in practice the guild overdeans and assemblies of the Three Members chose them and presented the prince with a *fait accompli*; the deans thus assumed greater powers under the Burgundians than before. Although rigid and at times fiscally

---

46. Blockmans, 'Wisselingsproces', 78–90; W.P. Blockmans, 'Mutaties van het politiek personeel in de steden Gent en Brugge tijdens een periode van regimewisselingen: Het laatste kwart van de 15e eeuw', *Bronnen voor de Geschiedenis van de Instellingen in België* (Brussels, 1977), 92–103.

47. *IAY* 3: 253; 4: 2, 4–5, 11.

48. *IAB* 3: 418–19; 4: 423.

49. *IAB* 4: 252–3; 5: 473, 475.

corrupt, the new regime worked. Civil conflicts at Ghent were much less severe after 1385 than before.[50]

Ghent also ran a chronic deficit. The major variable was the count's demands for money, but Ghent was more financially healthy than Bruges until 1453, when the fines exacted by the peace of Gavere forced the city to levy surcharges and rents. The statutory requirement that the count's officials audit the city books then became more than a formality.

INTERNATIONAL POLITICS AND THE MONEY SUPPLY

Flanders was particularly vulnerable to the problem of inadequate bullion supply that plagued Europe during the fifteenth century, for it had no native supplies of gold or silver, and most of what passed its borders was in foreign hands coming through Bruges. Surviving price series are drawn from large transactions and thus may not be an accurate reflection of conditions for the average consumer. The supply of petty or 'black' coins used for most small transactions was generally adequate to meet demand except between 1440 and 1470.[51]

The merchants, however, were hurt by the bullion famine. The Ghent mint ceased coining in 1392 and that of Bruges in 1402 and despite the Members' protests the mints were completely inactive until 1410. Local authorities at Bruges in 1399 tried to increase the amount of specie in circulation by prohibiting payment of bills of exchange by bank transfer, and between February 1400 and October 1401 and again between 1411 and 1416 merchants were ordered to settle all exchanges in bullion. The increased use of fiduciary money at Bruges thus reflected not only ingenuity but also inadequate money supply.[52]

Philip the Bold seems to have had a good understanding of the international monetary situation. The Flemish coin was devalued six times between 1384 and 1389, but each was a response to changes in the issues of France and the neighbouring states of the Low Countries,

50. Boone, *Gent en de Bourgondische hertogen*, 33–48.

51. John H. Munro, 'Deflation and the Petty Coinage Problem in the Late-Medieval Economy: The Case of Flanders, 1334–1484', *Explorations in Economic History* **25** (1988): 387–423, particularly 393, 404.

52. Munro, 'Deflation and the Petty Coinage', 414–15.

to avoid having Flanders flooded by cheap foreign coin, while the better Flemish coin was exported to pay for imported goods.[53]

In 1389, however, Philip ordered a sharp deflationary renforcement of the coin, strengthening silver 31.8 per cent and gold 41.7 per cent. This caused prices on Flemish cloth exports to rise, particularly since gold, which was used in international transactions, was deflated even more than silver. Prices in Flanders did not fall in proportion to the renforcement of the coin, and efforts to keep wages down led to disturbances. Furthermore, renforcement was not consistent, for debasements continued periodically through the fifteenth century. Between 1390 and 1416 the coin was strong, but the period 1416–33 was inflationary, again in response to French devaluations. The mints were again active during the periods of debasement to compensate for the need for more money.[54]

In May 1433 Philip the Good strengthened the coin and restricted the activities of deposit bankers, who were suspected of selling bullion to foreign mints. The Burgundian Netherlands were given a common coinage in 1433 based on the Flemish issue for values above the Flemish quarter groat. The Burgundians maintained a hard money policy until May 1466. Between 1433 and 1474 there was thus relative peace and a strong coinage. Since the cost of living was not high and wages generally outstripped price rises, Philip the Good's period was understandably remembered later as a period of prosperity. Thereafter, warfare, debasement and severe inflation, accentuated by silver imports from central Europe, caused serious problems. The renforcements were usually more substantial than the debasements, with the result that the long-range impact was minimal; the Flemish silver groat contained 0.97 grammes of silver in 1383, 0.54 in 1477.[55]

The Burgundian rulers usually involved the Four Members in coin questions. Peter Spufford has seen an embryonic Estates General developing in the Burgundian Netherlands as a result of the monetary

53. Pierre Cockshaw, 'A Propos de la circulation monétaire entre la Flandre et le Brabant de 1384 à 1390', *Contributions à l'histoire économique et sociale* 6 (1970): 105–41.

54. John H. Munro, 'Monetary Contraction and Industrial Change in the Late-Medieval Low Countries, 1335–1500' in *Coinage in the Low Countries*, 112; Munro, 'Mint Outputs, Money, and Prices in Late-Medieval England and the Low Countries', *Trierer Historische Forschungen* 7 (1984): 32.

55. Munro, 'Monetary Contraction and Industrial Change', 115; Munro, 'Petty Coinage', 395; Denis Clauzel, 'Comptabilités urbaines et histoire monétaire (1384–1482)', *RN* 63 (1981): 357–76; Munro, *Wool, Cloth, and Gold*, 81–2; John Day, 'The Great Bullion Famine of the Fifteenth Century', *Past and Present* 79 (1978): 3–54, reprinted in Day, *The Medieval Market Economy* (Oxford, 1987), 15–16, 42–3.

unification of 1433. Its abolition of individual coinages had to be ratified by each provincial assembly of estates. Since subsequent changes
had to be approved by all, it was easier to do it in one assembly, and
the first four meetings of the Estates General, between 1437 and 1461,
dealt almost exclusively with the coinage.[56]

Monetary policy and the English trade

Although Flanders was hurt more than England by trade stoppages,
good relations with Flanders were necessary for England, for Germans,
Brabanters and Lombards had to cross Flemish territory to get to the
Calais staple. In 1397, however, in response to the bullion shortage,
the English began requiring that wool purchases at Calais be made in
specie. Flemish and other wool buyers paid for their purchases in
Flemish coin, usually giving cash for one-third of the price, at Calais
and at the fairs of Bruges, Middelburg, Antwerp and Bergen-op-
Zoom. The rest would be payable later by bills of exchange at the fairs
or one of the Bruges banks. The staplers sent the money to England
by drawing bills of exchange to London mercers, who handled most
of the English import trade with the Low Countries. But the Calais
Ordinances of 1429 ordered a price rise and forced the staplers to take
only bullion or English coin in exchange for wool. This disrupted the
credit mechanism on which previous wool trading had been based, for
most drapers did not have enough coin to make wholesale purchases
in cash. This in turn forced the counts and Four Members again to
revalue Flemish coin in response to developments overseas.[57]

The Calais Ordinances caused a serious decline in the Flemish textile output, while prices rose sharply, although only on cloths made
with English wools. The average number of drapers' stalls rented in
the hall at Ypres between 1430 and 1433 dropped 30 per cent while
English wool exports to Calais were 32 per cent below the 1426–9
average and continued low for the rest of the century. This in turn
forced the 'new draperies' of Flanders, which had generally used
English wool, to switch to Spanish and Scottish. Although initially

---

56. Peter Spufford, 'Coinage, Taxation and the Estates General of the Burgundian
Netherlands', *Standen en Landen* **40** (Brussels, 1966): 65–70, 73–6; Blockmans, 'Vlaanderen 1384–1492', 212.

57. Munro, *Wool, Cloth, and Gold*, 84, 89–90; Eileen Power, 'The Wool Trade in
the Fifteenth Century' in Eileen Power and M.M. Postan (eds), *Studies in English Trade
in the Fifteenth Century* (London, 1933), 64–7.

disdained as an inferior product, by the 1460s more Spanish than English wool was being used at Ghent.[58]

The Flemish textile industries in the fifteenth century

We have seen that the Flemish textile industry underwent a serious crisis after 1275 that became much worse after 1360. There was some recovery in the early fifteenth century. Even at Ypres there was a substantial increase between 1410 and 1420 in the number of stalls rented in the cloth hall, and Ghent's tax farm yields on textiles increased 77 per cent between 1400 and 1430. During these years English wool exports rose while cloth exports declined. Much of the problem was the requirement that many Flemish textiles, which were closely regulated by their town guilds and city governments, use English wool, which was increasingly expensive and whose supply was decreasing sharply, particularly after 1429.[59]

Flemish cloth was made ruinously expensive by wool and dye prices and by high labour costs. The prices on eight of the nine most commonly exported Flemish textiles were twice as high as on English broadcloths, although still much lower than the finest Italian products. The expensive textiles were not monopolies of the Three Cities; the fine black cloths of Courtrai, Menen and Wervik, all light fabrics, were more expensive than the English, and that of Wervik was treble the English price. Cloth of Bruges and Ypres was more expensive at Krakau than that of the much smaller Brabantine centres of Mechelen and Herentals. There was a great disparity in cloth prices even among the smaller places, but most of it was dear.[60]

Some new markets were developing. Increasing amounts of Flemish cloth were being carried by the Germans to Poland and Russia, and Flemish cloth had an important market at Barcelona in the fifteenth century, especially *saies* of Wervik and cloth of Courtrai.[61] But by this

58. Munro, *Wool, Cloth, and Gold*, 96–8, 181; Munro, 'Monetary Contraction and Industrial Change', 117; Lloyd, *Wool Trade*, 263; Boone, *Gent en de Bourgondische hertogen*, 19.

59. Munro, 'Monetary Contraction and Industrial Change', 113; Thielemans, *Bourgogne et Angleterre*, 188–90, 197.

60. Blockmans and Prevenier, *In de ban van Bourgondië*, 113; C. Verlinden, *Brabantsch en Vlaamsch laken te Krakau op het einde der XIVe eeuw*, MKVA, Kl. Letteren, Jaargang 5, No. 2 (Brussels, 1943), 11–16; and more comprehensively Munro, 'Industrial Transformations', 142–8.

61. Verlinden, *Brabantsch en Vlaamsch Laken*, 9, 18–19; de Roover, 'Renseignements complémentaires', 64.

time the Three Cities were complaining less about the loss of foreign markets to the smaller centres; they seem to have been concerned more with the enormous domestic market within the cities and at the opulent Burgundian court. Tolls at the fairs show that the volume of internal trade within the Burgundian Netherlands nearly doubled between 1400 and 1480.

The concern to protect domestic manufacture was not limited to woollen cloth. In May and June 1407 the Four Members petitioned the chancellor to forbid the sale except at the fairs of not only foreign cloth but also trousers made from foreign cloth, and to prohibit the sale of foreign-made leather and shoes at Bruges, a request stated to affect notably Italian and German merchants. By September the count had evidently acceded, and the aldermen of Bruges sent letters to Nieuwpoort alleging that a large quantity of foreign shoes was being sold there contrary to the count's legislation.[62]

The great cities renewed their efforts to keep the smaller centres from imitating their speciality cloths. A major step was the ruling of 1407 that Bruges obtained from the count restricting textile manufacture in the Franc. Portions of it simply restate earlier statutes: every parish in the Franc was limited to one simple loom on which unsealed cloth could be made that could not be sold at the fairs or markets. Cloth made at Sluis could be sold only there. Raids against rural textiles resumed. Bruges also kept close watch over the annual village fairs in the Franc. The city even tried to stop the preparation of locally grown madder in the Franc, despite the Franc's protest that it had never been included in the staple.[63]

Agitation against rural textiles also continued around Ypres. On 10 March 1428 the count, to end the counterfeiting of Ypres cloth, forbade cloth making in any village of the castellanies of Ypres, Bailleul, Cassel and Warneton except those with formal textile privileges. The exceptions were that some villages might make coarse and short cloth with the native wool of the locality, and only for use of the family making it, never for sale. The number of looms permitted in each village was specified, and the restriction applied also to villages within 3 leagues of Ypres in which cloth had previously been made. Significantly, however, persons in these villages who had been making cloth could go to Ypres or to privileged places within a year, and the magistrates would give them the right of external bourgeoisie without exacting payment, which in a certain sense made the statute a dead

---

62. Zoete, *Handelingen*, 1: 215–16, 229.
63. *IAB* 3: 534–7; 4: 415–6; Zoete, *Handelingen*, 2: 922.

letter. In 1429 the count ordered his officials to warn the inhabitants of Nieuwkerken, Cassel and Bailleul that they could not sell cloth at the Torhout and Courtrai fairs.[64] The privilege of 1428 was quickly limited. The villagers were being accused of wholesale violations within the year. In 1431 the countess of Namur, who owned some of the villages in question, appealed Ypres's textile privilege to *parlement*, which finally ruled in 1446 that drapers of Nieuwkerken and Eeke could make the same types of cloth as before 1428.[65]

The medium-grade cloth of the small towns satisfied most domestic consumers, who no longer had to turn to the textiles of the Three Cities. They also continued expanding into foreign markets. They developed complex market mechanisms. In 1416, after property was seized from merchants of Toulouse at Douai, the victims informed the Four Members that they were 'good merchants at their innkeepers of Courtrai, Mechline, Wervik, Menen and other towns where they have customarily bought cloth each year'.[66]

The woollen industries of the smaller Flemish centres expanded in the early fifteenth century, but not enough to compensate for the loss of markets of the Three Cities; and after 1450 most declined, in part because they were more dependent on the increasingly volatile Hansards than were the larger centres. Veurne and Bergues are an exception. They expanded rapidly into *sayetterie* after 1450, taking up some of the slack when other smaller towns declined, but their trade was hardly immense, and as late as 1475 there were only two sealing days for *saies* per week.[67]

The Flemish linen industry

The Flemish linen industry continued to grow in the first half of the fifteenth century but declined in the second half, probably losing to competition from Hainault. The English obtained most of their linen at Antwerp and the other Brabant fairs, but combined Customs Accounts for London and Sandwich for the 1430s show that Flanders

64. *IAY* 3: 130–1, 138, 140–1. See comment of C.A.J. Armstrong, 'La Double monarchie France–Angleterre et la maison de Bourgogne (1420–1435): Le déclin d'une alliance' in Armstrong, *England, France and Burgundy in the Fifteenth Century* (London, 1983), 357–8.

65. *IAY* 3: 141, 146, 148–9, 191; van Caenegem, *Appels flamands*, 1: 507–9, 576–8.

66. Zoete, *Handelingen*, 2: 1085.

67. Van Houtte and van Uytven, 'Nijverheid en handel', 104; van Uytven, 'Terres de promission', 293–5; E. Coornaert, *Une Industrie urbaine du XIVe au XVIIe siècle: L'industrie de la laine à Bergues-Saint-Winoc* (Paris, 1930), esp. 14, 23, 25, 46–7, 54.

furnished 34 per cent of the total linen export of the Burgundian domains against 30 per cent for Brabant and 20 per cent for Hainault. But this represents a decline since the 1390s, when the Flemish share was 63 per cent of the Low Country linen entering London. The English in their turn carried Flemish linen as far away as Iceland.[68]

New sources of income

We have seen that the fishing trade along the Flemish coast helped to cushion some of the loss of income from textiles. The main centres of the Flemish herring trade were Nieuwpoort, Ostend, Biervliet and Dunkirk. The yield of the herring tax at Ostend grew 66 per cent between 1418 and 1434. The war with England after 1436 and the resulting piracy were a general disaster for the Flemish coast and the tax yield dropped catastrophically, but this was only a temporary setback for Ostend, which grew markedly between 1445 and 1480. It got a fish staple and the right to put the town mark on the tuns. In 1445 the count gave the town brokerage rights over fish, and by 1467 there were twenty-six innkeeper–brokers at Ostend, as the annual yield of the brokerage fee doubled in the 1460s.[69]

Other trades and industries had a more modest prosperity. Some of the 'decline' of Flemish textiles may be due to workers going into the manufacture of finished clothing as tailors or hat makers. The mercers of Ghent, purveyors of a variety of small items, some of them made locally, grew tremendously in the fifteenth century. Ghent developed an important leather trade, principally in gloves and purses.[70] Flemish jewellery had a good reputation in England. Although some towns had tapestry weaving in the fourteenth century, it became substantial only in the fifteenth, with guilds established at Oudenaarde in 1441 and shortly afterwards at Ghent and Bruges. There were 56 tapestry weavers at Bruges in the fourteenth century, 114 in the fifteenth. The industry spread to the rural areas around Oudenaarde and Geraardsbergen from mid-century, as linen working there declined.[71]

68. Thoen, Landbouwekonomie, 2: 980–9; Thielemans, Bourgogne et Angleterre, 225–7; E.M. Carus-Wilson, 'The Iceland Trade' in Power and Postan, Studies in English Trade, 175.

69. R. Degryse, 'De Crisis in de haringbedrijf te Oostende ende to Damme van 1437 tot 1441', ASEB 102 (1966): 53–68; Degryse, 'Het Begin van het haringkaken te Biervliet (+/- 1399)', ASEB 95 (1958): 72–81; Degryse, 'De Vlaamse Haringvisserij in de XVe eeuw', ASEB 88 (1951): 116–33.

70. Van Uytven, 'Terres de promission', 297.

71. Thielemans, Bourgogne et Angleterre, 295: Blockmans, 'Vers une société urbanisée', 89; Thoen, Landbouwekonomie, 2: 1014; Prevenier and Blockmans, Burgundian Netherlands, 448.

Curiously, despite the growing importance of the Flemish coast in fishing and navigation, the only significant Flemish shipbuilding centre was Dendermonde, which doubtless reflects the importance of Ghent's trade through Brabant and the grain imports from Hainault. Virtually everywhere in the Low Countries had intensive firearms production, but Flanders was outstripped by Brabant. The most important Flemish centre was Bruges, probably because of its access to foreign iron and artisans. Much activity at Bruges seems to have been in importing finished or semi-finished Italian pieces. Sluis, Damme, Lille and Ghent also had armourers.[72]

The decline of Ypres

The modest growth of new industries and trades cannot conceal the fact that both the absolute and relative economic position of Flanders declined seriously after 1385. The most conspicuous catastrophe was Ypres, the most dependent of the Three Cities on woollen textiles and the one with the most economically competitive hinterland. Hence the decline of the Flemish textile industry hurt Ypres more severely than Bruges, which had foreign trade, or Ghent, which had its grain staple and a more docile hinterland for which it could serve as a regional distribution centre. Ypres continued to be one of the Four Members, and its weaknesses may not have been immediately apparent abroad, but its political pretensions corresponded to no economic reality. While the Transport of 1325 had made Ypres responsible for 10.72 per cent of the count's taxes, in 1408 it was 8.58 per cent, and this may have been an overassessment.

The counts were not unsympathetic. In 1451 Philip the Good moved the Council of Flanders from Dendermonde, where it had been since 1446, to Ypres. His reasons were that Dendermonde was on the frontier, too small, and many people whose cases were being heard could not find lodging. Ypres, by contrast, had plenty of lodging and had so declined in wealth and population that he hoped this would revive it. But in 1464 the Council was moved again to Ghent. In 1474, with one-third of its houses empty and in ruins, the count further reduced Ypres's share in the *beden* to 4.31 per cent; virtually all other administrative units in the Westland and the town and castellany

---

72. Claude Gaier, *L'Industrie et le commerce des armes dans les anciennes principautés belges du XIIIme à la fin du XVme siècle* (Paris, 1973), 91.

of Courtrai were raised simultaneously, in most cases by at least 25 per cent. In 1486, in a suit to obtain exemption from the most recent subsidy, the Yprois claimed that only twenty-five to thirty drapers remained, population had declined to 5–6,000 and one-third of the inhabitants were begging.[73]

Totally apart from any question of rhetorical exaggeration to gain tax relief, the population of Ypres declined severely in the fifteenth century. The *Poorterieboek* of Ypres shows migration figures for the period 1352–79 averaging over 100 annually. The figure drops to 60 for the period 1383–7 and 29 for 1411–17. Single-year population figures for quarters of the city survive for five years during the fifteenth century. Rough extrapolations from the data suggest a population declining slightly from 10,736 in 1412 to 10,523 in 1431, then more rapidly to 9390 in 1437 and 7626 in 1491, then rising to 9563 in 1506.[74]

The aldermen tried to encourage migration to Ypres by relaxing some industrial regulations, but faced the hostility of the local guilds. In 1440 the city issued an ordinance that has not survived but that evidently involved reciprocity with some nearby villages. In 1463 the aldermen accused the candlemakers' guild of violating that ordinance by refusing to admit a man trained at Menen. The cloth workers may have been more realistic, at least by Maximilian's period. After a new prohibition against cloth making at Nieuwkerken and the environs, the regent noted in August 1484 that the aldermen of Ypres were urging drapers of the parishes in question to come to Ypres to exercise their trades and expressly freed them from prosecution for violating Ypres's textile monopoly.[75]

OVERSEAS TRADE

We have seen that the notion of a purely passive Flemish shipping trade is overdrawn, but the Flemish share in the southern French trade was diminishing. When Castilian piracy against Hanse ships became serious in 1432, some Germans started freighting their goods in Flemish

73. *IAY* 2: 254–5; 3: 206–7; 4: 13, 121–2.
74. H. Pirenne, 'Les Dénombrements de la population d'Ypres au XVe siècle (1412–1506): Contribution à l'histoire statistique sociale au moyen âge', *Vierteljahrsschrift für Sozial- und Wirtschaftsgeschichte*, 1 (1903): 1–32.
75. *IAY* 3: 254; 4: 89–90.

boats to conceal them from the Spaniards and justified it to their home governments by claiming that Flemish boats were better than German. Fewer Flemish boats left the port of London than those from Zeeland, but Flanders accounted for twice the number from Holland and one-quarter more than Brabant.[76]

Totally apart from the problem of the carrying trade, Flanders still had to import most strategic goods. It developed a ruinously negative trade balance with Italy, its only source of alum and the major supplier of many other dyes, minerals and edible spices. Genoa imported nearly three times as much value of goods from Flanders as it sold there in the early fifteenth century, but most of this was in goods not made in Flanders. While Flemish merchants remained active in trade with France, Scotland, Spain and Germany, the Italians handled the entire Flemish trade with Italy.[77]

Bruges and the Zwin markets

The major generator of foreign capital for Flanders in the fifteenth century was not exports but the commercial facilities and tolls at Bruges. Whenever foreign merchants left Bruges they had to return to get access to its money market and to trade conveniently with other foreigners. The general principle of medieval trade was that foreigners could not sell retail, nor directly to each other in the hostels; they had to use a local broker, and this was certainly followed at Bruges. In 1409 Bruges even tried to force all residents of Bruges, of whatever nationality, to take a sworn broker of Bruges with them when they left the city to sell cloth elsewhere in Flanders, an action that caused Ghent, Wervik and Courtrai to protest to the Four Members. In 1419 the Brugeois fined several Catalonians for violating this at Courtrai.[78] The London grocers imported garlic, cabbages, onions, apples, oranges and other fruits from France and Flanders. The Normans used Bruges for woad, spices, Castilian wool and Scottish products. Cod, pitch and rosin came from Germany through Flanders and on to Normandy.

76. Zoete, *Handelingen*, 1: 562; Beuken, *Hanze*, 93–4; E.M. Carus-Wilson, 'The Overseas Trade of Bristol' in Power and Postan, *Studies in English Trade in the Fifteenth Century*, 183–246; Thielemans, *Bourgogne et Angleterre*, 314ff.

77. Prevenier, 'Perturbations anglo-flamandes', 491; de Roover, 'Renseignements complémentaires', 63–4.

78. Zoete, *Handelingen*, 1: 379; 2: 1320, 1326, 1328.

Scandinavian wood became known in Normandy as 'wood of Flanders' because it was bought in such quantity at Bruges.[79]

Alum, which was available only through the Italians, was probably the single most important item traded at Bruges, for all northerners had to buy it there from the local brokers. The Hansards complained of alum cartels led by Bruges innkeepers in 1449; Flemish machinations caused alum prices to treble, and the aldermen of Bruges promised in 1457 to keep closer watch. Alum was the most important Norman acquisition in the Flemish port. Flemish trade with Normandy was subject to politically inspired interruptions, but it accounted for 12 per cent of the value of goods passing through the port of Dieppe in 1476–7. There is much less evidence of Bretons importing goods from Flanders, but in 1457 they accounted for 38 per cent of the number of boats at Sluis, although they were far behind the Scots and Portuguese in tonnage. Between 1450 and 1475 Bretons were cited fifty-two times by the water bailiff for various infringements of the staple. The Danes were important enough to the Bruges market to cause consternation when in 1416 some went to Zierikzee instead for fear of being arrested for debts owed to Flemings in Denmark.[80]

In addition to the international markets, the Zwin was an important centre for local trade. In 1408 some 1370 boats were certified to navigate the Lieve canal, which linked Ghent with Damme. In 1394 Bruges redeemed from the count an annual payment levied on all merchandise sold to foreigners during the second three days of the May fair, because the tax farmers who collected it had become so obnoxious that they were driving customers away. In 1408 the chancellor of Brabant asked the help of the Members because certain persons acting for lord Jan van Gistel had entered Brabant and robbed and abducted merchants from the area of Liège who were en route home from the fair of Bruges.[81]

79. Sylvia L. Thrupp, 'The Grocers of London: A Study of Distributive Trade' in Power and Postan, *Studies in English Trade*, 266.

80. O. Mus, 'De Brugse compagnie Despars op het einde van de 15e eeuw', *ASEB* **101** (1964): 100–1; Michel Mollat, *Le Commerce maritime normand à la fin du moyen âge: Etude d'histoire économique et sociale* (Paris, 1952), 38, 103–4, 124, 174; Henri Touchard, *Le Commerce maritime breton à la fin du Moyen Age* (Paris, 1967), 149, 194; Zoete, *Handelingen*, 2: 1089.

81. Boone, *Geld en Macht*, 176; *IAB* **3**: 296–8; Zoete, *Handelingen*, 1: 285.

The Hanse in Burgundian Flanders

Bruges is most famous for its Italian trade, but it had more trouble keeping the Germans happy. The treaty ending the blockade of 1388–92 obliged the Members to guarantee restitution of property stolen from Germans in Flanders. Channel piracy and the hostility of the various foreign groups towards one another made this liability a major embarrassment; in 1405 the Members had to pay enormous sums to four Germans for English wool lost to pirates at Nieuwpoort. The Flemings initially did what they could, but the Germans were so insistent that the Flemings right all their wrongs that Flemish efforts became increasingly perfunctory.[82]

Foreign populations in Flanders were largely rotating in the beginning as merchants accompanied their goods, but this was no longer the case by the early Burgundian period. The Four Members met in an extraordinarily long two-week session in January 1415 regarding foreign merchants, 'who in the past could not stay longer than forty days in Flanders doing business, but now they stay the entire year doing business against the common good of the land'. Foreigners were clearly disliked and their privileges of residence resented. At the same meeting the Members also discussed the running dispute between the Germans and the Scots; the Hanse had precipitated a crisis in Flanders in 1413 by refusing to buy cloth made with Scottish wool, which by then meant a considerable part of the output of the smaller centres. The Members noted that the decision damaged them and especially the 'common folk' who earned their livings with drapery.[83]

The Germans in Bruges were suspected of English sympathies, probably because they had the privileges of buying English cloth at Bruges as long as it was not resold to Flemish customers and of bringing English cloth bought elsewhere in transit through Flemish ports. In June 1436, as war fever mounted, the Germans were attacked in their hostels after a tavern altercation at Sluis, and several were killed. The Hanse moved its staple to Antwerp, returning in 1440 when Flanders had another grain shortage.[84]

82. Konrad Bahr, *Handel und Verkehr der deutschen Hanse in Vlaanderen während des vierzehnten Jahrhunderts* (Leipzig, 1911), 89–92; *IAB* 3: 524; J.H.A. Beuken, *De Hanze en Vlaanderen* (Maastricht, n.d.), 90; Zoete, *Handelingen*, 1: 140; 2: 748; *IAY* 3: 150–4.

83. Zoete, *Handelingen*, 2: 899–900, 1012–13.

84. Beuken, *Hanze*, 96–101.

Matters were generally quiet through the 1440s, but in 1450 the Hanse moved the staple to Deventer and declared a blockade, forbidding trade not only in Flemish goods but also in merchandise that had been in Flemish waters. The blockade was notably unsuccessful. The Hanse was in no position to blockade the entire Burgundian domain as well as Flanders. In 1452, realizing that Germans who were outside the Hanse, notably Nurembergers and Swabians, were using the absence of the Hanse to cut into the Flemish market, the League relaxed the blockade. Then in early 1453 the staple was moved to Utrecht, whose harbour was too shallow for larger boats. Negotiations dragged on until 1457, but this time the Hanse got none of its demands. Its old privileges were restored, but the demand of the Hanse to be able to negotiate with the Four Members without the count was rejected.

Although the blockade of the 1450s was unsuccessful, changes of German policy thereafter are harbingers of the future. As late as 1447 the Hanse had forbidden its members to purchase cloth except at Flemish or other staples, but in 1457 the Diet changed the staple obligation significantly: purchases of cloth and other staple goods had to be at the staple at Bruges *or* the fairs of Antwerp or Bergen-op-Zoom. German trade became less active thereafter, as many merchants used factors or even entrusted business to their former hostellers in Bruges.[85]

The English trade

The major items in Anglo-Flemish trade continued to be wool and smuggled English cloth. The concern with the domestic market prompted the Flemish policy forbidding the sale of English cloth in Flanders, since the Flemings knew that other foreigners could easily get access to the English product elsewhere. Although technically only the Hansards could bring packaged English cloth in transit through Bruges, in fact most of the others did so, and an ambiguous reference of 1414 suggests that the Hansards could have English cloth dyed in Bruges, which would mean unpacking it. Bruges, which could have benefited by free sales of English cloth, in February 1415 complained that English cloth was 'brought daily into the Zwin in many packages'. English cloth belonging to Germans was seized at Nieuwpoort in 1416 but was restored to its owners by the Four Members.[86]

85. Beuken, *Hanze*, 105–15, 150–3.
86. W. Brulez, 'Engels laken in Vlaanderen in de 14e en 15e eeuw', *ASEB* **108** (1971): 20–4; Zoete, *Handelingen*, 2: 913, 1044.

The Calais Ordinances of 1429 had damaged trade, and the changed diplomatic situation after 1435 was a disaster, but the Flemish cities needed the English trade too much to help Bruges's war against the count. By September 1436 Ypres was asking the count's permission to get wool at Calais, which was technically forbidden territory, and the other textile towns followed suit. By May 1437 the Four Members were trying to negotiate with England by using Hansards at Bruges as intermediaries. A three-year treaty was sealed on 29 September 1439: the Calais staple was open to Burgundian subjects. The English, Irish and Calaisiens got safe conduct in Flanders to deal with local and foreign merchants. There was to be free commerce in food, but not in arms, and trade in individual strategic items, such as grain, could be regulated by the prince.[87]

The treaty of 1439 began several years of relative quiet. The Calais Ordinances were revoked in 1442, then restored in 1445, which provoked another ban on English cloth between 1447 and 1452, this time in all the Burgundian domains. Philip the Good enforced this prohibition more strictly than its predecessors, refusing to allow the Hansards to buy English cloth at Bruges. English cloth exports fell by nearly half between 1447 and 1449, although factors other than Burgundian policy were striking the English market at this time. The English threatened to ban all imports from the Burgundian domains unless the prohibition on cloth sales in the Netherlands outside Flanders was revoked. Philip finally ended the ban on cloth in 1452 for Brabant and Holland–Zeeland, perhaps because by then the Germans were blockading Bruges and he could not afford two commercial wars at once. In 1459 Philip had to agree to ban from Flanders all English wool not bought at Calais, but the measure had little impact. When the English re-enacted the Calais Ordinances in 1463, Philip again prohibited English cloth.

Charles the Bold was less rigidly anti-English than his father. Final peace, however, came only in 1478 when the English revoked the Calais Ordinances, and the Burgundians reaffirmed their 1459 prohibition against the sale of all wool not bought at Calais. By this time, English cloth was so important in the trade of the other Burgundian domains, particularly Antwerp, that there was serious internal opposition to the bans; the merchants who dealt in English cloth were more important politically than the artisans whose markets were supposedly being protected. By 1482 English cloth was flooding the Low Countries, and

---

87. Thielemans, *Bourgogne et Angleterre*, 115, 121, 129–31.

the old Flemish draperies were overwhelmed. Since Flanders was still closed officially to it, the English took their cloth to Antwerp, underselling the Flemish and thus hastening the decline of Bruges. The ban on English cloth was ended officially in 1489.[88]

A fascinating vignette of English trade through Bruges and the negligible impact of the count's statutes is given by the ruling of the aldermen of Bruges on a suit of the English merchant William Cottesbrook against the heirs of Clais van der Buerze of Bruges in 1449. Cottesbrook had contracted at Bruges in 1434 to deliver English cloth to van der Buerze at the Antwerp market the next year and had also sold additional cloth to van der Buerze's factor at Antwerp. The heirs responded that Clais had never mentioned it and they 'had not found it in his account books'. The purchase of English cloth by a Fleming in Flanders for delivery outside was legally binding. Cottesbrook also alleged that English cloth had been delivered to van der Buerze at Bruges. The heirs admitted receiving some cloth from Cottesbrook's factor at Antwerp but denied the rest. They claimed the right as burghers to acquit themselves by oath. Cottesbrook said that this was insufficient, since in this instance a broker was present, and 'good proof can be found in his books'. The aldermen heard the testimony of the broker and examined his books, which sustained Cottesbrook.[89]

The Despars accounts

We have examined the mechanics of the exchange markets at Bruges in Chapter Ten. Insight into banking practices in the late fifteenth century, when Bruges was in serious decline, is given by the account books kept by the brothers Jan, Jacob and Wouter Despars between 1478 and 1499. Virtually all their business was between Lisbon and Bruges. Sugar from Madeira was their most important import, but they also trafficked in molasses, oil, raisins, figs and some woad and grain. They exported cloth from various Flemish communities, tapestries, mantles, coverlets, serges of Ghent and Antwerp, copper rings, fustian and bonnets. The Despars were resilient; when sugar prices declined in Flanders in 1485–6, they imported woad. When ties with Portugal were broken, and there was a food shortage in Flanders due

88. Munro, *Wool, Cloth, and Gold*, 133–42, 146–7, 175–7, 182; Munro, 'Monetary Contraction and Industrial Change', 116; Thielemans, *Bourgogne et Angleterre*, 129, 150–6; Munro, 'Industrial Protectionism', 251.

89. Thielemans, *Bourgogne et Angleterre*, Pièce justificative No. 6, 455–65.

to the civil war in 1489–90, they imported grain from Normandy.

The Despars had simply a family partnership, not a formal company, until after a severe crisis in Bruges in 1479–80 when prices dropped on sugar and molasses, and merchants were caught with large quantities for which they had paid a high price. After the crisis was over, Jacob Despars, the oldest brother and head of the firm, sent Wouter as his factor to Portugal (1480–7); before this, he had bought goods through other firms' agents. This trade was active; the Despars were in Portugal themselves, and their accounts show other Bruges merchants there.

Although the Despars began using the title 'company' after 1480, they were not a company on the Italian model, with central direction and book-keeping with the partners bringing capital into the firm and generally pledging not to do business outside it. Each brother kept his own books, and the partners were not restricted to dealing for the company. Wouter came back to Bruges in 1487 and 1492, and each time the books were closed and the company reformed. Jacob's death ended the partnership in 1500.[90]

The decline of Bruges

The Bruges municipal accounts show mammoth expenditures dredging the canals that gave access to the outports along the Zwin. The decline of Bruges became marked in the 1460s and catastrophic after the wars with Maximilian. The rise of Antwerp was hindered by the fact that the western Scheldt was peppered with numerous sandbanks and became navigable for large sea vessels only after the floods of 1375–6 and 1404. The aldermanic registers of Antwerp show that before 1400 most Flemings, except those who lived in the extreme northeast that was easily accessible to Antwerp, continued to use Bruges as the main source of dyes, even those coming down the Scheldt from France. But by 1426 so many Flemish merchants were attending the Antwerp fairs that the duke of Brabant warned them not to come to the next one, since he could not guarantee their safety due to a conflict between Antwerp and Bergen-op-Zoom.[91]

90. Mus, 'De Brugse compagnie Despars, 7–9, 16–20, 32–3, 36–9, 44, 79–81, 96–8.
91. W. Brulez and J. Craeybeckx, 'Les Escales au carrefour des Pays-Bas (Bruges et Anvers, 14e–16e siècles)', *Recueils de la Société Jean Bodin* **32** (Paris, 1974): 428; G. Asaert, 'De Handel in kleurstoffen op de Antwerpse markt tijdens de 15de eeuw', *Bijdragen en Mededelingen betreffende de Geschiedenis der Nederlanden* **88** (1973): 383, 391; *LAY* **3**: 119.

The declining receipts of the toll at Sluis are revealing. It was leased for £15,600 in 1380 and 1403, £16,800 in 1432 and 1440, £13,400 in 1464, then dropped more rapidly. In late 1463 the count authorized Bruges to sell rents, for the ordinary incomes of the city were less lucrative than before due to the decline of commerce, 'as is well known', and the decreasing depth of the harbour at Sluis was making it dangerous for merchants.[92] Bruges continued to be important for exporting native Flemish goods until about 1500. But the foreigners drifted towards Antwerp. The decisive change came after 1482. While as late as 1486–7, seventy-five boats still passed through Sluis, only twenty-three did so in 1499. Virtually all were Spanish or small Breton craft, with a few Portuguese and English.[93]

Antwerp offered economic advantages and privileges that Bruges could not match, including fairs in session for most of the year and the fact that it was a centre for trade between England and Germany, not only the Hanse but also the Rhine and southwest. By 1470 the Antwerp fairs had already lured so many merchants from Bruges that the court of Bruges was suspended during it. When Antwerp supported Maximilian in 1484, he offered inducements to foreigners to go there. Many returned to Bruges the next year, but virtually all of them left again when Bruges captured Maximilian in 1488. This time they stayed away. Between 1490 and 1493, the magistrates of Bruges negotiated feverishly with foreign deputations; but the few who succumbed to the blandishments were restricting their staples to certain goods and keeping the bulk of their operations in Antwerp. When the Hanse, the last of the foreign colonies to remain loyal to Bruges, moved most of its business in 1500, it symbolized the end of an era.[94]

92. Blockmans and Prevenier, *In de ban van Bourgondië*; *IAB* **5**: 438–9.
93. W. Brulez, 'Brugge en Antwerpen in de 15e en 16e eeuw: een tegenstelling?', *TG* **83** (1970): 15–37; van Uytven, 'Terres de promission', 282: *IAB* **6**: 275–6.
94. *IAB* **6**: 13; Maréchal, 'Départ de Bruges des marchands étrangers', 26–74.

CHAPTER THIRTEEN
A Burgundian Funeral and a Habsburg Epitaph: The End of Medieval Flanders, 1467–92

CHARLES THE BOLD (1467–77)

Philip the Good died on 15 June 1467 at Bruges. His long-estranged son Charles made his Joyous Entry into Ghent on 28 June. With characteristic tactlessness, Charles timed the ceremony to coincide with the return of a group of revellers from a religious festival. The two parties collided in a riot on the Friday Market. The rebels demanded an end to the demeaning restrictions and taxes imposed by the peace of Gavere in 1453 and restoration of Ghent's rights over its quarter. Charles got out of town only by promising concessions. But the following January he forced the entire magistracy of Ghent to ask his pardon for the riots. He then cashiered Philip the Fair's constitution of 1301 and announced that, as in other towns, the government of Ghent would thenceforth be named by his commissioners rather than town electors.[1]

While his father had followed a coherent and generally well-planned policy in limiting the autonomy of the Flemish cities, Charles's interventions became more frequent and often seemed petty or capricious. He altered the coinage in late 1467 without involving

---

1. Blockmans, 'Vlaanderen 1384–1492', 218; Richard Vaughan, *Charles the Bold: The Last Valois Duke of Burgundy* (London, 1973), 6–7.

the Four Members. He admitted in writing that he had little knowledge of Flemish affairs, but he appointed the dean of the fullers and even the doorkeeper of the town hall at Courtrai and asked the local government to ratify it. He intervened in the appointment of receivers, secretaries and clerks at Ghent, Oudenaarde, Aalst and Courtrai. In December 1473 Charles established the Great Council at Mechelen to hear appeals from lower courts when litigants wanted to bypass the Council of Flanders, a practice that Philip the Good had stopped around 1460.[2] The Four Members protested, but by this time they had little real power over the prince. As a result, the towns throughout his domains became serious enemies of the Burgundian regime.[3]

Charles was married three times. The last, to Margaret of York, sister of King Edward IV of England, was celebrated at Bruges in 1468 in a festivity that is often cited as an example of the concern of the Burgundian counts with pomp and ceremony. The count established Margaret and Mary, his daughter by his first marriage to Catherine of France, at Ghent almost continuously from the spring of 1473. Margaret seems to have played an active role in diplomacy and administration.[4]

By Charles's time, the hegemony that Flanders had enjoyed in the Low Countries was a thing of the past. Bruges was already losing place to Antwerp. The military fecklessness of the Flemings was as notorious now as their bellicosity had been in the eleventh century. Charles generally avoided using Flemish troops. He used some to garrison Abbeville, but they disliked serving outside Flanders and were near mutiny by the end of 1475. Accordingly, Charles spent even less time in Flanders than his ancestors had.

But the count's financial exactions in support of his grand designs against the French crown and in the eastern Netherlands became insupportable. The Four Members voted him enormous aids between 1473 and 1475 before rejecting a second request in 1475. Direct taxation in Flanders between 1472 and 1482 was triple the average of the previous fifteen years. In the tax of 1473 Flanders paid 25 per cent of the total, Brabant 22 per cent and Holland 18 per cent.[5]

2. Jan van Rompaey, *De grote Raad van de hertogen van Boergondie en het parlement van Mechelen, VKVA* **73** (Brussels, 1973).

3. *IAY* **3**: 285–6; Vaughan, *Charles the Bold*, 39–40; *IAB* **5**: 546.

4. Vaughan, *Charles the Bold*, 50, 234–5.

5. *IAB* **6**: 56; Vaughan, *Charles the Bold*, 415; Prevenier and Blockmans, *Burgundian Netherlands*, 274; Blockmans and Prevenier, *In de ban van Bourgondië,* 154; Blockmans, 'Vlaanderen 1384–1492', 220.

THE INCORPORATION OF FLANDERS INTO THE HABSBURG EMPIRE

The death of Charles the Bold at the battle of Nancy on 5 January 1477 was not announced officially until two weeks later. The Four Members of Flanders took action collectively and individually to reverse the tide of centralization that had cost them their autonomy. His heiress Mary, betrothed for some months to Maximilian of Habsburg, archduke of Austria, gave new privileges to Ghent on 30 January that annulled the restrictions placed on the city in 1453 and 1469. On 11 February Flanders got a privilege that has been called its first territorial constitution.

The Grand Privilege of 11 February 1477 promised judicial reform and replacement of the *parlement* of Mechelen with an itinerant court that would have no power in areas that were properly the prerogative of local authorities. The Chamber of Accounts, which Charles had moved to Mechelen, would be returned to Lille or some other place in Flanders. Free trade was guaranteed, and various new tolls were abolished. The twenty-five members of the Great Council were to be natives of Flanders, sixteen from 'Germanic lands' and nine from 'Walloon lands', and secretaries of the Council were to know both languages. Many provisions dealt with official corruption. The new duchess agreed not to farm or sell offices, grant church benefices to laymen or create new tolls. The competence of the Members was reaffirmed regarding aids, tolls and coin changes; but now there were only three Members, for Bruges had obtained the exclusion of the Franc. Taxes had to be voted unanimously by three Members, not by a majority. At the request of Bruges and Ghent, which evidently resented the tax concession of 1474 to Ypres, the Transport of 1408 was to be the basis of assessment, and taxes were to be levied at the place of residence, not at the site of the property concerned; thus rural property owned by burghers would be exempted.[6]

Open rebellion began at Ghent on 15 February. When a new council was installed three days later, reprisals began. In March, several officials were executed because they were held personally responsible

---

6. Maurice-A. Arnould, 'Les Lendemains de Nancy dans les "Pays de par deça" (janvier-avril 1477)' in W. Blockmans (ed.), *Het Algemene en de gewestelijke privilegiën van Maria van Bourgogne voor de Nederlanden, 1477* (Courtrai-Heule, 1985), 47–8; Blockmans, 'Breuk of continuiteit? De Vlaamse privilegien van 1477 in het licht van het staatsvormingsproces', *ibid.*, 97–123; see also *IAB* 6: 121–9.

for Charles the Bold's humiliation of the city in 1469. The guilds of Bruges also took arms. Their city obtained new charters on 30 March and 17 April.[7]

The new privileges established Bruges's lordship over the Franc and restored the rights abolished in 1438. By the charter of 30 March 1477 the Franc was definitely suppressed as the fourth Member, and the old restrictions on rural cloth making were confirmed. Foreign merchants were forbidden to buy at Antwerp, Bergen-op-Zoom or Calais to re-sell in Bruges. No trade might be practised within a league of the town except by masters who had been received in the corresponding guild of Bruges. The ancient subordination of Sluis and its guilds was restored. Burghers who bought wool at Calais were to bring it to Bruges before delivering it to their customers. Aldermen were to be chosen from the nine Members without interference from the prince. The charter of 21 April provided that the burgomaster of Bruges would be one of four commissioners who would oversee the renewal of the government of the Franc.[8]

By then, order had been re-established, and Mary married Maximilian by proxy. As her husband, Maximilian, who would become Holy Roman Emperor in 1493, acted as her guardian and became the recipient of Flemish hostility towards her Burgundian forebears. Mary herself seems to have been well liked. After December 1480, when Maximilian rejected Ghent's demand that he submit accounts to the Great Council before more *beden* were approved, the city boycotted assemblies called by the archduke or in which he participated. In February 1481 Ghent demanded control of the entire financial apparatus of the state and drew up a budget reflecting that claim. In late 1481 Ghent forbade its quarter to give any financial or military aid to the prince and tried to get the other Members to do the same. Maximilian yielded in April 1482, firing some councillors to whom the Members objected, and in return they gave him part of the aid he requested.

The agreement was of short duration. Mary of Burgundy died in a hunting accident soon afterwards, leaving a young son, Philip. Relations with Maximilian quickly reached a crisis. He called an Estates General at Ghent and tried to have them recognize him as Philip's guardian. Brabant took the lead in refusing, supported by the Flemings,

7. Blockmans, 'De "Constitutionele" betekenis van de privilegiën van Maria van Bourgondië (1477)' in *Privilegiën van Maria van Bourgogne*, 480–1.

8. *IAB* **6**: 140–4, 288, 147.

who said that Maximilian had reneged on his promise to conduct his foreign policy according to the wishes of the Estates General. The Flemish deputies also noted that under the terms of the marriage agreement of Maximilian and Mary, neither surviving party acquired rights on the lands of the other; yet Mary had designated her children as her heirs and Maximilian as their guardian shortly before she died, and by 30 April 1482 Flanders was alone in resisting Maximilian.

The situation was then complicated by an invasion of the Habsburg domains from France. Louis XI, blatantly bidding for Flemish town support against Maximilian, on 14 May 1483 restored the old textile monopoly of Ypres. On 24 May the bailiff of Amiens informed the king that angry inhabitants had chased him out of every village in which he had tried to proclaim it. The Four Members ordered the villages to cease resistance. On 30 August the White Hoods of Ghent forced the inhabitants of Nieuwkerken to admit that they had wrongfully made cloth in violation of the privileges of Ypres. On 1 October 1483 the Members again forbade the drapers of the villages of castellanies of Ypres, Warneton, Cassel and Bailleul to make cloth. On 6 February 1484 Maximilian issued a more general textile ordinance, citing complaints by foreign merchants as well as natives of imitation of the cloth of the Three Cities by the small centres.[9]

The towns of the West Quarter, joined quickly by the Members, asked Maximilian to defend Flanders against the French. His price was regulation of the regency, and despite the opposition of Ghent, the other Members on 23 December 1483 installed young Philip as count. The council of regency, comprising the relatives of the ruling dynasty and representatives of the Three Cities, sat at Ghent until 14 June 1485 and in effect governed Flanders. It legislated throughout the county, often at the request of local authorities. The legal situation of the van Artevelde period seemed to have been revived.

But conditions in Flanders continued to deteriorate. The French had made a treaty with the Flemish towns on 25 October 1484, and Maximilian responded by marching on Flanders from Brabant and quickly seized the important fortresses of Dendermonde and Oudenaarde. Charles VIII of France made new treaties with the towns on 5 and 26 February 1485.[10] Maximilian's control of the sea forced foreign nations to leave Bruges when hostilities resumed. Bruges was blockaded from Sluis from 5 March 1485 until the end of the year,

9. *IAY* **4**: 66–73, 77–9, 80–2.
10. *IAB* **6**: 251.

although Bruges capitulated in June and the foreigners returned.[11]

The peace of 28 June with the Four Members recognized Philip's claim as count and Maximilian's as his father and guardian. All of the archduke's exiled partisans were to be repatriated, privileges were confirmed and the administrative organization of Flanders remained unchanged. Maximilian gave a general amnesty, except for certain named persons, and the Estates General agreed to give him aid. But on 22 July he installed a German garrison at Ghent and revoked his confirmation of the city's privileges in the accord of 28 June, realizing that Ghent was his chief opponent. He restored the odious peace of Gavere, assuming the right to name all electors of aldermen and to choose the dean of the weavers from a list of three submitted by the guild. The towns and castellanies of eastern Flanders were withdrawn from the jurisdiction of Ghent. Ghent surrendered to him all seigneurial rights seized since 1477, notably those extracted from Mary in 1477 in violation of the peace of Gavere.[12]

The aldermen were rotated soon after the agreement of 28 June, and Ghent generally remained calm until a new revolution on 4 November 1487 returned the radicals to power. The other Members – now again including the Franc – tried to reconcile Ghent with Maximilian and asked him to convoke the Estates and come personally to Flanders. Instead, the prince called the towns and castellanies of Ghent's quarter to explain his grievances against Ghent. When Ghent formally allied with Charles VIII of France on 5 January 1488 in return for a confirmation of its privileges, then seized Courtrai the next week as the French invaded the Westland, the city was isolated within Flanders.

But Maximilian then dissipated his advantage by antagonizing Bruges. He asked the city government for a subsidy and soldiers to defend the frontiers. Bruges refused to act without consulting the other Members, for it did not want to antagonize Ghent, and it would not let Maximilian install a German garrison in the town gates. Because the other Members were supposed to mediate when one of them had a disagreement with the prince, Bruges and Ypres tried to reconcile Ghent with Maximilian, but the aldermen of Ghent refused, saying that they were defending the natural prince, Philip, against Maximilian and the Germans.

On 31 January 1488 Maximilian tried to leave Bruges but was stopped at all gates. He was imprisoned in his residence as guild

11. Mus, 'Despars', 51
12. *IAY* 4: 112–14, 115–16, 119.

militias took to the streets. New officials were named, and from 7 February Germans and anyone thought to sympathize with them were executed. The bloodbath at Bruges continued through the third week of March. Bruges then joined Ghent and asked Charles VIII for protection.[13]

Bruges began weakening by the end of March, but Ghent held on. Ypres objected both to holding Maximilian captive and to the alliance with the French. Maximilian's partisans held the Scheldt and Dender fortifications as well as Sluis and quickly moved westward, sacking towns as they went. The prince's father, the emperor Frederick III, brought an army, and the Germans were before Bruges by the beginning of May. On 10 May a peace was concluded on the basis of that of 1482. Two days later, a treaty inspired by the Grand Privilege of 1477 was made among the various provinces of the Low Countries, and Maximilian was released. He renounced the regency in Flanders and agreed that the county would be governed during Philip's minority by a council of the boy's maternal relatives, by the Three Members and by the Estates. During the regency, Maximilian would get an annual aid.

As soon as Maximilian was safely out of Bruges, however, he renounced this agreement as given under duress, and the war continued. Ghent initially found allies elsewhere in the Low Countries, but on 22 July 1489 Charles VIII agreed not to support the rebels. Bruges capitulated on 29 November 1490, but Sluis and Ghent held out until 1492.

The peace of Kadzand of July 1492 with Ghent is the terminal point of our story. It subjected the great cities to the central power. The duke's commissioners would renew the magistracies each year, and they and the aldermen would choose the other chief officials. The White Hoods of Ghent were suppressed, and the aldermen's jurisdiction was limited to the territory of the town except for payments owed to burghers on their rural estates. External burghers were restricted to the home quarter and were to be judged in their places of residence, not by the magistrates of Ghent, except in matters involving confiscation of property.[14]

Philip 'the Handsome', the son of Mary of Burgundy and Maximilian, married Joanna 'the Mad', daughter of Ferdinand and Isabella, who

13. R. Wellens, 'La Révolte brugeoise de 1488', *ASEB* **102** (1966): 5–36.

14. This brief summary of political events is based on Blockmans, 'Autocratie ou polyarchie? La lutte pour le pouvoir politique en Flandre de 1482 à 1492, d'après des documents inédits', *BCRH* **140** (1974): 257–368.

were creating a Spanish monarchy. Philip died prematurely in 1506. His son by Joanna, born at Ghent in 1500, was Charles V, who thus inherited the Burgundian empire from his father, would inherit Spain in 1516 from his maternal grandparents and would be elected Holy Roman Emperor in 1519 to succeed his paternal grandfather.

There is a cruel symmetry in the nearly simultaneous termination of the economic prosperity of Bruges and the political particularism of Ghent, twin pillars of egotistical privilege that had constituted the singularity of late medieval Flanders. Flanders, a place of poor natural resources, had become great by exporting manufactured cloth, but it had to import food as soon as its textile manufacturing began dominating the international market. As population grew, indigenous supplies of industrial raw materials also became inadequate, and more and higher-quality wools and dyes had to be imported. In the twelfth century, demand and supply were in symbiosis. During this period, the Flemish counts were among the greatest princes of Europe, dealing with the kings of England and France and the German emperor as their peers.

But during the thirteenth and fourteenth centuries the political impotence of the Flemish rulers in the face of the rivalry of two of Flanders' major suppliers, France and England, in combination with increased competition for cloth in overseas markets, created problems that were redressed to a degree by the growth of the service sector of the Flemish economy – the world market and financial network of Bruges and the development of Ghent as a regional commercial centre specializing in reconsigning French grain to destinations elsewhere in Flanders and the eastern Low Countries. Unfortunately, the greatness of Ghent and Bruges was achieved only through monopoly privileges that caused problems for the smaller communities and ultimately for the entire Flemish state and economy.

When the dukes of Burgundy became counts of Flanders and subordinated Flanders to broader strategic imperatives, and particularly when they realized how essentially weak Flanders was, the privileges of this essentially demand-driven world economy, caught between two states that had been Flanders' nearly equal rivals in the twelfth century but were vastly more powerful by the fifteenth, were first violated, then ignored and finally withdrawn. The services that had made Flanders great were not needed in the world of the colonial economy and the nation state.

History is full of ironies. Surely there is none greater than the fact that after the Flemings had spent nearly three centuries after 1206 fighting to keep their homeland from being absorbed by France, it became a possession of the Habsburgs of Spain.

Bibliography

This list includes only printed documents and historical literature that have been cited in the footnotes of this book or contributed significantly to its general conclusions. It is provided as a convenience to readers who may be confused by secondary references in the notes. It makes no claim to be a comprehensive list of the sources or literature available for the study of Flanders during the Middle Ages.

SOURCES

Annales Gandenses. Annals of Ghent. Translated from the Latin with Introduction and Notes by Hilda Johnstone. London: Thomas Nelson & Sons Ltd, 1951.

Appleby, John T. (ed.), *The Chronicle of Richard of Devizes of the Time of King Richard the First.* London: Thomas Nelson & Sons, 1963.

Baecker, Louis de (ed.), *Chants historiques de la Flandre 400–1650.* Lille: Ernest Vanackere, 1855.

Blockmans, W.P. 'Autocratie ou polyarchie? La lutte pour le pouvoir politique en Flandre de 1482 à 1492, d'après des documents inédits', *BCRH* **140** (1974): 257–368.

Blockmans, W.P. (ed.), *Handelingen van de Leden en van de Staten van Vlaanderen (1467–1477). Excerpten uit de rekeningen van de Vlaamse steden, kasselrijen en vorstelijke ambtenaren.* Brussels: Paleis der Academiën, 1971.

Boendale, Jan, *Brabantsche Yeesten. Collection des chroniques belges.* Brussels, 1839.

Boone, Marc, 'Particularisme gantois, centralisme bourguignon et diplomatie française. Documents inédits autour d'un conflit entre Philippe le Hardi, duc de Bourgogne, et Gand en 1401', BCRH **152** (1986): 49–113.

Brouwer, J. de, *Het Buitenpoortersboek van Geraardsbergen van 1396*. Brussels, 1954.

Caenegem, R.C. van (ed.), *Les arrêts et jugés du Parlement de Paris sur appels flamands conservés dans les registres du Parlement*, 2 vols. Brussels: Recueil de l'ancienne jurisprudence de la Belgique, 1966, 1975.

Caenegem, R.C. van, 'Het charter van Gwijde van Dampierre over de Gentse rechtspraak (10 Juli 1294)', BCRH **150** (1984): 415–36.

Caenegem, R.C. van and L. Milis, 'Kritische uitgave van de "Grote Keure" van Filips van de Elzas, graaf van Vlaanderen, voor Gent en Brugge (1165–1177)', BCRH **143** (1977): 207–57.

Caenegem, R.C. van and L. Milis, 'Edition critique des versions françaises de la "Grande Keure" de Philippe d'Alsace, comte de Flandre, pour la ville d'Ypres,' BCRH **147** (1981): 1–44.

Carolingian Chronicles. Frankish Royal Annals and Nithard's Histories. Translated by Bernhard Walter Scholz with Barbara Rogers. Ann Arbor: University of Michigan Press, 1970.

Cave, Roy C. and Herbert H. Coulson (eds), *A Source Book for Medieval Economic History*. Milwaukee, 1936.

Chaplais, Pierre (ed.), *English Diplomatic Documents*. 1: *1101–1272*. London, 1964.

Dekker, C. and J.G. Kruisheer, 'Een Rekening van de abdij Ter Doest over het jaar 1315', BCRH **133** (1967): 273–305.

de Pauw, N. and J. Vuylsteke (eds). *De Rekeningen der stad Gent. Tijdvak van Jacob van Artevelde, 1336–1349*. Ghent: H. Hoste, 1874–85.

de Pauw, N. (ed.), *Bouc van de Audiencie. Acten en Sentencien van den Raad van Vlaanderen in de XIVe eeuw*, 2 vols. Ghent: A. Siffer, 1901, 1903.

de Pauw, N. (ed.), *Cartulaire historique et généalogique des Artevelde*. Brussels: Commission Royale d'Histoire, 1920.

Des Marez, G. and E. de Sagher (eds), *Comptes de la ville d'Ypres de 1267 à 1329*. Brussels: Commission Royale d'Histoire, 1909–13.

Diegerick, I.L.A. (ed.), *Inventaire analytique et chronologique des chartes et documents appartenant aux archives de la ville d'Ypres*, 7 vols. Bruges: Vandecasteele-Werbrouck, 1853–68.

Encomium Emmae Reginae. Edited by Alistair Campbell. London: Royal Historical Society, 1949. Camden Society, Third Series, 72.

Espinas, G. and H. Pirenne (eds), *Recueil de documents relatifs à l'histoire drapière en Flandre*, 4 vols. Brussels: Commission Royale d'Histoire, 1906–24.

Galbert of Bruges, *The Murder of Charles the Good, Count of Flanders*. Translated with an Introduction and Notes by James Bruce Ross. New York: Columbia University Press, 1959, reprinted New York: Harper & Row, 1967. The translation is from Henri Pirenne (ed.), *Histoire du meurtre de Charles le Bon, comte de Flandre (1127–1128) par Galbert de Bruges* (Paris, 1891).

Gheldolf, A.E. (ed.) *Coutume de la ville de Gand*, Brussels: Coutumes des Pays et Comté de Flandre, 1868.

Gilliodts-Van Severen, L. (ed.), *Cartulaire de l'ancien Estaple de Bruges*, 6 vols. Bruges, 1904–6.

Gilliodts-van Severen, L. (ed.), *Cartulaire de l'ancien Grand Tonlieu de Bruges . . . Recueil de documents . . .*, 2 vols. Bruges, 1908–9.

Gilliodts-Van Severen, L. (ed.), *Inventaire des archives de la ville de Bruges*. Section première. *Inventaire des chartes*, 6 vols. Bruges: Edward Gailliard, 1871–6.

Gysseling, M. and A.C.F. Koch (eds), *Diplomata Belgica ante annum millesimum centesimum scripta*. Brussels: Belgisch Inter-Universitair Centrum voor Neerlandistiek, 1950.

Hariulf, *Vita sancti Arnulphi*. MGH, *Scriptores* 15. 2.

The Historical Works of Master Ralph de Diceto, Dean of London, edited by William Stubbs. (Rerum Brittannicarum Medii Aevi Scriptores (Rolls Series) Vol. 68, 2 vols). London: HMSO, 1876.

Herlihy, David (ed.), *Medieval Culture and Society*, New York: Harper and Row, 1968.

John of Hocsem, *Chronique*, edited by Godefroid Kurth. Brussels: Commission Royale d'Histoire, n.d.

Koch, A.C.F. 'Actes des comtes de Flandre de la période de 1071 à 1128', *BCRH* **122** (1957): 272–7.

Lair, Jules (ed.), *De Moribus et actis primorum Normanniae Ducum auctore Dudone Sancti Quintini*. Caen, 1868.

Limburg-Stirum, T. de (ed.), *Cartulaire de Louis de Male, comte de Flandre. Decreten van den grave Lodewyck van Vlaenderen, 1348 à 1358*, 2 vols. Bruges: Louis de Plancke, 1898–1901.

Pelsmaeker, P. de (ed.), *Registres aux sentences des échevins d'Ypres*. Brussels: J. Goemaere, 1914.

Pirenne, H. (ed.), *Chronique rimée des troubles de Flandre en 1379–1380*. Ghent: A Siffer, 1902.

Pirenne, H. (ed.), *Le Soulèvement de la Flandre maritime de 1323–1328*. Brussels: Commission Royale d'Histoire, 1900.

Prevenier, W., 'Briefwisseling tussen de vier Leden van Vlaanderen en Filips de Stoute, hertog van Bourgondië, en diens echtgenote Margareta van Male, over de inbreuken op de Vlaamse privileges door vorstelijke ambtenaren en instellingen (1398–1402)', *BCRH* **150** (1984): 506–22.

Prevenier, W. (ed.), *Handelingen van de Leden en van de Staten van Vlaanderen (1384–1405)*. Brussels: Commission Royale d'Histoire, 1961.

Prevenier, W. (ed.), *De oorkonden der graven van Vlaanderen (1191–aanvang 1206)*, 3 vols. Brussels: Paleis der Academiën, 1964.

Radulphi de Coggeshall Chronicon Anglicanum, edited by Joseph Stevenson (Rerum Brittannicarum Medii Aevi Scriptores (Rolls Series), vol. 66). London: HMSO, 1875.

Reynard the Fox and Other Mediaeval Netherlands Secular Literature. Edited and introduced by E. Colledge. Translated by Professor Adriaan J. Barnouw and E. Colledge. London: Heinemann, 1967.

Smet, J. de, 'Le Dénombrement des foyers en Flandre en 1469', *BCRH* **99** (1935): 105–50.

Smet, J. de, 'Le plus ancien livre de fiefs du Bourg de Bruges, vers 1325', *Tablettes des Flandres* **3** (1950): 69–87.

Thorndike, Lynn, *University Records and Life in the Middle Ages.* New York: Columbia University Press, 1944.

Trio, P., 'De Statuten van de laatmiddeleeuwse clericale O.L.V. Broederschap van de studenten van Parijs te Ieper', *BCRH* **148** (1982): 91–141.

Vercauteren, F. (ed.), *Actes des comtes de Flandre, 1071–1128*. Brussels: Palais des Académies, 1938.

Verhulst, A., 'Prijzen van granen, boter en kaas te Brugge volgens de "slag" van het Sint-Donatiaanskapittel (1348–1801)', in C. Verlinden *et al.*, *Dokumenten voor de geschiedenis van prijzen en lonen in Vlaanderen en Brabant* (Bruges: De Tempel, 1965), 2: 3–70.

Verhulst, A. and M. Gysseling (eds), *Le Compte Général de 1187, connu sous le nom de 'Gros Brief', et les institutions financières du comté de Flandre au XIIe siècle.* Brussels: Palais des Académies, 1962.

Vleeschouwers-Van Melkebeek, M., *Documenten uit de praktijk van de gedingbeslissende rechtspraak van de officialiteit van Doornik. Oorsprong en vroege ontwikkeling (1192–1300)*. Iuris Scripta Historica I. Brussels: Paleis der Academiën, 1985.

Vuylsteke, J. (ed.), *De Rekeningen der stad Gent. Tijdvak van Philips van Artevelde, 1376–1389*. Ghent: A Hoste, 1893.

Vuylsteke, J. (ed.), *Gentsche Stads- en Baljuwsrekeningen, 1280–1336*. Ghent: F. Meyer–van Loo, 1900.

Vyver, A. van de and Charles Verlinden, 'L'Auteur et la portée du *Conflictus ovis et lini*', *RBPH* **12** (1933): 59–81.

Werveke, Alfons van (ed.), *Gentse Stads– en Baljuwsrekeningen (1351–1364)*. Brussels: Commission Royale d'Histoire, 1970.

Werveke, H. van, 'Bronnenmateriaal uit de Brugse stadsrekeningen betreffende de hongersnood van 1316', *BCRH* **125** (1959): 431–510.

Wyffels, C., 'Twee oude Vlaamse ambachtskeuren: De Vleeschouwers van Brugge (2 December 1302) ende Smeden van Damme (eerste helft 1303)', *ASEB* **87** (1950): 93–109.

Zoete, A. (ed.), *Handelingen van de Leden en van de Staten van Vlaanderen (1405–1419). Excerpten uit de rekeningen der steden, kasselrijen en vorstelijke ambtenaren*, I *(24 maart 1405–5 maart 1413)*. Brussels: Paleis der Academiën, 1981; II *(10 maart 1413–7 september 1419)*. Brussels: Paleis der Academien, 1982.

LITERATURE

Acker, K.G. van, 'Geraard de Duivel: Poging tot belichting van een duisterfiguur', *HMGOG* **38** (1984): 3–15.

Acker, K.G. van, 'De "libertas castrensis operis" van Antwerpen en de Ottogracht te Gent', *HMGOG* **41** (1987): 1–9.

Acker, L. van, 'De Latijnse literaire cultuur in Noorden en Zuiden van circa 1050 tot circa 1350', *AGN* **2**: 328–42.

Algemene Geschiedenis der Nederlanden, 2nd edn. Utrecht: Fibula-Van Dishoeck, 1982.

Armstrong, C.A.J., 'Had the Burgundian Government a Policy for the Nobility?' in *Britain and the Netherlands, II: Papers Delivered to the Anglo-Dutch Conference, 1962*, edited by J.S. Bromley and E.H. Kossman (Groningen: J.B. Wolters, 1964): 9–32, reprinted in Armstrong, *England, France and Burgundy*, 213–36.

Armstrong, C.A.J., 'La Double monarchie France–Angleterre et la maison de Bourgogne (1420–1435). Le déclin d'une alliance', *Annales de Bourgogne* **37** (1965): 81–112, reprinted in Armstrong, *England, France and Burgundy*, 343–74.

Armstrong, C.A.J., *England, France and Burgundy in the Fifteenth Century* London: Hambledon Press, 1983.

Armstrong, C.A.J., 'The Language Question in the Low Countries: The Use of French and Dutch by the Dukes of Burgundy and their Administration', *Europe in the Middle Ages*, edited by J.R. Hale, J.R.L. Highfield and B. Smalley (London, 1965), 386–409, reprinted in Armstrong, *England, France and Burgundy*, 189–212.

Arnould, M.A. 'Les Lendemains de Nancy dans les "Pays de par deçà" (janvier–avril 1477)', in Blockmans, *Privilegiën van Maria van Bourgogne*, 1–95.

Asaert, G., 'De Handel in kleurstoffen op de Antwerpse markt tijdens de 15de eeuw', *Bijdragen en Mededelingen betreffende de Geschiedenis der Nederlanden* **88** (1973): 377–402.

Asaert, G., 'Scheepvaart en visserij', *AGN* **4**: 128–34.

Astaes, S., 'Het Waterwegennet ten noorden van Brugge van de XIe tot de XIVe eeuw', *HMGOG* **18** (1964): 3–17.

Auweele, D. van den, 'De Brugse gijzelaarslijsten van 1301, 1305 en 1328. Een comparatieve analyse', *ASEB* **110** (1973): 105–67.

Auweele, D. van den, 'De Evolutie van het recht in het Zuiden 12de–14de eeuw', *AGN* **2**: 145–63.

Avout, Jacques d', *Le Meurtre d'Etienne Marcel*. Paris: Gallimard, 1960.

Baeyens, H., 'De Bouwmeesters', *Flandria Nostra* **2**: 9–71.

Bahr, K., *Handel und Verkehr der deutschen Hanse in Vlaanderen während des vierzehnten Jahrhunderts*. Leipzig: Duncker & Humblot, 1911.

Baldwin, J.W., *The Government of Philip Augustus. Foundations of French Royal Power in the Middle Ages*. Berkeley and Los Angeles: University of California Press, 1986.

Barel, Y., *La ville médiévale. Système social. Système urbain*. Grenoble: Presses Universitaires de Grenoble, 1977.

Beardwood, A., *Alien Merchants in England 1350 to 1377. Their Legal and Economic Position*. Cambridge, Mass.: Medieval Academy of America, 1931.

Berings, G., 'Het oude Land aan de rand van het vroegmiddeleeuwse overstromingsgebied van de Noordzee. Landname en grondbezit tijdens de Middeleeuwen', *HMGOG* **39** (1985): 37–84.

Beuken, J.H.A., *De Hanze en Vlaanderen*. Maastricht: Uitgeverij 'Ernest van Aelst', n.d.

Bigwood, G., *Le Régime juridique et économique du commerce de l'argent dans la Belgique au Moyen Age*, 2 vols. Mémoires de l'Académie Royale de Belgique, Classe des Lettres, ser. 2, 14. Brussels: M. Lamertin, 1921–2.

Bigwood, Georges, 'Gand et la circulation des grains en Flandre, du XIVe au XVIIIe siècle', *Vierteljahrsschrift für Sozial- und Wirtschaftsgeschichte* **4** (1906): 397–460.

Blockmans, F., 'De zoogenaamde Stadskeure van Geeraardsbergen [sic] van tusschen 1067 en 1070', *BCRH* **106** (1941): 1–93.

Blockmans, F., *Het Gentsche Stadspatriciaat tot omstreeks 1302*. Antwerp: De Sikkel, 1938.

Blockmans, F., 'Le contrôle par le prince des comptes urbains en Flandre et en Brabant au Moyen Age', *Finances et comptabilités urbaines*, 287–338.

Blockmans, F., 'Peilingen nopens de bezittende klasse te Gent om-streeks 1300, I. Twee typen: Gilbert Utenhove en Wouter van der Meere', *RBPH* **15** (1936): 496–516.

Blockmans, F. and W.P., 'Devaluation, Coinage and Seignorage under Louis de Nevers and Louis de Male, Counts of Flanders, 1330–84', in Mayhew, *Coinage in the Low Countries*, 69–94.

Blockmans, W.P. (ed.), *Het Algemene en de gewestelijke privilegiën van Maria van Bourgogne voor de Nederlanden, 1477.* Standen en Landen 80. Courtrai-Heule: UGA, 1985.

Blockmans, W.P., 'De Bourgondische Nederlanden: de Weg naar een moderne staatsvorm', *Handelingen van de Koninklijke Kring voor Oud-heidkunde, Letteren en Kunst van Mechelen* **77** (1973): 7–26.

Blockmans, W.P., 'Breuk of continuiteit? De Vlaamse privilegien van 1477 in het licht van het staatsvormingsproces', in Blockmans, *Privilegiën van Maria van Bourgogne*, 97–123.

Blockmans, W.P., 'De "constitutionele" Betekenis van de Privilegiën van Maria van Bourgondië (1477)', in Blockmans, *Privilegiën van Maria van Bourgogne*, 473–94.

Blockmans, W.P., *Een middeleeuwse Vendetta. Gent 1300.* Houten: De Haan, 1987.

Blockmans, W.P., 'A Typology of Representative Institutions in Late Medieval Europe', *JMH* **4** (1978): 189–215.

Blockmans, W.P., 'De representatieve Instellingen in het Zuiden 1384–1482', *AGN* **4**: 156–63.

Blockmans, W.P., 'De Vermogensstruktuur in de St- Jakobsparochie te Gent in 1492–1494', in *Studiën betreffende de sociale strukturen te Brugge, Kortrijk en Gent in de 14e en 15e eeuw* (Heule: UGA, 1973), Standen en Landen 63, 139–98.

Blockmans, W.P., *De Volksvertegenwoordiging in Vlaanderen in de over-gang van Middeleeuwen naar Nieuwe Tijden (1384–1506). VKVA*, Kl. Letteren, 40, no. 90. Brussels: Paleis der Academiën, 1978.

Blockmans, W.P., G. Pieters, W. Prevenier and R.W.M. van Schalk, 'Tussen crisis en welvaart: sociale veranderingen 1300–1500', *AGN* **4**: 42–86.

Blockmans, W.P., 'Het Wisselingsproces van de Gentse schepenen tijdens de 15de eeuw', *HMGOG* n.s. **41** (1987): 75–96.

Blockmans, W.P., 'Le Régime représentatif et Flandre dans le cadre européen au bas Moyen Age avec un projet d'application des ordi-nateurs', *Studies Presented to the International Commission for the History of Parliamentary and Representative Institutions*, 1976.

Blockmans, W.P., 'Mutaties van het politiek personeel in de steden Gent en Brugge tijdens een periode van regimewisselingen: het laatste kwart van de 15e eeuw', in *Bronnen voor de geschiedenis van de instellingen in België*, Handelingen van het Colloquium te Brussel, 15–18. IV. 1975. Brussels: Algemeen Rijksarchief, 1977, 92–103.

Blockmans, W.P., 'Peilingen naar de sociale strukturen te Gent tijdens de late 15e eeuw', in *Studiën betreffende de sociale strukturen te Brugge, Kortrijk en Gent in de 14e en 15e eeuw*, Standen en Landen 54 (Heule: UGA, 1971), 215–62.

Blockmans, W.P., 'The Social and Economic Effects of Plague in the Low Countries 1349–1500', *RBPH* **60** (1982): 833–63.

Blockmans, W.P., 'Vers une Société urbanisée', in Witte, *Histoire de Flandre*.

Blockmans, W.P., 'Vlaanderen 1384–1482', *AGN* **4**: 201–23.

Blockmans, W.P. 'Het Wisselingsproces van de Gentse schepenen tijdens de 15de eeuw', *HMGOG* **41** (1987).

Blockmans, W.P. and Walter Prevenier, *In de Ban van Bourgondië*. Houten: Fibula, 1988.

Blockmans, W.P. and W. Prevenier, 'Armoede in de Nederlanden van de 14e tot het midden van de 16e eeuw: bronnen en problemen', *TG* **88** (1975): 501–38; English version abridged but amended as 'Poverty in Flanders and Brabant from the Fourteenth to the Mid-Sixteenth Century: Sources and Problems', *Acta Historiae Neerlandicae* (*Studies on the History of the Netherlands*) **10** (1978): 20–57.

Blok, D.P., 'De Frankische periode tot 880', *AGN* **1**: 288–304.

Blok, D.P., 'Hoofdlijnen van de bewoningsgeschiedenis', *AGN* **1**: 143–64.

Bonnaud-Delamare, R. 'La Paix en Flandre pendent la première Croisade', *RN* **39** (1957): 147–52.

Bony, Jean, *French Gothic Architecture in the Twelth and Thirteenth Centuries*, Berkeley: University of California Press, 1983.

Boone, M., 'Diplomatie et violence d'état. La sentence rendue par les ambassadeurs et conseillers du roi de France, Charles VII, concernant le conflit entre Philippe le Bon, duc de Bourgogne, et Gand en 1452', *BCRH* **156** (1990): 1–54.

Boone, M., *Geld en Macht. De Gentse stadsfinanciën en de Bourgondische staatsvorming (1384–1453)*. Ghent: Verhandelingen der Maatschappij voor Geschiedenis en Oudkeidkunde te Gent, 15, 1990.

Boone, M., 'Geldhandel en pandbedrijf in Gent tijdens de Bourgondische periode: politieke, fiscale en sociale aspecten', *RBPH* **66** (1988): 767–91.

Boone, M., *Gent en de Bourgondische Hertogen*. *VKVA*, Kl. Letteren 52, no. 133. Brussels: Paleis der Academiën, 1990.

Boone, M., 'De Gentse verplichte lening van 1492–1493', *BCRH* **147** (1981): 247–305.

Boone, M., 'Gentse financiële belangen te Biervliet 1382–1384. Naar aanleiding van een konfiskatiedossier', *AM* **33** (1982): 251–67.

Boone, M., 'Openbare diensten en initiatieven te Gent tijdens de late Middeleeuwen (14de–15de eeuw)', in *Het Openbare Initiatief van de Gemeenten in België. Historische Grondlagen (Ancien Régime)*. 11de Internationaal Colloquium, Spa, 1–4 sept. 1982. *Handelingen*. Brussels: Gemeentekredit van België, 1984. Historiche Uitgaven, no. 65, 71–114.

Boone, M., 'Het vorstelijk Domein te Gent (*ca*: 1385–*ca*. 1453): Speelbal tussen vorstelijke centralisatie en stedelijk particularisme?' *HMGOG* **42** (1988): 69–93.

Boone, M., Machteld Dumon and Birgit Reusens, *Immobiliënmarkt, fiscaliteit en sociale ongelijkheid te Gent, 1483–1503*. Courtrai-Heule: UGA, 1981. Standen en Landen, 78.

Boone, M., Marianne Danneel and Noël Geirnaert, 'Pieter IV Adornes (1460–ca 1496): een Brugs patricier in Gent', *HMGOG* **39** (1985): 123–147.

Boone, M., Thérèse de Hemptinne and W. Prevenier, 'Fictie en historische realiteit. Colijn van Rijsseles "De Spiegel der Minnen", ook een spiegel van sociale spanningen in de Nederlanden der late Middeleeuwen?' Koninklijke Soevereine Hoofdkamer van Retorica 'De Fonteine' te Gent, *Jaarboek* **34** (1984): 9–33.

Bovesse, J., 'Le Comte de Namur Jean Ier et les événements du comté de Flandre en 1325–1326', *BCRH* **131** (1965): 385–454.

Bovesse, J., 'Notes sur Harelbeke et Biervliet dans le cadre de l'histoire des Maisons de Namur et de France', *BCRH* **150** (1984): 453–74.

Bovesse, J., 'La Régence comtale namuroise et Flandre (juillet 1302–mai 1303)', *Liber Buntinx*, 139–65.

Braeckman, W., 'De Moeilijkheden van de Benedictijnerabdijen in de late Middeleeuwen: de Sint-Pietersabdij te Gent (*ca*. 1150–1281)', *HMGOG* **17** (1963): 37–103.

Bredero, A.H., 'Het godsdienstig leven circa 1050–1384', *AGN* **2**: 212–48.

Broecks, J.L., 'De Schilders', in *Flandria Nostra* **2**: 147–226.

Bronnen voor de Geschiedenis van de Instellingen in België, Handelingen van het Colloquium te Brussel, 15–18. IV. 1975. Brussels: Algemeen Rijksarchief, 1977.

Brooke, C.N.L. assisted by Gillian Keir, *London 800–1216: The Shaping of a City*. Berkeley and Los Angeles: University of California Press, 1975.

Bruin, C. de, 'De Letterkunde in de Nederlandse volkstaal tot omstreeks 1384', *AGN* **3**: 343–78.

Brulez, W. and J. Craeybeckx, 'Les Escales au carrefour des Pays-Bas

(Bruges et Anvers, 14e–16e siècles)', *Recueils de la Société Jean Bodin* **32** (Paris, 1974): 417–74.

Brulez, W., 'Brugge en Antwerpen in de 15e en 16e eeuw: een tegenstelling?' *TG* **83** (1970): 15–37.

Brulez, W., 'Engels laken in Vlaanderen in de 14e en 15e eeuw', *ASEB* **108** (1971): 5–25.

Buntinx, J., *De Audientie van de graven van Vlaanderen. Studie over het centraal grafelijk gerecht (c. 1330–c.1409)*. Brussels: Paleis der Academiën, 1949.

[Buntinx, J.], *Recht en Instellingen in de Oude Nederlanden tijdens de Middeleeuwen en de Nieuwe Tijd. Liber Amicorum Jan Buntinx*. Louvain: Louvain University Press, 1981.

Buntinx, W., 'De enquête van Oudenburg. Hervorming van de repartitie van de beden in het graafschap Vlaanderen (1408)', *BCRH* **134** (1968): 75–134.

Caenegem, R.C. van, 'Considérations critiques sur l'ordonnance comtale flamande connue sous le nom d'"Ordonnance sur les baillis"', *Actes du congrès international de la Société Italienne de l'Histoire du Droit. Venise 1967* (Florence: Olschki, 1971), 133–52.

Caenegem, R.C. van, 'Criminal Law in England and Flanders under King Henry II and Count Philip of Alsace', *Actes du congrès de Naples (1980) de la Société de l'Histoire du Droit*, 231–54.

Caenegem, R.C. van, 'Galbert of Bruges on Serfdom, Prosecution of Crime, and Constitutionalism (1127–28)', in *Lyon Essays*, 89–112.

Caenegem, R.C. van, 'Notes on Canon Law Books in Medieval Belgian Book-Lists', *Studia Gratiana* **12** (1967): 265–92.

Caenegem, R.C. van, 'Recht en politiek: de "precepta" van Graaf Filips van de Elzas voor de stad Gent uit het jaar 1178', in *Liber Buntinx*, 51–62.

Callebert, P., 'Ontstaan en vroegste geschiedenis van het kapittel te Eversam (1091–1200)', *ASEB* **107** (1970).

Calonne, S. and D. Clauzel, 'Conjoncture et société à Lille pendant la période bourguignonne', *RN* **56** (1974): 365–84.

Carus-Wilson, E.M., 'The Overseas Trade of Bristol', in Power and Postan, *Studies in English Trade in the Fifteenth Century*, 183–246.

Cauwenberghe, E. van, 'Bijdrage tot de financieel–economische evolutie van een vorstelijk domein in Vlaanderen: Deinze–Drongen (XIVe–XVIIe eeuw)', *ASEB* **207** (1970): 250–68.

Cauwenberghe, E. van, *Het vorstelijk domein en de overheidsfinanciën in de Nederlanden (15de en 16de eeuw). Een kwantitatieve analyse van Vlaamse en Brabantse domeinrekeningen*. Brussels: Historische Uitgaven Pro Civitate, ser. in 8vo, no. 61. Gemeentekrediet van België, 1982.

Cauwenberghe, E. van and Herman van der Wee, 'Productivity, Evolution of Rents and Farm Size in the Southern Netherlands Agriculture from the Fourteenth to the Seventeenth Century', in Herman van der Wee and Eddy van Cauwenberghe (eds), *Productivity of Land and Agricultural Innovation in the Low Countries (1250–1800)* (Louvain: Louvain University Press, 1978), 125–161.

Charles the Bald: Court and Kingdom, British Archaeological Reports, International Series 101 (Oxford, 1981).

Chédeville, A., 'De la Cité à la ville', in Georges Duby (ed.), *Histoire de la France urbaine*, 2. Paris: Seuil, 1980.

Childs, W.R., *Anglo-Castilian Trade in the Later Middle Ages*. Manchester: Manchester University Press, 1978.

Chorley, P., 'The Cloth Exports of Flanders and Northern France during the Thirteenth Century: A Luxury Trade?', *Economic History Review*, 2nd ser., **40** (1987): 349–79.

Clauzel, D., 'Comptabilités urbaines et histoire monétaire (1384–1482)', *RN* **63** (1981): 357–76.

Cockshaw, P., *Le Personnel de la chancellerie de Bourgogne–Flandre sous les ducs de Bourgogne de la maison de Valois*. Kortrijk-Heule: UGA, 1982. Standen en Landen, 79.

Cockshaw, P., 'A Propos de la circulation monétaire entre la Flandre et le Brabant de 1384 à 1390', *Contributions à l'histoire économique et sociale* **6** (1970): 105–41.

Coninck, C. de and W. Blockmans, 'Geschiedenis van de Gentse Leprozerie "Het rijke Gasthuis" vanaf de stichting (*ca* 1146) tot omstreeks 1370', *AH* **5** (1967): 3–44.

Contamine, Philippe, *War in the Middle Ages*. Oxford: Basil Blackwell, 1984.

Coornaert, E., *Un Centre industriel d'autrefois. La draperie–sayetterie d'Hondschoote (XIVe–XVIIIe siècles)*. Paris: Presses Universitaires de France, 1930.

Coornaert, E., *Une Industrie urbaine du XIVe au XVIIe siècle. L'industrie de la laine à Bergues-Saint-Winoc*. Paris: Presses Universitaires de France, 1930.

Cornelius, E., 'De Kunstenaar in het laat-middeleeuwse Gent. I. Organisatie en kunstproduktie van de Sint-Lucasgilde in de 15de eeuw', *HMGOG* **41** (1987): 97–128; II: De sociaal-economische Positie van de meesters van de Sint- Lucasgilde in de 15de eeuw', *HMGOG* **42** (1988): 95–138.

Corryn, F., 'Het Schippersambacht te Gent (1302–1492)', *HMGOG* **1** (1944): 165–204.

Courtenay, W.J., 'Token Coinage and the Administration of Poor Relief during the Late Middle Ages', *Journal of Interdisciplinary History* **3** (1972–3): 275–95.

Craeybeckx, Jan, *Un grand Commerce d'importation: les vins de France aux anciens Pays-Bas (XIIIe–XVIe siècle)*. Paris: SEVPEN, 1958.

Cuttino, G.P., *English Medieval Diplomacy*. Bloomington: Indiana University Press, 1985.

Danneel, M., 'Orphanhood and marriage in fifteenth-century Ghent', in Prevenier, *Marriage and Social Mobility*, 99–111.

Danneel, M., 'Quelques aspects du service domestique feminin à Gand, d'après les manuels échevinaux des Parchons (2ème moitié du XVe siècle', in Prevenier, *Sociale Structuren*, 51–72.

Day, J., *The Medieval Market Economy*. Oxford: Basil Blackwell, 1987.

Decavele, J., 'De Gentse Poorterij en Buitenpoorterij', *Liber Buntinx*, 63–83.

Decavele, Johan (ed.), *Ghent. In Defence of a Rebellious City. History, Art, Culture*. Antwerp: Mercatorfonds, 1989.

Declercq, C., 'De seculiere Geestelijken, mannelijke en vrouwelijke religieuzen te lande', *Flandria Nostra* **4**: 9–212.

Declercq, G., Nieuwe inzichten over de oorsprong van het Sint-Veerlekapittel in Ghent, *HMGOG*, **43** (1989): 49–102.

Declercq, G., 'Sekuliere Kapittels in Vlaanderen, 10de-begin 13de eeuw', *De Leiegouw* **28** (1986): 238–42.

Declercq, G., 'Wanneer ontstond het Sint-Donaaskapittel te Brugge?' *ASEB* **122** (1985): 245–57.

Degryse, L.M., 'Some Observations on the Origin of the Flemish Bailiff (*bailli*): The Reign of Philip of Alsace', *Viator* **7** (1976): 243–94.

Degryse, R., 'Het Begin van het haringkaken te Biervliet (+/- 1399)', *ASEB* **95** (1958): 72–81.

Degryse, R., 'Brugge en de organisatie van het loodswezen van het Zwin op het einde van de 15de eeuw', *ASEB* **112** (1975): 60–129.

Degryse, R., 'De Crisis in de haringbedrijf te Oostende ende te Damme van 1437 tot 1441', *ASEB* **102** (1966): 53–68.

Degryse, R., ''s Graven Domein te Nieuwpoort', *ASEB* **85** (1948): 70–111.

Degryse, R., 'De Nieuwpoortse Justiciarius en zijn opvolgers 1163–1302', *ASEB* **90** (1953): 131–9.

Degryse, R., 'Oude en nieuwe Havens van het IJzerbekken in de Middeleeuwen', *ASEB* **84** (1947): 5–40.

Degryse, R., 'De oudste Vuurbekens van de Vlaamse kust en nabijgelegen Noordzeeoevers (811–einde 16de eeuw)', I, *HMGOG* **36** (1982): 39–79.

Degryse, R., 'De Vlaamse Haringvisserij in de XVe eeuw', *ASEB* **88** (1951): 116–33.

Degryse, R., 'De Vlaamse Westvaart en de Engelse represailles omstreeks 1378', *HMGOG* **27** (1973): 193–239.

Degryse, R., 'Vlaamse Kolenschepen en Schonense Kaakharing te Newcastle upon Tyne (1377–1391)', *ASEB* **122** (1985): 157–88.

Demey, J., 'De Handarbeiders. I. De Middeleeuwen', *Flandria Nostra* **1**: 193–259.

Demey, J., 'De Vlaamse ondernemer in de middeleeuwse Nijverheid. De Ieperse drapiers en "upsetters" op het einde der XIIIe en in de XIVe eeuw', *Bijdragen voor de Geschiedenis der Nederlanden* **4** (1949): 1–15, reprinted Mus and van Houtte, *Prisma Ieper*, 143–56.

Demey, J., 'Proeve tot raming van de bevolking en de weefgetouwen te Ieper van de XIIIe tot de XVIIe eeuw', *RBPH* **28** (1950): 1031–48, reprinted Mus and van Houtte, *Prisma Ieper*, 157–70.

Demuynck, R., 'De Gentse oorlog (1379–1385). Oorzaken en karakter', *HMGOG* **5** (1951): 305–18.

Dept, G.G., 'Etude critique sur une grande inondation marine à la côte flamande (19 novembre 1404)', *Etudes d'histoire dédiées à la mémoire de Henri Pirenne par ses anciens élèves*. Brussels: Nouvelle Société d'Editions, 1937, 105–24.

Dept, G.G., *Les Influences anglaises et françaises dans le comté de Flandre au début du XIIIe siècle*. Ghent: Van Rysselberghe & Rombaut, 1928. Rijksuniversiteit te Gent, Works published by the Arts Faculty, no. 59.

Derville, A., 'Dîmes, rendements du blé et révolution agricole dans le nord de la France au Moyen-Age', *AESC* **42** (1987): 1411–32.

Derville, A., 'Les Draperies flamandes et artésiennes vers 1250–1350', *RN* **54** (1972): 353–70.

Derville, A., 'Le Grenier des Pays-Bas médiévaux', *RN* **69** (1987): 267–80.

Derville, A. (ed.), *Histoire de Saint-Omer*. Lille: Presses Universitaires de Lille, 1981.

Derville, A., 'Les Origines de Gravelines et de Calais', *RN* **66** (1984), no. 263: 1051–69.

Des Marez, G., *Etude sur la propriété foncière dans les villes du Moyen Age et spécialement en Flandre*. Ghent: H. Engelcke, 1898.

Des Marez, G., *La Lettre de Foire à Ypres au XIIIe siècle. Contribution à l'étude des papiers de crédit*. Brussels: Académie Royale, 1900.

Desportes, P., *Reims et les Rémois aux XIIIe et XIVe siècles*. Paris: A. & J. Picard, 1979.

Devliegher, L., 'De Bouwrekeningen van het stadhuis te Damme, 1461–1470', *ASEB* **102** (1966): 143–202.

d'Haenens, Albert, *Les Invasions normandes en Belgique au IXe siècle*. Louvain: Publications Universitaires de Louvain, 1967.

Dhanens, D., 'De plastische Kunsten in het Zuiden 1100–1384', *AGN* **2**: 250–76.

Dhanens, E., 'Sculpture and Painting before 1800', in Decavele, *Ghent*, 189–265.

Dhondt, J., Bijdrage tot het cartularium van Meesen (1065–1334), *BCRH* **106** (1941): 95–234.

Dhondt, J., 'Développement urbain et initiative comtale en Flandre au XIe siècle', *RN* **30** (1948): 133–156.

Dhondt, J., 'L'Essor urbain entre Meuse et Mer du Nord à l'époque mérovingienne', in *Studi in onore di Armando Sapori*, 1 (Milan, 1957): 55–78.

Dhondt, J., *Les Origines de la Flandre et de l'Artois*. Arras: Centre d'Etudes Régionales du Pas-de-Calais, 1944.

Dhondt, J., 'Steden in het landschap en stedelijk landschap', *Flandria Nostra* **1**: 55–85.

Doehaerd, R., 'Handelaars en Neringdoenden. I. De Romeinse Tijd en de Middeleeuwen', *Flandria Nostra* **1**: 357–407.

Dollinger, P., *The German Hansa*. Translated and edited by D.S. Ault and S.H. Steinberg. Stanford: Stanford University Press, 1970.

Doorselaer, A. van, 'De Romeinen in de Nederlanden', *AGN* **1**: 22–98.

Doudelez, G., 'La révolution communale de 1280 à Ypres', *Revue des questions historiques*, 1938, 58–78, 3–25; 1939, 21–70, reprinted Mus and van Houtte, *Prisma Ypres*, 288–394.

Douglas, David C., *William the Conqueror*. Berkeley: University of California Press, 1964.

Duby, Georges, *The Early Growth of the European Economy*. Ithaca, NY: Cornell University Press, 1974.

Dunbabin, J., *France in the Making, 843–1180*. Oxford: Oxford University Press, 1985.

Duverger, E., 'Tapijtkunst', *AGN* **4**: 339–41.

Duyper, J. de, 'De Abdij van de Duinen en Engeland gedurende de XIIe, XIIIe en XIVe eeuw', *ASEB* **88** (1951): 97–115.

Elslander, A. van, 'De Letterkundigen', *Flandria Nostra* **2**: 71–106.

Elslander, A. van, 'Literature', in Decavele, *Ghent*, 397–417.

Espinas, G., *La Draperie dans la Flandre française au Moyen Age*, 2 vols. Paris: Auguste Picard, 1923.

Espinas, G., *La Vie urbaine à Douai au Moyen Age*, 2 vols. Paris: Picard, 1913.

Espinas, G., *Les Origines du capitalisme. I. Sire Jehan Boinebroke, patricien et drapier douaisien (?–1286 environ)*. Lille: L. Raoust, 1933.

Favier, J., 'Enguerrand de Marigny en Flandre', *RN* **39** (1957): 5–20.

Fecheyr, S., 'Het Stadspatriciaat te Ieper in de 13e eeuw', in Mus and van Houtte, *Prisma Ieper*, 295–303.

Finances et comptabilités urbaines du XIIIe au XVIe siècle. Financiën en boekhouding der steden van de XIIIe tot de XVIe eeuw. Colloque International. Internationaal Colloquium. Blankenberge 6–9–IX 1962. Actes. Handelingen. Brussels: Pro Civitate, Collection Histoire, Historische Uitgaven in 8vo, no. 7, 1964.

Finot, J., *Etude historique sur les relations commerciales entre la France et la Flandre au Moyen Age.* Paris: Alphonse Picard, 1894.

Finot, J., *Etude historique sur les relations commerciales entre la Flandre & l'Espagne au Moyen Age.* Paris: Alphonse Picard, 1899.

Fixot, Michel, 'Une Image idéale, une réalité difficile: les villes du VIIe au IXe siècle', in G. Duby (ed.), *Histoire de la France urbaine*, 1. Paris: Seuil, 1980.

Flandria Nostra. Ons Land en Ons Volk, zijn standen en beroepen door de Tijden heen. Antwerp: Standaard Boekhandel, 1957–60. 5 vols.

Fossier, Robert, *La Terre et les hommes en Picardie jusqu'à la fin du XIIIe siècle.* Paris, 1968.

Fouret, Claude, 'La violence en fête: la course de l'Epinette à Lille à la fin du Moyen Age', *RN* **63** (1981): 377–90.

Fredericq, P., *De Secten der Geeselaars en der Dansers in de Nederlanden tijdens de 14de eeuw.* Mémoires de l'Académie Royale des Sciences, des Lettres et des Beaux-Arts de Belgique, vol. 53 (Brussels, 1896), no. 7.

Fromentin, Eugène, *The Masters of Past Time. Dutch and Flemish Painting from Van Eyck to Rembrandt.* Ithaca, NY: Cornell University Press, 1948.

Fryde, E.B., 'The Financial Resources of Edward III in the Netherlands', *RBPH* **45** (1967).

Fryde, E.B., *William de la Pole. Merchant and King's Banker (d. 1366).* London and Ronceverte: Hambledon Press, 1988.

Gaier, C., *L'Industrie et le commerce des armes dans les anciennes principautés belges du XIIIme à la fin du XVme siècle.* Paris: Société d'Edition 'Les Belles Lettres', 1973.

Ganshof, F.L., *La Belgique carolingienne.* Brussels: La Renaissance du Livre, 1958.

Ganshof, F.L., 'Le domaine Gantois de l'abbaye de Saint-Pierre-au-Mont-Blandin à l'époque carolingienne', *RBPH* **26** (1948): 1021–41.

Ganshof, F.L., 'La Flandre', in Ferdinand Lot and Robert Fawtier (eds), *Histoire des institutions françaises au Moyen Age* (Paris: Presses Universitaires de France, 1957), 343–426.

Ganshof, F.L., *La Flandre sous les premiers comtes*. Brussels: La Renaissance du Livre, 1943.

Ganshof, F.L. and G. Berings, 'De Staatsinstellingen in de Karolingische tijd', *AGN* **1**: 243–63.

Ganshof, F.L. and D.P. Blok, 'De Staatsinstellingen in de Merowingische tijd', *AGN*, **1**: 232–40.

Ganshof, F.L. and Adriaan Verhulst, 'Medieval Agrarian Society in its Prime: France, the Low Countries, and Western Germany', in *The Cambridge Economic History of Europe*. I. *The Agrarian Life of the Middle Ages*, 2nd edn. Cambridge: Cambridge University Press, 1966, 291–339.

Genicot, L.F. and H. van Liefferinge, 'De romaanse Bouwkunst in het Zuiden, 1000–1150', *AGN* **2**: 277–88.

George, R.H., 'The Contribution of Flanders to the Conquest of England, 1065–1086', *RBPH* **5** (1926): 81–99.

Gepts-Buysaert, R., 'De Beeldhouwers', *Flandria Nostra* **2**: 73–146.

Ghyssens, J., *Les petits Deniers de Flandre des XIIe et XIIIe siècles*. Brussels: Cercle d'Etudes Numismatiques. Travaux, 5, 1971.

Gilissen, J., 'Les Légistes en Flandre aux XIIIe et XIVe siècles', *Bulletin de la Commission Royale des Anciennes Lois et Ordonnances de Belgique* **15**, fasc. 3 (1939): 117–231.

Godding, P., *Le Droit privé dans les Pays-Bas méridionaux du 12e au 18e siècle*. Brussels: Palais des Académies, 1987. Académie Royale de Belgique. Mémoires de la Classe des Lettres, Coll. in 4o, 2e série, vol. 14, fasc.1.

Godding, P. and J.T. de Smidt, 'Evolutie van het recht in samenhang met instellingen', *AGN* **4**: 172–81.

Goethem, H. van, 'De Annales Gandenses: Auteur en Kroniek. Enkele nieuwe elementen', *HMGOG* **35** (1982): 49–59.

Greilsammer, M., 'Le Mariage en pays flamand: un "fait social total" ', in Prevenier, *Marriage and Social Mobility*, 69–98.

Grierson, P., 'The Relations between England and Flanders before the Norman Conquest', *TRHS*, ser. 4 (1941): 71–113.

Gucht, Katrien van der, 'Semmerzake (Gavere, O. Vl.): Merovingische Nederzettingsceramiek', *HMGOG* **35** (1981).

Gysseling, M., *Toponymisch Woordenboek van België, Nederland, Luxemburg, Noord-Frankrijk en West Duitsland (vóór 1226)* Brussels, 1960.

Gysseling, M., 'Germanisierung en tablgrens', *AGN* **1**: 100–15.

Gysseling, M., A. Verhulst and D.P. Blok, 'Landschap en bewoning tot circa 1000', *AGN* **1**: 99–164.

Haegeman, M., *De Anglofilie in het graafschap Vlaanderen tussen 1379 en 1435. Politieke en economische aspecten*. Standen en Landen, 90. Kortrijk-Heule: UGA, 1988.

Hanawalt, Barbara A. and Kathryn L. Reyerson (eds), *City and Spectacle in Medieval Europe*. Minneapolis: University of Minnesota Press, 1992.

Häpke, Rudolf, *Brügges Entwicklung zum mittelalterlichen Weltmarkt*. Berlin, 1908.

Harvey, P.D.A., 'The English Inflation of 1180–1220', *Past and Present* **61** (1973).

Hemptinne, T. de, 'Het Ontstaan van een lokaal scriptorium te Gentbrugge in het 2e kwart van de 14e eeuw', *HMGOG* **23** (1969): 3–12.

Hemptinne, T. de, 'Vlaanderen en Henegouwen onder de erfgenamen van de Boudewijns 1070–1214', *AGN* **2**: 372–98.

Herlihy, David, *Opera Muliebria. Women and Work in Medieval Europe*. Philadelphia: Temple University Press, 1990.

Hermesdorf, B.H.D., 'Ten hoofde gaan', *Vereeniging tot uitgaaf der bronnen van het oudvaderlandsch recht. Verslagen en Mededelingen* **11** (Utrecht, 1954): 17–50.

Herwaarden, J. van, 'De Nederlanden en het Westers Schisma', *AGN* **4**: 379–86.

Hodges, Richard, *Dark Age Economics*, Ithaca, N.Y.: Cornell University Press, 1982.

Hodges, Richard and David Whitehouse, *Mohammed, Charlemagne and the Origins of Europe. Archaeology and the Pirenne Thesis*. Ithaca: Cornell University Press, 1983.

Hoecke, W. van, 'De Letterkunde in de Franse volkstal tot omstreeks 1384', *AGN* **2**: 379–92.

Holsters, A., 'Moord en politiek tijdens de Gentse opstand', *HMGOG* **37** (1983): 89–111.

Houtte, J.A. van, *Bruges. Essai d'histoire urbaine*. Brussels: La Renaissance du Livre, 1967.

Houtte, J.A. van, 'Bruges et Anvers, marchés "nationaux" ou "internationaux" du XIVe au XVIe siècle', *RN* **34** (1952): 89–108.

Houtte, J.A. van., *An Economic History of the Low Countries 800–1800*. New York: St Martin's Press, 1977.

Houtte, J.A. van, 'Makelaars en waarden te Brugge van de 13e tot de 16e eeuw', *Bijdragen voor de Geschiedenis der Nederlanden* **5** (1950): 1–30, 177–97.

Houtte, J.A. van and R. van Uytven, 'Nijverheid en handel', *AGN* **4**: 87–111.

Howell, M., 'Marriage, Family and Patriarchy in Douai, 1350–1600', in Prevenier, *Marriage and Social Mobility*, 9–34.

Hugenholtz, F.W.N., *Drie Boerenopstanden uit de veertiende eeuw. Vlaanderen, 1323–1328. Frankrijk, 1358. Engeland, 1381. Onderzoek naar het opstandig bewustzijn*. Haarlem: H.D. Tjeenk Willink & Zoon, 1949.

Huizinga, J., *The Waning of the Middle Ages. A Study of the Forms of Life, Thought and Art in France and the Netherlands in the Dawn of the Renaissance.* New York: Doubleday, 1956.

Huyghebaert, N.N., 'De Meier van Zwevezele in de "Miracula S. Winnoci" ', *ASEB* **108** (1971): 213–29.

Huyttens, N., 'De Templiers in Vlaanderen', *HMGOG* **28** (1974): 47–57.

Jansen, H.P.H., *Middeleeuwse Geschiedenis der Nederlanden.* Utrecht and Antwerp: Spectrum, 1971.

Jansen, H.P.H., 'Handel en Nijverheid 1000–1300', *AGN* **2**: 148–86.

Jenkinson, H., 'William Cade, a Financier of the Twelfth Century', *English Historical Review* **28** (1913): 209–27, 731–2.

Kittell, Ellen E., *From Ad Hoc to Routine. A Case Study in Medieval Bureaucracy.* Philadelphia: University of Pennsylvania Press, 1991.

Koch, A.C.F., 'De Ambtenaren. I. De Middeleeuwen', *Flandria Nostra* **5**: 319–42.

Koch, A.C.F., 'Die flandrische Burgschaften', *Zeitschrift für Rechtsgeschichte. Germanistische Abteilung* **76** (1959).

Koch, A.C.F., 'Gérard de Brogne et la maladie du comte Arnoul Ier de Flandre', *Revue Benedictine* **70** (1960): 119–26.

Koch, A.C.F., 'Het Graafschap Vlaanderen van de 9de eeuw tot 1070', *AGN* **1**: 354–83.

Koch, A.C.F., 'Het Land tussen Schelde en Dender vóór de inlijving bij Vlaanderen (met een opmerking over het ontstaan van Oudenaarde)', *Handelingen van de Geschied- en Oudheidkundige Kring van Oudenaarde,* Feestnummer 1956, 56–73.

Koch, A.C.F., *De rechterlijke Organisatie van het graafschap Vlaanderen tot in de 13e eeuw.* Antwerp and Amsterdam: Standaard Boekhandel, n.d.

Koziol, G.G., 'Monks, Feuds, and the Making of Peace in Eleventh-Century Flanders', *Historical Reflections* **14** (1987): 531–49.

Krueger, H.C., 'The Genoese Exportation of Northern Cloths to Mediterranean Ports, Twelfth Century', *RBPH* **65** (1987): 722–50.

Labarge, M.W., *Women in Medieval Life. A Small Sound of the Trumpet.* London: Hamish Hamilton, 1986.

Laet, M. de, 'De Vlaamse aktieve handel op Engeland in de eerste helft van de 14e eeuw, aan de hand van de Customs Accounts', *Economische Geschiedenis van België,* 223–31.

Laleman, M.C. and Hugo Thoen, 'Prehistory–Sixth Century AD', in Decavele, *Ghent,* 23–35.

Lambrecht, D. and J. van Rompaey, 'De Staatsinstellingen in het Zuiden van de 11de tot de 14de eeuw', *AGN* **2**: 77–134.

417

Laurent, H., *Un grand Commerce d'exportation au Moyen Age. La draperie des Pays-Bas en France et dans les pays mediterranéens (XIIe–XVe siècle)*. Paris: E. Droz, 1935.

Law, Custom, and the Social Fabric in Medieval Europe: Essays in Honor of Bryce Lyon. Edited, with an Appreciation, by Bernard S. Bachrach and David Nicholas. Kalamazoo, Michigan: Medieval Institute Publications, 1990.

Lebecq, Stéphane, 'Les Cisterciens de Vaucelles en Flandre maritime au XIIIe siècle', *RN* **54** (1972): 371–85.

Lebecq, Stéphane, 'Dans l'Europe du Nord des VIIe–IXe siècles: Commerce frison ou commerce franco-frison?', *AESC* **41** (1986): 361–77.

Le Goff, Jacques, 'Ordres mendiants et urbanisation dans la France médiévale', *AESC* **25** (1970): 924–46.

Les Libertés urbaines et rurales du XIe au XIVe siècle. Vrijheden in de stad en op het platteland van de XIe tot de XIVe eeuw. Colloque International, Spa 5–8 IX 1966. *Actes*. Brussels: Pro Civitate, 1968.

Lloyd, T.H., *Alien Merchants in England in the High Middle Ages*. New York: St Martin's Press, 1982.

Lloyd, T.H., *The English Wool Trade in the Middle Ages*. Cambridge: Cambridge University Press, 1977.

Lucas, Henry S., 'The Great European Famine of 1315, 1316, and 1317', *Speculum* **5** (1930): 343–77.

Lucas, Henry S., *The Low Countries and the Hundred Years War, 1326–1347*. Ann Arbor: University of Michigan Press, 1929.

Luykx, T., *De grafelijke financiële Bestuursinstellingen en het grafelijke patrimonium in Vlaanderen tijdens de regering van Margareta van Constantinopel (1244–1278)*. VKVA, no. 39. Brussels: Palais der Academiën, 1961.

Luykx, T., *De Graven van Vlaanderen en de kruistochten*. Haaselt: Heideland, 1967.

[Lyon, Bryce], *Law, Custom, and the Social Fabric in Medieval Europe. Essays in Honor of Bryce Lyon*. Kalamazoo, Michigan: Medieval Institute Publications, 1990.

Lyon, Bryce and A.E. Verhulst, *Medieval Finance. A Comparison of Financial Institutions in Northwestern Europe*. Providence: Brown University Press, 1967.

Lyon, Bryce, *From Fief to Indenture. The Transition from Feudal to Non-Feudal Contract in Western Europe*. Cambridge, Mass., 1957.

Lyon, Bryce, 'Medieval Real Estate Developments and Freedom', *AHR* **63** (1957): 47–61.

Marechal, G, 'Armen- en ziekenzorg in de Zuidelijke Nederlanden', *AGN* **2**: 268–80.

Marechal, G. 'Het Sint-Janshospitaal in de eerste eeuwen van zijn bestaan', *800 Jaar Sint-Janshospitaal te Brugge* (Bruges, 1976): 41–75.

Marechal, G., *De sociale en politieke gebondenheid van het Brugse hospitaalwezen in de Middeleeuwen.* Kortrijk-Heule, 1978. Standen en Landen, 73.

Marechal, G., 'De Zwarte Dood te Brugge, 1349–1351', *Biekorf* **80** (1980), 377–92.

Marechal, J., 'Le Départ de Bruges des marchands étrangers (XVe et XVIe siècles)', *ASEB* **88** (1951): 26–74.

Marechal, J., *Geschiedenis van de Brugse Beurs.* Bruges, 1949.

Marechal, J., 'Het Weezengeld in de Brugse stadsfinancin van de Middeleeuwen', *ASEB* **82** (1939): 1–41.

Martens, M.P.J., 'Enkele middeleeuwse muurschilderingen te Gent, I. Gegevens op basis van kopieën; II: Gegevens op basis van documenten', *HMGOG* **39** (1985): 84–121; **40** (1986): 47–84.

Märtens, R., *Weltorientierungen und wirtschaftliches Erfolgsstreben mittelalterlicher Grosskaufleute. Das Beispiel Gent im 13. Jahrhundert.* Cologne and Vienna: Böhlau, 1976.

Mayhew, N.J., 'The circulation and imitation of sterlings in the Low Countries', in N.J. Mayhew (ed.), *Coinage in the Low Countries (880–1500).* The Third Oxford Symposium on Coinage and Monetary History. BAR International Series 54. Oxford, 1979, 54–68.

McDonnell, E., *Beguines and Beghards in Medieval Culture, with Special Emphasis on the Belgian Scene* (New Brunswick: Rutgers University Press, 1954).

McKitterick, R., *The Frankish Kingdoms under the Carolingians, 751–987.* London: Longman, 1983.

Mens, A., *Oorsprong en betekenis van der Nederlandse begijnen- en begardenbeweging.* Antwerp, 1947.

Mertens, J., *De laat-middeleeuwse Landbouweconomie in enkele gemeenten van het Brugse platteland.* Brussels: Pro Civitate, Reeks in 8vo, no. 27, 1970.

Mertens, J., 'De Brugse ambachtsbesturen (1363–1374, n.s.): een oligarchie', *Liber Buntinx*, 185–98.

Mertens, J., 'Les Confiscations dans la châtellenie du Franc de Bruges après la bataille de Cassel', *BCRH* **134** (1968): 239–84.

Mertens, J., 'De economische en sociale Toestand van de opstandelingen uit het Brugse Vrije, wier goederen na de slag bij Cassel (1328) verbeurd verklaard werden', *RBPH* **47** (1969): 1131–53.

Mertens, J., 'Enkele bepalingen omtrent bezaaing, beplanting en behuizing in laatmiddeleeuwse pachtcontracten voor het Brugse Vrije (XVde eeuw)', *ASEB* **108** (1971): 245–60.

Mertens, J., 'De Landbouwers in het Zuiden 1100–1300', *AGN* **2**: 105–22.

Mertens, J., 'Landbouw', *AGN* **4**: 12–41.

Mertens, J., 'Landschap en geografie in het Zuiden 1300–1480', *AGN* **2**: 40–7.

Mertens, R., 'Twee (Wevers)opstanden te Brugge (1387–1391)', *ASEB* **110** (1973): 5–20.

Messemaeker-de Wilde, G. de, 'De parochale Armenzorg te Gent in de late middeleeuwen', *AH* **18** (1980): 49–58.

Metcalf, D.M., 'Coinage and the Rise of the Flemish Towns', in Mayhew, *Coinage*, 1–23.

Mierlo, J. van, *Geschiedenis van de Oud- en Middelnederlandsche Letterkunde*. Antwerp, Brussels and Louvain: Standaard Boekhandel, 1928.

Milis, L., 'De Kerk tussen de Gregoriaanse hervorming en Avignon', *AGN* **3**: 166–211.

Milis, L., 'Kerstening en kerkelijke instellingen tot circa 1070', *AGN* **1**: 266–85.

Mollat, M. *Le Commerce maritime normand à la fin du moyen âge. Etude d'histoire économique et sociale*. Paris: Librairie Plon, 1952.

Monier, R., *Les Institutions centrales du comté de Flandre du IXe siècle à 1384*. Paris, 1943.

Monier, R., *Les Institutions judiciaires des villes de Flandre des origines à la Rédaction des Coutumes*. Lille: Valentin Bresle, 1924.

Monier, R., 'Le Recours au chef-de-sens, au moyen-âge, dans les villes flamandes', *RN* **14** (1928): 5–19.

Moore, E.W., *The Fairs of Medieval England. An Introductory Study*. Toronto: Pontifical Institute of Medieval Studies, 1985. Studies and Texts, 72.

Morimoto, Y. 'Problèmes autour du polyptyque de Saint-Bertin (844–859)', in Verhulst, *Grand domaine*, 125–51.

Morliou, Carla, 'De vroegste Geschiedenis van het Gentse St Agneeteconvent (1434–1454). Bijdrage tot de studie van de moderne Devotie in onze gewesten', *HMGOG* **38** (1984): 17–33.

Munro, J.H., 'Bruges and the Abortive Staple in English Cloth: An Incident in the Shift of Commerce from Bruges to Antwerp in the Late Fifteenth Century', *RBPH* **44** (1966): 1137–59.

Munro, J.H., 'Bullion Flows and Monetary Contraction in Late-Medieval England and the Low Countries', in J.F. Richards (ed.), *Precious Metals in the Later Medieval and Early Modern Worlds* (Durham, NC: Carolina Academic Press, 1983): 97–158.

Munro, J.H., 'Deflation and the Petty Coinage Problem in the Late-Medieval Economy: The Case of Flanders, 1334–1484', *Explorations in Economic History* **25** (1988): 387–423.

Munro, J.H., 'Economic Depression and the Arts in the Fifteenth-Century Low Countries', *Renaissance and Reformation* **19** (1983): 235–50.

Munro, J.H., 'Industrial Protectionism in Medieval Flanders: Urban or National?' in Harry A. Miskimin, David Herlihy and A.L. Udovitch (eds), *The Medieval City*. New Haven: Yale University Press, 1977, 229–67.

Munro, J.H., 'Industrial Transformations in the North-West European Textile Trades, c. 1290–c. 1340: Economic Progress or Economic Crisis?' in Bruce M.S. Campbell (ed.), *Before the Black Death. Studies in the Crisis of the Early Fourteenth Century* (Manchester, 1991).

Munro, J.H., 'The Medieval Scarlet and the Economics of Sartorial Splendour', *Cloth and Clothing in Medieval Europe. Essays in Memory of Professor E.M. Carus-Wilson*, edited by N.B. Harte and K.G. Ponting (N.P.: Heinemann Educational Books, 1983): 13–69.

Munro, J.H., 'Mint Outputs, Money, and Prices in Late-Medieval England and the Low Countries', *Trierer Historische Forschungen* **7** (1984): 31–122.

Munro, J.H., 'Monetary Contraction and Industrial Change in the Late-Medieval Low Countries, 1335–1500', in Mayhew, *Coinage*, 95–161.

Munro, J.H., *Wool, Cloth, and Gold. The Struggle for Bullion in Anglo-Burgundian Trade, 1340–1378*. Toronto: University of Toronto Press; Brussels: Editions de l'Université de Bruxelles, 1972.

Murray, J.M., 'The Failure of Corporation: Notaries Public in Medieval Bruges', *JMH* **12** (1986): 155–66.

Murray, J.M., 'Family, Marriage and Moneychanging in medieval Bruges', *JMH* **14** (1988): 114–125.

Murray, J.M., 'The Liturgy of the Count's Advent in Bruges from Galbert to the Van Eycks', in Hanawalt and Reyerson, *City and Spectacle*.

Murray, J.M., 'Housing, Real Estate and the Prince's Pauper in Four-teenth-Century Bruges', paper read at the 21st Annual International Congress on Medieval Studies, Kalamazoo, Michigan, May 1986.

Murray, J.M., 'The Commercial Comforts of Late Medieval Bruges' paper read at Midwest Medieval Conference, 1987.

Mus, O., 'Het Aandeel van de Ieperlingen in de Engelse wolexport, 1280–1330', *Economische Geschiedenis van België. Behandeling van de bronnen en problematiek*. Handelingen van het colloquium te Brussel, 17–19 November 1971 (Brussels, 1972), 233–59, reprinted in Mus and van Houtte, *Prisma Ieper*, 332–55.

Mus, O., 'De Brugse Compagnie Despars op het einde van de 15e eeuw', *ASEB* **101** (1964): 5–118.

Mus, O., 'Pieter de Maets, Stadsbouwmeester–ondernemer (Ieper, . . . /+1318)', *ASEB* **114** (1977): 339–60.

Mus, O. and J.A. van Houtte (eds), *Prisma van de Geschiedenis van Ieper*. Ypres: Stadsbestuur, 1974.

Nicholas, David, 'Crime and Punishment in Fourteenth-Century Ghent', *RBPH* **48** (1970): 289–334, 1141–76.

Nicholas, David, *The Domestic Life of a Medieval City: Women, Children, and the Family in Fourteenth-Century Ghent*. Lincoln: University of Nebraska Press, 1985.

Nicholas, David, 'Economic Reorientation and Social Change in Fourteenth-Century Flanders', *Past and Present* **70** (1976): 3–29.

Nicholas, David, 'The English Trade at Bruges in the Last Years of Edward III', *JMH* **5** (1979): 23–61.

Nicholas, David, 'The Governance of Fourteenth-Century Ghent: The Theory and Practice of Public Administration', in *Lyon Essays*, 235–60.

Nicholas, David, 'In the Pit of the Burgundian Theatre State: Urban Traditions and Princely Ambitions in Ghent and Bruges, 1360–1420', in Hanawalt and Reyerson, *City and Spectacle*.

Nicholas, David, 'The Marriage and the Meat Hall: Ghent/Eeklo, 1373–75', *Medieval Prosopography* **10** (1989): 22–52.

Nicholas, David, 'Medieval Urban Origins in Northern Continental Europe. State of Research and Some Tentative Conclusions', *Studies in Medieval and Renaissance History* **6** (1969): 53–114.

Nicholas, David, *The Metamorphosis of a Medieval City: Ghent in the Age of the Arteveldes, 1302–1390*. Lincoln: University of Nebraska Press; Leiden: E.J. Brill, 1987.

Nicholas, David, 'Of Poverty and Primacy: Demand, Liquidity, and the Flemish Economic Miracle, 1050–1200', *AHR* **96** (1991).

Nicholas, David, 'The Scheldt Trade and the "Ghent War" of 1379–1385', *BCRH* **144** (1978): 189–359.

Nicholas, David, 'Structures du peuplement, fonctions urbaines et formation du capital dans la Flandre médiévale', *AESC* **33** (1978): 501–27.

Nicholas, David, *Town and Countryside: Social, Economic, and Political Tensions in Fourteenth-Century Flanders*. University of Ghent: Publications of the Arts Faculty, no. 152. Bruges: De Tempel, 1971.

Nicholas, David, *The van Arteveldes of Ghent: the Varieties of Vendetta and the Hero in History*. Ithaca and London: Cornell University Press; Leiden: E.J. Brill, 1988.

Nicholas, David, 'Weert: a Scheldt Polder Village of the Fourteenth Century', *JMH* **2** (1976): 239–68.

Nicholas, Karen S, 'The Role of Feudal Relationships in the Consolidation of Power in the Principalities of the Low Countries, 1000–1300', in *Lyon Essays*, 113–30.

Noterdaeme, J., 'De vroegste Geschiedenis van Brugge, I. S. Salvatorskerk; II. O.L. Vrouwekerk', *ASEB* **112** (1975): 5–59.

Noterdaeme, J., 'De vroegste Geschiedenis van Brugge, III. De burcht van Brugge', *ASEB* **112** (1975): 171–204.

Noterdaeme, J., 'De vroegste Geschiedenis van Brugge, VI. Een ander "Oudburg" te Brugge', *ASEB* **114** (1977): 211–338.

Nowé, H., *La Bataille des éperons d'or*. Brussels: La Renaissance du Livre, 1945.

Nowé, H., *Les Baillis comtaux de Flandre. Des origines à la fin du XIVe siècle*. Brussels: Marcel Hayez, 1928.

Oost, A. van, 'Sociale Stratifikatie van de Gentse opstandelingen van 1379–1385. Een kritische benadering van konfiskatiedokumenten', *HMGOG* **29** (1975): 59–92.

Opll, F., *Stadt und Reich im 12. Jahrhundert (1125–1190)*. Cologne, Vienna and Graz: Hermann Böhlaus Nachfolger, 1986.

Pairon, E., 'De Financiën van de Sint-Baafsabdij in de 14e–15e eeuw', *HMGOG* **35** (1982): 61–79.

Palmer, J.J.N., *England, France, and Christendom, 1377–1399*. Chapel Hill: University of North Carolina Press, 1972.

Palmer, J.J.N., 'England, France, the Papacy and the Flemish Succession, 1361–9', *JMH* **2** (1976): 339–64.

Philippen, L.M.J., *De Begijnhoven. Oorsprong, geschiedenis, inrichting*. Antwerp, 1918.

Phillips, J.R.S., *The Medieval Expansion of Europe*. Oxford: Oxford University Press, 1988.

Pirenne, H., *Early Democracies in the Low Countries: Urban Society and Political Conflict in the Middle Ages and the Renaissance*. New York: Harper & Row, 1963.

Pirenne, H., *Histoire de Belgique*, I: *Des Origines au commencement du XIVe siècle*, 5th edn. Brussels: Maurice Lamertin, 1929; II: *Du Commencement du XIVe siècle à la mort de Charles le Témeraire*, 3rd edn. Brussels: Maurice Lamertin, 1922.

Pirenne, H., 'Les Dénombrements de la population d'Ypres au XVe siècle (1412–1506). Contribution à l'histoire statistique sociale au moyen âge', *Vierteljahrsschrift für Sozial- und Wirtschaftsgeschichte*, 1 (1903): 1–32, reprinted in Mus and van Houtte, *Prisma Ieper*, 359–90.

Pistono, S.P., 'Henry IV and the *Vier Leden*: Conflict in Anglo-Flemish Relations, 1402–1403', *RBPH* **54** (1976): 458–73.

Platelle, H., 'Esquisse de la vie religieuse de Lille au XVe siècle', *ASEB* **103** (1966): 125–77.

Platelle, H., 'La Violence et ses remèdes en Flandre au XIe siècle', *Sacris Erudiri* **20** (1971): 101–73.

Pleij, H., *Het Gilde van de Blauwe Schuit. Literatuur, volksfeest en burgermoraal in de late Middeleeuwen*. Amsterdam: Meulenhoff, 1979.

Poerck, G. de, *La Draperie médiévale en Flandre et Artois: Technique et terminologie*, 3 vols. Bruges: De Tempel, 1951.

Pounds, Norman J.G., *An Historical Geography of Europe, 450 BC–AD 1330*. Cambridge: Cambridge University Press, 1973.

Power, E. and M.M. Postan (eds), *Studies in English Trade in the Fifteenth Century*. London: Routledge & Kegan Paul, 1933.

Prevenier, W., 'Ambtenaren in stad en land in de Nederlanden. Socioprofessionele evoluties (veertiende tot zestiende eeuw)', *Bijdragen en Mededelingen betreffende de Geschiedenis der Nederlanden* **87** (1972): 44–59.

Prevenier, W., 'De Beden in het Graafschap Vlaanderen', *RBPH* **38** (1960): 330–65.

Prevenier, W., 'La Bourgeoisie en Flandre au XIIIe siècle', *Revue de l'Université de Bruxelles* 1978/4, 407–28.

Prevenier, W., 'Het Brugse Vrije en de Leden van Vlaanderen', *ASEB* **96** (1959): 5–63.

Prevenier, W., 'De laat-middeleeuwse vorstelijke kanselarijen als exponenten van een modern of archaisch staatsapparaat', *TG* **87** (1974): 202–10.

Prevenier, W., *De Leden en de Staten van Vlaanderen (1384–1405)*. Brussels: Paleis der Academiën, 1961.

Prevenier, W., 'En Marge de l'assistance aux pauvres: l'aumonerie des comtes de Flandre et des ducs de Bourgogne (13–début 16e siècle)', *Liber Buntinx*, 97–120.

Prevenier, W., 'Financiën en boekhouding in de Bourgondische periode. Nieuwe bronnen en resultaten', *TG* **82** (1969): 469–81.

Prevenier. W., (ed.), *Marriage and Social Mobility in the Late Middle Ages*. Handelingen van het colloquium gehouden te Gent op 18 april 1988. Ghent: Rijksuniversiteit te Gent, 1989.

Prevenier, W., 'Motieven voor leliaardsgezindheid in Vlaanderen in de periode 1297–1305', *De Leiegouw* **19** (1977): 273–88.

Prevenier, W., 'Officials in Town and Countryside in the Low Countries. Social and Professional Developments from the Fourteenth to the Sixteenth Century', *Acta Historiae Neerlandicae* **7** (1974): 1–17.

Prevenier, W., 'Quelques Aspects des comptes communaux en Flandre au Moyen Age', in *Finances et comptabilités urbaines du*

XIIIe au XVIe siècle. Colloque international, Blankenberge 6–9–IX–1962. Actes. Brussels: Pro Civitate, Collection Histoire in 8o, no. 7 (1964): 111–51.

Prevenier, W., 'Les Perturbations dans les relations commerciales anglo-flamandes entre 1379 et 1407. Causes de désaccord et raisons d'une réconciliation', *Economies et sociétés du Moyen Age. Mélanges Edouard Perroy*. Paris: Publications de la Sorbonne, 1973, 477–97.

Prevenier, W., 'De Verhouding van de Clerus tot de locale en regionale overheid in het Graafschap Vlaanderen in de late Middeleeuwen', *Sources de l'histoire religieuse de la Belgique. Moyen Age et temps modernes*. Bibliothèque de la Revue d'Histoire Ecclesiastique, fasc. 47. Louvain: Publications Universitaires de Louvain, 1968, 9–45.

Prevenier. W. and Wim Blockmans, *The Burgundian Netherlands*. Cambridge: Cambridge University Press, 1985.

Prevenier, W., Wim Blockmans *et al.*, 'Tassen crisis en welvaart: Sociale Veranderingen, 1300–1482', *AGN* **4**: 42–86.

Prevenier, W. and Marc Boone, 'The "city-state" dream', in Decavele, *Ghent*, 80–105.

W. Prevenier, R. van Uytven and E. van Cauwenberghe (eds), *Sociale Structuren en topografie van armoede en rijkdom in de 14e en 15e eeuw. Methodologische aspecten en resultaten van recent onderzoek*. Ghent: FKFO, 1986.

Primitifs Flamands Anonymes. Maîtres aux noms d'emprunt des Pays-Bas méridionaux du XVe et du début du XVIe siècle. Exposition organisée par la Ville de Bruges au Groeningemuseum 14 juin–21 septembre 1969. Tielt: Lannoo, 1969.

Puyvelde, L. van, *Un Hôpital au moyen âge et une abbaye y annexée. La Biloke de Gand. Etude archéologique*. University of Ghent: works published by the Arts Faculty, 57. Ghent, 1925.

Quicke, F., *Les Pays-Bas à la veille de la période Bourguignonne, 1356–1384*. Brussels: Editions Universitaires, 1947.

Reynolds, R.L., 'The Market for Northern Textiles in Genoa 1179–1200', *RBPH* **8** (1929): 831–51.

Ridder–Symoens, H. de, 'Possibilités de carrière et de mobilité sociale des intellectuels-universitaires au Moyen Age', *Proceedings of the First Interdisciplinary Conference on Medieval Prosopography Held at Bielefeld, 3–5 December 1982*. Kalamazoo: Medieval Institute Publications, 1986, 1–15.

Roggen, D., 'Gentsche Beeldhouwkunst der XIVe en der XVe eeuw', *Gentsche Bijdragen tot de Kunstgeschiedenis* **5** (1938): 51–73.

Rogghé, Paul, 'Het eerste Bewind der Gentse Hoofdmannen (1319–1320)', *AM* **12** (1961): 1–47.

Rogghé, Paul, 'Gemeente ende Vrient. Nationale omwentelingen in de XIVe eeuw', *ASEB* **89** (1952): 101–35.

Rogghé, Paul, 'De Gentse Klerken in de XIVe en XVe eeuw. Trouw en Verraad', *AM* **11** (1960): 5–142.

Rogghé, Paul, 'Het Gentsche Stadsbestuur van 1302 tot 1345. En een en ander betreffende het Gentsche Stadspatriciaat', *HMGOG* **1** (1944): 135–63.

Rogghé, Paul, 'Italianen te Gent in de XIVe eeuw. Een merkwaardig florentijnsch hostelliers- en makelaarsgeslacht: de Gualterotti', *Bijdragen voor de Geschiedenis der Nederlanden*, 1 (1946): 197–226.

Rogghé, Paul, 'De Politiek van Graaf Lodewijk van Male: Het Gentse verzet en de Brugse Zuidleie', *AM* **15** (1964): 388–441.

Rogghé, Paul, 'De Samenstelling der Gentse Schepenbanken in de 2e helft der 14e eeuw. En een en ander over de Gentse poorterie', *HMGOG* **4** (1950): 22–31.

Rogghé, Paul, 'Simon de Mirabello in Vlaanderen', *AM* **9** (1958): 1–52.

Rogghé, Paul, *Vlaanderen en het zevenjarig beleid van Jacob van Artevelde. Een critische–historische studie*, 2 vols. Brussels: A. Manteau, 1942.

Rogghé, Paul, 'De Zwarte Dood in de zuidelijke Nederlanden', *RBPH* **30** (1952): 834–7.

Rompaey, J. van, 'De Bourgondische Staatsinstellingen', *AGN* **4**: 136–55.

Rompaey, J. van, *De grote Raad van de hertogen van Boergondie en het parlement van Mechelen*. VKVA, no. 73. Brussels: Paleis der Academiën, 1973.

Rompaey, J. van, *Het grafelijke Baljuwsambt in Vlaanderen tijdens de Boergondische periode*. VKVA, no. 62 Brussels: Paleis der Academiën, 1967.

Roose, M. van, 'Twee onbekende 15de eeuwse dokumenten in verband met de Brugse "Beildesniders"', *ASEB* **110** (1973): 168–77.

Roosens, Heli, 'Traces de christianisation dans les centres urbains de l'ancienne Belgique', *RN* **69**: 1–15.

Roover, R. de, *The Bruges Money Market Around 1400*. Brussels: Paleis der Academiën, 1968.

Roover, R. de, 'Les Comptes communaux et la comptabilité communale de la ville de Bruges au XIVe siècle', in *Finances et comptabilités urbaines*, 86–102.

Roover, R. de, *L'Evolution de la lettre de change, XIVe–XVIIIe siècles*. Paris, 1953.

Roover, R. de, 'Le Marché monétaire au Moyen Age et au début des temps modernes. Problèmes et méthodes', *RH* **495** (1970): 5–40.

Roover, R. de, *Money, Banking, and Credit in Mediaeval Bruges. Italian Merchant-Bankers, Lombards, and Money–Changers. A Study in the Origins of Banking.* Cambridge, Mass.: Mediaeval Academy of America, 1948.

Roover, R. de, 'Renseignements complémentaires sur le marché monétaire à Bruges au XIVe et au XVe siècle', *ASEB* **109** (1972): 51–91.

Rossiaud, J., *Medieval Prostitution*, translated by Lydia G. Cochrane. Oxford: Basil Blackwell, 1988.

Rossiaud, J., 'Prostitution, Youth, and Society in the Towns of South-eastern France in the Fifteenth Century', in *Deviants and the Abandoned in French Society. Selections from the Annales* . . . IV (Baltimore: Johns Hopkins University Press, 1978).

Rouche, M., 'La Crise de l'Europe au cours de la deuxième moitié du VIIe siècle et la naissance des régionalismes', *AESC* **41** (1986): 347–60.

Ryckaert, M., 'Brandbestrijding en overheidsmaatregelen tegen brandgevaar tijdens het Ancien Regime', in *Bronnen voor de Geschiedenis van de Instellingen in België*, 247–56.

Ryckaert, M., 'De Brugse havens in de Middeleeuwen', *ASEB* **109** (1972): 5–27.

Sabbe, E., *De Belgische Vlasnijverheid*, I. *De zuidnederlandsche Vlasnijverheid tot het verdrag van Utrecht (1713)*. Bruges: De Tempel, 1943.

Sabbe, E., 'Grondbezit en landbouw, economische en sociale toestanden in de kastelenij Kortrijk op het einde der XIVe eeuw', *Handelingen van den Koninklijke Geschied- en Oudheidkundigen Kring van Kortrijk*, n.s. **15** (1936): 1–65.

Sabbe, J., 'De opstand van Brugge tegen graaf Robrecht van Béthune en zijn zoon Robrecht van Cassel in 1321–1322', *ASEB* **107** (1970): 217–49.

Sagher, E. de, 'Origine de la gilde des archiers de Saint-Sébastien à Ypres (1383–1398)', in *Prisma Ieper*, 420–39.

Sagher, H.H. de, 'L'Immigration des tisserands flamands et brabançons en Angleterre sous Edouard III', *Mélanges d'histoire offerts à Henry Pirenne par ses anciens élèves et ses amis à l'occasion de sa quarantième année d'enseignement à l'université de Gand, 1886–1926*, 2 vols. Brussels: Vromant & Col, 1926, 2: 109–26.

Schlesinger, W., 'Burg und Stadt', in *Aus Verfassungs- und Landesgeschichte. Festschrift zum 70. Geburtstag von Theodor Mayer*, 2. Lindau and Constance: Jan Thorbecke, 1955, 97–150.

Schofield, John, *The Building of London: From the Conquest to the Great Fire.* London: British Museum Publications, 1983.

Schouteet, A., 'Het Ambacht van de oudcleercopers te Brugge', *ASEB* **107** (1970): 45–87.

Schwarz, C. M., 'Village Populations According to the Polyptyque of St Bertin', *JMH* **11** (1985): 31–41.

Scollar, I., F. Verhaeghe and A. Gautier, *A Medieval Site (14th Century) at Lampernisse (West Flanders, Belgium)*. Bruges: De Tempel, 1970. Belgisch Centrum voor Landelijke Geschiedenis, no. 22.

Searle, Eleanor, *Predatory Kinship and the Creation of Norman Power, 840–1066*. Berkeley: University of California Press, 1988.

Simons, W., *Bedelordekloosters in het Graafschap Vlaanderen. Chronologie en topografie van de bedelordenverspreiding vóór 1350*. Bruges: Stichting Jan Cobbaut-Sint-Pietersabdij Steenbrugge, 1987.

Simons, W., 'Bedelordenvestiging en middeleeuws stadswezen. De stand van zaken rond de hypothese–Le Goff', *Tijdschrift voor Sociale Geschiedenis* **12** (1986): 39–52.

Simons, W., 'The Beguine Movement in the Southern Low Countries: A Reassessment', *Bulletin van het Belgisch Historisch Instituut te Rome* **59** (1989): 63–105.

Simons, W., *Stad en Apostolaat. De vestiging van de bedelorden in het graafschap Vlaanderen (ca. 1225–ca. 1350)*. VKVA, Kl. Letteren, jg. 49, no. 121. Brussels: Paleis der Academiën, 1987.

Sivery, G., *Les Comtes de Hainaut et le commerce du vin au XIVe siècle et au début du XVe siècle*. Lille: Publications du Centre Régional d'Etudes Historiques de l'Université de Lille, 1969.

Sivery, G., 'Histoire économique et sociale', in Trenard, *Histoire de Lille*, 1: 111–270.

Sivery, G., 'Les Débuts de l'économie cyclique et de ses crises dans les bassins scaldiens et mosans, fin du XIIe et début du XIIIe siècle', *RN* **64** (1982), 667–81.

Sivery, G., *Structures agraires et vie rurale dans le Hainaut à la fin du Moyen-Age*, 2 vols. Lille: Presses Universitaires de Lille, 1977, [1982].

Slicher van Bath, B.H., *The Agrarian History of Western Europe, AD 500–1850*. New York: St Martin's Press, 1963.

Smet, A. de, 'De Klacht van de "ghemeente" van Damme in 1280. Enkele gegevens over politieke en sociale toestanden in een kleine Vlaamse stad gedurende de tweede helft der XIIIe eeuw', *BCRH* **115** (1950): 1–15.

Smet, J. de, 'Brugse Leliaards gevlucht te Sint-Omaars van 1302 tot 1305', *ASEB* **89** (1957): 146–52.

Smet, J. de, 'De Repressie te Brugge na de slag bij Westrozebeke, 1 December 1382–31 Augustus 1384', *ASEB* **84** (1947): 71–118.

Smet, J. de, 'De Verbeurdverklaringen in het Brugse Vrije en in de smalle steden aldaar na de slag bij Westrozebeke (1382–1384)', *ASEB* **95** (1958): 115–36.

Smet, J.M., 'Passio Francorum Secundum Flemyngos. Het Brugse Spotevangelie op de nederlaag van de Fransen te Kortrijk (11 juli 1302)', *De Leiegouw* **19** (1977): 289–319.

Smith, C.T., *An Historical Geography of Western Europe before 1800.* New York: Praeger, 1967.

Sosson, J.P., 'A Propos des "travaux publics" de quelques villes de Flandre aux XIVe et XVe siècles: impact budgétaire, importance relative des investissements, technostructures, politiques économiques', in *Bronnen voor de Geschiedenis van de Instellingen in België*, 379–400.

Sosson, J.P., 'Die Körperschaften in den Niederlanden und Nordfrankreich: neue Forschungsperspektiven', in Klaus Friedland (ed.), *Gilde und Korporation in den nordeuropäischen Städte des späten Mittelalters* (Cologne and Vienna: Böhlau, 1984), 79–90.

Sosson, J.P., 'La Structure sociale de la corporation médiévale. L'exemple des tonneliers de Bruges de 1350 à 1500', *RBPH* **44** (1966): 457–78.

Sosson, J.P., *Les Travaux publics de la ville de Bruges, XIVe–XVe siècles. Les matériaux. Les hommes.* Brussels: Crédit Communal de Belgique, 1977.

Spufford, P., 'Coinage, Taxation and the Estates General of the Burgundian Netherlands', *Standen en Landen*, **40**. Brussels, 1966: 61–88.

Spufford, P., *Money and its Use in Medieval Europe.* Cambridge: Cambridge University Press, 1988.

Stafford, P., 'Charles the Bald, Judith and England', in M. Gibson and J. Nelson (eds), *Charles the Bald: Court and Kingdom*, 137–151.

Stein, W., 'Der Streit zwischen Köln und Flandern um die Rheinschiffahrt im 12. Jahrhundert', *Hansische Geschichtsblätter* **17** (1911): 187–215.

Strohm, R., *Music in Late Medieval Bruges.* Oxford: Clarendon Press, 1985.

Studien betreffende de sociale strukturen te Brugge, Kortrijk en Gent in de 14e en 15e eeuw, 3 vols. Heule: UGA, 1971–3. Standen en Landen 54, 57, 63.

Sturler, J. de, 'Le Passage des marchandises en transit par le duché de Brabant aux XIIIe et XIVe siècles. L'importance commerciale et maritime du port d'Anvers', *Annales du 30. Congrès de la Fédération Archéologique de Belgique.* Brussels, 1936, 155–76.

Sumberg, L.A.M., 'The "Tafurs" and the First Crusade', *Medieval Studies* **21** (1959).

Thielemans, M.R., *Bourgogne et Angleterre. Relations politiques et écon-*

omiques entre les Pays-Bas bourguignons et l'Angleterre, 1435–1467. Brussels: Presses Universitaires de Bruxelles, 1967. Université Libre de Bruxelles. Travaux de la Faculté de Philosophie et Lettres, tome 30.

Thoen, Erik, 'Het dagelijks leven van adel en ridderstand tijdens de 14de eeuw. Leefwijze en levensstandaard van Jan, heer van Oudenaarde (1373–1378)', *Gedenkboek 750 Jaar Pamelekerk* (Oudenaarde, 1985): 103–130.

Thoen, Erik, 'Historisch–Geografische Teksten bij het Kaartblad Oosterzele en Eeklo', *Project Historisch– Landschappelijke Reliktenkaarten van Vlaanderen*, Intern Rapports (RUG, 1987).

Thoen, Erik, *Landbouwekonomie en bevolking in Vlaanderen gedurende de late Middeleeuwen en het begin van de moderne tijden. Testregio: de Kasselrijen van Oudenaarde en Aalst (eind 13de–eerste helft 16de eeuw)*, 2 vols. Ghent: Belgisch Centrum voor Landelijke Geschiedenis, 1988.

Thoen, Erik, 'Een Model voor integratie van historische geografie en ekonomische strukturen in Binnen–Vlaanderen. De historische evolutie van het landschap in de Leiestreek tussen Kortrijk en Gent tijdens de Middeleeuwen', *Heemkring Scheldeveld* **19** (1990).

Thoen, Erik, 'Rechten en plichten van plattelanders als instrumenten van machtspolitieke strijd tussen adel, stedelijke burgerij en grafelijk gezag in het laat-middeleeuwse Vlaanderen. Buitenpoorterij en mortemain-rechten ten persoonlijken titel in de kasselrijen van Aalst en Oudenaarde, vooral toegepast op de periode rond 1400', *Machtsstructuren in de Plattelandsgemeenschappen in België en aangrenzenden gebieden (12de–19de eeuw). Handelingen.* Gemeentekrediet: Historische Uitgaven, ser. in 8, no. 77, 1988: 469–70.

Thrupp, Sylvia L., 'The Grocers of London: A Study of Distributive Trade', in Power and Postan, *Studies in English Trade.*

Tihon, C., 'Aperçus sur l'établissement des Lombards dans les Pays-Bas aux XIIIe et XIVe siècles', *RBPH* **39** (1961): 334–64.

Tits-Dieuaide, M.J., *La Formation des prix céréaliers en Brabant et en Flandre au XVe siècle.* Brussels: Editions de l'Université de Bruxelles, 1975.

Touchard, H., *Le Commerce maritime breton à la fin du Moyen Age.* Paris: Les Belles Lettres, 1967.

Toussaert, J., *Le Sentiment religieux en Flandre à la fin du Moyen Age.* Paris: Plon, 1960.

Trenard, L. (ed.), *Histoire de Lille*, I. *Des Origines à l'avènement de Charles-Quint.* Lille: Publications de la Faculté des Lettres et Sciences Humaines, n.d.

Trio, P., *De Gentse Broederschappen (1182–1580). Ontstaan, naamgeving, materiële uitrusting, structuur, opheffing en bronnen.* Verhandelingen der

Maatschappij voor Geschiedenis en Oudheidkunde te Gent, 16 (1990).

Tyghem, F. van, 'De gotische Bouwkunst in het Zuiden 1150–1500', *AGN* 2: 289–304.

Uytven, R. van, 'De Volmolen: Motor van de omwenteling in de industriële mentaliteit', *Alumni* 28 (1968): 62–4.

Uytven, R. van, 'La Flandre et le Brabant, "terres de promission" sous les ducs de Bourgogne?', *RN* 43 (1961): 281–317.

Uytven, R. van, 'Plutokratie in de "oude demokratieën" der Nederlanden', *Handelingen der Koninklijke Zuidnederlandse Maatschappij voor Taal- en Letterkunde en Geschiedenis* 16 (1962): 373–409.

Uytven, R. van, 'Stadsgeschiedenis in het Noorden en Zuiden', *AGN* 2: 188–253.

Uytven, R. van and W. Blockmans, 'Constitutions and their Application in the Netherlands during the Middle Ages', *RBPH* 47 (1969): 399–424.

Uytven, R. van and W. Blockmans, 'De Noodzaak van een geïntegreerde sociale geschiedenis. Het voorbeeld van de Zuidnederlandse steden in de late Middeleeuwen', *TG* 90 (1977), 276–90.

Vàczy, P., 'La Transformation de la technique et de l'organisation de l'industrie textile en Flandre aux XI–XIIIe siècles', *Studia Historica Academiae Scientiarum Hungaricae* 48 (1960): 3–26.

Vale, J., *Edward III and Chivalry. Chivalric Society and its Context 1270–1350*. Woodbridge: Boydell Press, 1982.

Vandermaesen, M., 'Artaud Flote, abt van Vézelay en raadsheer van de graaf van Vlaanderen. Triomf en val van een hoveling (1322–1332)', *HMGOG* 43 (1989): 103–127.

Vandermaesen, M., 'Het slot van Rupelmonde als centraal archiefdepot van het graafschap Vlaanderen (midden 13de–14de e.)', *BCRH* 136 (1970): 273–317.

Vandermaesen, M., 'Vlaanderen en Henegouwen onder het Huis van Dampierre 1244–1384', *AGN* 2: 399–440.

Varenbergh, E., *Histoire des relations diplomatiques entre le comté de Flandre et l'Angleterre au Moyen Age*. Brussels: C. Muquardt, 1874.

Vaughan, R., *Charles the Bold. The Last Valois Duke of Burgundy*. London: Longman, 1973.

Vaughan, R., *John the Fearless. The Growth of Burgundian Power*. London: Longman, 1966.

Vaughan, R., *Philip the Bold. The Formation of the Burgundian State*. Cambridge, Mass.: Harvard University Press, 1962.

Vaughan, R., *Philip the Good. The Apogee of Burgundy*. London: Longman, 1970.

Verberckmoes, J., 'Flemish Tenants-in-Chief in Domesday England', *RBPH* **66** (1988): 725–56:

Verbruggen, J.F., 'Beschouwingen over 1302', *ASEB* **93** (1956): 38–53.

Verbruggen, J.F., 'De Historiografie van de Guldensporenslag', *De Leiegouw* **19** (1977): 245–72.

Verbruggen, J.F., 'De Militairen', in *Flandria Nostra* **4**: 161–233.

Verbruggen, J.F., 'De Organisatie van de militie te Brugge in de XIVe eeuw', *ASEB* **87** (1950): 163–70.

Vercauteren, F., 'Une Parenté dans la France du nord aux XIe et XIIe siècles', *MA* **69** (1963): 223–45, translated as 'A Kindred in Northern France in the Eleventh and Twelfth Centuries', in Timothy Reuter (ed.), *The Medieval Nobility* (Amsterdam: North Holland, 1979).

Verhulst, A., 'The "Agricultural Revolution" of the Middle Ages Reconsidered', in *Lyon Essays*, 17–28.

Verhulst, A., 'An Aspect of Continuity between Antiquity and Middle Ages: The Origin of the Flemish Cities between the North Sea and the Scheldt', *JMH* **3** (1977): 175–206.

Verhulst, A., 'Die Binnenkolonisation und die Anfänge der Landgemeinde in Seeflandern', *Vorträge und Forschungen der Konstanzer Arbeitskreis* **7–8** (Constance, 1964): 447–60.

Verhulst, A., 'De Boeren, I: De Middeleeuwen', *Flandria Nostra* **1**: 87–122.

Verhulst, A., 'Bronnen en problemen betreffende de Vlaamse landbouw in de late Middeleeuwen (XIIIe–XVe eeuw)', *Ceres en Clio, zeven variaties op het thema landbouwgeschiedenis (Agronomisch–Historische Bijdragen,* 6). Wageningen, 1964, 205–35.

Verhulst, A., 'Castrum en Oudburg te Gent', *HMGOG* **14** (1960): 3–61.

Verhulst, A., 'Early Medieval Ghent between Two Abbeys and the Counts' Castle', in Decavele, *Ghent*, 37–59.

Verhulst, A., 'L'Economie rurale de la Flandre et la dépression économique du bas Moyen-Age', *Etudes Rurales* **10** (1963): 68–80.

Verhulst, A., 'Die Frühgeschichte der Stadt Gent', in *Die Stadt in der europäischen Geschichte. Festschrift Edith Ennen* (Bonn: Röhrscheid, 1972), 108–137:

Verhulst, A. 'Der frühmittelalterliche Handel der Niederlande und der Friesenhandel', in *Untersuchungen zu Handel und Verkehr der vor- und frühgeschichtlichen Zeit in Mittel- und Nordeuropa. III. Der Handel des frühen Mittelalters*. Abhandlungen der Akademie der Wissenschaften in Göttingen, Phil.-Hist. Klasse, dritte Folge, no. 150, 381–91.

Verhulst, A., 'Die gräfliche Burgenverfassung in Flandern im Hochmittelalter', in *Die Burgen im deutschen Sprachraum. Ihre rechts- und verfassungsgeschichtliche Bedeutung*. Vorträge und Forschungen der Konstanzer Arbeitskreis (Sigmaringen, 1976), 266–82.

Verhulst, A. (ed.), *Le grand Domaine aux époques mérovingienne et carolingienne*. Ghent: Belgisch Centrum voor Landelijke Geschiedenis, 1985.

Verhulst, A., 'De heilige Bavo en de oorsprong van Gent'. MKVA, Kl. Letteren, jg. 47, no. 1, 1985, 75–90.

Verhulst, A., *Histoire du paysage rural en Flandre de l'époque romaine au XVIIIe siècle*. Brussels: La Renaissance du Livre, 1966.

Verhulst, A., 'L'Historiographie concernant l'origine des villes dans les anciens Pays–Bas depuis la mort de Henri Pirenne (1935)', *Cahiers de Clio* **86** (1986): 107–16.

Verhulst, A., 'L'Intensification et la commercialisation de l'agriculture dans les Pays–Bas méridionaux au XIIIe siècle', in *La Belgique rurale du moyen-âge à nos jours. Mélanges offerts à Jean-Jacques Hoebanx* (Brussels, 1985), 89–100.

Verhulst, A., 'Kritische Studie over de oorkonde van Lodewijk IV van Overzee, koning van Frankrijk, voor de Sint-Pietersabdij te Gent (20 augustus 950)', *BCRH* **150** (1984): 274–327.

Verhulst, A., 'La Laine indigène dans les anciens Pays-Bas entre le XIIe et le XVIIe siècle. Mise en oeuvre industrielle production et commerce', *RH* **96** (1972): 281–322.

Verhulst, A., 'Leie en Schelde als grens in het portus te Gent tijdens de Xde eeuw', *Naamkunde* **17** (1985): 407–19. *Festbundel voor Maurits Gysseling . . .* Mededelingen van het Instituut voor Naamkunde te Leuven en van het P.J. Meertens-Instituut te Amsterdam, afdeling Naamkunde.

Verhulst, A., 'Note sur l'origine du mot flamand "kouter" (lat. *cultura*, fr. *couture*)', *Studi Medievali* **10** (1969): 261–7.

Verhulst, A., 'Occupatiegeschiedenis en landbouweconomie in het Zuiden, circa 1000–1300', *AGN* **2**: 83–104.

Verhulst, A., 'L'Organisation financière du comté de Flandre, du duché de Normandie et du domaine royal français du XIe au XIIIe siècle', in *L'Impôt dans le cadre de la ville et de l'etat* (Collection Histoire in 8o, no. 133, 1966), 29–41.

Verhulst, A., 'The Origins of Towns in the Low Countries and the Pirenne Thesis', *Past and Present* **122** (1989): 3–35.

Verhulst, A., 'Le Paysage rural en Flandre intérieure: son évolution entre le IXème et le XIIIème siècle', *RN* **62** (1980): 11–33.

Verhulst, A., *Précis d'histoire rurale de la Belgique*. Brussels: Editions de l'Université de Bruxelles, 1990.

Verhulst, A., 'Probleme der Stadtkernforschung in einigen flämischen Städten des Früh- und Hochmittelalters', in Helmut Jager (ed.), *Stadtkernforschung* (Cologne and Vienna: Böhlau, 1987), 279–95.

Verhulst, A., 'Saint Bavon et les origines de Gand', *RN* **68** (1986): 455–70.

Verhulst, A., *De Sint-Baafsabdij te Gent en haar grondbezit (VIIe–XIVe eeuw)*. VKVA, no. 30. Brussels: Paleis der Academiën, 1958.

Verhulst, A., 'La Vie urbaine dans les anciens Pays-Bas avant l'an mil', *MA*, 1986: 186–99.

Verhulst, A., 'De vroegste Geschiedenis van het Sint-Maartenskapittel en het onstaan van de stad Ieper', *HMGOG* **11** (1957): 31–48, reprinted Mus and van Houtte, *Prisma Ieper*, 476–95.

Verhulst, A. and D.P. Blok, 'De agrarische Nederzettingen', *AGN* **2**: 153–64.

Verhulst, A., 'Zur Entstehung der Städte in Nordwest-Europa' in *Forschungen zur Stadtgeschichte, Drei Vorträge, Gerda Henkel Vorlesung*. N.P.: Westdeutcher Verlag, 1986, pp. 25–33.

Verhulst, A. and D.P. Blok, 'Landschap en bewoning tot circa 1000', *AGN* **1**: 99–164.

Verhulst, A. and D.P. Blok, 'Het Natuurlandschap', *AGN* **1**: 116–42.

Verhulst, A. and R. De Blok-Doehaerd, 'Nijverheid en handel' (tot *ca* 1000)', *AGN*, **1**: 183–215.

Verhulst, A. and Georges Declercq in collaboration with Marie Christine Laleman, 'Early Medieval Ghent between Two Abbeys and the Counts' Castle', in Decavele, *Ghent*, 37–59.

Verhulst, A. and Th. de Hemptinne, 'Le Chancelier de Flandre sous les comtes de la maison d'Alsace (1128–1191)', *BCRH* **141** (1975): 267–311.

Verlinden, C., *Brabantsch en Vlaamsch Lakens te Krakau op het einde der XIVe eeuw*. MKVA, Kl. Letteren, jg. 5, no. 2. Brussels: Paleis der Academiën, 1943

Verlinden, C., 'Marchands ou tisserands? A propos des origines urbaines', *AESC* **27** (1972): 396–406.

Verlinden, C., *Robert Ier le Frison, comte de Flandre. Etude d'histoire politique*. Antwerp: De Sikkel, 1935.

Verplaetse, A., 'L'Architecture en Flandre entre 900 et 1200, après les sources narratives contemporaines', *Cahiers de civilisation médiévale* **7** (1965): 25–42.

Vleeschouwers-Van Melkebeek, M., *De Officialiteit van Doornik. Oorsprong en vroege ontwikkeling (1192–1300)*. VKVA, Kl. Letteren, 47, no. 117. Brussels: Paleis der Academiën, 1985.

Vocht, A. M. de, 'Het Gentse antwoord op de armoede: De sociale instellingen van wevers en volders in de late Middeleeuwen', *AH* **19** (1981): 3–32.

Walle, A.J. van de, *Het Bouwbedrijf in de Lage Landen tijdens de Middeleeuwen*. Antwerp: Nederlandse Boekhandel, 1959.

Warlop, E., 'De Keurbrief van het Brugse Vrije', *ASEB* **99** (1962): 161–86.

Warlop, E., *The Flemish Nobility before 1300*, 4 vols, translated by J.B. Ross and H. Vandermoere. Courtrai: G. Desmet-Huysman, 1975.

Watson, W.B., 'The Structure of the Florentine Galley Trade with Flanders and England in the Fifteenth Century', *RBPH* **39** (1961): 1073–91.

Waugh, Scott L., *England in the Reign of Edward III*. Cambridge: Cambridge University Press, 1991.

Wee, H. van der, *Historische Aspecten van de economische groei*. Antwerp and Utrecht: Nederlandsche Boekhandel, 1972.

Wee, H. van der, 'Structural Changes and Specialization in the Industry of the Southern Netherlands, 1100–1600', *EcHR* **28** (1975): 203–21.

Wee, H. van der, and Eddy van Cauwenberghe, 'Histoire agraire et finances publiques en Flandre du XIVe au XVIIe siècle, *AESC* **28** (1973): 1051–65.

Wellens, R. 'La Révolte brugeoise de 1488', *ASEB* **102** (1966): 5–52.

Werd, G. de, 'De laat-gotische Beeldhouwkunst', *AGN* **4**: 318–21.

Werveke, H. van, *Ambachten en erfelijkheid*. *MKVA*, Kl. Letteren, 4, no. 1. Brussels: Paleis der Academiën, 1942.

Werveke, H. van, 'La Banlieue primitive des villes flamandes', *Etudes Pirenne anciens élèves*, 389–401.

Werveke, H. van, 'De Bevolkingsdichtheid in de IXe eeuw. Poging tot schatting', 30e Congres van het Oudheid- en Geschiedkundige Verbond van België, Brussels, 1935. *Jaarboek* (Brussels, 1936), 107–16.

Werveke, H. van, *Burgus. Versterking of Nederzetting?* Brussels: Paleis der Academiën, 1965.

Werveke, H. van, 'Currency Manipulation in the Middle Ages: The Case of Louis de Male, Count of Flanders', *TRHS*, ser. 4, **31** (1949): 115–27.

Werveke, H. van, 'La Famine de l'an 1316 en Flandre et dans les régions voisines', *RN* (1959): 5–14.

Werveke, H. van, *Gent. Schets van een sociale geschiedenis*. Ghent: Rombaut-Fecheyr, 1947.

Werveke, H. van, *De Gentsche Stadsfinanciën in de Middeleeuwen*. Brussels: Paleis der Academiën, 1934.

Werveke, H. van, 'De Gentse Vleeschouwers onder het Oud Regime: Demografische studie over een gesloten en erfelijk ambachtsgild', *HMGOG* **3** (1948): 3–32.

Werveke, H. van, '"Hanze" in Vlaanderen en aangrenzende gebieden', *ASEB* **90** (1953): 5–42.

Werveke, H. van, *Jacques van Artevelde*. Brussels: La Renaissance du Livre, 1942.

Werveke, H. van, *De Koopman-ondernemer en de ondernemer in de Vlaamsche lakennijverheid van de Middeleeuwen*. *MKVA*, Kl. Letteren, 8, no. 4. Antwerp: Vlaamse Academie, 1946.

Werveke, H. van, *Kritische Studiën betreffende de oudste geschiedenis van de stad Gent*. Antwerp: De Sikkel, 1933.

Werveke, H. van, *Lodewijk Graaf van Nevers en van Rethel, zoon van de Graaf van Vlaanderen (1273?–1322). Een miskende figuur*. *MKVA*, Kl. Letteren, 20, no. 7. Brussels: Paleis der Academiën, 1958.

Werveke, H. van, *De Medezeggenschap van de knapen (gezellen) in de Middeleeuwse ambachten*. *MKVA*, Kl. Letteren, 5, no. 3. Brussels: Paleis der Academiën, 1943.

Werveke, H. van, *De Middeleeuwse hongersnood*. *MKVA*, 29, no. 3. Brussels: Paleis der Academiën, 1967.

Werveke, H. van, *De Muntslag in Vlaanderen onder Lodewijk van Male*. *MKVA*, Kl. Letteren, 11, no. 5. Brussels: Paleis der Academiën, 1949.

Werveke, H. van, *De omvang van de Ieperse lakenproductie in de veertiende eeuw*. *MKVA*, Kl. Letteren, IX, no. 2. Antwerp: Standaards-Boekhandel, 1947.

Werveke, H. van, 'Die Stellung des hansischen Kaufmanns dem flandrischen Tuchproduzenten gegenüber', in *Beiträge zur Wirtschafts- und Stadtgeschichte. Festschrift für Hektor Ammann* (Wiesbaden, 1965): 296–304.

Werveke, H. van, *Een Vlaamse Graaf van Europees formaat. Filips van de Elzas*. Haarlem: Fibula–Van Dishoeck, 1976.

Werveke, H. van, *De Zwarte Dood in de Zuidelijke Nederlanden (1349–1351)*. *MKVA*, Kl. Letteren, 12, no. 3. Brussels: Vlaamse Academie, 1950.

Werveke, H. van, 'La Contribution de la Flandre et du Hainaut à la troisième croisade', *MA* **78** (1972), 55–90.

Werveke, H. van, and A. Verhulst, 'Castrum en Oudberg le Ghent', *HMGOG* **14** (1960): 1–61.

Wightman, E.M., *Gallia Belgica*. Berkeley and Los Angeles: University of California Press, 1985.

Win, Paul de, 'The Lesser Nobility of the Burgundian Netherlands', in Michael Jones (ed.), *Gentry and Lesser Nobility in Late Medieval Europe* (New York: St Martin's Press, 1986), 95–118.

Winkel, J. te, *Maerlant's Werken, beschouwd als Spiegel van de dertiende eeuw*. Utrecht: H & S, 1979, reprint of original second revised edn, Ghent/The Hague, 1892.

Winter, J.M. van, 'Knighthood and Nobility in the Netherlands', in Michael Jones (ed.), *Gentry and Lesser Nobility in Late Medieval Europe* (New York: St Martin's Press, 1986): 81–94.

Winter, J.M. van, 'Adel, ministerialiteit en ridderschap 11de–14de eeuw', *AGN* **2**: 123–47.

Witte, Els (ed.), *Geschiedenis van Vlaanderen van de oorsprong tot heden. Histoire de Flandre des origines à nos jours.* Brussels: Renaissance du Livre, 1983.

Wolff, R. L., 'Baldwin of Flanders and Hainault, First Latin Emperor of Constantinople: His Life, Death, and Resurrection, 1172–1225', *Speculum* **27** (1952): 281–322.

Wyffels, C., 'Contribution à l'histoire monétaire de Flandre au XIIIe siècle', *RBPH* **45** (1967): 1113–41.

Wyffels, C., 'Hanse, grands marchands et patriciens de Saint-Omer', *Société Académique des Antiquaires de la Morinie. Mémoires* **38** (Saint-Omer, 1962).

Wyffels, C., 'Nieuwe Gegevens betreffende een XIIIde eeuwse "democratische" stedelijke opstand: de Brugse "Moerlemaye" (1280–81)', *BCRH* **132** (1966): 37–142.

Wyffels, C., 'Note sur les marcs monétaires utilisés en Flandre et en Artois avant 1300', *ASEB* **104** (1967): 66–107.

Wyffels, C., 'De Vlaamse handel op Engeland vóór het Engels–Vlaams konflikt van 1270–1274'. *Bijdragen voor de Geschiedenis der Nederlanden* **16** (1962): 205–18.

Wyffels, C., 'De Vlaamse Hanze van Londen op het einde van de XIIIe eeuw', *ASEB* **97** (1960): 5–30.

Ziegler, J., 'The *Curtis* Beguinages in the Southern Low Countries and Art Patronage: Interpretation and Historiography', *Bulletin de l'Institut Historique Belge de Rome* **57** (1987): 31–70.

Zoete, A., 'De Beden in het graafschap Vlaanderen onder Jan zonder Vrees en Filips de Goede', *Economische Geschiedenis van België. Behandeling van de bronnen en problematiek.* Handelingen van het Colloquium te Brussel 17–19 november 1971. Brussels: Algemeen Rijksarchief, 1972, 11–20.

Genealogical tables and maps

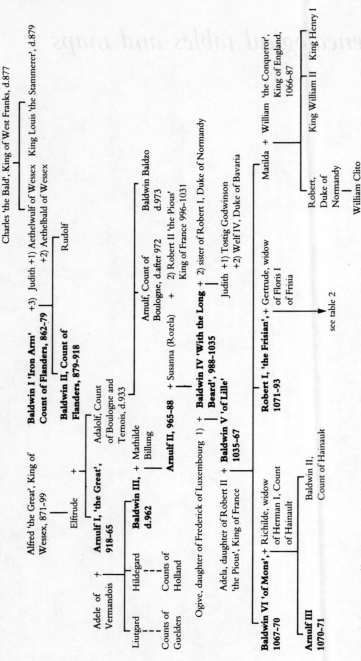

1. The Counts of Flanders, 862–1093 (*note*: the ruling Counts of Flanders are given in bold type)

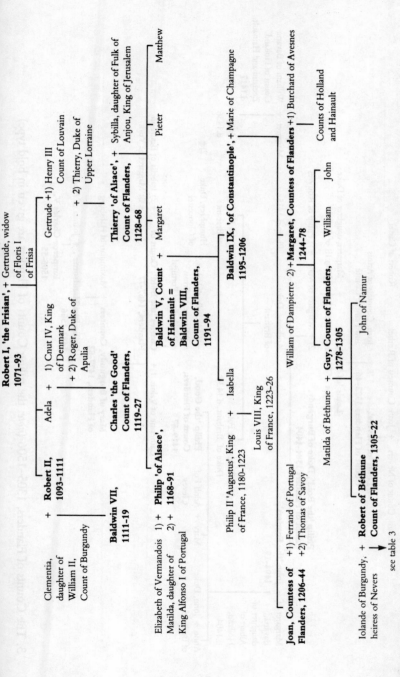

2. The Counts of Flanders, 1071–1322 (*note*: the ruling Counts of Flanders are given in bold type)

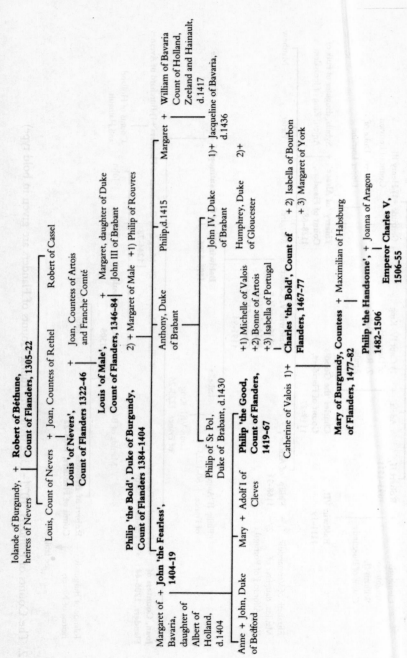

3. The Counts of Flanders, 1305–1506 (*note:* the ruling Counts of Flanders are given in bold type)

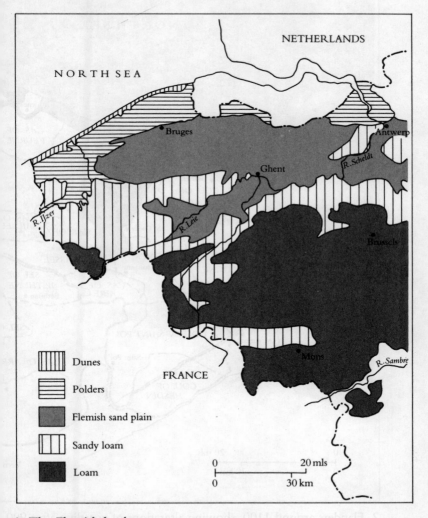

1. The Flemish landscape
After A. Verhulst, *Het Landschap in Vlaanderen in Historisch Perspectief* (Antwerp, 1965)

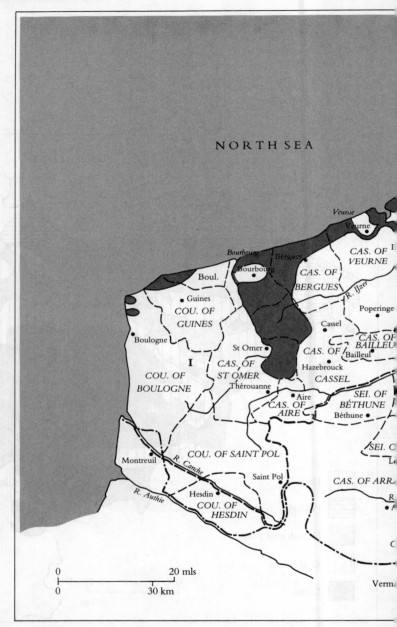

2. Flanders around 1100, showing alterations of coastline after 900
After F.L. Ganshof, *La Flandre sous les premiers comtes* (Brussels, 1943)

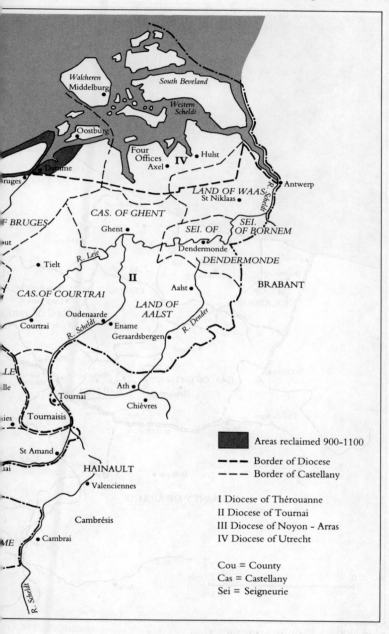

Areas reclaimed 900-1100

– – – Border of Diocese

– – – Border of Castellany

I Diocese of Thérouanne
II Diocese of Tournai
III Diocese of Noyon – Arras
IV Diocese of Utrecht

Cou = County
Cas = Castellany
Sei = Seigneurie

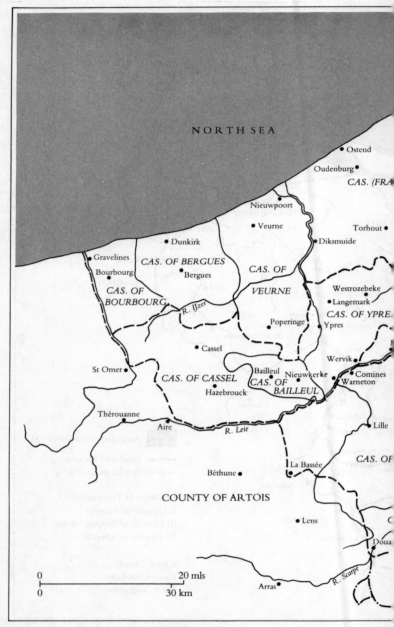

NORTH SEA

● Ostend

Oudenburg ●

CAS. (FRA

● Nieuwpoort

● Veurne

Torhout ●

● Dunkirk

Diksmuide ●

Gravelines ●

CAS. OF BERGUES

CAS. OF

Bourbourg ●

● Bergues

VEURNE

CAS. OF
BOURBOURG

Westrozebeke

● Langemark

CAS. OF YPRE

R. IJzer

● Poperinge

Ypres

● Cassel

Wervik ●

St Omer ●

CAS. OF CASSEL

Bailleul ● Nieuwkerke

● Comines

CAS. OF

● Warneton

Hazebrouck ●

BAILLEUL

Thérouanne ●

Aire ●

R. Leie

● Lille

● La Bassée

CAS. OF

Béthune ●

COUNTY OF ARTOIS

● Lens

Doua

0 _____ 20 mls
0 _____ 30 km

R. Scarpe

Arras ●

3. Flanders in the late Middle Ages
After H. Nowé, *Les Baillis comtaux de Flandre* (Brussels, 1928)

Borders of Castellanies

Borders of Quarters

Cas = Castellany

Sei = Seigneurie

Quarter of Bruges:
Castellanies of Bourbourg,
Bergues, Veurne and Bruges

Quarter of Ypres:
Castellanies of Cassel, Bailleul and Ypres

Quarter of Ghent
Castellanies of Courtrai,
Oudenaarde, Aalst, Oudburg,
the Land of Waas and the Four Offices;
and the Seigneurie of Dendermonde

Walloon Flanders
Castellanies of Lille and Douai

Index

457